SMALL BOATS, WEAK STATES, DIRTY MONEY

To

SAMANTHA

Without whose faith this book would never have been written

MARTIN N. MURPHY

Small Boats, Weak States, Dirty Money

Piracy and Maritime Terrorism in the Modern World

Columbia University Press
New York

Columbia University Press
Publishers Since 1893
New York   Chichester, West Sussex

Library of Congress Cataloging-in-Publication Data

Murphy, Martin N.
  Small boats, weak states, dirty money : Piracy and Maritime Terrorism in the Modern World /
Martin N. Murphy.
     p. cm.
  Includes bibliographical references and index.
  ISBN 978-0-231-70076-4 (cloth : alk. paper)
  ISBN 978-0-231-70077-1 (pbk : alk. paper)
  1. Maritime terrorism. 2. Piracy. 3. Hijacking of ships. I. Title.
  HV6431.M8746 2008
  364.16'4—dc22
                            2008037415

References to Internet Web sites (URLs) were accurate at the time of writing. Neither
the author nor Columbia University Press is responsible for URLs that may have expired
or changed since the manuscript was prepared.

12/10

CONTENTS

MAPS

FIGURES

TABLES

ACKNOWLEDGEMENTS

No book is the author's work alone. Like any author I am indebted to the people who have read it at the various stages of its development and whose comments, criticisms and encouragement have shaped its direction: Colin Gray, Geoffrey Till, Dale Walton, John Burnett, Dominick Donald and Richard Davey.

Many others have given me the benefit of their learning and experience. Of those I would like to single out Eric Ellen, the founder of the International Maritime Bureau. Without Eric's pioneering work driven, in no small part, by his indignation at the dismissive way many governments treat the risks and hazards seafarers face at the hands of maritime criminals, the scourge that is modern piracy would have taken far longer to reach public notice. Many seafarers directly or indirectly owe their lives to Eric's tireless work, and to that of his successor, Pottengal Mukundan, who guided my first steps in this field and who has answered my queries with great patience ever since.

The academic community that studies piracy, terrorism and disorder at sea is relatively small but growing quickly. When I began writing this book it was still just about possible to know most people in it but that is no longer the case. Over the years I have had conversations and correspondence with many in the field the fruits of which have ended up in these pages but I would like to mention especially Kim Hall, Rupert Herbert-Burns, Karsten von Hoesslin, Jonathan Howland, Peter Lehr, Catherine Zara Raymond, Michael Richardson, Vijay Sakhuja, Mark Valencia and Stan Weeks. I would like to extend particular thanks to Peter Chalk, Stefan Eklöf, Eric Frécon, Rohan Gunaratna and, above all, to Sam Bateman for his friendship and good humoured criticism. From the wider community of defence scholars I drew help and inspiration from Doug Farah, Eric Grove, Steven Haines, T.X. Hammes, Frank Hoffman, Tim Huxley, David Kilcullen, Peter Schwartz and Scott Truver.

Much of the study of this subject and even more of the practice revolves around legal definitions and interpretations. I am not a lawyer and without the help of Rosalie Balkin, Ron Barston, Brad Kierserman, James Kraska and 'Ash' Roach I would quickly have become lost. I would, however, like to extend especially heartfelt thanks to Sam Meneffee and Vaughan Lowe both of whom have an enviable ability to cut through the legal tangles to the heart of the issue.

The help I received from members of the naval, coast guard, police and intelligence communities has been vital. Several of those who gave their time so generously did it on the understanding that they would not be acknowledged publically but of those I can mention I would like to thank Kevin Creswell, Chris Dishman, Charlie Dragonette, Chris Fendt, John Morgan, David Pearl, Tony Rix and Bob Snodden. I would like to express my particular appreciation to Bruce Stubbs whose pride in his country and lifelong dedication to the cause of maritime security has now received rightful recognition.

Amongst the people with hand-on experience of shipping and the issues that surround this complex and fascinating business I wish to thank Peter Astbury, Rupert Aitkin, Steve Carmel, Joe Corless, Carina Dixon, David Fairnie, Chris Horrocks, Steven Jones, David Lentaigne, Andrew Linnington, Nigel Miller, Gordon Milne, Neil Roberts, Gavin Simmonds, Chris Trelawny, John Waite and Daryl Williamson.

Finally I would like to thank my editors but above all my wife, Samantha, without whose unflagging support this book would never have been written.

ABBREVIATIONS

AFP	Armed Forces of the Philippines
AIAI	Al-Ittihad al-Islami (Somalia)
AIS	Automatic Identification System
AMS	Automated Manifest System
ANFO	Ammonium Nitrate Fuel Oil mixture
ARPCT	Alliance for the Restoration of Peace and Counter-Terrorism (Somalia)
AQ	Al Qaeda
AQI	Al Qaeda in Iraq
ASAM	Anti-shipping Activity Message
ASCM	Anti-ship Cruise Missile
ASEAN	Association of Southeast Asian Nations
ASG	Abu Sayyaf Group
ASW	Anti-submarine warfare
ATS	Automated Targeting System
BLEVE	Boiling Liquid Expanding Vapour Explosion
CBP	US Customs and Border Protection
CINC	Commander -in-Chief
CJTF-HOA	US Combined Joint Task Force-Horn of Africa
CSI	Container Security Initiative
CTF	Coalition Task Force
C-TPAT	Customs-Trade Partnership Against Terrorism
DHS	Department of Homeland Security (US)
DIS	Defence Intelligence Staff (UK)
DPRK	Democratic People's Republic of Korea
DWT	Deadweight tonnage
ECDIS	Electronic Chart Display and Information System
EiS	"Eye in the Sky"
EOD	Explosive Ordnance Disposal

ETA	Euskadi Ta Askatasuna (Basque Homeland and Freedom)
ESO	External Security Organisation (Hizbollah)
EU	European Union
FARC	Fuerzas Armadas Revolucionarias de Colombia (Revolutionary Armed Forces of Colombia)
FBI	Federal Bureau of Investigation
FERIT	Far East Regional Investigation Team
FDN	Nicaraguan Democratic Force
FoC	Flag of Convenience
FP-25	Popular Forces of April 25
GAM	Gerakan Aceh Merdeka
GI	Al-Gama'a al-Islamiyya
GRP	Government of the Republic of the Philippines
GRT	Gross Registered Tonnage
HARTS	Harbour Craft Transponder System
HLH	"Hong Kong-Luzon-Hainan Island"
ICG	International Crisis Group
ICS	International Chamber of Shipping
IDF	Israeli Defence Force
IED	Improvised Explosive Device
IMB	International Maritime Bureau
IMO	International Maritime Organisation
IN	Indian Navy
IPSP	International Port Security Programme
IRA	Irish Republican Army
IRGCN	Iranian Revolutionary Guard Corps Navy
ISC	Information Sharing Centre (Singapore)
ISPS	International Ship and Port Facility Security code
ITOCG	UK International Terrorism and Organised Crime Group
IUU	Illegal, Unreported and Unregulated
IWAS	Irregular Warfare at Sea
JCC	Joint Cargo Committee
JCG	Japanese Coast Guard
JI	Jemaah Islamiyah
JIATF	Joint Inter-agency Task Force
JMSDF	Japanese Maritime Self-Defence Force
JTAC	UK Joint Terrorism Assessment Centre

JWC	Joint War Committee
KMM	Kumpulan Militan Malaysia
KSM	Khalid Sheik Mohammed
LMA	Lloyd's Market Association
LNG	Liquefied Natural Gas
LPG	Liquefied Petroleum Gas
LRIT	Long Range Identification and Tracking
LTTE	Liberation Tigers of Tamil Eelam
LOS	Law of the Sea
MALSINDO	MALaysia-Singapore-INDOnesia Trilateral Coordinated Patrol agreement
MANPADS	Man-portable Air Defence System
MARLO	US Maritime Liaison Office (Bahrain)
MDA	Maritime Domain Awareness
MEH	Marine Electronic Highway
MILF	Moro Islamic Liberation Front
MNLF	Moro National Liberation Front
MSTS	US Maritime Transportation Security Act
MTO	UK Maritime Trade Operations (Dubai)
NGA	National Geospatial Intelligence Agency
NOAA	National Oceanic and Atmospheric Administration
NSC	National Security Council
NUMAST	National Union of Maritime, Aviation and Shipping Transport Officers (now Nautilus)
OAE	Operation Active Endeavour
OECD	Organisation for Economic Cooperation and Development
OIC	Organisation of the Islamic Conference
ONI	Office of Naval Intelligence
PA	Palestinian Authority
PFLP	Popular Front for the Liberation of Palestine
PFLP-GC	Popular Front for the Liberation of Palestine–General Command
PIRA	Provisional Irish Republican Army
PLAN	People's Liberation Army Navy
PLF	Palestine Liberation Front
PLO	Palestine Liberation Organisation
PMC	Private Military Company

PRC	People's Republic of China
PRC	Piracy Reporting Centre
PSC	Private Security Company
PSI	Proliferation Security Initiative
ReCAAP	Regional Cooperation Agreement in Combating Piracy and Armed Robbery Against Ships in Asia
RDD	Radiological Dispersion Device
RMSI	Regional Maritime Security Initiative
RN	Royal Navy
RP	Republic of the Philippines
RPG	Rocket-propelled Grenade
RSN	Republic of Singapore Navy
SAFE	Securing America's Future Energy
SAR	Search and Rescue
SDV	Swimmer Delivery Vehicle
SICS	Supreme Islamic Council of Somalia
SLN	Sri Lankan Navy
SOE	Special Operations Executive
SOLAS	Safety of Life at Sea Convention
SPSS	Self Propelled Semi-Submersible
SUA	Convention for the Suppression of Unlawful Acts Against the Safety of Maritime Navigation
TCO	Transnational Crime Organisation
TEU	Twenty-foot Equivalent Unit (intermodal shipping container)
TFG	Transitional Federal Government (Somalia)
TNI	Tentara Nasional Indonesia
TOC	Transnational Organised Crime
UAE	United Arab Emirates
UAV	Unmanned Aerial Vehicle
UIC	Union of Islamic Courts
ULCC	Ultra Large Crude Carrier
UN	United Nations
UNCLOS	United Nations Convention on the Law of the Sea
UNCTAD	United Nations Conference on Trade and Development
UNSC	United Nations Security Council
US	United States

USCG	United States Coast Guard
USN	United States Navy
USV	Unmanned Surface Vehicle
UWIED	Underwater Improvised Explosive Device
VBSS	Vessel Boarding, Search and Seizure
VHF	Very High Frequency
VLCC	Very Large Crude Carrier
VTS	Vehicle Traffic Service
WBIED	Water-borne Improvised Explosive Device
WTO	World Trade Organisation

INTRODUCTION

Men prey upon each other. We can be sure that, given human nature, when the maritime Abel slipped his boat into the water for the first time the maritime Cain was close behind.

Piracy has its roots in the past but this book will address the piracy that is practiced today and what has been perceived as a new challenge, maritime terrorism. Ironically, despite its long history, contemporary piracy also appears to be viewed by many audiences as a new problem; as if the period which began at the end of the nineteenth century, when piracy became a nursery story and later was thrown up on the silver screen, formed an impervious barrier through which the reality of maritime depredation could not seep into the modern era.

This perception has been moulded partly by the elimination of piracy from the Atlantic and Mediterranean worlds (although it continued almost without interruption in Asia), and partly by changing legal definitions. Over the centuries piracy has taken several forms and been perpetrated for a range of reasons, but when the law on piracy was codified in the twentieth century the definition that was settled upon, which built upon thinking that had its origins in the nineteenth, restricted it to acts carried out for "private ends", which excluded piracy's political dimension. Consequently, when the first act of politically inspired piracy did occur, the hijacking of the *Santa Maria* in 1961, it caused consternation. Modern legal thinking was reluctant to label the act one of piracy and therefore, retrospectively, it was labelled terrorism.

Several commentators have rejected this categorical realignment. In the view of James Cable, the noted diplomat and naval historian, the difference between piracy and terrorism is artificial, one that is not recognisable in practice.[1] A similar view holds that piracy and terrorism are different

---

1   James Cable, *Navies in Violent Peace,* London: Macmillan, 1989, pp. 92-101.

activities separable legally and on the basis of motivation but that the line dividing them can become indistinct in practice.

This view has taken on particular force since the 9/11 attacks on targets in the United States. The sheer scale of those attacks appeared to presage a new age of mega-terrorism. The sea unquestionably offers scale. In the search for other possible scenarios that might match the 9/11 attacks in magnitude, attention was drawn to the vulnerability of the maritime trading system and the supposed ease with which ships could be hijacked and used to deliver large explosive devices into ports, some of which are located in or close to major cities. Examples were cited of pirates boarding and hijacking large ships in the Malacca and Singapore Straits. This evidence gave rise to the suggestion that pirates and terrorists might cooperate, or that pirates might teach terrorists the tricks of their trade. This book will question such a simple linkage and ask the reader to consider an altogether more complex picture.

In some ways it will be about definitions. Piracy, terrorism and a third phenomenon that will be touched upon, organised crime, are all contested concepts. So is the idea of weak states. State strength is obviously relative and derives from a number of sources that while largely material are also intellectual and moral. For the purposes of this study, weak states are those that in varying degrees lack the capability or will to secure the lives and property of their inhabitants from internal or external predation.[2] The aim, when it comes to piracy and terrorism, will be to determine, as far that is possible, whether or not each, separately or together, represent a threat to international security. Therefore, while it will look at the questions surrounding their definitions it will not attempt to resolve them, addressing instead the differences and commonalities between piracy and terrorism and, where relevant, between piracy, terrorism and organised crime.

"Contemporary" piracy can be dated most easily from 1983, which was the year when the International Maritime Organisation (IMO), the UN body with responsibility for maritime matters, first commented on the increased number of piracy attacks officially; whilst this is a useful datum point attacks took place before them, and these will be alluded to, as did the horrific ordeal of the Vietnamese "boat people", which will be dealt with at greater length. Maritime terrorism will be dated from the *Santa Maria* incident in 1961.

---

2   For those wishing to explore the subject of weak states in greater depth a good starting point is Stewart Patrick. 'Weak States and Global Threats: Fact or Fiction?' *The Washington Quarterly,* Spring 2006, pp. 27-53.

The two phenomena will be examined separately for two reasons: first, to avoid the temptation to invoke links where none exist; secondly, to ensure that each is seen in its own context because, as in so many fields touched by politics, context is all. For while it is natural to concentrate upon the sea when thinking about what threats pirates or maritime terrorists can pose, to do so is dangerously limited. Power in human affairs is based on the land. Power at sea is an adjunct to, or an extension of—but not a substitute for—power on land. The only reason that terrorists can use to justify employing their limited resources at sea is that it enables them to influence events on land more effectively. It is important, therefore, to place the acts that have taken place at sea in the wider context of terrestrial terrorism and ask how terrorist "effect" might be achieved from the sea, if at all.

The label "terrorism" is often applied too readily in what Professor Barry Buzan and his colleagues would regard as a form "securitisation".[3] Whatever the motive might be for the label's application, in most cases the groups involved in maritime "terrorism" approximate more closely to insurgents than to terrorists. Admittedly some of the acts these groups have perpetrated have been acts of terrorism, but most have not. Giving them the blanket label of "terrorism" serves only to obscure their purpose and their nature.[4] Terrorism is a tactic. Insurgency is an organised movement that, inspired by political, religious or even quasi-criminal motives, uses the methods of war and subversion to overthrown a government and achieve power.

Several of the factors that favour pirate activity also favour maritime insurgent/terrorist activity. This coincidence is important and will be examined in greater detail.

The overriding common factor is politics. While this might be obvious in the case of insurgency and terrorism, including the fact that weak states are less capable of resisting insurgent or terrorist infiltration, it is possibly less evident when it comes to piracy. Throughout history, however, the ebb and flow of pirate fortunes has been linked inextricably with the ebb and flow of power on land, with the power and policies of states and their

---

3   Barry Buzan, *et al, Security: A New Framework for Analysis.* Boulder and London: Lynne Rienner, 1998, pp. 23-6.

4   This point has been emphasised by David Kilcullen and Michael F. Morris in their two important papers which both provide a succinct summary of the differences between insurgency and terrorism and a strong argument in favour of treating al-Qaeda as an insurgent movement: Kilcullen, 'Countering global insurgency', *The Journal of Strategic Studies,* vol. 28, no. 4, Aug. 2005, pp. 597-617, and Morris, 'Al Qaeda as an insurgency', *Joint Forces Quarterly,* no. 39, Fourth Quarter 2005, pp. 41-50.

Piracy	Maritime Terrorism
Legal and jurisdictional opportunities	Legal and jurisdictional opportunities
Favourable geography	Geographical necessity
Conflict and disorder	
Under-funded law enforcement	Inadequate security
	Secure base areas
Cultural acceptability	Maritime tradition
	Charismatic and effective leadership
Permissive political environment	State support
Reward	Reward

Table 1. Factors favouring piracy and maritime terrorism

political leaders, strong as well as weak. In the past, as N.A.M. Rodger has pointed out, strong kings did not need piracy and suppressed it; weak kings tolerated it because they needed it to provide the men and the skills necessary in war.[5] This was as true in pre-colonial Asia as it was in Elizabethan England. In our own era the issues of sovereignty and the rights of nations are just as central to difficulties over piracy suppression as they were in the fifteenth century.[6] But money and the link between the wealth it can bestow and political power has also been central to piracy. "Piracy," Peter Earle has written, "has always benefited from the support of unscrupulous great men only too happy to receive bribes and cheap pirated goods at no risk to themselves".[7] The economic historian J.L. Anderson makes a similar point: "Throughout history, many officials at all levels of authority have found it expedient and usually profitable to ignore or even covertly to sponsor acts of piracy."[8] Once again, what was true historically of England, France and America in different periods has been recognisable in our own times in China, Indonesia, Somalia and other states.[9]

---

5   N.A.M. Rodger, *The Safeguard of the Sea: A Naval History of Britain, Volume One 660-1649*, London: HarperCollins, 1997, p. 116.

6   For an example of modern sensitivity see 'Jakarta sees foreign plot behind piracy charges', *The Business Times On-Line Edition*, 20 July 2004.

7   Peter Earle, *The Pirate Wars*, London: Methuen, 2003, pp. 20-1.

8   J.L. Anderson, 'Piracy and world history: an economic perspective on maritime predation' in C.R. Pennell, (ed.), *Bandits at Sea: A Pirates Reader*, New York: New York UP, 2001, p. 83.

9   On China see, for example, Nayan Chanda, 'Foot in the water', *Far Eastern Economic Review* (hereafter *FEER*), 9 March 2000; on Indonesia see, for example, Jon Vagg, 'Rough seas? Contemporary piracy in South East Asia,' *British Journal of Criminology*, vol. 35, no. 1, 1995, p. 63 and Tim Huxley, *Disintegrating Indonesia? Implications for Regional Security*, Adelphi Paper 349, Oxford: OUP for the IISS, 2002, p. 82.

Piracy is an organised crime. Even at its simplest it requires groups or gangs to carry it out. More profitable piracy requires larger and more sophisticated organisation. The most corrosive effect of organised crime is corruption, which as Thachuk and Tangredi argue, "is the main vehicle, and likely the most socially damaging activity, by which criminal gangs achieve their aims."[10] Phil Williams reaches the same conclusion: "Organised crime," he writes, "makes systematic use of corruption" and is an effect that has not been emphasised sufficiently.[11]

It is true that financial gain has undoubtedly been the main motivator for all types of criminal, including pirates, but neither has it been far from the minds of maritime insurgents and terrorists. To do what they do requires money. Short of funds since the main state sponsors of terrorism withdrew their support, insurgents and terrorists have, in many cases, adopted not only the methods but also the mores of organised crime. Crime corrupts, terrorism subverts and when they merge they do both.

Consequently, this book sets out to answer three questions:
1. What form does piracy take in the contemporary world?
2. What is maritime terrorism?
3. Are piracy and maritime terrorism similar or linked?

The aim is to test the proposition that piracy and maritime terrorism, separately or together, present a threat to international security.

---

10   Kimberley L. Thachuk and Sam J. Tangredi, 'Transnational threats and maritime responses' in Sam J. Tangredi (ed.), *Globalization and Maritime Power*, Washington DC: National Defence UP, 2002, p. 60.

11   Phil Williams, 'Combating transnational organized crime' in Carolyn W. Pumphrey (ed.), *Transnational Threats: Blending Law Enforcement and Military Strategies*, Carlisle, PA: US Army Wall College, Strategic Studies Institute, 2000, p. 186.

1

WHAT IS PIRACY?

A slippery concept

Piracy, very simply, is unlawful depredation at sea involving the use or threat of violence possibly, but not necessarily, involving robbery. It has been around for a very long time and this is how it was commonly understood for a very long time, certainly since the end of the seventeenth century.

Piracy, while not a political crime, has invariably been linked to politics and the expression of state power or, more commonly, weakness. This linkage has meant that the common notion of piracy has rarely been applied without some form of caveat or exemption that has changed its meaning. In the latter half of the twentieth century these changes—amounting almost to confusion—have grown as the number of states has grown and as each of these states has claimed (or been awarded by default) greater and greater jurisdiction over its territorial waters. This jurisdiction has been extended by international law through a succession of agreements without regard to the ability of many states to exercise proper authority over sea areas that can extend for hundreds of thousands of square miles and touch thousands of miles of coastline.

Lawyers and diplomats almost certainly would not accept the term "confusion". The UK House of Commons Transport Committee in its 2006 report on piracy certainly would. It wrote: "The absence of a single definition means that the classification of violent maritime incidents can become a matter of dispute and confusion."[1] Naval officers, coast guards and police officers charged with suppressing piracy almost certainly would

1   House of Commons Transport Committee, *Piracy*, HC 1026, London: The Stationery Office, 2006, p. 11.

7

accept it, and so would the victims. For them the act of piracy, which technically can only occur on the "high seas", compared to armed robbery at sea—which technically can occur only within territorial waters—is a distinction without a difference. Yet the English courts endorsed the definition of C.S. Kenny, the British jurist, that piracy was "any armed violence at sea which is not a lawful act of war" as recently as 1934 in the landmark decision, *In re Piracy Jure Gentium*.[2] J.L. Anderson echoed this definition when he characterised piracy as a "subset of violent maritime predation in that it is not part of a declared or widely recognised war".[3] The International Law Association in their 1970 Report defined piracy simply as "unlawful seizure or taking control of a vessel by violence, threats thereof, surprise, fraud or other means".[4] Furthermore, the International Maritime Bureau (IMB), which because it is a commercially funded organisation rather than an international body and therefore does not need to take undue account of the sensitivities of states, was able to define piracy pragmatically as "An act of boarding or attempting to board any ship with the intent to commit theft or any other crime and with the intent or capability to use force in the furtherance of that act."[5]

In contrast, the United Nations Law of the Sea Convention, 1982 (UNCLOS), surrounds its definition with restrictions and limitations. Article 101 describes piracy as:

(a) any illegal acts of violence or detention, or any act of depredation, committed for private ends by the crew or the passengers of a private ship or a private aircraft, and directed:

i. on the high seas, against another ship or aircraft, or against persons or property on board such ship or aircraft;

ii. against a ship, aircraft, persons or property in a place outside the jurisdiction of any State;

---

2   *In re Piracy Jure Gentium*, 1934 App. Cas 586, 598, *reprinted in* 3 BRIT. INT'L. CASES 836, 842 (1965) and cited in Malvina Halberstam, 'Terrorism on the high seas: The Achille Lauro, piracy and the IMO convention on maritime safety', *The American Journal of International Law*, vol. 82, no. 2, April 1988, p. 273.

3   Anderson, 'Piracy and world history', p. 82.

4   P.W. Birnie, 'Piracy: Past, present and future', *Marine Policy*, vol. II, no. 3, July 1987, pp. 170-1.

5   ICC-International Maritime Bureau, *Piracy and Armed Robbery Against Ships: Annual Report.* 1 Jan.-31 Dec. 2005, p. 3 [hereafter referred to using the formula ICC-IMB Piracy Report, date]

(b) any act of voluntary participation in the operation of a ship or of an aircraft with knowledge of facts making it a pirate ship or aircraft.[6]

This is the definition used by the International Maritime Organisation (IMO). The IMO is the United Nations agency with responsibility for maritime issues. The only people who are pleased are the pirates (one minute) or armed robbers (the next minute) as they skip from one side to the other of an invisible line that divides the high seas from territorial seas in order to evade capture.[7] Some of those seeking an explanation for this confusion would blame it on the greed and competitiveness of states. Some would perhaps go further and see the problem as being one that only an internationally agreed law can solve. Others, possibly, would feel that it is the perfect illustration of the limitations of international law and a demonstration in microcosm of how inadequate it can be in the face of practical challenges. It is salutary to recall that the rise of naval power during the nineteenth century—particularly the near ubiquity of the Royal Navy—coupled with the extension of colonies and imperial possessions around the globe meant that by 1925 it was possible to believe that piracy was obsolete.[8]

---

6   Available at http://www.un.org/Depts/los/convention_agreements/texts/unc-los/unclos_e.pdf, p. 61. There are many problems with this definition, perhaps the most serious of which is, as Rubin points out, under what legal system is piracy 'illegal': Alfred P. Rubin, 'Is piracy illegal?' *AJIL*, vol. 70, no. 1, Jan. 1976, pp. 92-5.

7   See, for example, Vijay Sakhuja, 'Maritime order and piracy', *Strategic Analysis*, vol. XXIV, no. 5, Aug. 2000, pp. 923-38 and Sam Bateman, 'Maritime transnational violence - problems of control and jurisdiction', Paper for seminar on 'Transnational crime' at the APCSS Biennial Conference, Honolulu, 16-18 July 2002; Peter Chalk, *Grey-Area Phenomena in Southeast Asia: Piracy, Drug Trafficking and Political Terrorism*, Canberra: Strategic and Defence Studies Centre, The Australian National University, 1997, p. 37. Possibly but not certainly: in 1926 one of the most notorious incidents in inter-war piracy took place when the *SS Sunning* was attacked between Amoy and Hong Kong: A.G. Course, *Pirates of the Eastern Seas,* London: Frederick Muller, 1966, pp. 219-27. In fact, piracy was suppressed through constant pressure, not as a result of any final defeat. A.W. Grazebrook points out that patrolling against piracy was the primary role of Britain's China Station right up until World War II. Grazebrook, 'Naval forces and the control of piracy in Southeast Asia', *Naval Forces*, vol. 6, no. 1, 1995, p. 58.

8   For example Birnie, 'Piracy: past, present and future', pp. 163-83 where she cites E.D. Dickinson, 'Is the crime of piracy obsolete?' *Harvard Law Review*, vol. 38, 1924-25, pp. 334-60. See also James Cable, *Gunboat Diplomacy 1919-1991* (3rd edn.), New York: St. Martin's Press, 1994, pp. 152-3.

Arguably the modern world could be content with the narrow UNCLOS definition. It focuses the attention of the international community on acts of maritime depredation in international waters. It leaves coastal states with an unambiguous responsibility to suppress such depredation in their own waters and to deal with coastal raiding as acts of murder and robbery under domestic law. This book rejects this approach. Piracy is complex and although governments and international organisations are adroit at defining problems out of existence, this does not make either the problem or the complexity go away. Piracy is distinguished by its mobility and by the often international character of both its perpetrators and its victims. UNCLOS attempted to encompass the crime of piracy but failed. Subdividing it permits states to respond differently (or not at all) to what is essentially a singular problem: the exploitation of a fluid medium for diverse but violent, criminal acts.

Piracy, politics and corruption

Throughout much of history the fortunes of piracy have been intertwined with the power, fortunes and policies of states, the one often rising as the other has fallen. States have used pirates but individual pirates have used their connections with states to advance their interests at the same time as they have advanced those of their patrons and protectors. By the late sixteenth and early seventeenth centuries piracy was so associated with England that it was known as "a nation of pirates". What was true of Elizabethan England became true elsewhere: France, pre- and post-Revolutionary America, the sultanates of the Trucial Coast and Southeast Asia, all were societies where private and public interests were often as intertwined as they are in many states today where piracy is allowed to flourish.

Mention of Asian pirates is important. Historical understanding of piracy, and navalism generally, is characterised largely by a narrow Western view. The world was "discovered" by European navigators. The same can be said about piracy. The "golden age of piracy" was a Western golden age. But it was far from alone. In 414 AD Shih Fa-Hsien, a Buddhist monk from Sri Lanka, recorded cases of piracy and marauding in the Malacca Straits and South China Sea.[9] Chinese sailors kept similar records.[10] From the thir-

---

9   Chalk, *Grey-Area Phenomena in Southeast Asia*, p. 23; Adam J. Young. *Contemporary Maritime Piracy in Southeast Asia: History, Causes and Remedies*. Singapore & Lieden: Institute of Southeast Asian Studies/International Institute for Asian Studies, 2007, p.26

10   Anderson, 'Piracy and world history', p. 92.

teenth through to the sixteenth centuries the *wakō* pirates equipped with large ships carrying up to three hundred men raided the coasts of China and Korea.[11] For the pirates of the Malay peninsula, Borneo and the Sulu islands, which form a chain linking Borneo with what is now the southern Philippines, piracy was an honourable profession, often driven by political and trading rivalries, that pre-dated the arrival of the colonial powers.[12]

The intertwining of private and public creates confusion. Confusion encourages corruption and out of corruption comes dependency. It creates ambiguities where none should exist. Elizabeth was not a weak monarch but she depended for the defence of her realm upon the sea power she could not afford. Inevitably, therefore, she depended upon ship-owners, financiers, commanders and merchants who were involved in maritime depredation to one degree or other. What was private interest and what was public often merged. As was noted earlier, a similar merger of interests has been recognisable in our own times in China, Indonesia and elsewhere.

Piracy in international law

Most law, even most international law, is jurisdictional: it requires a state to enforce it. This is how it came to be understood in the West, and particularly in England where interest in how law might apply to the sea was especially strong. The concept of closed seas—*Mare Clausum*—was driven in part by the need to control the activity of pirates or, perhaps more accurately, the piratical temptation experienced by many sea captains. Closed seas are a fine idea if you are the state doing the closing. They are not such a fine idea if you are a state with ships that want to cross the closed seas for the purposes of trade and in so doing run the risk of being accused of piracy and boarded. England's support for closed seas declined as its own trade expanded beyond the confines of the narrow seas it had come to dominate.

Freedom to trade requires the freedom to navigate without interference. Hugo Grotius was the first to formulate a new idea for the jurisdictional basis of law, *Mare Liberum,* which gradually found widespread favour based on a simple division of the sea between territorial waters—which were defined as a narrow belt over which the coastal state had jurisdiction—and the high

---

11   In Chinese *Wok'ou* in Japanese *Wakō,* both meaning roughly stunted men or dwarfs: Ralph T. Ward, *Pirates in History,* Baltimore: York Press, 1974, p. 162.

12   Course, *Pirates of the Eastern Seas,* pp. 84 & 90-1; Adam Young and Mark J. Valencia, 'Conflation of piracy and terrorism in Southeast Asia: Rectitude and utility', *Contemporary Southeast Asia,* vol. 25, no. 2, Aug. 2003, pp. 270-1.

seas, where no jurisdiction prevailed (except for that of the flag state over its own ships). This division was perceived to be of universal benefit. Pirates, who not only threatened this benefit but also attacked voyagers with fearful savagery, were branded as universal enemies, *hostis humani generis*. On the high seas, therefore, customary international law established piracy *jure gentium* whereby each state had the right and responsibility to arrest pirates and arraign them under its own domestic laws.

The notion of universality, however, was and is controversial. While some authorities argue that piracy was a universal crime others deny it ever could have been, pointing to the lack of an international criminal court or a specific treaty to which all countries were a party.[13] It is also a notion that has been misunderstood. As Eugene Kontorovich has demonstrated, piracy was not condemned for its heinousness. Therefore to draw parallels between it and modern crimes such as genocide is inaccurate.[14] Instead, it was a practical response to a shared problem. Grotius' re-formulation was quintessentially territorial. If its first aspect was to limit the extent of a state's territorial waters, its second was to strengthen the idea of a ship as an extension of a state's territory so that each one became, in effect, an "island of territoriality" on the ocean. States, however, were prepared to accept the encroachment on their sovereignty that the notion of a universal crime implied because pirates attacked ships of all states and answered to no one in a part of the world that was beyond the jurisdiction of any state. Consequently, what might be described rather inelegantly as "qualified universality" made sense in an era of few states and great empires, most of which shared a common heritage, with a largely common interest in trade and peaceful passage to distant colonies.[15]

Although the general idea that piracy was in some sense a "universal" crime was accepted, its interpretation and application in domestic legislation varied widely. Against this background, and in order to encourage some limit to this variation, it was hardly surprising that the League of Nations chose piracy to be one of the first offences for international codi-

---

13   See, for example, D.H.N. Johnson, 'Piracy in modern international law', *Grotius Society Transactions,* vol. 43, 1957, p. 69.

14   Eugene Kontorovich. 'The piracy analogy: Modern universal jurisdiction's hollow foundation', *Harvard International Law Review,* vol. 45, no.1, Winter 2004, pp. 183-237.

15   Martin N. Murphy, 'Piracy and UNCLOS: Does international law help regional states combat piracy?' in Peter Lehr (ed.) *Violence at Sea: Piracy in the Age of Terrorism,* New York: Routledge, 2007, p. 161.

fication. In 1926 the League's Committee of Experts for the Progressive Codification of International Law published its *Draft Provisions for the Suppression of Piracy*. These were arranged in eight articles that restricted piracy to the high seas, limited it to private acts, exempted politically motivated attacks and allowed states to make certain determinations about the status of belligerents. Partly because this *Draft* failed to secure widespread agreement it was taken no further. Instead a Group assembled by the Harvard Law School agreed to research the whole subject and in 1932 published its "Draft Convention on Piracy with Comments", now known more usually as the "Harvard Draft".[16] The Group's work was comprehensive, and if its ideas are not reflected in modern thinking to the degree that they deserve then the reasons for this are twofold. The first is practical: the type of piracy that concerned them most—high seas piracy—had almost completely disappeared. The Harvard drafters, on the other hand, never assumed that theirs would be the last word on the subject. On the contrary, they believed their work would be adjusted to suit changing circumstances. It has not been because of the second reason: complacency. This has had two aspects: the first is that piracy was seen as a problem out of history, of such little relevance to the modern world that if it did recur it could be dealt with easily; the second is that the rights and prerogatives of states have always and everywhere taken precedence over any measures to prevent and suppress the problem.

Both attitudes can be seen in the work of the International Law Commission that convened in 1949. The Commission's purpose was to prepare a comprehensive maritime law. Piracy was not its sole concern; it was merely one of many that jostled for the attention of the representatives of a large number of disparate and, in many cases, newly minted states.[17] The process concluded with the 1958 Law of the Sea Conference that adopted the High Seas Convention (HSC), Articles 14-21 of which dealt with piracy. These eight articles were based on the Harvard Draft, but the Conference adopted only those parts of the Draft recommended by the Commission and the Commission recommended only those that it thought the Conference would accept. As a result, many ideas from customary international law that the Harvard drafters had identified as useful were modified or

---

16　Harvard Research in International Law (hereafter called the Harvard Draft), 'Draft convention on piracy with comments', *AJIL*, vol. 26, Supplement, 1932, pp. 740-885.

17　Barry H. Dubner, *The Law of International Sea Piracy*, The Hague: Martinus Nijhoff, 1980, p. 38.

dropped. In James Cable's words the 1958 High Seas Convention "privatised piracy" and marked the date when the "rot set in".[18]

The piracy provisions of the High Seas Convention were incorporated almost without amendment (Articles 100-107) into the 1982 United Nations Law of the Sea Convention, generally referred to as UNCLOS. If the High Seas Convention was weak, UNCLOS was weaker. The narrow definitions of piracy that had been refined through the Harvard Draft and then the International Law Commission followed legal thinking that had developed over the previous century. This had restricted piracy to acts for "private ends" as regards purpose, and geographically to the high seas.[19]

Restricting the definition of piracy to "private ends" means that acts for "political ends" are excluded. This is not a serious problem providing that it is possible to distinguish clearly between the two and that acts for political ends are dealt with effectively under separate legislation. The fact is that they are not and, moreover, it is often impossible to separate the private from the political.

As far as purely criminal piracy is concerned, the new zonal provisions in UNCLOS exacerbated the existing geographical restriction. The new provisions expanded hugely the area of the seas that states could to varying degrees enclose. Territorial waters had generally been limited to three miles. In the years prior to UNCLOS there was pressure to widen this zone. Consequently the Convention agreed to a new limit not exceeding 12 nautical miles (22 kms). All states, moreover, could use the device of straight baselines (Article Seven) to increase their territorial waters further by smoothing coastal indentations and including bays and offshore islands, although the overall gain as a result of this "smoothing" was not substantial.[20] Most importantly, the right of hot pursuit into territorial waters without prior agreement was limited.[21] In addition the Convention recognised—but once again limited—the claims of several states to enclose straits used by international shipping, such as the Straits of Malacca. While the Convention guaranteed free navigation through these straits it

18   Cable, *Navies in Violent Peace*, p. 92.
19   For a history of these restrictions see Murphy, 'Piracy and UNCLOS: Does international law help regional states combat piracy?' pp. 159-63.
20   Birnie. 'Piracy: Past, present and future', p. 171.
21   For a fuller discussion of hot pursuit, reverse hot pursuit and the difficulties that the extension of the territorial limit has occasioned, see Burdick H. Brittin, 'The law of piracy: Does it meet the present and potential challenges?' in Eric Ellen (ed.), *Piracy at Sea*, Paris: ICC Publishing, 1989, pp. 164-5.

also placed that navigation at risk. By allowing them to be enclosed within territorial waters it handed control of what were often critical chokepoints to states that, in some cases, lacked the ability, resources and interest to maintain security and good order.

Enclosure was particularly egregious in the case of the archipelagic regime. Gaining recognition for this had been a prime negotiating objective of Indonesia and the Philippines. It allowed these states, and subsequently others, to bring vast ocean areas under their control that, in turn, compromised the operation of *jure gentium* notions of piracy.[22] As subsequent experience has demonstrated, in states where the central power is weak—for example Indonesia and the Philippines—this has proved to be a boon for pirates and a threat to everyone else.[23]

The international law of the sea also permits states to create an additional 12 nautical mile zone (above and beyond the 12-mile territorial limit) to a total limit not to exceed 24 nautical miles. This is known as the "contiguous zone". Seas within this zone are no longer unambiguously part of the high seas.[24] Although all states still have the legal right and obligation to detain any pirates caught in this zone under the high seas regime, a political equivocality has arisen. The fact that coastal states may exercise powers to enforce, for example, customs and sanitary regulations but not to control piracy under their own domestic legislation in this zone can give rise to political and operational ambiguities, which could in turn deter other states from enforcing the high seas regime within it.[25]

The difficulties for piracy suppression continue, for the wording of the articles relating to the 200-mile exclusive economic zone (EEZ) (Part IV, Articles 55-57) is also ambiguous when it comes to piracy.[26] Most commentators agree that, in accordance with Article 58(2), High Seas piracy

22   Birnie, 'Piracy: Past, present and future', pp. 171-2.

23   On this specific point and the obstacles to hot pursuit see Peter Chalk, 'Contemporary maritime piracy in Southeast Asia', *Studies in Conflict and Terrorism*, vol. 21, no. 1, 1998, p. 95.

24   See, for example, the argument advanced in Joel A. Doolin, 'The proliferation security initiative: Cornerstone of a new international norm', *NWCR*, vol. 59, no. 2, Spring 2006, p. 48.

25   International Law Commission, 'Convention on the Territorial Sea and Contiguous Zones, 1958' Article 24, available at http://157.150.195.3/LibertyX::vl r0EkRgQk0TiAM2b6HBwrEbgLbX; see also Birnie, 'Piracy: Past, present and future', p. 172.

26   See, for example, Zou Keyuan, 'Seeking effectiveness for the crackdown of piracy at sea', *JIA*, vol. 59, no. 1, Fall/Winter 2005, p. 122.

provisions apply fully in the EEZs, and that all states are allowed therefore to arrest and arraign any pirate found in them under the provisions of the Convention.[27] Other commentators are less certain. The reason is that the articles pertaining to piracy are in Part VI and, while Article 57 (of Part IV) makes it clear that all states are able to traverse EEZs for lawful purposes, it limits this by making them "subject to the relevant provisions of the Convention" without making clear what these provisions might be. This ambiguity is rooted firmly in the origins of the EEZ concept.[28] That this was not just a wording problem became apparent when attempts by the UNCLOS Drafting Committee to clarify its status were rejected. This unwillingness to seek clarity feeds fears that "thickening" jurisdiction, under which states seek to regulate activities within their EEZs more restrictively, "creeping" jurisdiction, whereby the seek to extend jurisdiction beyond the 200-mile EEZ limit, and the declaration of "security zones", which international law does not regulate or define adequately, will gradually transform the contiguous and economic zones into "quasi-territorial seas".[29]

---

27   See, for example, Barry H. Dubner, 'Human rights and environmental disaster—two problems that defy the 'norms' of the international law of sea piracy', *Syracuse Journal of International Law*, vol. 23, no.1, 1997, pp. 11-12; Justin Chenevier, 'Piracy under the law of the sea convention: Conceptual basis and practical limitations', *MLAANZ Journal*, vol. 15, Part 2, 1997, p. 53; H.E. José Luis Jesus, 'Protection of foreign ships against piracy and terrorism at sea: Legal aspects', *The International Journal of Marine and Coastal Law*, vol. 18, no. 3, 2003, p. 379; Sam Bateman, 'Piracy and the Challenge of Cooperative Security and Enforcement Policy', *Maritime Studies*, March/April 2001, pp. 14-15. In Vaughan Lowe's view, the EEZ counts as high seas for piracy purposes in line with Article 58(2). (Correspondence with author)

28   A thorough review of the history of the EEZ concept can be found in George V. Galdorisi and Alan G. Kaufman, 'Military activities in the exclusive economic zone: Preventing uncertainty and defusing conflict', *California Western International Law Journal*, vol. 32, 2002, pp. 257-68.

29   See, for example, Geoffrey Till, 'Coastal focus for maritime security', *Jane's NI*, May 1996, p. 16; Mihir Roy, 'The sea lines of communication: An Indian Ocean perspective' in Andrew Forbes (ed.), *The Strategic Importance of Seaborne Trade and Shipping*, Papers in Australian Maritime Affairs, no. 10. RAN Sea Power Centre, 2003, pp. 88-9; Juan Luis Suárez de Vivero and Juan Carlos Rodríguez Mateos, 'New factors in ocean governance: From economic to security-based boundaries', *Marine Policy*, vol. 28, Issue 2, March 2004, pp. 185-8; Justin Stares. 'EU seeks to extend territorial powers', *Lloyd's List*, 19 July 2006; and George V. Galdorisi and Alan G. Kaufman, *ibid.*, p. 254. See most particularly Wayne S. Ball, 'The Old Grey *Mare*, national enclosure of the oceans', *Ocean Development and International Law*, vol. 27, 1996, pp. 101-10 and Bernard H. Oxman's important paper 'The territorial temptation: A siren song at sea', *AJIL*, vol. 100, no. 4, Oct. 2006, pp. 830-51.

Piracy as an international interest

Common interests rarely result in common definitions or interpretations. The international piracy provisions might represent the lowest common denominator, but if they were to become a matter of dispute or modification, and their application consequently circumscribed, then—as Birnie has calculated—the net effect of UNCLOS would be that under its terms only 7%-15% of violent incidents at sea would be classified as piracy.[30] But why should the combination of a narrow definition of piracy and the erosion of the idea of the high seas be of serious significance? Most modern pirates, after all, are not like the buccaneers who prowled the high seas for their prey. They are land-based, venturing out to intercept shipping often no more than twenty miles from shore. In fact, almost all acts of modern piracy occur within the traditional limit of territorial waters in ports, harbours and anchorages. They are, therefore, a domestic criminal problem which should be dealt with under domestic law and in which the international community has no right to interfere.[31]

The argument fails on a number of counts. First and foremost, while the perpetrators might be domestic, the victims are often international. In many cases they are likely to be passing through, carrying international cargoes to international destinations; if not globally, say from the Persian Gulf to Japan, then regionally, perhaps from Singapore to Indonesia.[32] Freedom of navigation is a fundamental interest to all countries for trade and defence. It is a freedom that needs to be defended vigorously. Safeguarding this interest, including dealing with the small detail of piracy, cannot be left to the vagaries of different national interpretations.[33] Second, mobility: even

---

30   Birnie, 'Piracy: Past, present and future', p. 173. See also P.K. Mukherjee, 'Piracy, unlawful acts and maritime violence', *JIML*, vol. 10, no. 4, Aug.-Sept. 2004, p. 301 and, for a recent example, Bill Gertz, 'China enacts law extending its control', *Washington Times*, 27 Jan. 2003.

31   See I.D.H. Wood, 'Piracy is deadlier than ever', US Naval Institute *Proceedings*, vol. 126, no. 1, 2000, pp. 60-4. Also Michael Pugh, 'Piracy and armed robbery at sea: Problems and remedies', *Issues of Low Intensity Conflict*, vol. 2, no. 1, Summer 1993, pp. 1-18.

32   This notion of internationality is an important aspect of the Rome Convention. See Tullio Treves, 'The Rome Convention for the suppression of unlawful acts against the safety of maritime navigation' in Natalino Ronzitti (ed.), *Maritime Terrorism and International Law*, Dordrecht, Boston and London: Martinus Nijhoff, 1990, pp. 74-5.

33   Why then did the USA, which had held out for so long, finally sign the UNCLOS? According to George Galdorisi, it had nothing to do with suppression of

if the perpetrators are domestic they may sail their prizes into international waters; thereafter they might transfer the cargo to another vessel, or sail the entire ship to a second country to dispose of it and its cargo together or separately. Third, so long as the excuse of "political ends" is available there is always the risk that states will hide behind it in order to avoid taking action.[34] Fourth, no state wants to be known as having a piracy problem; consequently there is a considerable temptation to discourage incident reporting by demanding of any master and crew that reports an incident that they remain as witnesses while subjecting the ship to a long and expensive delay. Fifth, most states will only pay attention to piracy once it presents a threat to their interests; if not, they will do little or nothing even if it takes place off their own coasts. (The lack of response from local authorities, even to pleas for assistance, has been a theme that has run through IMB reports for many years.) Sixth, some states may be so poor, weak or corrupt that they lack the will or the means to tackle the problem even if their interests are affected. Finally, there is a class of crimes so heinous that they invite universal condemnation. This class includes genocide and the slave trade.[35] The popular view is that piracy is such a crime. While this might not be based on sound legal argument, nonetheless pirates' reputation for violence

---

piracy and therefore any concerns that might have been felt played no part in the decision. See Galdorisi, 'The United States and the law of the sea: Changing interest and new imperatives', *NWCR*, Autumn 1996. It did, however, have a great deal to do with achieving a consistent international regime and making sure that the USA was a participant so that it could influence the Convention's further development. It is therefore salutary to note that some states have, either when ratifying the Convention or through their domestic legislation, already interpreted the Law of the Sea differently. See Sam Bateman, 'Sea lane security', paper presented at the APEC High-Level Meeting on Maritime Security Cooperation held in Manila, 8-9 Sept. 2003, p. 11. Declarations made on signature, ratification, accession or thereafter can be found at http://www.un.org/depts/los/convention_agreements/convention_declarations.htm

34 See Wood, 'Piracy is deadlier than ever'. Young and Valencia make the point that some Southeast Asian states fear that the 1988 Convention for the Suppression of Unlawful Acts against the Safety of Maritime Navigation (SUA) could be expanded to allow hot pursuit into territorial waters. Most regional states have therefore failed to ratify it as they feel it only makes sense for states that have already established maritime dominance or possess secure maritime borders: Adam J. Young and Mark J. Valencia, 'Conflation of Piracy and Terrorism in Southeast Asia: Rectitude and Utility', *Contemporary Southeast Asia*, Vol. 25, No. 2, August 2003, p. 277.

35 See Doug MacKinnon, 'Transnational dimensions of maritime crime', paper presented at the Transnational Crime Conference, Canberra, March 2000, p. 2.

is well earned even today. Granted, many incidents involve only the threat of violence and in others there is no violence at all (in fact, if a ship is moored or if the crew are carrying out an intricate manoeuvre, pirates can often board and leave undetected) but in all too many cases piracy involves savage violence.[36] As Wood writes: "If the same rate of incidents and associated degree of lethality were to exist in international aerial hijackings, the world would react in a far more concerted and aggressive fashion".[37] Consequently, the international interest, if not paramount in every case, is substantial in many cases and cannot be easily superseded by domestic law and local enforcement devoid of an international dimension.

The practical problem is that pirates have never been prosecuted internationally. Until the middle of the last century all international law was law between states. Pirates are, quite obviously, individuals. Except in a very few cases, individuals can only be prosecuted under domestic law, but because definitions of piracy have varied from one state to another and continue to do so, what was defined as piracy in one jurisdiction might not have been piracy in another; in fact, in some jurisdictions, it might not even have been a crime, a situation that in some places is still true today.[38] At the most

---

36   For some recent examples, see as ICC Piracy Report, 2006, pp. 17-28.

37   See Wood, 'Piracy is deadlier than ever'. Peter Chalk makes the point that 'the human cost of pirate attacks is something that rarely receives the attention it deserves, largely because assaults are directed against less visible targets': See Chalk, 'Maritime piracy: A global overview', *Jane's IR*, vol. 12, no. 8, Aug. 2000, pp. 49-50. According to the ICC-IMB, acts of violence against crew and passengers increased from 58 in 1992 to 644 in 2003, dipping to 317 in 2006. See ICC Piracy Report, 2006, p. 10. That violence is a continuing trend is shown in 'Piracy takes a higher toll of seamen's lives', *ICC News*, 28 Jan. 2004, and 'Murder of four sailors marks violent start to shipping year 2004', *ICC New*, 13 Feb. 2004; Donald Urquhart, 'Nine missing as pirates throw crew overboard', *The Business Times On-Line Edition*, 16 July 2004. This trend appears to be continuing. Killings, which reached their highest level 2000, have been particularly numerous off Nigeria but also off the coasts of Vietnam, Bangladesh and the Philippines: see 'Killing by pirates on the rise', *BBC News* 26 July 2004. Young and Valencia, on the other hand, suggest that one of the main reasons for reporting a piracy incident is because violence has taken place and, consequently, the statistics may contain a bias that paints a picture of piracy as a more violent activity than it really is. However, they do agree that as the rewards of piracy have increased so the incentive to use greater violence has increased with them. Young and Valencia, 'Conflation of Piracy and Terrorism in Southeast Asia: Rectitude and Utility', p. 272.

38   India and Japan for example: on Japan see Susumu Takai, 'Suppression of modern piracy and the role of the navy', *NIDS Security Reports no.4*, NIDS, Tokyo, March 2003, p. 49, note 33; on India see William Langewiesche, *The Outlaw*

basic level, therefore, the international interest demands that nations enact uniform legislation in accord with international norms, perhaps along the lines modelled by the International Maritime Organisation (IMO) and the Comité Maritime International (CMI).[39] Uniformity, however, cannot be confined to legal definitions. It must include a uniformity of response and extend to associated legal mechanisms such as extradition. Although coastal states have an international duty to cooperate with flag states this is the limit of their obligation. Neither is required to take action and those open register ("flag-of-convenience") states where the income from the register is welcome, but the obligation to enforce regulations is not, might be keen to avoid it.

Simplicity of jurisdiction—or, at least, clarity of jurisdiction—is as essential as capability. As is the will to do something for, as Pugh writes, "whilst it may be relatively easy to codify the rights of states (to suppress piracy), the international community is disadvantaged when a state either turns a blind eye to pirates and armed robbers using its territory as sanctuary, or is unable to suppress the attacks through lack of resources."[40] Steel goes further. He points to the restrictive definitions enshrined in international law on one hand and, on the other, the reluctance of many states to face up to their legal and moral responsibilities. He concludes that it is "therefore possible to assert with some confidence that there is no international law of piracy at all, and also to suggest that there has never been any such law except in the unilateral projections of some states seeking to expand their jurisdiction, to safeguard their own trade or to establish imperial interests."[41] Uniform legislation, therefore, needs to be coupled

---

Sea, New York: North Point Press, 2004, p. 76.

39   With regard to the IMO see 'Combating piracy and armed robbery against ships–call for an international code', *IMO News,* no. 2, 1999, p. 11. In 2001 the IMO Assembly adopted the *Code of Practice for the Investigation of the Crimes of Piracy and Armed Robbery against Ships* in assembly resolution 922. The Code of Practice is available at http://www.imo.org/includes/blastDataOnly.asp/data_id%3D1880/984.pdf Also in 2001 the Comité Maritime International (CMI) adopted a *Model National Law on Acts of Piracy and Maritime Violence* which is available at http://www.comitemaritime.org/singapore2/singafter/modelgen/modelgen2.html

40   Michael Pugh, 'Is mahan still alive? State naval power in the international system', *Journal of Conflict Studies,* vol. 17, no. 2, Fall 1996, p. 8.

41   D. G. Steel, 'Piracy–can the order of the oceans be safeguarded?' *RUSI Journal,* Oct., vol. 140, no. 5, Oct. 1995, p. 20.

with a demonstrable willingness to prosecute and extradite perpetrators, not merely deport them.

Piracy: ancient and modern

The nature and purpose of piracy have not changed. The causal factors remain the same: the largely lawless space of the sea, favourable geography, weak or compliant states that provide sanctuary, corrupt officialdom that can benefit from and protect piracy, economic disruption that opens markets for stolen goods, and the promise of reward from the proceeds extracted either from the sale of rich cargoes or from seafarers and coastal communities too weak or isolated to defend themselves. These are little different from the factors that drove past Chinese, Mediterranean or Atlantic piracy; what occurs today cannot be decoupled from the piracy of the past. It is not a deracinated phenomenon. In the end it is states individually and collectively that determine whether piracy flourishes or fails. Piracy is a global phenomenon but not a global problem.

2

CONTEMPORARY PIRACY: THE WHO, THE WHY AND THE WHERE

Piracy is a global phenomenon but not a global problem. It is a phenomenon with many shared features, but how they are ordered and how they relate to one another is specific to each locality or region. There is an international dimension, which in some cases is significant, and when it is it is primarily political.

What are pirates after?

Pirates are criminals. They want money. At the lowest level they prefer cash, which they will take from ships' safes and from the crew. They will also take anything of value that can be sold readily and turned into money. They will take ships' stores such as paint and rope. They will take ships' equipment such as radios and navigational aids. They will take equipment from the crews' quarters such as televisions and DVDs. They will take the crews' personal possessions such as clothes and their valuables such as jewellery and watches. While they are doing these things there is always a risk they will take crew members' lives.

Piracy is a small group or gang crime. The idea of a lone pirate is slightly absurd. Being a gang crime, it has the quality of an enterprise. More organised pirate gangs steal larger and more valuable items including whole cargos. This could mean they will break into containers to get what they are looking for or, more usually, take control of a ship and unload its cargo—which will tend to be some sort of readily disposable commodity such as refined oil or metal bars—onto another ship or barge. They might then abandon the original ship, try to sell it or, in those cases where piracy merges with maritime fraud, use it to try and obtain other cargoes that they will then steal in turn. This is known as a "lost" or "phantom ship" fraud. In these cases a ship is registered on the basis of false information including the falsification of its previous names, tonnages, dimensions and owner's identity such that, once the crime has been committed, it is difficult and often impossible to trace it, its owners, its cargo and often its crew. Registration is facilitated by lax or corrupt registration authorities while ownership is hidden behind "paper companies" that are often set up only a few days ahead of an operation and based in temporary offices.[1] These sorts of sophisticated hijackings and frauds have been a feature of Far Eastern piracy, although incidents also occurred in the Mediterranean during the Lebanese civil war. Other pirates might simply steal boats or ships to sell. In 2006 the Indonesian authorities captured a gang that did this.[2] Pirates might also kidnap crew members for ransom; incidents such as this took place in the Malacca Straits and the Sulu Sea, and have also occurred off Nigeria. They can hijack whole ships and demand ransom for the ship, cargo and crew together, but because this requires a safe anchorage where the ship can be moored without any risk of its recapture, in recent years this form of piracy has been unique to Somalia.

Reasons for piracy

Piracy is a low-risk, criminal activity that pays well.[3] It occurs for one overriding reason: opportunity. It is often suggested that poverty is the main motivator, but this is simplistic.[4] Not everyone who is poor becomes a

1   ICC-IMB, 'Organised maritime crime in the Far East', Jan. 1991, p. 15.

2   Marcus Hand, 'Indonesia holds 16 over vessel hijacks', *Lloyd's List*, 30 June 2006; also ONI, Worldwide Threats to Shipping, Marine Warning Information (hereafter referred to as WWTTS Report), 6 July 2006, Paragraph D.1. [Reports are available at http://www.nga.mil/portal/site/maritime/]

3   As one researcher wrote, 'little is know about the motivations of modern-day maritime pirates, mainly because few are ever caught...' John L. Worrall, 'The routine activities of maritime piracy', *Security Journal*, vol. 13, no. 4, Oct. 2000, p. 45.

4   John S. Burnett, *Dangerous Waters: Modern Piracy and Terror on the High Seas*. New York: Dutton, 2002, p. 117. He notes that the increase in Malacca Straits and South China Sea piracy coincided with the Asian financial crisis of the 1990s. Peter Chalk, 'Threats to the maritime environment: Piracy and terrorism', *Presentation to RAND Stakeholder Consultation*, 28-30 Oct., 2002, p. 3, while acknowledging the same correlation adds that the crisis also meant that regional states were forced to reduce the resources they made available for surveillance. If anything this problem became worse after 9/11, which focused security measures on land. As a consequence, countries such as the Philippines and Indonesia had

criminal. Furthermore, to draw the conclusion that because people are poor
they will try piracy as readily as they will turn to street crime or vehicle theft
overlooks the inherent difficulty that men cannot survive or operate at sea
without specific skills and in the absence of even a rudimentary support
network to sustain them.

Economic dislocation has, however, had a role. Significant changes in
trade flows have driven piracy in the past and even today changes in circumstances have encouraged some to try their hand. The criminologist Jon Vagg
points out that "developing economies frequently suffer high crime rates,
partly because development leads to structural changes in the economy and
the dislocation of segments of the working population".[5] The consequence of
uncontrolled migration from areas of low investment to areas of high investment can reach the point where the numbers of migrants outstrip the available employment. People who have been given the hope of a new life have
seen that hope dashed; furthermore, in the process of uprooting themselves
and moving to live amongst strangers they have left behind the social and
family networks than might have sustained them through disappointment.
The men who Eric Frécon calls the "new" pirates on the Indonesian island of
Batam are arguably one product of such migration.[6]

The Batam Industrial Development Authority (BITA) was created under President Suharto in 1978 to turn the island into a major industrial
and free trade zone. Suharto appointed his then protégé—and eventual
successor—B.J. Habibie to be its head. Along with the factories and harbours came golf courses, resorts and hotels designed to attract Singapore's
money and commercial spirit, the Batam development also attracted Singaporeans eager to let their hair down.[7] It became, in Peter Gwin's words,
Singapore's "dark sister".[8] The proximity of the city-state, coupled with the

---

even fewer resources to spend at sea. Chalk, interview with author, Aug. 2004.
More recently the Minister Mentor of Singapore, Lee Kuan Yew, has put the
problem of piracy in the Malacca Straits down to poverty on the Indonesian side
and, while acknowledging that opportunity is a factor, claimed that the problem
will only be solved once the problem of poverty has been solved. Marcus Hand,
'Poverty blamed for piracy', *Lloyd's List,* 23 June 2006.

5   Vagg, 'Rough seas?' p. 66.

6   Eric Frécon, 'Piracy and armed robbery at sea along the malacca straits: Initial
impression from fieldwork in the Riau Islands' in Graham Gerald Ong-Webb
(ed.), *Piracy, Terrorism and Securing the Malacca Straits,* Singapore: ISAS, 2006,
p. 72.

7   'Sex trade and exploitation in Batam and Bintan', *AP,* 4 Dec. 2000.

8   Peter Gwin, 'Dark passage', *National Geographic,* vol. 212, no. 4, Oct. 2007, p.

laissez-faire attitude Habibie encouraged, brought in legitimate investment mainly from Singapore, Japan and Taiwan but also less welcome elements: prostitution, gambling, organised crime and corrupt money. The corruption that welcomed these investments was home grown.[9] As was the way under Suharto, Habibie, his family and his associates made a great deal of money.[10] The poor from other parts of Indonesia who rushed to what promised to be an El Dorado ended up chasing too few jobs.[11] Some turned to crime, including piracy. Data from arrest records during the 1990s shows that most pirates were men in their thirties with secondary school education who came from other parts of Indonesia.[12] Frécon describes the life of Marcus Uban (not his real name), who drifted from Timor to Jakarta and then, like so many others, was lured to Batam where he eventually became a pirate. "Singapore was rich; we were poor," Uban told Frécon;[13] to escape "a miserable kampong life...we targeted cargo ships."[14] Gwin in his investigation described men with similar experiences lured to piracy partly for the money but also, as one put it, because "it is fun, an adventure, like James Bond".[15] One that would lead to a "happy, happy" time: after major hijackings the pirates would spend their money on the expensive delights of Jakarta; after attacks on smaller ships they would end up in the clubs and karaoke bars of Batam.[16] Poor kampong dwellers almost certainly lacked the skills necessary to board ships, but the Batam development arose close to old pirate haunts such as Nagoya (known formerly as "Lubak Bajak" or

137.

9   'Now, Habibie Inc.', *Asiaweek*, 5 June 1998; Jeffrey A. Winters. 'Notes on B.J. Habibie', 1 March 1998.

10   Jose Manuel Tesoro, 'En route to Jakarta', *Asiaweek*, 4 Sept. 1998; Johan Lindquist, 'Modern spaces, wild places and international hinterlands: The cultural economy of decoupling and misrecognition', *Anthropology Today*, vol. 16, no. 3, June 2000, pp. 15-17.

11   Stefan Eklöf. *Pirates in Paradise*. Copenhagen: NIAS Press, 2006, p. 48; Frécon, 'Piracy and armed robbery at sea along the Malacca Straits, p. 72.

12   *Ibid.*, pp. 48-9, pp. 75-6.

13   *Ibid.*, p. 71.

14   Richel Langit-Dursin, 'Indonesia key to end piracy in Malacca Straits', *The Jakarta Post*, 6 Aug. 2006; Frécon, *Ibid.*, p. 71.

15   Gwin, 'Dark passage', p. 146.

16   *Ibid.*, pp. 136 & 147. The temptations of dissolute living often extended to their paymasters. As the IMB commented, 'Much of the money goes to maintain luxurious lifestyles', ICC-IMB, 'Organised maritime crime in the Far East', p. 33.

the "pirate mire") where the practice was well established and the skills did exist.[17] Former pirates, as Frécon discovered when he visited the islands in 2002, were not averse to teaching a younger generation: one group reportedly travelled from Palembang in the province of South Sumatra to become "apprentices".[18]

This group would not have been unusual; the coast of South Sumatra is another pirate area and several pirates captured in the Riau islands in the 1990s came from there.[19] The experience of Syaiful Rozi bin Kahar appears to be indicative: he moved from South Sumatra to Batam in 1981; after drifting for a while from job to job he was introduced to Abdul Rachman, a taxi boat driver who doubled as a pirate at night. Rozi joined his gang first as the man who bailed water from the boat before graduating to a raider. He eventually became the chief of the most successful pirate gang on the island. Rozi described Rachman and two others, Mohammad Rasim and Adi Buldog (*sic*), as the first generation of modern gang leaders who possessed at least some understanding of modern cargo vessels acquired, in at least one case, from personal experience as a crew member. They based themselves in Belakang Padang, a group of small islands north of Batam and close to the Phillip Channel.[20] Rozy is also described by Frécon, who mentions him as a "Robin Hood" character who built a mosque and walkways in the village, together with another pirate, Winang, who moved his base from Belakang Padang to the north of Jemaja in the Anambas archipelago where he would operate amongst the local fishermen for several months at a time before he and his gang returned to their families in South Sumatra.[21] Frécon reports that Rozy was murdered and Winang also died mysteriously, but below

---

17   Frécon, 'Piracy and armed robbery at sea along the Malacca Strait', p. 72.

18   *Ibid.,* p. 71.

19   Eklöf, *Pirates in Paradise,* p. 49.

20   *Ibid.,* pp. 49-50 (based on a report in the Indonesian journal *Tempo,* 28 Aug. 1993).

21   For the accounts of Rozy and Winang see Eric Frécon, 'Pirates set the straits on fire: Causes and contexts of the pirate arsons in the Malay Archipelagos since the nineties', paper prepared for the conference on 'Maritime piracy in Southeast Asia' hosted by the Konrad Adenauer Foundation, Kuala Lumpur, 13-15 July 2006, p. 31. He is also mentioned in Frécon, 'Piracy and armed robbery at sea along the Malacca Strait', pp. 71-2 where he is named 'Nasrul'. On Winang's peripatetic pattern see Eric Frécon, 'Piracy in the Malacca Straits: Notes from the field', International Institute for Asian Studies (IIAS) *Newsletter,* Number 36, March 2005, p. 10. Also author's correspondence with Eric Frécon , Nov. 2007.

them was a second layer of experienced subordinates who could in turn draw on a third layer consisting of local fishermen, taxi boat operators, petty criminals and the like.[22] As of 2005, Buldog and his brother had control of six or seven gangs on the island, each of about eight pirates, and although his brother reportedly remained, Buldog himself retired in comfort to a town in East Java.[23]

Sustained predation requires, at the very least, men like Rozi and Winang with organisational and leadership skills. While these gangs are nowhere near as powerful or as well-resourced as the gangs that hijack whole ships, they nonetheless exist on the same continuum as they are better equipped than ordinary fishermen and can have contacts in the legitimate business world and arrangements with corrupt officials. Organised gangs capable of conducting it as a business have dominated piracy in the past and the same is true today.[24] Organised gangs are sensitive to risk: they have capital employed and want to protect it just as any business would. The extent to which piracy is organised is therefore important.

There are seven major factors that encourage piracy, lessen the risk of capture or detention and help protect pirate capital:

1. Legal and jurisdictional opportunities
2. Favourable geography
3. Conflict and disorder
4. Under-funded law enforcement/inadequate security
5. Permissive political environments
6. Cultural acceptability/maritime tradition
7. Reward

These reasons act and react with and on each other, and although one might predominate at any one time and in any one place they are all usually

---

22   Eric Frécon, 'Belakang Padang and Jemaja: Two Indonesian islands plagued by piracy', paper presented at the IIAS conference on 'Ports, pirates and hinterlands in East and Southeast Asia: Historical and contemporary perspectives' held in Shanghai, 10-12 Nov. 2005, p. 4.

23   On Roziy's murder see Frécon, 'Piracy and armed robbery at sea along the Malacca Strait', p. 72; on Buldog see Frécon, 'Pirates set the Straits on fire', p. 25 (where he refers to him as 'Bulldog'), and 'Piracy and armed robbery at sea along the Malacca Strait', pp. 77-8 (where he refers to him as 'Deddy'). Also correspondence with the author, Nov. 2007.

24   Anderson, 'Piracy and World History', p. 84; OECD,, Security in Maritime Transport: Risk Factors and Economic Impact, Directorate for Science, Technology and Industry, July 2004, p. 13.

present to some degree; the cards remain the same but the deck is shuffled differently.[25]

Legal and jurisdiction opportunities. The legal and jurisdictional difficulties faced by law enforcement agencies, which were examined in Chapter One and revolve largely around issues relating to state sovereignty, are significant in lowering the risk factor wherever piracy is a problem. These difficulties exist in national and international law. The weaknesses with the international Law of the Sea (UNCLOS) treaty's approach to piracy can be summarised as:

- The restriction of the definition of piracy to "private", as opposed to "public" or "political" acts, which excludes the actions of terrorists and insurgents
- The geographical restriction of piracy to the high seas
- A mechanism to enable hot pursuit into a state's territorial waters
- The "two-ship" requirement that excludes internal seizure from the definition of piracy
- The lack of a requirement that states enact domestic anti-piracy legislation
- The lack of a requirement that states cooperate in anti-piracy measures
- The lack of an mechanism to penalise states that do not fulfil their anti-piracy obligations
- The lack of a disputes procedure.

However, if legal impediments were the only factor then piracy would be far less widespread.

Favourable geography. The popular image of piracy—courtesy of Hollywood—is of a fast ship bearing down on a slow, lonely merchantman on the high seas, an image that in turn derived from the so-called "golden age of piracy" when pirates did indeed sail from the West Indies and the Atlantic seaboard of North America to the Indian Ocean and back, plundering as they went. In reality and for the most part, piracy has taken place close to coasts or, at most, in the narrow seas that adjoin them such as the Caribbean, the Mediterranean, the English Channel or the South China Sea.

---

25   In his analysis in 'Rough seas?' Vagg concurs with three of these—opportunity, cultural acceptance, and official corruption/state sanctioning—and adds a fourth, economic dislocation. Frécon in 'Pirates set the Straits on fire' recognises four—geography, tradition, lack of security and socio-economic motivations—and adds a fifth, legal causes, in 'Jolly Roger over Southeast Asia: History of the resurgence of the sea piracy', unpublished English translation, 2005, pp. 94-111. Also, Young 'Contemporary Piracy in Southeast Asia', pp. 57-113.

This was certainly the method of Muslim and Asian piracy over centuries. Much the same applies today: contemporary piracy is land-based and concentrated in a limited number of areas, principally the narrow seas close to Southeast Asia, the Bay of Bengal, Somalia and Tanzania, the West African coast (Nigeria in particular) and parts of South America.[26]

Piracy is only sustainable in places that offer a combination of rewarding hunting grounds, acceptable levels of risk and proximate safe havens.[27] Ships that are stationary in ports, harbours or anchorages are the favoured targets. In most cases the level of thieving is minor, although it can be violent and is always distressing to the victim. More than one expert has characterised this type of attack as "maritime mugging".[28]

When ships are under way, attacks take place in the narrow seas generally but straits, bays, estuaries and archipelagos, where vessels are forced to move close to shore for navigational or commercial reasons, offer the best opportunities.[29] Narrow seas are more crowded than the high seas, which means there are more targets. Crowded seas also force large ships to move slowly, which means they are easier to board and find it more difficult to take evasive action. In most cases what proximity to land does not mean is that calls for help will be answered quickly or at all. While it is true that Malaysia and Singapore have striven to improve their response times in those parts of the Malacca and Singapore Straits for which they are responsible, in most other piracy prone areas seamen should assume that any call for assistance is likely to be ignored.

Conflict and disorder. Piracy—and criminality at sea generally—can thrive when coastal regions are troubled by war or civil disturbance, or their aftermath. The piracy that plagued the Gulf of Thailand between 1975 and the early 1990s fed on the refugees fleeing the imposition of Communist rule

---

26   The criminologist David Carter describes piracy as a 'unique example of geographic organized crime': Carter, 'International organized crime: Emerging trends in entrepreneurial crime' in Patrick J. Ryan and George E. Rush (eds), *Understanding Organized Crime in Global Perspective: A Reader,* Thousand Oaks, CA and London: SAGE, 1997, p. 140.

27   See Jack A. Gottschalk and Brian P. Flanagan, *Jolly Roger with an Uzi: The Rise and Threat of Modern Piracy.* Annapolis: Naval Institute Press, 2000, p. 3.

28   For example, Jayant Abhyankar, deputy director of the IMB, quoted in *ibid.*, p. 88.

29   For a definition of 'narrow seas', particularly in the naval sense, and the related terms of 'coastal waters', 'shallow waters' and 'confined waters' see Milan N. Vego, *Naval Strategy and Operations on Narrow Seas,* London & Portland: Frank Cass, 1999, pp. 5-7.

after the Vietnam War. Lebanon during the civil war from 1975 to 1990 became a haven for criminal activity; "unofficial" ports sprang up along the coast to handle stolen cargo and refit stolen ships.[30] Similarly the sundering of Somalia into warring fiefdoms following the collapse of General Mohamed Siad Barre's dictatorial regime in January 1991 appears to have triggered the country's piracy problem.[31]

Underfunded law enforcement/inadequate security. Many states find it impossible to sustain adequate levels of security in their coastal waters.[32] In Southeast Asia the financial crisis of the 1990s meant that regional states were forced to reduce the resources they would have allocated to surveillance. After 9/11 the problem became worse as attention was focused on security on land, which meant that states such as Indonesia and the Philippines had even less available to spend on security at sea.

Inadequate state funding and training for enforcement organisations, whether these are the judiciary, police, coast guard or navy, allows pirates the freedom to operate. Many states simply cannot afford the personnel, equipment, and command and control apparatus that is required or, like Indonesia, believe what resources they do have should be expended on other priorities.[33] The police post on the pirate island of Belakang Pedang, for example, was equipped with only two under-powered wooden boats and

---

30   Barbara Conway. *The Piracy Business.* London: Hamlyn Paperbacks, 1981, p. 15; also Barbara Conway, *Maritime Fraud,* London: Lloyd's of London Press, 1990, pp. 56-7.

31   The first recorded piracy incident off Somalia took place on 12 Jan. 1991 and involved a ship named the *MV Naviluck.* According to the report it was attacked by three boatloads of pirates off Xaafuun. Three of the crew were taken ashore and killed. The remainder were forced overboard and were later rescued by a trawler. National Geospatial Intelligence Agency, 'Anti-Shipping Activity Message', 1991-4 [hereafter referred to using the formula 'NGA ASAM', Ref. no. Reports are available at http://www.nga.mil/portal/site/maritime/]. Although this was the first piracy report as such, the waters off Somalia had clearly become lawless before then. In 1989 there was a report of Somali Nationalist Movement (SNM) boats seizing three ships. The SNM was the movement that eventually overthrew the Barre regime. General Aideed was one of its leaders. NGA ASAM 1989-19, 5 Dec. 1989.

32   Thomas B. Hunter, 'The growing threat of modern piracy', US Naval Institute *Proceedings,* vol. 125, no. 7, July 1999, p. 75.

33   With regard to Indonesia see, for example, the comments of Eric Frécon in Langit-Dursin, 'Indonesia key to end piracy in Malacca Straits'.

the four Indonesian Navy personnel assigned to the police post on Jemaja had no boats at all.[34]

Enforcement is expensive; there are huge sea areas to be covered which require boats and aircraft well-equipped with radar, communications and, above all, trained and honest crews, shore-based command and coordination facilities, reliable information about ship movements and cargoes, and sound local knowledge of the waters and the weather, coupled with reliable intelligence about pirate activity. To be truly effective, however, surface search and interdiction need air support for surveillance, reconnaissance and, if necessary, deployment of police or marines who can be dropped onto suspect craft. None of this is cheap and, to all intents and purposes, none of the cost can be recovered from the crews and ship-owners it is designed to protect.[35] In 1989 an official from Nigeria, an OPEC member and one of the world's most important oil exporting countries wrote:

We recognise that large resources have to be diverted from areas of pressing need, particularly in the developing economies of the west coast of Africa for [the purpose of piracy control]. The question therefore is how many countries faced with the problem can afford the cost of effective policing of their territorial sea, not to mention their EEZ and contiguous zone. In the Nineteenth century Great Britain's supreme control of the sea allowed her to use her naval strength and massive wealth to suppress piracy, [but now the Law of the Sea] "imposes on coastal states, regardless of their resources, an undue burden for providing security in large stretches of sea".[36]

It is against this background of limited resources that Indonesia, and to a lesser extent Malaysia, have sought to use Article 43 of UNCLOS as a lever to persuade states whose ships use the Straits of Malacca to contribute to the cost of security. This Article, which was drafted with the Malacca Straits in mind specifically, encourages states that use straits to cooperate with the states that border them to provide navigational and safety aids

34　Frécon, 'Pirates set the Straits on fire', p. 26; also 'Piracy and armed robbery at sea along the Malacca Straits', pp. 73-4.

35　In 1992, for example, Indonesia, Malaysia and Singapore adopted a policy of aggressively patrolling the Straits of Malacca, which resulted in the virtual elimination of pirate activity. Despite this success it had to be abandoned after six months because it was so expensive. See Hunter, 'The growing threat of modern piracy', p. 75. On the issue of non-recovery of costs see Sam Bateman, Catherine Zara Raymond and Joshua Ho, 'Safety and security in the Malacca and Singapore Straits', Policy Paper, Singapore: IDSS, May 2006, p. 6 and Lee Cordner, 'Maritime terrorism: The next "soft target"', *Defence and Foreign Affairs Daily*, 9 Dec. 2003.

36　Office of the Defence Attaché, Permanent Mission of Nigeria to the United Nations, 'Piracy control in Nigeria's territorial seas' in Ellen, *Piracy at Sea*, p. 222.

and other improvements, and to prevent, reduce and control pollution. Conferences held in Singapore in 1996 and 1999 brought user and coastal states together with the IMO and others to examine cooperative arrangements. It was agreed, consensually, that it was inequitable to expect the coastal states to bear all the responsibility for maintaining the Straits, that the user and coastal states should seek suitable cooperative arrangements and that funding mechanisms should be developed in order to fulfil the Article's requirements.[37] In fact, as far as the Straits are concerned, the limited range of technical activities which the Article covers have been funded by Japan (and Japan alone), through the Nippon Foundation, for the past 35 years, to the tune of around $100 million. Much of this equipment is now coming to the end of its service life. It is probably no coincidence that while Japan was prepared to be the sole benefactor so long as it was the primary beneficiary of safe passage through the Straits, the fact that China and other competitors such as Taiwan and South Korea are now equally dependent on secure passage through the Straits for their oil supplies might have prompted the Nippon Foundation to once again float the idea that user states should contribute to the cost. If a legal basis is needed it would likely be Article 43 (rather than an attempt to create a *sui generis* solution), although just how it could work remains unclear. Nonetheless, the Foundation appears confident that an agreement will be reached before the end of the decade.[38]

---

37   Murphy, 'Piracy & UNCLOS', p. 170. Lim Teck Ee, 'Straits of Malacca and Singapore: Past, present and future co-operation', presentation to the Maritime Institute of Malaysia Conference, Kuala Lumpur, Malaysia, 12 Oct. 2004. See also Sam Bateman, 'The regime of straits transit passage in the Asia Pacific: Political and strategic issues' in Donald R. Rothwell and Sam Bateman, *Navigational Rights and Freedoms and the New Law of the Sea,* The Hague, Boston and London: Martinus Nijhoff Publishers, 2000, p. 101 and Bateman, 'Sea lane security', p. 9.

38   Marcus Hand, 'Pay-as-you-go safety scheme for Malacca Strait', *Lloyd's List,* 2 June 2006 and 'Paying for passage: A new paradigm in maritime safety', *Lloyd's List,* 14 June 2006; Clarence Fernandez, 'Malacca Strait users may have to pay fees–experts', *Reuters,* 2 Aug. 2006; Sharidan M. Ali, 'Straits users should be taxed', *The Star Online,* 7 Aug. 2006; Abd Rahim Hussin, 'The management of the Straits of Malacca: Burden sharing as the basis for co-operation', paper presented at the MIMA International Maritime Conference, Awana Porto Malai, Langkawi, Malaysia, 4-5 Dec. 2005; Bateman, *et al,* 'Safety and security in the Malacca and Singapore Straits', p. 27; Vijay Sakhuja, 'Malacca: Who's to pay for smooth sailing?' *Asia Times,* 16 May 2007 and 'Footing the bill', *Shiptalk,* 17 May 2007.

This confidence was strengthened by the outcome of an IMO conference convened in Kuala Lumpur in September 2006 at which a number of user states, including China, India and the United States, pledged support for a variety of maritime safety projects for the Malacca Straits such as wreck removal, hazardous incident response capacity, a project to demonstrate the feasibility of installing AIS transponders on small ships, navigational aids replacement, and a tide and wind management system.[39] It was suggested before the conference that the littoral states might ask for security assistance, but when the measures were announced none, with the possible exception of the AIS responder demonstration programme, were security related.[40] Although much of this support was more rhetorical than actual, it did appear that progress was made.[41] The IMO Secretary-General, Efthimios Mitropoulos, moreover made it clear that there was no plan to make ship owners pay a toll for using the Straits.[42] Since the conference concluded, however, Indonesia has suggested that a special fund should be

---

39   Joshua Ho, 'The IMO-KL meeting on the Straits of Malacca and Singapore', IDSS *Commentaries*, 5 Oct. 2006; Marcus Hand, 'Landmark deal for Malacca Strait safety', *Lloyd's List*, 19 Sept. 2006. Since the conference, Malaysian ship owners have put forward the view that a voluntary finding arrangement will not prove workable and will have to be made mandatory, but without making it clear how this could be achieved. Marcus Hand, 'Malaysian owners call for mandatory Malacca security funding', *Lloyd's List*, 3 Oct. 2006.

40   'Straits users welcomed to participate in maritime security–Najib', *Bernama.com*, 18 Sept. 2006; '31 nations agree to make Malacca Strait safer for navigation', *The Star Online*, 20 Sept. 2006; 'Littoral states key to Malacca safety', *Fairplay*, 20 Sept. 2006. The push to install AIS Class B transponders on small craft continued after the conference closed. Sharidan M. Ali, 'Reducing risks posed by small vessels', *The Star Online*, 9 Oct. 2006.

41   Marcus Hand, 'Funding sought for $1000m Malacca Strait safety projects', *Lloyd's List*, 21 Sept. 2006; 'Steps towards a safer strait', *Lloyd's List*, 26 Sept. 2006. Some agreements were reached in 2007: Marcus Hand, 'Users pledge to fund Malacca Strait safety', *Lloyd's List*, 6 Sept. 2007.

42   Marcus Hand, 'No tolls in Malacca Strait for owners–Mitropoulos', *Lloyd's List*, 20 Sept. 2006. But concerns appear to persist. 'Owners oppose Malacca levy', *Fairplay*, 1 Dec. 2006; Marcus Hand, 'Nippon Foundation calls for Malacca fund', *Lloyd's List*, 15 March 2007; Marcus Hand, 'Singapore owners demand consultation on Malacca fund', *Lloyd's List*, 19 March 2007; Marcus Hand, 'Shipowners refuse to pay for Strait security', *Lloyd's List*, 13 June 2007. These concerns appeared to have been justified. In Sept. 2007 the IMO's Mitropoulos appeared to adjust his position when he called on 'all parties' to consider their 'social responsibilities' and give thought to making 'voluntary contributions': Chew Wai Yee, 'IMO calls on industry to fund Strait safety', *Lloyd's List*, 5 Sept. 2007. See 'Paying to stay safe', *Lloyd's List*, 12 Sept. 2007 for objections to this suggestion and its possible implications.

established for security purposes exclusively.[43] Safety and environmentally related cooperation took a step forward in September 2007 when the three littoral states agreed to establish a formal "Cooperative Mechanism" which was implemented in May 2008.[44]

At the same time fingers have been pointed at the shipping industry for not doing enough to protect its own ships. Clearly, sensible precautions can and should be taken when ships pass through known piracy areas such as standing extra watches, priming fire hoses so they are ready to be used to douse suspicious small craft if they come too close, and fitting secure locks to doors.[45] More sophisticated equipment such as high-voltage "fences" installed out board of the ship's rail and electronic tracking devices are also available. This equipment, however, is far too expensive for the operators of most of the small ships that constitute pirates' most common prey.

The alternative is to allow ships' crews to exercise their right of self-defence. Almost nobody wants this to happen.[46] Many states place severe restrictions on what arms can be carried (if any) while the ISPS Code demands that any arms on board be declared when entering a port. The primary purpose of carrying arms would be to deter. If, however, the crews laid down their arms and surrendered then the concept of arming crew would lose credibility.[47] If fire were exchanged—particularly across an in-

---

43   'Jakarta proposes Straits' safety fund', *The Star Online*, 2 Oct. 2006.

44   S. Ramesh, 'Malaysia, Indonesia and Singapore set up cooperative mechanism', *ChannelNewsAsia*, 4 Sept. 2007. The suggestion was quickly made that this might provide a model for other coastal areas: Marcus Hand, 'Framework could be copied in other regions', *Lloyd's List*, 7 Sept. 2007. The UN has suggested that this mechanism could also enable user states and the shipping industry to be involved and 'make contributions': 'UN-backed project to boost safety, security in vital Malacca shipping lane', UN News Service, 18 Sept. 2007. In May 2008 the three littoral states announced the inauguration of the Cooperative Mechanism for the Straits of Malacca and Singapore. 'Malaysia, Singapore and Indonesia implement cooperative mechanism to safeguard Straits'. *Bernama*, 27 May 2008.

45   John M. Glionna, 'A friendly voice, when pirates strike', *LA Times*, 13 Nov. 2006. See also Janet Porter, 'Maersk on course to tackle piracy', *Lloyd's List*, 22 Jan. 2008.

46   Clarence Fernandez, 'World body opposes weapons on ships to fight piracy', *Reuters AlertNet*, 19 Sept. 2006. The current IMO guidance is contained in IMO. MSC/Circ.623/Rev.3, 29 May 2002, p. 9 available at http://www.imo.org/includes/blast_bindoc.asp?doc_id=941&format=PDF. For a contrary view, albeit confined to cruise ships, see Nigel A. Collett, 'Firearms and piracy: The case for a change in practice', *Seaways*, Jan. 2007, pp. 15-17.

47   Steven W. Haines, 'Criminal violence at sea: Observations on the threat and

ternational border from one jurisdiction to another—the legal difficulties would worsen and multiply if there were fatalities. There are practical difficulties too: time would need to be set aside for training which would need to be repeated regularly if the crew were not to become more of a danger to themselves than to any pirate who attempted to get on board. Nor do merchant crewmen want to deal with the tiresome business of declaring the arms they are carrying every time they visit a port. They no longer see themselves as fighters.

Nonetheless, some of the fishing boats operating illegally off Somalia are clearly armed and in South East Asia some ship owners—particularly the owners of vulnerable vessels such as tugs, barges, dredgers and oil rigs under tow—are reported to have taken matters into their own hands and contracted with private security companies (PSCs) to provide either on-board armed guards or escort vessels.[48] These companies assert that their presence alone, whether it is in the form of an on-board guard force or a clearly identifiable escort vessel, is sufficient to deter pirates.[49] To date at least there is nothing in the public domain to show that this belief has ever been tested.[50] Pottengal Mukundan of the IMB has reportedly said that he believes guards, armed or not, have only a limited deterrent effect, although they have apparently been employed successfully by Filipino tuna fishermen to deter pirates from stealing their catches. Little is known about the companies' actual activities, as compared with their claims and press rumours.

However, in a letter to the *Jakarta Post*, the managing director of Background Asia Risk Solutions (BARS) provided some detail. He explained that his company concentrated on route planning, the provision of early warning to the appropriate authorities if an attack occurred and the execution of unspecified "measured tactics and strategies to suppress the attack", actions that would presumably be in line with the right to self-defence, while waiting for the authorities' response. Companies also appear to be in-

appropriate responses' in B.A.H. Parritt (ed.), *Violence at Sea*, Paris: ICC Publishing, 1986, pp. 99-100.

48   With regard to Somalia see 'Battle against illegal fishing off east Africa's coast', *The Economist*, 3rd August 2006. For a useful introduction to PSC operations in Southeast Asia see Carolin Liss, 'Private security companies in the fight against piracy in Asia', Perth, Western Australia: Murdoch University, *Working Paper no. 120*, June 2005.

49   *Ibid.*, p. 6.

50   Mark J. Valencia, 'Mercenaries in the Strait of Malacca', *The Jakarta Post*, 28 July 2005..

volved in risk assessment, crew training, the recovery of hijacked vessels and their crews, and fishery protection.[51] One commentator has suggested that the various PSCs appear to have performed successfully and therefore, to a degree at least, are operating in cooperation with the states bordering the Malacca Straits, the Java Sea and around the southern Philippines.[52] Given the questions that have been raised about their activities, this is certainly the message that various companies have endeavoured to put across. Singapore has admitted that it has licensed a small number of companies to operate in its waters which, because it only claims a three-mile territorial limit, are very small, but Malaysia and Indonesia have not.[53] The two countries initially issued stern warnings against such practices but their subsequent responses, particularly those of Malaysia, became less rigid in the light of the concerns being expressed by the often internationally-owned companies operating vulnerable shipping in the region.[54] The pattern now appears to be that these states are "informed" about planned operations, money changes hands and "permission" is granted, though rarely in writing.[55] The essence is discretion. Malaysian authorities reacted angrily to two articles about PSC operations that appeared in the *Straits Times* in April 2005 and the discovery in May of that year that one PSC, Glenn Defense Marine, had conducted an exercise on board its ship the *Glenn Braveheart* while it

51   Liss, 'Private security companies', p. 3; see also 'Private navies combat Malacca Strait pirates', *WorldNetDaily,* 31 July 2005.

52   Ian Barclay, 'Private sector helps ease piracy fears in Malacca Strait', *Lloyd's List,* 4 July 2006.

53   Karl Malakunas, 'Armed escorts in high demand at sea', *The Peninsula* (Qatar), 12 May 2005; Sira Habibu and Nik Khusairi Ibrahim, 'Shocker over private armies patrolling straits', *Lloyd's List,* 22 Dec. 2005.

54   Malakunas, 'Armed escorts'; 'Armed escort boats to be detained', *Bernama. com,* 26 April 2005; 'Malaysia warns Straits gun guards', *The Standard,* 28 April 2005; 'Indonesia rules out private armed escorts in Malacca Strait', *Bloomberg.com,* 2 May 2005; 'Malaysia warns on private marine escorts', *MarineLog. com,* 2 May 2005; '3 Malacca Strait govts weigh allowing ships to carry arms', *Straits Times,* 15 May 2005; Marcus Hand, 'Malaysian premier rejects private armed escorts in Malacca Strait', *Lloyd's List,* 23 May 2005 and Sharidan M. Ali, 'Secure passage via Straits', *The Star Online,* 21 Aug. 2006. See also Graham Gerard Ong, 'A case for armed guards on ships', *Straits Times,* 26 May 2005 and Morten Hansen, 'Security in maritime Southeast Asia: Private solutions to public problems', IDSS *Commentaries,* 4 May 2005.

55   Carolin Liss, 'Maritime security in Southeast Asia: between a rock and a hard place?' Murdoch University, Asia Research Centre *Working Paper no. 141,* Feb. 2007, p. 18.

was moored in Malaysia's most important port, Port Klang.[56] The company immediately suspended operations pending "clarification".[57] Within a matter of days Malaysia conceded that provided such companies abided by the requirements of the international straits regime it had no authority to control the operations of PSCs in international waters, but was nonetheless only willing to allow them to "pass through" Malaysia's territorial waters under strict conditions.[58]

Permissive political environment. To flourish, piracy requires not only weak law but also lax law enforcement.[59] This laxity is almost always the consequence of state weakness. In the absence of a hegemonic power this has been the normal condition on the high seas throughout most of human history.

Most conflicts cause refugee flows. The Vietnam War was no exception. When it ended in the mid-1970s it left behind a permissive environment that ended in tragedy. The imposition of Communist rule in 1975 led people to flee Vietnam. Many left by sea, so many, in fact, that they became know as the "boat people".[60] The international response—driven largely by guilt—was initially sympathetic but while they were at sea the refugees were sailing in a political vacuum. From almost the very beginning those fleeing what had been South Vietnam were preyed upon by pirates. This predation was well known but no systematic attempt was made to suppress it. The Socialist Republic of Vietnam had unequivocal standing in international law to act, or to ask others to act, to protect its citizens but did nothing, although it took vigorous action if pirates attempted to use its own territorial waters.[61] That said, Communist navy boats did commit acts

56   David Boey, 'Ship owners using hired guns', *Straits Times,* 8 April 2005; Tracey Sua, 'For hire: Guardians of the sea', *Straits Times,* 15 April 2005; Catherine Zara Raymond, conversation with author, Sept. 2006. Also Marcus Hand, 'Malaysian premier rejects private armed escorts'.

57   Malakunas, 'Armed escorts in high demand at sea'.

58   R. Corrigan, 'Malaysia to allow armed escorts in Malacca Strait', *Sea Watch,* May/June 2005, p. 14.

59   A point confirmed by Pottengal Mukundan in his interview with the author, April 2004.

60   See, for example, Bruce Grant, *The Boat People: An 'Age' Investigation,* Harmondsworth: Penguin, 1979; Nghia M. Vo, *The Vietnamese Boat People, 1954 and 1975-1992,* Jefferson, NC & London: McFarland & Co., 2006; Scott McKenzie, 'Vietnam's boat people: 25 years of fears, hopes and dreams', *CNN.com,* ND; Martin Woollacott, 'The Boat People', *The Guardian,* 3 Dec. 1977.

61   Vo, *The Vietnamese Boat People,* p. 144.

of piracy.[62] Other states had no standing to act directly.[63] As the willingness of Western states to resettle victims declined, so the nations of Southeast Asia became less receptive to the victims' plight.[64] Malaysia and Singapore gained a notorious reputation for turning boats away.[65] The attitude of the Thai authorities could best be described as ambivalent. On the one hand they tried to house the refugees and aid their resettlement.[66] On the other, while it might be true that investigations were hampered by an apparent code of silence in tightly knit fishing communities,[67] passivity on the part of the police, navy and judiciary at the national level led to speculation that the pirates might have benefited from some form of semi-official sanction.[68] By 1980, for example, courts in Thailand were handing down three-day prison sentences to fishermen who tried to help the refugees by towing their boats to shore.[69] Even though many boats sneaked past the patrols on their second attempt, some were forced back into the arms of pirates who saw profit in robbery, pleasure in brutal and often repeated rape, and escape from the consequences of what they had done in wholesale murder.[70]

This evil episode started quietly enough. Most of the pirates were Thai fishermen. That does not mean that these men were transformed from innocents to criminals overnight. Nor is it meant to imply that most fishermen are pirates or potential pirates; more often they are victims.[71] None-

---

62   Nhat Tien, Duong Phuc and Vu Thanh Thuy, *Pirates on the Gulf of Siam: Report from the Vietnamese Boat People Living in the Refugee Camp in Songkhla, Thailand*, San Diego: Boat People SOS Committee, 1981, p. 33.

63   J.L. Anderson, 'Piracy and World History', p. 98.

64   Grant, *The Boat People*, p. 63.

65   *Ibid.*, p. 63; Nhat Tien, *et al.*, *Pirates on the Gulf of Siam*, pp. 57-8; 'Save us! Save us!' *TIME*, 9 July 1979.

66   Tien, *Ibid.*, p. 57.

67   John McBeth, 'Thailand's part-timers in terror', *FEER*, 1 Feb. 1980, p. 27

68   Grant, *The Boat People*, p. 64; Nhat Tien, *et al.*, *Pirates on the Gulf of Siam*, pp. 51 & 53; Eklöf, *Pirates in Paradise*, pp. 26-7 & 30.

69   'Piratical murders and rape at sea', *TIME*, 9 Nov. 1981.

70   'Facing a 'Liquid Auschwitz', TIME, vol. 114, no. 1, 2 July 1979; '71 boat people feared dead in pirate attack off Malaysia', *New York Times*, 9 Aug. 1989. The "push-offs" apparently gave the signal that it was permissible to attack the Vietnamese boats with even greater violence. Murray Hiebert. 'Sink or swim?' *FEER*, 23 February 1989.

71   I.G. Hyslop in 'Contemporary Piracy', in Ellen, *Piracy at Sea*, p. 16 reports that 'Thai fishermen have been accused of attacking, and in some cases throwing overboard, Malay and Bangladeshi fishermen - several hundred disappeared in recent years...Thai fishermen are themselves victims of violent attacks–some-

theless, in Southeast Asia generally, the distinctions between fishermen, smugglers, illegal traders and pirates can be blurred and the exercise of extreme violence is not uncommon.[72] In the beginning fishermen came to the assistance of the refugees, who often set sail in boats that were barely seaworthy. Once the rumour spread that they had dollars, valuables and even gold on the board—and the refugees sometimes paid in a form of beaten gold called "*tael*" because they had no Thai currency—then, starting around the second half of 1979, the attacks began.[73] Even then Jack Bailey, an ex-US Army colonel who headed a rescue operation, estimated that only 300 vessels, around two per cent of the Thai fishing fleet, became involved.[74] Fishing boats working alone became groups of two or three boats working together using radio to coordinate their assaults, often by forming rings perhaps ten miles in diameter which closed once a refugee boat had entered the trap.[75] The evidence of radios and radar, larger boats and automatic weapons suggested to Bailey that as early as 1980 the pirates were becoming professional and, moreover, enjoyed the protection of corrupt local officials.[76] In June 1979 a US estimate suggested that just under a third of all refugee boats were attacked, but only a few years later another estimate suggested that this proportion had grown to two-thirds.[77] Some boats were boarded more than once; in one well-documented case a boat was attacked ten times, several were attacked 24 times and there is a record of one boat being attacked 47 times.[78]

The pirates turned the uninhabited Ko Kra Island, about 55 miles (80 kms) off the Thai mainland, into a dumping ground for their victims to which they returned repeatedly for orgies of rape.[79] The suggestion has

times by Kampuchean, or other, pirates, and sometimes by Vietnamese government forces'.

72   Grant, *The Boat People*, p. 64.

73   Vo, *The Vietnamese Boat People*, p. 142; Grant, *Ibid*, p. 63; Roger Villar. *Piracy Today: Robbery and Violence at Sea since 1980*. London: Conway Maritime Press, 1985, pp. 33-6.

74   Eklöf, *Pirates in Paradise*, pp. 18-19.

75   Vo, *The Vietnamese Boat People*, p. 143; Grant, *The Boat People*, p. 65.

76   Eklöf, *Pirates in Paradise*, p. 24; Bernard D. Nossiter, 'Thai piracy against boat people seems relentless', *New York Times*, 7 May 1980.

77   Grant, *The Boat People*, p. 65.

78   Vo, *The Vietnamese Boat People*, p. 144; Grant, *The Boat People*, p. 65; Nhat Tien et al., *Pirates on the Gulf of Siam*, pp. 53-4. Also James P. Sterba, 'The Agony of Vietnam Refugee Boat 0105', *New York Times*, 25 July 1979.

79   Nhat Tien et al., *Pirates on the Gulf of Siam*, pp. 8-14, 27-9, 32-5, 71-3 &

been made that this was a deliberate ploy designed to demean the women and prepare them for a life in Bangkok's brothels,[80] to which an unknown number were sold.[81] One victim of multiple rapes ran into the long grass to escape her tormentors. Unwilling to search for her they set the grass alight. She preferred to burn rather than surrender.[82] On more than one occasion, Thai police and naval vessels passed by and even anchored without responding to the refugees' pleas for help.[83] In at least one case the crews came ashore, forced the refugees to strip naked and then left.[84] Reportedly after 1982 and the introduction of UNHCR-initiated anti-piracy measures, the number of attacks declined but the violence only became worse, common enough for the acronym "RMP", which stood for "raping, murdering and pillaging", to appear regularly on US case histories.[85] Engines were sabotaged; holes were smashed in hulls and often, once the pirates had returned to their own boat, they turned it around and rammed it into the refugees' craft to make sure it sank.[86] The killing, in other words, had become premeditated.[87] By 1989 the suspicion was that hard-core criminals with possible wider connections to organised crime had replaced or were now working in league with the professional pirates and what remained of the fishermen pirates.[88] The whole shameful episode ended not as a result of state action but because the prey stopped coming.

When and where such permissive environments exist within states and their territorial waters, therefore, they generally come about either because the political environment is corrupt locally or nationally and allows illegal activity to take place for its benefit; or because law enforcement is under-

81-7; Henry Kamm, 'Thai pirates kill 70 'boat people'', *New York Times*, 11 Jan. 1980.

80   Eklöf, *Pirates in Paradise*, p. 23.

81   *Ibid.*

82   Douglas Stewart, *The Brutal Seas: Organised Crime at Work*, Bloomington, IN and Milton Keynes, UK: Author House, 2006, p. 281.

83   Vo, *The Vietnamese Boat People*, pp. 147-8; McBeth, 'Thailand's part-timers in terror'.

84   Nhat Tien *et al.*, *Pirates on the Gulf of Siam*, p. 11.

85   Vo, *The Vietnamese Boat People*, p. 144; Grant, *The Boat People*, p. 65.

86   Vo, *The Vietnamese Boat People*, p. 151; Grant, *The Boat People*, p. 66; Nhat Tien *et al.*, *Pirates on the Gulf of Siam*, pp. 10, 27 & 54.

87   Vo, *The Vietnamese Boat People*, p. 151.

88   *Ibid.*, p. 150; Conway, *The Piracy Business*, pp. 17 & 89-90; Eklöf, *Pirates in Paradise*, p. 24.

funded and lacks the resources to deal with it. Often, of course, both conditions apply simultaneously. Because the police are under-funded (which usually means under-paid) they connive with criminals in order to make a living. Whatever the reason, a supportive, criminal infrastructure can develop which is able to feed pirate groups with intelligence and equipment, and dispose of stolen goods, and even entire cargoes, if necessary.[89]

Corrupt law enforcement officials are a feature of all areas affected by piracy. They are certainly a problem in Thailand, the Philippines and even parts of Malaysia along the Malacca Straits and Sabah, where local fishermen are regularly confronted by demands for money or fish. There is a suspicion that some fishermen fail to report attacks because they are fearful the police are involved and might well take revenge.[90] However, the jurisdiction with the most notorious reputation currently is Indonesia. Elements of the Indonesian police and navy have been involved in piracy for years but the central authorities have ignored the problem. To take one example: everyone in Belakang Padang knows who the pirates are but the police have no interest in arresting them. On the contrary the police are, according to Eric Frécon, "not only tolerant of the criminal activities of the pirates but…also accomplices and act as bodyguards."[91] The Indonesian authorities appear to give the impression that they are prepared to tolerate small-scale piracy, and even piracy on a larger scale if it has sufficient political protection, providing it is not linked to insurrectionist groups such as GAM. A stance perhaps best encapsulated by the daughter of the central government official responsible for Belakang Padang, who married the leader of a pirate gang.[92]

Cultural acceptability. Piracy can only take root in areas with a maritime tradition and the skills that go with it, an important fact that is often over-

---

89   Examples can be drawn from around the world: on China see, for example, Chanda, 'Foot in the water'; Jon Vagg, 'Rough seas?' pp. 63-80, and on the *Anna Sierra* case, Samuel Pyeatt Menefee,. *TMV* Jane's SR. Coulsdon: Jane's Information Group, 1996, p. 72; on Indonesia see, for example, Michael Richardson, 'Crackdown on piracy', *Asia-Pacific Defence Reporter* Oct.-Nov. 1992, and on military involvement in particular, Huxley, *Disintegrating Indonesia?* p. 82; on Brazil see, for example, Gottschalk & Flanagan, *Jolly Roger with an Uzi*, pp. 60 & 62; on West Africa see *ibid.*, p. 64 and Hyslop, 'Contemporary Piracy', pp. 8-10.

90   Liss, 'Maritime security in Southeast Asia', p. 6.

91   Langit-Dursin, 'Indonesia key to end piracy in Malacca Straits'.

92   Frécon, 'Piracy and armed robbery at sea along the Malacca Straits', pp. 74-5 and 'Pirates set the Straits on fire', pp. 27-8.

looked. Trading patterns are one factor that helps to determine this accept-ability: it is possible that piracy has deeper roots in Southeast Asia than in West Africa because important trading routes have bisected Southeast Asian archipelagos for centuries, making piracy there a way of life that has been established for generations, often on a clan or family basis.[93] For example, in the Tausug communities of the Sulu archipelago that stretches between the southern Philippines and Borneo, piracy "was encouraged among the men, and associated with highly regarded virtues".[94] The maritime expertise of the Tamil Tigers, who have probably engaged in piracy to support their insurgency, is founded on a centuries-old Tamil maritime trading tradition based on the port of Velvettiturai.[95] The Riau-Lingga archipelago, which lies a short distance south of Singapore, is a notorious piracy centre today but it has been one since long before the colonial powers arrived in the early nineteenth century.[96] In some communities, however, where every-one knows everyone else's business or where intimidation prevails, drawing the line between social acceptability and social peace might be difficult.[97]

The promise of reward. No opportunity, however great, would be exploit-ed without the promise of reward, and piracy can be "a highly lucrative venture", as the OECD points out.[98] The buccaneers preferred cash; most modern pirates prefer the same. Reward is relative, and sums that might appear paltry to people on even moderately comfortable incomes in the West are well worth the risks involved to the people from the pirate com-munities involved. There are numerous reports from all around the world of paint being stolen from lockers and rope from decks. Jon Vagg, how-ever, analysed the *cash* takings from 83 pirate attacks in Indonesian waters

---

93   See Menefee, *TMV*, p. 132 on the existence of 'pirate societies' in South East Asia, the Red Sea and—arguably—the Caribbean; the societal acceptability of piracy in South East Asia has been noted by several writers including Vagg, 'Rough seas?' pp. 67-8; Hyslop, 'Contemporary piracy', pp. 12 & 28 and Pugh, 'Is Mahan still alive?' p. 2. Stefan Eklöf, on the other hand, argues that the roots of Riau piracy lie in recent, rapid social and economic change driven by the expansion of global capitalism: Eklöf, *Pirates in Paradise,* p. 58.

94   Eklöf, *Ibid.,* p. 41.

95   Anthony Davis, 'Tiger international: How a secret global network keeps Sri Lanka's Tamil guerrilla organization up and killing', *Asiaweek,* 26 July 1996.

96   On the history of Riau-Lingga piracy see Ger Teitler, 'Piracy in Southeast Asia: A historical comparison', *MAST,* vol. 1, no. 1, 2002, p. 69; for a description of Riau-Lingga piracy more recently see Vagg, 'Rough seas?' pp. 69-74.

97   Frécon, 'Pirates set the Straits on fire', p. 25.

98   OECD, *Security in Maritime Transport,* p. 14.

over the 1991-92 period (there is little reason to believe that, apart from inflation, the value of the rewards have changed greatly since the time of the study): attackers in 21 cases got away with nothing, 35 made off with between $100 and $5,000 while 22 got their hands on sums ranging from $5,000 to over $20,000. His analysis suggests that in at least 30 per cent of cases pirates got away with over $1,000, which even if split amongst a gang, was a good return for a night's activity in a country where the 1991 per capita income was $638.[99] In 1997, during the Asian financial crisis, a factory worker on Batam in Indonesia could earn around $320 per month with overtime. On the basis of one pirate's confession in 1993 in which he claimed to earn around $270 for his part in a pirate raid, the Swedish academic Stefan Eklöf estimates that by 1997 it was reasonable to assume a gang member could expect to take home between $500 and $700 from each attack.[100]

As noted earlier, these cash thefts can be supplemented by the sale of portable equipment from the ship such as binoculars, DVD players, radio and radar sets, plus whatever valuables the pirates may find on the crew personally and in their quarters, such as jewellery and watches. Peter Chalk has suggested that on the basis of this wider "take" the average now is more like $10,000.[101] On the same basis Mark Valencia has quoted a figure of between $5,000 and $15,000.[102] In fact, one of the reasons why the number of pirate attacks, particularly against large international carriers, might be dropping but the seriousness of the attacks against other craft might be increasing is that, in direct response to the theft of money from ships' safes, large ships now carry much less cash than they once did. Shipping companies and ships' captains have now joined other travellers and put their trust in the international banking system and the ubiquity of the credit card.[103]

---

99   Vagg, 'Rough seas?' pp. 73-4.

100   Eklöf, *Pirates in Paradise,* pp. 100-1.

101   Chalk, interview with author, Aug. 2004. Also Anthony Davis, 'Piracy in Southeast Asia shows signs of increased organisation', *Jane's IR,* vol. 16, no. 6, June 2004, p. 38, where he quotes Noel Choong of the PRC suggesting a range of $10-20,000.

102   Mark J. Valencia, 'Piracy and terrorism in Southeast Asia: Similarities, differences and their implications' in Derek Johnson and Mark Valencia. *Piracy in Southeast Asia: Status, Issues and Responsibilities.* Singapore: ISEAS, 2005, p. 80.

103   P. Mukundan, interview with author, 2005; Stefan Eklöf, 'Piracy: Real menace or red herring?' *Asia Times Online,* 4 Aug. 2005; *Latitudes,* vol. 33, Oct. 2003,

However, the pickings only become really rich when the pirates take over a ship entirely (hijackings) and sell the cargo. These thefts can be bulk cargoes such as oil and petroleum products, which are often siphoned off into another tanker, or the contents of shipping containers about which pirates often appear to have prior knowledge. Ship hijackings have been a feature of Southeast Asian piracy. The alternative is to kidnap and ransom the crew, which has been the principal objective of the most active Somali pirates.

In the end, pirates are criminals and while the tone might be sneering the assessment of Gray and his colleagues is correct: "For most, piracy is a low-risk, high-paying job when compared to other lines of work they qualify for".[104]

What types of ship are attacked?

It is natural that the press should report attacks on large ships. Unfortunately this gives the impression that large vessels on international voyages are the pirates' prime targets. They are not. Attacks on such ships in such circumstances certainly occurred during the 1990s, particularly in Southeast Asia, but few have taken place more recently, perhaps because when they pass through known pirate areas now they do so in a state of high alert. Nonetheless, because crew numbers have been reduced large ships remain vulnerable.[105] Smaller crews mean more work for those who remain, which in turn leads to higher levels of fatigue.[106] When large

---

p. 26.

104 Jim Gray, Mark Monday and Gary Stubblefield. *Maritime Terror: Protecting Yourself, Your Vessel and Your Crew against Piracy.* Boulder: Sycamore Island Books, 1999, p. 11.

105 Chalk, 'Maritime terrorism in the contemporary era: Threat and potential future contingencies' in *The MIPT Terrorism Annual, 2006,* Oklahoma City: National Memorial Institute for the Prevention of Terrorism, pp. 22-3.

106 The House of Commons Transport Committee refers to the UK Department for Transport, Maritime Accident Investigation Branch 2004 annual report which points to fatigue rates at 'elevated levels' and various poor working practices that are all 'classic symptoms of fatigue': House of Commons Transport Committee, *Piracy,* p. 21. On the problems created by the reduction in crew numbers see also Roger Villar, *Piracy Today,* p. 11 and Chalk, 'Threats to the maritime environment: Piracy and terrorism', *Presentation to RAND Stakeholder Consultation,* 28-30 Oct., 2002, p. 5. One ship-owner even complained of the additional cost of paying crews to stand extra watches. Michael Vatikiotis and James Bartholomew, 'Raiders of Riau: Alarming surge in attacks on shipping', *FEER,* vol. 155, no. 26, 2 July 1992, p. 14.

ships are attacked pirates in the Straits and elsewhere seem to favour bulk carriers, probably because they have low freeboards (that is to say there is a short distance between the waterline and the deck).[107]

Despite this vulnerability, pirates on the whole prefer to attack smaller ships. A study of actual attacks in the Malacca Straits between 2000 and 2005 showed a general reduction in assaults on ships above 20,000 GRT.[108] Tug and barge combinations appeared to be particularly vulnerable.[109] The crews of smaller ships also tended to be more at risk from kidnapping. During the period of the study, 26 abductions took place on smaller vessels compared with five on vessels over 1,000 GRT.[110]

The study also highlighted the fact that most attacks are on local craft rather than on international vessels passing through the area.[111] This pattern accords with historical experience: the majority of victims of Malay piracy were generally local people or merchants from China and Indochina. In 1824, which was a year when pirates were particularly active, only one British ship was attacked. During the 1840s, when around a dozen British ships were reported lost to pirates, seven were looted after they ran aground and the rest simply lost without trace.[112] Even during the period at the end of the eighteenth century, when the south China coast was under the sway of pirate "confederations", European opium ships, which were rich prizes, were avoided because they were better armed,

---

107   Bateman *et al.*, 'Safety and security in the Malacca and Singapore Straits', , p. 22; Thomas Turner, 'Bulk carriers 'top of pirate hit list'', *Lloyd's List,* 9 May 2006; on the particular vulnerability of ships with low freeboards see, for example, Hunter, 'The growing threat of modern piracy', p. 72 and Burnett, *Dangerous Waters*, p. 119-33, who recounts the sometimes ludicrous measures crews take to minimise it.

108   Sam Bateman *et al.,* 'Sea Lane Security', p. 22. The study did not, however, indicate how small ships needed to be before they no longer interested pirates. In his study Mark C. Farley suggests the great majority of attacks were against commercial vessels over 500 tons: Farley, 'International and regional trends in maritime piracy, 1989-1993', Monterey: Naval Postgraduate School, Masters Thesis, 1993, p. 12. During the second quarter of 2000, 20 per cent of the attacks on vessels in Southeast Asia occurred against medium-sized ships (i.e. up to 10,000 GRT) or large ships (i.e. over 20,000 GRT): Jane Chan and Joshua Ho. 'Report on armed robbery and piracy in Southeast Asia, 2nd Quarter 2007', S. Rajaratnam School of International Studies, Maritime Security Programme, ND.

109   'Worrying trend as pirates turn attention to tugs', *Lloyd's List,* 11 Dec. 2006.

110   Sam Bateman *et al.* 2006, *ibid.,* p. 21.

111   *Ibid.,* p. 22.

112   Anderson. 'Piracy and world history', pp. 92-3 and note 49, p. 103.

and although some European ships were attacked the pirates preferred to prey upon the more numerous and poorer, but relatively defenceless, local craft.[113]

Methods of attack and boarding

Attacks against ships at anchor demand the ability to approach ships quietly. Attacks mounted when ships are underway at sea clearly require additional skills. The perpetrators need to be able to approach ships undetected and then board them while they are still moving. Mark Farley, a lieutenant commander in the US Navy who analysed Office of Naval Intelligence (ONI) data on piracy from 1989 to 1993, found that stationary ships were boarded successfully over 90 per cent of the time and that figure dropped to 62 per cent when ships were underway.[114]

The most vulnerable vessels are those that move slowly, have low freeboards, and because of size or draft restrictions are unable to manoeuvre freely. Pirates in Southeast Asia, although their religious observance appears to be slight, prefer to avoid attacking during Ramadan and when the moon is full. According to the accounts given to Frécon, they often drink and even take morphine before leaving to dull the sense of danger.[115] If this is insufficient, many of them also believe that local spirits can make them invisible or even immune to bullets.[116] They tend to depart their villages at around 20.00 and return around 02.00. They often blend into the nocturnal fishing fleets by fishing, or pretending to fish, as they size up the situation.[117]

The most common boarding method, and certainly the one that is practiced most frequently in Southeast Asia, is to approach to the stern of a ship using a fast boat. In Southeast Asia this is usually a small fishing boat, called a *pancung* in Indonesia, often equipped with more than one outboard motor and crewed by seven or eight men, which because of its weight and

---

113   *Ibid.*, pp. 97-8.

114   Farley, 'International and regional trends in maritime piracy', p. 23. He also noticed that whether ships were stationary or not over 80 per cent of successful boardings took place at night, compared with 40 per cent during the day. This might have changed as pirates have become more willing to use firearms to stop ships.

115   Frécon, 'Pirates set the Straits on fire', p. 35.

116   Frécon, 'Piracy and armed robbery at sea along the Malacca Straits', pp. 79-80; also Gwin, 'Dark passage', p. 139.

117   Frécon, 'Pirates set the Straits on fire', p. 35 and 'Piracy and armed robbery at sea along the Malacca Straits', p. 79.

shape is able to cut through a ship's wake unlike lighter, fibreglass boats.[118] If the target is equipped with radar this exploits the radar "blind-spot" (called "sector blanking") caused by the ship's funnel. However, because most pirate craft are not metal-hulled and are easily lost by radar amidst the wave clutter, this approach is more likely dictated by the lower freeboard at the stern of favoured vessels, while the curve of the ship's hull at this point hides the pirates from sight once they are alongside. A grappling device made from metal or shaped from a mangrove root is attached to a rope or more of-ten a long bamboo pole (or poles lashed together), which when hooked over the stern rail allows the pirates to pull themselves up.[119] The disadvantage with this approach is that the turbulence associated with the ship's screw can make any approach and subsequent station holding extremely difficult and hazardous.[120] Boardings have been known to take place at speeds of up to 18 knots.[121] A variation on this approach is to drive a boat against the side of a ship. When this is done a vacuum is created and the pirate boat holds fast to the ship's side. But there is danger in this method too, for if the ship rolls heavily it can turn the boat over.[122] An alternative, which was only been used infrequently because of the risks involved, and only in Southeast Asia when boats lacked the power to catch and then hold station with a moving vessel, was to position two boats either side of the bow of an approaching ship and, by stringing a cable between two, allow the ship's momentum to draw the boats against the hull which was again scaled using long poles or ropes.[123]

118   Robert Stuart. *In Search of Pirates: A Modern-Day Odyssey in the South China Sea*. Edinburgh and London: Mainstream Publishing, 2002, p. 194; Gwin. 'Dark passage', p. 146.

119   Frécon, 'Piracy and armed robbery at sea along the Malacca Straits', p. 79. The pirate Gwin interviewed claimed he and his companions (who described them-selves as 'jumping squirrels') used this method to put five men aboard a ship in a minute: Gwin, 'Dark passage', pp. 146-7.

120   Rupert Herbert-Burns, 'Compound piracy at sea in the early twenty-first cen-tury: A tactical to operational-level perspective on contemporary, multiphase piratical methodology"' in Peter Lehr (ed.), *Violence at Sea: Piracy in the Age of Terrorism*, New York: Routledge, 2007, p. 106; Gwin, 'Dark passage', p. 147 reports that because the whole gang depend on the skill of the '*tekong*' who pilots the boat, he is paid the largest share of the money.

121   IMB, 'Special piracy report', June 1992, p. 8.

122   Stuart, *In Search of Pirates*, p. 195.

123   Anthony Davis, 'Piracy in Southeast Asia shows signs of increased organisation', p. 38. For an example of this tactic see NGA ASAM 2003-194, 30 May 2003; also Herbert-Burns, 'Compound piracy at sea in the early twenty-first century', p. 106.

Scaling a ship's side is not easy. For this reason most boardings of this type are undertaken at night and in calm conditions.[124]

To circumvent these restrictions more direct and violent methods, which to some observers suggested some form of military training, have become increasingly common. The first has been used in parts of Southeast Asia: the use of multiple, fast-moving boats that weave in front and around a target in an attempt to distract the watch-keepers and force the ship to slow down sufficiently for other members of the gang to board the ship using grappling hooks. The second has been used in Southeast Asia and Somalia: the use or threat of gunfire aimed at the bridge to force ships to stop and lower a ladder. Herbert-Burns makes the point that small calibre weapons would be unlikely to penetrate steel or the armoured glass of bridge windows (but could be sufficiently intimidating to achieve the desired effect), which would require either heavy-calibre machine guns or rocket-propelled grenades; and pirates have used both types of weapons, off Somalia in particular. However, firing any sort of weapon from a moving boat with any accuracy is extremely difficult.[125] One major incident occurred in 2003 when 50 pirates in two boats armed with assault rifles fired on the Taiwanese-registered *MV Dong Yih* for two hours in the Malacca Strait off Aceh in an attempt to force it to stop. They failed; the 2,600-ton ship loaded with fish escaped, although the captain was wounded and over 100 bullets had riddled the superstructure.[126]

The cost of piracy

No systematic study of the cost of piracy has been undertaken.[127] Accurate assessment is made difficult by the lack of standard measures or even definitions. This makes it hard to know what is being included in any calculation

124   Herbert-Burns, 'Compound piracy at sea in the early twenty-first century', p. 107.

125   *Ibid,*, p. 110.

126   *Ibid.*, p. 109; also Melody Chen, 'Captain tells pirate story', *Taipei Times,* 12 Aug. 2003 and Rupert Herbert-Burns and Lauren Zucker, 'Drawing the line between piracy and maritime terrorism', *Jane's IR,* vol. 16, no. 9, Sept. 2004, p. 33.

127   Peter Chalk: 'No empirical work has been done on the cost of piracy, certainly in comparison with the cost of suppression.' Interview with author, Aug. 2004. According to a leading insurer, '…there are no reliable figures documenting the economic consequences': 'Piracy-threat at sea: A risk analysis', Munich Re Group *Knowledge Series,* 22 Sept. 2006, p. 37.

and what is not.[128] The IMB in a confidential report issued in 1991, comments that it is difficult "to quantify losses incurred by insurers" or even to establish precisely how many ships are involved in maritime crime in Southeast Asia. Furthermore, the "precise number of (phantom ship) incidents is impossible to ascertain with many cases of individual cargo losses being dealt with locally".[129] Therefore estimates vary wildly. Alan Chan, the Managing Director of the Singapore-based Petroships which owned the *Petro Ranger*, a ship hijacked in 1998 on a voyage from Singapore to Vietnam, believes that piracy adds about $500 million to the shipping industry's costs each year as a result of higher insurance premiums, delays and additional on-board security.[130] Chalk suggests that the cost to the shipping industry is at least $1 billion per year.[131] John Burnett, the author of *Dangerous Waters*, cites the estimate of the US-based analyst John Brandon that financial losses from maritime crime amount to as much as $16 billion.[132] Gray, Monday and Stubblefield quote the same figure as Burnett but describe it as the total for piracy and maritime fraud.[133] Gal Luft and Anne Korin also suggest $16 billion but say this covers the loss of ships and cargo and rising insurance charges.[134] The journalist Peter Goodspeed reports a suggested figure of $23 billion. The naval strategist Vijay Sakhuja advances a figure of "some $25 billion" and the Southeast Asian historian James Warren "about $25 billion" as the cost of piracy to the world economy.[135]

---

128   For a discussion of some of these problems see M. Bruyneel, 'Current reports on piracy by the IMO and IMB–a comparison', paper prepared for the People and the Sea II Conference organised by the Centre for Maritime Research (MARE) and the IIAS, Amsterdam, 4-6 Sept. 2003.

129   ICC-IMB, 'Organised maritime crime in the Far East', pp. 9-10.

130   Eric Ellis, 'Piracy on the high seas is on the rise in South-East Asia', *Fortune*, 29 Sept. 2003.

131   Peter Chalk, *Non-Military Security and Global Order: The Impact of Extremism, Violence and Chaos on National and International Security*, London: Macmillan, 2000, p. 50.

132   Burnett, *Dangerous Waters*, p. 70.

133   Gray *et al.*, *Maritime Terror*, p. 1

134   Gal Luft and Anne Korin, 'Terrorism goes to sea', *Foreign Affairs*, vol. 83, no. 6, Nov./Dec. 2004, p. 62.

135   Peter Goodspeed, 'Not since Captain Kidd has piracy been so rife', *National Post*, 3 Aug. 2001; Vijay Sakhuja, 'Sea piracy: India boosts countermeasures', Institute of Peace and Conflict Studies *Article no. 987*, 14 March 2003; James Warren is quoted in Jane McCartney, 'Asian piracy costs $25 bln a year, says expert', *Reuters*, 11 Dec. 2002 and David Osler, 'Global piracy bill hits $25bn'. *Lloyd's List*, 11 December 2002.

The marine lawyer Michael McDaniel suggests the cost of cargo crime and piracy should be combined, which results in a figure closer to $50 billion.[136] By way of comparison estimated losses from cargo theft worldwide range from $30 to $50 billion annually, mostly from trucks.[137]

At the high end at least these figures appear fanciful. The US maritime intelligence specialist Charles Dragonette brands Luft and Korin's estimate as one that "does not stand up to simple arithmetic". According to the IMB there were 445 reported incidents of actual and attempted attacks in the year to which Luft and Korin refer, which, as Dragonette points out, means that the average loss per incident amounts to a preposterous $38 million.[138] The reinsurance company Munich Re report that in 1998 the "reputed average loss per reported attack was in the order of €50,000" (approximately $60,700).[139] In that year the IMB reported 202 actual *and attempted* attacks. Calculating on the basis of Munich Re's "reputed" figure the loss that year amounted to $12.3 million (excluding indirect costs such as contractual penalties or additional crew pay). Even if any of these estimates are accurate the amounts are still miniscule compared to an estimated 2005 total worldwide maritime commerce figure of around $7.8 trillion. On a more limited geographical scale the value of the trade that passes through the Malacca Straits each year has been put at well over $500 billion and is probably nearer $2 trillion. Even an estimate taken on the basis of the worst year (2000) when 75 attacks took place, and doubling this number to allow for unreported cases, suggests—assuming an average "take" of $5,300 per attack—a total loss of only $795,000. This equates to between 0.001 and 0.002 per cent of the value of goods transported through the Straits.[140] If the much higher average "take" of $10,000 is accepted the total loss would still only amount to $1.5 million. During 2007-8, several very large ransom

---

136 Quoted in Robert Malone, 'Dangerous waters', *Forbes.com*, 25 July 2006.

137 OECD, *Security in Maritime Transport*, p. 10.

138 Charles H. Dragonette, 'Lost at sea' (Letter to the Editor), *Foreign Affairs*, vol. 84, no. 2, March/April 2005, p. 175. As Stefan Eklöf points out, however, if the figure is based on the 332 *actual* attacks that were recorded that year, then the average loss figure should be even higher at $48 million: Eklöf, *Pirates in Paradise*, p. 108, note 29.

139 'Piracy-threat at sea: A risk analysis', p. 19.

140 The figure of $5,300 per attack is based on the figure of $5,000 cited in IMB, 'Piracy and armed robbery against ships: A special report', July 1997, p. 29, which was repeated by IMB's Jayant Abhyankar and quoted in Gottschalk and Flanagan, *Jolly Roger with an Uzi*, p. 88, adjusted for inflation over the intervening period. Calculation in Eklöf, *Pirates in Paradise*, p. 99.

payments were reportedly made to recover ships and their crews hijacked in Somalia.[141] Nonetheless, although an individual ship owner with insufficient insurance cover could be ruined by a single large payment if a ship were to be held for ransom and thereby prevented from working for any length of time, the estimated losses for the shipping industry as a whole remain insignificant. As Gottschalk and Flanagan point out, so long as losses remain at this negligible level "businesses engaged in maritime commerce will have little incentive to take the steps necessary to eradicate, or even to seriously combat, the piracy problem".[142]

One reason for the substantial variation among the figures is that analysts disagree about what to include. Counted among the more tangible possible costs are insurance, those relating to delays and re-routing, and increased freight rates.[143] [144] For states that harbour pirates, however unwillingly, there are also the less tangible costs associated with loss of reputation, loss of harbour fees from bunkering services and even cruise ship visits, suppressive measures and environmental damage. Nonetheless, these are merely possibilities: in modern times "no known trade has ceased or been re-routed".[145]

Insurers, in fact, play a crucial, if hidden, role. By spreading the risk and shielding the individual ship-owner, insurance can enable governments to ignore the problem of piracy for longer. On the other hand, the insurance industry can apply pressure swiftly and decisively whenever it believes the

141   For example: 'Official: Pirates were paid $1.2M ransom', *AP,* 27 April 2008.

142   Eklöf, *Pirates in Paradise,* pp. 93-4.

143   Markets can react dramatically following a well-publicised incident such as the 2002 suicide boat attack on the MV *Limburg* in Yemeni waters; according to Neela Banerjee and Keith Bradsher, 'A vulnerable time to be moving oil by sea', *New York Times,* 19 Oct. 2002, insurance rates for tankers passing through Yemeni waters tripled in the aftermath of the attack. However, it is important not to overstate the consequences. As far as insurance is concerned generally, marine underwriters to date have, in the main, been able to treat piracy as a low to medium-level nuisance. See Jonathan Ignarski, 'Piracy, law and marine insurance' in Ellen, *Piracy at Sea,* p. 187. This position appears to be continuing: Vivian Schlesinger, 'Piracy not hitting insurance rates', *Journal of Commerce Online,* 13 Jan. 2003.

144   Dana R. Dillon argues that these increased costs as a result of piracy act as a non-tariff trade barrier. Also the costs of using the most dangerous ports can be sufficiently high to discourage ship-owners from taking cargo there, which is, in effect, a form of economic boycott. Dana R. Dillon, 'Piracy in Asia: A growing barrier to international trade', The Heritage Foundation *Backgrounder,* no. 1379, 22 June 2000, p. 2.

145   Dragonette, 'Lost at sea', p. 174.

risks are becoming unacceptably high; when that has happened in the past it has been insurers who have pressed hardest for action. However, the regularly repeated assertion that piracy leads directly to higher insurance premiums appears to be unsupportable.[146] Although the industry does recognise that piracy is a problem it does not regard it as serious; in fact it does not even account for piracy claims separately. Maritime disorder generally, however, it does see as a serious issue.[147]

Other, less tangible, costs result from the diversion of investment into security and away from more productive activity. There can be diversion into active measures such as electric fences around ships' rails and even armed escorts, or more passive measures such as improved communications and alarms. Looking even more broadly, it is necessary to take into account the disruption to the efficient operation of the economy and the disincentive effect that pirate activity can have on the business community to continue or expand their activities, or for new entrants to come into the market.[148] Once again, all these considerations are largely hypothetical.

One cost that is far from hypothetical is the human cost in terms of numbers killed and traumatised.[149] It must never be forgotten although all too often this appears to be the case.[150] Seafarers even on large ships are apprehensive and even afraid when they pass through pirate-prone areas. Those that have suffered attacks are often unwilling to return to sea.[151] Security is primarily the responsibility of shipping companies but

---

146   *Ibid.*, p. 175.

147   See M.J. Peterson, 'An historical perspective on the incidence of piracy', in Ellen, *Piracy at Sea*, pp. 42-3; also Martin N. Murphy, 'Slow alarm: The response of the marine insurance industry to piracy and maritime terrorism', *Maritime Studies*, no. 148, May/June 2006, pp. 1-14.

148   Anderson, 'Piracy and world history', p. 85.

149   Gottschalk and Flanagan, *Jolly Roger with an Uzi*, pp. 20-1; Eric Ellen, 'Bringing Piracy to Account', *Jane's NI*, April 1997, p. 29. Margaret Ryan, 'Captain counts the cost of piracy', *BBC News*, 2 Feb. 2006. The IMB is reluctant to put a price on piracy because, in its view, it detracts from the real cost—the danger to crews: Pottengal Mukundan, interview with author, April 2004.

150   Interview with Captain John Swain, Dec. 2007. Douglas Stevenson, a director of the Seamen's Church Institute of New York and New Jersey, makes the point that crew members who have been the victims of piracy are compensated for the loss of their belongings but never for the long-term effects of the physical and mental trauma, which although the precise numbers are unknown, can be so severe that they leave the industry: Michael Grey, 'Stevenson says victims of piracy must be offered structured support regime', *Lloyd's List*, 25 May 2007.

151   'Captain tells of fear and loathing on the high sea', *Lloyd's List*, 13 Oct. 2005.

although they have developed defensive procedures and even training, all too often they do not appear to take the problem sufficiently seriously, an attitude which may be based on the fact the ships, cargoes and even crews are insured, which limits any loss. In this the industry appears to share the interests of the littoral and flag states in not addressing the problem with the honesty it demands. Seafarers are due as much protection as everyone else from their own governments and the governments through whose waters they sail. Yet they often do not get it. According to Andrew Linington of NUMAST (now renamed Nautilus following a merger with its Dutch equivalent), between 1995 and the middle of 2006, 3,284 seafarers were held hostage, 617 were threatened on board ship, 463 were injured, 349 were killed, 208 suffered actual assault, 112 were kidnapped or held to ransom and 164 are missing presumed dead.[152] In a subsequent survey conducted among 350 of the union's members in the UK and Denmark, 32 per cent admitted to being "very" concerned and 41 per cent "mildly concerned" about piracy (27 per cent were unconcerned). Unsurprisingly those who were "very" concerned sailed regularly through piracy-prone areas. More alarmingly, 22 per cent had been on a ship that had been involved in a piracy incident or an attempted attack, in some cases more than once.[153] The cost of piracy, in other words, is not purely economic.

State piracy

All the piracy that has been considered up to this point, even privateering, has had a common theme: the desire for financial gain. However, there is another form: the use of maritime depredation by a state for the purposes of policy. Arguably it has occurred, albeit rarely. Because the purpose behind these attacks is not actual or intended robbery (*animus furandi*) they have not been regarded as piracy, as it is a widely held misapprehension that such intention is essential. The issue is again one of "private" versus "public" ends. The writers of the Harvard Draft retained the "private ends" requirement, although they did not define it. Dubner describes their decision as one of "expediency" because it meant that they could avoid such difficult political questions as immunity, asylum, insurgency and belliger-

---

Chalk, *Non-Military Security and Global Order,* p. 66. One concrete example is that of the Master and Chief Engineer of the *Alondra Rainbow.*

152   Andrew Linnington, conversation with author, Aug. 2006..

153   Marcus Hand, 'Survey reveals human cost of piracy', *Lloyd's List,* 14 June 2007.

ency.[154] If the distinction between "private" and "public" is to be eroded then the possibility of state piracy needs to be addressed. It is worth recalling that Kenny, as noted already, defined piracy as any armed violence at sea which is not a lawful act of war.[155] Unfortunately, it is no longer current practice between states to "declare" war. In some cases, what amounts to a state of belligerence is over so quickly that one side is able to amass the force necessary to achieve a limited objective before withdrawing behind inviolable borders or calling in international mediation. Piracy, or at least the simulation of piracy, can enable states to achieve objectives that might otherwise only be attainable through open conflict. The mode of attack could vary between "hit-and-run" tactics and the steady drip of repeated, low-level incidents. The first has been employed and the second has possibly been attempted.

The most famous examples of "hit-and-run" tactics have been the seizure of the USS *Pueblo* by North Korea in 1968 and the seizure of the SS *Mayaguez* by the Khmers Rouges in 1975. In both cases the extent of the territorial limit was an issue. In both cases the United States only recognised a three-mile international limit whereas the coastal states involved both claimed limits of 12 miles.[156] In both cases the US ships were sailing within the territorial limits claimed by the coastal states, limits that were not recognised by the US. The position was complicated further in the case of the *Mayaguez*, as the US did not recognise the Khmers Rouges as the legitimate government of Cambodia. In both cases the ships were accused of spying. In both cases the subsequent view was that, under the current interpretation of international law, neither was an act of piracy as private ends were entirely absent.[157] Under many past interpretations of customary international law they would have been.

A straightforward alternative to the "private ends" requirement is to treat all depredations at sea as piracy unless approved by due authority. It is to be regretted that the International Legal Committee and its successors

---

154   Dubner, *The Law of International Sea Piracy*, pp. 62-3; Dubner, 'Human rights and environmental disaster', pp. 19-20.

155   Cited in Birnie, 'Piracy: Past, present and future', p. 166.

156   Stephen B. Finch, Jr. 'Pueblo and Mayaguez: A legal analysis', *Case Western Reserve Journal of International Law*, vol. 9, 1997, p. 88.

157   Birnie, 'Piracy: Past, present and future', p. 176; Menefee, *TMV*, p. 58. In Paul Wilkinson's view the *Pueblo* hijacking was a 'clear case of state use of international terrorism at sea': Paul Wilkinson, 'Terrorism and the maritime environment' in B.A.H. Parritt (ed.), *Violence at Sea*, Paris: ICC Publishing, 1986, p. 28.

did not choose this formulation, as it is the one that stems most logically from the pirate-privateer distinction. In 1927, for example, the Permanent Court of International Justice held that "the distinctive mark of piracy is independence or rejection of State or equivalent authority". However, this somewhat begs the question of what constitutes due authority. Is it the apparent authority or one that lies behind it, with enough of a gap between the two to allow for plausible deniability? This was the issue raised by the depredations carried out by Chinese maritime police and customs boats in the South China Sea in the 1990s, a history that also illustrates how the steady drip of repeated, low-level incidents could be used to advance state policy. It also lay behind the suspicion that pirate gangs and regional syndicates in the same area had benefited from Chinese financial and material support as an indirect way of exerting maritime claims.[158]

The South China Sea contains many areas where states are in conflict. It is also the focus of a Chinese expansionist drive. Although some maritime boundary disputes are a hangover from the colonial era, the overwhelming reason for this drive and for potential conflict is the belief that the undersea strata contain economically recoverable quantities of oil and gas. In the early 1990s this belief gave rise to several violent clashes, usually over the ownership of various islets and reefs in the Spratly group, many of which are barely visible at high tide but which, under UNCLOS, are key to gaining control of these sub-sea resources.[159] At the same time these clashes took place there were also, between 1993 and 1995, strong and persistent allegations that the PRC was using piracy as another way of asserting its sovereignty in the South China Sea; as a senior Indonesian naval officer put it: "We suspect that the Chinese are deliberately staging this piracy, using their navy, as another way to assert their sovereignty".[160] A Philippine report talked about a "renegade" task group of three ships, two of them

158 Chalk, *Non-Military Security and Global Order*, p. 60. William M. Carpenter and David G. Wiencek, 'Maritime piracy in Asia' in William M. Carpenter and David G. Wiencek, *Asian Security Handbook: An Assessment of Political-Security Issues in the Asia-Pacific Region*, Armonk, NY and London: M.E. Sharpe, 1996, pp. 83-4.

159 For background on the disputes see Stewart S. Johnson, 'Territorial issues and conflict potential in the South China sea', *Conflict Quarterly*, vol. IV, no. 4, Fall 1994, pp. 26-44. On the specifically economic dimensions of the disputes see Federico Bordonaro, 'The importance of the Spratly Islands', *PINR*, 28 Nov. 2006.

160 Michael Vatikiotis and Michael Westlake, 'Gunboat Diplomacy', *FEER*, 16 June 1994, p. 22.

with the same bow-mounted serial number 04420, operating from bases in Shantou, Kityoung and Senwei.[161] Similar allegations also circled around Chinese activity in waters off Hong Kong, which was then under British control. In one month alone around twenty ships were harassed or seized on leaving the colony while transiting waters claimed by the mainland government. "It is not yet clear," Michael Pugh wrote at the time, "whether this represents the assertion of jurisdiction claims or whether the security officials are engaging in criminal activities."[162] The US Department of Energy in its report wrote that the incidents that had taken place "suggest the possibility of a number of things other than piracy: harassment…official or non-official attempts to interdict commerce…extra-territorial anti-smuggling operations by a national government; organized crime activities disguised as military operations; unsanctioned military operations by rogue military units; (and) terrorism."[163]

The commonly accepted interpretation now is that it was more likely opportunistic provincial officials who were responsible for attacks both around Hong Kong and in the South China Sea, and they stopped when the central government reasserted its control.[164] The explanation is credible. Goods were smuggled into China on vessels that declared their destination was Vietnam and Chinese officials, who were allowed to keep up to half of all goods seized, began to stop ships on the margin of Hong Kong territorial waters and even within them.[165] That, however, was not how events appeared at the time.[166] This activity might just as well have stopped be-

161   'Rogue units of Sino Navy behind piracy'. *Philippine Daily Inquirer,* 21 February 1996.

162   Pugh, 'Piracy and Armed Robbery at Sea', pp. 2-3. See also 'China accused of piracy', *Lloyd's List,* 11 March 1994, p. 11. The Hong Kong Government reportedly compiled a report on these incidents for the IMO which indicated that Chinese security forces were engaging in "piracy". Although it was passed to the IMO it was never published. Paul Richardson and Jim Mulrenan. 'Hong Kong piracy report "updated" after withdrawal'. *Lloyd's List,* 27 May 1993.

163   US Department of Energy, Office of Intelligence, Office of Threat Assessment, 'Piracy: The threat to tanker traffic', Number 2, March 1993, p. 5, Note 5.

164   Ji Guoxing asserts very strongly that all the problems that occurred in the early 1990s were the fault of 'rogue' officials and 'were not 'a deliberate PRC exercise of extra-territorial sovereignty": Ji Guoxing, 'SLOC Security in the Asia Pacific', Asia-Pacific Centre for Security Studies: *Centre Occasional Paper,* Feb. 2000, p. 12.

165   Michael Westlake, 'Hot pursuit', *FEER,* 16 June 1994, pp. 26. See also 'HK gives Hainan piracy warning', *Lloyd's List,* 18 March 1993.

166   Chalk, *Grey-Area Phenomena in Southeast Asia,* pp. 30-2; also Greg Torode,

cause Beijing put an end to a programme that was no longer delivering the desired outcome. Frankly, we are unlikely to obtain a definitive answer.

Similar incidents occurred in the Persian Gulf following the invasion of Iraq in 2003. On several occasions between 2004 and 2007, armed craft "representing themselves as the Iranian authorities" committed acts of piracy in the northern Gulf "up to and including extortion and armed robbery".[167] These might have been the acts of local or provincial commanders taking advantage of Iraqi weakness and Coalition caution. They might not. They might have been something towards which the central government in Tehran was prepared to turn a blind eye, or which it was ready even to condone, as it probed its opponents' capabilities and resolve. In the same period sailors from the Australian Navy successfully countered an Iranian kidnap attempt in 2004, and British Navy sailors and marines were captured in 2004 and 2007, demonstrating that there were elements within the Iranian government prepared to undertake such probing actions.[168] In Southeast Asia during the periods of the Malayan "Emergency" (1948-60) and the later "Confrontation" (1963-66), when the Sukarno government was attempting to destabilise the newly-formed Malaysian Federation, there was evidence that the Indonesian government was condoning—if not necessarily controlling—sea raiding.[169] More recently Indonesian officials in coastal provinces have reportedly blamed officials in Jakarta for failing to understand maritime matters and to control elements in the military, a situation that is the reverse of what occurred in China, although in the Indonesian case there has been no suggestion that government employees supported piracy for anything other than criminal reasons. In all three cases, however, "rogue" officials could, whatever the truth might be, claim to be operating with "due authority" while the regime could exploit the opportunity for "plausible denial". In any state which lacks (in modern parlance) "transparency", and where the ostensible chain of command might not be the real chain of command, it is all too easy for one part of a regime to blame another.

'HK exposes China piracy', *South China Morning Post,* 16 March 1994.

167 David Osler, 'Pirates pose as Iranian officials', *Lloyd's List,* 29 June 2006. See also Maritime Liaison Office (MARLO) Bahrain, MARLO Advisory Bulletin 04-06, 15 June 2006 at http://www.marlobahrain.org/advisory-004-06.htm

168 'Aussie crew 'fended off' Iranian gunboats', *The Australian,* 22 June 2007; 'Iran seizes UK vessels and crew', *BBC News,* 21 June 2004; 'UK sailors captured at gunpoint', *BBC News,* 23 March 2007.

169 Pugh, 'Piracy and armed robbery at sea', p. 2.

These ambiguities are not confined to totalitarian or weak states. In 1985 agents of the French government sank the *Rainbow Warrior* in Auckland harbour. This Greenpeace ship had been leading the protest against French nuclear testing in the South Pacific. The French government initially denied responsibility. Unfortunately a photographer, Fernando Pereira, was trapped on board and drowned. His death prompted the New Zealand police to mount a major investigation. The capture of the agents involved led, eventually, to an embarrassing admission by the French Prime Minister, that they had, in fact, been operating under the orders of the DGSE, the French intelligence service.[170]

The thought of state piracy makes people uncomfortable. Partly this is because the idea of states being involved in the sponsorship or direction of a crime that for many is close to being a crime against humanity is repugnant. In addition it is a hybrid, it fits no neat category. At one extreme it could be a device to advance state interests under the guise of criminal activity. At the other extreme it could be a criminal device disguised as state policy: in other words, a form of state-organised or state-tolerated crime because the state that sponsors it is to some degree a criminal enterprise or has links to criminal interests. In this guise it could, from the outside, be difficult to distinguish from the organised criminal piracy described below. Indeed, it could be its end product.

How many attacks are there and who counts them?

Four organisations publish regular reports on piracy activity: the International Maritime Bureau (IMB) which issues a weekly incident report and a quarterly and an annual report;[171] the International Maritime Organisation (IMO) which issues monthly reports, quarterly summaries and an annual summary;[172] the UK DIS International Terrorism and Organised Crime Group (ITOC) Maritime Branch which issues a monthly "Worldwide Threats to Shipping Report";[173] and the US Office of Naval Intelligence (ONI) that issues weekly "Worldwide Threats to Shipping" reports that feed into the US National Geospatial Intelligence Agency's (NGA) Anti-

---

170   Menefee, *TMV*, pp. 57-8; Scott C. Truver, 'Maritime terrorism 1985', US Naval Institute *Proceedings*, May 1986, pp. 163-5 and James Hepburn, *The Black Flag*, London: Headline, 1995, pp. 209-29.

171   http://www.icc-ccs.org/prc/piracyreport.php

172   http://www.imo.org/home.asp

173   http://www.rncom.mod.uk/maritime/WWTS/apr06/index.cfm

Shipping Activity Message (ASAM) database.[174] The IMO, the ITOC and the ONI all rely on the IMB for a majority of their incident reporting. The IMB receives reports directly from ships or the owners of ships that have been attacked or suspect they have been targeted for attack. It is important to note that the IMB only publishes the initial incident report and neither conducts nor tracks subsequent investigations. The IMB is a branch of the International Chamber of Commerce that established the Bureau in 1979 with the remit to combat maritime fraud. In 1992 the IMB in turn established the Piracy Reporting Centre (PRC) in Kuala Lumpur in response to the increasing number of piracy attacks in Southeast Asia. It is now the international recognised collection point for piracy reports and statistics, although it has no official standing. In addition, a new government-sponsored reporting centre, the Information Sharing Centre (ISC), was opened in Singapore in December 2006.

Before 1992 the piracy picture is patchy and confused. This is mainly because at the time few saw it as a problem. Although the IMB has reports of attacks dating back to the early 1970s, piracy only made it onto the international agenda in 1983 when the IMO passed a resolution that noted "with great concern the increasing number of incidents involving piracy and armed robbery."[175] The resolution was prompted by the "alarming" growth in the number of attacks on ships anchored at night off the coast of Nigeria awaiting a berth in vastly overcrowded ports.

In order to gain some understanding of what piracy was taking place before 1992 it is necessary to refer to two overlapping sources: the IMO and the work of an individual researcher, Mark Bruyneel. Bruyneel's aim was to put together all the available figures, to place them side-by-side in order to see if there was any consistency or pattern, and to push the start date of the problem as far back as the figures would allow. This turned out to be 1978 and his study covered the period from then until 2000. For the period 1979-84 he relied on Roger Villar's book, *Piracy at Sea; Robbery and Violence at Sea since 1980*, but Villar provided very limited data and, as Bruyneel comments, "prior to 1980 records were either not kept or have not been retained on file in sufficient numbers". Between 1984 and 1990 Bruyneel drew on data from the Federation of American Scientists (FAS), which compiled its data from the Anti-Shipping Activity Messages that were in turn held in a database created and managed by the National

---

174   http://www.nga.mil/portal/site/maritime/

175   See IMO, 'Piracy and armed robbery at sea'.

Imagery and Mapping Agency's (NIMA) Maritime Safety Information Centre for the US Maritime Administration (MARAD).[176] The NIMA is now known as the National Geospatial Intelligence Agency (NGA) and, as noted above, draws its data from the ONI. From 1990 to 1992 Bruyneel used data from the International Maritime Organisation (IMO), the International Maritime Bureau (IMB) and the United Nations. From 1992 onwards, he used the commonly accepted figures from the IMB's Piracy Reporting Centre to produce the following graph:[177]

Between 1983 and 1985 the IMO commissioned the IMB to prepare three annual reports.[178] Although the MSC only instructed the Secretariat

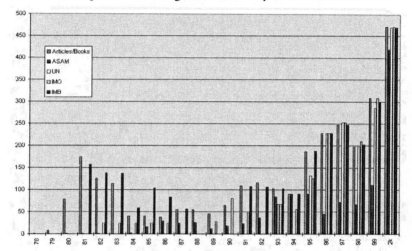

Figure 1: Piracy Statistics, 1978-2000 Compiled by Mark Bruyneel; updated 28 November 2001

to publish piracy statistics starting in 1995, it has recorded them since 1984 divided by region. It updates the accumulated data and publishes them in graph form in its annual summary. Bruyneel has noticed that discrepancies

---

176   FAS ASAM postings are available from 1985 to 1999. Refer to http://www.fas. org/irp/world/para/pirates.htm

177   For full details see Mark Bruyneel, 'Modern-day piracy statistics', 7 Feb. 2001.

178   Samuel Pyeatt Menefee, 'Under-reporting of the problems of maritime piracy and terrorism: Are we viewing the tip of the iceberg?' in Maximo Q. Mejia, Jr (ed.), *Contemporary Issues in Maritime Security*, Malmö: WMU Publications, 2005, p. 246.

between the IMO's monthly and annual figures mean that they are not wholly reliable.[179]

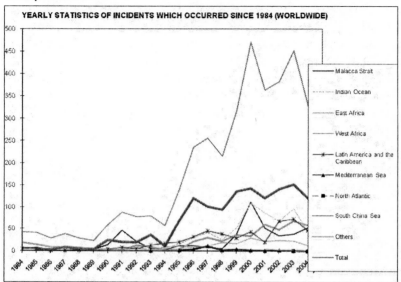

Figure 2. Yearly statistics of piracy incidents worldwide 1984-2005 Source: International Maritime Organisation, 2006

Year	Malacca Straits	Indian Ocean	East Africa	West Africa	South America & Carib	Med	South China Sea	Other	Total
1984	7	2	0	18	5	0	0	0	32
1985	7	0	2	14	5	0	3	0	31
1986	3	3	0	8	1	0	3	0	18
1987	8	5	0	7	1	0	8	0	29
1988	6	2	0	3	2	0	6	0	19
1989	4	4	0	2	0	0	4	0	14
1990	14	3	1	4	4	0	24	0	50
1991	46	1	1	3	8	0	20	0	79
1992	21	5	6	12	5	0	19	0	68
1993	6	4	1	9	13	1	36	0	70
1994	3	6	9	2	17	0	11	0	48
Totals	125	35	20	82	61	1	134	0	458

Table 2. Total number of recorded incidents, 1984-1994. Source: International Maritime Organisation, 2006

The data underlying this graph are as follows:

---

179   Bruyneel, 'Current reports on piracy by the IMO and IMB'.

Bruyneel's analysis from 1978, and the IMO data starting in 1984, show a broadly equivalent picture. However, little can be inferred from either except that the problem was insignificant throughout the 1980s, increased somewhat in the early 1990s and increased again starting around 1995.

Bruyneel's figures are global. The IMO records what it calls "incidents" that are probably only actual attacks. The figures are broken down regionally and suggest some interesting variations, but the numbers are too small to draw any conclusions. The IMB reported a global total of 239 actual and attempted attacks in 2006.[180] This might not appear to be many, and might seem to be well down on the peak of 469 attacks in 2000 (see table below), but, then again, how many is enough?

1995	1996	1997	1998	1999	2000	2001	2002	2003	2004	2005
188	228	247	202	300	469	335	370	445	329	276

Table 3. Total number of recorded actual and attempted attacks, 1995-2005. Source: International Maritime Bureau, 2006

It is generally accepted that the piracy figures produced by the International Maritime Bureau's PRC are more reliable than those available previously. Trying to establish their statistical significance, however, is not easy. The annual data provide insufficient data points. To be worthwhile the analysis needs to be based on quarterly figures as a minimum. The IMB has not retained its data in quarterly form. This means that no analysis can go back further than 1995, which is when the IMO started their quarterly breakdown. Over the period 1995 to 2005 the IMO recorded the following:

1995	1996	1997	1998	1999	2000	2001	2002	2003	2004	2005
154	183	305	193	283	501	335	422	341	322	249

Table 4. Total number of recorded actual and attempted attacks, 1995-2005. Source: International Maritime Organisation, 1995-2005

Even a simple analysis of the IMO data by quarter requires several assumptions across multiple variables. A visual inspection of the data by quarter suggests a trend of an increasing number of incidents from 1995 to 2000 and a decline thereafter to 2005. A trend line can be drawn which suggests an increase in the underlying number of incidents from around 26 per quarter in 1995 to 108 per quarter in 2000 and then a fall to around 60 per quarter in 2005. Such a trend fits the data reasonably well with 80 per cent of the observations falling within 29 of the trend. It also shows a

---

180   ICC-IMB, ICC-IMB Piracy Report, 2006, Table 1, p. 5.

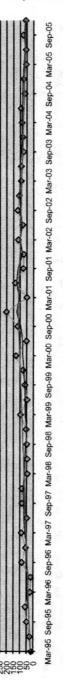

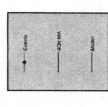

Figure 3. Total number of actual and attempted attacks, 1995-2005, analysed by quarter. Author's calculation. Source: International Maritime Organisation, 1995-2005

clear amount of variation above and below this trend line. Statements that piracy increased by 168 per cent between 1993 and 2005 can be misleading because they give the impression that piracy was continuing to rise in 2005, whereas the trend line in the IMO data suggests the number of incidents was falling.[181] What we do know, however, is that piracy has waxed as well as waned throughout history and, given the number of political, economic, social and law enforcement variables (and even natural variables of which the 2004 Asian tsunami was merely the most dramatic) that affect modern piracy, there is no reliable way of telling what direction the global trend might take in the future however sophisticated the statistical analysis.[182]

Weaknesses with the figures

There are three problems with these statistics: their accuracy and reliability; the problem of where the ships are when the attacks take place; and the failure to take full account of regional variations and trends.

The first is fundamentally a problem of collection which gives rise in turn to problems of analysis and categorisation. The second is debatable and can be dealt with briefly. The third is in some respects a problem of perception. The global figures are the figures that are reported in the press. These are the figures everyone points to. In reality they are barely important because, as highlighted earlier, piracy is a global phenomenon but not a global problem. The most important thing to understand is what is happening locally and regionally.

First, how accurate are the figures? Quite simply, no one can be sure. The IMB depends upon self-reporting. The figures are therefore self-selected. Ship-owners and ships' masters choose whether or report an incident or not. Also, because the PRC was established in Southeast Asia in response to what was seen at the time as a largely Asian problem, incidents in other regions were probably under-represented in the early years. Regardless of these problems, the IMB remains the main source of reports and is likely to remain so. Some observers have suggested that the ISC based in Singapore might reduce dependence on IMB incident reports, which in their opinion are not merely impaired by their self-selecting bias but can also suffer from exaggeration and misinterpretation.[183]

---

181   House of Commons Transport Committee, *Piracy*, p. 3.

182   Villar, *Piracy Today*, p. 10. Villar's view was it might wax and wane but that the general trend was upward.

183   Bateman *et al.*, 'Safety and security in the Malacca and Singapore Straits', p. 23.

The Information Sharing Centre (ISC) was established as part of the Regional Cooperation Agreement in Combating Piracy and Armed Robbery Against Ships in Asia (ReCAAP) ratified in June 2006.[184] Each ReCAAP signatory has its own designated point of contact, which receives incident reports and transmits them to the ISC. The ISC provides greater detail on incidents than the IMB, follows up the incident reports, and records and monitors the law enforcement response. The ISC claims that its coordination and enforcement role distinguishes it from the IMB. Nonetheless it does gather and collate regional piracy statistics.[185] Moreover, although its activities have been praised,[186] doubts have also been raised about how effective it will prove to be, not least because it is necessarily as reliant on incident reporting as is the IMB and, indeed, appears to make considerable use of IMB incident reports itself. The first doubt arises because neither Malaysia nor Indonesia are signatories (although they have stated they will sign eventually, this appears to be a distant prospect) and it is hard to see how the centre will be able to operate effectively without them.[187] The second comes from the suspicion that, as the centre is under governmental control, unwelcome reports might be suppressed and the statistics exposed to political influence or "adjustment". The third could be related to the second: even if an incident has been reported to a local authority, there is no guarantee it will be passed to the centre.[188]

---

184   'Anti-piracy agreement signed by 11 Asian countries', *The Star Online*, 21 June 2006; 'Asia unites against piracy', *Strategypage.com*, 1 July 2006; T. Rajan, 'Singapore to open anti-piracy coordination centre', *Straits Times*, 23 Nov. 2006; 'Factsheet on the regional cooperation agreement on combating piracy and armed robbery against ships in Asia'; Jackson Sawatan, 'Piracy information centre launched in S'pore', *Bernama.com*, 29 Nov. 2006; Noor Mohd Aziz, 'Boost for maritime security with launch of information sharing centre in Singapore', *ChannelNewsAsia*, 29 Nov. 2006; T. Rajan, 'Pirate attack? Team in S'pore will alert 14 nations', *Straits Times*, 30 Nov. 2006.

185   ISC reports can be found at http://www.recaap.org/publish/recaap/reports.html

186   Marcus Hand, 'ReCAAP success in Asia prompts call for expansion', *Lloyd's List*, 29 Feb. 2008.

187   See, for example, 'Indonesia determined to postpone ratification of Malacca Strait pact', *Antara News Agency*, 25 Sept. 2006. Also Donald Urquhart, 'Time to close the piracy gap', *The Business Times*, 29 Nov. 2006. Ian Story reports that both countries were piqued that Singapore, with which they have an uneasy relationship, had been chosen to host the ISC. Ian Storey. 'Securing Southeast Asia's Sea Lanes: A Work in Progress'. *Asia Policy*, No. 6, July 2008, pp. 114-5.

188   The PRC has been under pressure almost since its inception. For more information on the ReCAAP centre see Marcus Hand, 'IMB fights back over potential

There are already signs of confusion within the system. Some of the reports it receives from local sources have often not been reported to the IMB. In other cases, captains have reported incidents to both organisations, which because of time delays have resulted in the same incident being reported as occurring at different times and in different locations. More worrying is that some captains are now reporting directly to the ISC and not to the IMB, which has injected a further element of uncertainty into the figures.[189] Despite these difficulties it is nonetheless important to acknowledge that the Centre represents "the first time that governments in East, Southeast and South Asia have institutionalised their cooperation in combating piracy and armed robbery against ships in the form of a permanent body with full-time staff".[190]

There is a widely held suspicion that it is at least possible—in fact, more then likely—that under-reporting or mis-reporting hides the full extent of the piracy problem.[191] In 1998 the UK Defence Intelligence Staff estimated that the number of incidents could be 200 per cent higher than those that are reported. At the same time the Australian DIO issued a report that put the number of reported incidents at between 20 and 70 per cent below actual levels.[192] The Nippon Foundation in its 1999 survey of attacks on Japanese shipping in the Malacca Straits suggested that the number of at-

new Asian anti-piracy centre', *Lloyd's List*, 26 May 2006; also 'Regional agreement against maritime piracy to take effect in September', *Peoples Daily Online*, 21 June 2006; Marcus Hand, 'Asian alliance to fight piracy goes ahead despite dissenters', *Lloyd's List*, 22 June 2006; 'Anti-piracy agreement wins approval', *Fairplay*, 22 June 2006; ONI. WWTTS Report, 5 July 2006.

189   Marcus Hand, 'Piracy alert wrangle leads to loss of life fears', *Lloyd's List*, 25 April 2007; 'Double vision on piracy', *Fairplay*, 10 May 2007. The ISC, however, denies there is a problem. Marcus Hand, 'Agencies deny rift over piracy reporting', *Lloyd's List*, 3 May 2007.

190   Joshua Ho, 'The security of sea lanes in Southeast Asia', *Asian Survey*, vol. XLVI, no. 4, July/Aug. 2006, p. 570.

191   The IMB in its own comment on the figure for 2005 states: 'Though the attack numbers have dropped, the IMB would like to stress that many actual and attempted cases also go unreported.' ICC-IMB Piracy Report, 2005, p. 16.

192   UK DIS figure from Defence Intelligence Analysis Staff, 'Maritime piracy today', Classified. London: Ministry of Defence, 10 July 1998, p. 1; Australian DIO figure from Defence Intelligence Organization 'Maritime piracy: Rough seas ahead?' Classified. Canberra, Australia: Department of Defence, Oct. 1996, p. 3, both quoted in US Office of Naval Intelligence and US Coast Guard Intelligence Coordination Centre, *Threats and Challenges to Maritime Security 2020*. Prepared by 1 March, 1999, p. 16.

tacks could be ten times the level actually reported.[193] I.R.Hyslop suggests the share of incidents going unreported is "likely to be at least half, and may in some cases be as high as ninety per cent".[194] Anthony Davis reports an estimate that only one in eight incidents are reported; Peter Chalk believes "most" attacks go unreported; the IMB Piracy Reporting Centre in Kuala Lumpur suggests between two-thirds and a half; the International Transport Workers Federation suggests half; Birnie suggests half; while in Sam Bateman's view it is only some. Bateman also believes that the scale of the increase may be exaggerated because, as with any crime, people will only report it if it is acknowledged to be a problem and many incidents, particularly petty ones, may well have gone unreported in the past.[195] The reality is that the percentage of incidents that are unreported or misinterpreted as piracy is completely unknown.

On the other hand, agreement is widespread as to why under-reporting or misreporting takes place: most brutally, the witnesses might be dead;[196] secondly, states or ports do not want to be branded as having a piracy problem and therefore may not record or report an incident;[197] thirdly, shipping companies have an incentive to keep quiet for fear of the harm it might do to their reputations (including the fact they may have taken insufficient precautions), the concern that crews might demand additional payments for sailing into or through pirate-prone areas, the expense that accompanies

---

193 Nippon Foundation, *Survey on Acts of Piracy and Armed Robbery against Japanese Shipping Companies,* 1999. Cited in House of Commons Transport Committee, *Piracy,* p. 12. Original available only in Japanese.

194 Hyslop, 'Contemporary piracy', p. 5.

195 Davis, 'Piracy in Southeast Asia shows signs of increased organisation', pp. 37-8; Chalk, 'Threats to the maritime environment', p. 4; the PRC figures is cited by Burnett, *Dangerous Waters,* p. 165; ITWF estimate cited in Chalk, *Non-Military Security and Global Order,* p. 60; Birnie, 'Piracy: Past, present and future', p. 173; Bateman, 'Maritime Transnational Violence', p. 4. In his interview with the author (June 2004), Bateman made the point that reporting is a question of balance; under-reporting in one area is probably balanced by over-reporting in another. In his interview (April 2004) the IMB Director, Pottengal Mukundan, would only venture that the under-reporting was 'substantial'. In Mark Valencia's opinion, few incidents are reported (interview with author, Aug. 2004). See also Young and Valencia, 'Conflation of piracy and terrorism', pp. 271-2.

196 John Grissim, 'Pirates again stalking the seven seas', *The World Paper,* May 1997.

197 Between 1992 and 1995, for example, Hong Kong gained a reputation for 'extreme danger' which led NUMAST and the Japanese Shipowners Association to threaten to redirect shipping away from the port. Chalk, *Grey-Area Phenomena in Southeast Asia,* p. 26.

any investigation when ships are delayed (and which in several jurisdictions might be corrupt or incompetent anyway)—and even, in the case of kidnappings, because of actual threats.[198] Crews and ship owners have been intimidated in other ways: in one incident reported to the IMB, a ship was boarded by men who were almost certainly Indonesian servicemen; the IMB dutifully reported the incident to the Indonesian authorities shortly afterwards but were then contacted by the ship-owners, who asked that the matter not be pressed as they and their ships had a continuing need to enter Indonesian ports and territorial waters and did not wish to suffer official reprisals.[199] States are amongst the most reluctant reporters: "The very countries that are so forward in their protest about statistics are shrinking violets when it comes to reporting...acts in their own waters."[200] Finally, according to a previous head of the Piracy Reporting Centre, John Martin, several shipping associations have written into their manuals of procedure that ship attacks should not be reported at all.[201] In short, the piracy that is reported is the piracy no one can ignore.[202]

The second question affecting the reliability of the statistics is, where are ships when they are attacked? As noted earlier, most attacks on ships occur when they are in, or close to, ports. Of the 239 actual or attempted pirate

---

198   *Ibid.,* pp. 28-9. Also Jayant Abhyankar, 'Piracy–a growing menace', paper presented at the Okazaki Institute conference, 'Combating piracy and armed robbery at sea: Charting the future in Asia-Pacific waters', 24-5 March 2001, Bangkok, p. 4.

199   In addition see, for example, Chalk, 'Contemporary maritime piracy in Southeast Asia', pp. 89-90; Villar, *Piracy Today,* pp. 13-14; Hyslop, 'Contemporary piracy', p. 12 and p. 17, where he stresses the underestimation of the number of human victims; Philippe B. Moulier and Ethan Casey, 'Pirates? What pirates?' *US News & World Report,* 23 June 1997, pp. 33-4; Edward G. Agbakoba, 'The fight against piracy and armed robbery against ships', International Maritime Organisation, ND; Michael S. McDaniel, 'Modern high seas piracy', presentation to the Propeller Club of the United States, 20 Nov. 2000, p. 14. On threats following kidnapping see Burnett, *Dangerous Waters,* p. 311, endnote 51. On costs incurred by ship owners also Gottschalk and Flanagan, *Jolly Roger with an Uzi,* p. 99. Both Chalk, *Grey-Area Phenomena in Southeast Asia,* p. 28 and Wood, 'Piracy is deadlier than ever', quote a figure of $25,000 per day as the average cost of a ship held up in port. McDaniel. 'Modern high seas piracy', p. 14 suggests a range of between $10,000 and $50,000 per day.

200   Menefee, 'Under-reporting of the problems of maritime piracy and terrorism', p. 248.

201   Chalk, *Grey-Area Phenomena in Southeast Asia,* pp. 28-9.

202   Peter Chalk, interview with author, Aug. 2004. See also US ONI & USCG, *Threats and Challenges to Maritime Security, 2020,* p. 16; Farley, 'International and regional trends in maritime piracy', pp. 2-3.

attacks recorded by the IMB in 2006 nearly 63 per cent took place when ships were berthed (15) or at anchor (135).[203]

As far as the IMO is concerned these attacks are not piracy but, in accordance with the UNCLOS definition, armed robbery against ships. For the IMB they are acts of piracy.[204] The IMB is unwilling to concede any distinction between different types of piracy because it is reluctant to privilege one form over another. Nonetheless, there is a case for separating piracy against ships that are berthed from piracy elsewhere. While such robberies can be deeply distressing they are not necessarily injurious physically to the victim, and, because they are often mounted from the quayside or launched from boats that draw alongside when the ship is tied up, they are effectively port crimes mounted in the main by the same people or gangs that pilfer and steal from warehouses and containers. There is some concern, furthermore, that their inclusion can be used to undermine the credibility of the way incidents are reported and the statistics recorded, by distracting attention from the more serious and usually more frightening crimes that are committed when ships are either anchored awaiting a berth or underway at sea. Incidents when ships were berthed accounted for six per cent of the total in 2006 and 17 per cent in 2002.[205] It is possible that this decrease might be due to improved port security brought about by the International Ship and Port Facility Security Code (ISPS) that entered force in July 2004.[206] On the other hand, given the inconsistent and all too often poor standard of implementation of the Code by ports, including major international hub ports, this should not be assumed.[207]

Stefan Eklöf argues that all piracy committed against ships berthed or at anchor in the vicinity of a port should be considered port crimes and goes on to suggest that port crimes and sea-based crimes require very different counter-measures: port crimes require better security measures to defeat

203   ICC-IMB Piracy Report, 2006, p. 9.

204   That attacks in port can be considered acts of piracy was reaffirmed in 2005 by the High Court of Singapore in the case of *Bayswater Carriers vs. QBE Insurance* when the judge held that piracy had been committed because the ship was 'at sea' within the port and that—most important—the necessary element of force had been present. David Martin-Clark, 'Case notes: Bayswater carriers Pte. Ltd. V. QBE Insurance (International) Pte. Ltd.', 2005.

205   ICC-IMB Piracy Report, 2006, p. 9 and ICC-IMB Piracy Report, 2002, p. 9.

206   See http://www.imo.org/Newsroom/mainframe.asp?topic_id=583&doc_id=2689

207   Hugh O'Mahony, 'Mitropoulos voices fears over ISPS Code inconsistencies', *Lloyd's List*, 30 Nov. 2006.

them while sea-based crimes require better international cooperation. This might be too black-and-white. The crews of ships at anchor are as vulnerable to intimidation and violence as ships at sea. Ships are moored away from dockside security and lights.[208] In many anchorages the maritime police fail to respond to calls for help and, even if they do, inevitably take time to arrive. This gives pirates the opportunity to commit their crime and make good their escape.

The final problem about the statistics, mentioned above, is that they are affected by regional variations and trends. Piracy occurs in comparable locations around the world for similar but not the same reasons. They form what Menefee has termed "pirate clusters".[209] It is important, therefore, to recognise regional differences, and this lack of recognition is one of the problems with the piracy statistics as they are published currently. The IMB figures are organised by country, reflecting the fact that most piracy nowadays takes place within, or close to, a country's territorial waters rather than on the open ocean. Whilst the Bureau's methodology is perfectly logical, to a degree it obscures the mobility of pirates and, consequently, can hide regional, as opposed to purely national, patterns. The IMO, on the other hand, does agglomerate its figures regionally, but the regions are so large that the contribution of each individual country—and therefore the success or failure or its anti-piracy efforts—is hidden.[210] From a global perspective piracy over the ten years from 1995 to 2005 might have gone up and then gone down, but variations in the number of *reported* attacks occurring in the waters of individual states or between specific states over the same period have been much more dramatic, certainly when expressed in straight-line percentage terms. To keep these variations in proportion it is therefore important to also look at the actual number of reported incidents. To take two examples: piracy off Nigeria increased by 1,600 per cent, that is to say from one incident in 1995 to 16 in 2005, while piracy in the Straits of Malacca and Singapore taken together increased by 433 per cent over the same period, which meant that the number of incidents

---

208 Herbert-Burns, 'Compound piracy at sea in the early twenty-first century', p. 102

209 Samuel Pyeatt Menefee, 'Scourges of the sea: Piracy and violent maritime crime', 1 *Marine Policy Reports,* vol. 13, Spring 1989, p. 16.

210 Samuel Pyeatt Menefee comments that the 'IMO offers regional breakdowns of statistics, but has been reluctant to call a spade a spade and offer similar national breakdowns': Menefee, 'Under-reporting of the problems of maritime piracy and terrorism', p. 247.

climbed from six to 26, which is still a very small number compared to the number of annual ship transits.

Six regions will be reviewed in detail: Southeast Asia, South China Sea, Bay of Bengal-Bangladesh, South America, East Africa and West Africa. The aim is to situate the factors that favour pirates in context and to lay the ground for the discussion in the next chapter about the differences between common and organised piracy.

Southeast Asia

Southeast Asia is the ideal environment for piracy and one where pirate traditions go back virtually uninterrupted to the fifth century. In the nineteenth century Sir Henry Keppel, who in his rise to become Admiral of the Fleet twice led expeditions against Asian pirates, wrote: "As surely as spiders abound where there are nooks and crannies, so have pirates sprung up wherever there is a nest of islands."[211] Warren has written in a similar vein that it was "the case at the end of the Eighteenth century, and it remains the case at the end of the Twentieth, that geography remains a sinister ally of the modern Southeast Asian pirates".[212] More incidents take place in this region than anywhere else. It is one where pirates can use a maze of islands, reefs, corals, shifting shoals and sandbars that require intimate knowledge to navigate safely in order to escape. It is a region where pirates can hide in the creeks, small rivers and mangrove swamps that puncture the coast, and amongst the thousands of other small craft that ply their innocent trade between islands; in the case of the Malacca Straits estimates suggest they are crossed by 80,000 people and fished by 10,000 boats every day.[213] It is a region where the will to suppress piracy varies significantly between states; Indonesia, the state where the most pirate incidents take place, displays the least interest in its suppression.[214] In parts of Indonesia and the Philippines it is likely that pirates can blend into the local population without undue

---

211   Philip Gosse, *The History of Piracy,* New York: Tudor Publishing, 1946 (orig. pub., 1932), p. 1. Frécon makes a similar point in 'Pirates set the Straits on fire', pp. 21-3.

212   James F. Warren, 'A tale of two centuries: The globalisation of maritime raiding and piracy in Southeast Asia at the end of the eighteenth and twentieth centuries', National University of Singapore, Asia Research Institute *Working Paper Series,* no. 2, p. 12.

213   Bronson Percival, interview with the author, June 2006.

214   Langit-Dursin, 'Indonesia key to end piracy in Malacca Straits'.

fear of betrayal.[215] It is, moreover, a region where the piracy phenomenon can truly be described as *regional*: not just for the reason that pirates can cross maritime boundaries—some of which are still disputed—to throw off their pursuers, but because pirates can cross these boundaries to hijack a ship in the waters of one state and dispose of its cargo in another, while the men who control these sophisticated pirate operations are most probably, and evidence suggests quite deliberately, based in a third state.

Indonesia. Indonesia is an archipelagic state intertwined by narrow seas. It covers a vast area, over large parts of which the writ of the central government runs only tenuously, if at all, and which claims a coastline of about 50,000 miles (81,000km), approximately twice the circumference of the Earth. Even the Indonesian government is unsure how many islands make up the archipelago.[216] Although Indonesia is concerned about maritime security generally, issues other than piracy tend to receive more attention, particularly piracy against ships passing through its waters.[217] Smuggling of people and goods and the degradation of the maritime environment through overfishing are much higher concerns. In 2002 the Indonesian government estimated that illegal fishing, for example, was costing the country over $4 billion a year.[218] An estimate in 2003 of the value of fish taken by Thai fishermen alone put the figure at between $1.2 and $2.4 billion.[219] These problems and priorities go a long way to explaining why

215   As ONI comment: 'Past reporting from officials state that pirate gangs operating off the coast were viewed as latter day Robin Hoods by some of the villagers in the region.' ONI WWTTS Report, 6 July 2006, Paragraph D.2.

216   Ed Davies, 'Indonesia counts its islands before it's too late', *Reuters*, 16 May 2007; 'Indonesia to register small islands names to UN August 18', *TEMPO Interactive*, 23 July 2007.

217   John F. Bradford, 'Japanese anti-piracy initiatives in Southeast Asia: Policy formulations and the Coastal State responses', *Contemporary Southeast Asia*, vol. 26, no. 3, 2004, pp. 497-9. The fact that, according to the IMB, only one per cent of the traffic transiting the Malacca Straits actually trades with Indonesia could influence its attitude to Malacca Straits security. Cited in House of Commons Transport Committee, *Piracy*, Ev. 28.

218   Stefan Eklöf, 'Piracy: A critical perspective', International Institute for Asian Studies *Newsletter*, no. 36, March 2005. This is a very vague estimate. In 2006 Dr Tommy Wagel of the Arafura and Timor Sea Expert Forum admitted it could be anywhere between $2 billion and $4 billion per year. David Weber, 'Illegal fishing cost Indonesia $2 billion a year: expert', *ABC Online*, 12 May 2006. For an authoritative report on the problem world-wide see 'The global extent of illegal fishing', a report prepared by MRAG and Fisheries Center, University of British Columbia, April 2008.

219   Anucha Charoenpo, 'Illegal Thai fishing robbed Indonesia off (sic) billions

it recorded the highest number of incidents of piracy—50 in 2006, 21 per cent of the global total. In fact its unenviable position at number one remained unchallenged from 1991, when 55 incidents were recorded until 2007. The majority of attacks in Indonesian waters outside the Malacca Straits (and the Gelasa Straits, see below) tend to take place in or close to ports: the main concentrations appear to be around Subaraya, Gresik, Jakarta (Tanjong Priok), Balikpapan, Samarinda and Belawan.[220] These tend to be of the petty variety involving the theft of money, personal possessions or ships' equipment; however, the pirates usually come armed, if not with guns then with long knives.

That corruption is a common problem amongst agencies in the region charged with maritime law enforcement has been touched upon already. The fact that it is endemic in the Indonesian political and military system needs to be emphasised. The Indonesian military are not financed by taxation alone. They are at least partly, and probably largely, self-financing. The proportion that comes from outside sources is unclear but could be as much as 75 per cent.[221] Any military that is not funded entirely from the public purse (as in China where the PLA owns many businesses) is not wholly answerable to its civilian masters, and this has unquestionably been the case in Indonesia. Much of this income comes from legitimate businesses owned by the military, although the revenue often bypasses the treasury.[222] Another stream derives from protecting or guarding the operations of major multinational companies, particularly in the mining and energy sectors, that have been designated "vital national assets", an enforced arrangement that one company executive branded "one grand national extortion racket".[223] The rest comes from mafia-style criminal activity including protection rackets for gambling and prostitution, bribery and the imposition of corrupt "taxes". This criminal proportion might well

---

of catches and cash', *South East Asian Press Alliance,* 2003. Also Brian Fegan. 'Plundering the sea'. *Inside Indonesia,* January-March 2003.

220 Chalk, *Non-Military Security and Global Order,* p. 70; Davis, 'Piracy in Southeast Asia shows signs of increased organisation', pp. 39-41.

221 Human Rights Watch, 'Too high a price: The human rights cost of the Indonesian military's economic activities', vol. 18, no. 5 (c), June 2006, pp. 4-5; Tony Sitathan, 'Cash-strapped military recipe for corruption', *Asia Times,* 15 March 2003; Andreas Harsono, 'Nationalism and sea piracy in the Malacca Strait', Keynote speech presented to the 'Maritime piracy in Southeast Asia' conference held at Hotel Equatorial, Kuala Lumpur, 14 July 2006.

222 Human Rights Watch, 'Too high a price', p. 2

223 *Ibid.,* pp. 46-7.

be increasing because, as Human Rights Watch point out, "many military business ventures have been great failures" and have contributed "only modest sums to help cover unbudgeted expenses", which has meant that the network of "informal and illegal military economic activities that are more hidden and more difficult to control" has spread.[224] The central command of Tentara Nasional Indonesia (TNI), the Indonesian armed forces, is only able to oversee the activities of the military enterprises. The security activities are generally managed at the provincial command level, leaving the remainder, the criminal activities, to the lowest level of command and even to individuals. For example, an Army sergeant based in Merauke in Papua opened a bar with dozens of prostitutes and used the income to help pay for his troops' meals.[225] At sea this criminal activity might well have meant active engagement in, or "taxation" of, pirate activity. Fishermen on the Malaysian side of the Malacca Straits, for example, have claimed they have been forced to pay "protection" money to Indonesian officials. Ships and their owners can also be forced to pay "protection" fees when they visit Indonesian ports: the researcher Carolin Liss recounts an incident of a ship-owner, whose vessel had been arrested for illegal dumping, paying $200,000 "compensation" to navy officials to obtain its release.[226] Andreas Harsono, who now heads the Pantau Foundation, a media think tank in Jakarta, holds the view that "directly or indirectly, the 900-kilometer Malacca Strait is a source of funding potential...for the Indonesian military. They could increase patrol (sic) to minimize crimes—when the international communities are screaming—but also to give green-light signals to their underworld links."[227]

The Philippines. Indonesia's neighbour the Philippines is also an archipelagic state, and one which appeared to be close to rivalling it in terms of piracy incidents in 1996 when it experienced 39 attacks (compared with 57 in Indonesia) including sophisticated and organised criminal hijackings, but it had only four attacks in 2004 and apparently none in 2005. Eric Ellen and others have cast doubt on the reliability of these figures.[228] The

---

224   *Ibid.,* p. 3.

225   Harsono, 'Nationalism and sea piracy in the Malacca Strait'.

226   Liss, 'Maritime security in Southeast Asia', p. 8.

227   Harsono, 'Nationalism and sea piracy in the Malacca Strait'.

228   The Philippine figure may be a clear case of under-reporting. According to Eric Ellen, the then Director of the IMB, there were 143 cases of piracy in Philippine waters in 1993, none of which were reported. Chalk, *Grey-Area Phenomena in Southeast Asia,* p. 29, and ICC-IMB Piracy Report 2005, Table 1,

Philippines is as troubled by corruption, terrorism and under-funded law enforcement as Indonesia. The armed forces and law enforcement agencies of both countries have struggled to control maritime crime regardless of what the official spokesmen say.[229]

The work of Eduardo Ma R. Santos, a retired Vice-Admiral in the Philippine Navy, would appear to support this. His figures reinforce the suspicion that the number of pirate attacks in Philippines waters has been far higher than the figures reported to the IMB. To take the first four years of this century as an example, the IMB reported a total of 39 attacks, whereas Santos suggests there were 461.[230] In an interesting NGA ASAM report 2006-146, dated 22 May 2005, of a fishing boat boarded off the Isla de Higantes which was found to be carrying a group that included a local policeman, the Provincial Police Chief Charles Calima is recorded as claiming that pirates and hijackers "usually" used deception, which would imply that attacks are, contrary to the published figures, a common occurrence.[231] These deception tactics, which include disguising boats and crew as police or coast guards, and luring victims by simulating engine trouble or distress, are no different from those used by pirates everywhere.[232]

Casual killing of fishermen and local traders appears to be a regular feature of many attacks throughout the Philippine-Indonesia-Malaysia "tri-border" region where Philippine Mindanao and Malaysian Sabah are effectively linked by the Sulu island chain that separates the Sulu from the Celebes Seas. ONI, in their report on the discovery of the fishing boat *James Bond* found drifting with two bodies aboard in April 2004, note that murder in such cases is "relatively common" although "seldom reported".[233] A passenger vessel, travelling to Polilio Island off Luzon on 17 March 2008 with 10 passengers and five crew, was commandeered by two of the passengers. They shot dead three crewmembers including the

---

p. 5. The IMB reported three attacks in the first half of 2006: ICC-IMB Piracy Report, 2006, Table 1, p. 5.

229   Edith Regalado, 'NSA: RP can't police sea lanes between Mindanao, Indonesia', *The Philippine Star,* 16 Oct. 2006; 'Navy overwhelmed by pirates in Malacca Strait', *Tempo Interactive,* 30 Nov. 2006.

230   Eduardo Ma R. Santos 'Piracy and armed robbery against ships in the Philippines' in Graham Gerald Ong-Webb (ed.) *Piracy, Terrorism and Securing the Malacca Straits.* Singapore: ISAS, 2006 , p. 40 (Chart 3.1).

231   Also recorded in ONI. WWTTS Report, 14 June 2006, Paragraph K.6.

232   Santos, 'Piracy and armed robbery against ships in the Philippines', p. 41.

233   NGA ASAM, 2004-100, 17 April 2005

captain, tied their bodies to the anchor and threw them overboard before shooting and injuring the other two crewmembers, one of whom threw himself over the side, before fleeing in a motor boat.[234] In Eklöf's view the Sulu region, in terms of violence and human suffering, is probably the most dangerous maritime area in the world.[235] It has a long piracy tradition.[236] Pirate activity was never suppressed to any great extent during the Spanish colonial period, although US forces countered it effectively during the period of American occupation from the end of the Spanish-American War until 1941. After the end of the Second World War and the granting of Philippine independence, piracy quickly returned and by the late 1970s had reached the point where the waters of the Sulu and Celebes Seas were, in Warren's view, more pirate-infested than any others.[237] Davis, writing in 2004, suggested there were six pirate groups operating in the region, all of which moved between Malaysia and the Philippines using the international border as a defence mechanism. They were all armed, some of them heavily—the Moley Uwah Group, for example, was reported to be equipped with a GPMG and M-79 grenade launchers—and some had links with the Abu Sayyaf Group (ASG).[238]

An important aspect of piracy in this region is the attention pirates have paid to coastal settlements. Some have been raided and others forced to pay protection money: 20 raids were mounted on coastal settlements in British North Borneo in 1962, one of the most brutal of which was visited on the logging camp at Kunak;[239] from the 1970s through to the 1990s other coastal settlements in Sabah such as Semporna, which was assaulted twice in 1996 and again in 2000, and Lahad Datu, were hit regularly the raiders concentrating on banks, shops and airline offices in a pattern that was repeated in 1995 when the Abu Sayyaf Group (ASG) ransacked the Philippine town of Ipil.[240] Whether criminal gangs or insurgent groups

---

234 ICC-IMB Weekly Piracy Report, 18-24 March 2008.

235 Eklöf, *Pirates in Paradise*, p. 43.

236 James Francis Warren, *Iranun and Balangingi: Globalization, Maritime Raiding and the Birth of Ethnicity*, Quezon City: New Day Publishers, 2002; Warren, 'A tale of two centuries', pp. 2-14; Eklöf, *Pirates in Paradise*, pp. 9-13.

237 Eklöf, *Pirates in Paradise*, pp. 36-44; Warren. 'A tale of two centuries', p. 17.

238 Anthony Davis, 'The Sulu Triangle', *Jane's IR*, vol. 16, no. 6, June 2004, p. 40.

239 Eklöf, *Pirates in Paradise*, pp. 38-9.

240 On the Semporna raids see Warren, 'A tale of two centuries', p. 18 and Eklöf, *Pirates in Paradise*, p. 112. Frécon suggests the town was also assaulted in 1952 and 1954. Frécon , 'Jolly Roger over Southeast Asia', p. 138. Eklöf refers to the

perpetrated the attacks on Semporna and Lahad Datu is still uncertain although the Philippines authorities have accused insurgent groups of coastal raiding.[241] Whatever their allegiance in the main these attacks are likely to have perpetrated by the Muslim inhabitants of the Sulu islands. In a despatch from the British embassy in Manila written in 1949, the writer lamented the decline in the professionalism of the Philippine police following the American withdrawal, commenting that the "result among the Moros is, I fear, that they are reverting to type and are again finding in piracy and smuggling an easy way of making a living".[242] On the other hand, the account Chong Chee Kin gives of one raid on Semporna suggests that at least some of the raiders could have been local criminals. The residents talked about recognising some of their attackers and said they came from a poor village on the outskirts of the town. They talked also of the raiders coming when they were short of money and of hitting smaller communities on the multitude of smaller islands, sometimes every week, for "rice, food and fruits". Significantly, they saw no point in reporting these incidents to the police.[243]

Ships up to the size of small freighters and ferries have been attacked. Cargo was stolen; passengers were robbed and, in cases where the whole vessel was taken, passengers and crew were forced to jump over the side.[244] In 1985 an attempt was even made on a cruise ship, the *Coral Princess*, with 260 passengers on board, the pirates only fleeing when a coast guard cutter made a fortuitous appearance.[245] On other occasions pirates were accused of sabotaging navigational aids to lure ships aground in order to make their cargo easier to plunder.[246]

1954 raid in 'The return of piracy: Decolonization and international relations in a maritime border region (the Sulu Sea), 1959-63', Lund University Centre for East and South-East Asian Studies *Working Paper no. 15*, 2005, p. 4. On Lahad Datu see 'A tide of pirates', *Asiaweek*, 27 May 1988, pp. 27-8; Frécon , 'Jolly Roger over Southeast Asia', p. 138; and Hyslop, 'Contemporary piracy', p. 18.

241 Eklöf, *Pirates in Paradise*, p. 113.

242 Cited in Eklöf, *Pirates in Paradise*, p. 37 and more fully in Eklöf, 'The return of piracy: Decolonization and international relations', p. 4.

243 Chong Chee Kin, 'Attack is no surprise for Semporna folk', Unpublished communication, 29 April 2000.

244 Eklöf, *Pirates in Paradise*, p. 42; Warren, 'A tale of two centuries', p. 17.

245 Geoffrey Murray, '20th century pirates roam the seas of Southeast Asia', *Christian Science Monitor*, 9 June 1986.

246 Warren, 'A tale of two centuries', p. 17; 'The Jolly Roger still flies', *TIME*, 31

The wide availability of firearms of all types, including AK-47s and M-16s following the end of the Vietnam War, which overlapped with the beginning of the Moro National Liberation Front (MNLF) insurgency in the southern Philippines in 1972, meant that pirates were usually armed and used their weapons without compunction to force ships to stop and kill whoever was on board.[247] Accounts of the brutality meted out almost defy belief: the slicing off of ears, the shooting of knee-caps to make swimming impossible and, in one case, the decapitation of every member of a boat's crew, leaving their heads dangling in the water at the end of fishing lines where they were discovered later by coast guards.[248]

Whilst many such incidents appeared to be related to the age-old pirate desire to eliminate witnesses, many others were linked to extortion rackets. It is hard to be sure the extent to which this criminality and violence was linked to the Muslim separatist movements, first the MNLF and then, subsequently and additionally, the MILF and the ASG, and also the New People's Army (NPA) revolutionary movement—the military wing of the Communist Party of the Philippines—but because all are known to have raised funds from sea robbery and extortion, their involvement is likely to have been considerable.[249] In 1988 35 gangs of indeterminate motivation were known to be operating, in addition to the Ambak Pare gang that was almost certainly part of the MNLF.[250] By 2003 the number of known gangs had dropped to 17: two in Luzon, three in the Visayas, eleven in Mindanao and one between Palawan and Malaysia. Six of these gangs were either linked to or actual members of the MILF.[251] "Piracy in this region," writes Menefee, "is often hard to distinguish from politically based maritime violence."[252] In the southern Philippines, during the 1980s and 90s at least, pirates were one element in a mix of "corrupt politicians, manipulative traders, smuggling and dynamite-fishing syndicates" many of whom were drawn from the Tausug, a Muslim ethnic group predominant in the

---

July 1978.

247   Eklöf, *Pirates in Paradise*, p. 43; 'The Jolly Roger still flies'.

248   'A tide of pirates', p. 28.

249   Santos, 'Piracy and armed robbery against ships in the Philippines', p. 42; Hyslop, 'Contemporary Piracy', pp. 16-17. For useful description of the NPA see 'New People's Army', *Jane's TSM*, 6 June 2006.

250   'A tide of pirates', p. 28

251   Santos, 'Piracy and armed robbery against ships in the Philippines', p. 44.

252   Menefee, *TMV*, p. 83.

area.[253] Between 1992 and 2004 Santos reports that 3,916 people and 1,574 vessels were attacked: of the vessels 193 were stolen; of the people 431 died, 189 were wounded and 426 are still missing. Although these figures are for the Philippines as a whole the overwhelming number of incidents were concentrated in the Sulu and Celebes Seas with smaller numbers occurring off Manila, northern Luzon and some ports in the Visayas.[254]

Vietnam. In contrast to the apparent decline in pirate activity in Philippine waters shown by published figures, activity in Vietnamese waters has become regular since 2000, with ten attacks in 2005 and a high of fifteen in 2003. Most attacks appear to have been mounted against vessels moored in Hong Gai, Haiphong, Vung Tau and Ho Chi Min City (Saigon), but Vietnamese fishermen have been subject to brutal attacks by what are claimed to be organised pirate groups based in Cambodia, Thailand, Indonesia and Malaysia.[255]

Malacca and Singapore Straits. The picture in the Malacca and Singapore Straits is rather different. Because free passage through the Straits is a vital interest to so many countries, which has meant that they have been the subject of close attention over a long period,[256] the impression has arisen that Straits piracy is representative of piracy worldwide. This is not the case. At the lowest level much of it is akin to Indonesian piracy. However, what is distinctive about Straits piracy is its variety, epitomised by the Riau islands where, according to the provincial Head of Operations for the Indonesian Marine Police, there were three groups operating in 2005: the first was made up of small gangs of robbers trying to earn a living; the second, based on Batam, went after tug boats, which were then sold; the third was armed and organised and targeted larger ships, especially tank-

---

253   Ralph Johnstone, 'The Sea Gypsies: Hard times for a vanishing Philippine tribe', *Asiaweek,* 21 April 1993, p. 47; also Eklöf, *Pirates in Paradise,* pp. 40-1.

254   Santos, 'Piracy and armed robbery against ships in the Philippines', p. 39.

255   Tran Dinh Thanh Lam, 'Pirates plague Vietnamese fishermen', *Asia Times Online,* 12 Nov. 2002. In 2007 Cambodia's Prime Minister Hun Sen admitted he was 'very concerned' that Cambodia could become 'a safe shelter for terrorists in maritime areas' and that he intended his country should cooperate with its neighbours to combat 'terrorists and cross-border criminals': 'Cambodia beefs up maritime security against terrorists, cross-border criminals', *People's Daily Online,* 28 Nov. 2007.

256   For an early example see Kathryn Davies, 'Modern-day pirates use speedboats to raid Southeast Asian sea lanes', *Christian Science Monitor,* 18 Sept. 1981. Also Hyslop, 'Contemporary piracy', pp. 12-15.

ers with foreign flags.[257] In addition the Straits have also experienced the sort of incidents that are common in the Philippines: crew kidnapping, insurgency-related piracy and coastal raids.[258]

Because the Straits are narrow and crowded, almost all types of attack have taken place in international shipping lanes and sparked concerns that they might affect the free flow of trade. This might seem surprising, even alarmist given that, in proportion to the volume of ship movements through the Straits, the chances of suffering a pirate attack are extremely low: Eklöf calculated that based on 200 ships transits a day in 2004 (a figure that *excludes* intra-strait traffic) the probability of an attack was less that 0.2 per cent.[259] Sam Bateman and his colleagues in their study that covered the period from 2000 to 2005 estimated the proportion to be between 0.06 per cent and 0.19 per cent of *total* traffic, the bulk of which moved between local ports.[260] The concerns arose however because, despite this low probability, most of the attacks were mounted on vessels on the move in waters that are narrow and crowded, where sudden changes in the weather and the configuration of the channels demand that crews exercise great care and attention if ships are to be navigated safely.[261] The fear was, and remains, that a large ship or one carrying a hazardous cargo might be left without bridge control and collide with another, so blocking or polluting a key channel.

---

257   'Indonesia identifies three groups in sea crimes', *Channel News Asia,* 31 May 2005.

258   Kidnapping and insurgency-related piracy are dealt with elsewhere. On coastal raiding during the 1980s see the brief mention in Murray, '20th century pirates roam the seas of Southeast Asia'.

259   Eklöf, *Pirates in Paradise*, p. 99. The figure of 200 transits is based on a variety of ship types but *excludes* intra-strait traffic. This figure accords with the 1999 Japan Maritime Research Institute study which found that 75,510 ships over 1,000 GRT transited the Straits in that year. Cited in Bateman *et al.*, 'Safety and security in the Malacca and Singapore Straits', p. 13. According to the Marine Department Peninsula Malaysia, transit traffic through the Straits increased from 43,964 ships in 1999 to 63,636 ships in 2004, an increase of 30.9 per cent. According to this source the 2004 total included 14,144 coastal barter trade movements and 1,131 transverse ferry movements. Cited in Hussin, 'The Management of the Straits of Malacca: Burden Sharing as the Basis for Co-operation', pp. 4-5.

260   Bateman *et al.*,, 'Safety and security in the Malacca and Singapore Straits', p. 20.

261   For a brief summary of the geographical and meteorological characteristics of the Malacca and Singapore Straits see J. Ashley Roach, 'Enhancing maritime security in the Straits of Malacca and Singapore', *JIA*, vol. 59, no. 1, Fall/Winter 2005, pp. 98-100.

Malacca and Singapore Straits: Counter-piracy activity and cooperation. The littoral states of the region, individually and collectively, have struggled to overcome the factors that have encouraged piracy. There can be no question that significant financial resources need to be spent on boats, aircraft, surveillance assets and personnel if the pirates' ability to exploit the region's favourable geography is to be overcome. Nonetheless other, less tractable, obstacles have prevented states from taking effective action and engaging in fruitful cooperation:

1. Complacency that the problem of piracy has been exaggerated, mainly by foreigners. In Indonesia, at least, this is reinforced by the belief that the benefits of piracy suppression do not justify the costs because most of the shipping that is attacked is foreign owned.

2. Resentment that even though the international community has, through a United Nations convention, granted states control over critical straits and huge ocean areas with all their resources, the international states that use these waters simply for transit do not contribute to the cost of security.

3. Corruption that can exist anywhere on a spectrum from the lowest level, where it might involve port officials supplying information, to the highest, where politically powerful figures can provide protection and influence what resources are devoted to the fight.

4. Political priorities that place the need for national cohesion and economic development ahead of piracy suppression; that can in fact view piracy suppression as an irrelevance.

5. Rivalry between states to demonstrate that the piracy problem lies in another state's waters; this led Indonesia, for example, to accuse Malaysia of conspiring with the IMB to "massage" its piracy statistics by locating the majority of incidents on the Indonesian side of the Straits.[262]

6. Fear that what has been won by international agreement can be taken away: that the pressure to adopt definitions of piracy (such as the IMB's) could, if adopted, lead to the erosion of national sovereignty over territorial waters and the "internationalisation" of straits. This, in turn, could be seen internally as a slight on national sovereignty and be used by opponents to stir up political discord.

7. Failure to acknowledge that piracy is a land-based problem which demands effective and sustained land-based policing and political attention if it is to be suppressed.

---

262 Bradford, 'Japanese anti-piracy initiatives in Southeast Asia', p. 499.

Cooperation between states requires the conjunction of perceived self-interest and political maturity. The primary obstacle that inhibits inter-state cooperation anywhere is concern over sovereignty. This is one that is felt acutely in Southeast Asia. The states of the region are young and artificial, to the extent that they are based on colonial-era territories. Neither characteristic is conducive to political self-assurance. The consequence has been that cooperation has been all too often seen as a possible diminution of hard-won sovereignty.[263] Hence, while some purely national measures have been put in place, and some largely symbolic bilateral agreements concluded, the most significant national and regional initiatives to tackle the problem of piracy have come about in response to external promptings: first, the Regional Cooperation Agreement on Combating Piracy and Armed Robbery against Ships in Asia (ReCAAP), which was initiated by Japan starting in 2001 and established mechanisms to achieve international cooperation;[264] secondly, the Regional Maritime Security Initiative (RMSI) proposed by the United States in 2004, which, while it was never implemented because regional states were wary of greater US involvement in their affairs, drove them to take much needed action;[265] thirdly, the 2005 decision of the Joint War Committee of Lloyd's to designate parts of the Malacca Straits to be areas of "Perceived Enhanced Risk" (PER), which put (or threatened to put) an economic cost on Southeast Asian piracy, one that the governments of the littoral states of the region could not disguise,

---

263 Murphy, 'Piracy and UNCLOS: Does international law help regional states combat piracy?' p. 167; John F. Bradford. 'Shifting the Tides against Piracy in Southeast Asian Waters'. *Asian Survey*, Vol. XLVIII, No. 3, May/June 2008, p. 489.. For an example of how these concerns can enter domestic politics and even be used to influence elections see D. Arul Rajoo, 'Foreign powers eyeing Straits of Melaka, says Chandra Muzaffar', *Bernama*, 6 March 2008. For a useful discussion of both the theoretical issues, and the history of the cooperative efforts that have been attempted or undertaken see Ruijie He. 'Ganging up on the Jolly Roger in Asia: International Cooperation and Maritime Piracy'. Cambridge, MA: Massachusetts Institute of Technology. BS/MS thesis, June 2008.

264 Roach, 'Enhancing Maritime Security in the Straits of Malacca and Singapore', p. 106.

265 See, for example, Ioannis Gatsiounis, 'Malaysia tweaks its terror compass', *AsiaTimes.com*, 25 June 2004, and John F. Bradford, 'The growing prospects for maritime security cooperation in Southeast Asia', *NWCR*, vol. 58, no. 3, Summer 2005, pp. 82-3, where he writes, 'it seems one motivation for their development was to exclude the United States and, to a lesser extent, Japan from a direct, visible role in Strait of Malacca security'. Also Storey. 'Securing Southeast Asia's Sea Lanes', pp. 115-6.

manipulate or ignore.[266] The Committee's decision complemented the external political pressure. Measures that might never have been agreed, or if agreed never or only partially implemented, or if implemented not funded adequately or sustained, went ahead, and the chances are reasonable that they will be kept in place until they have brought the threat from disorder in the Straits under greater control.[267] Taken together these various measures can be grouped under national, bilateral and multilateral measures.

(1) National measures: Singapore is the richest littoral state, and because it depends most on free movement through the Straits has invested heavily in its navy and maritime police. In addition it has built an integrated surveillance and information network for tracking suspicious maritime movements, randomly escorts high-value merchant vessels in its waters, and has redesignated shipping lanes to minimise convergence between such vessels and small boats.[268]

Malaysia has taken several steps to improve security. In 2000 the Royal Malaysian Marine Police established an anti-piracy task force equipped with 20 fast strike boats and four rigid inflatable boats and formed a tactical commando unit intended to operate alongside Malaysia's other special forces.[269] The retirement of Prime Minister Mahathir Mohamed accelerated the introduction of constructive measures and the prospect (but not the guarantee) that suggestions for multilateral cooperation would be ac-

---

266 Murphy, 'Piracy and UNCLOS: Does international law help regional states combat piracy?' p. 174. On the background to the JWC's decision see Murphy, 'Slow alarm: The response of the marine insurance industry to the threat of piracy and maritime terrorism', pp. 7-10.

267 Ramadas Rao and Tony Chan, 'Malacca nations shocked into anti-pirate action', *Fairplay*, 11 Aug. 2005; 'Money Talks', *Fairplay*, 17 Aug. 2006; Thomas, 'Malacca Straits a 'war risk zone'? Lloyd's should review its assessment', IDSS *Commentaries*, 19 Aug. 2005, p. 2; 'New Malaysian coastguard to crack down on Malacca Strait piracy', *Lloyd's List*, 12 Oct. 2005; 'Malaysia to step up anti-piracy patrols in Malacca Strait', *Forbes.com*, 9 Feb. 2006; 'New fleet chief vows to combat piracy', *The Jakarta Post*, 18 Feb. 2006; Marcus Hand and James Brewer, 'Malacca Strait declared a high risk zone by Joint War Committee', *Lloyd's List*, 1 July 2005. Several private interviews with the author, Aug. 2005-Feb. 2006. See also the comments of Rupert Atkin, who was Chairman of the JWC at the time the decision was taken to declare the Strait an area of PER: Rupert Atkin, 'Role of insurers key to beating piracy' (Letter to the Editor), *Lloyd's List*, 18 July 2007. The need for the pressure to be maintained is a point that continues to be made by the IMB. For example, ICC-IMB Piracy Report, 2005, p. 16.

268 Ho, 'The Security of Sea Lanes in Southeast Asia', p. 567.

269 *Ibid.*, p. 566.

cepted more readily.[270] The intense nationalism and espousal of "Asian values" that characterised Mahathir's time in office from 1981 to 2003, which undermined anti-piracy cooperation with other states, was replaced with the more open and decisive attitude of Abdullah Badawi's government. In 2005 it announced its intention to build a chain of radar stations along its side of the waterway,[271] and later in the same year formed the Malaysian Maritime Enforcement Agency (MMEA), the equivalent of a coast guard, by bringing together elements from several existing agencies such as the Marine Police, Customs and Immigration departments.[272]

Steps taken by Indonesia include the establishment of naval command and control centres in Batam in the Riau islands and Belawan in northern Sumatra in 2004.[273] By the end of 2008 eight radar stations donated by the US were due to be in operation along the eastern coast of Sumatra.[274]

(2) Bilateral measures: these have been taken between all three littoral states at various times. In 1992 the Indonesia-Singapore Coordinated Patrols were established, involving a direct communications link between the two navies and coordinated patrols undertaken every three months. A similar arrangement was concluded at the same time between Indonesia and Malaysia.[275] However, Bradford reports that bilateral coordination "amounted to little more than exchange of schedules, to which in many cases partners did not adhere".[276] More promisingly a joint radar surveillance system known as

---

270   The US RMSI programme, for example, was rejected in 2004 (despite being discussed openly for months) whereas neither Malaysia nor Indonesia protested when the US and Indian navies escorted high value cargoes through the Malacca Straits in 2001 and 2002. Bradford, 'The growing prospects for maritime security cooperation in Southeast Asia', p. 74.

271   'Malaysia to boost Malacca Strait security with 24-hour radar system', *Channel NewsAsia*, 11 March 2005.

272   'Malaysian Maritime Enforcement Agency' available at http://www.mmea.gov. my/hocgmy/mmea.htm; 'Malaysia's own coast guards by Nov.', *The StarOnline*, 20 June 2005.

273   Bernard Kent Sondakh, 'National sovereignty and security in the Strait of Malacca', Presentation to the Maritime Institute of Malaysia Conference, Kuala Lumpur, Malaysia, 12 Oct. 2004, pp. 8-9.

274   'New radar system to boost Malacca Straits security near completion', *Japan Today*, 13 June 2007.

275   Ho, 'The security of sea lanes in Southeast Asia', p. 568; Hunter, 'The growing threat of modern piracy', p. 75.

276   Bradford, 'The growing prospects for maritime security cooperation in Southeast Asia', p. 66.

Project SURPIC was launched in 2005 to enable Indonesia and Singapore to share a common operating picture of traffic in the Singapore Straits.[277]

(3) Multilateral measures. Regional states were unwilling to enter multilateral arrangements until 2004 when the US advanced its RMSI proposal. The littoral states' immediate response was to sign the MALSINDO (MALaysia-Singapore-INDOnesia) trilateral patrol agreement,[278] supplemented in 2005 by an aerial surveillance agreement dubbed "Eye in the Sky" (EiS).[279] Together they form the Malacca Straits Security Initiative (MSSI).[280] The three participating countries (which Thailand has also announced it will join eventually[281]) each currently contribute two maritime patrol aircraft sorties per week, each flying no less than three miles from any coast. Each aircraft carries a team consisting of one officer from each country. The on-board team advises of any suspicious contacts and the country in whose waters the incident has been observed can activate a patrol. The three countries signed a further agreement in 2006 to establish a Joint Coordinating Committee (JCC) to bring both the maritime and aerial patrols under a single umbrella to expedite information exchange.[282] The final multilateral initiative, whilst not related to security directly, is the IMO-sponsored Marine Electronic Highway (MEH) Project, which aims to provide electronic

277   'Singapore, Indonesia launch sea surveillance system', *Vietnam News Agency,* 27 May 2005.

278   MINDEF Singapore News Release, 'Launch of trilateral coordinated patrols–MALSINDO Malacca Straits coordinated patrol', 20 July 2004; Bradford, 'The growing prospects for maritime security cooperation in Southeast Asia', p. 68 comments that this initiative, although it came about as a reaction to a proposed external programme, was the 'first significantly operationalised multilateral cooperation in Southeast Asia to develop without an extraregional partner.'

279   MINDEF Singapore News Release, 'Launch of the Eye in the Sky (EiS) Initiative', 13 Sept. 2005; Graham Gerald Ong and Joshua Ho, 'Maritime air patrols: The new weapon against piracy in the Malacca Straits', IDSS *Commentaries,* no. 70, 13 Oct. 2005; Catherine Zara Raymond. 'Piracy in Southeast Asia: New trends, issues and responses', IDSS, *Working Paper* no. 89, Oct. 2005, pp. 15-17; S. Ramesh, "Eyes in the Sky' initiative launched for Malacca Strait security', *Channel NewsAsia,* 13 Sept. 2005; Storey. 'Securing Southeast Asia's Sea Lanes', p. 116.

280   Rajeev Sawhney, 'Redefining the limits of the Straits: A composite Malacca Straits security system', IDSS *Commentaries,* 18 May 2006.

281   'Thailand will join anti-piracy patrols in the Malacca Strait', *TNA,* 17 Aug. 2007; 'Thailand to join patrols of Malacca Strait to help boost maritime security', *AP,* 25 Aug. 2007.

282   'Three littoral states agree to set up joint coordinating committee', *Business Times,* 22 April 2006.

navigation charts for the straits, including tidal and current data on a real time basis, AIS shore stations, and to operate a model MEH system for tankers equipped with Electronic Chart Display and Information Systems (ECDIS).[283] Shortage of funds has slowed implementation of the project, even though Korea has made a substantial contribution.[284]

Both MALSINDO and EiS, however, have substantial weaknesses to the point where their effectiveness can be questioned.[285] Catherine Zara Raymond has reported suggestions that EiS in particular is largely "for show".[286] Ian Storey was to unable to draw out from the crews of EiS patrol aircraft how they could, from the air, determine intention amongst the hundreds of small boats using the Straits and thus be able to identify "suspicious activity".[287] Only 17 vessels are currently assigned to the MALSINDO patrols although at least 24 are required. In the main they are manned by junior crews. They have not been given the right of "hot pursuit" into another state's territorial waters. All questions relating to "hot pursuit" are still governed by the existing bilateral agreements, while Malaysia and Singapore still have no agreement to cover such eventualities.[288] In every case chasing boats must "hand over" to a vessel from the state into which the pirates have fled. Similar capacity and procedural difficulties beset the EiS initiative. The current programme calls for eight sorties per week whereas effective coverage demands 10 sorties *per day*. Questions have also been raised about the effectiveness of the surveillance equipment carried on board the aircraft as pirate boats have small radar and heat signatures that can only be detected using highly sensitive apparatus.[289]

---

283 Koji Sekimizu *et al.*, 'The marine electronic highway in the Straits of Malacca and Singapore–An innovative project for the management of highly congested and confined waters', *Tropical Coasts,* July 2001.

284 Roach, 'Enhancing maritime security in the Straits of Malacca and Singapore', p. 107.

285 Ioannis Gatsiounis, 'Pirates mock Malacca Straits security', *AsiaTimes.com,* 9 April 2005; Nachammal Raman, 'Three nations coordinate flights to spy on Malacca pirates', *Christian Science Monitor,* 17 Aug. 2005; Liss, 'Maritime security in Southeast Asia', p. 11.

286 Catherine Zara Raymond, 'Piracy in Southeast Asia: new trends, issues and responses', *Harvard Asia Quarterly,* 9 Feb. 2006.

287 Storey. 'Securing Southeast Asia's Sea Lanes', p. 119.

288 Ho, 'The security of sea lanes in Southeast Asia', p. 572.

289 Ong and Ho, 'Maritime air patrols: The new weapon against piracy in the Malacca Straits'.

Joshua Ho, the Coordinator of the Maritime Security Programme at Singapore's Institute of Defence and Security Studies, has written that although "the functional cooperation between the navies of the three littoral countries is excellent at the tactical level," this does not extend fully to the operational level. He suggests that this is because each country adopts a different approach to command and control: Malaysia's is centralised, Indonesia's is decentralised and Singapore's is coordinated, which impedes performance, decision making and, in particular, interdiction activity.[290]

The primary effect of these patrols is deterrence.[291] As Burnett points out: "Unless pirates are caught in the act...it is impossible to charge them with the crime",[292] although the cases of the *Nepline Delima* in 2005 and the *Kraton* in 2007 suggest that pirates can be caught in the act on occasion[293]. In 2005, for instance, only one of the 101 reported cases of actual or attempted piracy incidents in the waters of Indonesia, Malaysia, the Malacca Straits, and the Singapore Straits resulted in the arrests of the perpetrators.[294] Notably, the apprehension of the pirates was not a direct result of any of the coordinated patrols. Their very presence, however, may encourage fishermen and others to report suspicious activity that will enable the patrols to build an intelligence picture of the Straits and, on occasion, to receive a tip-off that might lead directly to an arrest.

---

290 Joshua Ho, 'Managing the peace-conflict continuum: A coast guard for Singapore?' IDSS *Commentaries*, 28 Nov. 2005. Also Yun Yun Teo, 'Target Malacca Straits: Maritime terrorism in Southeast Asia', *Studies in Conflict and Terrorism*, vol. 30, no. 6, June 2007, pp. 542-55.

291 Kim Hall, 'Consensus and cooperation between littoral states and user nations in combating maritime piracy and violence in the Malacca Straits', University of Cambridge, MPhil Thesis, 2006, pp. 59-60; Storey. 'Securing Southeast Asia's Sea Lanes', p. 125..

292 Burnett, *Dangerous Waters*, p. 179.

293 In the *Nepline Delima* case, recounted in detail in Gwin, 'Dark passage', pp. 136-7 & 148-9, a crew member was able to escape and alert the Malaysian authorities who intercepted the ship before it left their territorial waters. See also ONI WWTTS Report, 22 June 2005, Paragraph K.2. In 2007 the 2,500 dwt product tanker the *Kraton* was hijacked south of Bintan. The master was able to alert the Indonesian authorities who were able to use a tracking system to search for the vessel. When it was boarded the 14 pirates on board were arrested. Marcus Hand, 'Indonesia detains pirates for tanker hijacking': *Lloyd's List*, 26 Sept. 2007. Also ONI WWTTS Report, 22 Sept. 2007, Paragraph K.1.

294 ICC-IMB Piracy Report 2005, pp. 33-43 and 61-3.

The various counter-measures have had an uneven effect. Nonetheless, since they were implemented pirate activity in the Straits has shown a sharp decline. The Malacca and Singapore Straits, which together suffered 80 attacks in 2000, recorded only 19 attacks in 2005. Whether this decline was due to these new arrangements or not, there were no attacks in the early months of 2006 and the hope was expressed that the problem had been curbed if not eliminated.[295] Attacks, however, resumed in April 2006 with five between then and July and a further attempted attack in October.[296] The status of the security arrangements by the end of 2007 was that although information sharing had unquestionably improved, active cooperation remained limited largely to exercises because each littoral state continued to be highly protective of its territorial waters and national intelligence.[297] Although Malaysia claimed that the patrols had reduced the number of incidents to "zero per cent" attacks nonetheless continued albeit at a significantly reduced level.[298] The IMB recorded seven attacks during the period between January and December 2007 which prompted Chan and Ho to comment that the "Malacca and Singapore Straits remain a high risk area of water" and for Chan to question, in 2008, "how effective current regional efforts to combat piracy and armed robbery are to eradicate the long standing problem within these

---

295   Stefano Ambrogi, 'Pirate attacks on the wane', *Reuters*, 7 May 2005, where he reports the note of caution sounded by the IMB. As Bradford writes "there is insufficient direct evidence to correlate them positively with the apparent drop in piracy rates". Bradford. 'Shifting the Tides against Piracy in Southeast Asian Waters', p. 482.

296   On the 2006 incidents see Eileen Ng, 'Pirates attack UN ships near Indonesia', *The State*, 4 July 2006; Simon Montlake, 'Japanese ship foils pirate attack', *Guardian Unlimited*, 4 July 2006; Siti Rahil, 'Japan ship's crew tell of harrowing brush with pirates', *Kyodo News*, 5 July 2006; 'Pirates attack three ships off Indonesia', *Reuters*, 5 July 2006; and 'Pirate attacks in Malacca Strait', *BBC News*, 4 July 2006. On the wider implications of these attacks see David Boey, '3 pirate attacks off Aceh in 2 days spark alarm', *The Straits Times*, 5 July 2006; Marcus Hand, 'Attacks hit bid to end Malacca war risk rating', *Lloyd's List*, 5 July 2006; Donald Urquhart, 'New Malacca pirate attacks raise concern', *Business Times*, 5 July 2006; 'Rebels become Malacca pirates', *Fairplay*, 3 Aug. 2006. On the Oct. attack see 'Piracy returns to the Malacca Straits', *Fairplay*, 10 Oct. 2006.

297   Denise Hammick, 'Turning the tide', *Jane's DW*, vol. 44, no. 47, 21 Nov. 2007, p. 21;

298   Marcus Hand, 'Joint patrols cut Malacca attacks to 'zero per cent'', *Lloyd's List*, 144 April 2008.

waters."[299] It is worth noting that in April 2008 pirates boarded a Thai tanker, the *Pataravarin 2*, off Singapore but after robbing the crew left the vessel apparently disappointed that it was carrying jet fuel rather than the diesel that they were expecting to find.[300] Diesel has been a traditional target for organised pirate gangs in the region because, as been noted already, it is easy to sell on the local black market. This attack, moreover, possibly reflects a return towards more organised attacks, a pattern noted by Chan and Ho in their first report in 2008.[301]

International attention on Malacca and Singapore Straits piracy has always focused on the threat to international shipping. What has generally been ignored has been attacks on local shipping, fishing craft in particular, and there is no reason to believe that the number of attacks on these vessels has declined. In July 2006 the official Malaysian news agency, Bernama, carried a report that the fishermen from the village of Parit Jawa in Johore had stopped going to sea because pirates attacked them regularly, often with automatic weapons. While the pirates never attacked when police patrols were in the area, the villagers said they rarely filed incident reports because they did not want to be "burdened by police investigation that could mean being interviewed seven or eight times." The pirates were described as "foreigners", which was presumably a euphemism for Indonesians.[302] In a second village, Hutan Melintang, which is home to a 900-vessel fleet, a fishing boat has been attacked on average every month. Since the 1970s the local fishermen have complained that "lost commands", that is to say rogue elements of Indonesian police and navy, have been responsible for around half the attacks but, because nothing has been done to stop them, predation has become a way of life and an easy way to make a living.[303] In his address to a maritime security

299   ICC-IMB Piracy Report, 2007, Table 1, p. 5. Jane Chan and Joshua Ho, 'Report on armed robbery and piracy in Southeast Asia 2007', S. Rajaratnam School of International Studies, Maritime Security Programme, 31 Jan. 2008, p. 7. Jane Chan. 'Southeast Asia Maritime Security Review, 2nd Quarter 2008'. S. Rajaratnam School of International Studies, Maritime Security Programme, ND.

300   Achadtata Chuenniran, 'Pirates rob Thai tanker crew', *Bangkok Post*, 288 April 2008; 'Heavily-armed pirates attack, Thai, South Korea ships', *Channel NewsAsia*, 30 April 2008. ONI WWTTS Report, 30 April 2008, Paragraph K.3.

301   Jane Chan and Joshua Ho, 'Report on Armed Robbery and Piracy in Southeast Asia, 1st Quarter 2008', S. Rajaratnam School of International Studies, Maritime Security Programme, ND, p. 2.

302   'Piracy: Fishermen reluctant to go to sea', *Bernama.com*, 21 July 2006.

303   Langit-Dursin, 'Indonesia key to end piracy in Malacca Straits'; also Carolin

conference in 2007 the Malaysian Inspector-General of Police, Tan Sri Musa Hassan, talked about a "criminal phenomenon" of extortion in the Malacca Straits where pirates were forcing fishermen to pay a "ransom" in exchange for "safe fishing certification". He added that, although the problem was confined currently to a limited number of areas, it was becoming rampant.[304]

However, as Liss points out, fishermen in some case leave themselves open to depredation. As traditional grounds become less productive fishermen are tempted to fish illegally either in the waters of other states or in protected areas such as national parks. In no position to call either for protection or to report the incident subsequently, they are easy prey for corrupt police, naval personnel and pirates.[305]

Nor was this harassment confined to the Malaysian side of the Strait. In 2003 the North Sumatran owner of a small fishing fleet told the *Jakarta Post* that different groups of pirates would demand protection money which could add up to Rp 4 million (about $440 in 2007 dollars) per boat per day. In 2004 the director of the North Sumatra Fishery Office claimed that at least 30 fishing vessels, 15 of them Indonesian, had been attacked off North Sumatra and Aceh in the first third of the year and that two-thirds of the province's fishing fleet—8,000 boats—were tied up because of the piracy threat.[306]

There is, therefore, little reason to take comfort from, or to become complacent about, the sort of improvements that appear to have occurred in the Malacca and Singapore Straits.[307] Piracy's signal characteristic is its mobility. As fishermen follow fish so pirates follow prey. Vijay Sakhuja likens pirates to sharks and says that "like sharks...they breed and show up more often in some regions than others...piracy moves around, and its centre of gravity keeps shifting (but) pirate-plagued areas remain

---

Liss, 'The roots of piracy in Southeast Asia', *Austral Policy Forum*, 07-18A, 22 Oct. 2007, who reports that fines can be paid at sea, in which case the fishing boat is allowed to go, or the boats can be taken to Indonesia where they can be detained for months as negotiations are conducted.

304 'Melaka Straits must be kept safe from maritime terrorism, says IGP', *Bernama*, 12 June 2007.

305 Liss, 'The roots of piracy in Southeast Asia'.

306 Eklöf, *Pirates in Paradise*, p. 54.

307 For example, Felix Soh, 'Straits of Malacca now free of pirate attacks'. *Straits Times*, 13 April 1996

active".[308] Piracy attacks in the Straits might have gone down but few of the perpetrators have been caught, and given piracy's endemic nature there must be at least a suspicion that the gangs are biding their time.[309] Pottengal Mukundan, the director of the IMB, said in 2007 that "we know the gangs are there...The moment they feel that law enforcement have taken their eye off the ball and are looking somewhere else and have no time for piracy, surely the attacks will come back."[310] It appears, for example, that at least some of the pirate activity that used to take place in the Malacca Straits has transferred to other piracy "blackspots", one close to the Natuna Islands in the South China Sea and another in the Gelasa Strait between Bangka and Belitung Islands.[311] In 2008 the IMB warned that between March and June five ships had been attacked in the vicinity of the Anambas Islands, part of the Nantuas.[312] Some local gangs in the Malacca Straits would lack the skill, equipment or motivation to move so far. However, the gang led by Winang, mentioned earlier, that came from South Sumatra but based itself amongst the fishing people of Jemaja for months at a time, illustrates that mobility is possible, while organised crime operations would hire local labour as they needed it. Karsten von Hoesslin, another researcher who has conducted fieldwork in the region, suggests that the Bhudil Synil gang, which used to be based on Batam, transferred their operation to Lombok, and Bobby's Gang began attacking shipping in the Gelasa Strait and the Java Sea.[313] Given also that in order to improve policing in one area the law enforcement agencies would probably have moved assets from another, local gangs in the denuded

308 Vijay Sakhuja, 'Indian Ocean and the safety of sea lines of communication', *Strategic Analysis,* vol. XXV, no. 5, Aug. 2001.

309 Simon Montlake, 'Hard times for pirates in busy world waterway', *Christian Science Monitor,* 30 Oct. 2006; Robin Brant. 'Tackling rising threat of piracy'. *BBC News,* 23 May 2008.

310 Clarence Fernandez, 'Strait nations urged not to relax piracy vigil', *Reuters,* 15 June 2007. Also Marcus Hand, 'Keep up pressure on pirates, urges IMB', *Lloyd's List,* 12 May 2006 and Storey. 'Securing Southeast Asia's Sea Lanes', p. 120 on concerns that the littoral states lack the resources to maintain the initiative.

311 Gelasa Straits are sometimes spelt Gerasa and even Gaspar on some maps. For a report on a 2006 attack see Akihiro Ishihara, 'JCG seeks foreign help in probe of pirate attack', *Daily Yomiuri Online,* 20 June 2006; also IMB reports.

312 Marcus Hand. 'Pirate attack warning at Anambas Islands'. *Lloyd's List,* 9 June 2008.

313 Karsten von Hoesslin. Interview with author, March 2008.

area could well be tempted to exploit the opportunity presented by the newly permissive environment.

Whatever the circumstances, however, so long as littoral states retain a reactive stance, pirates retain the initiative. In 2007 for example, Datuk Jalaluddin, the chief of the Malaysian marine police, complained that if information about an incident took hours to arrive it gave the pirates time to make their escape, but admitted that even if they were given timely advice they would still take between 30 minutes and an hour to respond.[314]

South China Sea

Although Indonesia's position on the international league table has remained largely unchanged, the piracy problem in the waters of other states has ebbed and flowed. Like all crime statistics it is likely that the number of piracy reports (and thus the number of recorded incidents) has increased as awareness of the problem had grown. Grounds for sug-

Rank	1995	2000	2005
1	Indonesia	Indonesia	Indonesia
2	China/HK/Macau	Malacca Straits	Somalia
3	Philippines	Bangladesh	Bangladesh
4	Brazil	India	Nigeria
5	Somalia	Malaysia	India
6	India	Ecuador	Malacca Straits
	Iran	Gulf of Aden/Red Sea	
7	"HLH"*	Philippines	Gulf of Aden/Red Sea
		South China Sea	Iraq
		Nigeria	Vietnam
8	Sri Lanka		Jamaica
9	Malaysia		

Table 5. Sea areas with the highest number of piracy incidents Selected years 1995-2005. Source: International Maritime Bureau, 2006, "Hong Kong-Luzon-Hainan Island"

gesting this come from the fact that the proportion of attacks reported from *outside* East and Southeast Asia grew from 38 per cent in 1995 to 51 per cent in 2005. It is also true that in 1983 it was the problem of piracy off West Africa (see below) that first caught the IMO's attention,

---

314   V. Shankar Ganesh, 'Malaysian, Indonesian police to up anti-piracy operations in Straits of Malacca', *New Straits Times*, 18 June 2007.

not piracy in Asia.[315] Therefore there is some value in looking at how the rankings have changed at five-year intervals.

Between 1993 and 1995 the second focus after Indonesia was the South China Sea, Hong Kong and Macau, and the so-called "Hong Kong-Luzon-Hainan Island (HLH) triangle".[316] [317] Numerous incidents occurred, several of which indicated the involvement of organised criminal gangs.[318] However, the most noteworthy characteristic was the involvement of official Chinese patrol craft. The political aspect of this episode was discussed earlier. Chinese vessels, possibly connected to the regional government or military administration on Hainan Island off China's southern coast, knowing that cigarettes being smuggled into China were brought in by ship from Singapore, ventured far out into the South China Sea to intercept and detain vessels, purportedly in order to enforce "Chinese" customs duties. One example was the *Hye Mieko*, which reported that it was hijacked off the Cambodian coast by a boat resembling a Chinese Customs launch and forced to accompany it 1,000 miles to Shanwei in Guandung Province. There the Chinese authorities charged the vessel with attempting to smuggle its cargo of cigarettes into China. The boat and its cargo were promptly seized.[319] Other seizures, however, undermined the anti-smuggling argument.[320] For example, a Singapore-flagged freighter, the *Vosa Carrier*, was seized by what the crew described as a Chinese military patrol craft while en route from Hong Kong to Haiphong in Vietnam in 1997. They were forced to sail the ship to the Chinese port of Hui Lai and then to Pao Tai where they were deprived of food, water and sleep and forced to sign false confessions before their cargo worth $2.5 million was confiscated.[321] In

315   ICC-IMB Piracy Report, 2005, Table 1, p. 5.

316   Chalk, *Grey-Area Phenomena in Southeast Asia*, pp. 29-30.

317   In 1985 Roger Villar identified 1) West Africa, 2) Singapore, 3) Gulf of Siam and Thailand, 4) Philippines, 5) Central and South America. In 1989 Samuel Menefee identified 1) West African piracy, 2) Malacca and Singapore Straits piracy, 3) Philippines maritime violence, 4) 'Boat' People, 5) Attacks on Haitian refugees. See Villar, *Piracy Today*, pp. 91-146 and Menefee, 'Scourges of the sea: Piracy and maritime crime', p. 16.

318   Menefee, *TMV*, p. 70.

319   Dubner, 'Human rights and environmental disaster', p. 8; Menefee, *TMV*, p. 71; Jayant Abhyankar. 'Maritime fraud and piracy', *TOC*, vol. 4, no. 3-4, Autumn/Winter 1998, p. 192; IMB, 'Piracy and armed robbery against ships', p. 39. NGA ASAM 1995-104, 23 June 1995.

320   Vatikiotis and Westlake, 'Gunboat Diplomacy', p. 23.

321   'The bloody cost of inaction', *Fairplay*, 3 Sept. 1998, p. 24; 'China: Miscel-

1991, 15 pirates who claimed to be part of the PLAN demanded that a loaded tanker, the *World Bridge,* should stop and be searched. When the master refused they threw explosives onto the deck and fired at the hull before giving up.[322] In fact one of the notable characteristics of piracy in the South China Sea during this period, certainly when compared with piracy in Southeast Asia, was the number and weight of firearms in evidence, including rocket launchers, whereas Southeast Asian pirates largely employed edged weapons but firearms only occasionally.[323] Finally, an insight into the extent of the links between these hijackings by naval or police vessels and organised crime was given by the discovery of the *East Wind,* a Panamanian freighter that had been seized by the Chinese authorities in 1992, adrift in the Pacific in 1993 with 527 Chinese migrants on board who were apparently being smuggled to the US.[324]

As suggested earlier, it is not clear why this activity ceased around 1995. Leaving the political suggestions to one side, one explanation is that Beijing reined in the local administration because it was conscious that the activity was harming China's reputation internationally and, perhaps more pertinently, because the rise of lawlessness and corruption was a challenge to its own authority.[325] It claimed that if official craft were involved they came from "rogue units",[326] and certainly denied that the customs launch

---

laneous; Conainers confiscated from Singapore vessel by China'. *Lloyd's List,* 18 Nov. 1997; Eric Ellen. 'Is there an even darker side to China Sea piracy?' *Lloyd's List,* 18 December 1997. NGA ASAM 1998-21, 11 Oct. 1997. Other seizures included the *Havkong* taken to Shen Zeng, the *Asian Friendship* which was sailed to Shanwei and the *Anabas* which was taken to an unspecified destination. Eric Ellen. 'Shipowners naïve to think that paying ransom will stop vessel seizures'. ICC *Commercial Crime International,* March 1998, p. 4; On the *Asian Friendship* specifically see Niall Fraser, 'China: Mainland accussed of ship hijack', *Lloyd's List,* 29 Nov. 1997.

322   Menefee, *TMV,* p. 69. NGA ASAM 1992-25, 25 Sept. 1992. The explosives were later identified as very large fireworks. 'South China Sea pirates extend range', *Lloyd's List,* 30 Sept. 1992, p. 2.

323   US Department of Energy, 'Piracy: The threat to tanker traffic', p. 6.

324   William M. Carpenter and David G. Wiencek, 'Maritime piracy: A growing threat in the Post-Cold War World' in Thomas C. Fitzhugh III (ed.), *International Perspectives on Maritime Security.* Charlotte, NC: Maritime Security Council, 1996, p. 232.

325   David Rennie, 'China orders military to wage war on killer pirates', *Daily Telegraph,* 27 Nov. 1999.

326   Vatikiotis and Westlake, 'Gunboat diplomacy', p. 23; Paul Richardson, 'China explains 'piracy attacks", *Lloyd's List,* 18 March 1994, p. 12; Lind Choy, 'Official link to pirates rejected', *South China Morning Post,* 19 March 1994.

involved in the *Hye Mieko* incident was on official business.[327] However, the breakneck growth in the Chinese economy that started around this period, which appeared to weaken the central government's control over its provincial officials, made China the favoured destination for black market goods. Factory managers desperate to make their quotas were apparently willing to buy the raw materials they needed anywhere they could find them, no questions asked. Consequently, the waters of Southeast Asia as far south as the Malacca Straits experienced an unusually high number of major ship hijackings from the early 1990s to the early 2000s; the cargoes vanished without trace, the assumption being that most of them ended up in the rapidly expanding factories of China's coastal belt. Interestingly, the hijacking of the *MT Steadfast* and two other vessels in December 2005 prompted ONI to comment:

These incidents appear to represent a form of piracy not reported since China's crackdown on black-market activity starting in 1998, wherein a ship is targeted for seizure at its load port and the cargo is taken to some destination, where arrangements for disposal have already been concluded. The complexity of the operation suggests transnational players at the ship selection and cargo-disposal ends of the operation. In these types of cases, crew and ship owner complicity must be considered, since they have no immediate financial interest in the cargo, per se. Since the crackdown on the illegal Chinese markets, hijackers have experienced difficulty disposing of their cargos. If the *Steadfast* is indeed hijacked and is not rapidly located and its cargo recovered, or traced, this could be a sign that criminal gangs have solved their problem with disposal of stolen goods.[328]

In fact the *Steadfast* was recovered quickly.[329] Nonetheless the problem has by no means gone away. In October 2006 a tanker carrying 1,800 tonnes of diesel was stolen off Dubai. In November it turned up for sale in Singapore minus its cargo and its crew.[330] In September 2007 a 2,500-dwt product tanker, the *Kraton,* was hijacked on a voyage within Indonesia from Palembang to Cilacap with the apparent intention of diverting it to Malaysia. The pirates failed to disable the ship's tracking system, which enabled the Indonesian authorities to recapture the vessel.[331]

---

327   Menefee, *TMV*, p. 71.

328   NGA ASAM 2006-7, 19 Dec. 2005; see also Marcus Hand, 'Chemtanker feared hijacked', *Lloyd's List*, 22 Dec. 2005.

329   Marcus Hand, 'Joint alert forces pirates to flee hijacked tanker', *Lloyd's List*, 29 Dec. 2005.

330   'Phantom ship sale', *Shiptalk.com*, 27 Nov. 2006.

331   Marcus Hand, 'Indonesia detains pirates for tanker hijacking', *Lloyd's List*, 26

Bay of Bengal – Bangladesh

As Vijay Sakhuja noted, the volume of piracy attacks at the northern end of the South China Sea declined such that the centre of gravity swung westwards towards the Bay of Bengal and the Arabian Sea.[332] The IMB's figures appeared to confirm this: India recorded five attacks in 2006, which was down from 35 in 2000, but on par with the five it recorded in 1992. The problem, however, has become most serious off Bangladesh. According to IMB figures there were two attacks in 1994 but the number increased steadily until, between 2000 and 2005, Bangladeshi waters were the most dangerous after Indonesia's.[333] In 2006 47 attacks were recorded, only three fewer attacks than in Indonesia.[334] In reality the number of pirate attacks was probably significantly more. Menefee, who undertook a detailed study of Bangladeshi piracy in 2003, which drew on local as well as international reports of the problem, suggests that the number of boats attacked was probably 75 per cent more than was recorded by either the IMB or the IMO.[335]

Piracy in Bangladesh started in the early 1980s. It is concentrated in two areas: firstly around the port of Chittagong, which has an unenviable reputation for organised crime, corruption and poor management; the suspicion of collusion between the Chittagong port authority employees and the pirates will not go away. Secondly, the estuarial region in the southwest.[336] Although most of the attacks have been of the petty variety, as in Indonesia long knives are much in evidence and a strain of viciousness runs through the reports stretching back many years. In 1982, for example, eight of the eleven-man crew of a trawler were tied in sacks by 30 pirates and thrown overboard to drown. The pirates kept the fishermen's catch, worth $30,000.[337] In 1995

Sept. 2007; ICC-IMB Piracy Report, 2007, p. 30.

332   Sakhuja, 'Indian Ocean and the safety of sea lines of communication'.

333   Although there were no attacks in the Malacca Straits in the first three months of 2006, in 2004 it appeared that the focus was swinging back in that direction with a 33 per cent rise in incidents in the first half of 2004, whereas the number of attacks in Indian and Bangladeshi waters fell: 'Malacca sea piracy on rise', *CNN.com*, 25 July 2004.

334   ICC-IMB Piracy Report, 2006, p. 5.

335   Menefee, 'Under-reporting of the problems of maritime piracy and terrorism', p. 249.

336   Nazimuddin Shyamol, 'Mafia syndicates growing in Ctg port', *The Independent* (Bangladesh), 14 May 2006; 'Corruption charges cheat Chittagong port sell-off', *Fairplay*, 1 June 2006.

337   Menefee, *TMV*, p. 51.

another group of 30 pirates boarded another fishing vessel, the *Aliya,* and forced the crew over the side, 30 of whom are believed to have drowned.[338] The level of violence has actually increased; the use of guns has been reported, and incidents of kidnapping, mainly of fishermen, appear to be on the rise.[339] This could be because of clan rivalries over access to fishing grounds. The seriousness of the attacks can be gauged from the fact that between April and June 2006 six fishermen were killed and 200 trawlers looted of fish, nets, engines and fuel oil. Forty fishermen were abducted and 100 others injured. The most notorious pirate gang leaders are reputed to operate from secret dens in the deep forest and saltwater swamps of the Sunderbans that cover the lower part of the Ganges delta.[340] In August 2003 the *Bangladesh Observer* quoted local fishermen who had told the paper that ten groups of pirates were operating in the Sunderbans, often fighting between themselves for domination.[341] It is reported that the Bangladeshi authorities are now mounting a campaign to suppress pirate activity.[342] Although reports of arrests are scarce, in August 2006 Alauddin, the leader of the infamous "Alauddin Bahini" gang, was shot and killed in a shootout with police.[343] As in so many areas, the role of corrupt officials and police connivance is mentioned regularly in reports.[344]

South America

While the main concentration of piracy incidents (65 per cent of all piracy attacks world wide, 2001-2005) occurs in an arc around the Southeast Asian peninsula and its offshore archipelagos, i.e. from the "HLH" triangle through the Philippines and Indonesia to the Bay of Bengal, they also oc-

---

338 Chalk, *Non-Military Security and Global Order,* p. 74; Menefee, *TMV,* p. 52.

339 See, for example, the report of 28 fishermen being abducted by 13 pirates in NGA ASAM 2006-136, 15 May 2006. Not that the pirates always have it their own way. In 2003 the IMB reported that villagers had attacked and lynched 28 pirates on the Noakhali coast south of Chittagong. ICC-IMB Piracy Report for 1 Jan.-31 Dec. 2003, p. 25.

340 ONI, WWTTS Report, 21 June 2006, Paragraph H.2.

341 Menefee, 'Under-reporting of the problems of maritime piracy and terrorism', p. 255

342 'Bangladesh Coast Guard and Navy begin drive against pirates', *Narinjara News,* 18 July 2006; ONI, WWTTS Report, 19 July 2006, Paragraph D.1.

343 ONI, WWTTS Report, 23 Aug. 2006, Paragraph D.1.

344 Menefee, 'Under-reporting of the problems of maritime piracy and terrorism', pp. 253 & 254.

cur elsewhere. In South America, between 1997 and 2002, the waters off Ecuador witnessed an attack about once a month. These were concentrated in the vicinity of Guayaquil, a city where separatist pressures had both weakened the power of central government authority and encouraged corruption amongst local law enforcement agencies.

Brazil has had a serious piracy problem in the past with a high of 17 attacks in 1995. The IMO brought substantial pressure to bear on the Brazilian government that responded by improving maritime security, focusing its attentions on the ports of Rio de Janeiro and, in particular, Santos (where corruption in the police force was rife), which between 1994 and 2000 were especially dangerous. A suspiciously high proportion of the attacks appeared to be well organised and targeted against specific vessels and cargoes.[345] The attack on the LPG carrier *Isomeria*, which was boarded while it was discharging its cargo at Santos in January 1998 by four pirates carrying Uzi sub-machine guns (who injured the second officer during the subsequent shoot-out with police), was perhaps the most noteworthy incident.[346] By the mid-2000s Santos was once again experiencing problems, with an upsurge in attacks on container ships.[347] However, attacks were not restricted to these ports alone. In 2001 the internationally renowned sailor Sir Peter Blake was murdered on board his yacht as it lay at anchor awaiting customs clearance near the mouth of the Amazon.[348] Although, pirate attacks in Brazilian waters overall have been reduced, they have not been eradicated; there

---

345   Chalk, *Non-Military Security and Global Order,* p. 71.

346   'Officer shot in pirate attack', NUMAST *Telegraph,* vol. 31, no. 2, Feb. 1998, p. 1; Michael Fabey, 'Sitting ducks', *Latin Trade,* Sept. 1999; Countryman & McDaniel Vessel Loss Dispatches, Jan. 1998 available at http://www.cargolaw.com/presentations_casualties_a.html#nov_98. Also NGA ARAM 1998-1, 9 Jan. 1998 where it is noted that this was the first time the Brazilian authorities successfully apprehended perpetrators in Santos.

347   Rob Ward, 'Piracy attacks on boxships erupt again in Santos port', *Lloyd's List,* 17 Nov. 2006; ONI WWTTS Report, 6 Dec. 2006, Paragraph D.3.

348   The attack took place near Macapa. For a description of the attacks see 'Peter Blake–Murder on the Amazon', *Latitude 38,* Jan. 2002. See also John Simpson, 'Death on the Amazon sheds light on modern-day piracy', *Sunday Telegraph,* 9 Dec. 2001 and Andrew Downie and Tim Jeffery, 'Blake's killers are jailed', *Daily Telegraph,* 20 June 2002. See also Burnett, *Dangerous Waters,* p. 85. In the relevant ASAM, 2001-329 dated 5 Dec. 2001, ONI point to circumstantial evidence that raises the question whether pirates carried out the attack or Blake was instead murdered because his environmental campaigning might have upset certain Amazonian business interests.

were two in 2005, seven in 2006 and continuing problems in Santos which meant that by 2008 its ISPS certification was in jeopardy.[349]

Piracy in the Caribbean did not come to a happy end with Jack Sparrow. Piracy incidents occur regularly throughout the region from Suriname and Guyana—where the attacks appear to be mounted primarily against fishermen, some of them involving vicious violence—westwards along the coast of Venezuela to Colombia, where they involve yachts and ships at anchor off ports such as Maracaibo, Cartagena and Barranquilla. Reports of ships being boarded while anchored off the port of Kingston, Jamaica, became more frequent starting in 2003 and sufficiently worrisome by 2006 for the IMB to suggest that it should be declared a piracy "hotspot". This was disputed vigorously by port officials, who were possibly concerned that the reports could damage the plan to develop Kingston as a cargo transshipment centre.[350]

Yacht piracy

Yacht piracy can occur anywhere.[351] A 2006 report pointed to the trade in yachts stolen off France from where they were run across the Mediterranean to Malta or Tunisia. There they were repainted before being sailed to the Black Sea to be sold to the newly rich of Russia and the Ukraine.[352] However, it has been a particularly frequent occurrence in Caribbean wa-

---

349 ICC-IMB Piracy Report for the period 1 Jan. to 31 Dec. 2006, Table 1, p. 5. Robert Ward, 'Piracy could cost Santos ISPS certification', *Lloyd's List*, 9 April 2008.

350 ICC-IMB Piracy Report 2006, Table 1, p. 5; 'No piracy in Jamaica waters, official says', *Reuters AlertNet* 26 May 2006. It is also worth noting that, contrary to the official position, local fishermen have been complaining about piracy attacks and that Jamaican waters have been over-fished. There is also concern as to whether or not Jamaica has the resources to defend its maritime domain. See Michael Burke, 'Difficult decisions', *Jamaica Observer*, 29 June 2006. For a report detailing pirate attacks on Jamaican fishing boats see ONI WWTTS Report, 12 July 2006.

351 See, for example, Klaus Hympendahl (tr. Martin Sokolinsky). *Pirates Aboard!* Dobbs Ferry: Sheridan House, 2005; also Burnett, *Dangerous Waters*, pp. 1-8. The yachting fraternity draw on a number of websites to keep abreast of piracy risks. The two main ones are http://www.noonsite.com/General/Piracy and http://www.yachtpiracy.org/en/dangerous_regions.htm. Interestingly builders of 'super' yachts are now incorporating increasingly sophisticated levels of security: Ricky Barrett. 'Builders arm boats to chase off pirates', *The Sun News*, 10 Aug. 2006.

352 Henry Samuel, 'Gendarmes hunt down Riviera boat thieves', *Daily Telegraph*, 14 July 2006.

ters, from the coast of Venezuela northwards up the island chain to the Bahamas and the coast of Florida; that is to say, along the island-hopping drug smuggling route from South to North America. In most cases when drug runners are involved they kill or kidnap those on board and then sell or sink the yacht after one trip to minimise the risk of detection. The US authorities suspect that over the years many more yachts have disappeared than have been reported.[353] Of the 610 American yachts that went missing between 1970 and 1974 for example , 44 matched the profile of the yachts drug runners looked for; 202 people linked to these specific losses remain missing.[354]

East Africa – Somalia

Outside Asia, it is in the waters around Somalia that the pirate presence has been greatest over the past few years. Although its precise origins are unclear, the problem began in the region in the early 1990s as an aspect of the generalised disorder that followed the overthrow of the socialist dictator Muhammad Siad Barre by clan-based warlords. The consequence of that disorder is that the land area of Somalia is split three ways politically between the break-away republic of Somaliland which abuts Djibouti in the northwest, the break-away region of Puntland in the northeast, and the south which is nominally controlled by the UN-recognised Transitional Federal Government (TFG) but is actually divided between various warlord groupings.

In 1995, the IMO reported the case of the *Bonsella*, attacked in September 1994 by a party of 26 pirates posing as coastguards, who for six days used it as a base from which to attack other ships.[355] In 1997 the IMB reported that an armed faction seized the MV *Baharihindi* and sailed it to Garad on the east coast. It was released after a $200,000 ransom had been paid but not before the third officer had been shot in the stomach.[356] By

---

353 Chalk, *Non-Military Security and Global Order*, pp. 72-3.

354 Menefee, *TMV*, p. 98.

355 IMO MSC/Circ. 698, 30 June 1995, p. 3; also Nick Ryan, 'Wave of terror', *The Scotsman 'Weekend'*, Aug. 1997; Michael McDaniel, 'Modern high seas piracy'. For a detailed account see NGA ASAM 1995-8, 9 Oct. 1994.

356 IMB, 'Piracy and armed robbery against ships', p. 16; 'The bloody cost of inaction', pp. 24-25.

1998, two thirds of all maritime abductions worldwide were taking place in the Gulf of Aden close to Somalia.[357]

Much Somali piracy appears to have its roots in fishing disputes: the absence of any effective authority operating along Africa's longest national coastline has meant that fishing vessels from Europe and East Asia can exploit the area's rich marine resources at the expense of locals, causing dangerous tensions.[358] Some commentators argue that the main source of piracy in the region is armed groups, formed by local fishermen in response to unregulated fishing by foreign fishing vessels, which subsequently become pirate gangs.[359] Certainly the issue is cited by those accused of piracy: the Somalis captured by the US navy ship USS *Gonzalez* in March 2006 apparently claimed to be defending local fishermen by 'taxing' illicit foreign trawlers, as did the attackers of the *Dongwon-ho* the following month.[360]

In 2000, there were 23 incidents of piracy recorded in the Red Sea-Aden-Somalia region, a third of the African total.[361] This level was sustained through 2001 but this was also the year of the US's *Operation Enduring Freedom* in Afghanistan. Fearing that high-ranking members of al-Qaeda would attempt to escape via Pakistan and the Arabian Peninsula to the Horn of Africa, the US assembled the multinational Coalition Task Force (CTF) 150 to patrol the northern Arabian Sea from the Pakistani coast to Somalia. The number of reported piracy incidents declined. In 2004, only ten incidents were recorded but this turned out to be only a brief respite. In 2005 pirate attacks resumed in earnest off the Somali coast, fueled by continuing warlordism on land.

Somali piracy appears to be a hybrid of common and organised pirate types. At sea Somali pirates have tended to employ basic methods and haphazard planning. On shore their tactic of hijacking vessels and holding

---

357 Chalk. *Non-Military Security and Global Order,* p. 75.

358 Scott Coffen-Smout, 'Pirates, warlords and rogue fishing vessels in Somalia's unruly seas', ND; also 'US captures 13 Somali 'pirates', *BBC News,* 19 March 2006.

359 Abdulkadir Khalif, 'How illegal fishing feeds Somali piracy', *The East African* (Nairobi) 15 Nov. 2005 and Karsten von Hoesslin, 'Taiwan and piracy along the Horn of Africa', *Taiwan Journal,* 24 Feb. 2006.

360 On the *Dongwon-ho,* see Bo-Mi Lim, 'Militants who seize S. Korea ship off Somalia say they're defending against illegal fishing', *NCTimes.com,* 5 April 2006.

361 For more details about African piracy see Peter Chalk, 'Africa suffers wave of maritime violence', RAND *Commentary,* 2001.

them, along with crew and cargo, to ransom is relatively sophisticated.[362] The lawless conditions in Somalia, where it is possible to moor a ship beyond the reach of rescue or retaliation, make it an ideal place for ransom-based piracy to thrive. The ransom income of Somali pirates has probably been substantial. For example, the most successful group, the Xarardheere-based 'Somali Marines', apparently demanded $1m and eventually settled for $800,000 for the return of the *Dongwon-ho*, a South Korean tuna fishing vessel captured in April 2006.[363]

It was this group that was behind the attack in November 2005 on the Bahamas-flagged, US-operated cruise liner *Seabourn Spirit*. The ship was sailing about 100 miles off the coast, well within the area that the IMB and ONI advised ships to avoid, when it was attacked and chased by a group of pirates firing automatic rifles and rocket-propelled grenades. It managed to increase speed and escape but the incident drew the attention of the world's media to the issue of Somali piracy.[364] The attack on the *Seabourn Spirit*, being an assault on a passenger ship under US ownership and, as such, an object of international attention, prompted the IMO to raise the issue of piracy at the UN Security Council in the hope of obtaining a UNSC resolution.[365] The attempt was only partially successful. In March 2006 the Security Council issued a statement which stated that member states with naval vessels in the vicinity should be vigilant and "take appropriate action to protect merchant shipping, in particular the transportation of humanitarian aid, against any such act, in line with international law".[366] The response of the US government was much more robust. Whereas prior to

---

362   It is worth taking note of the press release issued by Andrew Mwangura of the Seafarers' Assistance Programme, Mombasa, Kenya, on 8 Feb. 2006.

363   ONI WWTTS report, 26 April 2006. Paragraph H.8; NGA ASAM 2006-91, 4 April 2006.

364   Amongst the many accounts see, for example, 'Cruise ship repels Somali pirates', *BBC News,* 5 Nov. 2005; 'Pirates attack cruise ship', *CBS News,* 5 Nov. 2005 and 'Somalia: Liner docks after pirate attack', *New York Times,* 8 Nov. 2005. Also ONI WWTTS report, 30 Nov. 2005, Paragraph H.4; NGA ASAM 2005-340, 5 Nov. 2005. Unfortunately the attack sparked speculation that it had been mounted by terrorists. 'Missile 'embedded in US cruise ship", *WorldNetDaily,* 7 Nov. 2006.

365   Stefano Ambrogi.'IMO asks Security Council to act on Somalia piracy', *Reuters AlertNet,* 28 June 2007.

366   See 'Somalia: Security council urges action over piracy off the coast of Somalia in line with IMO assembly resolution', *Cargo Security International,* 17 March 2006; also Richard Meade, 'Cruise attack sparks UN action', *Fairplay,* 10 Nov. 2005.

the attack CTF 150 had focused on counter-terrorism, afterwards the US navy, with the support of its Coalition partners, adopted a more aggressive posture towards piracy starting late in 2005.

Much attention was devoted to curbing the activities of the 'Somali Marines', which during its first active period, from 2005 to 2006, was the most effective pirate gang operating off Somalia. It stood out because it was willing to venture far out to sea. In 2004, the IMB advised ships to sail at least 50 nautical miles (93 km) from the coast, preferably further, but by autumn 2005 had increased this to 150nm (278 km).[367] Even these distances did not appear to be far enough. In mid-November 2005, a general cargo vessel reported that it was chased for one and a half hours 390nm (720 km) out to sea.[368] Despite the warnings, ships continued to sail closer to the coast than was advisable.

Nonetheless, the success of this pirate group in locating targets at these ranges, and their maritime competence in general, should not be exaggerated. Some attempted attacks reported as taking place 200nm (370 km) or more from the coast, including the supposed chase at 390nm noted above, could have been cases of masters, fearing a pirate attack, confusing at a distance the sight of a fishing ship deploying its nets with a mother ship preparing to deploy fast boats.[369] The presence of the US Navy, including two high profile interceptions by US warships, the first in January 2006 when the USS *Winston S. Churchill* intercepted the *Al Bisarat*, a captured dhow that was being used as a 'mother ship', the pirate crew of which were prosecuted successfully by Kenya, and the second in March when the pirates' fire was returned by two US ships, the USS *Gonzalez* and the USS *Cape St George*, which left the pirate boat involved burning and one pirate dead, had some success in restricting the 'Somali Marines' activities to coastal waters by deterring the group from entering international shipping lanes although it could not prevent their incursions entirely.[370]

---

367   'Somalia's dangerous waters', *BBC News*, 26 Sept. 2005; see also US Department of Transportation. 2005. Maritime Administration (MARAD), MARAD Advisory 05-03, 28 Oct., which advised ships to maintain a distance of 200nm from the coast. Available at http://www.marad.dot.gov/headlines/advisories/ADV_0503.htm.

368   Marcus Hand, 'Somali pirates move even further from the coast', *Lloyd's List*, 14 Nov. 2005; interview with IMB director Pottengal Mukundan, 2005.

369   For more details on this type of fishing vessel see http://www.fao.org/figis/servlet/vesseltype?fid=150 and http://www.fao.org/figis/servlet/geartype?fid=249

370   On the first interception see, 'Somali pirates detained by US Navy', ICC-IMB, 24 Jan. 2006; 'US Navy captures Somali 'pirates'", *BBC News*, 22 Jan. 2006;

In May and June 2006, the warlords' rule collapsed and the Islamic Courts Union (ICU) established control in several towns, including Mogadishu. The ICU took steps to suppress the pirates, who had operated under the protection and possible direction of the warlord forces that opposed them, by shutting down their bases.[371] Fearing the prospect of rising Islamist influence, US-backed Ethiopian forces defeated the ICU in December 2006 and removed it from power. Following the collapse of ICU rule, there were signs of renewed pirate activity. In December 2006, the ONI reported that a cargo ship, the *Sheila McDevitt,* had encountered a suspected pirate vessel 120nm (222 km) off the coast the previous month,[372] and early in 2007 there was a report that pirates were re-assembling at Xarardheere, the 'Somali Marines' former base.[373] Although it is believed that four (and maybe five) pirate groups have been operating at any one time, the suspicion is that it is the reinvigorated 'Somali Marines' that have been responsible for most, if not all, of the large scale piracy that has taken place off Somalia in the period between the ICU's collapse in 2006 and early 2008.

Reports issued in April and May 2007 indicated that pirate activity had resumed in the shipping lanes with an attack on a bulk carrier, the *Ibn Younos,* recorded around 200nm (370 km) from the coast.[374] Although

---

David Osler, 'US Navy seizes suspect pirate vessel off Somalia', *Lloyd's List,* 24 Jan. 2006; Louise Hansen, *et al,* 'US prowls Africa's coasts to extinguish threat from pirates', *The Virginian-Pilot,* 21 March 2006; Marc Lacey, 'Another Somali distinction: Its perilous coast', *International Herald Tribune,* 2 July 2006. Also ONI WWTTS report, 25 Jan. 2006, Paragraph D.1. On their successful prosecution in Kenya see 'Piracy suspects found guilty', 2006. *Reuters,* 26 Oct. 2006. See also David Pearl. 'Safan Al Bisarat Hijacking: A MOTR Case Study'. *ONI Quarterly,* April 2008, pp. 9-11. On the second interception see Cathy Jenkins, 'US ships in Somali pirate clash', *BBC News,* 18 March 2006; 'US Navy fights pirates off E. Africa', *CBS News,* 18 March 2006; 'US Navy returns fire on suspected pirates', *WorldNet Daily,* 18 March 2006. See also 'Somali militiamen say US fired first', *CBSNews,* 19 March 2006. The US announced subsequently that in this case it had decided against prosecution: 'Alleged pirates freed after US declines to prosecute', *Mail & Guardian Online,* 2 May 2006.

371   United Nations. 'Report on the Monitoring Group on Somalia pursuant to Security Council Resolution 1676', Nov. 2006, pp. 30 & 41-42.

372   ONI. WWTTS Report, 3 Jan. 2007, Paragraph H.3; NGA ASAM 2007-3 and 2007-14, 19 Dec. 2006. Also 'Piracy resurgence feared off Somalia', *Fairplay,* 11 Jan. 2007.

373   Aweys Osman Yusuf, 'Somali pirates gather at the coastal town of Haradhdere', *Shabelle Media Network,* 26 Jan. 2007. Also ONI WWTTS Report, 31 Jan. 2007, Paragraph D.1.

374   ONI WWTTS Special Advisory, 17 May 2007; NGA 2007-108, 14 May

CTF 150 remained active in the area it, like any maritime patrol, could only have a limited deterrent and constabulary effect given the vast sea to be covered.[375] It also became apparent that the pirates were using satellite phones and GPS navigation equipment, and, through their connections with land–based warlord groups, had access to heavier weapons.[376] Given the distances from land at which interceptions were made, it was plain that the formations of two or three skiffs that the pirates used had to be transported to the search areas by on mother ships that were sufficiently anonymous to be able to merge with ordinary shipping traffic.[377] To prolong their time in the search areas, the 'mother ship' concept was sometimes extended by using one of the skiffs in a three-skiff deployment to transport fuel for the other two.

The pirates were also able to exploit the reluctance of Coalition forces to enter Somali territorial waters without the permission of the Somali Transitional Federal Government (TFG).[378] In June 2007 the USS *Carter Hall*, correctly identifying that a Danish freighter, the *Danica White*, that had been hijacked in heavy seas 130nm (210 km) off the coast, was under the control of pirates, fired shots intended to disable the vessel. Unable to continue firing because the pirates used crewmembers as human shields, it broke off pursuit once the ship had crossed the Somali territorial limit.[379] The *Danica White* and her crew were released in August. Unusually, the Danish government admitted a ransom had been paid, a move that was immediately condemned as a naïve encouragement for further hostage tak-

---

2007; 'Pirates open fire on cargo ship: Malaysian watchdog warns key routes threatened', *AP,* 15 May 2007.

375   'Pirates moving into deep sea', *Lloyd's List,* 22 May 2007.

376   Anthony Mitchell. '4 suspected Somali pirates arrested', *Washington Post,* 27 Feb. 2007; Helmoed-Roemer Heitman. 'Attacks underline escalation of Somali piracy threat', *Jane's DW,* 30 May 2007; Audrey Gillan. 'Guns, grenades and GPS: the brutal reality of Somalia's pirates', *The Guardian,* 12 June 2007; 'Piracy plagues Somali waters', *Forbes,* 19 Nov. 2007.

377   Marcus Hand. 'Somalia pirates using 'mother vessel' tactics', *Lloyd's List,* 18 May 2007; Katharine Houreld. 'Anti-piracy coalition turns their sights on elusive Somali mother ship', *AP,* 1 Dec. 2007.

378   Jon Rosamond. 'Boarding party: Pursuing pirates to the world's end', *Jane's NI,* vol. 112, no. 6, July/Aug. 2007, p. 14.

379   NGA ASAM 2007-133, 1 June 2007. Jeremy Clarke. 'Danish ship and crew hijacked off Somalia–official', *Reuters AlertNet,* 3 June 2007; Andrew Scutro. 'Amphib lights up, but loses Somali pirates', *Navy Times,* 7 June 2007 and Marcus Hand. 'IMB sounds red alert over Somalia piracy', *Lloyds List,* 11 June 2007.

ing.[380] The amount paid was never revealed but the pirates were known to have demanded $1.5 million.[381] In a subsequent incident in October 2007, however, the US Navy received permission to enter Somali territorial waters in pursuit of a Japanese-owned chemical tanker loaded with benzene, the *Goldon Nori*, which had been hijacked in the Gulf of Aden. The USS *Porter* succeeded in sinking the pirates' skiffs, which were being towed behind the tanker, but could not prevent the tanker itself being sailed to a point 380nm (704km) further south. Once there it remained moored, under US Navy observation, until it and its crew were released in December, shortly after the pirates issued a demand for a $1 million ransom and the US Navy began to block supplies reaching the ship from the shore.[382]

Even now, most Coalition navies, because they lack law enforcement powers and experience, are reluctant to capture pirates unless there is a good chance that a government in the region will accept jurisdiction. Transporting suspects back to face charges in home courts presents significant logistical problems and although most cases would be justicable providing the requisite domestic legislation was in place, evidentiary concerns and subsequent human rights appeals could raise costs and place the final outcome of a prosecution in some doubt. The consequence of this reluctant is that the territorial waters of weak and failed states, of which Somalia is the prime example, continue to provide pirates with safe havens in the majority of cases.

What the presence of Coalition warships did appear to do was to influence the pirates to gradually shift the geographical focus of their attacks away from the Indian Ocean coast of Somalia towards the Gulf of Aden.[383] The waters off the Gulf coast, which is also the northern coast of Puntland, are trafficked more heavily than those along the east coast which means there are more potential targets and despite the fact there are also more Coalition warships active in the area, more opportunities to hide their craft

---

380   'Rewarding piracy', *Arab News*, 24 Aug. 2007.

381   David Osler. 'Pirates release Danica White', *Lloyd's List*, 23 Aug. 2007.

382   ONI WWTTS Report, 31 Oct. 2007, Para H.2. Kate Wiltrout. 'Navy helps foil pirates' attack on merchant ships off E Africa', *Hampton Roads Pilot*, 31 Oct. 2007; 'US ships block supplies to hijacked Japanese tanker', *Agence France-Presse*, 5 Dec. 2007; Laura Clout. 'Somali pirates threaten to kill tanker crew', *Daily Telegraph*, 11 Dec. 2007; 'Somali pirates free Japan tanker', *BBC News*, 12 Dec. 2007.

383   Andrew Spurrier. 'Anti-piracy chief calls for stronger Somalia security', *Lloyd's List*, 10 April 2008.

amongst the larger number of local fishing craft.[384] In fact, in the case of the *Le Ponant* discussed below, the pirates initially hijacked a legitimate Yemeni fishing boat and used it as their base ship while they waited for a suitable target. Once this had been identified, the pirates boarded their skiffs and allowed the fishing vessel to make its escape.[385]

In March 2007 a small cargo ship, the MV *Rozen*, was hijacked and its crew held for ransom off the northeast coast of Puntland as it returned from delivering UN relief supplies. The *Rozen* incident was of significance because the attack took place off the town of Bargal, where the ship was subsequently anchored, which is located very close to the Horn. It indicated that the 'Somali Marines' were prepared to hunt for targets in the Gulf of Aden, which they reached by hugging the Puntland coast thereby staying within Somali territorial waters for the duration of their transit from their bases further south.[386] It also brought into the open the suspicion, which had been circulating for months (if not years), that senior members of the Puntland administration, some of whom also held senior positions in the TFG, were actively involved in piracy; a suspicion that was not allayed by the arrest of four pirates from the *Rozen* when they came ashore for food.[387] Despite the close attentions of a US warship, the pirates retained control of the ship until April when they surrendered it in exchange for the payment of an undisclosed ransom.[388]

---

384   Houreld. 'Anti-piracy coalition turns their sights on elusive Somali mother ship'.

385   'Pirates used 'good conduct guide' in French yacht siege: source', *Agence France-Presse*, 17 April 2008; Andrew Spurrier. 'France opens proceedings against Le Ponant pirates', *Lloyd's List*, 18 April 2008. See also NGA ASAM 2008-85, 4 April 2008.

386   NGA ASAM 2007-46, 25 Feb. 2007. 'Pirates hijack UN ship near Somalia', *Agence-France Presse*, 26 Feb. 2007. Coincidentally, in June 2007, sites close to Bargal that were suspected of being used by al-Qaeda operatives were targets for US naval gunfire: 'US attacks Somali 'militant base'', *BBC News*, 2 June 2007; Salad Duhul, 'GET SOME! Destroyer bombards militants', *AP*, 3 June 2007.

387   'Pirates halt Somali aid shipments', *BBC News*, 21 May 2007; ICC-IMB. Piracy Report 1 Jan.-31 March 2007, p. 23. Cathy Majtenyi, 'Suspects in ship hijacking arrested in Somalia', *NewsVOA.com*, 27 Feb. 2007; Mitchell, '4 suspected Somali pirates arrested'; See also Said Shiiq, 'Puntland: The epicenter of Somalia's piracy and human trafficking', *Garowe Online*, 28 Dec. 2007 and Xan Rice, 'How savage pirates reign on the world's high seas', *The Observer* (London), 27 April 2008.

388   Cathy Majtenyi, 'Warship heading to ship hijacked off Somalia's northern coast', *NewsVOA.com*, 26 Feb. 2007; Betsy Pisik, 'US sends warship against sea pirates', *The Washington Times*, 27 Feb. 2007. 'Somali pirates release hijacked food aid ship', *Environmental News Service*, 9 April 2007; Jeremy Clarke, 'Two

Similarly in February 2008, a Danish-owned tug boat, the *Svitzer Korsakov*, was hijacked off the northeast coast en route to the Russian Far East by a group calling itself the 'Ocean Salvation Corps'. This group, which sailed the tug to Eyl on the eastern coast just inside Puntland but close to the border with southern Somalia, was generally assumed to be the 'Somali Marines' using a new name in an effort to improve their poor international image.[389] Interestingly, the pirates ordered that the tug be moored in water too shallow for US navy ships apparently in expectation that they would intervene or, as did occur, an attempt would be made to isolate their prize from shore-based support.[390] It was released in April following the payment of a $680,000 ransom.[391] In the same month a pirate group, not believed to be the 'Somali Marines', hijacked a French luxury yacht, the *Le Ponant*, in the Gulf of Aden triggering the most robust, counter-piracy response seen to date. The vessel was sailed to the town of Garacad, south of Eyl, where it was greeted by about 70 townsfolk who were paid about $50 each for their help.[392] A ransom demand for $2 million was made but once this was delivered and the yacht released, a French helicopter-borne Special Forces team captured six men believed to be part of the gang or their associates, recovered a portion of the ransom, believed to be no more than $200,000, and transported the captives to France to stand trial.[393]

One of the questions about Somali piracy that remains unresolved is where does the ransom money go? The 'foot soldiers' who conduct the actual hijackings in most cases see relatively little of it although the amounts

---

ships hijacked off Somali waters released', *Reuters,* 7 April 2007.

389   'Pirates hijack Danish-owned ship off Somali coast', *AP,* 4 Feb. 2008; David Osler, 'Svitzer tug hijack 'linked to environmental group'', *Lloyd's List,* 5 Feb. 2008. See also NGA ASAM 2008-39, 1 Feb. 2008.

390   Anita Guidera, 'My private hell on the high sea', *Irish Independent,* 29 March 2008; 'US Navy fires at Somali hijackers of Russian ship', *Reuters,* 12 Feb. 2008. For background on the US engagement rules see Tony Perry, 'Low-key war on pirates becomes more perilous', *LA Times,* 28 March 2008.

391   Karsten von Hoesslin. Correspondence with author, April 2008. Most press reports rounded the amount up to $700,00. 'Anger at Somali pirates' ransom', *BBC News,* 18 March 2008.

392   Spurrier, 'France opens proceedings against Le Ponant pirates'.

393   'Somali pirates seize French yacht', *BBC News,* 4 April 2008; John Lichfield, 'French commandoes seize Somali pirates after yacht hostages freed', *The Independent,* 12 April 2008; Katrin Bennhold, 'Piracy, kidnapping and rescue off the Somali coast', *International Herald Tribune,* 15 April 2008; 'Pirates used 'good conduct guide' in French yacht siege: source'; Spurrier, 'France opens proceedings against Le Ponant pirates'.

quoted in the press are a fortune by local Somali standards: The *Le Ponant* hijackers were reported to have been paid between $11,000 and $20,000 each; Andrew Mwangura of the Mombasa-based Seafarers' Assistance Programme suggested pirate gunmen could earn between $10,000 and $30,000 per year; while a pirate calling himself Muse claimed to have made $90,000 which he blew on cars and women in two months.[394] Local people are almost certainly paid a share either to tolerate the pirates' presence, or for services and supplies as demonstrated in the *Svitzer Korsakov* case, or, as with the *Le Ponant*, for guarding the vessel.[395]

But the bulk of the money goes elsewhere. Since 2005, payment methods have become more sophisticated although not in every case; the ransom for the *Le Ponant* in 2008 was reportedly paid in cash handed over in Somalia. However, as far as the Somali Marines are concerned, while they were prepared to accept cash when they hijacked the *Feisty Gas* in 2005, later payments were made in Mombasa and then in Dubai where intermediaries became used to doing business with a smartly-dressed Somali woman who, once the payment was secured, made a phone call authorizing the ship's release. The Dubai connection, and other indications, suggested that business interests based outside Somali, who were almost certainly connected to senior Somali political figures, were financing and ultimately benefiting from the hijackings.[396] According to Andrew Mwangura, the proceeds that were not spent by the pirates and their commanders on cars and drugs were invested by the local warlords and their business partners in various ventures such as illegal fishing and human trafficking, the charcoal trade, mining, and the production and distribution of the local narcotic known as khat.[397] Although it has been asserted frequently there is no evidence that al-Qaeda "dominates" Somali piracy, or even takes a share of the proceeds.[398]

In June 2008 the UN Security Council passed Resolution 1816 which condemned and deplored piracy off the coast of Somalia and urged states to

---

394   Spurrier, 'France opens proceedings against Le Ponant pirates'; Rice, 'How savage pirates reign on the world's high seas'; and Elizabeth A. Kennedy, 'Somali pirates find booming business', *AP,* 23 April 2008.

395   'Somalia: Tension in coastal town after pirate clashes, 1 killed', *Garowe Online,* 14 Feb. 2008; 'Pirates used 'good conduct guide' in French yacht siege: source'.

396   Rice, 'How savage pirates reign on the world's high seas'.

397   Sungata West, 'Piracy Revenues Financing Warlords in Somali Insurgency', The Jamestown Foundation *Terrorism Focus,* vol. IV, Issue 42, 19 Dec. 2007.

398   Damien McElroy, 'UK to attack al-Qa'eda pirates', *Daily Telegraph,* 29 Nov. 2007.

take action to deter pirate activity in cooperation with the TFG. It allowed foreign naval forces to enter Somalia's 12-mile territorial limit in pursuit of pirates and called on all states with an interest to cooperate in "investigation and prosecution" of suspected pirates.[399] This Resolution was undoubtedly welcome. It added a new element of deterrence and, providing a naval vessel was close enough to an incident to be able to render assistance, gave international navies greater freedom to take action if their national engagement rules allowed them to do so. However, it will not solve the problem of Somali piracy which is rooted in the failure of the Somali state and the deep divisions in Somali society which the UN has neither the political will nor the resources to address.

West Africa—Nigeria

On the west coast there is a general problem of piracy around the Gulf of Guinea excluding Nigeria (ranging from a high of 32 attacks in 2001 and 2002 to a low of nine attacks in 2005). The problem extends northwards towards Sierra Leone and Senegal, and south to the Congo River. It is in Nigerian waters, however, that the problem is worst.[400] In 2003 there were 39 attacks in Nigerian waters. In 2004 the number of attacks fell in line with the reduction worldwide but Lagos, because of the dramatic but temporary fall in the number of attacks in Chittagong, became the most dangerous port in the world. In 2006 there were 12 attacks.[401]

There is always a risk in speculating what form or direction piracy might take in any specific area or at any particular time. Nonetheless, a number of factors appear to be in place in Nigeria that point to a possible increase in pirate activity and maritime crime. Furthermore, the level of corruption and the manifest willingness of the ruling People's Democratic Party to rig elections in its favour feed Nigeria's instability to the point where some observers suggest it might become a failed state.[402]

The Niger delta region is a maze of waterways covering about seven per cent of Nigeria's land area. Before the 1970s Nigeria experienced only a

---

399   United Nations Security Council. Resolution 1816 (2008). 2 June 2008; 'Navies to tackle Somali pirates'. *BBC News,* 2 June 2008; Marcus Hand. 'UN Security Council comes down on Somali pirates'. *Lloyd's List,* 3 June 2008.

400   For background on West African piracy in the 1980s see Hyslop, 'Contemporary piracy', pp. 8-12.

401   ICC-IMB Piracy Report, 1 Jan. to 31 Dec., 2006, Table 1, p. 5.

402   International Crisis Group, 'Nigeria: Failed elections, failing state?' Africa Report no. 126, 30 May 2007.

few scattered attacks concentrated almost entirely around Lagos, although some did take place in the delta region around Port Harcout, Bonny, Warri and Calabar.[403] As the oil boom gained momentum in the mid-1970s, and a fleet of ships carrying construction materials that was christened the "cement armada" began to mass offshore waiting for berths, pirate attacks on the waiting ships and wholesale theft of goods from ports began.[404] Much of this activity, at least at the outset, was of the petty variety; in one incident in 1983, for example, a group of female pirates stole clothes from a ship's laundry.[405] It quickly became more organised. Pirates began to operate in gangs of 20 or 30 and their boats began to appear with outboard motors, items that were too expensive for ordinary fishermen to afford.[406] Ships' captains became convinced that the gangs were being guided with inside information, the product of collusion between the pirates and some port authority and customs officials.[407] Stolen goods quickly ended up in Lagos shops and street markets; one importer was astonished to see his goods on sale before they were due to be unloaded from the ship.[408] The most frequent victims were familiar pirate targets: small ships, particularly those under 300 tons with small crews and low freeboards, although at least one large ship, a 12,000-ton Panamanian registered freighter, disappeared off Nigeria in 1978.[409] As the size of the gangs increased so did the violence or the threat of violence; there were reports of ships being boarded by 40-50 pirates at a time and attacks involving up to 12 boats.[410] Until the attack

403   'Prior to 1970 (armed robbery in Nigerian waters) was virtually unheard of', Office of the Defence Attaché, 'Piracy control in Nigeria's territorial seas', p. 220.

404   On the cement ships see 'The cement block', *TIME,* 27 Oct. 1975; also John Darnton, 'Pirates plying Nigerian Seas', *New York Times,* 9 Jan. 1977; Office of the Defence Attaché, 'Piracy control in Nigeria's territorial seas', p. 220.

405   Hyslop. 'Contemporary piracy', p. 8 and 'The IMB chronology of pirate attacks on merchant vessels, 1981-1987', Entry 413, in Ellen, *Piracy at Sea,* p. 257. The ship's name was, perhaps appropriately, the *Amazona.*

406   Villar, *Piracy Today,* p. 16; Darnton, 'Pirates plying Nigerian seas'.

407   Darnton, 'Pirates plying Nigerian seas'; Gregory Jaynes, 'Pirates of Lagos: Once an annoyance, now a major threat', *New York Times,* 14 March 1981.

408   Darnton, 'Pirates plying Nigerian seas'

409   Darnton, 'Pirates plying Nigerian seas'; 'Freighter disappears off Africa', *New York Times,* 21 Jan. 1978.

410   On the incident involving 40-50 men (*Tey Kaiser*) see Villar, *Piracy Today,* p. 101; on the 12 boat attack see *ibid.*, p. 102 (*Nigerian Brewer*)–each boat was reported to have had 5-6 pirates on board, which would have meant the raiding party totalled between 60 and 72 men.

on the *Lindinga Ivory* in 1979, when the ship's master was killed and all 14 members of the crew injured, the Nigerian authorities appeared to be quite unwilling to intervene.[411] Despite supposedly "drastic steps" little change was noticeable.[412] During the first quarter of 1981, Lagos roads was experiencing between three and 12 attacks *a day.*[413] However, that appeared to be the high point of the problem. By the following year the number of attacks had apparently tailed off substantially. Although the Nigerian government attributed this to improved law enforcement, external observers suggest it was probably due to the decline in the oil price, which reduced the number of available targets.[414]

Piracy and maritime crime generally remained quiescent in Nigerian waters until the mid-1990s. When it returned the raiders' tactics and techniques remained much the same except that high-speed motorboats generally replaced canoes driven by paddles or small outboards, while knives, machetes and the occasional firearm were supplemented in many cases by automatic weapons. Three aspects were, however, radically different: first, while attacks in Lagos roads continued, pirate attacks increased in the 27,000 square miles (70,000 sq km) of rivers, creeks and swamps that make up the Niger delta; second, the motivation for the attacks ceased to be simply criminal and become a mixture of criminal, inter-tribal and political, with always the strong suspicion that many of the political claims were merely rhetoric to clothe the criminal and inter-tribal; third, the purpose of an increasing percentage of the attacks was no longer robbery but kidnap-and-ransom and even sabotage. Whilst Nigerian piracy, like piracy elsewhere, had always demonstrated a degree of organisation a new, more organised and purposeful element was introduced into the equation.

The delta, which was always rich in oil, was now also rich in resentment.[415] This stemmed from the belief that the federal government had

---

411   Villar, *Piracy Today*, p. 16.

412   *Ibid.*, pp. 16-17.

413   *Ibid.*, p. 102

414   Menefee, *TMV*, pp. 111-12; Villar, *Piracy Today*, p. 22; Office of the Defence Attaché, 'Piracy control in Nigeria's territorial seas', p. 220.

415   Simon Robertson, 'Nigeria's deadly days', *TIME*, 14 May 2006; Dulue Mbachu, 'The poverty of oil wealth in Nigeria's delta', ISN *Security Watch*, 3 Feb. 2006; International Crisis Group, 'The swamps of insurgency: Nigeria's delta unrest', *Africa Report no. 115*, 3 Aug. 2006; Ike Okonta, 'Niger Delta: Behind the mask', *Pambazuka News*, 26 Oct. 2006; Chibuike Rotimi Amaechi. 'Fundamental causes of maritime insecurity'. A lecture delivered to a workshop on combating piracy and armed robbery at sea organised by the Joint Stand-

taken too great a share of the oil wealth and left local communities with too little. Shell made the first oil discovery in Nigeria in 1956. Other companies were granted concessions in the early 1960s. A violent civil war was waged between 1967 and 1970 when what had previously been called the Eastern Region, home of a good deal of the country's oil production, attempted to secede from Nigeria to form the Republic of Biafra. In 1979 Section 40 of the new constitution declared that all the country's oil and gas was Federal property; the formula for division of the federal revenue from these resources among the federal, state and local governments has been amended several times and is a major political issue. Oil revenues in 1979 accounted for 82 per cent of the Federal government's income. As of 2000 little had changed: 40 per cent of Nigeria's GDP, 83 per cent of Federal government revenues and 98 per cent of export earnings were generated by the oil industry. At the same time Nigerian agricultural production for export or industrial use plummeted: exports of cocoa, groundnuts and rubber all fell, and while Nigeria had been self-sufficient in food under British administration, by the early 1980s considerable quantities had to be imported. All these changes were accompanied by the rise in central government and police powers.[416]

Very few in the delta region benefited from the revenue increased oil production generated. Most people across Nigeria regarded successive governments as corrupt but in the delta, which was effectively paying for this corruption, militant groups began to emerge. The region is far from being ethnically homogeneous: there are many tribes, including the Ogonis, Ijaws and Urhobos. Militant youth organisations such as the Odua Peoples Congress (OPC) and the Movement for the Survival of the Ogoni People (MOSOP) were formed in the early 1990s.[417] Similar groups had emerged

---

ing Committee of the Nigerian Maritime Administration and Safety Agency (NIMSA) and the Nigerian Navy at Abuja, and published by *The Tide Online*, 6 May 2008'.

416   Obi Ebbe ranks Nigeria, alongside other states such as Mobuto's Zaire and Duvalier's Haiti, as a "predator state" where politicians and criminals ally to amass wealth and ensure their own survival. He describes how the 'oil boom' has fed this corruption and led to the neglect of the agricultural sector. Obi N.I. Ebbe, 'Slicing Nigeria's "National Cake"' in Roy Godson (ed). *Menace to Society: Political-Criminal Collaboration Around the World*. New Brunswick & London: Transaction Publishers, 2003, pp. 137 & 143-4.

417   For details on other groups see Ike Okonta, 'MEND: Anatomy of a people's militia', *Pambazuka News*, 2 Nov. 2006. On the OPC which was founded to seek peaceful change but later spawned an armed militant group see MIPT Group Profile, 'Odua People's Congress'. MOSOP remains committed to peaceful

much earlier in the Ijaw areas, where resentment was particular strong.[418] In 1998 Ijaw youths formed the Ijaw Youth Council (IJC) a direct action campaign for "freedom, self-determination and justice". Other Ijaw groups to emerge subsequently have been Niger Delta People's Volunteer Force (NDPVF) in 2003, and the Niger Delta Vigilante (NDV). When they came into conflict in 2004 the Nigerian government intervened on the NDV's side.[419] This was apparently because it was at least possible that the founder of the NDPVF, Mujahid Dokubo-Asari, who was involved in the foundation of the IYC, became its president with the help of the Rivers State governor, Peter Odili, who wanted to use Dokubo-Asari to split the movement. Dokubo-Asari denied involvement with Odili,[420] and established the NDPVF, a move that allegedly led Odili to employ the NDV to counter his activities.[421] The most significant group, the Movement for the Emancipation of the Niger Delta (MEND), emerged after Dokubo-Asari's arrest in 2005,[422] a coincidence that led to the suspicion that it and other splinter groups were made up of former NRPVF fighters.[423] Okonta dates its birth to a government raid in February 2006 on the Ijaw village of Okerenkoko. MEND, he suggested, was not a formal organisation but a loose coalition of armed militias, many of them motivated by local grievances, that coordinated their activities under a collegiate leadership. They exploited mobile phones and internet connections, and their knowledge of the maze of creeks which link the Delta clans all the way from Port

---

change despite the execution of its founder Ken Saro-Wiwa and eight other activists following a questionable trial in 1995: Mbachu, 'The poverty of oil wealth in Nigeria's delta'.

418   Okonta. 'Niger Delta: Behind the mask'

419   Human Rights Watch, 'Rivers of blood: Guns, oil and power in Nigeria's rivers state', Briefing Paper, Feb. 2005.

420   International Crisis Group. 'The swamps of insurgency: Nigeria's delta unrest', p. 21.

421   Erich Marquardt, 'Mujahid Dokubo-Asari: The Niger Delta's Ijaw leader', The Jamestown Foundation *Terrorism Monitor*, vol. V, Issue 15, 2 Aug. 2007, pp. 2-3.

422   Senan Murray, 'The shadowy militants of Nigeria's delta', *BBC News*, 10 May 2007.

423   Marquardt, 'Mujahid Dokubo-Asari: The Niger Delta's Ijaw leader', p. 3; 'Intelligence brief: M.E.N.D. escalates instability in Nigeria', *PINR*, 27 April 2006. See also MIPT Group Profile, 'Movement for the emancipation of the Niger Delta'.

Harcourt to Warri, to mount hit-and-run raids and kidnappings.[424] The irregular warfare specialist John Robb has on the other hand suggested that MEND, far from being an organisation built on local support, hires "experts and fighters mostly from criminal gangs and tribal warrior cults to do their operations".[425] Political student cults are certainly an element in the conflict.[426] The truth appears to lie somewhere between the two: Dokubo-Asari has admitted that MEND was based partially on NDPVF fighters but subsequently accused another founder member, Henry Okah, of manipulating and controlling the organisation for profit through his access to arms, and appears to have had a hand in his extradition from Angola and arrest by the Nigerian authorities.[427]

The upshot is that various politico-criminal groups operating in the Delta have been fed by, and in turn have fed, the resentment of the region's population but the line between the political and the criminal is almost impossible to draw.[428] They have become major players in the kidnapping of oil workers and the theft of crude oil, a crime referred to using the term 'bunkering', which is also the term used throughout the maritime world to describe refuelling ships and which often takes place at sea.[429] Okonta has

---

424   Okonta, 'MEND: Anatomy of a people's militia'.

425   Quoted in Noah Shachtman, 'Inside the *Brave New War*, Part 1', *Wired* Blog Network, 16 May 2007.

426   Bestman Wellington, 'Nigeria's cults and their role in the Niger Delta insurgency', The Jamestown Foundation *Terrorism Monitor*, vol. V, Issue 13, 6 July 2007, pp. 8-10; also Okonta, 'MEND: Anatomy of a people's militia' and Ebbe, 'Slicing Nigeria's "National Cake"', p. 154.. For further detail on the criminal activities see Bestman Wellington, 'Origin of the Niger Delta's Deewell and Deebarn militias', The Jamestown Foundation *Terrorism Monitor*, vol. V, Issue 18, 27 Sept. 2007, pp. 10-12.

427   Dulue Mbachu. 'Niger Delta: 'Robin Hood' has a face', ISN *Security Watch*, 26 March 2008.

428   The Governor of Rivers State, Chibuike Rotimi Amaechi, in a generally fair minded analysis written in 2008, placed threats to maritime security in the Delta region in three categories: militant political activists, criminal thugs, and community bounty hunters. He went on the explain that there was a 'thin, often overlapping, line between these groups. An attacker may one day kidnap an oil worker in order to buy a flashy car; the next day he may join a raid by a militant group and, on the third day, hijack a rig to generate cash for his chief or to get jobs, a new hospital or generator for his village.' Amaechi. 'Fundamental Causes of Maritime Insecurity'.

429   Robertson, 'Nigeria's deadly days'. Dan Isaacs, 'The Nigerian Delta's troubled waters', *BBC News*, 20 Feb. 2006; 'Nigeria's shadowy oil rebels', *BBC News*, 21 Feb. 2006; 'The elephant in the room', *Fairplay*, 7 Sept. 2006; John C.K. Daly, 'Nigeria continues to slide towards instability', The Jamestown Foundation *Ter-*

suggested that criminal bunkering "had been practiced for decades in [sic] the high seas by powerful government officials in collaboration with oil workers" but that it was the proliferation of small arms in the Warri area in the late 1990s that caused it to grow rapidly. In his view it was fringe elements in these militarised youth groups who tapped into oil pipelines, in collaboration with organised criminal syndicates, and who were recruited subsequently by politicians to intimidate opponents and rig elections.[430] In September 2006 Nigerian officials estimated production losses were running at around 800,000 barrels per day owing to militant attacks and pipeline leaks.[431] Other reports suggest that theft alone accounted for 100,000 barrels daily.[432] Some estimates put the annual value of the oil lost at $1.5 billion.[433] Different sources suggest that the country's crude oil production has been cut by 25 or 30 per cent.[434] Small-scale thieves steal an unknown quantity: it is not uncommon to see small boats loaded with jerry cans plying local waters. The major groups, however, tap into pipelines and siphon oil off into barges.[435] In some cases, where pipelines bridge streams or creeks, an oil barge is apparently positioned below the pipe, which is then punctured.[436] One barge was reportedly recovered with 250,000 tonnes on board; although as this is the amount "lifted" by a VLCC, the report must be regarded as somewhat of an exaggeration.[437] Much of the stolen oil is transported in barges to ships, known as "depot ships", waiting offshore and then sold to illegal oil traders (who in turn sell it in other parts of West Africa and on the international oil market).[438] The Nigerian navy claimed,

rorism Monitor, vol. 4, no. 24, 14 Dec. 2006; Mike Pflanz, 'Nigerian rebels threaten new wave of kidnaps', Daily Telegraph, 7 Feb. 2007.

430   Okonta, 'MEND: Anatomy of a people's militia'.

431   'Attack shuts down Shell Nigerian output', Lloyd's List, 10 Oct. 2006.

432   'Nigeria: Report says Nigerian waters the most deadly', IRIN, 27 July 2004.

433   ONI, WWTTS Report, 21 June 2006.

434   'The elephant in the room'; Daly, 'Nigeria continues to slide towards instability'.

435   Alex Last, 'Tempting riches of Nigeria oil crime', BBC News, 30 Aug. 2006. Nigeria's naval secretary, Commander Olasaad Ibrahim, made the estimate of the daily loss: see 'South Africa, Nigeria take lead against piracy', Fairplay, 22 Sept. 2005.

436   Helmoed-Römer Heitman, 'Forgotten 'wars'', Jane's DW, vol. 41, no. 38, 22 Sept. 2005, p. 27.

437   'Navy seizes 250,000 tons of fuel barges', BNW News Blog, 11 Jan. 2006.

438   Tony Carnie, 'Oil piracy and gas dragons', Alexander's Gas & Oil Connections, 27 May 2005; 'Nigerian oil fuels Delta conflict', BBC News, 25 Jan. 2006.

in September 2007, to have arrested 236 such ships over a three-year period and in May 2008 was ordered by the Nigerian Federal government to
attack any ship caught in Nigerian territorial waters trying to lift oil from
the Niger delta illegally.[439] Among the goods bought with the proceeds
are arms, which are also brought in by sea.[440] Dokubo-Asari, the leader
of the Niger Delta People's Volunteer Force, admitted his organisation
had stolen from oil pipelines and used the revenue to buy arms. He was
reported as saying: "We are very close to the international waters and it's
very easy to get weapons."[441] Oil deals are often paid for in arms.[442] Oil
thefts also provide the funds to bribe police and security officials.[443] Oil
thefts, moreover, might not be the only source of funds for arms; reports
suggest that drugs from South America have been routed through the delta
and that the presence of drugs has meant, inevitably, that some criminal
groups have developed drug habits of ther own that they need to pay for.[444]
Although the Nigerian Navy does mount patrols and make arrests, it is
fair to say that, given the level of corruption in the armed forces and the
lack of resources at their disposal, Nigerian territorial waters are effectively
ungoverned space.[445]

It cannot be said for certain that the region's politico-criminal groups
are involved in piracy specifically, but the general level of militant activity
has undoubtedly generated instability in an area where water has been and
remains the principal medium of transport and communication: an instability that has in turn led to an increase in attacks on ships at sea, river-craft,

---

439   Kingsley Omonobi, 'Navy arrest 236 ships for illegal bunkering, other vices in
       three yrs', *Vanguard,* 18 Sept. 2007; Segun James. 'FG orders attack on illegal
       vessels in Nigerian waters', *This Day,* 5 May 2008.

440   Henry Okah, who trained as a marine engineer and was employed by Nigeria's
       national shipping line for many years, was apparently engaged in buying a ves-
       sel when he was detained in Angola. Mbachu. 'Niger Delta: 'Robin Hood' has
       a face'.

441   'Nigeria: Report says Nigerian waters the most deadly'.

442   Marquardt, 'Mujahid Dokubo-Asari: The Niger Delta's Ijaw Leader', p. 3.

443   'The elephant in the room'.

444   Dulue Mbachu. 'The West Africa-South America drug route', ISN *Security
       Watch,* 28 Feb. 2008

445   Sean Kane. 'Threat to safety rises on Nigeria piracy inaction', *Lloyd's List,* 2 April
       2008. For a broader review of the West African littoral as an unogoverned space
       see Kevin A. O'Brien; and Theodore W. Karasik, 'Case Study: West Africa' in
       Angel M. Rabasa. *Ungoverned Territories: Understanding and Reducing Terrorism
       Risks.* Santa Monica: RAND, 2007, pp. 173-205

oil platforms and the boats that service them. The region's "waterborne crimes", as Menefee has written, "resist easy interpretation. This is more than a question of government claim and tribal counterclaim: the number of 'players' in the region makes assigning responsibility for any particular action tricky… Additionally, the sources available cannot exactly be called impartial."[446] Within these limitations Menefee has provided an account of maritime crime in the delta region from 1997 through to 2006.[447] He describes an increasing tempo of lawlessness as gangs of young men attempt to coerce oil companies into paying ransoms and "compensation" for oil pollution—the worst incidents of which, the oil companies claim, have been perpetrated by the gangs themselves.[448] Oil industry vessels of all sizes, including tankers, support craft, barges and oil rigs, have been hijacked or attacked, their cargoes stolen and their crews kidnapped. In 2000 Ijaw "militants" stormed two Royal Dutch Shell oil rigs located in the delta's mangrove swamps, taking 165 employees hostage before releasing them in exchange for talks.[449] MEND is unquestionably involved in the abduction of oil workers and bomb attacks on oil installations.[450] Rumours circulating early in 2007 suggested that ransoms of around $800,000 were being paid for each victim.[451] For his part, Dokubo-Asari has, since his release from custody, publicly condemned the rise of criminality and branded kidnap-

---

446   Samuel Pyeatt Menefee, 'Delta blues: maritime and riverine crime in the Nigerian delta', paper delivered to the International Symposium on Coastal Zone Piracy, World Maritime University, Malmö, Sweden, 14 Nov. 2006, p. 11.

447   *Ibid.*, pp. 11-30.

448   *Ibid.*, p. 12; Robertson. 'Nigeria's deadly days'.

449   NGA ASAM 2000-158, 31 July 2000 .

450   Last, 'Tempting riches of Nigeria oil crime'; 'The Elephant in the room'; Okonta, 'MEND: Anatomy of a people's militia'; 'Resentment is mounting in oil-rich Niger Delta', *Alexander's Gas & Oil Connections*, 6 April 'Piracy report says Nigerian waters most deadly', *IRINnews.org*, 23 Sept. 2005; 'Unrest hits oil facilities in Niger Delta', *New York Times*, 23 Sept. 2005; Dino Mahtani, 'Attacks feared on Nigerian oil facilities', *Financial Times*, 23 Sept. 2005; 'Worse Nigerian violence seen', *Fairplay*, 24 Aug. 2006; 'Militants set to target Niger Delta oil firms', *Lloyd's List*, 6 Nov. 2006; Pflanz, 'Nigerian rebels threaten new wave of kidnaps'. The massive explosion in 2006 that left 200 dead tragically illustrated the risks involved in siphoning off oil: 'Gasoline pipeline blast kills up to 200 in Nigeria', *CNN.com*, 13 May 2006. The first *publicised* kidnap-and-ransom episode occurred in 2003 involving the *Maersk Shipper*, although it was almost certainly not the first to have taken place. NGA ASAM 2003-141, 15 April 2003.

451   Pflanz, 'Nigerian rebels threaten new wave of kidnaps'.

ping in particular as "evil. It has brought easy wealth, laziness, criminality in our midst. It has destroyed the moral fabric of the Ijaw man."[452]

Nonetheless kidnapping is almost endemic in Nigeria, a hazard that comes with doing business in the country. Criminals entered the game along with the militias and started to move up the scale from violent armed robbery to the theft of whole ships, either for their cargo or to be used to transport stolen oil.[453] Vessels have also been sabotaged: in January 2008, for example, two remotely-controlled explosive devices were detonated on board the *Golden Lucy* shortly after it had discharged 7,500 tonnes of fuel at Port Harcourt. Although MEND claimed it was an act of militancy, the tanker was boarded as it drifted upriver after the explosion during which time the remains of its cargo were stolen, it was stripped of equipment and set alight again. Even after the owners paid a ransom, another militant group attacked the ship when it was under tow. Then, when the ship was finally salved, the local Nigerian authorities demanded several thousand dollars 'compensation' for reasons ranging from port dues to fire fighting assistance.[454] Non-oil vessels have also been attacked: in 1999, for example, the *Vega*, a 3,000 ton reefer, was strafed with heavy-calibre machine gun fire in the Escravos River by the occupants of a speedboat who were dressed in military uniforms; in 2008 the attack on the *Spar Gemini*, a bulk carrier, raised further concerns.[455] Even though attacks have forced some river craft to travel in convoy under naval or police escort,[456] it is likely that members of the armed forces have perpetrated some of the attacks themselves.[457] The Nigerian navy admitted that some of their officers, including a rear admiral, had been involved in at least one oil-bunkering cartel.[458]

---

452   Marquardt, 'Mujahid Dokubo-Asari: The Niger Delta's Ijaw leader', p. 4.

453   'The elephant in the room'.

454   NGA ASAM 2008-14, 11 Jan. 2008. Austin Ekeinde. "Rebels bomb tanker in Nigeria, exports spared', *Reuters*, 11 Jan. 2008; Kelvin Ebiri. 'Explosion rocks ship in Port Harcourt', *The Guardian* (Lagos), 12 Jan. 2008; 'Blast tanker finally leaves Bonny River', *Lloyd's List*, 13 March 2008.

455   NGA ARAM 1999-65, 11 July 1999; David Osler. 'Nigerian pirate attack on bulker fuels new fears'. *Lloyd's List*, 17 July 2008.

456   Heitman, 'Forgotten 'wars'', p. 27.

457   Menefee, 'Delta blues', p. 15.

458   'Nigerian navy ousts 10 officers for smuggling oil', *Reuters Africa*, 27 July 2007.

In a development that echoes Somali piracy, it is possible that MEND fighters and criminal groups have struck further out to sea with raids occurring on ships and fixed installations around 100km (62 miles) from the coast.[459] In June 2008 MEND attacked Shell's Bonga field, Africa's largest, located 120km (75 miles) offshore. Although the raiding party failed to reach their stated objective, the control room where the flow is coordinated, Shell was nevertheless forced to halt production amounting to ten per cent of its total Nigerian output. MEND subsequently issued a statement saying the attack was mounted to demonstrate that the offshore oil platforms that had been developed after 2005 to reduce the security risks faced by multinational oil companies when working in the Delta, and which were considered beyond the group's range, were now vulnerable and that further attacks would be mounted in the future.[460] If MEND's claims are true then this attack represents a substantial escalation in the conflict and one that the Nigerian Navy, given its limited resources, may find difficult to counter.[461]

The suggestion has also been made that Delta militants and criminals might strike outside Nigerian's borders. In 2002, the International Court of Justice transferred sovereignty over the Bakassi peninsula from Nigeria to Cameroon. The peninsula had been the subject of a border dispute between the two countries. Local residents, however, rejected the Court's decision and threatened to declare independence.[462] Shortly before Nigerian troops withdrew in August 2006, two local militant groups together with MEND announced the area would secede. In late 2007, men in Nigerian military uniforms, attacked a Cameroonian army outpost killing around 20 Cameroonian soldiers.[463] In June 2008 a group of men described as "pirates" fired on a Cameroonian patrol; three members of the

---

459   The elephant in the room', *ibid.*

460   Russell Hotten. Nigerian militant's step up attack against Shell's oilfields'. *Daily Telegraph*, 19 June 2008; 'Nigerian attack closes oilfield'. *BBC News*, 20 June 2008; Dulue Mbachu. 'Niger Delta: Nowhere to Hide'. ISN *Security Watch*, 27 June 2008.

461   John C.K. Daly. 'Nigeria's Navy Struggles with Attacks on Offshore Oil Facilities'. The Jamestown Foundation *Terrorism Monitor*, Vol. 6, No. 14, 10 July 2008, pp. 7-8

462   Dulue Mbachu. 'Nigeria: Tensions over Bakassi Peninsula'. *ISN Security Watch*, 21 July 2008.

463   '20 Cameroun soldiers die in Bakassi', *Daily Trust* (Abuja), 14 Nov. 2007; Edem Edem. 'Pirates kill 21 Camerounian soldiers', *Leadership* (Abuja), 14 Nov. 2007.

patrol managed to escape but six were captured and later found dead.[464] Although it is suspected that the attack in 2007 was a multi-million dollar arms deal that went wrong, MEND appears to have been involved and, it has been suggested, they or other groups are prepared to mount attacks on targets in other nearby states and even planned to invade Equatorial Guinea and overthrow its government.[465]

Oil extraction and the official corruption it has engendered have disrupted the region's traditional economic activities of hunting, farming and fishing. Pirates in particular have, in the words of the Nigerian Trawler Owners Association (NITOA), been "ravaging Nigeria", such that "most of the boats were tied down at jetties" as a consequence.[466] In 2008 fishermen's leaders stated that the problem had extended from its point of origin in the Niger delta as far up the coast as Lagos.[467] The piracy that has been practiced in the delta's rivers and coastal waters is unrelated to the piracy that was practiced previously and is related instead to the current politico-criminal struggle over the region's oil revenues, which gives militants, and criminals and militants acting as criminals, and corrupt officials, all they cover they need to carry out their activities.[468]

For different reasons, the piracy on the west and east coasts of Africa demonstrates one constant in pirate activity: that the line between the political and the criminal is hard to draw. In fact it is virtually indistinguishable, particularly in those states where political power is criminal power and where to be a successful politician it is often useful to be a successful criminal first.

---

464   Tansa Musa. 'Cameroon says "pirates" seize six in Bakassi attack'. *Reuters Alert-Net*, 11 June 2008; 'Abducted Cameroonians found dead'. *BBC News*, 14 June 2008.

465   Mbachu. 'Niger Delta: 'Robin Hood' has a face'; 'Delta militants deny Bakassi raid'. *BBC News*, 15 November 2007.

466   ONI. WWTTS, 14 July 2006. Also 'Fish trawlers decry pirate activities', *The Vanguard*, 5 May 2006 and Ifeyinwa Obi, 'Fish on the run: How pirates attacks on fishing trawlers hike price of fish', *The Vanguard*, 2 March 2008.

467   Bukola Olatunji. 'Operators withdraw trawlers over pirates' attacks', *This Day* (Lagos), 4 Feb. 2008; 'Pirates paralyse economic activities in Ibeno', *The Vanguard*, 13 Feb. 2008; Sarah Simpson, 'A rise in pirate attacks off Nigeria's coast', *Christian Science Monitor*, 20 March 2008. Omoh Gabriel, *et al.* 'Renewed piracy attacks: fish scarcity looms, Nigeria may loose $600m export earnings'. *Vanguard*, 2 June 2008. Also Amaechi. 'Fundamental causes of maritime insecurity'.

468   Menefee, 'Delta blues', p. 30.

Global phenomenon, local problem, diffuse challenge

Piracy is not a global problem. In almost every case it is a local problem. Contemporary pirates cross local borders—from Indonesia to Singapore, from Malaysia (Sabah) to the Philippines (Sulu and Mindanao), from Bangladesh to Burma—but only rarely do they travel further and exploit opportunities regionally. A number of factors limit their willingness to move away from home waters: the information edge about ship movements, police patrol patterns and weather all decline with distance, while the protection provided by corrupt local officials or police is lost. Admittedly, the availability of new technology—particularly the steadily falling cost of more powerful and more reliable boat engines—by reducing the time it takes pirates to reach their targets, has almost certainly extended their operational areas, and the falling cost of newer technologies such as GPS and satellite phones might expand these still further. Pressing beyond these boundaries, however, requires craft with greater range and sea-going qualities than they generally possess and an organisation that can provide intelligence and fulfil logistical requirements at a distance. When long range piracy has occurred these requirements have been fulfilled in three ways: first by "rogue" naval or coast guard forces, of which perhaps the most audacious has been the Chinese units that operated as far south as southern Vietnam in the early 1990s; secondly by gangs capable of hijacking large ships and navigating them to distant harbours to dispose of the cargo; and thirdly by the use of mother ships capable of deploying smaller attack craft, a tactic that has been employed off Somalia. What needs to be determined are the factors that encourage pirates to take these risks and the support structures that need to be in place to reduce the risks to an acceptable level.

The re-emergence of piracy in the 1980s caught many observers by surprise. This is puzzling because by the early 1980s a decade or more had passed since the colonial empires had been replaced by young states with less security capacity, different political agendas, and new economic priorities. The issue of economic dislocation was raised earlier in relation to the proposition that poverty is a cause of piracy and it was argued that while poverty (or unemployment) was quite possibly a contributory factor it was not the primary cause given the particular demands of maritime operations. Economic dislocation, however, has other effects of which the creation of new markets, or the opening of old ones to new sources of supply, are amongst the most important. In some cases the cost of satisfying this new demand legally might be high enough to create an opportunity for criminal entrepreneurs.

Philip Gosse in one of the most famous books written about piracy, *The History of Piracy,* described a pirate cycle: "First a few individuals from amongst the inhabitants of the poorer coastal lands would band together in isolated groups...and attack only the weakest merchantmen. Next would come the period of organisation, when the big pirates either swallowed up the little pirates or drove them out of business." When these organisations reached the size of independent states what "had been piracy then for a time became war" until one side defeated the other, reducing the defeated once again to the status of outlaws.[469]

This book has chosen to focus on modern piracy, but it is arguable that the main factors that encourage pirate gangs to form have remained largely constant over time. The exigencies of maritime operation mean that piracy is always an organised crime and Peter Lupsha's developmental model based on American experience suggests three stages that approximate to Gosse's cycles: the "predatory" stage epitomised by street gangs which engage in extortionate violence, using its proceeds largely for their own consumption; the "parasitical" stage, in which gangs become more organised and create a network capable of providing a range of illicit products and services on a scale large enough to justify (and necessitate) the corruption of officials and the influencing of elections; and, finally, the "symbiotic" stage where syndicates exist alongside legitimate businesses and state actors in a mutually beneficial relationship.[470] In an Asian setting, the Royal Hong Kong Police described a very similar structure of professional "criminal gangs", whose members may or may not be Triad; "multicrime syndicates" involved in diverse and overlapping criminal activities, locally and internationally, in complex organisational structures involving both legitimate and illegitimate activities; and "criminal enterprises", which differed from the multicrime syndicates only insofar as their members had distanced themselves from their Triad allegiances and from any day-to-day criminal involvement.[471]

469   Gosse, *The History of Piracy,* pp. 1-2.

470   P. Lupsha, 'Organized crime' in William G. Bailey (ed.), *The Encyclopaedia of Police Science,* (2nd edn.), New York: Garland Publishing, 1995, pp. 494-5.

471   James J. McKenna, Jr., 'Organized crime in the former royal colony of Hong Kong' in Ryan and Rush (eds)., *Understanding Organized Crime in Global Perspective: A Reader,* pp. 207-8.

In past ages maritime predation could be the source of great wealth. Given the wealth that can be earned from the criminal trades in drugs and migrants, fraud and counterfeit goods, the opportunities in piracy are relatively less appealing then they once were. Nonetheless, for gangs with specialist skills the rewards remain attractive and for other criminal organisations opportunities for piracy can emerge out of their use of the sea for other purposes including the smuggling of drugs, arms and people. Consequently, whereas in Gosse's model piracy was the source of the wealth that enabled pirate gangs to expand to the point where they reached the political or symbiotic stage, now it is more likely that the source of wealth lies elsewhere and gangs who have access to it look on piracy as a subsidiary or opportunistic investment. One exception to this appears to be Somalia where piracy has been an important source of income for some warlords. The other is piracy undertaken by naval, police and customs units which has taken place most noticeably in China, Indonesia, Iran and Nigeria.

The UN advanced a straightforward definition of organised crime in 1993 as "...a form of economic commerce by illegal means, involving the threat and use of physical force, extortion, corruption, blackmail and other methods, and the use of illicit goods and services".[472] This explanation which is broadly economic is not, however, without its challengers, and two other theories have been put forward: the political interpretation advances the idea of illegal states within states similar to the Mafia; the sociological interpretation lays stress on the idea of weak, particularly immigrant, groups, excluded economically from the host society, combining for protection and to exploit illegal markets which are the only ones open to them. However, it is the economic interpretation that is favoured generally. It views organised crime as akin to business in that it exists to exploit clandestine markets, employs many of the disciplines of business, and often has connections with legal enterprises such that the boundaries between the two can be blurred. These explanations are not mutually exclusive.[473] In fact, each one probably reflects part of the truth. What is unquestionable is that if large criminal organisations are to survive they

---

472   UN General Assembly, 'Ninth United Nations congress on the prevention of crime and the treatment of offenders. Discussion guide', Vienna: UN, A/Conf. 169/PM.1, 27 July 1993, p. 8.

473   Alex P. Schmid, 'The links between transnational organized crime and terrorist crime', *Transnational Organized Crime*, vol. 2, no. 4, Winter 1996, pp. 42 & 44; Roy Godson and William J. Olson, 'International organized crime', *Society*, vol. 32, 1995, pp. 20-2.

require large incomes and the flexibility to respond to the emergence of new and profitable opportunities.

In our own era we have become familiar with more flexible organisational structures such as "flat" management and networks. In their legal and illegal forms they have been able to exploit the speed and security of modern travel, communications and money transfers to quickly move an organisation's assets to where they can generate the greatest returns. In their illegal forms, particularly, they have proved adept at exploiting loyalties that exist within ethnic groups (such as the Tamils and Chinese) that have left their homelands and settled abroad. In some cases the "windows of opportunity" that such criminal organisations wish to exploit might last for only a few years before the pressures that reduce profitability in all markets, such as decline in demand and the availability of substitutes, and the special factors that affect illegal markets, such as the costs imposed by police and law enforcement activity, make them less attractive. The exploitation of such transient markets requires not merely liquid capital and adaptive organisational forms but access to a flexible pool of labour that possesses the relevant skills.

Organised pirate activity does not start spontaneously. Gosse's "organised" pirates, perhaps best epitomised by Morgan in the Caribbean, the Barbary pirates in the Mediterranean and the pirate fleets, commanded first by Ching Yih and after his death by his wife Ching Yih Saou, that terrorised shipping off the south China coast at the beginning of the nineteenth century,[474] emerged out of or absorbed simpler organisational structures. Similarly, the period since 1983 has witnessed two quite distinct episodes of organised piracy characterised by a high level of organisational skill and international reach: first there was the wave of hijacking and "phantom ship" frauds starting in Southeast Asia around 1992, and second, the ship-and-crew hijackings focused on the town of Xarardheere on the central eastern coast of Somalia that emerged seemingly out of nowhere in mid-2005, retreated in the face of ICU suppression in mid-2006, but quickly resumed early in 2007 once the ICU had been defeated. Neither episode would have been possible unless there were already existing groups of common pirates available for employment as "foot soldiers".[475]

---

474   On Morgan see Gosse, *History of Piracy*, pp. 154-61; on the Chinese pirates see Dian H. Murray. *Pirates of the South China Coast*, Palo Alto: Stanford UP, 1987; Harry Miller, *Pirates of the Far East*. London: Robert, Hale & Co, 1970, pp. 120-3.

475   This is not say that if the opportunities exist and the entry-costs are low enough,

Little concrete information is available about how the Xarardheere-based pirates have operated. In Southeast Asia, however, organised criminals have used intermediaries to hire individual pirates and, latterly, whole gangs to execute their operations.[476] In 2003 a pirate leader named Husni told *Latitudes* magazine that his business was picking up because:

These days we work on a contractual basis. All we have to do is wait for an order to come in, with the coordinates of where the ship is to be attacked. Our forces go in, take the ship and capture the sailors. Then the replacement crew (a group of professional sailors) comes in to deliver the ship to the customer.[477]

The local pirates therefore serve as a labour pool that can be called upon when needed; once a hijack has been completed, they are left behind. As another pirate, who called himself Anderson, told the journalist Tom McCawley: "We're just the grunts".[478] Frécon recounts the example of a pirate organiser, a Singaporean Chinese named Chen, who brought pirates to an island in the Anambas archipelago from where they raided shipping for a number of months.[479] There is, in other words, a link between piracy at the lowest level and piracy at the highest; between what can be described as "common piracy" and "organised piracy", between attacks on local fishermen and local boats and attacks on international traffic. What is not clearly understood is now these links are maintained and what sparks them into life. However, as Samuel Pyeatt Menefee has put it: "It seems reasonable to assume that piracies which today affect international trade have arisen in a *milieu* in which local piracy is viewed as a successful business", and that if littoral states do not tackle incidents of low-level piracy and the links,

---

the traffic could flow the other way and common pirates might seek to emulate more organised gangs. This appears to have taken place off Somalia where the highjacking of the French yacht the *Le Ponant* and the Spanish trawler the *Playa de Bakio* in the 2008 were perpetrated by seemingly less well-organised groups. In both cases the ransom was delivered to the hijacked vessels in cash, a perilous arrangement but one that was used by the 'Somali Marines' in their formation phase. The crew of the *Playa de Bakio* told reporters that they watched the pirates collect the $1.2 million ransom in plastic bags and divide it up in front of them on the deck of their ship. 'Somali pirates "received ransom onboard Spanish boat"'. *Agence France-Presse*, 29 April 2008.

476   Eklöf, *Pirates in Paradise*, p. 82. Pottengal Mukunden, interview with author, 2004.

477   *Latitudes*, p. 26. An almost identical account appears in Alex Perry, 'Buccaneer tales in the pirates' lair: From island hideaways brigands plague Asia's shipping lanes as they have for generations', *TIMEasia. com*, 20-27 Aug., 2001.

478   Tom McCawley, 'Sea of trouble', *FEER*, 27 May 2004, p. 52.

479   Frécon, 'Piracy and armed robbery at sea along the Malacca Straits', p. 77.

real or potential, between local and transnational groups not tracked, then littoral and user states will be blinded to the rise of maritime transnational crime as "attacks on fishing boats, if not checked, lead in time to attacks on supertankers".[480]

---

480   Menefee, 'Under-Reporting of the Problems of Maritime Piracy and Terrorism', p. 257.

3

CONTEMPORARY PIRACY: IRRITATION OR MENACE?

Pirate typology

In 1993 the IMO attached extracts from a working group report on piracy in the Malacca Straits to its Maritime Security Committee Circular 622 (MSC/Circ. 622). Following discussions with interested parties, the report made the judgement that an armed attack on a fishing boat could "hardly be counted in the same league as an armed attack on a VLCC off Raffles Light". Deliberately disregarding attacks on vessels below 100 GRT, it concluded that piracy in the area could be divided into three categories and that these categories were also applicable elsewhere:

"Low-level armed robbery" (LLAR): an opportunistic attack mounted close to land.

"Medium-level armed assault and robbery" (MLAAR): piracy carried out further from shore, often in narrow sea lanes, and therefore a more serious hazard to shipping with a high chance that violence will be used and crew members murdered.

"Major criminal hijack" (MCHJ): well resourced and practiced operations in which violence would commonly be employed to take over and steal not merely the money or cargo on board a ship but the ship itself.[1]

---

1   International Maritime Organisation, 'Piracy And Armed Robbery Against Ships: Recommendations to Governments for combating piracy and armed robbery against ships', *Maritime Safety Committee Circular 622* (MSC/Circ. 622), 22 June 1993, Annex: Extracts from the Report of the IMO Working Group on the Malacca Strait Area, paragraphs 4-8. See also Edward Fursdon, 'Sea Piracy–or Maritime Mugging?' *INTERSEC,* vol. 5, no. 5, May 1995, p. 166, where he attributes the classifications to the IMB. It has never used them. P Mukundan, conversation with author May 2006.

Peter Chalk suggests a similar, more geographically based categorisation: harbour/anchorage attacks, attacks against vessels on the high seas or in territorial waters and hijackings of commercial vessels on the high seas (including the phantom ship phenomenon).[2]

Neither categorisation is entirely satisfactory. Both place the emphasis too firmly on piracy in the maritime context. There is no denying that piracy has its most visible effects at sea and pirate activity can compromise maritime safety and security. Piracy, however, "crosses the beach". It is as much a land-based activity as a maritime activity. Its origins are on land, its bases and its markets are on land, and many of its most pernicious effects are felt on land. That said, the degree to which it affects events on land depends largely on the degree to which it is an organised activity with links to other organised crime, or to official or political corruption, that is to say to the modern day equivalent of Peter Earl's "unscrupulous men".[3]

Anderson proposes a more satisfactory categorisation from a historical perspective. He sees three types based on what he calls piracy's form or expression: parasitic, which feeds on successful maritime trade or wealthy littorals; episodic, which comes about as the result of the weakening of large-scale political power and the consequent distortion in trading patterns; and intrinsic, in which piracy is a component part of a society's fiscal or commercial life.[4] When applying his own criteria to current circumstances he suggests that "piracy committed on commercial shipping, although perhaps organised by criminal groups and essentially parasitic, can have elements of intrinsic predation" because pirates and their vessels are able to blend into local shipping and local communities might "knowingly give them shelter and support".[5] This is almost certainly the case among many remote, coastal communities in Southeast Asia. It is also worth remembering the claim of some Somali pirate groups that they were levying "taxes" on ships using their waters, and while this might, in many cases, have been a clever conceit it is no different from what other societies, also branded as piratical, have done in the past.[6]

---

2 Chalk, 'Threats to the Maritime Environment', p. 4. See also Wood, 'Piracy is Deadlier than Ever'; and Young and Valencia. 'Conflation of piracy and terrorism'.

3 Earle, *The Pirate Wars*, pp. 20-1.

4 Anderson, 'Piracy and World History', pp. 86 & 93-4.

5 *Ibid.*, p. 98

6 *Ibid.*, p. 83. See also Alfred P. Rubin. *The Law of Piracy* (2nd edn.), Irvington-on-Hudson: Transnational Publishers, 1998, pp. 21-2.

However, James Warren's argument that there are similarities between Southeast Asian piracy at the end of the eighteenth and twentieth centuries, coinciding on both occasions with booms in trade with China, opens up the economic perspective: that at least some of the piracy in the region might be episodic and rise and fall in response to market demand in China or elsewhere.[7] Given, however, that common pirates prey on local and not international traffic, and given that they lack the resources to supply the Chinese market directly, the market stimulus must apply at a higher and more organised level—one that appreciates that there is a profit to be made in stealing cargoes in the waters of Southeast Asia states with weak law enforcement regimes and disposing of them in China with correspondingly weak or corrupt customs and border protection. In the case of Somalia the pirates are clearly extracting a profit from the almost total absence of effective law enforcement, either on land or in the country's adjacent waters, by kidnapping seafarers from wealthier states, an opportunity that has been facilitated greatly by modern high-speed communication and fund transfer mechanisms.

Therefore, when thinking about the problem of *contemporary* piracy in terms of its potential impact on national or international security, a more flexible typology might have greater practical application. When evaluating how much piracy represents a threat to *security*, as opposed to maritime safety, in a particular country or region, or internationally, two assessments must be made. The first is an assessment of the country or region's vulnerability. The second is an assessment of the threat posed. Generally speaking, the more organised pirate activity becomes the more the threat increases.[8] Vulnerability must therefore be measured against the degree of pirate organisation in a given area and the ability of that organisation to gain access to sometimes distant markets, for a risk assessment to be made. Against this background, pirate organisation can be assessed on a scale that ranges from common criminal piracy to highly organised criminal piracy.

Assessments of this kind are undertaken by a number of governmental and commercial bodies in different parts of the world. Very broadly, the interests that are affected by piracy and are interested in its control or sup-

---

7   Warren, 'A tale of two centuries', p. 1.

8   Young and Valencia reach a similar conclusion: "Piracy encompasses a wide range of criminal behaviour (that) corresponds to an escalating scale of risk and return (as) does the apparent degree of organisation of the attackers". Young and Valencia, p. 272. See also Young. *Contemporary Maritime Piracy in Southeast Asia*, pp. 3, 65

pression are the trading community (ship owners, operators and their customers who are interested in supply security), the insurance industry, littoral states, major international trading nations (the "user" states) and, once they are engaged, naval powers. Piracy affects different interests in different ways. In the real world, each interest that is threatened by piracy makes an assessment of its seriousness based on its own, largely subjective, criteria. These assessments might achieve a degree of objectivity and consistency by assigning numerical values to them, and by revisiting them regularly, but they are all, in the end, subjective and open to challenge. Each interest assesses the threat piracy presents on its own matrix. This might include the location of the attacks, the types of vessel that are subjected to attack and what is taken from them, the scale of the losses, the sustained level of violence, the threat to free navigation and, perhaps most important, the damage piracy might inflict on the reputation or political standing of the state or its government. Each interest "weights" these criteria according to its own priorities, but given that the attitude of states is the key to any response, it is the last that is likely to have the most influence on policy. More recently—since the attacks of 9/11 and the attempted sinking of the USS *Cole* and the *Limburg*—it is the real or suspected link between piracy and terrorism that has tended to overshadow all others.

Vulnerability assessment

Assessing vulnerability is akin to assessing beauty: much of it lies in the eye of the beholder. Any assessment needs to take account of the "to what", "by whom", "for whom" and "why" factors and mistakes are easily made. The physical features of an area, such as the width and depth of a channel, or weather patterns such as the prevalence of storms or fog, are generally known and their effects on a region's susceptibility to piracy, and the extent to which they together have consequences for its security, can more or less be calculated. However, most vulnerability assessments must also take account of less tractable human factors, such as corruption and morale, which are notoriously hard to judge. Even if a coast guard is well equipped, for example, is that equipment in working order and are the crews motivated sufficiently to do their jobs? Therefore, as much as the particular physical circumstances of each area need to be recognised, so too do the differences in history, culture and political priorities that can mean different interest groups—say littoral states and user states, or shipping companies and their insurers—viewing the same conditions very

132

Factors	Internal Security	International Security
Criticality of waterways, trade or access routes		
International traffic volume	Low	High
Vulnerability to interruption	Low	High
Absence of alternative routes	Low	High
Type of traffic		
Oil & gas	Low	High
Nuclear materials	Low	High
Naval and military movements	Low	High
Environmental sensitivity		
Impact on economic activity e.g. loss of fishing	High	Low
Impact on wildlife/eco-system	High	(Low)
Littoral state stability		
Weak		*
Strong	*	
Littoral state security/law enforcement capacity		
Inadequate		*
Adequate	*	
Maritime safety capability		
Inadequate		*
Adequate	*	
Local tolerance of piracy activity (cultural acceptability)		
High		
Low		*
	*	
Official/political links with crime organisations		
High		*
Low	*	
Integrity of the criminal justice system		
High	*	
Low		*
Level of international security/justice cooperation		
Ad-hoc		*
Institutionalised	*	
Insurgent/terrorist groups activity		
High		*
Low	*	

Table 6. Vulnerability Assessment Table: Local conditions that make piracy a potential problem within and beyond the territorial waters of a littoral state

differently. Assessments, in other words, are bound to differ and shared conclusions are usually a compromise.

When attempting to assess the vulnerability of specific locations from an international security perspective, the factors listed in Table One are likely to be the most significant. For current purposes the factors have been drawn only indicatively; for practical purposes they would need to be defined more tightly. Where the answers can be located in the left-hand column then the issues will generally be ones that affect international interests slightly, if at all, and can therefore be left to littoral states to deal with. As the answers tend towards the right-hand column then they will begin to affect the interests first of neighbouring states, then regional states and finally extra-regional states to the point where the issues can be regarded as being of international concern. Responses to these issues will in turn escalate from the neighbourly to the international. The most worrying escalation occurs if, during its transition from the left-hand column to the right, an issue moves from being a security concern to being the focus of a real or potential security dispute; that is, it moves from being of little or no political importance to one with high political implications. Examples of the latter include the pirate attacks on the Vietnamese boat people, which caused tensions among Malaysia, Singapore, Thailand and Vietnam and between these countries and the international community; also the pirate attacks off Somalia in 2006 and once they re-started again in 2007 that have attracted the attention of the UN.

Threat assessment

Threat is also difficult to measure, though perhaps less so than vulnerability. Piracy patterns in particular areas, even the capabilities of particular groups, are often known. What are usually less well understood are the connections the gangs might have to wider organised crime networks, politicians, and just possibly insurgent or terrorist organisations, and how these are likely to influence the gangs' activities and reach. Nonetheless, a general principle stands that as the capabilities of a gang increase or criminality in an area becomes more organised, so the threat to *international* interests is likely to become more substantial; on the Table it would begin to move from the left-hand column to the right. A highly organised gang would be able to pursue larger and more significant targets, such as oil tankers, and dispose of their cargoes, or hostages, and obtain hostage payments, with consequently greater potential financial and social impact, than a less organised gang. Ultimately, these effects could undermine the political stability of a vulnerable state either directly, via corruption, or indirectly, via the fiscal strain imposed by the need for larger and better-equipped security forces. Such instability potentially presents a risk to national and regional security and has international implications if it affects security in the vicinity of vital international "hub" ports or in regions with valuable natural resources such as oil, minerals or even fish. Table Seven indicates

Threat characteristics	Common Criminal Piracy	Organised Criminal Piracy
Attack location		
Ports & harbours	*	
Anchorages	*	
Coastal waters	*	*
High seas		*
Target identification		
Opportunity	*	
Intelligence-based planning		*
Target interception		
Opportunity	*	
Information-led interception		*
"Sleeper"		*
Attack persistence		
Long	*	
Short		*
Objectives		
Theft of cash	*	
Theft of crew possessions	*	
Theft of small craft incl. yachts	(*)	Specialised
Theft of cargo		*
Theft of ships		*
Theft of ships & cargo		*
K&R		*
"Phantom ship" fraud		*
Environmental threat		
Risk of consequential damage	High	Low
Violence		
Propensity to use or threaten violence	Mid to High	High
Access to markets		
Local	*	
International		*
Links to insurgent/terror groups		
None to occasional	*	
Frequent to integrated		*
Level of political or official support		
Low-level to none	*	
Medium to High		*
Links to organised crime		
None to occasional	*	
Frequent to integrated		*

Table 7. Threat Assessment Table

characteristic patterns of "common" piracy and "organised" piracy, that is to say piracy often undertaken in association with, or under the leadership of, wider criminal networks, and gives a sense of the contexts within which each pirate type will tend to operate.

Attack location. The location of attack is a useful differentiator between common and organised piracy. Common criminal piracy is an activity that takes place close to coasts, in the main when ships are stationary in port or anchored just offshore waiting to load or unload cargo.[9] Common pirates use speed and their knowledge of local waters to evade capture and prosecution and some will cross jurisdictional boundaries.[10] Most organised criminal piracy takes place outside ports in anchorages or, more often, over-the-horizon in international waters. Organised pirates exploit freedom of navigation, jurisdictional boundaries and their official status (if they have it) to escape, to move hijacked vessels—or cargo stolen and then offloaded onto another vessel—into another jurisdiction for disposal.[11] When it comes to the growing phenomenon of maritime kidnap-and-ransom (K&R), sophisticated organisation is generally apparent. Clues suggesting this come from reports of victims being moved between multiple locations; in the case of the crew kidnapped from a Japanese tug, the *Idaten,* this involved six moves from boat to boat before they reached land.[12] In other cases, particular those involving the island of Batam but at other locations as well, captured crew have been detained on the property of people who quite obviously possess both wealth and status.[13]

Target identification. In the vast majority of cases, common pirates put to sea on the lookout for small vessels, vessels with low freeboards such as oil tankers or bulk carriers (although rarely over 20,000 GRT), or those that

---

9   Out of 445 attacks reported in 2003, 242 took place when ships were either berthed or at anchor. ICC-IMB Piracy Report, 2003, Tables 4 & 5, pp. 8-9; of the 263 attacks reported in 2007, 145 took place in berths and anchorages. ICC-IMB Piracy Report 2007, Tables 4 & 5, pp. 10-11.

10   See Young and Valencia, 'Conflation of piracy and terrorism'.

11   McCawley, 'Sea of trouble', p. 51. For accounts of the trans-shipment of oil cargoes at sea see, for example, Gray *et al., Maritime Terror,* p. 19 on the cases of the *Petro Ranger, Atlanta 15 and Tioman 1.* See also 'Oil piracy proves growing menace to tanker traffic in South China Sea', *Oil and Gas Journal,* 18 Oct. 1999, pp. 23-5, which makes the point that 'sophisticated networks of black-market crude oil dealers throughout the region enable them to dispose of oil products worth millions of dollars relatively quickly'. In addition to the ships mentioned by Gray *et al.* it cites the cases of the *MT 1* and the *President.* The article goes on to point out that the sophisticated level of pirate organisation, including the use of speedboats, machine guns, radar and jamming equipment, suggests some military involvement.

12   'Pirates attack Japanese-owned ship in Malacca Straits', *Kyodo News,* 4 April 2005.

13   Private information, Aug. 2005.

have taken insufficient anti-piracy measures and thus present them with an opportunity to board. It is possible that corrupt port officials, who have access to cargo manifests, may identify high-value cargoes and pass this information to pirates who consequently target specific ships and, occasionally, specific containers.[14] Frécon suggests that even mid-level organised gangs on Bintan are able to listen in to VHF.[15] Both common and organised pirates can benefit from political or official support; in the case of common piracy this tends to come from local officials and law enforcement officers who provide information or protection in exchange for bribes or a cut of the proceeds.

Organised pirates do not leave things to chance. They know what they are looking for because in most cases they will have a buyer waiting or know buyers who would be interested. The information they need can, in many instances, be acquired quite legitimately from Lloyd's and port ship movement bulletins. In others they use information obtained corruptly from either official or commercial sources to identify specific cargoes, or to target vessels that will be particularly vulnerable either because of the route they will take or their lack of precautions.[16]

Target interception. Common pirates can attack their targets using either direct methods, which often involve the use of firearms to persuade their targets to heave-to, or surreptitious methods, which involve boarding their target as silently as possible. Organised pirates can do the same. They can also employ deceptive techniques such as disguising their boats and themselves as police, coast guards or members of armed services. This can be especially effective if they *are* members of such services. Organised pirates have been known to place an accomplice aboard (a "sleeper") to sabotage the vessel or its defences, to transmit updates of its position and to help the gang get on board.[17] The "sleeper" who was on board the *Nepline De-*

---

14   McDaniel, 'Modern high seas piracy', p. 12 and Ken Cottrill, 'Modern marauders: Pirates on the South China Seas use high-tec weapons', *Popular Mechanics*, no. 12, 1997, and Fabey, 'Sitting ducks', refer to reports of pirates coming aboard with computer printouts of where specific cargo is stored.

15   Frécon, 'Piracy and armed robbery at sea along the Malacca Straits', p. 78.

16   Chalk, 'Threats to the maritime environment', p. 7 suggests that such groups rely on intelligence from brokers and operators across several countries to provide them with current information on cargoes, ships, routes and buyers, as well as government counter-measures.

17   'Terror on the high seas–A spreading plague', *DEBKANet-Weekly* Special Report, 14 Aug. 2002. Perry, 'Buccaneer tales in the pirates' lair', provides a detailed description of a hijacking involving a 'sleeper'.

lima when it was hijacked in 2005 sent text messages to the raiding party reporting the ship's speed, course and position. Most importantly he told the gang when he would be on watch and almost certainly was responsible for disabling the Ship's Security Alarm System (SSAS).[18] By using multiple identities and false papers "sleepers" usually have little trouble finding work on other ships, which for the right price they will also betray.[19]

Attack persistence. Common and organised pirates may press their attacks with equal vigour. Ships currently have a number of non-violent measures they can employ to discourage boarding: speed, manoeuvre, "fishtailing" to create a violent wake, or the use of powerful lights, noise and water from their high-pressure hoses. Persistence, however, motivated by the belief the victim can be made to stop as a result of terror or exhaustion, appears to be an indicator either of common criminal piracy—some ships have been chased and harried for hours—or rogue military forces using government vessels to launch pirate attacks.[20] Organised pirates are more likely to be able to mount their assault quickly and effectively because they are likely to have good intelligence on a ship's course and defensive capabilities, have the resources to mount more effective deceptions, employ heavier firearms and be able to either place a "sleeper" on board, or know which seamen are open to offers.

Objectives

Common piracy targets, in the main, cash and the personal belongings of the crew or passengers and items of ships' equipment, although small items of cargo have been taken on occasion. Common pirates have been known to hijack small vessels: fishing boats are attacked regularly, and in some areas yachts can be prize targets because they have few defenders, are easy to board and, ton for ton, usually carry large quantities of cash and valuables.[21] Common pirates will then take what they can and leave. Once organised pirates are on board they will obviously take cash and anything else that comes to hand, but their main purpose is either to steal the cargo, which often means stealing the entire vessel, or, more recently, to kidnap

---

18   Gwin, 'Dark passage', p. 136. Also NGA ASAM 2005-208, 13 June 2005.

19   Gwin, 'Dark passage', p. 139.

20   US Department of Energy, 'Piracy: The Threat to Tanker Traffic', p. 6.

21   Gray *et al., Maritime Terror,* p. 3.

138

members of the crew. In Somalia, the pirates hijacked the ship and the crew together for a combined ransom.

Organised piracy is looking for substantial profits. It appears that these can be earned in four ways: cargo theft, ship and cargo theft, cargo fraud, and kidnap-and-ransom. Cargo theft occurs when the ship is highjacked and the cargo transferred to another ship or barge at sea before the ship is sent on its way. Ship and cargo theft is similar but the ship is disguised and re-registered before being sailed to a port where the cargo is sold. The ship can then be sold to an unsuspecting buyer or even, in some cases, for scrap.[22] Small vessels can be taken to remote bays or harbours where the cargo can be offloaded and the ship cut up. Larger ships can be stripped of their components while ships of any size can be simply abandoned and allowed to rust away undetected.[23] One of the first examples of this type of piracy took place in 1990 with the hijacking of the *Marta* on a voyage from Thailand to Korea. The pirates knew exactly where the ship would be and had made detailed plans for its hijacking and disposal. The ship's name and appearance were changed and it was sailed to an unknown port where accomplices, using forklifts, took two and a half days to transfer its cargo to a waiting barge. It was then taken out to sea again at which point the crew and the master were separated. The master was taken hostage and released independently to ensure that the crew, who were allowed to sail the ship to Bangkok once the pirates left, obeyed their instructions. During the hijacking one of the pirates admitted that the *Marta* was their sixth successful hijacking, a series that might have begun with the *Thai Wong* in 1986.[24] The most notorious cases have been the *Cheung Son* (which is dealt with in more detail below), the *Anna Sierra* and the *Alondra Rainbow*.[25]

A party of thirty pirates hijacked the *Anna Sierra* in 1995 in the Gulf of Thailand. Parts of the ship were repainted and it was renamed the *Artic Sea* and re-registered in Honduras. About half the crew were set adrift on a makeshift pontoon (and fired upon by the pirates as they drifted away) while the other half were forced to leave the ship in rough weather aboard a life raft. The ship was sailed to Beihai in Guangxi Province in China where its $4 million cargo of sugar, which had already been sold to local interests in

22 See ICC-IMB Piracy Report, 2003, p. 24.

23 Ryan, 'Captain counts the cost of piracy'.

24 Menefee, *TMV*, p. 80. Also ICC-IMB, 'Organised maritime crime in the Far East', pp. 75-6.

25 For the history of this form of piracy see Abhyankar, 'Maritime fraud and piracy', pp. 187-91.

a pre-arranged deal at well below the market price, was due to be unloaded. While in the harbour it was identified by the IMB which proved the ship had been stolen. Nonetheless, the Chinese authorities allowed the pirate crew to slip away, impounded the cargo, demanded a "docking fee" of $350,000 for the ship's release and then eventually sold the cargo themselves without compensating the rightful owners.[26] In the end the *Anna Sierra* was never released and remains in the harbour at Beihai, little more than a rusting hulk.[27]

Jayant Abyankar asked the pertinent question, "Is the...*Anna Sierra* case the result of inefficiency and infighting amongst the seemingly inept Chinese authorities concerned, or part of a deeper plot to cover up China's participation in criminal activity?"[28] In fact both factors were probably involved. Ken Blyth was the Australian master of another ship, the *Petro Ranger,* which was hijacked in 1998. In his case the Chinese Marine Police became suspicious, boarded his ship and arrested his hijackers.[29] Their intervention might well have saved his life. Nonetheless he recognised, after sitting through numerous interviews, that the various parts of the Chinese government were in conflict. The attitude of the People's Liberation Army (PLA) and the Marine Police was that the incident could embarrass China and therefore the pirates who had taken his ship should be punished. The People's Security Bureau (PSB) appeared to be under the control—or influence—of the local authorities which almost certainly had links to, and benefited from, the pirates' activities.[30] As if to confirm this ambiguous po-

26   NGA ASAM 1995-123, 13 Aug. 1995. Dubner 'Human Rights and Environmental Disaster', p. 7. Five further descriptions of this case are to be found in Seth Faison, 'Pirates, with speedboats, reign in China Sea port', *New York Times,* 20 April 1997; John Grissim, 'The hijacking of the Anna Sierra', *The World Paper,* May 1997; Abhyankar, 'Maritime fraud and Piracy', pp. 187-92; IMB, 'Piracy and armed robbery against ships: A special report', pp. 33-9 and Mark Bruyneel, 'Tale of a modern pirate gang', 21 Nov. 2000.

27   Jack Hitt, 'Bandits in the global shipping lanes', *The New York Times Magazine,* 20 Aug. 2000.

28   Jayant Abhyankar, 'The case of the Anna Sierra' in Ellen, *Shipping at Risk,* p. 279.

29   Ken Blyth (with Peter Corris), *Petro Pirates: The Hijacking of the Petro Ranger',* St Leonards, NSW: Allan & Unwin, 2000, pp. 54-5. Also NGA ASAM 1998-33, 17 April 1998 and Charles Glass, 'The new piracy', *London Review of Books,* vol. 25, no. 24, 18 Dec. 2003.

30   Blyth, *Petro Pirates,* particularly pp. 71-8 & 104. Herman, the pirate leader, also suggested that the crews of the two vessels that came alongside the *Petro Ranger* to remove its cargo were manned by Chinese naval personnel, although

sition, the pirate's leader was beaten brutally ("he looked like he'd aged ten years"), yet a few months later he and his gang were all quietly released.[31] The Chinese refused to explain why.[32] A few months after that five of the gang were spotted off the Malaysian coast once again working as pirates.[33] Similarly, among the 16 pirates who hijacked the *Tenyu* and killed its crew in 1998 (see below) and who were also released by the Chinese authorities, at least two were identified as members of the *Anna Sierra* gang that had been let go in 1997.[34] At about the same time that the crew of the *Tenyu* lost their lives, officials in China apparently began to recognise that the country had such a significant interest in economic growth that it needed to adapt to the modern world and play by the rules of global trade. The central authorities began to reassert control over provincial interests in a campaign that drove the most successful and high profile smuggler, Lai Changxing, into exile in 1999. According to prosecutors, Lai's organisation had revenue of $6.4 billion between 1996 and 1999 alone. Lai himself admits to paying bribes (or "gifts" as he preferred to call them) to public security and customs officials amounting to $2 million between 1991 and 1997.[35] Despite Lai's demise, the old ways of doing business are unlikely to

---

Blyth speculates that they may have come from the PSB: *ibid.*, p. 47. Even after his arrest, Herman was confident that a bribe would secure his release: *ibid.*, p. 76.

31 Sandra Speares. 'IBM condemns pirates' release'. *Lloyd's List*, 19 Oct. 1998. Matthew Flynn. 'China promises crackdown as it strives to escape image of a safe haven for pirates'. *Lloyd's List*, 24 February 1999.

32 Two explanations have been advanced: the first, incredibly, was that there was insufficient evidence. 'Indonesians deported due to lack of evidence: China'. *Agence France-Presse*, 29 October 1998. The second was that, according to Zou Keyuan, there was no extradition treaty in place: Zou, 'Seeking effectiveness for the crackdown of piracy at sea', p. 129. This argument is somewhat undermined by the fact that China was a signatory to the SUA Convention, which is arguably applicable in this case, that encourages states to consider extradition even when no formal treaty is in place. Blyth suggests a deal was agreed: Blyth, *Petro Pirates*, pp. 114 & 140-4.

33 Hitt, 'Bandits in the global shipping lanes'.

34 'Dead men tell no tales', *The Economist*, 16 Dec. 1999; 'China frees "Anna Sierra" hijackers'. *Lloyd's List*, 11 Feb. 1997; Flynn. 'China promises crackdown as it strives to escape image of a safe haven for pirates'.

35 See Susan V. Lawrence, 'A city ruled by crime', *FEER*, 30 Nov. 2000 and Hannah Beech, 'Smuggler's blues', *TIMEAsia*, 7 Oct. 2002. For a more detailed account of this extraordinary individual and the *milieu* that allowed him to operate see Oliver August., *Inside the Red Mansion: On the Trail of China's Most Wanted Man*, New York: Houghton Mifflin Company, 2007.

disappear in China for, as a US State Department officer put it, if money is involved, it is "not always clear how devoted they are [to making changes] when push comes to shove".[36]

The case of the *Alondra Rainbow* illustrates many of the methods of organised piracy and also many of the problems of international law enforcement even when a state is willing to act. In October 1999 the ship loaded a cargo of aluminium ingots valued at $10 million at the Indonesian port of Kuala Tanjung. The cargo was due to be delivered to Japan. Within hours of the ship leaving the port and while it was heading down the Straits of Malacca a 15-man pirate gang made up of Malays, Indonesians, Thais, Chinese and possibly other nationalities hijacked it. Their arrival was the result of detailed planning. The gang had been assembled on the Indonesian island of Batam by a professional recruiter who in turn took his orders from a criminal boss. The boss' nationality was reputedly Chinese but this could not be determined accurately as he only communicated by telephone. The boss, or the syndicate he represented, had hired an old freighter, the *Sanho*.[37] The pirates boarded this ship off Jakarta and sailed it up the Malacca Strait to Kuala Tanjung where it anchored, waiting for the *Alondra Rainbow* to leave. When it did, the *Sanho* either left the anchorage first or followed. When night fell a fast boat was launched that carried the gang to the stern of their target. It is possible that the gang were in contact with a "sleeper" aboard who lowered the ropes they used to shinny up to the deck. Equally, they could have thrown grappling hooks over the rail. What is known is that once on board they took over the bridge. They blindfolded the crew and locked them in the messroom. They stole their passports plus their personal papers and valuables. The ship's safe was broken into and the cash removed. It seems likely that while this was happening the ship was not under proper control. The pirates came equipped

---

36   Hitt, 'Bandits in the global shipping lanes'. Doubts exist not merely about China's law enforcement methods but about its judicial processes as well. See, for example, James Brewer, 'London Club tells members to be wary of Chinese legal system', *Lloyd's List*, 10 July 2006.

37   The use of freighters as support vessels is not uncommon. The MV *Pulau Mas* is noted below. Another was the MV *Polaris* which was certainly in use in 1997. It only used this name during a hijack. At other times it used its registered name. Its only cargo was a large speed boat which was hidden in the hold but interestingly it was sometimes accompanied by a fishing boat which was used to scout out victims and observe them in port. Arms were delivered to the ship prior to an attack and were thrown overboard before it entered another port. Private correspondence.

with pistols and knives and used them to threaten any crew member who refused to obey their orders. This threat undoubtedly had an effect: the previous year the *Tenyu,* another Japanese-owned freighter also carrying a cargo of aluminium ingots, had disappeared after departing from the same port, to be discovered three months later in the Chinese port of Zhangijana on the Yangtze River with a new name, a new Honduran flag and a new cargo of palm oil.[38] The original cargo had disappeared, as had the original crew of 15. The presumption was that they had been murdered.[39]

At some stage someone with ship handling experience took control on the bridge. The ship slowed and the *Alondra Rainbow*'s crew, still blind-folded, were marched up on deck. They thought they were going to be pushed overboard. Instead, the blindfolds were removed and they were forced to jump across to another ship, probably the *Sanho,* which had been brought alongside. After seven days at sea the crew were forced into the *Alondra Rainbow*'s own life raft, which appears to have been brought along for the purpose, and set adrift. The pirate ship left them and has never been found. With no sails or means of propulsion the life raft drifted. The crew had no way of telling where they were but they had ten flares. Whenever they saw a ship they fired off a flare. Not one ship stopped. On the tenth day, a Thai fishing vessel approached them. Because pirates are believed to have deceived seafarers into stopping by posing as distressed mariners, the fishermen treated them with extreme suspicion and only took them to Phuket once their story had been verified.

In the meanwhile the *Alondra Rainbow* had been sailed through the busy Singapore Strait towards the Malaysian port of Miri in Borneo. On the way it had been renamed the *Global Venture* and its funnel had been repainted. At Miri it transferred nearly half its cargo of aluminium ingots to another freighter, the *Bansan II,* an operation that must have taken several days. This ship then sailed to Subic Bay in the Philippines, changing its name to the *Victoria* on the way. There the cargo was successfully sold. The insur-ers subsequently tried to recover what they could through the Philippine courts but failed. The police investigation got nowhere. When the *Alondra*

---

38   'Dead men tell no tales'; also Burnett, *Dangerous Waters,* Note 43, p. 38. NGA
       ASAM 1998-61, 27 Sept. 1998.

39   Langewiesche, *The Outlaw Sea,* pp. 54-5; Michael Richardson, 'India and
       China set sights on piracy', *International Held Tribune,* 23 Nov. 1999; Corey
       Bousen. '*Tenyu* crew feared murdered'. *Lloyd's List,* 30 December 1998; Yoshi-
       hikio Yamada, 'Defending Asian seas from marauding by pirates', The Tokyo
       Foundation *Japanese Dynamism no. 6,* March 2004.

Rainbow, a.k.a. *Global Venture*, set sail from Miri it was now overdue at its original destination and the ship's owners had informed the IMB which in turn issued an international alert.

On 13 November a ship answering the *Alondra Rainbow*'s description was spotted off the southwest coast of India. The IMB contacted the Indian authorities who agreed to take action, which was remarkable given that the ship was owned by Japanese interests, registered in Panama, crewed by Filipinos, and had been pirated off Indonesia. Perhaps they did not realise what they were getting themselves into. An Indian Coast Guard vessel chased the ship. It was joined later by a more heavily armed Indian Navy corvette after the *Alondra Rainbow*, which was now named the *Mega Rama*, refused to even slow down despite being hit repeatedly by gunfire. It stopped finally when confronted by the corvette's heavier armament. When the Indians were able to board they discovered the pirates had burned every incriminating document, including their own passports, and had opened the sea valves in an attempt to sink the ship.[40] Only prompt action by Indian Navy divers prevented it from going down. The ship was towed to Mumbai. On the way a number of the pirates were reported to have confessed, but these confessions were deemed inadmissible at their trial. They claimed they were beaten up, a claim that was denied, although one was somehow shot in the leg.

Their trial started finally in 2001. The first problem that arose was that India had no law prohibiting piracy. Relevant legislation dating from the time of the British Raj was found eventually but given that Indian law had in the meanwhile been codified questions arose as to whether it was still in force. Consequently, to be sure of a conviction, the prosecuting authorities charged the men with a catch-all list of crimes. The trial dragged on in the Mumbai Sessions Court until 2003 when the men were convicted successfully and sentenced to seven years' imprisonment. In 1999 the IMB, which had emphasised the need for international cooperation and the importance of political will if piracy was to be defeated, said it was "fantastic to see the Indian authorities act under the auspices of international law to intercept the ship."[41] All the authorities concerned now congratulated each other on a job well done.

---

40   Suspicions exist that the original cargo was bartered for arms to be supplied to the LTTE. NGA ASAM 1999-114, 22 Oct. 1999.

41   'International cooperation beats modern-day pirates', IMB, 24 Nov. 1999.

Sadly, however, this was not the end of the case. In March 2005 the Mumbai High Court overruled the Session Court and acquitted all the accused. The High Court appeared to have concerns about the process and over the fact that neither the Master of the *Alondra Rainbow,* who had twice travelled from Japan to confirm that the *Mega Rama* really was the *Alondra Rainbow* and to testify as to what had happened, nor the Chief Engineer was prepared to identify any of the pirates, apparently because they feared reprisal. Like so many victims of piracy, they have never gone to sea again.[42]

Improved security measures, greater awareness of the problem amongst harbour authorities and shippers, the introduction of the IMO Ship Identification Numbering Scheme under which a unique number is affixed in a prominent position on a ship's superstructure,[43] the Continuous Synopsis Record of the ship's history including flag and registration details,[44] and the widespread installation of SSAS[45] have meant that gangs involved in this form of theft have become more ingenious. On 10 July 2006 the MV *Kimtrans Mega-Lift* left Pangkalbalam on Indonesia's main tin producing island, Bangka, for Singapore loaded with about 800 tons of tin ingots; on 12 July the ship was hijacked and the crew abandoned in a small boat; the following day the ship was seen sinking. Reports indicate that pirates intentionally sank the vessel in shallow water to hide it from the authorities, so that they themselves could later dive and salvage the valuable cargo. Only a gang with considerable technical knowledge and transnational connections to ensure of its disposal could have undertaken such a complex operation.[46]

---

42   This account of the *Alondra Rainbow* case is based on the very full description in Langewiesche, *The Outlaw Sea,* pp. 46-61 & 70-81. See also Michael Richardson, 'India and China set sights on piracy'. On the decision of the Mumbai High Court to acquit see R.S. Vasan, 'Alondra Rainbow revisited: A study of related issues in the light of the recent judgement of Mumbai High Court', South Asia Analysis Group *Paper no. 1379,* 13 May 2005 and Vijay Sakhuja, 'Maritime legal conundrum', Institute of Peace and Conflict Studies *Paper no. 1778,* 29 June 2005.

43   'IMO ship identification number scheme'; also Stephen Jones, *Maritime Security: A Practical Guide,* London: The Nautical Institute, 2006, pp. 210-11.

44   International Maritime Organisation, 'IMO adopts comprehensive maritime security measures', ND

45   Jones, *Maritime Security,* pp. 211-12.

46   ISC, 'Report for December 2006', p. 10. The ship did trigger its SSAS. NB: this incident was not reported to the IMB.

The attack was similar to two others. The first was mounted on the *MV Prima Indah* hijacked on 30 September 2005 three hours after departing Bangka, also for Singapore. It was reported to be transporting 660 tons of tin worth an estimated $4.7 million. The crew was set adrift in a fishing boat and later landed safely on an island. The vessel was later spotted sunk off Bangka in about 35 metres (115 feet) of water, not far from where it began its journey. The second incident involved the *MV Inabukwa*, hijacked on 22 April 2005 off the Lingga Islands. Pirates, armed with guns, ordered the crew to sail the tin-laden ship to Pasir Gudang port, in Malaysia's southern Jahor state. The vessel was reported to be carrying a cargo of at least 575 tons, worth an estimated $4.6 million. The vessel docked in Pasir Gudang port for two days while the crew unloaded the tin into a warehouse under threat of being killed if they did not cooperate. On 25 April the pirates ordered the ship back to Indonesian waters and escaped in a speedboat, leaving the crew uninjured. After the incident was reported, authorities checked the warehouse and found the cargo of tin intact.[47] ONI noted the similarities between these incidents and the hijacking of the *MV Steadfast* in their report on the latter, discussed earlier.[48]

Cargo fraud takes several forms.[49] Only one is related to piracy directly, the so-called "phantom-ship" phenomenon that mixes fraud with theft.[50] A "phantom ship" is one that has been registered with a phantom identity using the temporary registration procedure in which all the details of previous names, tonnage, dimensions and ownership details are fictitious.[51] Although "phantom ship" scams can be undertaken using compliant crews,

---

47 See NGA ASAM 2005-140, 22 April 2005 on the *MV Inabukwa* and ASAM 2005-309, 30 Sept. 2005 on the *MV Prima Indah*. It is of interest that the *MV Inabukwa* was the victim of a previous pirate hijacking in 2001 while lifting $1.2 million of tin plates from Pangkalbalam to Singapore. In this incident, the cargo was untouched and only the crew's accommodation was raided. NGA ASAM 2001-98, 15 March 2001.

48 NGA ASAM 2006-07, 19 Dec. 2005.

49 Like all crime, it adapts to exploit new opportunities. Although the number of fraudulent scuttles may have declined, trade frauds have increased with buyers and sellers often working in collusion with banks: 'Maritime crime changes with time', *Fairplay,* 3 Oct. 2006.

50 The 'phantom' or 'ghost' ship is, in fact, another British innovation of the Victorian era. See Hepburn, *The Black Flag*, pp. 286-7 for the story of Herbert Rennie Smith.

51 ICC-IMB, 'Phantom ships', July 1994, paragraphs 3.1, 5 & 7.

something that was suspected in the cases of the *Marta*, *Thai Wong*[52] and *Steadfast*, and can be perpetrated as forms of "deviation" or "documentary" frauds,[53] they can also begin as piratical hijacks in which the ship's own crew is replaced (which often means killed) by the hijackers' own men who are mostly Burmese, Thai or Filipino.[54] The IMB suggested that piracy as a method of acquiring the necessary ships—as compared with outright purchase, chartering, transfer of ownership within or between criminal syndicates and reviving vessels that have been reported as total losses—might well have been triggered by the rising price of ships on the second-hand market in the late 1980s.[55] The incidents began in exactly the same way as a ship and cargo theft or a scuttle fraud, with the theft of a ship complete with its cargo, but instead of the cycle ending with the sale, abandonment or sinking of the ship it was retained, its name was changed and in some cases its appearance was altered, after which it was used to lure another cargo.[56] Several incidents of "phantom ship" fraud took place off Lebanon during the civil war (1975-90) and the IMB identified a further case in the Mediterranean, once again with Lebanese connections, in 1999.[57] However, the area most associated with the scam was Southeast Asia, where the first incidents were noticed in the 1970s. The number of incidents there grew progressively each decade until they came to an abrupt end in the early years of the new century. The origins of the practice appeared to lie in a plague of hull and cargo insurance frauds perpetrated in the region in the 1970s. The insurance industry mounted its own inquiry (known as FERIT, see below) and introduced measures that were successful in reducing this problem, but the gangs responsible, although known, were never brought to trial. In most cases it was the same gangs that went on to perpetrate the more sophisticated "phantom ship" hijackings from the mid-1980s to 2002.[58]

52   I.R. Hyslop, 'Contemporary piracy', p. 18.

53   ICC-IMB, 'Organised maritime crime in the Far East', pp. 21-4 & 26-8.

54   ICC-IMB, 'Phantom ships', paragraph 3.5.

55   ICC-IMB, 'Organised maritime crime in the Far East', pp. 16 & 43.

56   Menefee, *TMV*, p. 126; Conway, *The Piracy Business*, p. 20; OECD, *Security in Maritime Transport*, p. 14.

57   Menefee, *TMV*, p. 126-7; Conway, *The Piracy Business*, pp. 15-17. On the 1999 Mediterranean case see 'Investigation discovers first phantom ships in the Mediterranean for 15 years', ICC *Commercial Crime International*, vol. 16, no. 11, April 1999, p. 1.

58   For detail on the origins and background of the 'phantom ship' phenomenon and how it evolved out of the previous hull and cargo frauds see Abhyankar, 'Maritime fraud and piracy', pp. 175-83. Also ICC-IMB, 'Organised maritime

The ships that were targeted for these "phantom ship" frauds carried cargo that could be disposed of easily on the black market such as frozen prawns, diesel, kerosene, refined palm oil, plywood, rubber and metals.[59] After each successful fraud the ship was again repainted, renamed and sent into another port with new documentation to look for another shipper who was in a hurry to move a consignment. This was in turn loaded aboard the ship, which disappeared once more. Most of these thefts were believed to be to order, but not all, and when the ship involved was carrying a mixed cargo there would be goods the gangs could not dispose of immediately. If that was the case the cargo was offloaded, usually onto barges in international waters, and then stored in warehouses on land, in some cases—it was reported—on the Malaysian peninsula close to Singapore and in other cases in remote locations such as the Zamboanga area in the Philippines and places in China.[60] During the Lebanese civil war it was reputed that surplus goods were stored on "floating warehouses", two ships of around 10,000 tons which sailed in international waters and from which goods were "called off" by middlemen as buyers were found.[61] In other cases the stolen cargoes were sold to unsuspecting buyers via "shell" companies.[62]

Examples of "phantom ships" include the *Global Mars*, hijacked off Malaysia in 2000, and the *Silver Med*, hijacked in the Philippines in 1998.[63] Earlier examples include the MV *Taiyo Maru* (1987), the MV *Bona Vista*

---

crime in the Far East', pp. 5-6 where the authors say it is 'unfortunate' that because there were so few prosecutions and no real attempt to 'thoroughly investigate the apparent crimes' FERIT had found that 'a number of fraudsters have been able to remain within the industry and later to re-emerge, together with others, to face the industry with serious maritime crime problems'. Also ICC-IMB, 'Phantom ships', paragraph 10.3.

59 ICC-IMB, 'Organised maritime crime in the Far East', p. 19; ICC-IMB, 'Phantom ships', paragraph 3.11.

60 Abhyankar, 'Maritime fraud and piracy', p. 180. ICC-IMB, 'Organised maritime crime in the Far East', pp. 23-4; ICC-IMB, 'Phantom ships', paragraphs 3.12, 8.2 & 8.3.

61 Conway, *The Piracy Business*, p. 16.

62 Tim Whiteman, 'Ship held after spate of deviations', ICC *International Cargo Crime Prevention*, vol. 5, no. 12, April/May 1988.

63 The *Global Mars* was hijacked off Malaysia and later recovered in southern China. See Mark Bruyneel, 'The MT Global Mars attack', April 2000; NGA ASAM 2000-294, 24 Feb. 2000. On the *Silver Med* hijacked from Manila see Menefee, *TMV*, p. 83 and ICC-IMB, 'Organised maritime crime in the Far East', p. 68. Also NGA ASAM 1988-28, 15 Sept. 1988. For a fuller (but by no means comprehensive) list see ICC-IMB, 'Phantom ships', paragraphs 2.1 & 2.2.

1 (1988), the MV *Pacific Fortune* (1993), the MV *Windsor III* (1994) and the MV *Samudra Samrat* (1995) which was hijacked by the same syndicate that pirated the *Anna Sierra*.[64] Astonishingly, each "phantom ship" could go through the cycle perhaps three times a year for up to three years and, in the case of the *Doo Yang Jade,* nine changes of identity in two and a half years.[65] In most cases the cycle came to an end not because the pirates were apprehended, but because they had no interest in maintaining the physical fabric of the ships they had stolen; consequently the critical components, such as the engines, deteriorated to the point where the ships became unusable commercially. This was the moment when they could begin a new life smuggling people, guns or drugs.[66] Over the course of their working lives each "phantom ship" could generate millions of dollars of revenue—the IMB estimates $50 million annually—for the gangs involved.[67] While such events were relatively rare they took place regularly and at a frequency that

---

64   ICC International Maritime Bureau. 'Solving the Problems of Piracy and Phantom Ships'. October 1997, Paragraph 2.

65   P. Mukundan. Interview with author, April 2004. On the *Doo Yang Jade* see P. Mukundan, 'Cargo frauds', presentation to the International Union of Marine Insurers Annual Conference, London, 10-14 Sept. 2000; Hepburn, *The Black Flag,* pp. 293-7 and ICC-IMB, 'Organised maritime crime in the Far East', pp. 70-1. In contrast, the Panama-registered *Natris,* which was hijacked in 2002, traded successfully as the Belize-registered *Paulijing* for three years before it was apprehended in 2005: Marcus Hand, 'Flags of convenience are 'assisting criminals", *Lloyd's List,* 3 Nov. 2005.

66   P. Mukundan, interview with author, April 2004. See also OECD, *Security in Maritime Transport,* p. 14; Chalk, *Grey-Area Phenomena in Southeast Asia,* p. 32; Bertil Linter, *Blood Brothers: The Criminal Underworld of Asia,* New York: Palgrave Macmillan, 2003, pp. 302-3; 'Phantom vessels the latest tactic in Asian piracy', *South China Morning Post,* 22 July 1994; and Kevin Sullivan and Mary Jordan, 'High-tec pirates ravage Asian seas', *Washington Post,* 5 July 1999. For published descriptions of the 'phantom ship phenomenon' and cargo scams see Burnett, *Dangerous Waters,* pp. 218-19; 'Dead men tell no tales'; Greg Torode, 'Probe into stolen ship racket leads to HK firm', *South China Morning Post,* 25 July 1994. See also 'Organised crime takes to the high seas, ICC report finds', *ICC News* report, 4 Feb. 2002. Samuel Pyeatt Menefee also notes that the gangs involved usually have a wide range of criminal interests: Menefee, *TMV,* p. 127, a point amplified by Langewiesche, *The Outlaw Sea,* pp. 51-2.

67   IMB earnings estimate quoted in Chalk, 'Maritime piracy: A global overview', p. 49; *The Economist* suggested $40 million; 'Dead men tell no tales'*;* Ali M. Koknar, 'Piracy and terrorism are joining forces and creating troubled waters for the maritime industry', *Security Management Online,* June 2004, suggests that the 'take' from each hijacking may range from $8 million up to $200 million and that, as a consequence, such hijackings are very much the work of organised criminal gangs.

increased until it reached the 2002 peak.[68] Why they stopped is unknown. The assumption was that, like the hijacked cargoes, most of the "phantom ship" cargoes also ended up in China and therefore the Chinese authorities put a stop to the practice while at the same time refusing to admit that it had ever happened.[69] However, in January 2006 the IMB reported that an Indonesian ship, the MV *Alfa Gemilang*, had been hijacked along with its cargo on a voyage from Sampit on the southern coast of Kalimantan to Belawan in northern Sumatra. The hijack gang had been allowed on board as passengers. Most of the ship's crew were landed on Tawi-Tawi Island in the Philippines, after which the ship disappeared with three members of the crew still on board.[70]

The complete ship hijack in which the gang is looking for a ransom for the ship and the crew together has in the past few years been unique to Somalia, as has been described already. Kidnap-and-ransom of the crew alone, while far from being a new crime, has occurred in three areas: first, the Sulu Sea where the criminally and politically motivated groups in effect continued the centuries-old slave raiding traditions of the Sulu pirates; secondly, starting early in 2002, at both the northern and southern ends of the Malacca Straits;[71] thirdly, Nigeria where it became increasingly common as the political situation in the Niger delta region deteriorated.

In the Straits the ships that were attacked were fishing boats or vessels with low freeboards such as small tankers or cargo vessels, none of which had large crews or could be defended effectively.[72] Most of these craft were local but the most famous case, also mentioned earlier, involved a Japanese tug, the *Idaten*. This took place in March 2005 when a gang of 15 pirates armed with RPGs, AK47 and M16 automatic rifles kidnapped two Japa-

---

68 With regard to the relative rarity of hijacking see Gottschalk and Flanagan, *Jolly Roger with an Uzi*, p. 91. On the reduction in 2003 see ICC Piracy Report 2004, p. 16. Also 'Piracy takes a higher toll of seamen's lives'.

69 One case where they have done is that of the *Siam Xanxai*. In Feb. 2003 a court in Shantou sentenced ten Indonesian pirates to jail for hijacking this Thai-registered tanker in Malaysian waters in 1999 and bringing it to Chinese waters. The pirates falsified the ship's documents. The ship plus its cargo, valued at $1 million, was returned to its Thai owners: Sakhuja, 'Maritime legal conundrum' and Richardson, 'India and China set sights on piracy'.

70 ICC-IMB Piracy Report 2006, p. 18.

71 Davis, 'Piracy in Southeast Asia', p. 39.

72 See, for example, 'Pirates free Indonesian hostages', *BBC News*, 19 March 2005. Also Bateman *et al.*, 'Safety and security in the Malacca and Singapore Straits', p. 21.

nese and a Filipino.[73] The ferocity of the Japanese reaction, at least equal to that which had attended the hijacking of the *Alondra Rainbow* in 1999, probably prompted their early release. It also drew international attention to the problem, which in turn sparked local law enforcement activity that precipitated a rapid decline in kidnappings.[74]

The incidents at the northern end of the Straits were ascribed generally to GAM, the Aceh separatist movement. There was no question that the piracy in the area became more organised in 2003, around the time when GAM was separated from its funding sources on land as a result of more vigorous counter-insurgency activity by the Indonesian armed forces.[75] It also true that kidnap-and-ransom largely supplanted the theft of petty cash or cargo.[76] Substantial sums of money were demanded: reportedly up to $150,000 for a crew member and up to $250,000 for a captain, although the amounts the pirates received were more likely to be in the $10-20,000 range.[77] That said, evidence of GAM's guilt was never conclusive. The group itself denied it was responsible.[78] When the upsurge of criminality began the Indonesian government did not respond, treating it very much as business as usual until the early months of 2005 when the *Idaten* was attacked and the complaints from neighbouring states and international shipping became too shrill to be ignored. The general but unspoken assumption in the region was that common pirates, and quite possibly members of the Indonesian armed forces, had been behind at least some of attacks and that the Aceh insurgency, although it almost certainly contributed to the problem, served as another useful cover for criminality.[79] In 2006 the IMB ex-

---

73   Vijay Sakhuja, 'The sea muggers back in the Malacca Straits', South Asia Analysis Group, *Paper no. 1300*, 23 March 2005; and Yamada, 'Defending Asian seas from marauding by pirates'. Also NGA ARAM 2005-88, 14 March 2005.

74   Refer also to the comment in ONI, WWTTS Report, 6 April 2005, Paragraph D.2.

75   Kate McGeown, 'Aceh rebels blamed for piracy', *BBC News*, 8 Sept. 2003.

76   McGeown, 'Aceh rebels blamed for piracy'; also Raymond, 'Piracy in Southeast Asia'.

77   Confidential interview, July 2005; Davis, 'Piracy in Southeast Asia', p. 39; Raymond, 'Piracy in Southeast Asia'.

78   'Indonesian rebels deny carrying out pirate attacks in Malacca Strait', *Channel NewsAsia*, 17 March 2005; 'GAM says it will not attack ships in Malacca Straights [*sic*]', *Islam Online*, 7 Sept. 2001.

79   Martin N. Murphy, 'The blue, green and brown: Insurgency and counter-insurgency on the water', *Contemporary Security Policy*, vol. 28, no. 1, April 2007, pp. 68-9.

pressed concern that an attack in June on two landing craft carrying aid to Aceh under charter to the UN, and an attack a few days later in July on the Japanese freighter *Island Oasis*, were intended kidnappings because they both occurred in daylight and the attackers were heavily armed.[80] Later in July three ex-GAM members were arrested in connection with the attack on the UN ships.[81]

Whoever was responsible for the incidents at the northern end of the Straits, the kidnappings at the southern end of the Strait, and certainly the *Idaten* case, were undoubtedly the work of criminal gangs based mainly on the Indonesian island of Batam. Throughout the Straits as a whole, 31 incidents involving kidnapping were reported between 2000 and 2005.[82] Nor have kidnappings stopped: in August 2007 a tug towing a barge laden with steel billets was attacked between Penang and Belawan by a ten-man gang who took the master and chief engineer, releasing them later in the month after a ransom had been paid.[83] It is assumed, furthermore, that many other incidents were never notified out of concern for the captives' safety as crew members were reportedly killed when ransom demands were not met.[84] This points to another important difference between kidnappings in Southeast Asia and Somalia: in Somalia victims lives have been threatened only rarely because they could be easily held captive in one place for months if necessary without any fear that they would escape or be rescued.[85] In Southeast Asia they needed to be moved regularly to avoid de-

---

80   'Piracy attacks spark crew concerns', *Fairplay*, 5 July 2006; Marcus Hand, 'Piracy experts fear Malacca Strait attacks will set new kidnap agenda', *Lloyd's List*, 12 July 2006. According to the NGA report, the pirates who assaulted the landing ships claimed to be GAM. NGA ASAM 2006-165, 3 July 2006.

81   'Indonesian navy arrests tsunami aid pirates in Aceh', *Reuters*, 26 July 2006; 'Rebels became Malacca pirates'.

82   Davis, 'Piracy in Southeast Asia', p. 39.

83   NGA ASAM 2007-204 , 13 Aug. 2007. Also Marcus Hand, 'Pirates kidnap tug crew in Malacca Strait', *Lloyd's List*, 14 Aug. 2007; 'Pirates free Indonesian sailors', *ABC Radio Australia*, 27 Aug. 2007.

84   Reports on crew members being killed can be found in Marcus Hand, 'Piracy attacks leave owners facing ransom cover dilemma', *Lloyd's List*, 24 June 2005; Stephen Fidler and Arlen Harris, 'Attacks are raising security and insurance concerns', *Financial Times*, 23 June 2005; Simon Montlake, 'Pirates ahead!' *Christian Science Monitor*, 18 March 2004.

85   In July 2007 there were reports that a crew member of a Taiwanese trawler, the *Ching Fong Hwa 168*, had been killed because the pirates had become impatient about the ransom negotiations: ONI, Worldwide Threats to Shipping Mariner Warning Information, 11 July 2007, Paragraph H.7. This report was

tection. The crew of the *Idaten* was moved from boat to boat and then between various small islands, including one that was described as "isolated", which was possibly in Indonesia, then forced to trek through jungle before finally being released off southern Thailand six days after the hijacking took place, once the ransom of $461,000 had been paid.[86] It is likely that only a well-organised and well-resourced organisation with good negotiating skills and an international spread could have executed such an operation successfully.[87] Consequently, the longer kidnapped crews were held the greater the risk became. Any deal for their release usually had to be concluded within a few weeks, after which the likelihood they would be killed increased. The probability, therefore, is that because hijacking Western and Japanese seafarers can draw unwelcome publicity, and despite the example of the *Idaten*, most of the incidents in the Straits of Malacca involved "local" kidnappings and "local-to-local" negotiations.[88]

Environmental risk. Because common piracy is unguided and uncoordinated and therefore more accident-prone, it presents a potentially greater threat of disruption to economically vital waterways, and of environmental damage to the fishing grounds and fragile ecosystems that adjoin shipping channels in many regions, than organised piracy.[89] Common pirates tend to raid ships. If these raids occur when the ship is underway the crews can be distracted such that control of the ship is lost for a time. In other cases, when crews have been imprisoned and have only been able to free them-

---

confirmed subsequently, making it the first incident when Somali pirates intentionally killed a hostage since piracy emerged as a serious problem on the central east coast in 2005. For a full account of the incident see 'Survivors of pirate attack speak out', *AP,* 15 Nov. 2007.

86   Manuel L. Quezon, III, 'Could terrorists use the strait of disquietude to wreak havoc?' *Arab News,* 25 March 2005. As a point of interest, this report claims that the 'going rate' for ransom was 10 million yen (about $90,000) which was about what was paid in this case.

87   Herbert-Burns, 'Compound piracy at sea in the early twenty-first century', pp. 100 and 112.

88   *Ibid.,* p. 112.

89   There is an interesting parallel here between current piracy and historical privateering. As Janice E. Thompson writes: 'With British privateers out of control in 1758, insurance company loses mounted. The government responded by placing a minimal [*sic*] size on privateering vessels and required that privateers post a proper security. This eliminated the 'little fishermen-privateers', who were most out of control, and improved the conduct of the larger ones.' Janice E. Thompson, *Mercenaries, Pirates and Sovereigns: State-building and Extraterritorial Violence in Early Modern Europe,* Princeton: Princeton UP, 1994, p. 70.

selves after the pirates have gone, or their navigation and communications equipment has been stolen or destroyed, ships have been out of control for longer. They have become what are called "rogue" ships. In either case there is an obvious risk of collision or grounding. If the ships involved are carrying hazardous cargoes, or if the incidents occur in constricted waters where the risk of colliding with a ship carrying such a cargo is clearly higher, there is an additional potential risk of serious explosion or significant marine pollution.

The governments of Malaysia and Singapore, and external observers, rate the risk of environmental disaster as high as, or higher than, any other potential consequence of piracy.[90] As Peter Chalk points out many people, in Southeast Asia particularly, depend upon the bounty of the sea.[91] In 1991, for example, the *Eastern Power*, a fully laden Panamanian-flagged VLCC steamed out of control for 15-20 minutes following a pirate attack in the crowded Phillips Channel south of Singapore.[92] In 1992 the single-hulled *Valiant Carrier*, loaded with furnace oil, steamed on fire and out of control close to the Sumatra coast after it was attacked by pirates south of Singapore.[93] Although a crew member was able to alert the engine room which cut all power, meaning that the ship was drifting rather than making way, the crew were only able to regain full control of the ship less than one mile short of reefs.[94] In 1999 pirates boarded the *MT Chaumont*, a fully laden VLCC, and although bridge control was not lost it too steamed down the narrow and crowded Phillips Channel for 35 minutes as the crew were assaulted in their quarters.[95] Most spectacularly, in 1992 another single-hulled oil tanker, the *Nagasaki Spirit*, released around 14,000 tons of crude oil when it collided with a container ship, the *Ocean Blessing*. Investigators believed the accident happened because pirates either kidnapped the crew of the *Nagasaki Spirit* or the ship was fired upon forcing the crew

---

90   Davis, 'Piracy in Southeast Asia', p. 37.

91   Peter Chalk, interview with author, Aug. 2004. Mark J. Valencia also rates environmental disaster as a serious risk: interview with author, Aug. 2004.

92   Dubner, 'Human rights and environmental disaster', p. 6. Also 'Oil piracy proves growing menace to tanker traffic in South China Sea', p. 25 which refers to the ship being without bridge control for ten minutes.

93   NGA ASAM 1992-14, 24 April 1992..

94   Burnett, *Dangerous Waters*, pp. 54-71; IMB, 'Special piracy report', p. 9 and 'Oil piracy proves growing menace to tanker traffic in South China Sea', p. 24.

95   Burnett, *Dangerous Waters*, pp. 146-7 and Note 30, p. 307; McDaniel, 'Modern high seas piracy', p. 14. NGA ASAM 1999-55, 2 March 1999.

to abandon ship, which meant that it was out of control when the collision took place.[96] This, however, could not be proved, as there were no survivors. Fire had virtually destroyed both ships.[97]

Violence

There is no distinction to be drawn between common and organised pirates when it comes to violence; both are ready to kill their victims on the principle that dead men tell no tales. According to the IMB Piracy Reporting Centre, most reported attacks "can now be expected to involve casualties of one sort or another".[98] Gottschalk and Flanagan recount incidents of pirates talking, not only about killing and torturing their victims, but even about how much they despised them.[99]

Perhaps the most gruesome case occurred in 1998, when pirates pulled sacks over the heads of all 23 crew members of the MV *Cheung Son* and then shot, stabbed, but mainly clubbed them to death before throwing them over the side.[100] Six of the bodies turned up in fishermen's nets off Shantou. The main reason why the pirates were caught was that one of them took and kept a photograph, uncovered during a routine police check, of the party they held amongst the corpses before they weighed them down and threw them away.[101] Although the vessel itself has never been found the pirates, who apparently presented themselves as Chinese customs officials on an anti-smuggling mission, were convicted in what the *Beijing Morning Post* described as the biggest case of robbery and murder in 50 years of Communist rule.[102] Thirteen of them were executed.[103] The most curious aspect of the case was that the ship was carrying low-value

---

96 The distress message from the *Nagasaki Spirit* said: 'Have been fired upon and now have fire in nos 5 and 6 central tanks. Abandoning vessel immediately...': Stewart, *The Brutal Seas*, p. 299.

97 Burnett, *Dangerous Waters*, pp. 134-42 and Gottschalk and Flanagan, *Jolly Roger with an Uzi*, p. 113,

98 Chalk, 'Maritime piracy: A global overview', p. 47; Hitt, 'Bandits in the global shipping lanes'.

99 Gottschalk and Flanagan, *Jolly Roger with an Uzi*, p. 24..

100 Chalk, 'Maritime piracy: A global overview', p. 47; Glass, 'The New Piracy'..

101 Andrew Chang, 'Terror on the waves', *ABC News.com*, 29 Jan. 2001.

102 'Dead men tell no tales'; Langewiesche, *The Outlaw Sea*, p. 57; Sakhuja, 'Maritime legal conundrum'. For an account of the outcome of the trial see Vu Kim Chung, 'Thirteen pirates sentenced to death', *Penguin Star*, 22 Dec. 1999.

103 'China executes 13 pirates', *People's Daily Online*, 29 Jan. 2000.

furnace slag. The suspicion was that the slag was dumped and the ship used instead to transport an illegal Chinese arms shipment.[104] The barbarity that took place was, however, nothing new. South China Sea pirates have a long history of extreme violence (as epitomised by the horrific experiences of the "boat people").[105]

Almost the equal of the *Cheung Son* case but much more mysterious was that of the 17,000 dwt freighter the *Errica Inge*. When brought to Guangzhou to be broken up in 1992 it arrived bearing the name *Hai Sin* and in a refrigerated section in one of its holds, from which the power had long since been turned off, the breakers discovered ten charred and rotting corpses. Forensic examination determined that the bodies were probably Caucasian, which suggested they had been the crew of a cargo ship on an international voyage. Eric Ellen, who investigated the case, remains convinced that the bodies could well have been those of the crew of the *Nagasaki Spirit* which collided with the *Ocean Blessing* (as described above).[106] Forty-four seamen died as a result of the collision, 16 of whom were unaccounted for. That the *Ocean Blessing* was under attack appears highly likely and the collision could well have occurred as a consequence: "Her speed changes and zigzagging as observed by others, were consistent with manoeuvres to shake-off a boarding party".[107] There is no evidence that the bodies found on the *Errica Inge* were those of the missing men but Ellen contends that it is hard to imagine where a similar group could have come from. It is quite conceivable that the *Errica Inge*, which investigations have shown was operating as a "phantom ship" in the vicinity at the same time (possibly under the name *Palu III*), could have picked up the burned bodies, which showed no signs of foul play. "Phantom ships" are known to have been operated by crews who were unaware of the ships' real purpose and if this was true of the *Errica Inge*, the crew might therefore have picked up the bodies because they would have seen it as their duty to do so. How-

104 'Dead men tell no tales'.

105 Villar, *Piracy Today*, pp. 29-30.

106 Eric Ellen, conversation with author, Sept. 2007. Burnett, *Dangerous Waters*, p. 141. For a full account of the *Errica Inge* case see Stewart, *The Brutal Seas*, pp. 285-302.

107 Comment made by the head of the Liberian ship registry's investigative team, Captain Chadwick, and cited in Stewart, *The Brutal Seas*, p. 300. According to Frank Wiswall 'the accident followed reports from other nearby mariners that the *Ocean Blessing* was being operated in an erratic manner, and that radio transmissions were broken and irregular.' Quoted in Tanya Mitchell, 'Mariners face growing threat from pirates', *Village Soup*, 29 Sept. 2006.

ever, once the criminal operators were made aware that the bodies were on board they might have been left with no option but to dispose of the ship as rapidly as possible. One of the few facts known for certain about the case is that the company that sold the *Hai Sin* never existed.[108]

Other acts of violence, such as those suffered by Captain John Swain of the *Stolt Eagle* who lost three fingers fighting off pirates, Captain Donny Montiero of the *Valiant Carrier* whose infant daughter was knifed by pirates during the attack on his ship, and Captain John Bashforth murdered by pirates on board his ship the *Baltimar Zephyr* have been noted by officers and crews alike.[109] Their resulting apprehension when traversing pirate-prone sea areas was reflected in the *Nautilus* survey mentioned above.

Access to markets

Pirates need trustworthy intermediaries to dispose of stolen goods and convert foreign currency. In those parts of the world where pirates are regarded as Robin Hood-style benefactors of the poor, such as coastal villages in Indonesia and the Philippines, perhaps simple barter suffices. Robbers who steal marine equipment and sundries and valuables from crews' quarters can probably sell them in local maritime yards and directly into local communities without many questions being asked.

It is the gangs that steal whole cargoes, or ships, or ships and cargoes together that need larger markets, which in many cases are located well away from where the hijackings take place. The speed with which goods are disposed of would suggest that buyers are in place before the cargo is hijacked; in fact, that the cargoes are almost certainly stolen to order. The cases of the *Anna Sierra*, the *Tenyu*, and the *Alondra Rainbow* all demonstrate this. In the case of the *Petro Ranger*, which has also been touched on already, the tanker met two others at sea to which much of the cargo was transferred and was waiting to discharge the remainder when the Chinese maritime police intervened.[110] It is likely that piracy on this scale will fluctuate according to market demand and will continue, or resume, when

108 Stewart, *The Brutal Seas*, p. 296.

109 On John Swain see Burnett, *Dangerous Waters*, pp. 106-7. On the knife attack on Donny Montiero's child see Burnett, *Dangerous Waters*, p. 65. On John Bashforth see Stewart, *The Brutal Seas*, p. 8.

110 Blyth, *Petro Pirates*, pp. 54-5; Hitt, 'Bandits in the global shipping lanes'; Eklöf, *Pirates in Paradise*, p. 74.

buyers can obtain what they want from pirates more cheaply than they can from legitimate suppliers.

Risk is the deciding factor. Legal and illegal markets are not the same. Pino Arlacchi, a senior official of the UN Office for Drug Control and Crime Prevention, has made the point that "...some of the dynamics of criminal markets are substantially different from those that drive legal markets. Illegal enterprises can resort to the use of violence and intimidation (and can) also corrupt those who uphold the law and those who are in a position to manipulate public institutions."[111] This point resonates with two made by the IMB: first, that the "phantom ship" syndicates were "extremely dangerous" and prepared to use violence; second, that the problem was attributable to the opening of China in the early 1980s, which caused a surge in demand for goods. When all this was coupled with both the mainland regime's lack of experience in dealing with the outside world, and its refusal to admit Taiwan to international bodies—which effectively created a safe haven for fraudsters—the risks criminals faced were reduced substantially.[112] On the other hand the Chinese experience from mid-1998 onwards, when the government decided to crack down on smuggling and piracy-related maritime crime, suggests that, providing there is sufficient political will, governments and law enforcement organisations can increase the risk to buyers of pirate goods more effectively than they can increase the risk to the pirate themselves. Providing this is true, it is likely that this type of piracy can be controlled or ended more readily when the groups and organisations that buy from pirates are disrupted or their operations are discouraged by land-based police activity, political pressure, sentencing policy and international cooperation. As David Pearl, Maritime Armed Crime Analyst at the Office of Naval Intelligence has written, "the reality is that combating piracy on the high seas is the least desireable and least cost-effective tactic".[113] It was perhaps nervousness on the part of the buyer in the *Steadfast* incident, induced by just this sort of pressure, that brought it to a close. The pirate gang involved unloaded the cargo into a warehouse but it was never collected.[114] Dragonette made the point that pirates were "failing to find a market

---

111   Pino Arlacchi, 'The dynamics of illegal markets' in Phil Williams; and Dimitri Vlassis, (eds), *Combating Transnational Crime: Concepts, Activities and Response*, Abingdon and New York: Frank Cass, 2001, pp. 7-8.

112   ICC-IMB, 'Phantom ships', paragraphs 1.8 & 1.9; Flynn. 'China promises crackdown as it strives to escape image of a safe haven for pirates'.

113   David Pearl. 'ONI and Combating Piracy'. *ONI Quarterly*, April 2008, p. 4.

114   Hand, 'Joint alert forces pirates to flee hijacked tanker'.

for stolen goods" and were being denied the "peace and quiet in which to process their spoils."[115] A point echoed by Joe Corless, of the investigators Gray Page when he commented that: "Without China, the phantom-ship problem would die out".[116] It is therefore at least arguable that the sharp decline in attacks on large ships in the Malacca Straits and elsewhere in Southeast Asia since about 2002 owed more to the anti-smuggling and counter-corruption drives in China than to more vigorous patrolling and aerial surveillance in the Straits themselves.

Links to insurgent or terrorist groups

There is no clear evidence that any pirate group has cooperated with or has links to any insurgent or terrorist organisation. Pirates' skills are not unique; they are shared by other groups such as fishermen and former naval personnel who might be more prepared to work with terrorists.[117] This lack of evidence has not, however, dampened continuing speculation.[118] It has not put an end to "uncritically repeated myths, half truths, and unsupportable assertions of an alleged nexus of piracy and terrorism."[119]

One report, for example, that came in for particular criticism was carried by *The Economist*, and amplified subsequently by Gal Luft and Anne Korin in their article for *Foreign Affairs*: that the pirates who had attacked the chemical tanker *Dewi Madrim*, off Sumatra in March 2003, had behaved unlike other pirates and in fact had acted more like terrorists.[120] They had taken control of the ship for about an hour and during that time altered course and altered speed, as if they were learning to control it or to understand its handling characteristics; treating it, in other words, as if it were a "flight training school for terrorists".[121] "Pirates" do not need to know these

115 Charles H. Dragonette, 'Maritime legends', *Bulletin of the Atomic Scientists*, vol. 62, no. 5, Sept./Oct., 2006, p. 17.

116 Christopher Donville. 'Yo-ho-ho and an M16'. *Bloomberg*, December 1997, p. 41. Interview with Joe Corless, July 2008.

117 Sam Bateman, 'Assessing the threat of maritime terrorism: Issues for the Asia-Pacific region', *Security Challenges*, vol. 2, no. 3, Oct. 2006, p. 81.

118 Chalk, 'Maritime terrorism in the contemporary era', pp. 23-4.

119 Dragonette, 'Lost at Sea', p. 174.

120 'Peril on the sea', *The Economist*, 4 Oct. 2003, pp. 67-8; Luft and Korin, 'Terrorism goes to sea', p. 67; also 'Terror threat swells at sea', *WorldNetDaily.com*, 8 June 2004; and Patrick Goodenough, 'Maritime security takes centre stage in SE Asia', *CNSNews.com*, 29 June 2004. ONI, WWTTS, 2 April 2003, Paragraph K.1.

121 Glass, 'The new piracy'.

things. Nor do they generally leave with little of value if they have had the time and opportunity to find and take what they want. The conclusion that was drawn was that they were learning to control a ship in the same way that the 9/11 hijackers had learned to fly aircraft and, quite possibly, with a similar suicidal purpose in mind. This account of what happened originated with the London-based defence and security consultancy, Aegis Defence Services, that suggested "something altogether more sinister" than a pirate attack had taken place.[122] The problem was that the ship owner contradicted this report. He denied that the captain had been kidnapped, said that little of value had been taken and expressed his view that the attack was unquestionably the work of pirates. Extensive inquiries by the IMB and other interested agencies could find no evidence to support the contention that terrorists had been involved.[123] What happened was that pirates boarded the ship and proceeded to take what they could. This took time. In order to avoid hitting other ships or running aground the pirates manoeuvred the ship. They then left.[124] For their part Aegis Defence Services subsequently issued a second report, which warned that terrorists could either adopt pirates' tactics or "piggyback" on pirates' raids. They went on to write that "the threat is not from traditional commercial pirates, but from a new breed of maritime terrorist, whose skills evolve from a conventional piracy base".[125] To date there are no grounds for believing this is true.

Nonetheless, while it would seem the theories that pirates might use their expertise to teach terrorists how to hijack vessels for the purposes of attacking ports or undermining trade are currently without foundation, changes to the financing of many terrorist groups over the past twenty years has brought about some cooperation and even convergence between insurgent

---

122 Aegis has consistently refused to publish the report or even the section dealing with this incident. Interested agencies appear to have obtained copies and this quote is from Dragonette, 'Maritime legends', p. 18.

123 P. Mukundan, interview with author, 2004; Dragonette, 'Lost at sea', p. 175. Dominick Donald, Senior Analyst at Aegis, in his interview with the author in 2004, claimed that *The Economist* had quoted the report with much of the qualifying material removed. The point Aegis wanted to emphasise was that, in their view, the behaviour of the 'pirates' was hard to explain without taking into account a terrorist motive. See also Keith Bradsher, 'Attacks on chemical ships in Southeast Asia seem to be piracy, not terror', *New York Times*, 27 March 2003.

124 Dragonette, 'Maritime legends', p. 18. NGA ASAM 2003-97, 26 March 2003..

125 Quoted in Goodenough, 'Maritime security takes centre stage in SE Asia'.

and terrorist groups and organised crime networks, creating a potential *indirect* link between terrorism and organised piracy. Also, the presence of pirate activity in a locality can confuse police and intelligence efforts aimed at tracing terrorists, and distract investigators from their proper targets. The fact that some insurgent groups that have engaged in terrorism—such as the LTTE in Sri Lanka, GAM in Indonesia, MNLF and ASG in the Philippines, MEND in Nigeria—have also used piratical methods to raise money contributes to this opacity.

Level of official support and corruption

Common piracy flourishes in weak and "failed" states. Common piracy can be suppressed, or at least contained, by on-shore police work supported by vigorous maritime patrolling. Weak states often can afford neither. Where they can, the forces nominally responsible for suppressing piracy might nonetheless be in league with the pirates or, in some cases, actually *are* the pirates, which appears to have been the case, on occasion, in Indonesia.[126] Various factors can bring this corruption about, such as cultural acceptability, inadequate pay, lack of supervision, or clan or ethnic differences which prompt local officials to support members of their own community rather than the central government.

Organised pirates can benefit from the support of those in power. Major hijackings and "phantom ship" frauds can make men rich, reason enough for corrupt officials and politicians to offer criminals their help. The subject's sensitivity means the evidence is naturally scarce but analysts of maritime crime, and others who are concerned about maritime security, believe that organised pirates in most pirate-prone areas have benefited from the protection of senior provincial officials, police officers, or even nationally known politicians.[127]

The Corruption Perceptions Index calculated annually by the Internet Centre of Corruption Research scores countries between 10 (highly clean) and 0 (highly corrupt). All of the countries highlighted as having a piracy problem or providing a market for pirated goods scored low on the 2006 Index: China 3.3, Philippines 2.5, Indonesia 2.4, Nigeria 2.2, Bangladesh

---

126   Mark Huband. 'WMRC report blames Indonesian corruption for rise in piracy in Southeast Asian waters', *Financial Times*, 14 Feb. 2004.

127   ICC IMB, 'Organised maritime crime in the Far East', p. 37: 'One factor inhibiting the availability of information is the high-level patronage, both political and personal, which some syndicates enjoy, giving them a high degree of protection'.

2.0 (Somalia no data but 2.1 in 2005). By way of comparison, two countries that suffer from the effects of piracy but are taking action against it score more highly: Malaysia 5.5 and Singapore 9.4.[128]

Even in cases of the most basic common piracy, people other than the pirates will know about their activities, will benefit from them or be forced to tolerate them.[129] The more money a gang makes the more sophisticated its methods need to become in order to manage and protect its operations; inevitably more people will come under its influence, many of them willingly, forming the modern equivalent of Peter Earl's "unscrupulous men" prepared to bend the rules for a profit. These men are to be found not only in the states bordering pirate seas but in developed countries because, as Louise Shelley points out, much of the profit of transnational crime flows overseas to states where criminals could not operate without the expertise of local bankers, lawyers and accountants who either serve, or fail to exercise due diligence over, their client's activities.[130]

Links to organised crime

Piracy is as much a land-based activity as it is a marine activity. In fact, so long as states persist in seeing piracy as largely sea-based, rather than a land-based problem with a maritime dimension, then it will continue to flourish. Experience throughout history has shown that pirates cannot survive without land-based support. The crucial difference between common and organised piracy is not to be found at sea but in the scale and sophistication of the networks that sustain them from the land, the social and political effects these networks have there and, consequently, the nature of the political environment that tolerates or even supports piracy and other criminal activity. Corruption becomes more important to piracy the more connections a gang has to wider criminal networks: corruption and organised crime are rarely separable.

Defining organised crime is a difficult as defining piracy or terrorism. The Global Action Plan against Organised Crime, adopted at the World Ministerial Conference held in November 1994, did not define it but did list what it regarded as its six principal characteristics: a group organised to commit crime; links that enable leaders to control it; the use of violence,

---

128   The Index is available at http://www.icgg.org/corruption.cpi_2006_data.html

129   Vagg, 'Rough seas', pp. 65 & 68-9.

130   Louise I. Shelley, 'Unraveling the new criminal nexus', *Georgetown JIA*, Winter/Spring 2005, p. 6.

intimidation and corruption to earn profits or control territories or markets; the ability of a group to launder its proceeds of illicit activities and use these to infiltrate the legitimate economy; its ability to expand into new activities and beyond its own national borders; and, finally, its ability to cooperate with other organised crime groups. The more elements of this description a group displays, the more it could be said to be an organised crime group.[131]

The skills and assets of organised piracy gangs are likely to be of interest to diversified transnational criminal organisations (TCOs) or, to give them their alternative name, transnational organised crime (TOC) groups. Given their inherent mobility and flexibility, ships and boats can perform a multiple of roles. A fishing boat can serve legal and illegal fishermen just as well;[132] it can also be used as an attack boat or be used to smuggle drugs, arms or migrants. With care it can do any of these things without changing its appearance or its operating pattern enough to arouse suspicion.

Colombian drug smugglers have demonstrated the level of sophistication that criminals have already attained in their use of the sea. In order to reach the United States, narcotics smugglers appear to use two methods. The first employs a combination of commercial-sized vessels and "go-fast" speedboats. Commercially-sized vessels sail west of the Galapagos Islands to points as far as 2,000nm (3,700km) from the Colombian or Ecuadorian coasts where they transfer the cocaine to go-fast boats, typically about 50 feet (15m) in length with closed hulls and powered by three or four inboard or outboard engines, which then run for the coasts of Mexico and Central America guided by GPS and refuelled on the way from pre-positioned, makeshift tankers.[133] Alternatively the drugs are taken to inlets along the Colombian coast where they are loaded aboard go-fast boats that then run directly to destinations in Central America and Mexico. These

---

131   Schmid, 'The links between transnational organized crime and terrorist crime', pp. 43-4. Also Louise Shelley, John Picarelli and Chris Corpora. 'Global crime inc' in Maryann Cusimano Love, *Beyong Sovereignty: Issues for a Global Agenda* (2nd edn.), Belmont: Wadsworth Publishing, 2003, pp. 145-7.

132   Illegal fishing is a serious problem in northern Australian waters, for example. The Australian fisheries minister, Eric Abetz, 'says the boats were purchased by organised crime gangs and staffed by Indonesian villagers': 'Australia detains more Indonesian boats', *ABC Radio Australia*, 17 July 2006 and 'Australia links organized crime to illegal fishing'. *Reuters*, 26 May 2008.

133   Chris Kraul, 'Ecuador's divided loyalties', *LA Times*, 15 Jan. 2007; Jeffrey J. Hathaway and Terry R. McGee, 'MDA support to the drug war', *Coast Guard Proceedings*, Fall 2006, pp. 17 & 18.

go-fasts, which are usually painted blue to blend with the sea and sit low in the water to minimise radar contact, also need to be refuelled from pre-positioned boats in order to complete their journey.[134] To facilitate the boats' landfall Mexican cartels are reported to have bought coastal farms, in Nicaragua for example, to provide themselves with secure sites in the knowledge that the Nicaraguan navy has few assets with which to interdict their operations.[135] The Mexican navy is similarly ill-equipped and ill-trained to deal with this organised criminal onslaught.[136]

While weak or "failed" states can provide pirates with useful sanctuary and secure operating bases, they are very unlikely to be the headquarters of the "organising minds". These will be elsewhere. Even if the pirates, the "dumb infantry" in these operations, are caught, and even if the trail of suspicion leads back to the "organising mind" the complexity of international extradition, coupled with the fact that the act of piracy itself would have been perpetrated in international waters, means these "organising minds" are effectively immune from prosecution. In addition, they may well have some form of political influence, and can therefore count on benign indifference or even either open or tactic political protection.[137] The journalist Abby Tan quotes Freddie Clemo, a British marine insurance agent based in Manila, speaking about the problem in 1996: "Everyone's in it. Governments are openly against piracy. But so many rice bowls are involved. [Governments] don't want to break them."[138]

Little of what is known about the organised crime groups involved in piracy has entered the public domain. The "organising minds" behind some pirate groups or, at least, some pirate activity appear to be individuals or syndicates that almost certainly engage in legitimate business as well. In other cases the "organising mind" appears to be a TOC group. In Asia suspicion has been directed at both Chinese Triads and Japanese *yakuza*, but the prime movers behind piracy might well be local and less well-known "mafias" based in several states. In every case, piracy appears to be one of a number of criminal activities alongside, or subordinate to, others such

134 Andrew Selsky, 'Cocaine smugglers using high-tec boats', *AP,* 7 Nov. 2005.

135 Héctor Tobar, 'Drug smugglers reroute shipments via Central America', *LA Times,* 4 March 2007.

136 'Mexican navy reorganized for fighting drug trafficking', *Contralinea,* 1-15 Jan. 2008.

137 Anderson, 'Piracy and world history', p. 84

138 Abby Tan, 'In Asian waters, sea pirates eschew eye patches, steal ships via Internet', *Christian Science Monitor,* 13 June 1996.

as human smuggling, arms running and drug trafficking. In 1989, for example, Eric Ellen claimed that ships could be stolen "to order" in Manila harbour and that if an "extra" fee was paid the necessary documents could be obtained without difficulty from a "flag-of-convenience" state. He suggested that the gangs involved in ship stealing were also involved in drug running, rackets exploiting the "boat people" and, quite possibly, "phantom ship" frauds.[139]

One of the men involved was "Captain" Emilio Changco. He is suspected of organising every major ship hijacking and "phantom ship" fraud in Philippines waters between 1980, when the MV *Comicon* and her 25 crew disappeared, until 1992, when he was arrested and the hijackings stopped.[140] In the years in between he could be contacted in a hotel overlooking Manila Bay from where he organised ship hijackings, including the disposal of the crews, for which he charged around $300,000.[141] It was said that clients could stand at his hotel window and choose which ship they wanted.[142] Amongst the ships, numbering at least nine and very probably more, that Changco, who worked with his brother Cecilio,[143] was known to have hijacked were the *Isla Luzon*, taken off Mindanao in 1989 and identified by chance a year later in Puzan, South Korea renamed the *Nigel*; the *Silver Med*, seized in 1988, which went through four names changes between its capture in September and its recovery by Philippines Customs in January 1989; and the *Tabangoa*, captured in 1991, which was sold later in Singapore as the *Galilee*. Changco died while trying to escape from prison. He apparently climbed over a wall and was observed running away, an account which aroused suspicion because he suffered from bone cancer and walked with a cane. Following his death questions were obviously raised about what he might have been prepared to reveal.[144]

---

139   McDaniel, 'Modern high seas piracy', p. 12.

140   Abhyankar, 'Maritime fraud and piracy', p. 179. On the *Comicon* see ICC-IMB, 'Organised maritime crime in the Far East', p. 20.

141   Abhyankar, 'Maritime fraud and piracy', p. 179; Menefee, *TMV*, p. 84; although he does not mention Changco by name he describes his *modus operandi* clearly.

142   ICC-IMB, 'Organised maritime crime in the Far East', p. 19.

143   For further details on the Changco brothers' operations see the court testimony at Republic of the Philippines Supreme Court, GR no. 111709, 30 Aug. 2001.

144   Hepburn, *The Black Flag*, pp. 291-2; Teresa Albor,. 'Killers on the high seas'. *Sunday Morning Post*, 2 May 1993 and conversation with Eric Ellen, Sept. 2007. For fuller descriptions of the ships taken see Abhyankar, 'Maritime fraud

Transnational crime groups have in many cases adopted management methods similar to those of modern business. They have the ability to operate flexibly, to seek out opportunities that offer the least resistance and therefore potentially the greatest profit. In those periods when piracy is the subject of intense law enforcement interest in its areas of operation, or when the markets for pirated goods offer insufficient reward (perhaps also because of police pressure), then they can invest in other criminal or even legitimate activities until law enforcement attention has moved elsewhere.[145]

The relationship between the "organising mind" and the pirates varies between countries and between regions. In Bangladesh local mafias appear to be heavily involved. In Somalia the assumption has been that the pirates were answerable to a very small number of warlords, who were involved in the country's politics, and who were involved in their turn with others at the country's highest political levels and overseas. In Nigeria corruption is so endemic that identifying what groups might exercise control and on whose behalf is almost impossible.[146] What is known is that Nigerian criminal activity is widespread not just within Nigeria but across Africa, Europe and North America and is sufficiently well organised to have won powerful shares in major criminal activities such as fraud, counterfeiting, drug running, gambling, prostitution and oil "bunkering".[147]

In Southeast Asia, when vessels have been hijacked and, in some cases, turned into "phantom ships", fraud and piracy can merge. In June 1979 the Salvage Association set up an ad-hoc working party called FERIT (Far East Regional Investigation Team) which later that year published its confidential, industry report.[148] The team was funded by various marine insur-

---

and piracy', pp. 178-9; Menefee, *TMV,* pp. 83-4, and on the *Silver Med* specifically Carpenter and Wiencek, 'Maritime piracy in Asia', pp. 82-3. See also ICC-IMB, 'Phantom ships', section 6; ICC-IMB, 'Organised maritime crime in the Far East', pp. 72-3 on the *Isla Luzon* and p. 68 on the *Silver Med.* Also NGA ASAM 1989-6, 1 July 1989 on the *Isla Luzon.*

145   Tamara Makarenko, 'Transnational crime and its evolving links to terrorism and instability', *Jane's IR,* Nov. 2001, p. 24; Mark Galeotti, 'The new world of organised crime', *Jane's IR,* Sept. 2000, p. 47.

146   Last, 'Tempting riches of Nigeria oil crime'.

147   Jonathan Winer, 'Nigerian crime: Testimony before the House Sub-committee on Africa of the House International Relations Committee', Washington, DC, 11 Sept. 1996.

148   F.E.R.I.T. Report. ND. This report is extremely difficult to obtain, however, George Lauriat, 'Awash in an ocean of dollars', *FEER,* 16 Nov. 1979, pp. 66-9 provides a reliable account of its main points.

ance interests including Lloyd's and consisted of an insurance company claims manager, a Salvage Association Special Officer, an average adjuster and a maritime lawyer, with other investigators co-opted as required.[149] It focused on hull loss, that is to say the physical loss of a ship, and what it defined as "cases where cargo interests have colluded with hull interests in a total loss".[150] It did not look at the other major form of fraud, documentary fraud, which exploits the chain of documents that are exchanged between buyers and sellers to trigger payments and deliveries.[151] Moreover Lauriat makes the point that because the report did not consider items beyond its immediate concern, it paid no attention to illegal migration or what was then referred to as "refugee traffic", even though such movements "are very much part of the overall regional maritime problem".[152] In all it investigated over 60 cases of suspicious loss, 48 of which were subject to closer scrutiny, and as a result 27 came to be regarded as highly suspect.[153] From this analysis the team was able to build a picture of the typical vessel used by the fraudsters: 84 per cent flew the Panamanian flag and were over 15 years old, while 65 per cent were under 3,000 GRT.[154] The later "phantom ships" had a similar profile: in the majority of cases they were poorly maintained, between 15 and 20 years old, and generally flew either the Panamanian or the Honduran flag.[155]

"Phantom ship" scams depend on documents. They therefore overlap with documentary frauds.[156] The pirate gangs involved need to be able to re-register their prizes quickly and without question. Consequently, the corruption such gangs engender is experienced not only in the state that suppliers the hijackers and the state where the goods are sold but in the state that connives in supplying the gang with a new flag and a new set of documents. At this level piracy is akin to white-collar crime. If the sort of measures that are being taken to limit money laundering and to rein in the unregulated offshore banking sector were taken against unscrupulous flag

---

149   F.E.R.I.T. Report, paragraphs 2.2 & 2.3.

150   *Ibid.*, paragraphs 4.2.1–4.2.3; Conway, *The Piracy Business*, pp. 91-2.

151   *Ibid.*, paragraph 4.2.1

152   Lauriat, 'Awash in an ocean of dollars', pp. 67-8.

153   F.E.R.I.T. Report, paragraph 4.1.4.

154   *Ibid.*, paragraphs 4.1.4 & 7.1-7.3 and Appendix 2; Lauriat, 'Awash in an ocean of dollars', p. 66.

155   ICC-IMB, 'Phantom ships', paragraph 3.10.

156   Abhyanker, 'Maritime fraud and piracy', p. 175; Conway, *The Piracy Business*, p. 92.

of convenience states, this would place a significant obstacle in the way of organised piracy.[157]

The social effects of the crimes involved and the corruption they engender can unsettle major states and destabilise weaker ones. In a combined report, the United States Coast Guard and the US Navy's Office of Naval Intelligence wrote that TOC groups "can not only adversely affect civil society, but they can also threaten the power and sovereignty of the states in which they operate...and can be more destabilising than the activities of revolutionary or terrorist groups".[158] In 1999 Andreas Harsono, the Indonesian investigative journalist, wrote an article entitled "Dark alliance rules the high seas". In it he concluded that Indonesian piracy was "controlled by a dark alliance between pirates and the Indonesian coastal patrol and other maritime officials".[159] He went on to identify a "Mr Wong" as a pirate organiser and linked him specifically to the case of the 399 DWT tanker *MT Pulau Mas* which, when raided, was found to be carrying handcuffs, face masks, knives, fake documents, paint and other paraphernalia, everything, in fact, that would be needed to carry out a "phantom-ship" takeover.[160] "Wong" (or David Wong as Burnett calls him[161]), a Singaporean whose real name was (or might have been) Chew Cheng Kiat, was charged with the *Atlanta* and *Petro Ranger* hijackings.[162] Like the Filipino Captain Chang-

---

157 Peter Chalk, interview with author, Aug. 2004. See also Conway, *The Piracy Business*, p. 21; Michael Richardson, 'Crimes under flags of convenience', *Maritime Studies*, no. 127, Nov./Oct. 2002, pp. 22-4. As Abhyankar makes clear in 'Maritime fraud and piracy', pp. 178 & 180, temporary registration is absolutely crucial to the success of the 'phantom ship' scam; among other things, it can protect the criminals from any legal proceedings the rightful owners might attempt to bring.

158 ONI/USCG, *Threats and Challenges to Maritime Security 2020*, p. 15. Phil Williams, 'Transnational criminal organisations and international security' in John Arquilla and David Ronfeldt, *In Athena's Camp: Preparing for Conflict in the Information Age*, Santa Monica, RAND, 1997, pp. 315-37 reaches a similar judgement.

159 Andreas Harsano, 'Dark alliance rules the high seas', *The Nation* (Bangkok), 13 April 1999.

160 See also McDaniel, 'Modern high seas piracy', p. 12 on the *Pulau Mas* and its links with twenty-one ship hijackings which involved the use of 'sleepers'. Also MacKinnon. 'Transnational dimensions of maritime crime', pp. 8-9.

161 Burnett, *Dangerous Waters*, p. 226.

162 Andreas Harsono, 'Mr. Wong: Pirate or law-abiding citizen?' 13 April 1999; Stuart, *In Search of Pirates*, p. 139 (based on an account published in the Batam-based daily newspaper *Sijori Pos*). Stuart reports that the original Mr. Chew was apparently a labourer who had lost his Singapore passport and identity card in

co, Wong, who was arrested in 1998, was a middleman, a facilitator, who worked for what Commander (subsequently Rear-Admiral) Sumardi, the Commandant of the *Guskamla Armabar* that apprehended him, described as a "Big Boss in China" who had men "not only here, but also in Hong Kong, the Philippines and other places".[163] This chimes with some of what the writer of another, longer, anonymous article also entitled "Dark alliance rules the high seas" (undated) suggested first, that "there is no justice in Indonesia in the Western sense" and that Wong may have been set up by the Indonesian military;[164] second, that "most of the pirate operations are run by ethnic Chinese businessmen with family ties to China from pre-Communist days"; thirdly, that the real 'Mr Bigs' were amongst the richest men in Asia who had connections with the region's leading politicians particularly, in the past, from Indonesia, and through them to leading Western politicians and national leaders. The suspicion was that several of these major, if shady, figures had family connections to Fujian province, which coincidentally had long Triad and piracy traditions.[165]

Malaysia in 1997: *ibid.*, p. 143. When Stuart interviewed Wong's lawyer, even he admitted he was not sure of his client's real name. It could, he said, be Chow Kah Pong: *ibid.*, p. 177. For detail on the *Atlanta* hijack see NGA ASAM 1998-11, 18 Nov. 1997; also 'Oil piracy proves growing menace to tanker traffic in South China Sea', pp. 23-4.

163 Stuart, *In Search of Pirates*, pp. 140-1. A 'Guskamla Armabar' is a 'command of Joint Operations (that) normally consists of the Navy, Police, Immigration and Customs and Excise and is headed by the Navy': *Ibid.*, p. 142. Also Burnett, *Dangerous Waters*, pp. 226-7.

164 Wong himself asserted that he had been hired to sail the *Pulau Mas* to Johore in Malaysia, but while the vessel was at anchor, members of the Indonesian Navy (or men dressed in Navy uniforms) and three known criminals boarded it, threatened him with a gun and demanded S$50,000. When he refused to pay they ordered him to sail the vessel back to Batam where the police arrested him for piracy a few days later. Stuart, *In Search of Pirates*, p. 174. According to Harsono the boarding took place at Johor Baru and the man who demanded the money was an ex-employee of 'Wong's' named Franky Kansil: Harsono, 'Nationalism and sea piracy in the Malacca Strait'. According to 'Wong's' own account to Stuart the man was a Navy informant: Stuart, *In Search of Pirates*, p. 174. One of the most intriguing aspects of the case was how long Franky had been working for the Navy because, by its own admission, it had been tracking the *Pulau Mas* for seven months but the ship had always been able to slip away, which raises the question about whether or not 'Wong' was tipped off about its intentions. Franky, moreover, disappeared shortly before 'Wong's' trial: *ibid.*, p. 178.

165 For more on those traditions see Lintner, *Blood Brothers*, p. 93.

The leader of the gang that hijacked the *Petro Ranger,* an Indonesian ship's captain named Herman, appeared to confirm elements of this account. Before the Chinese Marine Police boarded the ship he told Blyth that he worked for a syndicate with four principals based in China, Hong Kong, Indonesia, and Singapore where they all possessed sufficient political and financial influence to be able to avert trouble if it arose. Their organisation was clearly well run: it had been operating for ten years and had permanent employees and a capital base of several million dollars.[166] It had penetrated the ship owner's head office, knew exactly when the ship would sail, where it would go and what load it would be carrying. It knew the personal details of Blyth and most of the crew including where they lived, together with details of their wives and children. It had secured all the necessary documents including new registration documents for the ship, new bills of lading and documents identifying the pirates as the legitimate crew. It had buyers for the cargo.[167] Gwin met a similar gang leader, also an Indonesian ship's captain, know to him as "Jhonny", who worked for both legitimate companies and criminal organisations and who had moved from Indonesia to Hong Kong during the 1980s to work for a Chinese crime syndicate. His estimate was that 75 per cent of all hijackings were inside jobs involving the ship's crew and often the captain, and that they were commissioned by shipping agents who had buyers looking for specific cargoes.[168]

Wong's lawyer, in his conversation with Robert Stuart, echoes much of this account. Wong, he said, was a member of a pirate syndicate. His boss was based in Hong Kong and apart from Wong had other men in Jakarta

---

166   Blyth, *Petro Pirates,* p. 24.

167   *Ibid.,* p. 24-5. Also Hitt, 'Bandits in the global shipping lanes', and 'Dead men tell no tales'. Burnett makes the point that these and similar reports are based on Blyth's own account and that he could be covering the fact that he might not have taken the precautions Petroships required Masters to take to prevent hijackings. He argues that all the information which, in Blyth's view, the pirates could only have obtained from internal company sources could in fact have been obtained publicly. He concedes, however, that Wong admitted having his own man aboard the *Petro Ranger,* which was his normal practice. Burnet, *Dangerous Waters,* pp. 227-9.

168   Gwin, 'Dark passage', pp. 138-9. This accords with the assessment made in ICC-IMB, 'Organised maritime crime in the Far East', pp. 18 & 35 with regard to shippers and underwriters. Herman, the leader of the gang that hijacked the *Petro Ranger,* began his career as a maritime criminal scuttling ships for Chinese ship-owners in Indonesia so that they could claim the insurance: Blyth, *Petro Pirates,* p. 25.

and, possibly, Malacca.[169] Harsono alleges that the man in Hong Kong was a businessman who had connections in Johore and Taipei.[170] Wong's advantage was that he was a shipping agent who knew exactly what ships, with what cargoes going to what destinations were passing through the Malacca and Singapore Straits and could bribe a crew member to give him precise details of the ship's position. If he judged the ship could be taken he instructed his Indonesian gang to attack.[171]

The profile Harsono and Stuart draw of Wong and the shady organisation that lay behind him bears a close resemblance to the picture Jayant Abhyanker paints of the criminals responsible for "phantom ship" frauds. The "syndicate theory" had been circulating in Far Eastern shipping circles for three years before the FERIT report's publication. Received wisdom suggested that Taiwanese ship-owners, using Hong Kong agents, had combined with Singapore and Bangkok-based cargo interests to scuttle ships for the insurance money.[172] The FERIT investigators were initially sceptical because of the elaborate organisation necessary but quickly changed their minds.[173] Their report was the first to suggest that serious maritime fraud and hijackings might be the responsibility of not one large syndicate but up to five smaller syndicates involved in hull fraud and three involving cargo which exchanged information about what the Report described as the "latest 'techniques'".[174] The Report's authors admit that "a great deal" of information obtained from regional police forces about individual assured and individual claims was omitted in case it compromised either criminal or civil proceedings.[175] Lauriat, however, who appears to have been well-briefed, asserts that the syndicate's members were Chinese or of Chinese origin, including gangsters from Fujian as well as others from Guangdong and Shanghai, and that there was also evidence that these groups had in-

---

169   Frécon, who also interviewed Wong, observes 'the 'shady business partners' of Mr Wong, who lead the triad from their offices in East Asian cities, are even more mysterious and seem to have left him alone': Frécon, 'Piracy and armed robbery at sea along the Malacca Straits', p. 70.

170   Harsano, 'Mr Wong: Pirate or law-abiding citizen?'

171   Stuart, *In Search of Pirates*, pp. 176-7.

172   Lauriat, 'Awash in an ocean of dollars', p. 67.

173   F.E.R.I.T. Report, paragraphs 4.1.1 & 4.1.2; Lauriat, 'Awash in an ocean of dollars', p. 67.

174   *Ibid.*, paragraph 4.3.

175   *Ibid.*, paragraphs 3.7 & 3.8.

terests in the movement of drugs and migrants.[176] Furthermore, that these men also had substantial shipping, banking and insurance interests across Southeast Asia.[177]

The links between the syndicates that were subject to the FERIT investigation and those involved in the "phantom ship" frauds have never been revealed, but the IMB were confident that "some members of the syndicates were associated with the companies named in the FERIT report (and) undoubtedly...have obtained from their previous employment large numbers of contacts and deep knowledge in these illegal dealings".[178] Previously, in "Organised Maritime Crime in the Far East", the IMB had expressed the view that the majority of the organised gangs were Chinese or of Chinese origin from China, Hong Kong, Taiwan, Singapore, Thailand, Malaysia and Indonesia where they also had legitimate business interests. One member of the Hong Kong syndicate reputedly managed the letter of credit organisation of an important Hong Kong bank.[179] *The Economist* reached a similar conclusion, suggesting that four Asian syndicates had the requisite level of transnational expertise to make high seas piracy work on a regular basis.[180] Retired Rear Admiral P.P. Sivamani of the Indian Navy also suggested there were four based in Singapore, Jakarta, Bangkok and Hong Kong that had effectively divided the waters of Southeast Asia between them.[181] John Burnett concurs, adding that they had subsidiary operations in every littoral country in the region stretching from Burma to China and often divided the proceeds of a hijacking between them.[182] Noel Choong of the IMB suggests the syndicates are divided along ethnic lines: three Chinese syndicates originating in Guangzhou, Fujian and Shanghai but controlled by businessmen located in Hong Kong, Indonesia, the Philippines and Thailand, and a fourth, Indian syndicate preying

176   Lauriat, 'Awash in an ocean of dollars', p. 67 & p. 68.
177   Abhyanker, 'Maritime fraud and piracy', p. 181.
178   ICC-IMB, 'Phantom ships', paragraph 10.3.
179   ICC-IMB, 'Organised maritime crime in the Far East', p. 32; ICC-IMB, 'Phantom ships', paragraph 9.2.
180   'Dead men tell no tales'.
181   P.P. Silvamani, 'The LIMOs are here to stay', *Navy Despatch*, Dec. 2005, p. 11.
182   Burnett, *Dangerous Waters*, p. 219.

mainly on shipping in the Andaman Sea.[183] The UK government suggested there were five.[184]

Details about these four (or five) groups and the connections between them remain sketchy at best. Each gang recruited exclusively from its own ethnic base, making them hard to penetrate, and their level of organisation was described as "frightening".[185] Furthermore, they rarely operated on their home territory. The Hong Kong gang, for example, generally used hotels in Singapore and Bangkok.[186] As the IMB wrote: "It is a fact, that the gangs operating these frauds do not fear the individual investigations and…will continue to move from one jurisdiction to another carefully avoiding any area where they feel they may be at risk…It would be an understatement to describe these syndicates as 'confident'."[187] Perhaps because of censorship or an unwillingness to acknowledge the presence of ethnic Chinese crime organisations, very little information emerges from Indonesia, Malaysia or Singapore about any of their activities.[188] The weakness with the FERIT process was that although the likely perpetrators and their methods were identified, as mentioned previously they were not arrested.[189] All the insurers could do was refuse to insure goods carried in any ship that met the

183 Eklöf, *Pirates in Paradise*, pp. 72-3. Also ICC-IMB, 'Phantom ships', paragraphs 9.3-9.5. The hijacking most associated with the Indian syndicate were those of the MV *Iskander* (1993) and the MV *Elenora 8* (1994). ICC International Maritime Bureau. 'Solving the Problems of Piracy and Phantom Ships', Paragraph 8.2.

184 Jo Dillon, 'UK leads attack on piracy', *The Independent*, 27 Aug. 2000.

185 ICC-IMB, 'Organised maritime crime in the Far East', pp. 37 & 42. The ICC-IMB report 'Phantom ships', paragraph 9.3 points out that 'like all Chinese, the dialect spoken seems to play an important role in determining the composition of these groups'.

186 ICC-IMB, 'Organised maritime crime in the Far East', p. 34.

187 *Ibid.*, pp. 13 & 14.

188 Glenn E. Curtis, *et al.*, 'Transnational activities of Chinese crime organizations', a Report prepared for the Federal Research Division, Library of Congress, Washington, DC: Federal Research Division, Library of Congress, April 2003, p. 39. Also Roy Godson. 'The Political-Criminal Nexus and Global Security' in Godson, *Menace to Society*, pp. 5-6 where he highlights the fact that "more powerful PCNs (members of what he describes as the 'political-criminal nexus') in China facilitate PCNs in other parts of the world" through their involvement in a number of criminal activities including piracy and that, moreover, such groups exploit their ability to operate across borders using some areas as safe havens, others as transit regions and others for services such as meetings and the production of false documents.

189 Abhyankar, 'Maritime fraud and piracy', p. 181.

likely profile, which appeared to work as no scuttles were recorded for the ten years following the report's publication.[190] Abhyankar points out that in addition to their subsequent involvement in "phantom ships" scams, these gangs, like those profiled in the FERIT report, were also suspected of being involved in drug and migrant smuggling and of having close connections with the members of regional governments and even one of the region's royal families.[191] Or, as Tom McCawley put it: "syndicates...(that) operate across borders, stealing in one port and selling in another." Burnett suggested that they engaged in a diverse range of activities in addition to ship hijacking including the smuggling of narcotics, illegally mined timber and other commodities—even human cargo; anything, in short, that drew a profit on the black market.[192] They were almost certainly involved in the wave of illegal Chinese emigration to the US, UK, Australia and Canada that began in the late 1990s.[193] The leader of the gang that assaulted the *Baltimar Zephyr* in the Gaspar Strait in 1992, and killed its British master, turned up a decade later smuggling illegal migrants into the United Kingdom.[194] These gangs, known as *she-tou* or, more commonly, "snakeheads", were based in Fujian, Hong Kong and other parts of southern China.[195] The ship that became the *Golden Venture*, which ran aground off Long Island in 1993 with a cargo of 300 illegal migrants from Fujian province, had been hijacked in Southeast Asia and its crew apparently killed.[196] Conway

190 Eric Ellen, 'The dimensions of international maritime crime' in Martin Gill (ed.), *Issues in Maritime Crime: Mayhem at Sea,* Leicester: Perpetuity Press, 1995, p. 8.

191 Abhyanker, 'Maritime fraud and piracy', pp. 180-2; Burnett, *Dangerous Waters,* p. 212 & 218; on the drug connection see also Conway, *The Piracy Business,* p. 90 and ICC-IMB, 'Organised maritime crime in the Far East', p. 34; on the regional royal family see ICC-IMB, 'Phantom ships', paragraph 9.9.

192 McCawley, 'Sea of trouble', p. 51. This willingness to look for profit in anything now extends to the trade in endangered species and animal parts such as ivory and bears' paws. Wildlife and drug smuggling can even come together. Some snakes have been discovered stuffed with packets of cocaine. See Arthur Max, 'Crime syndicates smuggling wildlife', *AP,* 7 June 2007 and 'Endangered cargo', *Shiptalk,* 29 May 2007.

193 'Dead men tell no tales'; Burnett, *Dangerous Waters,* pp. 219-22.

194 Confidential information, June 2006. NGA ASAM 1992-33, 11 Dec. 1992. For more on the ship hijack see Douglas Stewart, 'Perils of the sea–Baltimar Zephyr' in Ellen, *Shipping at Risk,* pp. 9-15 and Stewart, *The Brutal Seas,* pp. 1-23.

195 Burnett, *Dangerous Waters,* p. 219.

196 *Ibid.*; Julia Preston, 'Smuggling immigrants just a sideline, court told', *Interna-*

points to the close association between the fraudulent losses and a limited number of shipping agencies and brokers, plus the fact that the same names cropped up repeatedly as captains and crew members.[197] In contrast, it is rare for seafarers who have really been attacked by pirates to go to sea again. As she says the "theme of interlocking cargo, ship owning and chartering interests is the dominant one in investigations of suspicious losses in the Far East".[198]

While the issue of ethnicity is a contentious one in organised crime studies, time and again, organised crime movements have begun in ethnic diasporas through which they have extended their influence back to their countries of origin.[199] The Chinese connection with Indonesian piracy is primarily ethnic; as Stuart writes, "the ethno-economic structure and hierarchy of piracy...was (as demonstrated by the Wong case) the perfect arrangement: the Chinese, with their obsessive passion for money and their renowned business acumen, formed the syndicate operation; while the Indonesians and Malays, with their more easy-going laissez-faire 'Third World' attitude, plus their maritime skills, provided the crews and logistics."[200]

The examples of the *Anna Sierra* and the *Petro Ranger*, amongst many others, show, however, that the risk organised piracy presents is not confined to weak states; on the contrary, China itself had a piracy problem in the 1990s, one that might or might not have been separate from the incidents in the South China Sea that gave rise to accusations of "state" piracy. Peter Chalk pointed out that at the time numerous maritime bodies claimed officials in southwest China were involved heavily in maritime crimes: "There is a widespread belief that major criminal syndicates retain close links with, or have access to, corrupt government officials, particularly in southern China", although he admitted that "the question of Chinese

---

tional Herald Tribune, 24 May 2005.

197   Conway, *The Piracy Business*, p. 93.

198   *Ibid.*, p. 125.

199   Sebastyen Gorka, 'The 'new' threat of organised crime and terrorism', *Jane's TSM*, 1 June 2000. Galeotti, however, makes a more nuanced point: 'Organised crime,' he writes, 'is becoming increasingly inclusive; people and groups with the right skills, contacts or territories can be accepted within the network so long as they can operate within the dominant culture,' although 'what is emerging is not a process of 'gang expansion' but rather greater traffic between networks of gangs from a variety of ethnic groups.': Galeotti, 'The new world of organised crime', p. 51.

200   Stuart, *In Search of Pirates*, pp. 178-9.

complicity in piracy remains highly contentious". Given the willingness of the Chinese government to penalise and ostracise its critics, this is perhaps not surprising.[201] In March 1994 the government of the then British sovereign territory of Hong Kong passed a report to the IMO implicating Chinese security forces and government officials in nearly half of the piracy attacks on shipping in the South China Sea over the previous 18 months.[202] Smuggling is the prototypical organised crime.[203] In the 1990s China was the world's biggest market for smuggled goods.[204] Although the Chinese government now appears to be cracking down on pirate activity because it wishes to be regarded as a legitimate trading nation, that does not necessarily mean its ports and markets are places where pirate goods cannot be disposed of in the same way that New York and Baltimore provided eager buyers from goods taken on the "pirate round".[205] The nature of the Chinese political system means there is little separation between the political and the commercial.[206] The imperative is economic growth. How that is achieved is secondary. In fact the relationship between the political and the commercial can become so close that, as Jayant Abhyankar pointed out, the cargo stolen from the MV *Harpers* that was hijacked in 1993 was stored under armed guard at an army camp in Guangxi province while in 1994 a car carrier, the *Tequila*, was tracked on radar as it was accompanied by two

201 Chalk, 'Maritime piracy: A global overview', pp. 49-50. See also Neil Renwick and Jason Abbott, 'Piratical violence and maritime security in South East Asia', *Security Dialogue*, vol. 30, no. 2, June 1999, pp. 186-7.

202 Kevin Murphy, 'Hong Kong links China to bulk of sea piracy', *International Herald Tribune*, 17 March 1994.

203 Schmid, 'The links between transnational organized crime and terrorist crime', p. 47.

204 'Dead men tell no tales', 1999 *ibid.* Also McCawley, 'Sea of trouble' and Torode, 'Probe into stolen ship racket leads to HK firm'.

205 On the steps China is taking to improve maritime security see Zhang Shouguo, 'China–Playing an active role in fulfilling maritime security obligations', presentation to OECD Workshop on Maritime Transport, Paris, 4-5 Nov. 2004. However, its drive for international respectability has not stopped it being a destination for stolen raw materials. See Malcolm Moore, 'Record copper prices power China's black market demand for hot metal', *Daily Telegraph*, 17 June 2006.

206 Shuntian Yao, 'Privilege and corruption: The problems of China's Socialist market economy', *American Journal of Economics and Sociology*, vol. 61, no. 1, Jan. 2002, p. 282. For a comment on China's broader corruption problems see Friedrich Wu, 'China's losing battle against corruption', IDSS *Commentaries*, 17 Oct. 2006.

small speed-boats into an area off limits to all but official Chinese vessels.[207] Nor does it mean that as one market closes others do not open, even if they lack the scale of the one they replace: at the same time that Chinese ports were open to illegal cargoes others were being disposed of in the northern Philippines, and it appears that pirate goods are now making their way to India and Iran.[208] Organised piracy, in other words, is one manifestation of organised crime which, when linked to corruption and weak governance, is a far more insidious threat.

Contemporary piracy: irritation or menace?

The discussion began with an assertion that contemporary piracy is a global phenomenon but not a global problem. In fact this can be narrowed down still further. Piracy is a potential threat to all seafarers in the areas where it occurs. While piracy attacks do occur in many places around the globe, contemporary piracy is concentrated in a only a few areas that to some extent shift over time: in the early years of this century these areas have been found in an arc that runs from the Philippines through Indonesia and the southern South China Sea, up the Malacca Straits, then jumps to the Bay of Bengal with a special focus off Bangladesh. It has been particularly vigorous along the Indian Ocean coast of Somalia and has continued without interruption in the Gulf of Aden and southern Red Sea. Scattered attacks have occurred around the Gulf of Guinea from the Congo to Guinea but concentrated mainly off Nigeria. Sporadic piracy has taken place around the coast of South America, the main concentrations being between Suriname and Colombia, off Peru, and the port of Santos in Brazil. A large ship passing through any piracy-prone area runs a low risk of being attacked, especially if it takes precautions, although the fear of attack takes its toll

---

207   Abhyankar, 'Maritime fraud and piracy', p. 180. Also Abhyankar. 'Phantom ships' in Ellen, *Shipping at Risk*, p. 64. Investigators showed that the MV *Harpers* had changed its name five time in six months. ICC-IMB, 'Phantom ships', paragraph 2.2. On the *Tequila* see Greg Torode. 'Hijacked ship might be at Chinese base', *SCMP,* 22 March 1994.

208   On the northern Philippines see Tan, 'In Asian waters, sea pirates eschew eye patches, steal ships via Internet'; also Burnett. *Dangerous Waters,* pp. 216-17 on the *Inabukwa* discovered in 'Salumagi, a remote town in Ilocus Sur known to be a favourite place for smugglers to land with motorcycles and electronic goods'. On Iran and India see Warren, 'A tale of two centuries', p. 23 and his quoted remarks in Osler, 'Global piracy bill hits $25bn'. The *Alondra Rainbow* was close to India when it was intercepted.

on crews. The communities that have been affected most are local seafarers such as fishermen, and villages and small ports in pirate areas.

The factors that cause or sustain piracy are common but the deck is shuffled differently in each area. The overriding factor, however, is opportunity. Of the other factors one—geography—is immutable. Another—cultural acceptance—is deeply rooted in parts of Southeast Asia but probably less so in others such as Nigeria. Poverty is only important where it coincides with propitious geography. The legal framework, while not immutable, changes only slowly particularly if international law is involved. When it is and changes are necessary then a semblance of urgency can be injected into the process through the involvement of a powerful state exercising its interest through bilateral agreements.

The other factors are more changeable. The most important is a permissive political environment. If the political will to suppress or control piracy is missing for whatever reason, then piracy will continue. It will persist so long as the benefits outweigh the risks. The most common reason for the lack of political will is state weakness. Piracy and weak states go together. Organised crime more generally can destabilise weak states through the corruption and violence it engenders, as has already been demonstrated in the cases of El Salvador and Guatemala beginning in the early 1990s, and can unsettle stronger ones, as happened in Italy in the early 1990s and which appears to have happened in Mexico and Peru.[209] The Inter-American Development Bank esti-

---

209   For an account of the Italian experience see Alexander Stille, *Excellent Cadavers: Mafia and the Death of the First Italian Republic*, New York: Vintage Books, 1996. On the American experience see Max G. Manwaring, *Street Gangs: The New Urban Insurgency*, Carlisle, PA: US Army War College, Strategic Studies Institute, March 2005, pp. 7 & 12-15. For background on the Central American gangs see Max G. Manwaring, *A Contemporary Challenge to State Sovereignty: Gangs and Other Illicit Transnational Criminal Organizations in Central America, El Salvador, Mexico, Jamaica and Brazil*, US Army War College, Strategic Studies Institute, Dec. 2007, pp. 12-23; Clare M. Ribano, 'Gangs in Central America', Congressional Research Service *Report for Congress*, RL34112, 2 Aug. 2007; and Federico Brevé, 'The Maras: A Menace to the Americas', *Military Review*, July-Aug. 2007, pp. 88-95. For the situation in Mexico see Manwaring, *A Contemporary Challenge to State Sovereignty*, pp. 23-33; George W. Grayson, 'Mexico and the Drug Cartels', Foreign Policy Research Institute *E-Notes*, Aug. 2007; Martha Lauer, 'Mexican Drug Policy: Internal Corruption in an Externalized War', Council on Hemispheric Relations *Press Release*, 26 June 2007; Sarah Miller Llana, 'With Calderón in, a new war on Mexico's mighty drug cartels', *Christian Science Monitor*, 22 Jan. 2007; 'Calderon changes Mexico's drug war strategy', *AP*, 14 May 2007; Matt Levitch, 'Cartels lash out at Mexican crackdown on drug trafficking', *Christian Science Monitor*, 16 May 2007; Mark Stevenson, 'Mexico: Drug gangs using terror tactics', *AP*, 18 May 2007;

mates that crime costs Central American countries 14.2 per cent of GDP including law enforcement, healthcare, expenditure on social programmes and lost foreign investment.[210] Iduvina Hernandez, a Guatemalan political analyst, has explained that the goal of organised crime is to control the political system: "If they can control a small town, they can build a landing strip there and use it as a base. If they have someone in Congress, all the better."[211] Similar problems exist in India. In rural states such as Bihar and Uttar Pradesh, *"sensas"*, which for the most part are caste-based private armies of gangsters, have largely taken over the political system.[212] In Brazil the prison based criminal organisation Primeiro Comando da Capital (PCC), which has its primary power base in São Paulo, has organised large civil disturbances and is paying for the education of future politicians, law-

---

Sarah Miller Llana, 'Escalating drug war grips Mexico', *Christian Science Monitor*, 23 May 2007; Howard LaFranchi, 'Mexico seeks anti-drug aid from US', *Christian Science Monitor*, 8 Aug. 2007; Manuel Roig-Franzia, 'Mexican drug cartels threaten elections', *Washington Post*, 5 Jan. 2008; Ioan Grillo, 'Mexico's narco-insurgency', *TIME*, 25 Jan. 2008; 'Marching as to war', *The Economist*, 31 Jan. 2008; Daniel Borunda, 'Drug cartels possess more firepower, technology'. *El Paso Times*, 2 June 2008; "Mexico drug traffickers make car bomb', *Reuters AlertNet*, 16 July 2008 and Adam Thompson, 'Drug cartels "threaten" Mexican Democracy', *Financial Times*, 13 July 2008; The violence and turmoil in parts of Mexico have also been felt in the US: 'Mexican drug commandos expand ops in 6 US states', *WorldNetDaily*, 21 June 2005. Jerry Seper, 'Mexican mercenaries expand base into US', *The Washington Times*, 1 Aug. 2005; Robert J. Lopez, *et al.*, 'Gang uses deportation to its advantage to flourish in US', *LA Times*, 30 Oct. 2005; Richard A. Serrano, 'Border violence pushes north', *LA Times*, 19 Aug. 2007; Samuel Logan and M. Casey McCarty, 'Violence on the US-Mexico Border', ISN *Security Watch*, 29 Jan. 2008; Manuel Roig-Franzia, 'From Mexico, drug violence spills into US', *Washington Post*, 20 April 2008; and on the wider political ramifications both north and south of the border see David Francis, 'As violence grows along border, Congress debates funding for fighting Mexican drug cartels', *World Politics Review*, 7 March 2008. On Peru see Sarah Miller Llana, 'Violent cartel culture now threatens Peru', *Christian Science Monitor*, 3 April 2007.

210   Anna Gilmore, 'Gang Warfare', *Jane's IR*, vol. 19, no. 7, July 2007, p. 50.

211   Marc Lacey, 'Drug gangs use violence to sway Guatemala vote', *New York Times*, 4 Aug. 2007. Also Samuel Logan, 'Governance in Guatemala increasingly threatened by organized crime', *PINR*, 19 Oct. 2007.

212   John P. Sullivan, 'Terrorism, crime and private armies' in Robert J. Bunker (ed.), *Networks, Terrorism and Global Insurgency*, Abingdon and New York: Routledge, 2005, p. 77; 'Private caste armies in Bihar', South Asia Terrorism Portal; Peter Foster, 'Burgeoning lawlessness in India's Wild East', *Daily Telegraph*, 20 March 2007.

yers and security officials.[213] The four days of violence that it unleashed on São Paulo in 2006 was described in one report as looking more like a "guerrilla offensive with multiple fronts".[214] Where piracy is an element it too can, as Peter Chalk has observed, "play a...role in undermining and weakening political stability by encouraging corruption among elected government officials".[215]

While the act of piracy takes place at sea (or on the water), its effects on land are more insidious. Piracy is a group activity and groups require organisation. More organised groups are able to mount larger and more profitable operations. The more sophisticated the attacks, the more sophisticated the scams. Greater sophistication entails a wider network of contacts to provide documents, dispose of the goods, provide political protection, and transfer the profits to be used in other markets for possibly other criminal purposes or to be invested in legitimate businesses. England, Ireland, France, North America, North Africa and China are amongst the places that historically have played host to the markets for pirate goods and the shadowy networks that financed, supported and benefited from them. More recently similar major markets have reappeared in China. Smaller, almost local markets have continued to survive across Southeast Asia and appear to operate in Nigeria and Bangladesh. The networks that feed them appear to have no difficulty in operating. Without official connivance and the corruption that goes with it these markets and networks would find it hard to survive and the problem of piracy would be an irritation rather than a menace. So long, however, as organised crime and political corruption coexist to hamper effective law enforcement on land, as they have been able to do in states such as Indonesia, the Philippines and Nigeria, so long as pirates benefit from the jurisdictional jealousy of states that often hinders cross-border cooperation and "hot pursuit", and so long as they are able to exploit the jurisdictional and law enforcement ambiguities of the high seas, then the problem of piracy will continue, and where it has links to organised crime its effects will extend well beyond the area or even the state where the at-

213   Samuel Logan. 'Brazil's P.C.C.: The true power behind the violence', *PINR*, 24 May 2006 and Manwaring, *A Contemporary Challenge to State Sovereignty*, pp. 40-6. 'Brazil's mighty prison gangs', *BBC News*, 15 May 2006 reports that the group learnt to use revolutionary language and organisational methods from left-wing guerrillas that its members met in prison.

214   Marcelo Soares and Patrick J. McDonnell, 'Inmates unleash a torrent of violence on Brazilian city', *LA Times*, 16 May 2006.

215   Chalk, 'Maritime piracy: A global overview', p. 50.

tacks take place to other states where the proceeds can be used to fund other crimes and subvert other polities through corruption. In international security terms, in terms of the number of attacks compared with the number of ship movements and the threat they pose to the free movement of goods, piracy attacks at sea might be an irritation, but they are usually terrifying for the victims, are often violent, and are linked to events on land by a half-hidden chain of menace that can have consequences for regional and international security.

4

MARITIME TERRORISM

The leap from the criminal to the political is usually—as one would hope—one of some magnitude. However, as this book has suggested, piracy throughout history has had a political connection. The transition from organised criminal piracy to politically driven piracy is the third of Gosse's pirate cycles. In his terms, of course, it is the transition to pirate states or republics, but in our age, when political power can be more diffuse and political violence is often characterised by irregularity, then the most obvious parallel is with insurgent or terrorist use of the sea. Perhaps unjustifiably, it is maritime terrorism that has given rise to the greatest concern.

What is terrorism?

Terrorism is a tactic. It is used by a wide variety of groups, including insurgents, front organisations for legitimate states and even criminals who believe it will advance their interests. For some groups terrorism is the only tactic they use; for others it is just one amongst several, including assassination, guerrilla war, information warfare, propaganda, political agitation, representative politics and welfare provision. This distinction is important and it is only for the sake of brevity that the term "terrorist" is used here rather than "a group that uses terrorism".

Terrorism in the broadest sense is a form of violent coercion.[1] What makes it special—and especially terrifying—is that the violence used vio-

---

1   Thomas Schelling articulated this view; see Martha Crenshaw, 'Theories of terrorism: Instrumental and organisational approaches' in David C. Rapoport (ed.), *Inside Terrorist Organisations* (2nd edn.), London and Portland, OR: Frank Cass, 2001, p. 13. For a similar interpretation see Richard K. Betts, 'The soft underbelly of American primacy: Tactical advantages of terror', *Political Science Quarterly,* vol. 117, no. 1, 2002, p. 20.

lates social taboos, either through its ferocity or by its indiscriminate nature.[2] Terrorism is the public and systematic use of this "extranormal" or "extramoral" violence against combatants and non-combatants in situations short of conventional war to provoke fear and impose unacceptable costs through the loss of life, property or prestige, mainly and ostensibly for political purposes; and to gain the publicity that will amplify these acts, such that they appear more consequential than they often are.[3] To be successful terrorists must inflict or threaten to inflict intolerable damage, ideally but not necessarily on targets that symbolise their opponents' power, in order to highlight the limits or fragility of that power.[4] Their opponents' armed forces, intelligence services and police, for example, each one of which represent and protect their opponents' power, are obvious targets. Classic guerrilla theory maintains they should be attacked to provoke a disproportionate reaction that alienates them from the people they ostensibly protect, but attacks also deter recruits from joining these services, and can make them appear ineffective if their response is slow and cumbersome.

The threat to inflict intolerable damage can often be effective on its own. Propaganda is a weapon in all wars but of disproportionate significance in irregular war. It is in the mind that the terrorist achieves his effect: the essence of terrorism is the breaking of the enemy's will through the exploitation of fear.[5] The reason for this is simple: no terrorist group has sufficient material resources to wear down and defeat a strong government through the application of conventional force. Al Qaeda and the groups that share its ideology, and others such as Aum Shinrikyo, which together can be labelled "annihilation terrorists", are very interested in killing large numbers of people. For them mass murder is as important, and as satisfying, as the psychological result. For other groups the number of people they kill or the material damage they inflict can be almost incidental, providing the way they die or the response to their deaths generates sufficient psychological

---

2   Martha Crenshaw, 'The strategic development of terrorism', paper delivered at the annual meeting of the American Political Science Association, New Orleans, Aug./Sept. 1985, p. 4.

3   David Rapoport uses the terms 'extranormal' and 'extramoral' to describe violence that 'goes beyond the convention or boundaries particular societies establish to regulate coercion': David C. Rapoport, 'Messianic sanctions for terror', *Comparative Politics,* vol. 20, no. 2, 1988, p. 196.

4   'Intolerable' is relative. What may be an unsustainable level of death and destruction in one conflict might be bearable in another.

5   John Gearson, 'The nature of modern terrorism' in Lawrence Freedman (ed.), *Superterrorism: Policy Responses,* Oxford: Blackwell, 2002, p. 8.

effect. The object is to encourage the people, institutions and allies that their opponent needs or values to withdraw their support and by so doing undermine the opponent's will to resist. Terrorists can win by making their opponents defeat themselves or by making the cost of defeating them so high politically that the opponent is forced to seek an accommodation.[6]

Consequently, terrorism needs targets the loss or destruction of which will resonate psychologically with the target audience (but are not so valuable as to provoke overwhelming retaliation), and the means to communicate their destruction to that audience preferably in the most direct way. In this sense television and terrorism were made for each other. These conditions can be fulfilled at sea or on waterways but only with difficulty. The reason why they have not been exploited at sea to any great extent, to date at least, is that they can be exploited more easily on land. For the majority of terrorist groups operating today, maritime activity is unnecessary; there are only a few groups for whom maritime operations are driven by a strategic or operational imperative.

What is maritime terrorism?

Maritime terrorism is terrorism that takes place at sea, on inland water, or against places that are touched by water such as ports and coastal infrastructure.[7] In terms of its aims, objectives and strategic design it is no different from the terrorism that takes place on land or in the air.

Terrorist attacks at sea – the story so far

The number of terrorist attacks at sea has been extremely small as a proportion of the number of terrorist attacks overall.[8] According to the RAND Terrorism Chronology Database and the RAND-MIPT Terrorism Incident Database, incidents of maritime terrorism have amounted to only two

---

6   See N.O. Berry, 'Theories on the efficacy of terrorism' in Paul Wilkinson and Alasdair M. Stewart (eds), *Contemporary Research on Terrorism*, Aberdeen UP, 1987, pp. 293-306. For similar views see also Colin S. Gray, 'Thinking asymmetrically in times of terror', *Parameters*, Spring 2002, pp. 7-9 and Gearson, 'The nature of modern terrorism', p. 23.

7   The working group of the Council for Security Cooperation in the Asia Pacific (CSCAP) offers a similar definition: Sophia Quentin, 'Shipping activities: Targets of maritime terrorism', *MIRMAL*, Issue no. 2, 20 Jan. 2003.

8   Since the 1960s there have been less than 200 maritime terrorist incidents compared with over 10,000 terrorist incidents in total: Anthony Davis, 'Piracy and terrorism should not be conflated', *Jane's IR*, vol. 16, no. 8, Aug. 2004, p. 57.

per cent of all the terrorism incidents recorded over the past thirty years.[9]
[10] The first recognised incident was the hijacking in 1961 of the cruise ship
the *Santa Maria*, seized while sailing from Curaçao to Miami, by a small
group whose purpose was to inspire a revolt against the Portuguese dictator, Salazar, by capturing the Spanish island of Fernando Pó and using it as
a base to attack the Angolan capital of Luanda.[11] Led by Henrique Galvão,
who had a long history of opposition to Salazar and the Portuguese colonial
presence in Africa, the group proclaimed they were insurgents, which in
an era still largely unexposed to international terrorism caused confusion.
If they were insurgents they were not pirates and therefore could not be
treated as such.[12] US warships that had been ordered to intercept the ship
actually turned away when told the hijacking was "political".[13] The *Santa
Maria* hijacking resulted in one death.

In a long forgotten incident another cruise liner, the *Sanya*, was sunk in
Beirut harbour in 1973 by the Fatah unit Black September. The ship was
carrying 250 American tourists to Haifa in Israel. There were no casualties.
Interestingly, a limpet mine was used for the attack.[14]

---

9   Chalk, 'Maritime terrorism in the contemporary era', p. 21.

10 Looking further back, the maritime analyst Charles Dragonette suggests there
     were 500 incidents of maritime 'terrorism', which he defines very broadly as
     'politically-motivated violence at sea', between 1945 and 1996: Charles H.
     Dragonette, 'Maritime terrorism: Underway as before?' in Thomas C. Fitzhugh,
     III (ed.), *International Perspectives on Maritime Security*, Charlotte, NC: Mari-
     time Security Council, 1996, p. 160.

11 G.O.W. Mueller and Freda Adler, *Outlaws of the Ocean*, New York: Heart Ma-
     rine Books, 1985, pp. 162-4; John P. Cann. *Brown Waters of Africa: Portuguese
     Riverine Warfare, 1961-1974*, St. Petersburg, Fl: Hailer Publishing, 2007, pp. 5
     & 14-15.

12 For further details see Menefee, *TMV*, pp. 90-4; B.A.H. Parritt, *Security at Sea:
     A Practical Guide*, London: The Nautical Institute, 1991, pp. 15-17; Gottschalk
     and Flanagan, *Jolly Roger with an Uzi*, pp. 35-6; Brittin, 'The law of piracy',,
     pp. 159-63 and Dragonette, 'Maritime terrorism: Underway as before?', pp.
     160 & 163-4, where he describes the incident as the first 'planned' attack on
     a passenger ship, to differentiate it from the *Achille Lauro* and the unfortunate
     case of the *Dara*, a British ship blown up close to Dubai in April 1961, prob-
     ably because it was being used by Omani separatists to transport a bomb to its
     eventual target; 236 people lost their lives: *Ibid.*, p. 161.

13 Brittin, 'The law of piracy', pp. 159-60 and Samuel Pyeatt Menefee, 'Piracy,
     terrorism, and the insurgent passenger: A historical and legal perspective' in
     Natalino Ronzitti (ed.), *Maritime Terrorism and International Law*, Dordrecht,
     Boston and London: Martinus Nijhoff Publishers, 1990, pp. 56-8.

14 Mueller and Adler, *Outlaws of the Ocean*, p. 165; 'Islamic terrorism timeline',
     Entry for 4 March 1973; MIPT Incident Profile: Black September attacked

The Achille Lauro *attack.* The most famous attack of all was mounted on the *Achille Lauro* in 1985. It was, however, a failure and, most probably, a mistake. Terrorists from the Abu Abbas faction of the Palestine Liberation Front (PLF) boarded the ship at the start of its voyage in Genoa.[15] Several explanations have been advanced to explain their objectives. One suggestion is that they aimed to ram the ship into the oil installations at the Israeli port of Ashdod, the ship's destination. Perhaps the most persuasive was that their aim was not to hijack the ship but to wait until the passengers had disembarked and, while they waited to board buses for a tour of the Holy Land, massacre some of them and bargain for the lives of the remainder in exchange for PLF prisoners held by Israel.[16] However, shortly after the ship left Alexandria where, thankfully, the majority of passengers had disembarked for an overland trip, a member of the cabin staff interrupted them while they were cleaning their weapons. Caught *in flagrante*, so to speak, they made the best of a bad job, took over the ship, separated the passengers by nationality and threatened to kill a hostage every hour until their demand for the release of Palestinian terrorists held by Israel was met. They selected two passengers for death but only one was killed, 69-year-old Leon Klinghoffer, a wheelchair-bound American Jew whose body was tossed over the side.[17] Israel refused to negotiate. In the absence of another plan the terrorists secured a deal with Egypt, surrendering the ship in return for safe passage to Tunis. The United States, however, was not party to the

---

Maritime Target, 4 March 1973; Menefee, *TMV,* p. 32 where he refers to the *Sounion-Sana.* Katz, who refers to the ship as the SS *Soniyon,* and Lorenz suggest that the mine might have detonated prematurely as Black September later claimed it was designed to explode when the ship reached Haifa. Samuel M. Katz, *Guards Without Frontiers,* London: Arms and Armour Press, 1990, p. 155 and Akiva J. Lorenz, 'The threat of maritime terrorism to Israel', *Intelligence and Terrorism Information Center at the Israel Intelligence Heritage and Commemoration Center,* 1 Oct. 2007, p. 7.

15   The PLF was itself made up of three factions only one of which, that led by Abbas, was loyal to Yasser Arafat, the head of the PLO. Michael K. Bohn, *The Achille Lauro Hijacking: Lessons in the Politics and Prejudices of Terrorism,* Washington, DC: Potomac Books, 2004, p. xv.

16   Katz, *Guards Without Frontiers,* pp. 172-3. Lorenz points out that PLF internal documents refer to the hijacking as the 'Ashdod port operation': Lorenz, 'The threat of maritime terrorism to Israel', p. 14.

17   The terrorists were keen to take on reinforcements and killed Klinghoffer in an attempt to pressure Syria into allowing the ship to dock at one of its ports. Dragonette, 'Maritime terrorism: Underway as before?', p. 166 and Bohn, *The Achille Lauro Hijacking,* p. 10.

deal and forced the hijackers' plane to land at a NATO airfield in Italy.[18] The Italians, while they arrested the actual hijackers, knowingly allowed the terrorist leader, Mahmoud Abul Abbas, to escape. The end, in other words, was unsatisfactory for everyone. The US did not gain because it wanted to try Klinghoffer's murderers under US jurisdiction. The international community did not gain because, while the hijacking led directly to the 1988 UN Convention for the Suppression of Unlawful Acts Against the Safety of Maritime Navigation (SUA), this is a flawed agreement as discussed below. The terrorists did not gain either, for although the event demonstrated the publicity that could be generated, and that damage could be inflicted on the tourist industry, it also showed how difficult it is for hijackers to make a successful escape from a ship. Nonetheless, as Samuel Pyeatt Menefee notes, the case of the *Achille Lauro*, "like the *Potemkin* mutiny, will continue to be an icon in discussions of violent maritime crime".[19]

The City of Poros, Nile cruise boats and Chechen hijacking. In contrast to the *Santa Maria* and the *Achille Lauro*, the attack on the *City of Poros* south of Athens in 1988 was much bloodier. Eleven people died and 98 were injured when three Arab passengers tossed grenades and sprayed the ship with automatic fire. The origins and purpose of the attack remain unclear. Islamic Jihad claimed responsibility and there is evidence that the Abu Nidal organisation was involved.[20] It is possible that this bloody incident was

---

18   For background on how this was accomplished see Terry White, *Swords of Lighting: Special Forces and the Changing Face of Warfare,* London: Brassey's, 1992, p. 239.

19   Menefee, *TMV,* pp. 11, 29 & 33-36 and Bohn, *The Achille Lauro Hijacking,* pp. 1-19 on the hijacking itself and pp. 20-44 on the interception and capture of the terrorists. There have been several other accounts including, for example, Parritt, *Security at Sea,* pp. 13-15; Bruce Hoffman, *Inside Terrorism,* London: Gollancz, 1998, p. 145; Brittin, 'The law of piracy', pp. 163-5; Paul Wilkinson, 'Navies in a terrorist world', *Jane's NR,* 1987, pp. 170-2; Dragonette, 'Maritime terrorism: Underway as before?', pp. 165-6; and Cable, *Navies in Violent Peace,* pp. 94-5. On the specific point about it being a military success but a political failure for the US see Charles T. Eppright, "Counterterrorism' and conventional military force: The relationship between political effect and utility', *Studies in Conflict and Terrorism,* vol. 20, no. 4, 1997, p. 341.

20   Dominique Chambon, 'Once a terrorist, always a terrorist', *International Review,* Winter 1993-94 cites French reports that Abu Nidal carried out the attack at the behest of Libya, while Kupperman and Kamen suggested that Abu Nidal undertook the attack to grab hostages which they would then have used to stop Greece extraditing to Italy Mohammed Rashid, a terrorist wanted in connection with the 1982 bombing of a Pan Am flight from Tokyo to Honolulu: Robert H. Kupperman and Jeff Kamen, 'Greece, haven for terrorists', *New York*

not an attack at all but a shoot-out between two rival terrorist groups,[21] although Menefee suggests the intention was to seize hostages in exchange for terrorists held in Israeli jails and in this sense the action was akin to the hijack of the *Yori,* a Greek freighter, in Karachi harbour in 1974.[22] The *City of Poros* was the last passenger ship to be attacked at sea (until Somali pirates attacked the *Seabourn Spirit* in 2005), although others have been attacked on the Nile between 1992 and 1996 by al-Gama'a al-Islamiyya, which was the same group that massacred tourists at Luxor in 1997.[23] That is not to say that cruise ships may not become targets in the future. When Al Qaeda's chief of maritime operations, Abd al-Rahim al-Nashiri, was captured he was, according to press reports, found with a 180-page dossier that listed cruise ships as one of the group's "targets of opportunity".[24]

On the other hand attacks have been mounted against ferries. Interestingly, another theory regarding the *City of Poros* attack suggested that it might have had its origins in a 1986 plan to attack a ferry in the English Channel, which was abandoned when the British and French stepped up their security.[25] In 1996 Chechen rebels seized a ferry, the *Avrasya,* on its way from Trabzon in Turkey to Sochi in Russia and took the 220 passengers hostage in an attempt to force Russian forces to lift their siege of 250 Chechens trapped in the Dagestani village of Pervomayskoye.[26] The hijack-

Times, 16 Dec. 1988. However, a report in a Danish newspaper suggested that the firing was, in fact, a shoot-out between Abu Nidal terrorists and Mossad agents, the last act of a drama that had started when Mossad blew up a car in Athens that was to have been driven on board the ferry. 'Danish newspaper explains City of Poros slaughter', *Washington Report on Middle Eastern Affairs,* Oct. 1988, p. 39.

21   Confidential information.

22   Menefee, *TMV,* p. 32.

23   Menefee, *TMV,* p. 40 and Bob Newman, 'Terrorists feared to be planning subsurface naval attacks', *CNSNews.com,* 3 Dec. 2002.

24   See 'Al-Qaeda new tactics, targets ocean liners', CSIS *Transnational Threats Update,* vol. 2, no. 4, Jan. 2004, pp. 3-4; Newman, 'Terrorists feared to be planning sub-surface naval attacks'; Zachary Abuza, 'Terrorism in Southeast Asia: Keeping Al-Qaeda at bay', The Jamestown Foundation *Terrorism Monitor,* vol. II, Issue 9, 6 May 2004, p. 5; according to Koknar, 'Piracy and terrorism are joining forces', the document specified cruise ships of over 140,000 tons with more than 5,000 passengers as the preferred target. In 2008 there were only two ships that came close to meeting al-Nashiri's reported criteria.

25   Menefee, *TMV,* pp. 36-8 and Parritt, *Security at Sea,* p. 17.

26   Dragonette, 'Maritime terrorism: Underway as before?', p. 166.

ers sailed the ferry to the mouth of the Bosporus where they surrendered after being denied permission to pass through.[27]

The Superferry 14 *attack and other attacks on ferries in the Philippines.* The deadliest ferry attack to date took place in the Philippines, involving the 10,000-ton *Superferry 14* which suffered an explosion and subsequent fire as it left Manila Bay in 2004. The explosion killed 63 people and of the 717 people who jumped overboard a further 53 died or were presumed dead.[28] Although this was the worst incident, attacks on ferries are a common occurrence in Philippine waters; most have been carried out by terrorist groups such as the ASG and MNLF, usually in an attempt to extort money from ferry operators.

All these attacks have one thing in common. At no time was there any sense that any terrorist group had grasped how attacks from the sea could significantly affect events on land.

Seafarers' attitudes

The 2007 Nautilus survey on seafarers' attitudes to piracy also asked similar questions about their attitudes to terrorism. Many of those expressing concern worked on passenger ships or ferries; 27 per cent said they were "very" concerned and 61 per cent they were "mildly" concerned. Overall, 53 per cent saw terrorism as the major threat compared to 43 per cent who saw piracy as more worrying.[29]

The current and developing legal regime. The difficulties encountered by the legislators of many countries when trying to categorise terrorism are multiplied many times when the attempt is repeated in the international arena. The only way in which contentious issues can be dealt with effectively is to remove contentious terms and labels and replace them with specific offences designed to address, say, the smuggling of narcotics or nuclear material about which it is hard for states to disagree. The result of such a step-by-step process is that progress towards an effective international anti-terrorism regime has inevitably been slow.

27   Menefee, *TMV*, pp. 40-1; 'Ship hijacked as Chechen siege expands', *CNN World News*, 16 Jan. 1996.

28   Michael D. Greenberg, *et al.*, *Maritime Terrorism: Risk and Liability,* Santa Monica: RAND, 2006, p. 95. Human Rights Watch, 'Lives destroyed: Attacks against civilians in the Philippines', July 2007, pp. 12-15.

29   Hand, 'Survey reveals human cost of piracy'.

The United Nations Convention on the Law of the Sea (UNCLOS) draws a distinction between acts committed for "private ends" and those committed for "political ends". The requirement that a pirate act has to be committed for "private ends" has its origin in the distinction between piracy and privateering. The latter was piracy under license. Providing privateer captains abided by the conditions of their licenses, they were virtually immune from prosecution. This immunity was recognised by all states including those of their victims. Although the Declaration of Paris of 1856 abolished privateering, the distinction between private and public ends was maintained because courts (and states) wanted to differentiate between piracy and acts of maritime depredation carried out by insurgents or rebels. This distinction was drawn repeatedly by jurists and in court judgements. The case of *Bolivia v. Indemnity Mutual,* a case heard before the English Courts in 1909, is regarded as seminal.[30] By affirming that a loss as a result of a rebel incident was not piracy, as public ends were being pursued not private, it shaped the definition of piracy for twentieth-century international jurisprudence. The consequence of this continuing distinction is that so-called "political" acts are excluded, including those that involve internal seizure, as in the case of the *Achille Lauro,* or are perpetrated by states, as in the case of the USS *Pueblo.*[31] Above all, of course, because "political" acts are excluded from the piracy provisions, UNCLOS cannot be used against terrorists.

In the wake of the *Achille Lauro* seizure, the IMO prepared a study of the problem of terrorism on board or against ships. This led in 1988 to the Convention for the Suppression of Unlawful Acts Against the Safety of Maritime Navigation, now referred to more often as the SUA or "Rome" Convention. Based on aviation precedents, it was designed to deal with politically motivated violence at sea.[32] There is a widespread and not wholly

---

30   Timothy H. Goodman, "Leaving the Corsair's name to other times': How to enforce the law of sea piracy in the 21st Century through regional international agreements', *Case Western Reserve Journal of International Law,* vol. 31, no.1, 1999, pp. 147-8.

31   It was P.W. Birnie who noted that UNCLOS took no account of the 1970 International Law Association Report that defined piracy simply as 'unlawful seizure or taking control of a vessel by violence, threats thereof, surprise, fraud or other means'. Johnson, who was the rapporteur, felt that both internal seizures and hijackings should also be defined as piracy. Birnie, 'Piracy: Past, present and future', pp. 170-1. See also Natalino Ronzitti, 'The law of the sea and the use of force against terrorist activities' in Ronzitti. *Maritime Terrorism and International Law,* p. 2.

32   For a full discussion of the Convention and the thinking that underlay the approach taken see Treves. 'The Rome Convention', pp. 69-90.

erroneous assumption that the SUA is concerned solely with terrorist acts. In fact the word "terrorism" does not occur in the text. The drafters, quite sensibly, decided that defining terrorism was too sensitive, too political and too much of a waste of time to be attempted and therefore adopted the term "unlawful acts" as an acceptable euphemism. Consequently, the Convention addresses specific actions, such as ship seizure and violence by those on board, that could result in physical injury, or damage to the ship or its cargo. Because it took as its models the Hague and Montreal Conventions against aircraft hijacking it has two important differences compared to the piracy provisions found in UNCLOS: first, the SUA Convention is applicable everywhere, even in territorial waters, *providing* the ship under attack is coming from or proceeding to an international destination; secondly, state parties must enact domestic legislation to make Convention offences punishable under their laws:[33] the main aim of the Convention is legal prosecution, not physical prevention; its central purpose is to ensure that states either prosecute or extradite. It does not, in contrast to treaty and customary law on piracy, recognise or authorise preventative police activity at sea. Furthermore, it is not relevant if the violence on board is insufficient to compromise maritime safety, it is inapplicable to the intra-state coastal traffic that accounts for so many maritime movements in the world's territorial and archipelagic waters, and it is not, of course, applicable to non-signatory states which, unfortunately, include Somalia and many of the states in Asia where concern about maritime terrorism and piracy is most acute.[34] The result has been that, apart from one minor case in US waters, SUA has never been invoked.

If the *Achille Lauro* seizure sparked a legal rethink, then 9/11 ignited a counter-terrorism revolution. In the maritime domain this resulted in two important changes. The most immediate was the adoption of the US-inspired International Ship and Port Facility Security (ISPS) Code. Although this started life as an initiative in the G8, it built upon existing parts of the 1974 Safety of Life at Sea (SOLAS) Convention and gained international

---

33   Roach, 'Enhancing maritime security in the straits of Malacca and Singapore', p. 105.

34   See Robert C. Beckman. 'Combatting piracy and armed robbery against ships in Southeast Asia: The way forward', *Ocean Development and International Law*, vol. 33, 2002, pp. 321-2 & 329; R.R. Churchill and A.V. Lowe, *The Law of the Sea* (3rd edn.), Manchester UP, 1999, p. 211; Luis Jesus, 'Protection of foreign ships against piracy and terrorism at sea', pp. 391-4; Halberstam, 'Terrorism on the high seas', p. 292.

legal force because it was implemented as amendments to Chapters V and XI of that Convention. Since 1 July 2004 these amendments now apply to all vessels over 300 Gross Registered Tons (GRT) on international voyages and to ports servicing international traffic. The aim of the Code is to introduce a risk management approach to ship and port security, an approach that has worked in the fields of safety and environmental protection, largely successfully, for over a decade. In both these fields success has depended on making changes to often entrenched attitudes and working practices, changes that take time to have effect and are engendered almost entirely as a consequence of sustained managerial pressure. On the basis of this experience, it is likely that ISPS will succeed only if owners and managers in the ship and port industries are convinced that the increased costs that are an inevitable concomitant of such changes will either yield commercial benefits or be borne equally by competitors, not just in their own countries but around the globe. It will also succeed only once an active, day-to-day commitment to security has been accepted, and demonstrated, by seamen and port workers at all levels, whatever their training or background. Results to date have therefore been patchy but progress is being made.

The second change was a substantial increase in the number of activities covered by the SUA Convention, coupled with the introduction of provisions to allow the boarding of vessels suspected of involvement in terrorist activity. The previous reluctance to recognise or authorise preventative constabulary activity at sea was set aside. While it was the IMO Legal Committee that brought these revisions forward for consideration, they were based in large part on US practice. An important element of this was the concept of "deemed permission". This had emerged out of the experience the US gained from the operation of 23 agreements with Caribbean and Central American states (plus the UK). These agreements enabled it to board flag vessels of those countries, if it believed they were being used to smuggle narcotics. Some of these were so-called "shiprider" agreements whereby an official of a signatory state travelled aboard a US ship, available to grant immediate permission to board when a suspect vessel was intercepted. In others cases the flag state was asked for permission to board if one of its flag vessels came under suspicion; if the flag state had not responded within a specified time (usually two or four hours) then permission was deemed to have been given. In the case of the UK, the US was given permission in advance to board any UK flagged vessel within a designated sea area.

In 2003 the Aruba Agreement, or to give it its full title, "The Agreement concerning cooperation in suppressing illicit maritime and air trafficking in narcotic drugs and psychotropic substances in the Caribbean area, 2003", was signed, although at the time of writing it still lacks sufficient ratifications to come into force. This was a multilateral agreement that supplemented but did not replace these bilateral agreements. Most Caribbean states were involved in the negotiations that led up to the Agreement plus four external powers with Caribbean territories, the US, the UK, France and the Netherlands. The anticipated benefit of the additional multilateral agreement is that states in addition to the US who are parties to it, and have the requisite naval or coast guard assets, can enforce its provisions. However, because the US has more naval assets in the region than any other state, the bilateral agreements remain the most important. Significantly, the Agreement makes a simple distinction between territorial waters and the high seas, and permits signatories to engage in reverse hot pursuit (or "pursuit and entry" in US parlance) of suspect vessels under certain conditions. This is valuable because the geography of the region meant that, heretofore, "go-fast" boats could move up the island chain all the way from the South American coast to Florida, safe in the knowledge that if they were spotted by a law enforcement vessel (which was likely to be that of an external power), they could run for the territorial waters of a small island state and shelter there safely as the pursuing ships could not follow them. The various bilateral agreements, and the multilateral Aruba Agreement, have stripped away that sanctuary. The weakness of the Aruba Agreement is that because of sovereignty concerns, instead of following the simplest course—that a state by ratifying the agreement allows the vessels of external powers free access to its territorial waters when in pursuit of narcotics smugglers—states prior to ratification can choose from a "menu" of options that range from the fact that the agreement itself constitutes the necessary permission, through "shiprider" arrangements, to case-by-case notification to "deemed" permission. This is not entirely satisfactory but it does mean that the communication channels and procedures that have been established between states can make permission easier to obtain, and could also prove useful in other cases such as piracy or terrorism, even though neither the bilateral nor the multilateral agreements cover either specifically.[35]

---

35   For a full discussion of the Agreement see William Gilmore, 'Agreement concerning co-operation in suppressing illicit maritime and air trafficking in narcotic drugs and psychotropic substances in the Caribbean area, 2003', London: The Stationery Office, 2005.

The Aruba Agreement grew out of, and built upon, the 1988 United Nations Convention against Illicit Traffic in Narcotic Drugs And Psychotropic Substances. It incorporated lessons from it. Perhaps the most pertinent with regard to ship-boarding was that the 1988 "Drug Trafficking" Convention requires states to extend their domestic counter-narcotic legislation to ships of their own flag. On the other hand, it allows them, but does not require them, to extend that legislation to foreign nationals on foreign or "stateless" vessels transiting their territorial waters. The fact that many states have not introduced the legislation necessary to cover foreign nationals on such ships is not unusual: states tend to implement the mandatory parts of any agreement but do not make use of the discretionary powers those agreements often give them. Unfortunately, this can make nonsense of whatever has been agreed. A successful arraignment depends on the necessary domestic legislation being in place. The consequence of such omissions for the 1988 Convention has been that if ships that fall into either category are suspected of transporting narcotics, and boarded under its terms, it was possible that foreign nationals and stateless persons could not be arrested even if narcotics were found. The Aruba Agreement closed this lacuna. All parties to the Agreement are required to enact legislation covering foreign and stateless vessels within their jurisdiction. International law learns as its goes along and is developing all the time. Therefore, if the Aruba Agreement can be seen as an advance on the 1988 "Drug Trafficking" Convention, it can also be seen as a stepping stone towards the revision of the 1988 SUA Convention.

The most important change introduced by the 2005 Protocols to the SUA Convention was that it became an offence under Article 3*bis* to intimidate or coerce a state and to use a vessel as a platform for the discharge of an explosive, radiation or BCN (Biological, Chemical, Nuclear) weapon. It also became an offence, under the same article, to use a vessel to transport such weapons or their components and precursors knowing that they are intended to cause harm. Just as required under the original 1988 SUA Convention, signatory states must make prohibited acts criminal under their own national laws and take whatever steps are required to ensure they can be enforced. Furthermore, under Article 8*bis,* ships can be boarded if there are grounds for believing they have contravened Article 3. However, while this new ship-boarding provision reflects elements of US experience, as with the multilateral Aruba Agreement, and in contrast to many of the individual bilateral agreements that the US has signed with Caribbean states, the details of US practice have not been accepted wholeheartedly. The new Protocol contains numerous safeguards and restrictions and, critically, the default position is that boarding can only take place if the flag state gives its permission. Ships remain "islands of territoriality" on the sea. Nonetheless, flag states can agree in advance, by notifying the Secretary-General of the IMO, that under Article 8*bis*.5(e), if the boarding state has not received permission within four hours such permission is deemed to be given, and under Article 8*bis*.5(f) a state can also agree in advance that its permission is given without the need for a response. In fact, under Article 13, states can make whatever arrangements they wish to realise the intent of the Protocol. These changes were adopted in October 2005 and now await the necessary ratifications to come into effect. However, to place these new arrangements in perspective, the rules for boarding and inspecting fishing vessels under the "Straddling Fish Stocks Agreement" are—as Rüdiger Wolfrum, a member of the International Tribunal on the Law of the Sea has pointed out—less onerous than those required to inspect ships for suspected terrorist activity.[36]

A global threat on the global medium?

The USS Cole *attack.* In October 2000, the *Arleigh Burke*-class destroyer USS *Cole* was severely damaged and nearly sunk in Aden harbour. Seventeen US servicemen died and 39 were injured. One of the most advanced warships afloat, designed to protect carrier battle groups, proved incapable of defending itself against two men in a rubber dinghy packed with a 500lb. (227 kg) shaped charge, even though it was on full "Bravo" alert, with armed guards on deck. It has been suggested that the *Cole* was unlucky, that it was simply in the wrong place at the wrong time, but this assertion is difficult to sustain in the face of the numbers of warnings that were received. In 1997, the NSC had sent a memo to the Pentagon warning specifically about risks to US ships in port. The US Navy had access to the wealth of other intelligence about Al Qaeda. In particular, as General Tommy Franks admitted, CENTCOM had long anticipated frogman and

---

36   'Agreement for the implementation of the provisions of the UN Convention on the law of the sea relating to the conservation and management of straddling fish stocks and highly migratory species, 1995'; Rüdiger Wolfrum, 'Fighting terrorism at sea: Options and limitations under international law', Twenty-eighth Doherty Lecture organised by the Center for Oceans Law and Policy, University of Virginia School of Law, Charlottesville, Virginia, delivered in Washington, DC, 13 April 2006, p. 14.

small boat attacks against Navy ships. Despite this his predecessor as regional CINC, General Anthony Zinni, had approved the decision to refuel in Yemen.[37]

Most importantly, this was not the terrorists' first attempt. In January 2000 the same terrorist cell used the same technique to attack the USS *The Sullivans,* a destroyer from the same class as the *Cole.* The attack failed because they overloaded the skiff, which foundered in shallow water before it reached the ship.[38] More importantly, they learned from their failure: before the second attempt the cell, according to Gunaratna, rehearsed the operation, conducted a dry run to ensure the attack boat would not sink again and even tested the explosives.[39]

Al Qaeda and the link to 9/11. The *Cole* attack was undoubtedly the work of Al Qaeda. Like the attacks on the US embassies in east Africa in 1998, and

---

37   The National Commission on Terrorist Attacks upon the United States, *The 9/11 Commission Report: Final Report of the National Commission on Terrorist Attacks upon the United States* (authorized edn.), New York and London: W.W. Norton & Company, 2004, pp. 190-5 [hereafter referred to as *The 9/11 Commission Report*]; Daniel Benjamin and Steven Simon, *The Age of Sacred Terror,* New York: Random House Trade Paperback, 2003, pp. 323-4; Peter L. Bergen, *Holy War, Inc: Inside the Secret World of Osama bin Laden,* London: Weidenfeld & Nicholson, 2001, pp. 202-4; Richard A. Clarke, *Against All Enemies: Inside America's War on Terror,* London: The Free Press, 2004, pp. 222-3, particularly on the failures of inter-service communication that allowed the ship to be exposed to unnecessary risk in the first place; Rohan Gunaratna, *Inside Al-Qaeda: Global Network of Terror,* London: Hurst, 2002, p. 49 and pp. 140-1, where he recounts that bin Laden was so delighted by the success of the attack he actually composed a poem in its honour and recited it at the wedding of his son; Shaul Shay, *The Red Sea Terror Triangle,* New Brunswick & London: Transaction Publishers, 2007 (orig. pub. 2005), pp. 125-8; Raphael Perl and Ronald O'Rourke, 'Terrorist Attack on the USS Cole: Background and Issues for Congress', *Congressional Research Service,* 30 Jan. 2001 (RS20721); and Harold W. Gehman Jr., *Lost Patrol: The Attack on the USS Cole,* US Naval Institute *Proceedings,* vol. 127, no. 4, April 2001, pp. 34-7 on the inquiry that followed the attack and the preventive measures that can be taken in the future. See also 'Blast holes US warship', *BBC News,* 12 Oct. 2000; ''Asymmetric warfare', the USS Cole and the Intifada', *The Estimate,* vol. XII, no. 22, 2000, pp. 1-3; Daniel V. Smith, 'Terrorist attack on the *USS Cole*', *JINSA Online,* 13 Oct. 2000.

38   Benjamin and Simon, *The Age of Sacred Terror,* pp. 31-3; Clarke, *Against All Enemies,* p. 213; Gunaratna, *Inside Al-Qaeda,* pp. 49 & 140; David Fairnie, interview with author.

39   Rohan Gunaratna, 'The threat to the maritime domain: How real is the terrorist threat?' in Richmond M. Lloyd (ed.), *Economics and Maritime Strategy: Implications for the 21st Century.* Proceedings of a workshop sponsored by the William B. Ruger Chair at the Naval War College, Newport, RI, 6-8 Nov. 2006, p. 85.

the attacks that would follow in 2001 on the targets in the United States itself, it demonstrated what a new generation of Islamist militants were capable of planning and executing, coupled with their willingness to exploit the freedoms of globalisation: freedom to move internationally, freedom to communicate cheaply, securely and almost instantaneously; freedom to raise funds around the world rapidly and anonymously; freedom to study the technology of the West (often at Western universities and at Western expense) and to turn that knowledge against the teachers. However, it took the 9/11 tragedies in New York and Washington to finally make the world aware of the horrific moral universe which that capability was designed to serve.

Conceptually, however, none of these attacks, not even the attacks of 9/11, was very different from other terrorist "spectaculars". The attacks on New York and Washington did not represent a fundamental innovation in terrorist methods, nor did they herald a significant change of direction. Instead they built on the tried and tested foundation of terrorist tactics: surprise and simplicity executed by means of known and straightforward technology, coupled with the ability to observe and then exploit weaknesses in the target's security. It was the scale and audacity of the attack and, once it became apparent, the scale and international reach of the group behind it that took people's breath away. President George W. Bush claimed that those events changed the world; they did not, but the reaction to them did.[40]

It was the elements of scale and international reach which, when taken together, led people to look for other possible scenarios where acts on a similar scale could be carried out. The sea certainly offers scale. It is perhaps not surprising, therefore, that some of that speculation focused on the maritime domain. Two main reasons have been extended as to why terrorists might mount attacks on water: first, that the seas are a largely unregulated space which, in the case of weak states that are unable to police their territorial waters effectively, extends right up to coast; secondly, that major ports are inherently difficult to secure if they are to work efficiently; thirdly, few terrorist incidents have occurred at sea and therefore, by some unaccount-

---

40   Louise Richardson, *What Terrorists Want: Understanding the Enemy, Containing the Threat*, New York: Random House, 2006, p. 167. Also Robert Jervis, 'An interim assessment of Sept. 11: What has changed and what has not?' *Political Science Quarterly*, vol. 117, no. 1, 2002, pp. 37-54.

able law of averages, it is the turn of ships and seafarers to provide the next vehicle and the next set of victims.[41]

The attacks of 9/11 have a number of dimensions in terms of the targets and methods and it is instructive to use the assaults on New York and Washington to identify major elements in a successful terrorist attack, and then transfer those elements to the maritime domain in order to see how they might be replicated at sea. The 11 September attackers exploited the inherent features of aircraft to turn them into guided weapons without any form of modification. The targets on that fateful day were iconic symbols of American power. The Twin Towers were also an economic target; their destruction imposed a serious but not unsustainable cost on the American economy. The Pentagon was transparently a military target. They were both, of course, also mass casualty targets.

Categories of maritime targets

With these elements in mind the possibilities for terrorism at sea can be broken down into four broad categories:

1. Ships as iconic targets
2. Ships as economic targets
3. Ships as mass casualty targets
4. Ships as weapons.

Commentators and analysts have also looked at *how* ships could be attacked and where.

Obviously, the only land-based targets that can be attacked by a ship directly are on the shore—in other words, ports or fixed seabed structures such as oil terminals or production platforms. Ships could, however, be used to transport men, money or equipment that can then be used to attack land targets; in other words they could be used as delivery vehicles for weapons. While ships can be attacked anywhere they can travel, terrorists are not navies and therefore, for practical reasons, are unlikely to mount external attacks against ships unless they are in a port or a short distance from

---

41   See, for example, the comments made by Dr Tony Tan, the Deputy Prime Minister of Singapore, quoted in Joshua Ho, 'Maritime counter-terrorism: A Singapore perspective', paper presented at the Observer Research Foundation Maritime Counter-Terrorism Workshop, 29 –30 Nov. 2004, p. 4; Glass, 'The new piracy'; also Peter Grier and Faye Bowers, 'How al-Qaeda might strike the US by sea', *Christian Science Monitor*, 15 May 2003.

the coast. Some of the possibilities in these categories have been realised already by terrorists while other remain only potential threats.

Ships as iconic targets. Until the end of the Second World War the size of a nation's merchant marine was one measure of its power. Each ship was representative of the state whose flag it flew. That link has now been broken. Most ships today are registered in states that offer the ships' owners some regulatory, cost or tax advantage. Few cargo ships, therefore, are so closely linked with any state, or so obviously serving the interests of that state, that an attack on the ship would be seen as an attack on the flag state.

Warships, however, are different.[42] Apart from the attack on the USS *Cole,* which epitomised this, several other actual, attempted or planned attacks have taken place: the attempted attack on the USS *The Sullivans* in Aden in 2000, the planned attacks on a US warship in Singapore uncovered in 2001, the planned attacks that were to have been mounted from Morocco in 2002 on US and British warships in the Straits of Gibraltar, and the attempted attack in 2005 on the USS *Ashland* and USS *Kearsage* while on a visit to the Jordanian port of Aqaba.[43] It is possible that other planned or attempted attacks on warships have been disrupted.[44] Although it would not have involved a ship it is worth noting that, according to the operative tasked with the mission, Ibn Yahya al-Libi (who escaped from US detention at Bagram Air Base in Afghanistan in 2005 and is now one of Al Qaeda's most senior leaders[45]), one of the operations that Abd al-Rahim

42   Auxiliaries could also fall into this category and have the advantage, from the terrorists' perspective, of being much less heavily armed.

43   For references on the *Cole* attack and the attempted attack on *The Sullivans* see above. On the Singapore and Gibraltar attacks see below. For the Aqaba attack see 'Jordanians hunt rocket suspects', *BBC News,* 20 Aug. 2005; 'Jordanians find rocket launcher used in attack on US ships', *New York Times,* 20 Aug. 2005; Tim Butcher, 'Missile attack on US ship in Jordanian Red Sea port', *Daily Telegraph,* 20 Aug. 2005; 'Zarqawi 'link to Jordan rockets'', *BBC News,* 24 Aug. 2005.

44   Barbara Starr, 'Sources: Warships targeted by Al-Qaeda', *CNN.com,* 21 Nov. 2002.

45   On the escape see Mark Tran, 'Terror suspects escape US Afghan base', *The Guardian,* 11 July 2005; on his subsequent position within al-Qaeda see Sami Yousafzai and Ron Moreau, 'Al Qaeda family feud', *Newsweek,* 30 July 2007. Also Michael Scheuer, 'Abu Yahya al-Libi: Al Qaeda's theological enforcer–Part 1', The Jamestown Foundation *Terrorism Focus,* vol. IV, Issue 25, 31 July 2007 and Part 2, vol. IV, Issue 27, 14 Aug. 2007; Michael Moss and Souad Mekhennet, 'Rising leader for next phase of al-Qaeda's war', *New York Times,* 4 April 2008.

al-Nashiri, the leader of the cell that attacked the *Cole* and the *Limburg* (see below), was planning prior to his capture was an attack on the headquarters of the US Fifth Fleet in Bahrain.[46]

Cruise ships, although they might be seen primarily as potential mass-casualty targets, when carrying large numbers of Americans or Israelis have an iconic status because of the nationality of those on board. Some cruise ships, such as the Cunard-owned *Queen Mary 2* and *Queen Victoria*, have an iconic status simply because of what they are and the privilege they represent.[47] The economic effects if a major cruise ship were attacked successfully could also be extremely damaging.[48]

Ships as economic targets. Al Qaeda's strategy has an economic dimension.[49] In a tape released in 2004 bin Laden suggested the group had a "policy (of) bleeding America to the point of bankruptcy."[50] The al-Qaeda ideologue, Abu Mus'ab al-Suri, echoed this when he wrote about denying the West access to Muslim markets and raw materials.[51] Oil is its obvious focus. In Christopher Blanchard's view it is based on a "sophisticated consideration of the economic and military vulnerabilities of the United States and its allies, particular with regard to the role of Middle Eastern oil…" He goes on to point out that bin Laden has spoken regularly of the economic effects of terrorist attacks and talked about the need for the Arab world to retain its oil reserves, "as a great and important economic power for the coming Islamic state", and the effectiveness of economic boycotts. He suggests that it is possible al-Qaeda could adopt a more protracted, attrition strategy

---

46   Oliver Burkeman, 'US captures key al-Qaeda suspect', *Guardian Unlimited,* 22 Nov. 2002; 'US hopes al-Qaeda captive will reveal future plots', *USA Today,* 22 Nov. 2002.

47   'The QE2 threat and the symbolic value of cruise ships', STRATFOR *Daily Terrorism Brief,* 13 April 2006. On the other hand Dragonette, 'Maritime terrorism: Underway as before?', p. 169 makes the point that the era of 'ship as symbol' is over and that even the *QE2* was honoured more by rumours than by actual threats.

48   For a thorough assessment of those affects see Greenberg, *et al., Maritime Terrorism,* pp. 79-85.

49   Matthew Hunt, 'Bleed to bankruptcy: Economic targeting tactics in the global jihad', *Jane's IR,* Jan. 2007, pp. 14-17. For background on economic targetting by terrorist groups see James M. Lutz. 'Terrorism as Economic Warfare', *Global Economy Journal,* Vol. 6, No. 2, 2006..

50   'Bin Laden: Goal is to bankrupt the US', *CNN.com,* 1 Nov. 2004.

51   Brynjar Lia, *Architect of Global Jihad: The Life of Al-Qaida Strategist Abu Mus'ab al-Suri.* London: Hurst & Co, 2007, pp. 398-401.

based on attacks against economic targets and critical infrastructure such as oil facilities and pipelines.[52]

Tankers are certainly part of the oil industry's critical infrastructure. Almost exactly two years after the attack on the USS *Cole,* the *Limburg* (now the *Maritime Jewel*), a Very Large Crude Carrier (VLCC), was struck, again off Yemen. On the morning of the attack a threat from bin Laden to "target key sectors of your economy until you stop injustices and aggression" was broadcast by Arabic satellite television, and during a later recording he praised the attack explicitly.[53]

The *Limburg*, like the *Cole,* was attacked by a small, fast-moving craft packed with explosives—probably, once again, a shaped charge. The boat detonated against the side of the ship blowing a hole between six and eight metres (20-26 feet) deep in the outer hull, (although only about one square metre (11 square feet) in the inner hull). The tanker was partly loaded with 400,000 bbl of crude oil (it was en route to load a further 1.5 million bbl) which formed a slick 45-miles (72km) long beside the Yemeni coast. The timing of the attack, when the ship was picking up a pilot and therefore almost stationary, and in the early morning when few crew were on watch, indicates good research.[54] Again, Al-Qaeda carried out the attack. Again,

---

52   Christopher M. Blanchard, 'Al Qaeda: Statements and evolving ideology', Congressional Research Service, *Report for Congress* RL32759, 20 June 2004, p. 12.

53   'Bin Laden hails anti-Western attacks', *BBC News*, 14 Oct. 2002. Attacks on cruise ships would also affect the tourist industry. For details on the immediate effects following the *Achille Lauro* incident see Bohn, *The Achille Lauro Hijacking,* p. 153.

54   For accounts of the attack and the reluctant acknowledgement by Yemen of al-Qaeda involvement see, for example, 'Craft 'rammed' Yemen oil tanker', *BBC News*, 6 Oct. 2002; Philip Smucker, 'We were bombed, says oil tanker captain', *Daily Telegraph,* 8 Oct. 2002; 'Yemen ship attack was terrorism', *BBC News* report, 13 Oct.; 'Militant 'planned attacks' in Gulf', *BBC News*, 23 Dec. 2002; 'Limburg saboteurs had inside information', *ICC News*, 19 June 2003; Shay, *The Red Sea Terror Triangle,* pp. 128-30; and Gunaratna, 'Threat to the maritime domain: How real is the terrorist threat?' p. 86. Al Qaeda also drew attention to the operation's cost effectiveness, pointing out that the suicide boat only cost $1,000 and comparing this to the cost of an oil tanker: 'Al Qaeda, tanker insurance rates, mines among key war concerns', *Oil and Gas Journal,* 31 March 2003. In this connection it is worth noting that the USS *Cole* took 14 months to repair at a cost of over $250 million: Michael Richardson, *A Time Bomb for Global Trade: Maritime-related Terrorism in an Age of Weapons of Mass Destruction.* Singapore: Institute of Southeast Asian Studies, 2004, p. 18 and John C.K. Daly, 'Al Qaeda and maritime terrorism (Part I)', The Jamestown Foundation *Terrorism Monitor,* vol. 1, no. 4, 24 Oct. 2003, p. 2.

intelligence warnings had been received; in September the US Navy had alerted shipping about possible attacks against oil traffic.

The *Limburg* attack did have an economic effect but most of it fell on Yemen. Insurance rates for ships calling at Yemeni ports increased immediately and substantially. As a direct consequence, shippers of all types of goods shunned Yemeni ports; throughput of containers fell from 43,000 TEUs in September 2002 to 3,000 TEUs in November and then almost ceased; three thousand port workers were laid off. The rates were reduced after six months for two reasons: first, because it became clear that the tactic was unlikely to be repeated; secondly, because the Yemeni government issued Lloyd's with a letter of credit to cover any subsequent losses up to an agreed limit. The OECD estimated that Yemen's economic losses equalled one per cent of the country's 2001 GDP. The cumulative losses for the port were, however, so substantial that the Singapore-based port operator PSA withdrew from the project and handed its share back to the Yemeni government.[55]

The wider affects of the attack were much more limited. The oil price increased by 1.3 per cent within hours but fell back quickly, admittedly in a period of slack demand. In a tight oil market, one that was also troubled by the affects of political turbulence particularly in the Middle East, that outcome might not be so benign. Nonetheless, to be able to inflict economic hardship of sufficient severity to bring about a change of policy, a terrorist group would need to reduce world oil supply by a significant amount. Prior to his capture al-Nashiri was also reportedly planning an operation to attack several oil tankers as they passed through the Straits of Hormuz.[56]

---

55   Murphy, 'Slow alarm', p. 4; Richardson, *A Time Bomb for Global Trade,* pp. 70-1; Rashmi Jain, *Securing the Port of New York and New Jersey: Network-Centric Operations Applied to the Campaign Against Terrorism,* Appendix 1-4, Stevens Institute of Technology, 2004, p. 4.

56   Al-Nashiri was reportedly the 'mastermind' behind both attacks. For a biography of al-Nashiri go to http://en.wikipedia.org/wiki/Abd_al-Rahim_al-Nashiri. On his importance and his role within al-Qaeda see *The 9/11 Commission Report,* pp. 152-3; on his capture see 'Top al-Qaeda operative arrested', *CNN.com,* 22 Nov. 2002; "Al Qaeda Gulf chief" held by US', *BBC News,* 22 Nov. 2002; 'Suspected Qaeda chief cooperating', *CBS News,* 22 Nov. 2002; and 'Al-Qaeda operative talking', *CNN.com,* 23 Nov. 2002. There is some suspicion that in Yemen he worked with the Aden-Abyan Islamic Group: Koknar, 'Piracy and terrorism are joining forces', and 'Aden-Abyan Islamic Army', *GlobalSecurity. org,* ND. Concern was raised when several members of the group escaped from a Yemeni jail in 2006: Francis Harris, 'Terrorist alert over Yemen jail breakout', *Daily Telegraph,* 6 Feb. 2006; also Andrew McGregor. 'Al-Qaeda's Great Escape in Yemen', The Jamestown Foundation *Terrorism Focus,* vol. III, Issue 5, 7 Feb. 2006. This escape was the reason why Yemen was returned to the Lloyd's Joint

He was presumably hoping that if he sank several ships close together these would block the Straits for a sufficient period of time to bring about the necessary market disruption.[57] One tanker sinking and probably even several tanker sinkings would not be enough (although they would certainly provoke a howl of environmental rage).

There are disadvantages in mounting attacks on economic targets at sea. From a terrorist's point of view, tankers have the advantage of being isolated and vulnerable once they leave a protected anchorage; the disad-

---

War Committee list of 'at risk' areas for the first time since the listing was lifted following the *Limburg* attack. For details on the escapees' whereabouts see Gregory D. Johnsen, 'Tracking Yemen's 23 escaped jihardi operatives–Part 1', The Jamestown Foundation *Terrorism Monitor*, vol. V, Issue 18, 27 Sept. 2007, pp. 5-7. The central figure in this escape was Jamal al-Badawi who had escaped previously from another prison in 2003. The escape in 2006 was made through a tunnel dug between the prison and a nearby mosque by sympathisers burrowing into the prison from the outside. For domestic political reasons the government of President Saleh dealt leniently with both detainees and escapees as part of a policy designed to discourage them from committing militant acts within the country's borders. This stance, coupled to the procedural obstacles that had been put in the way of the original FBI investigation of the *Cole* bombing, led the US government to become increasingly frustrated with Yemen's excessive generosity towards those it viewed as international terrorists. See Craig Whitlock, 'Probe of USS Cole bombing unravels', *Washington Post*, 4 May 2008 and Ali H. Soufan, 'Coddling terrorists in Yemen', *Washington Post*, 17 May 2008.

57   President Bush included a number of maritime incidents in the list of thwarted terrorist attacks issued in 2005: Peter Baker and Susan B. Glasser, 'Bush says 10 plots by al-Qaeda were foiled', *The Washington Post*, 7 Oct. 2005. Amongst them he alluded to a disrupted attempt to attack ships in the Straits of Hormuz. This was probably the attempt by al-Nashiri to launch small attack craft from a mother ship. For a report on this plan see Julian Borger, 'Plot to sink warship on 9/11', *The Guardian*, 21 Feb. 2003. Also private information, Oct. 2005. The President may also have been referring to the attack on the USNS *Walter S. Diehl*, an American naval oiler, which on 23 April 2002 repelled an attack as it traversed the Straits of Hormuz. Whether this was the work of terrorists or pirates or a practice run by the IRGCN could not be determined: Newman, 'Terrorists feared to be planning sub-surface naval attacks' and Adam Geibel, 'Cyclones, Firebolt and the Persian Gulf pirates', *Strategy Page*, 22 Oct. 2003. However, private sources have indicated to the author that the attack amounted to a substantial assault. Contrary to press reports that mentioned six boats, a total of 40 boats were actually involved, most of which were organised in three waves to distract the crew's attention to one side of the ship while the final wave of six speedboats approached from the starboard direction, among which was hidden a boat carrying what appeared to be a suicide bomber. This wave was also spotted and driven off. Several other similar or attempted attacks on USNS ships have occurred in the Gulf, all of which have been denied by US authorities.

vantages are that they require specific skills to attack successfully and that several successful attacks may be required to achieve the desired economic disruption.[58] From simulations conducted by Securing America's Future Energy (SAFE), it is estimated that a four per cent global shortfall in daily supply would result in a 177 per cent increase in the price of oil.[59] Oil supplies and prices are currently underpinned by Saudi Arabia's excess capacity. Any significant disruption in that supply, which is already coming under pressure as world consumption increases, would put a serious strain on the global economy.[60] Kubarych in his review of the global economic response to the oil "shocks" of the past 30 years, makes a similar point. He argues that although the effect of the oil price rise that began in 2002 has so far been less damaging that the original "shock" of 1973-75, these supply constraints, coupled with rising demand from economies such as China and India, mean that the oil market is becoming tighter.[61] Given this vulnerability but at the same time recognising every terrorist group's need to conserve resources, it makes more sense for them to attack production facilities, export terminals and refineries directly even though they are likely to have higher levels of security and might well be actively defended. If such attacks succeeded, however, the effect that could be achieved might be extremely serious, depending on the state of the global market.[62]

This is indeed what terrorist groups have tried to do. Multiple attacks were mounted against oil installations in Iraq, including 366 recorded attacks on pipelines between 2003 and 2007 that seriously reduced that country's oil production and pushed back its reconstruction process.[63] In 2002 al-Qaeda reportedly planned to attack the Saudi refinery and loading

---

58   Ed Blanche, 'Terror attacks threaten Gulf's oil routes', *Jane's IR*, vol. 14, no. 12, Dec. 2002, p. 7.

59   Hunt, 'Bleed to bankruptcy', p. 15.

60   *Ibid.*, p. 15. The UAE has made plans to build pipelines and terminals that will enable it to circumvent the Straits in the event of a blockage: Matt Chambers, 'Just in case', *Wall Street Journal*, 27 Aug. 2007.

61   Roger Kubarych, 'How oil shocks affect markets: Consider the five most recent scenarios', *The International Economy Magazine*, Summer 2005.

62   Neal Adams, *Terrorism and Oil*. Tulsa: PennWell, 2003; Adam Porter, 'Global refinery shortage shifts power balance', *BBC News*, 2 Oct. 2005.

63   'Attacks cripple Iraq oil exports', *BBC News*, 15 June 2004; John C.K. Daly, 'The Threat to Iraqi oil', The Jamestown Foundation *Terrorism Monitor*, vol. 2, no. 12, 17 June 2004; 'Insurgent attacks on Iraq's oil sector', *Reuters Foundation AlertNet*, 8 June 2006. Statistic on pipeline attacks from Hunt, 'Bleed to bankruptcy', p. 15.

complex at Ras Tanura.[64] A successful attack on this facility could potentially take out ten per cent of the world's traded energy supply.[65] In 2006 it attacked the huge Saudi export facility at Abqaiq using a combination of suicide car bombers and gunmen in a failed attempt to break through the main gate.[66] The result was a $2 increase in the oil price.[67] Later in 2006, oil facilities in Yemen were struck.[68] In 2007 Saudi Arabian security forces arrested 100 men who had been trained in Iraq and were apparently planning to attack oil facilities in the Kingdom.[69] So far, however, there has only been one attack on a maritime-based facility. In April 2004 a dhow and two other, smaller boats approached the Al-Basra (previously known as Mini al-Bakr) and Khawr al-Amaya oil terminals located about six miles (10 km) off Basra, through which all of Iraq's oil exports pass. An interception boat was sent to investigate the dhow. As it pulled alongside the dhow exploded, killing three US sailors. The two smaller craft then ran towards the terminals at high speed but, unlike the boat that attacked the *Limburg*, exploded before they made contact.[70] Reportedly a fourth boat

64   Blanche, 'Terror attacks threaten Gulf's oil routes', p. 7.

65   Analysts have suggested this might be achieved by using a passenger jet to dive bomb the site. Hunt, 'Bleed to bankruptcy', p. 17.

66   'Al Qaeda says it hit Saudi oil facility', *Aljazeera.net*, 25 Feb. 2006; 'Q&A: Saudi oil attack', *BBC News*, 24 Feb. 2006; 'What if?' *The Economist*, 27 May 2006. Simon Henderson, 'Al-Qaeda attack on Abqaiq: The vulnerability of Saudi oil', the Washington Institute for Near East Policy *PolicyWatch no. 1082*, 28 Feb. 2006 makes the point that Abqaiq has been built with a great deal of redundancy built in and would therefore be difficult to knock out completely. Fighter aircraft are reported to be on quick reaction alert to intercept any attempted aerial attack.

67   Hunt, 'Bleed to bankruptcy', p. 16

68   Chris Heffelfinger, 'Al-Qaeda oil attack thwarted in Yemen', The Jamestown Foundation *Terrorism Focus*, vol. III, no. 37, 26 Sept. 2006, pp. 3-4; 'Qaeda claims Yemen oil attacks, vows more strikes', *Reuters*, 7 Nov. 2006; Dominic Moran, 'Al-Qaida' hits back in Yemen', ISN *Security Watch*, 17 Nov. 2006.

69   Damien McElroy, 'Saudi Arabia arrests over 100 terror suspects', *Daily Telegraph*, 29 Nov. 2007.

70   Louis Miexler, 'Oil terminal attack costs Iraq $28m', *AP*, 25 April 2004; 'Blasts target Iraqi oil terminals', *BBC News*, 25 April 2004; Philip Sherwell and Colin Freeman, 'Suicide boats close oil port as 42 die in Iraq', *Sunday Telegraph*, 25 April 2004; Josh White and Bradley Graham, 'US to change tactics after Gulf attacks', *The Washington Post*, 27 April 2004; James Glanz, '15 miles offshore, safeguarding Iraq's oil lifeline', *New York Times*, 6 July 2004; Daly, 'The threat to Iraqi oil'.

was involved, which might well have had a command function.[71] The then leader of Al Qaeda in Iraq, Abu Musab al-Zarqawi, claimed responsibility for the incident. Oil prices rose but fell back quickly as they had done after the *Limburg* attack.[72] These facilities are now heavily guarded.[73] It is not, however, inconceivable that further attacks in pursuit of an economic agenda might be mounted in the future because it is known, for example, that Salifist Islamist groups observe and record ship movements in and out of key ports, and monitor the sailing schedules published on company websites.[74]

Ships as mass-casualty targets. This is the category of attack that few people want to talk about. With the major exception of the 2006 RAND study, the literature is remarkably free of references to the possibility.[75] A successful attack on a cruise ship would, however, serve terrorist purposes very well, particularly if the ship itself constituted a prestige target, for example the *Queen Mary 2*.[76] Ever since the *Achille Lauro* incident terrorist watchers have been waiting for such an incident, particularly as around 78 per cent of cruise passengers are from North America.[77] So far none have occurred, although plans for an attack on an Israeli cruise ship in 2005 when it was due to call at the port of Mersin in Turkey were disrupted at an advanced stage.[78]

---

71   'Oil terminal to open after suicide attack', *The Age*, 26 April 2004.

72   'Oil prices rise on fears of attacks on Iraqi resources', *Taipei Times*, 27 April 2004.

73   Jim Garamone, "Ring of steel' encircles Iraqi oil platforms', Armed Forces Information Service *News Article*, 15 July 2006; Jennifer H. Svan, 'Iraq's oil industry: Guarding a nation's future', *Stars and Stripes*, 22 Oct. 2006; Chip Cummins, 'US digs in to guard Iraq oil exports', *Wall Street Journal*, 12 Nov. 2007.

74   Private information.

75   Greenberg, *et al.*, *Maritime Terrorism*, esp. pp. 73-89; 'Security experts say cruise ships a soft target'; *The Houston Chronicle*, 20 Nov. 2001. There is a similar comment in John Mintz, '15 freighters believed to be linked to Al Qaeda', *The Washington Post*, 31 Dec. 2002. Also Chalk, 'Maritime terrorism in the contemporary era', pp. 26-7.

76   See Ben English, *et al.*, 'Al Qaeda targeting ocean liners', *FOX News*, 30 Dec. 2003; also 'Cunard confirms indications of terrorist threat to QM2 but says security is adequate', *Aon Counter-terrorism and Political Risk report*, 8 Jan. 2004.

77   William B. Ebersold, 'Cruise industry in figures', *Business Briefing: Global Cruise 2004*, pp. 15-16.

78   Murad Sezer, 'Terror suspect: 'I was going to attack Israeli ships", *USA Today*, 11 Aug. 2005; 'The ongoing threat to cruise ships', *Stratfor*, 14 Dec. 2005;

Significant numbers of dead, injured and traumatised passengers would be a hugely satisfying outcome for any terrorist organisation, but would be hard to achieve. Cruise ships are well built. They are double-hulled and, although they cannot be subdivided entirely, have a large number of watertight compartments. An attack using multiple small boats equipped with shaped charges might compromise enough subdivisions to cause the ship to take on water but it would be highly unlikely to sink. However, if the intention was simply to create fear and pandemonium then even a single small boat delivering a shaped charge in a manner similar to the *Limburg* assault could be effective. The noise of the explosion would be deafening. A huge amount of heat and smoke would be given off and it is almost inevitable that large numbers of passengers would be injured (and possibly killed) in the resulting panic and during the subsequent evacuation.[79] An attack could also be mounted using a limpet mine (otherwise known as a "parasitic device") and, although Michael Greenberg and his RAND colleagues regard such an attack as unlikely, this is precisely how the *Sanya* was sunk in Beirut in 1973 (see above).[80]

Alternatively, gunfire and rocket-propelled grenades (RPGs) could be directed at the deck, bridge and accommodation, either when the ship was stopped in the water as the result of an IED attack or if it was moving slowly in congested waters. When handled accurately RPGs are undoubtedly capable of smashing though cabin windows and damaging internal fittings, as was demonstrated during the pirate attack on the *Seabourn Spirit*.[81] If passengers or crew were in range they could suffer fragmentation injuries. If explosive or incendiary warheads were used the damage could be even greater.

Cruise ships also offer the opportunity for internal attack, either by bombing, suicide bombing or mass hostage taking. All three would almost certainly depend upon terrorists posing as passengers or infiltrated as crew, or a combination of the two. Attacks would probably be more difficult to execute if the target was a prestige ship. Airport-type screening has been introduced for passengers and crew of such vessels. The vulnerability may remain in the case of less prestigious vessels where the percentage screened

'Al-Qaida suspect says Taliban financed failed plot on Israeli ship', *AP,* 21 Feb. 2006.

79   The potential for injury as the result of normal operations is, apparently, considerable: 'Hundreds injured in cruise ship lurch', *Daily Telegraph,* 20 July 2006.

80   Greenberg, *et al., Maritime Terrorism,* pp. 78 & 87.

81   'I beat pirates with a hose and a sonic cannon', *BBC News,* 17 May 2007.

prior to boarding appears to be considerably less.[82] Since the *Achille Lauro*, cruise ship security has been stepped up in other ways and now includes defensive measures that range from X-ray checks of baggage to hull inspections, although the rigour with which these measures are applied can vary.[83] The verification of crew members' credentials is now common practice, although the service staff that board at tourist destinations are not usually subject to similar checks.[84]

The assumption is that the Mediterranean and the Caribbean would be the most likely venues; the Caribbean especially as it is the largest cruise market where it is certain that the vast majority of passengers will be American and the American media will not have to travel far to record their death and suffering. There is consequently every likelihood that the scenes of distress would be enough to affect the industry as a whole and perhaps even shut it down (or shut parts of it down) at least for a time.[85] Furthermore, if an attack was perpetrated successfully on a major cruise ship carrying large numbers (and Royal Caribbean's *Freedom of the Seas* and Cunard's *Queen Mary 2* can accommodate over 3,000 passengers and 1,000 crew), serious questions would be asked about the prior knowledge of the relevant intelligence services and the coast guard rescue response, which if not well executed could erode confidence in governmental competence in ways similar to the impact the 2004 Madrid train bombings had on the Aznar administration.[86]

82 RAND reports that the figure could be as low as 2 per cent: Greenberg, *et al.*, *Maritime Terrorism*, p. 76. Several cruise lines employ plain-clothes security staff to confront any terrorist attack, including ex-British Army Gurkhas: see Bill Glenton, 'A sea change required on security risks', *Financial Times*, 7 Sept. 2002; also 'I beat pirates with a hose and a sonic cannon'.

83 RAND's research suggests that baggage is not normally checked before it is transferred to customers' cabins. Greenberg, *et al.*, *Maritime Terrorism*, p. 76. See also Don Walsh, 'Tourism and terrorism: A difficult journey ahead for the cruise ship industry', *Sea Power*, Dec. 2002 for a description of the risks confronting the industry together with implemented or suggested counter-measures. Also Glenton, 'A sea change required on security risks', who points out that many merchant vessels carry passengers, too few of whom are checked adequately.

84 Greenberg, *et al.*, *Maritime Terrorism*, p. 76.

85 Murphy, 'Slow alarm', pp. 10-11; Greenberg, *et al.*, *Maritime Terrorism*, pp. 81-5. For specific comments on Caribbean port security see General Accountability Office, 'Port security in the Caribbean Basin', presented to the Cognizant Committee as required by the SAFE Port Act of 2006, 13 April 2007.

86 Conversation with Peter Chalk, July 2007. Also Peter Chalk. *The Maritime Dimension of International Security: Terrorism, Piracy, and Challenges for the United*

Evidence to date, however, indicates that it is extremely difficult to take and *hold* a ship with a large number of passengers and crew on board for any length of time if that is the terrorists' objective. However, although the general assumption is that a significant number of terrorists would be required to overcome resistance and subdue the large number of passengers and crew, this need not be the case. Depending on the configuration of the ship, it might be possible for a small number of terrorists to gain control by commandeering the bridge and isolating vulnerable passenger groups such as children. Nonetheless, more men would be required to control a ship than an aircraft. Time would be against the attacker because the resolution of the crew and passengers would return once the initial shock of capture had passed and on board any ship there are multiple opportunities for disruption and harassment. The crew of the *Santa Maria*, for example, opened taps throughout the ship to reduce the amount of fresh water on board.[87]

On the other hand cruise ships also appear to be vulnerable in another regard. While it might be possible to disable any ship, including a warship, at least temporarily by introducing chemical or biological agents into the food or water supply, cruise ships appear to be especially vulnerable given the number of incidents that occur apparently in the normal course of events.[88]

Ferries offer similar mass casualty opportunities to cruise ships as the *Superferry 14* bombing demonstrated (see above), and possibly better opportunities for mass hostage taking.[89] Although they generally lack the iconic quality of cruise ships this is not the case everywhere: an attack on ferries crossing the English Channel, the ferries operating in the Puget Sound and around Vancouver, in the vicinity of New Orleans and in the New York/New Jersey area all have this status. River cruise boats, such as those operating on the Nile, the Rhine or the Seine through Paris, have similar features.

Ferries, like trains and buses, are open-access forms of transportation. Compromising that access, other than to the most limited extent, would undermine their ability to transport large volumes of passengers and freight efficiently. Their open access, however, makes them vulnerable to terrorist

---

States. Santa Monica: RAND, 2008, p. 37.

87   Dragonette, 'Maritime terrorism: Underway as before?', pp. 166, 167 & 169.

88   For a list of incidents recorded from 2002 onwards see http://www.cruisejunk-ie.com/. Also Greenberg, *et al.*, *Maritime Terrorism*, p. 79.

89   Paul Rothman, 'Passenger ferries could be prime terrorist target', *Access Control & Security Systems*, 1 Oct. 2003 reports that, according to a USCG study, large passenger ferries received the highest risk assessment score amongst 80 maritime terrorist scenarios.

attack by passengers bringing arms or explosives on board or, perhaps more especially, from explosives brought on board in larger quantities by truck or car.[90] Trucks can be screened for explosive content. Regular commercial traffic can be inspected away from the port area and given a security certification to speed them through, which allows attention to be focused on irregular and unknown movements. Screening private car traffic is much more difficult and depends to a much greater extent on profiling and the vigilance of port security staff.[91] Prior intelligence and monitoring the activity of likely perpetrators is, however, paramount. In 2000 the Basque terrorist group ETA tried to place a large car bomb on the Valencia-Ibiza ferry, and in 2001 an apparent plot by the same group to bomb the *Val de Loire* Plymouth to Santander car ferry was disrupted.[92] The intention in 2000, it was reported, was to blow up the ship while it was still in port, while the 2001 attack was apparently intended to provoke a mass evacuation of the ship before the bomb was detonated remotely. A plot by an unspecified group to target a ferry between Algeciras in Spain and Morocco was reportedly detected at an early stage in 2005.[93] Another plan by ETA to attack another ferry, the *Pont Aven,* that also sailed the Plymouth-Santander route, was reported to have been disrupted in 2007.[94]

The consequences of a major explosion on board a ferry once it had left harbour could be catastrophic. Because large, open decks are required to permit the rapid loading and unloading of vehicles, such vessels are not subdivided into water-tight compartments, and if water does penetrate these spaces to a depth of no more than a few inches, they become subject to what is called "free surface effect" whereby even a relatively small volume of water, if it begins to flow from side to side, has the potential to destabilise and thus capsize a ship.[95] This was the cause of the *Herald of*

90 Eric Lipton, 'Trying to keep the nation's ferries safe from terrorists', *New York Times,* 20 March 2005.

91 John Steele, 'The problem of policing ferries', *Daily Telegraph,* 12 July 2007.

92 Emma Daly, 'ETA warns tourists of Spain risk', *International Herald Tribune,* 31 March 2001; Isambard Wilkinson, 'Eta plot to bomb Plymouth ferry foiled in Spain', *Daily Telegraph,* 21 June 2001.

93 Brian Reyes, 'Prisoner accused of Gibraltar ferry terror plot', *Lloyd's List,* 30 March 2005.

94 Edward Owen, 'Eta plot to bomb Plymouth ferry foiled', *Daily Telegraph,* 12 July 2007.

95 On 'free surface effects' see http://en.wikipedia.org/wiki/Free_surface_effect. Under the Stockholm Agreement the car decks of ferries must now be capable of being flooded to a depth of 50 cm (about 20 inches) without the ship capsiz-

Free Enterprise (1987) and *Estonia* (1994) ferry disasters when 193 and 852 people lost their lives respectively.[96]

Ships as weapons. The suggestion that large or medium-sized ships could be used as weapons has gained considerable currency.[97] The idea is a scaling-up of the actual use of civilian airliners as weapons in the 9/11 attacks, and reports that other similar attacks have been contemplated or even planned.[98] The reasoning has been that if two relatively small objects, airliners, could cause so much destruction through a combination of kinetic energy (that is to say the energy generated by an object in motion) and the destructive power of the fuel they carried, then ships which are self-evidently large

---

ing. James Sturcke, 'Herald of sea changes', *The Guardian*, 6 March 2007. For a summary of other risks to ferries see Greenberg, *et al.*, *Maritime Terrorism*, pp. 95-8.

96   On the *Herald of Free Enterprise* see http://en.wikipedia.org/wiki/Herald_of_Free_Enterprise; on the *Estonia* see http://en.wikipedia.org/wiki/MS_Estonia; Langewiesche, *The Outlaw Sea*, pp. 125-95 and Stewart, *The Brutal Seas*, pp. 49-84.

97   See, for example, Blanche, 'Terror attacks threaten Gulf's oil routes', p. 10.

98   For example, the 1994 plan by the Algerian GIA to crash a plane fully laden with fuel into the Eiffel Tower in Paris: for details on this disrupted attack and other examples see Rohan Gunaratna, 'Terror from the sky', *Jane's IR*, Oct. 2001, pp. 6-9; a second example was the plot codenamed 'Oplan Bojinka' driven by the man behind the 1993 World Trade Center attack, Ramzi Yousef, to blow up a number of airliners in mid-air over the Pacific. The Abu Sayyaf Group (ASG) supported this plot. See Maria A Ressa. *Seeds of Terror.* New York: Free Press, 2003, pp. 26-40; Zachary Abuza, *Balik Terrorism: The Return of the Abu Sayyaf,* Carlisle, PA: US Army War College, Strategic Studies Institute, Sept. 2005, pp. 6-7. On the links between the Air France attack and Ramzi Yousef see Evan Kohlmann, 'Missed opportunities: the Dec. 1994 Air France hijacking', *Global Terror Alert*, 2004; see also Paul J. Smith, 'Transnational terrorism and the Al-Qaeda model: Confronting new realities', *Parameters*, Summer 2002, pp. 33-4; Benjamin and Simon, *The Age of Sacred Terror*, pp. 20-6; Simon Reeve, *The New Jackals: Ramzi Yousef, Osama bin Laden and the Future of Terrorism*, London: André Deutsch, 1999, pp. 77-91; Simon Reeve and Giles Foden, 'A new breed of terror', *The Guardian*, 12 Sept. 2001. In 2003 there were intelligence reports that al-Qaeda intended to hijack an aircraft in Eastern Europe and crash it into a terminal at Heathrow Airport and possibly London's Canary Wharf tower; see 'US claims al-Qaeda planned to crash planes in UK', *Daily Telegraph* (expat edn.), 22 June 2006. On a wider front the UK considered the hypothetical scenario of a Soviet civil aircraft being used to deliver an atomic bomb on a suicide mission and the need to shoot it down: Jeremy Black. *The Dotted Red Line: Britain's Defence Policy in the Modern World*, London: The Social Affairs Unit, 2006, p. 70. Not that everyone was convinced: see Julian Borger, 'Hijackers fly into Pentagon? No chance, said top brass', *The Guardian*, 15 April 2004.

objects could, if laden with suitably volatile cargoes, cause commensurately more. Their obvious limitation, of course, is that they can only be usefully detonated in ports or a very limited number of vital waterways.

The use of ships as weapons is nothing new. The most direct method is to sail a ship into a port and blow it up. The picture that is often painted of the potential risk is akin to that of the "hellburners of Antwerp", the fire ships designed by the Italian Giambelli, packed with explosive, which when they blew up during the siege of 1585 famously destroyed almost everything within a half-mile (0.8km) radius.[99] The correlation between aircraft-as-weapon and ship-as-weapon is straightforward and as a result terrorists no longer have strategic surprise. However, provided terrorists could mount any intended operation in secret they would have operational and tactical surprise. Even if the defenders' suspicions are aroused they can still succeed through the judicious use of diversion and deception. A good example is the British raid on Saint-Nazaire in 1942 when the old destroyer HMS *Campbeltown*, loaded with four and a half tons of demolition charge in her bows, was driven into the gates of the dry dock and exploded. As William McRaven explained: "Surprise was achieved through deceptive signalling, and after surprise was lost, time to the target was under five minutes."[100]

Once a terrorist ship is inside a harbour there is almost nothing unprepared defenders can do to prevent an explosion, and two historical examples demonstrate just how devastating the effects can be if the explosive charge is detonated successfully. The first occurred on 6 December 1917 when the French munitions ship *Mont Blanc*, carrying over 2,500 tons of benzol fuel, TNT, picric acid and gun cotton, blew up Halifax harbour. Over 1,600 people were killed immediately. All communications with the city were cut in a subsequent snowstorm. The eventual death toll rose to over 2,000, with perhaps up to 9,000 injured, including between 200 and 600 people who lost their sight.[101] To provide a gruesome comparison, an

99 Garrett Mattingley, *The Defeat of the Spanish Armada*, London: Pimlico, 2000, p. 293; 'Military science in Western Europe in the sixteenth century', ND, p. 27 available at http://www.drizzle.com/~celyn/jherek/16thMilSci.pdf.

100 William H. McRaven, *Spec Ops: Case Studies in Special Operations Warfare, Theory and Practise.* Novato CA: Presidio Press, 1996, pp. 158-9. This raid was, of course, carried out by a large and highly trained military and naval force that had practiced extensively and benefited from a diversionary air raid.

101 Laura M. MacDonald, *Curse of the Narrows*, New York: Walker & Company, 2005, pp. 60-73. Also http://www.collectionscanada.ca/05/0518/05180202/051 8020203_e.html; and Gottschalk and Flanagan, *Jolly Roger with an Uzi*, p. 110.

estimated 2,752 people lost their lives as a result of the 9/11 assaults on the Twin Towers.[102]

The explosion in Texas City in 1947 involved another French vessel, the *Grand Camp*, an ex-Liberty ship. It was preparing to sail with a cargo of 2,300 tons of ammonium nitrate fertiliser bound for Europe.[103] The cause of the explosion has never been positively determined. It may have been a discarded cigarette. It could equally have been the way the ammonium nitrate had been manufactured and packed in paper sacks, which meant that even though the ammonium nitrate was not primed, conditions on board the ship were conducive for spontaneous combustion. Large quantities of ammonium nitrate are known to be unstable if stored incorrectly.

Whatever the cause a fire started on board which could not be extinguished. When a ship is on fire it is standard procedure to tow it out to sea but in this case the plan was implemented too late. An hour after the fire started the cargo exploded with a force that could be heard 150 miles away, shattered windows in Houston 40 miles away and sent a shockwave that was felt 250 miles away in Louisiana. The shockwave engulfed the nearby Monsanto Chemical plant in fire. This spread, via pipelines, to other plants in the surrounding area. A second ship, the *High Flyer*, was also in port, loaded with sulphur and 1,000 tons of ammonium nitrate. Attempts to tow it away failed and later that day it exploded with even greater force. Estimates put the number of dead at over 600, with 3,500 injured and property to the value of $67 million ($6.7 billion at 2007 values) destroyed.[104] Interestingly, a stack of ammonium nitrate on the quayside did not explode, probably because it was loosely packed.

Later, in the shadow of 9/11, it was the report on the *Dewi Madrim* that crystallised fears about the use of large ships as weapons. As recounted in Chapter Three, parallels were drawn between this unverified activity and the use the 9/11 hijackers made of American flight schools but these were always loose at best. Ships are not standardised to anything like the same degree as aircraft; knowledge gained handling one ship is not necessarily

---

102 Phil Hirshkorn, 'New York reduces 9/11death toll by 40', *CNN.com*, 29 Oct. 2003.

103 According to Michael Richardson the ammonium nitrate aboard the *Grand Camp* had been manufactured originally as an explosive and altered subsequently: Richardson, *A Time Bomb for Global Trade*, p. 47.

104 For full accounts of the disaster see 'The Texas City disaster'; Richardson, *A Time Bomb for Global Trade*, p. 47-8 and Gottschalk and Flanagan, *Jolly Roger with an Uzi*, p. 111.

transferable to another.[105] The 9/11 targets were directly accessible in level flight; the pilots did not need to manoeuvre their craft skilfully near an airport. In many cases maritime hijackers would have to manoevre a large ship in the crowded waters of a port to be able to bring their "floating bomb" near enough to a target. Aegis in their report apparently suggested that terrorists could "capture tug boats and tow... (a tanker) into a busy international port...and detonate the ship's contents" an elaborate scenario that appears to be fraught with technical difficulties.[106] Even if terrorists did not hijack ships but used ones they already owned there are simply, from the terrorists' point of view, too many things that can go wrong.[107]

The quantities of ammonium nitrate being traded between the world's ports are certainly sufficient to tempt any terrorist. Unadulterated ammonium nitrate is an agricultural fertiliser. Ammonium nitrate when mixed with a small quantity of explosive such as TNT or Semtex is a military explosive. Timothy McVeigh used just two tons, i.e. 0.1 per cent of the quantity on board the *Grand Camp*, to blow up the Federal office building in Oklahoma City in 1995, although the version he used was probably mixed with nitromethane, a motor racing fuel that is more potent than ANFO (see below).[108] On 22 February 2003 the *Cefalonia* ran aground in the mud off Pittsburg, CA loaded with 27,000 tons of the fertiliser.[109] It was trapped for three days before tugs could pull it free. The lower Mississippi is the world's largest bulk commodity port area. In 1997 almost 400,000 tons of ammonium nitrate floated past the city of New Orleans on its way upriver. Rotterdam also has significant fertiliser traffic passing through its narrow entrance channel.[110] The US and other OECD countries imported 1.6 million tons in 2000, mostly by sea.[111]

---

105   Dragonette, 'Lost at Sea', p. 175.

106   Dragonette, 'Maritime legends', p. 18.

107   With regard to the use of ships that they might own or charter see Richardson, *A Time Bomb for Global Trade*, p. 33. For a long time it was believed that Al Qaeda operated its own 'fleet'. Although there is no doubt that the organisation and its offshoots do have ready access to marine assets when they need them, the idea that it operates its own fleet is now generally discounted. Private information, April and Sept. 2005.

108   'In depth: Toronto bomb plot; ammonium nitrate', *CBC News*, 5 June 2006.

109   Paul Rogers, 'Bay at risk for chemical disaster', *The Mercury News*, 19 Feb. 2004

110   OECD, *Security in Maritime Transport*, p. 12.

111   Richardson, *A Time Bomb for Global Trade*, p. 45

In most of its forms ammonium nitrate is stable and needs to be "primed" with diesel oil to create a mix known as ANFO before it can be detonated. The ratio is approximately 95 per cent ammonium nitrate to 5 per cent fuel oil and a quantity of explosive has to be added to serve as a trigger.[112] If terrorists hijacked an ammonium nitrate carrier its cargo would not, of course, be primed. The 9/11 model suggests that the terrorists' first recourse would be to use the priming agent that is on board already: the ship's own fuel.

In practical terms it is hard to see how this could be done. Large ships use low speed diesel engines, which use two types of fuel. When running at sea they use fuel oil. Fuel oil is a heavy, low volatility, low viscosity, tar-like substance that needs to be heated before it can be used. When ships manoeuvre in harbour they use medium diesel, which is similar to the fuel used in truck motors. Large transoceanic cargo ships will carry about four thousand tons of fuel oil for the voyage and between six hundred and one thousand tons of diesel oil for harbour manoeuvring. Because fuel oil is not easy to pump it is only the diesel on board that could be used to prime an ammonium nitrate cargo and the quantities carried are likely to be insufficient to prime a large amount, particularly as, in practice, the mixture needs to be over-primed in order to guarantee it will explode. Smaller ships below 3,000 GRT use medium-speed diesel engines, which do use diesel oil, and the quantity of ammonium nitrate they could carry would be quite enough to cause a devastating explosion. However, as with large ships, there is no direct connection between the fuel bunkers and the holds and therefore the diesel would need to be pumped from one to the other using hoses. The only hoses that are likely to be carried are for fire fighting. Even if the length of hose was sufficient to stretch from the bunkers to the hold, the bore of fire hoses is small, which would restrict the flow and prolong the transfer time.

An alternative method could be to draw off diesel from a tanker or barge brought alongside prior to the bombing run.[113] This could be done at sea ('bunkering') if the condition were sufficiently calm, otherwise it would

112　OECD, *Security in Maritime Transport,* p. 12; Nic Fleming, 'The cheap and easy recipe for bombs', *Daily Telegraph,* 31 March 2004. According to the European Fertiliser Manufacturers Association, ammonium nitrate can also be 'degraded' by the addition of coal, grain or sawdust as well as oil. See European Fertiliser Manufacturers Association, 'Guidance for sea transport of ammonium nitrate based fertilisers', 2004, p. 6; also 'ANFO' at http://en.wikipedia.org/wiki/ANFO

113　David Fairnie, interview with author.

need to be done in a port, harbour or sheltered bay. Seafarers tend to notice strangers and unusual activity in waters with which they are familiar, particularly if the work is undertaken by men whose appearance is distinctive in some way. If the target was in a country with an adequately funded and alert coast guard then it is likely such activity would be reported and quickly investigated.

To be truly effective, moreover, the primer needs to be distributed thoroughly throughout the fertiliser. Whatever method was used to introduce a primer the mixture would be crude, bearing in mind the large volume of a ship's cargo, unless the terrorists were able to use a crane or digger of some sort. Despite these doubts there is always the risk that, providing the terrorists were able to detonate it, the sheer volume of material might be enough to overcome this problem. Two further points, however, are also worth making. First, ammonium nitrate is anhydrous, so that mixing it on or near water could jeopardise its effectiveness because its explosive potential declines once it becomes wet. Secondly, the agricultural grade is less suitable for making into ANFO than the explosive grade. Given that terrorists dislike risk, and the risk of failure in an attempt to transform fertiliser grade ammonium nitrate into an explosive at sea is high, the likelihood of its use as the explosive contents of a ship bomb is relatively low.[114]

Terrorists could, of course, hijack a ship transporting ready-assembled ANFO. In 2003 the Greek authorities intercepted the freighter *Baltic Sky* that claimed to be en route from Tunisia to Sudan. On board they discovered 750 tons of ammonium nitrate based explosive plus 8,000 detonators.[115] To find such a large quantity on one ship was, in their view, "extremely rare" and, according to the Greek Minister of Shipping (in something of an exaggeration), "tantamount to the power of an atomic bomb".[116]

The Halifax and Texas City explosions were huge. But ports that are large enough to accommodate large ships are themselves large places and

---

114 See Christine Gorman, 'How garden-variety fertilizer becomes killer bombs', *TIME*, vol. 145, no. 18, 1 May 1995, on industrial and amateur mixing methods and the rather sorry results that can obtain when the mixing has been insufficient.

115 ANFO is the commercially manufactured version of the ammonium nitrate/fuel oil mixture. It is widely used because it is more powerful than dynamite yet much more stable. .

116 Jonathan Howland, 'Hazardous seas: Maritime sector vulnerable to devastating terrorist attacks', *JINSA Online*, 1 April 2004, p. 2; 'Greece traces route of seized ship', *CNN.com*, 24 June 2003; Richardson, *A Time Bomb for Global Trade*, pp. 45-6.

hard to destroy. The alternative to ANFO would be conventional explosive. Obtaining it in the quantities necessary is no easy matter. Admittedly, however, terrorists have moved large shipments of explosive by sea in plastic form and as assembled bombs. With Libyan help the Provisional IRA was transporting two tons of Semtex aboard the *Eksund* (out of a total arms delivery of 150 tons) when the French authorities intercepted it in 1987.[117] Prior to 2007 the LTTE had lost at least three ships, the *Yahata,* the *Ahat* and the *Comex-Joux 3,* to explosions, the first two self-detonated to avoid capture and the third destroyed by Sri Lankan aerial attack, but most are assumed to have got through.[118] Michael Richardson, for example, names the *Swene,* which successfully delivered sixty tons of TNT and RDX in 1994 and the *Stillus Limassol* that landed 32,400 mortar bombs in 1997.[119]

That said, blowing up people and things is only one option. Gassing people is another. Although terrorists groups have shown an interest in acquiring or making their own chemical agents none, with the exception of the Aum Shinrikyo group which attempted to release poison gas on the Tokyo subway in 1995, have pressed this interest to the point of production.[120] The assumption therefore must be that terrorists are more likely to look for commercially available chemicals that are toxic and flammable and transported regularly in large quantities, such as Vinyl Chloride Monomer (VCM), Methyl Chloride, Ammonia and Propylene Oxide. In 1995, for example, a tanker loaded with about 18,000 tons of pressurised anhydrous ammonia lost control of its steering and came close to crashing into the Golden Gate Bridge. If the tanks had ruptured, thousands of people could potentially have been poisoned.[121]

117   Peter Foster, 'Arms seized as terrorists are set free', *Daily Telegraph,* 29 July 2000; Stewart, *The Brutal Seas,* p. 322.

118   Davis, 'Tiger international'.

119   Richardson, *A Time Bomb for Global Trade,* p. 26. See also G.H. Peiris, 'Secessionist war and terrorism in Sri Lanka: Transnational impulses' in A.P.S. Gill and Ajai Sahni, *The Global Threat of Terror: Ideological, Material and Political Linkages,* New Delhi: Bulwark Books for The Institute of Conflict Management, 2002, pp. 111-12 and Raymond Bonner, 'Tamil guerrillas in Sri Lanka: Deadly and armed to the teeth', *New York Times,* 7 March 1998.

120   For a discussion of Aum Shinrikyo and the responses to its use of poison gas see, for example, Hoffman, *Inside Terrorism,* pp. 121-4; Mark Juergensmeyer, *Terror in the Mind of God* (3rd edn.), Berkeley and London: University of California Press, 2003, pp. 103-18; Walter Lacqueur, *No End To War: Terrorism in the Twenty-First Century,* New York and London: Continuum, 2003, pp. 144-5.

121   Rogers, 'Bay at risk for chemical disaster'.

A true parallel with 9/11, however, would be to exploit the destructive potential of a ship's cargo without augmentation.[122] In this scenario oil and gas are painted as presenting the most serious risk. The destructive power of both is obvious. Despite this their weapon potential is open to some doubt. The primary problem is how to get them to explode or ignite or, more particularly, how to get them to explode or ignite on demand.

Crude oil is not like gunpowder. The oil on the *Torrey Canyon*, for example, that ran aground off the Cornish coast in 1967, only burned once it had been subject to massive air attack, including the use of napalm.[123] Refined oil is less difficult to ignite—particularly gasoline, kerosene and, obviously, aviation spirit—but is usually transported in smaller quantities.[124] Crude oil vapour, which is often vented during a voyage and is present in empty tanks, presents a greater danger. Therefore, rather than tankers "in load" it can be empty tankers that represent a risk if they are not rendered safe ("inerted") correctly, or tankers with some tanks full and others empty, as was the case with the *Limburg*.[125] However, even if the cargo or the va-

---

122   It is noteworthy that amongst the information taken from Muhammed Naeem Noor Khan's computer was that Al Qaeda had indeed investigated whether an oil tanker could be used as a weapon: Peter Foster, 'Secret arrest yielded 'treasure trove'', *Daily Telegraph*, 3 Aug. 2004.

123   '1967: Bombs rain down on *Torrey Canyon*', *BBC News* On This Day, 29 March 1967. According to the report the RAF and RN dropped 62,000 lbs of bombs, 5,200 gallons of petrol, 11 rockets and large quantities of napalm. Despite the huge fire and tower of smoke this caused, which could be seen 100 miles away, the ship refused to sink.

124   The accidental explosion at the Buncefield oil depot north of London in 2005 demonstrated the explosive and destructive potential of refined oil products. The depot was reported to be storing 7.7 million gallons of refined petrol, paraffin and, possibly, aviation fuel (compared to a total capacity of 16 million gallons), a portion of which was ignited. However, although the explosion was heard 100 miles away and resulted in a fire that was described as the 'possibly the biggest incident of its type in Europe since 1945', only two people were seriously injured. See, for example, Sally Pook, 'It's like a vision of doomsday', *Daily Telegraph*, 12 Dec. 2005 and 'Clues destroyed as inferno rages', *BBC News*, 12 Dec. 2005.

125   When crude oil is discharged from a tank volatile gasses remain. A spark can ignite these and set off an explosion. To prevent this happening tanks are rendered inert by pumping exhaust gases—which consist mainly of carbon dioxide—from the ship's engines into the empty spaces. On the relevance of this to the *Limburg* see Rupert Herbert-Burns, 'Terrorism in the early 21st century maritime domain' in Joshua Ho and Catherine Zara Raymond, *The Best of Times, The Worst of Times: Maritime Security in the Asia-Pacific*, Singapore: World Scientific Publishing/IDSS, 2005, p. 165.

pour does ignite, the tanker's hull is likely to contain the lateral force of any explosion, thus forcing most of the destructive energy skywards.[126]

Liquefied Natural Gas (LNG)[127] is largely methane with smaller fractions of ethane and propane that has been cooled to minus 163 degrees Celsius (minus 260 degrees Fahrenheit) to form an odourless, non-toxic liquid. Cooling the gas reduces it to 1/600 of its volume which makes it economical to transport over distances in excess of 3,000 kilometres (around 1,800 miles) and practical to move by sea. When it has been returned to its gaseous state it is supplied to industrial and residential customers as "natural gas". It is valued because it burns with a high radiant heat and, depending on the methane content, little smoke. It can be dangerous.

Concerns have risen because of the dramatic increase, both actual and planned, in the volume of LNG traded internationally and the consequent increase in the number of LNG tankers plying the world's sea routes.[128] In 2003 there were approximately 1,153 LNG and LPG tankers in the world's fleet (compared with over 16,000 oil tankers of a similar capacity).[129] Of these, 151 were LNG tankers.[130] On the basis of figures available in 2006, it took 34 years for the world's fleet to reach 100 ships; the next 100 were built over eight years; the expectation was that the two years following would see another 100 more.[131] LNG is safe if handled properly. The ships used to transport it are usually amongst the best built, best run and best maintained in the fleet. There is little danger while the LNG is on the ship. Since 1952 there have been several accidents involving LNG carriers but none have led to LNG ignition.[132] The terminals where the gas is discharged and regasified are usually isolated and all are subject to regulations that stipulate the distance between the complex and human habitation, including the well-known terminal at Everett, near Boston, MA that has

126   Private information, Aug. 2005.

127   This section and the one following are based on Martin N. Murphy, 'Tanker terror: The unfounded fear of liquefied gas ships', *Jane's IR*, vol. 19, no. 12, Dec. 2007, pp. 20-4.

128   'Liquid natural gas terrorism', *Jane's TSM*, 12 Sept. 2007; John McLaughlin, 'LNG is nowhere near as dangerous as people are making it out to be. Perception is the problem', *Lloyd's List*, 8 Feb. 2005.

129   OECD, *Security in Maritime Transport*, p. 12; UK P&I Club Issue 8, 'The carriage of liquefied gasses'.

130   US Energy Information Administration, 'World LNG shipping capacity expanding', 2004.

131   'Gas fleet up 50% in two years', *Fairplay*, 6 July 2006.

132   Richardson, *A Time Bomb for Global Trade*, p. 44.

caught the attention of several commentators,[133] as this is the point on the transportation cycle where the risks are greatest.[134]

LNG does not explode; or, to be precise, the chance that it would explode in an unconfined space is extremely small and could only occur under the most extreme conditions. Methane, the primary component of natural gas, is relatively insensitive to initiation compared to heavier hydrocarbons. Explosive test data show that unless the vapour contains more than to 20 per cent ethane and propane it will not detonate in open air.[135] As LNG is typically purified until it is more than 90 per cent methane, this eventuality is unlikely. If LNG vapour was to explode then, historical experience suggests it would need to be confined and contain the requisite fractions of ethane and propane. Even then the chance of triggering an explosion using an external explosive device is remote.[136]

If LNG is to be used as a weapon a series of steps need to take place, each one of which has to be successful even though each one has a significant chance of failure. The tank containing the LNG has to be breached. Sufficient liquid has to be released to form a pool. This must not be ignited immediately. Instead it needs time to warm and form a cloud that must rise and drift over an area where it could cause damage. Once this cloud hits a suitable ignition source it must be within the flammability range and that range must be maintained consistently through the cloud such that the flame can burn back to the pool, which is the fuel source, where it will form a "pool fire".

It is the science of LNG that makes so many aspects of this possible sort of attack questionable. Once LNG has spilt from a ship's containment vessel it begins to warm. At minus 162 degrees Celsius (minus 259 degrees Fahrenheit) it will begin to return to its gaseous form and mix with air. LNG becomes flammable when the air-fuel mixture is between 5.3 and 14%. If the liquid is released in a quantity large enough not to vaporise immediately it may form a pool of LNG on the surface of the water (al-

133   Stephen Flynn, *The Edge of Disaster*, New York: Random House, 2007, pp. 20, 27-8 & 32-4; Clarke, *Against All Enemies*, p. 15; and James A. Fay, 'Spills and fires from LNG and oil tankers in Boston Harbour', 26 March 2003.

134   There have been 13 serious accidents at LNG plants since 1944. Paul Parfomak, 'Liquefied natural gas (LNG) infrastructure security: Background and issues for congress', *Congressional Research Service*, 16 March 2005, RL32073, p. 11.

135   G.A. Melham, *et al.*, 'Managing LNG risks: Separating the facts from the myths', ioMosaic Corporation *White Paper*, Aug. 2006, p. 4.

136   *Ibid*, pp. 6-7.

though wind and wave action mean that this is not inevitable), and this, if ignited, would form what is known as a "pool fire". Such a fire would emit very high level of radiant heat; estimates of the distance at which burns from a pool fire would occur after 30 seconds' exposure range from 500 metres (500 yards) to 2,000 metres (1.25 miles); the 2004 study by the US Department of Energy's Sandia Laboratories suggests about 1,600 metres (approximately 1 mile) beyond which, it suggests, the public safety impact would in most cases be low.[137] Differing assumptions about the breach size, the number of tanks involved, the volume of the spill, essential LNG fire properties and environmental conditions explain the variations. In the opinion of many experts a pool fire, particularly one over water, is, because of thermal effects, the most serious LNG hazard.[138]

If a pool did form but ignition was avoided at that stage, the gas would warm and rise to form a "plume" that would drift with the wind. Standard procedure would be to evacuate everyone upwind to behind line-of-sight shelter of such a release. If those portions of the "plume" that were within the gas-air flammable range ignited, the expectation is that the fire would burn back from the ignition source to the pool in a manner known as "deflagration", which is a sub-sonic burning movement through the gas cloud (as compared to "detonation", which is a supersonic movement that generates much greater over-pressure). The fire would ignite any readily flammable objects in its path but although the assumption is often made that the gas cloud would drift a considerable distance, it seems more likely that it would encounter an ignition source before it penetrated far into a populated area. LNG vapours are also less dense than air and as they warm will eventually rise and disperse above most ignition sources. Asphyxiation and cryogenic effects from the extremely cold gas cloud might be a risk to workers very close to a release but for everyone else the risk would be very low, lower even than the burn hazard.

A "super-sized" pool fire can be extinguished. However, given that it would only burn so long as there was gas available, and given the high radiant heat, it usually makes sense to let it burn itself out.[139] Moreover, the

---

137   Sandia National Laboratories. 'Guidance on risk analysis and safety implications of a large liquefied natural gas (LNG) spill over water', *Sandia Report*, Dec. 2004 (SAND2004-6258), p. 19 [hereafter referred to as the *Sandia Report*].

138   Parfomak, 'Liquefied natural gas (LNG) infrastructure security', p. 9.

139   It is frequently asserted that LNG fires cannot be extinguished: see for example Fay, 'Spills and fires from LNG and oil tankers in Boston Harbour', p. 2; Jerry

heat emitted has only been measured in relatively small-scale experiments. Small pool fires emit relatively little smoke. The size of the fire envisaged as a result of a tanker breach would mean that sufficient heat would be emitted to vary the heat characteristics observed in small fires. The effect of smoke on heat flux in fires where the pool exceeds 35m (115 feet) in diameter is theoretical and has never been verified in large-scale experiments.[140]

The question of heat transfer also appears to be misunderstood (or misrepresented). It takes time for heat to go from one object to another, depending on a range of factors including distance, thermal conductivity, humidity and density. Hence, while the temperature of a flame may be extremely high, the temperatures of surrounding objects will not rise for some time, if ever. Candles burn at a temperature only slightly less than LNG, yet if one is left burning in a cold church, for example, it will not prevent the worshippers from shivering. It simply does not transfer its heat quickly enough to make a discernable difference to its surroundings and to overcome all the sources of heat loss.

Terrorists are averse to failure and dislike risk. They want to feel sure that if they mount an attack there is a strong likelihood that it will succeed. Depending on the vagaries of a "pool" that would be affected by sea conditions, a gas cloud that would move with the whim of the wind and would probably rise quickly above most human habitation and, if it did not warm sufficiently to rise above that habitation, would probably be ignited before it penetrated it to any depth, would appear to fall into the high risk category. Gas clouds might drift for 20 miles (32km) or more over the sea or over desert but the chance they would do this over a town or city before hitting an ignition source is extremely unlikely.

Releasing the gas is a highly technical undertaking and manoeuvring a large LNG ship would require a crew and tugs; therefore, if terrorists are to succeed in breaching a ship's tank it is likely they will do so with a device that is itself an ignition source, such as an explosive-laden boat.[141] A 2002

Havens, 'Terrorism: Ready to blow?' *Bulletin of the Atomic Scientists,* vol. 59, no. 4, 2003, pp. 16-18; and Flynn, *The Edge of Disaster,* p. 32. This is, however, incorrect.

140 Gordon Milne, Lloyd's Register of Shipping; interviews with author, Dec. 2005 and April 2007; Havens, 'Terrorism: Ready to blow?' There is a powerful case for mounting experiments on a larger scale. Interestingly, one operator has offered to donate a sacrificial ship for just such an experiment, although some cynics have suggested this is merely a way of avoiding disposal costs: 'Explosive proof of gas safety', *Fairplay,* 25 May 2006.

141 Davis, 'Piracy and terrorism should not be conflated'.

report by Lloyd's Register of Shipping examined the possible outcomes of a missile or small boat attack on an LNG tanker at the Everett terminal. It concluded that under certain circumstances it was possible a loss of containment could occur as a result of shock action, and that this loss could present a hazard.[142] However, it went on to say that any resulting fire would be less serious than that which could result from a petrol or LPG release.[143] The reason for this is that a missile or bomb would ignite the escaping gas immediately it passed through the breach or, at worst, in close proximity to the ship, and no "plume", or "long distance delayed ignition flammable cloud", would form.[144] It is also possible that the fire would be confined to the contents of one tank and not engulf the whole ship.[145] It has been suggested that cryogenic damage could result in the cascading failure of adjacent tanks.[146] This is possible but whether or not the resulting effects would be significantly worse than a single tank fire is open to doubt. The fire would burn longer but it would not burn any hotter.

Other studies have not concurred with this assessment and uncertainty will characterise this debate until large-scale tests are undertaken.[147] For that reason, LNG ships are at present only allowed into ports under strict supervision and are under close guard whilst they are there, even though the *Sandia Report* concluded that risks from accidental spills are small and the risks from intentional acts can be contained.[148] On the balance of prob-

---

142 E. Waryas (Lloyd's Register America, Inc.), 'Major disaster planning: Understanding and managing your risk', paper presented to the Fourth National Harbor Safety Committee Conference, Galveston, TX, 4 March 2002, pp. 11 & 24.

143 *Ibid.,* p. 12.

144 Gordon Milne, interviews with author, Dec. 2005 and April 2007; Parfomak, 'Liquefied natural gas (LNG) infrastructure security', p. 9; Havens, 'Terrorism: Ready to blow?'

145 Gordon Milne, interviews with author, Dec. 2005 and April 2007. On the possibility of cascading failure see *Sandia Report,* p. 15; Ben Raines and Bill Finch, 'Study talks about possible LNG disaster as result of accident', 12 July 2003.

146 Ben Raines and Bill Finch, 'LNG study: explosions possible', *Mobile Register,* 7 Dec. 2003.

147 Parfomak, 'Liquefied natural gas (LNG) infrastructure security', p. 12; Ben Raines and Bill Finch, 'Holes in LNG study', *Mobile Register,* 4 Dec. 2003..

148 On the security arrangements see Parfomak, 'Liquefied natural gas (LNG) infrastructure security', pp. 13-19; *Sandia Report,* p. 14. Immediately following 9/11 the USCG prevented an LNG ship from entering Boston harbour. No reason was given apart from heightened security. See 'LNG Matthew banned from Boston', *MarineLog.com,* 27 Sept. 2001; Stephen E. Flynn, 'The unguarded homeland' in James F. Hoge, Jr. and Gideon Rose, *How Did This Happen?*

abilities, therefore, while LNG presents an accident risk, that quality alone does not make it an obvious terrorist weapon.

Liquefied Petroleum Gas (LPG), because it detonates with an associated damaging pressure wave, has somewhat greater potential as a weapon. It is a hydrocarbon gas which can be predominantly propane or predominantly butane or a mixture of both. If liquefaction is undertaken at atmospheric pressure it must be reduced to minus 42 degrees Centigrade (minus 44 degrees Fahrenheit), but it can also be stored in liquid form under pressure of about eight atmospheres without the necessity of cooling.[149]

Very few risk studies have been carried out on LPG, certainly on large-scale events. Most of the data has been extrapolated from LNG studies.[150] Because LPG can be transported under pressurised rather than refrigerated conditions, which can be the case with LPG ships, then if a shipboard tank containing the liquid under pressure were to be breached, it would vaporise very rapidly. Such a sudden drop in pressure can cause the liquid to boil, which releases vapour. This, in turn, triggers a greater wave of overpressure which may cause the vessel to fragment. As with any terrorist attack, however, an ignition source is likely to be present and therefore, as LPG is flammable, the rapidly-expanding gas would form a fireball in which a blast wave would pass through the burning gas. The consequences of such explosions can be extremely serious.

However, this outcome is not guaranteed. For example, on 12 October 1984 the fully laden Panamanian-registered LPG carrier the *Gaz Fountain*, which was similar in construction to an LNG carrier, was struck by

---

Terrorism and the New War, Oxford: PublicAffairs, 2001, p. 185; Clarke, *Against All Enemies*, p. 15. The publication of the *Sandia Report* has not dissuaded port authorities and many opinion formers, particularly those that might be affected by the construction of new LNG terminals, from being extremely nervous of LNG operations. Husick and Gale, for example, posit a scenario that they suggest could circumvent current port security precautions: Lawrence A. Husick and Stephen Gale, 'Planning a Sea-borne Terrorist Attack', *Foreign Policy Research Institute*, 21 March 2005; while Richard A. Clarke reviewed a variety of terrorist attack methods: Richard A. Clarke, 'LNG Facilities in Urban Areas: A Security Risk Management Analysis for Attorney-General Patrick Lynch, Rhode Island', Good Harbor Consulting, May 2005, Ref: GHC-RI-0505A. Clarke, who has built up a well-paid consultancy practice that advises on the dangers of LNG shipments, has been accused of exaggerating the risks: 'Well-paid fear-mongering', *The Providence Journal*, 26 Nov. 2006.

149   James A. Fay, 'Risks of LNG and LPG', *Annual Review Energy*, vol. 5, 1980, p. 91.

150   *Op. cit.*, pp. 92 & 101.

three armour-piercing Maverick missiles launched from an Iranian aircraft, after loading 20,000 tons of pressurised butane and propane at Ras Tanura.[151] Two of the missiles exploded on or above the deck, causing little damage, but the third penetrated the deck creating a six-metre square (65 square feet) hole in a butane tank.[152] The attack occurred outside the port. Although the containment system was breached, fire-fighting vessels were able to extinguish the huge jet fires and save the ship and most of the cargo.[153] Arguably, however, the consequences could have been much more serious if the missile had penetrated the side of the vessel, rather than the roof of a tank, as LPG could have spilled onto the water causing a pool fire.[154] In 1986 AS-12 missiles struck the Panamanian-registered *Leegas*. Her rear tank exploded, causing a major fire, which wrote off the vessel.[155] There have been six other incidents in which LPG carriers have been fired on by 4.5 inch shells or RPGs. In each case the damage was minor.[156]

What is probably the most serious incident on record took place in November 1974 when the *Yuyo Maru 10*, a combination LPG/oil products tanker loaded with butane and propane in the fully refrigerated tanks and naphtha in the wing tanks, collided with a bulk carrier in Tokyo Bay. Naphtha spilled from a 24 metre (80 foot) gash that extended below the water line. The naphtha ignited immediately and enveloped most of both vessels; as a consequence, 34 crew members from both vessels died. LPG vented from the safety valves and burned continuously. The fire spread to the other Naphtha tanks. Yet although this fire could not be contained no rupture or explosion of the LPG tanks took place, despite the collision damage, and the fierce and continuous burning continued until the ship was sunk using naval gunfire and torpedoes.[157]

151   Martin S. Navias and E.R. Hooton, *Tanker Wars: The Assault on Merchant Shipping during the Iran-Iraq Crisis, 1980-1988*, London: I.B. Tauris, 1996, p. 84; Anthony H. Cordesman and Abraham Wagner, 'The tanker war and the lessons of Naval Conflict', CSIS *Working Paper*, 26 Sept. 1993, p. 8.

152   Parfomak, 'Liquefied natural gas (LNG) infrastructure security', p. 13.

153   Society of International Gas Tanker & Terminal Operators (SIGTTO), 'Safe havens for disabled gas carriers' (3rd edn.), 2003, p. 12. No LNG tankers were hit during the Iran-Iraq 'Tanker War'. This incident might be the one that OECD and Michael Richardson refer to as an LNG attack. OECD *Security in Maritime Transport*, p. 12; Richardson, *A Time Bomb for Global Trade*, p. 43.

154   Parfomak, 'Liquefied natural gas (LNG) infrastructure security', p. 13.

155   Navias and Hooton, *Tanker Wars*, p. 144 plus private information.

156   Private information, July 2006.

157   SIGTTO, 'Safe havens for disabled gas carriers', pp. 9-10.

The assumption that underlies all the examples examined above is that, as in 9/11, terrorists will hijack or otherwise take over the vessel they need for their mission. There is an alternative: they could buy or charter a ship that was involved in the trade regularly and wait for an appropriate cargo, or buy or charter a ship and buy the cargo they want. They could put their own crew on board and, if they could find a discreet location, could possibly take whatever time they needed to make their preparations. With ammonium nitrate they could use a simple post-hole auger to drill holes at intervals in the cargo, which they could then fill with diesel oil. They could use the auger or a digger for additional mixing. If a volatile gas carrier was used it could be brought into a terminal area where the valves could be opened to release the gas (although this is a complex operation in itself). Providing the wind was blowing in the right direction it might be possible to site a detonation source ashore at the optimum height to ignite the gas cloud as it passed over the target.

There are three major problems with the buy or charter scenario. First, terrorist organisations are frugal and conscious of costs. The attacks on 9/11 are generally believed to have cost around $300,000, perhaps $500,000 at most; the attack on the USS *Cole* and the Madrid bombings both cost around $50,000; the 7/7 attacks on London are estimated to have cost no more that $1,000; while the *Superferry 14* attack possibly cost no more than $400.[158] Any ship would need to be in good condition to avoid arousing suspicion. LNG carriers are hugely expensive, and even the smaller LPG ships or bulk carriers cost between $6 and $30 million. None of this, of course, might be an obstacle to a state or a state-sponsored terrorist organisation.

Secondly, even if a ship could be chartered for less money, the organisation would still need to find a master and a trained crew. This requirement is particularly pressing if the aim is to use a gas carrier, as releasing the gas is a specialist undertaking. If they were sufficiently determined, however, there is no reason why a terrorist group could not acquire or develop the necessary skills and infiltrate a sufficient number of its members into a legitimate crew.[159] It would probably take ten years or more, but it is still

---

158   'Al-Qaeda operations are rather cheap', *The Economist*, 10 April 2003, p. 45; Michael Buchanan, 'London bombings cost just hundreds', *BBC News*, 3 Jan. 2006; *Superferry 14* estimate by Peter Chalk, conversation with author July 2007.

159   Donna J. Nincic, 'The challenge of maritime terrorism: Threat identification, WMD and regime response', *The Journal of Strategic Studies*, vol. 28, no. 4, Aug. 2006, pp. 629-30.

likely to be easier to train a suicide bomber to be a Master than it would be to persuade a Master to be a suicide bomber.[160] Finally, there is the problem of carrying off the deception throughout the period of cargo loading, departure, the voyage and arrival at the target port. However dedicated they were the crew would have to perform all the normal tasks of ship handling without any apparent perturbation for many days, possibly weeks. The 9/11 hijackers only had to keep their nerve for an hour or so. The number of people involved and the timescale of the operation would probably make detection by intelligence agencies hard to avoid. For these reasons, the buy and even charter options are unlikely to be exercised, particularly in the case of oil or gas carriers.

Other ways in which large ships could be used as weapons have also been suggested. First, for example, an oil tanker could be run aground deliberately to cause oil pollution serious enough to close ports or even critical chokepoints such as the Straits of Malacca or Hormuz, although is it unclear how such action would serve known terrorist objectives.[161] Its disruptive potential is also questionable: during the first Gulf War, Iraq discharged between 834,000 and 1,500,000 tonnes of crude oil into the northern Persian Gulf without achieving noticeable military or strategic effect. Tanker spills are much smaller: the *Amoco Cadiz*, for example, released 223,000 tonnes, the *Exxon Valdez* 37,000 tonnes.[162] Metrological and hydrographical factors obviously mean that different types of oil spilled in different quantities in different places have different effects; however, it is unlikely that terrorists could *block* a chokepoint using pollution alone, although they could cause some temporary disruption, forcing vessels to

---

160   Conning a large ship is not a task that can be learned quickly (nor can it be accomplished without a skilled crew). However, in his address to the conference on 'Civilian effects of maritime homeland security' held at the University of Hull, 23 Sept. 2004, Howard Goodrick of Farriby Marine pointed out that a seafarer can start as a deckhand and become the Master of a cargo ship in eight years, a span that was, and possibly still is, within Al Qaeda's planning horizon. Qualifying an LNG Master is likely to take longer.

161   Luft and Korin, 'Terrorism goes to sea', p. 66. Authorities in the vicinity of the Malacca Strait continue to issue warnings about the dangers of vessel hijacking and the economic effects of blocking the sea lane: 'Terrorism still a threat in Malacca Strait: KL's police chief', *JoyoNews*, 12 June 2007; 'Terror, piracy still threaten Malacca Strait–Malaysian exec', *Agence France-Presse*, 2 Sept. 2007.

162   See 'Major oil spills' available at http://www.abelard.org/news/archive-oil1-2.htm

divert until the spill has been cleared, and serious damage to fisheries and low-lying coastal regions.[163]

Secondly, a large ship could be used as a blockship, or possibly several large ships could be sunk in a coordinated pattern, to prevent movement through a narrow strait or harbour entrance. There are grounds for believing that this method could be effective and that terrorists have considered using it to attack the Suez Canal, which was blocked by mines and war debris between 1967 and 1975.[164] Manoeuvring a large ship to the optimum location deliberately would demand considerable technical skill, patience and luck (and in most cases would be impossible without the assistance of tugs).[165] Such action could potentially cause severe disruption but, providing the necessary lifting gear is available, wrecks do not necessarily present long-lasting obstacles.[166] In 2004 the Russian-owned, Liberian-flagged tanker *Tropical Brilliance* ran aground in the Suez Canal as a result of steering gear failure. The Canal was blocked for less than two days and the non-maritime press only took notice because the incident was blamed for the shortage of "Playstation 2" units in the run-up to Christmas.[167]

---

163   On the possibility of using ships to commit environmental terrorism see Chalk, *Non-Military Security and Global Order*, p. 27 and, more generally, Elizabeth L. Chalecki, 'A new vigilance: Identifying and reducing the risks of environmental terrorism', *Pacific Institute for Studies in Development, Environment, and Security*, Sept. 2001.

164   Private information, Aug. 2005.

165   Bateman, 'Assessing the threat of maritime terrorism: issues for the Asia-Pacific region', p. 85.

166   Dennis Blair and Kenneth Lieberthal, 'Smooth sailing: the world's shipping lanes are safe', *Foreign Affairs*, vol. 86, no. 3, May/June 2007, p. 11. However, it is worth considering the case of the MV *Tricolor*. This 109m-long Ro-Ro car carrier with a gross deadweight of around 50,000 tonnes was struck in fog in the English Channel in Dec. 2002 by a container ship, the MV *Kariba*. The *Tricolor* sank and came to rest on the Channel bottom but was only partially submerged at low tide. Continuing heavy fog prevented an immediate salvage operation and although other shipping was alerted the wreck was struck the following day by the MV *Nicola*, which was eventually pulled free. To avert any further collisions the French navy positioned a guard ship close to the wreck. Unfortunately this precaution was not enough to prevent the wreck being struck again seventeen days later by the MT *Vicky*, which was also freed. The *Vicky* was loaded with 70,000 gallons of kerosene. The wreck of the *Tricolor* was lifted finally in Aug. 2003. See http://www.cargolaw.com/2003nightmare_tricolor.html; 'Inquiry into Channel collision', *CNN.com*, 2 Jan. 2003 and 'Ship hits submerged cargo vessel', *BBC News*, 1 Jan. 2003.

167   'Russian oil tanker jams Suez Canal', *Mosnews*, 8 Nov. 2004; 'Christmas shortage due to Suez blockage', *I.T.Vibe*, 7 Dec. 2004. A cargo ship that blocked

Finally, large ships could be used as "kinetic" weapons in their own right to be driven into ports or, more likely, other ships in ports with volatile or dangerous cargoes to trigger some destructive event. This would only be feasible in ports without a narrow entrance channel and where the assistance of neither a tug nor a pilot was required (although even a pilot is likely to agree to whatever is suggested if he has a gun to his head). The United States appears to be particularly vulnerable in this regard; for example, parts of the ports of New York/New Jersey, Baltimore, Los Angeles/Long Beach, San Diego, and Seattle where ships heading for the southern berths pass downtown. Big ships, however, are not merely hard to control but require a crew. The logistics of managing anything much bigger than a large motor cruiser are therefore of a different order from hijacking an aircraft. Given the current levels of airport security, ships are undoubtedly easier to board than aircraft; the terrorists' problem is how to direct that control once they have it, and how to disguise the fact that they have it, because as soon as a ship stops behaving normally it will attract attention and, if weapons are available, possibly become a target itself.

The alternative, of course, would be to attack ships using small craft rather than a less manoeuvrable larger ship, either when they are entering a harbour, with the aim of blocking the entrance, or again when vessels are discharging volatile cargoes, quite possibly with the aim of triggering the sort of "chain reaction" that characterised the Texas City disaster. Experience with the *Limburg* has shown that for such an operation to be successful there would almost certainly need to be a coordinated attack using several fast-moving boats in order to deliver the requisite weight of explosive. Interestingly this appears to have been the planning behind the April 2004 attack on the two Iraqi oil terminals off Basra, examined above. The similarities between these attacks and the ones mounted against the USS *Cole* and the *Limburg* indicate that lessons had been learnt and the necessary skills transferred from Yemen to the Gulf.[168] Deception, disguise and diversion, which were so vital in the Saint Nazaire raid, appeared to be important elements here too: there are grounds for believing that the role of the dhow in the Basra attack, which exploded when approached, was to divert

---

the Canal in 2006 was moved within twenty-four hours: 'Suez Canal reopens after blockage', *BBC News*, 9 Feb. 2006; also Chalk, 'Maritime terrorism in the contemporary era', p. 28.

168   David Fairnie, interview with author, 2004. See also 'Al Qaeda statement claims Iraq boat attack', *Aljazeera.com*, 26 April 2004.

the attention of the terminals' defenders, and in that it almost succeeded.[169] In Western harbours these elements could be achieved using the apparently innocent activity of private yachts, speedboats or other pleasure craft to distract attention from, or camouflage the intentions of, an attack boat—a tactic that has been used by the Sea Tigers who have hidden suicide boats amongst fishing boats in order to infiltrate closer to their targets.[170]

The weapons and methods of maritime terrorists

Clearly no one can be sure that Khalid Sheikh Mohammed (KSM), the architect of 9/11, and al-Nashiri, Al Qaeda's so-called maritime "mastermind", would not have found a way of using large ships if they had not been captured. It is known that both considered the use of large ships for attack purposes.[171] When it came to it, however, they used small boats.

Small boats. The reason for the use of small boats is straightforward: terrorists are cautious. While it is true that they are constantly adapting known and trusted tactics to new targets, developing existing weapons and technology and looking at new technology, they are doing so across a relatively narrow range.[172] Terrorists have a surprise advantage but a re-

---

169   David Fairnie, interview with author.

170   On Sea Tiger deception methods see Martin N. Murphy, 'Maritime threat: Tactics and technology of the Sea Tigers', *Jane's IR*, vol. 18, no. 6, June 2006, pp. 7 & 8. On US concerns see 'Coast Guard chief: Attack by small boats still possible', *Philadelphia Inquirer*, 8 July 2004; Caroline Drees and Edgar Ang, 'US at risk from boats packed with explosives', Reuters, 1 June 2006; Eleanor Stables, 'Mines, small boats may pose threat to US ports', *CQ Homeland Security*, 14 May 2007; Eleanor Stables, 'DHS to increase focus on threat poised by small watercraft', *CQ Homeland Security*, 19 June 2007; Breanne Wagner, 'Government lacks clear plans to ID small vessels used as terrorist weapons', *National Defense*, Nov. 2007.

171   *The 9/11 Commission Report*: on KSM see pp. 145-50; on al-Nashiri, pp. 152-3; on KSM's consideration of large ships, private information, Sept. 2005; on al-Nashiri's plans see Richardson, *A Time Bomb for Global Trade*, pp. 18-20.

172   For comments on their tactical conservatism see, for example, Hoffman, *Inside Terrorism*, p. 198; Grant Wardlaw, *Political Terrorism: Theory, Tactics and Counter-measures* (2nd edn.), Cambridge UP, 1989, p. 192; Chalk, 'Maritime terrorism in the contemporary era', p. 21; Peter Chalk, 'Past experience of maritime terrorism', *Jane's IR*, vol. 14, no. 12, Dec. 2002, p. 8; also Paul Wilkinson, 'Technology and terrorism', *Terrorism and Political Violence*, vol. 5, no. 2, Summer 1993, pp. 4-5 who, whilst agreeing that terrorists might be tactically conservative, shows they are prepared to embrace technical innovation. See also Craig Whitlock, 'Homemade, cheap and dangerous: Terror cells favour simple ingredients in building bombs', *Washington Post*, 5 July 2007.

source disadvantage. Instead of interpreting this as an opportunity to exploit the surprise advantage to the limit, they more often view it as a risk that if things go wrong they will miss their chance. Consequently, they prefer adaptation or incremental adjustment to revolutionary change. This rule applied to the 9/11 attacks. Aircraft hijacking was a proven terrorist procedure. Aircraft as suicide weapons had been thought of by terrorists already and had been demonstrated by Japanese *kamikaze* tactics during the Second World War.

Small boats are terrorists' preferred choice for external attack. They are often fast and if not fast can accelerate rapidly, which is often more important. They are highly manoeuvrable. They can be hard to detect because they sit low in the water and often possess a low or non-existent radar signature. They are inexpensive enough to be used in multiples, so that they can mount attacks from different directions, and are anonymous enough to be hidden amongst other small craft such as fishing vessels or pleasure boats.[173] While most attacks using small boats have been carried out using suicide operatives, craft of this size could be adapted for remote operation in the future.

Some ships, such as the Philippine inter-island ferries, have been attacked using planted bombs; a few, such as the *Sanya*, have been attacked using mines or limpet mines, but the majority of maritime terrorist strikes to date have been carried out using small boats.[174] The USS *Cole* and the French tanker *Limburg* were struck by small boats equipped with IEDs. Al Qaeda's exemplars, the Sea Tiger branch of the Sri Lankan LTTE separatist movement, have used small boats in "swarms" and for the majority of their suicide missions.[175] The attack on the *Cole* was a copy of the Sea Tigers' suicide attacks on the Sri Lankan naval ship *Edithara* in 1990, which was badly damaged, and the surveillance command ship *Abeetha*, hit off Point Pedro

---

173   James Pelkofski, 'Before the storm: Al Qaeda's coming maritime campaign', US Naval Institute *Proceedings*, vol. 131, no. 12, Dec. 2005, p. 22; also Chalk, 'Maritime terrorism in the contemporary era', p. 28.

174   Pelkofski, 'Before the storm', p. 22.

175   Walter Jayawardhana, 'Tamil Tiger leader says Osama bin Laden-led al Qaeda copied terrorist tactics from Liberation Tigers of Tamil Eelam', *Go2lanka. com*, 12 Dec. 2002; see also Rohan Gunaratna, 'Sea Tiger success threatens the spread of copycat tactics', *Jane's IR*, vol. 13, no. 3, March 2001, pp. 12-16. Although largely discounted, other reports have suggested that the links between the LTTE and al-Qaeda might amount to more than emulation. Rashmee Z. Ahmed, 'Osama hand in glove with LTTE', *The Times of India*, 22 Sept. 2001.

in 1991, which sank.[176] The LTTE attacked and sank the SLN offshore patrol vessel the *Sagarawardene* in a similar fashion in 1994.[177] The attack on the Basra oil terminals was attempted using small boats.[178] The planned attacks on NATO warships transiting the Straits of Gibraltar in 2002, as well as the attacks planned in 2003 and 2005 on Israeli cruise ships calling at Turkish ports, were to have been carried out using small boats.[179]

Small boats have disadvantages. Although a small boat appears to be analogous to a car, in fact the number of steps (or "evolutions") needed to prepare a boat for a bomb run are considerably more than are necessary to prepare a car or truck. A discrete preparation area is required. Undertaking the necessary work in a port of harbour would risk discovery. A car might be rigged in a garage but a boat would require more space and would then need to be taken to a slipway or beach to be launched. Suitable sites tend also to be used by smugglers and other criminals and are therefore generally known and watched by the police. Small boats, furthermore, cannot operate in adverse sea-states. They can be disabled or destroyed relatively easily, although this is true only if the requisite weapons and the men with the training to handle them are available. Fast-moving boats, particularly

---

176   Murphy, 'Maritime threat: Tactics and technologies of the Sea Tigers', pp. 7 & 10; V. Suryanarayan, 'Sea Tigers–threat to Indian security', *The Hindu*, 28 July 2004; Gunaratna, 'The threat to the maritime domain: How real is the terrorist threat?' p. 88. On the LTTE's maritime capability generally see Anthony Davis, 'Tamil Tigers seek to rebuild naval force', *Jane's IR*, March 2005, p. 39 and two articles by Rohan Gunaratna: 'The asymmetric threat from maritime terrorism', *Jane's NI*, Oct. 2001, pp. 24-9, and 'Trends in maritime terrorism–the Sri Lankan case', *Lanka Outlook*, Autumn 1998, pp. 27-9.

177   Atul Bharadwaj, 'Maritime aspects of Sri Lankan conflict', *Journal of Indian Ocean Studies*, vol. 8, no. 3, Dec. 2000, p. 242 & 245.

178   Jonathan Howland, 'Counter maritime terror, US thwarts attacks, builds up foreign navies', *JINSA Online*, 17 June 2004; 'Raid disrupts Iraqi oil exports', *BBC News*, 25 April 2004.

179   On Gibraltar see, for example, Daly, 'Al Qaeda and maritime terrorism (Part I)', pp.1- 2; Vijay Sakhuja, 'Casablanca: Al Qaeda's maritime node', Institute of Peace and Conflict Studies, *Article no. 1039*, 21 May 2003; Gunaratna, 'The threat to the maritime domain: How real is the terrorist threat?', p. 86; 'Morocco 'uncovers al-Qaeda plot'', *BBC News*, 11 June 2002; also the reports in the compendium edition of the Gibraltar *Panorama* for w/c 6 June 2002: 'Claim that al-Qaeda team visited Gibraltar' and 'Terror plan in Gibraltar Strait'. On Turkey see, for example, 'Istanbul bombing suspects charged', *BBC News*, 25 Feb. 2004; 'Syrian admits Israeli cruise ship plot in Turkey', *International Herald Tribune*, 12 Aug. 2005; Sezer, 'Terror suspect: 'I was going to attack Israeli ships''; Gunaratna, 'The threat to the maritime domain: How real is the terrorist threat?', pp. 84 & 87; also private information, Aug. 2005.

if they are operating in numbers and approaching from several directions, have proved hard to hit even by trained marksmen. When the Royal Navy deployed to the Gulf in 2003, small boat attacks mounted by Al Qaeda operatives were regarded as the biggest threat they might face.[180] The US Navy subsequently issued a similar warning with a particular emphasis on oil supplies.[181]

From the terrorist perspective, small boats are simple, cheap, easy to handle, fast (or innocently slow) and anonymous enough to be able to mingle inconspicuously with other small marine traffic while at the same time being capable of delivering a useful weight of ordnance. A Rigid-hulled Inflatable Boat (RHIB) or small recreational craft should be capable of delivering the equivalent of a car bomb, between 250 and perhaps as much as 2,200 pounds (0.11 to 1 tonne); a large recreational boat should be able to deliver the equivalent of a truck bomb—6,600 pounds, up to about 27 tons (3 to 25 tonnes), although at the upper range these loads would have a serious effect on a boat's performance; quantities of explosive greater than twenty-seven tones would ordinarily require a small freighter. To provide some comparison, the 7/7 rucksack bombs in London each weighted around 22 pounds (10 kilos); the *Cole* bomb was probably around 500 pounds (227 kilos), while of the two most infamous truck bomb attacks, the bomb used to demolish the Marine Corps barracks in Beirut in 1983 weighed about six tons (5.4 tonnes) and that used in the attack on the Khobar Towers in Dhahran, Saudi Arabia, in 1996 was around 12 tons (10.8 tonnes).

Small boats are also more appropriate to the less "spectacular", less ambitious and more opportunistic attacks that appear to be the method of choice across much of the terrorist spectrum.[182] Large attacks take time to plan and prepare and if mounted in North America, Australia, Singapore or most of Europe run a more significant risk of detection given the higher prevailing alert levels. Western intelligence and police services talk

---

180   'Al Qaeda biggest threat to navy', *BBC News*, 10 March 2003.

181   Stefan Ambrogi, 'US Navy says al Qaeda poses major threat from sea', *Reuters AlertNet*, 3 July 2006.

182   On the change from 'spectacular' attacks to less ambitious targets see, for example, Brian Michael Jenkins and Gregory F. Treverton, 'Misjudging the Jihad: Briefing Osama on all the war's wins and losses', *San Francisco Chronicle*, 13 Nov. 2005; Raphael Perl, 'Trends in terrorism', *Congressional Research Service*, 21 July 2006 (RL33555); Robert Block, 'How terrorists' goals may be melding', *Wall Street Journal*, 6 July 2007.

regularly of disrupted terrorist operations and although the number and scale of those operations is rarely revealed, there is little reason to doubt that possible attacks have been thwarted. In response, terrorist groups have shortened their operational cycle in an attempt to avoid detection.[183] The result has been generally less well-planned, but also less disruptive, attacks. Nonetheless, terrorist groups can be highly adaptable and it cannot be assumed that this situation will continue; in fact, the plots to hijack multiple aircraft after they left London's Heathrow Airport in 2006 and to attack Frankfurt Airport in 2007 both demonstrated that al Qaeda remains intent on mounting "spectacular" operations and, despite the huge international intelligence and police effort that has been assembled against it since 2001, has rebuilt much of the necessary capability.[184]

Small boats also have their limitations. Hitting a target with any accuracy, even one that is stationary, is difficult. It is most unlikely that one small craft could sink a large ship. The attack on the *Limburg*, which involved only one suicide craft that caused serious but not irreparable damage, suggests that the coordinated action of several small boats is required to deliver the requisite weight of ordnance to achieve what the military call a "mission kill", at least on a ship of that size. This is exactly what the Sea Tigers did when they employed a "swarm" of small craft to sink the *Saga-rawardana*, the SLN's largest warship, in 1994.[185] Such attacks require detailed planning and extensive practice. In states with vigilant internal security preparing the boats, launching them undetected, conducting practice runs, manoeuvring them in restricted spaces such as harbours or operating them at sea in other than calm conditions are highly risky and demanding activities. The *Limburg* attack also demonstrated that an explosive charge detonated against the outer hull of a double-hulled vessel would not necessarily breach the inner hull, meaning that the damage caused would not necessarily disable the ship. The suggestion has been made that maritime terrorists could solve this problem by mimicking developments in land attacks whereby one car or truck bomb is used to breach the target's defences,

---

183   Private information, Dec. 2005.

184   Tim Shipman, 'Bin Laden sidelined as al-Qaeda threat revives', *Sunday Telegraph*, 16 Sept. 2007; Con Coughlin, 'Al Qaeda 'as strong today as it was on 9/11", *Daily Telegraph*, 13 Oct. 2007.

185   Murphy, 'Maritime threat: tactics and technologies of the Sea Tigers', p. 10; Gunaratna, 'The asymmetric threat from maritime terrorism', p. 28; Vijay Sakhuja, 'The dynamics of LTTE's commercial maritime infrastructure', Observer Research Foundation *Occasional Paper*, April 2006.

paving the way for a second which drives through the debris before being detonated closer to the target causing the maximum damage.[186] Replicating this tactic at sea, particularly if the target was still moving or able to defend itself, would be extremely difficult. An immediate follow-on attack would run into turbulence and back-wash, a vessel attempting an attack after a short delay would have to take aim at a breach that might already be partially submerged or shrouded by flames and smoke, and one after a longer delay might be observed and destroyed.

Sinking a vessel, however, may not be necessary; disabling it or damaging it sufficiently to capture the media's attention may be all that is required, as the attack on the *Cole* demonstrated. A supertanker drifting in a narrow sea lane with oil pouring from its ruptured tanks might not be enough to close a Strait, waterway or harbour entrance but it might grab the world's headlines, following the precedent set by the *Limburg* (although that attack barely made it to the front pages). The sight of a white cruise ship, its hull blackened by fire, coupled with the eye-witness accounts of the traumatised passengers who heard the massive explosion, might be enough to shut down an industry overwhelmed by the subsequent insurance claims. A large yacht loaded with enough high-performance explosive might be able to damage or temporarily close one of the Panama Canal locks. Exposed and vulnerable beaches, resorts, shopping malls and industrial plants could be assaulted by raiding parties landing from small boats. All of these are more likely scenarios than the use of large ships as weapons.

Naval mines. Small craft equipped with Improvised Explosive Devices (IEDs), a combination that is known as a Water-borne Improvised Explosive Device (WBIED), undoubtedly present currently the most substantial maritime terrorist threat. The more discreet but very effective supplement, or alternative, is the mine. As the US commander of the amphibious task force off Wonsan during the Korean War, Rear Admiral Allen E. Smith, said: "We have lost control of the sea to a nation without a navy, using pre-World War I weapons, laid by vessels utilised at the time of the birth of Christ." It is hard to better this as a description of maritime asymmetric warfare.[187]

---

186   'Group claims attack: Double suicide bombings', *AP,* 25 April 2007.

187   Edward J. Marolda, 'Mine warfare', Naval Historical Center, 26 Aug. 2003. See also Scott C. Truver, 'Mines and underwater IEDs in US Ports and Waterways: Context, threats, challenges and solutions', *NWCR,* Winter 2007, p. 109.

Their efficacy was demonstrated in 1984 when, between 9-10 July and 20 September, some twenty vessels struck anchored mines in two areas of the Red Sea, the first at the southern end close to the Bab el-Mandeb strait and the other at the northern end close to the entrance to the Suez Canal. Further incidents occurred right up until April 1985 when the Panamanian-registered bulk carrier *Mariner II* struck the final mine and sank. As early as August 1984 Islamic Jihad claimed responsibility. Later in the month the Egyptian authorities accused Libya and Iran and later, on the basis of the evidence available, fixed the blame entirely on Libya. It was later proved that Libyan naval personnel had sown the mines from a ship named the *Ghat* (or *Ghada*) which had transited the Suez Canal, sailed down the Red Sea and then returned, taking rather more time than usual to make the voyage.[188]

The most sophisticated modern naval mines are expensive devices.[189] Many of them are considered to be beyond the financial reach and operational capability of any terrorist group that lacks anything less than substantial state sponsorship or support. Nonetheless, as Scott Truver points out, more than 30 countries produce mines and 20 export them. Increasingly "even highly sophisticated weapons are available on the black market, usually on a cash-and-carry basis".[190] Examples include the Italian-made Marta that costs around $15,000, one of which nearly sank the USS *Princeton*, and the Argentine M-80 multiple influence weapon, both of which are sophisticated, affordable and available. Moreover, Underwater Improvised Explosive Devices (UWIED) are easy and cheap to make.[191] In April 2004 a crude device, consisting of explosive packed into plastic tubes wrapped in trash bags to give them buoyancy (and so small that an observer who might have seen it being thrown into the water could well have thought it was a bag of rubbish being thrown away), was discovered floating in Lake Pontchartrain in Louisiana. The intended target might have been the

---

188   For a full review of this episode see Scott C. Truver, 'Mines of August: An international whodunit', US Naval Institute *Proceedings*, vol. 111, no. 5, May 1985, pp. 95-117. Also Truver, 'Mines and underwater IEDs in US ports and waterways', p. 111 and Menefee, *TMV*, p. 44.

189   For a brief summary of their capabilities see Truver, 'Mines and underwater IEDs in US ports and waterways', pp. 108-9.

190   *Ibid.*

191   *Ibid.*

presidential candidate John Kerry, who planned to make a campaign trip on the lake.[192]

However, it is the older naval mine that remains, in many ways, the perfect maritime terrorist weapon. It satisfies the terrorist requirement for the maximum return on investment. These mines can be made even more dangerous than they appear if they have been upgraded internally with more sophisticated technologies which can present particular problems to Explosive Ordnance Disposal (EOD) divers and technicians.[193]

There are four methods of detonation: contact, pressure, acoustic and magnetic (combinations of which can be built into a single device). Possibly the most famous peacetime mining incident occurred in the Corfu Channel in 1946, when two Royal Navy ships struck moored Albanian mines, with the loss of 45 British lives.[194] More recently, the US frigate the *Samuel B. Roberts* struck an Iranian moored contact mine in 1988.[195] The device was designed in Russia when Nicholas II was Tsar and last modernised in 1939. It cost the Iranians about $1,500 and inflicted around $96 million in damage. The presence of mines of the same design, but this time manufactured by Iraq, were enough to "stall the world's greatest Navy in its tracks in February 1991" and dissuade it from undertaking an amphibious assault on the Iraqi forces occupying Kuwait.[196]

A further advantage is that while naval mines can be cheap to manufacture and plant, they are expensive and time-consuming to remove. It is estimated currently that it would take a mine counter-measures (MCM) team about ten days to deploy by air from the United States and become fully operational, and between 30 and 60 days for a seaborne force to do the same. Mines can be planted quickly and surreptitiously in large numbers. Experience has shown that they are extremely effective area denial weapons. Before an MCM team can arrive terrorists can use mines to try and force ships—or a particular ship—into killing zones where they can be

---

192   *Ibid.*, p. 111; Grace V. Jean, 'Improvised explosive devices: Could they threaten US ports?' *National Defense*, Jan. 2008.

193   Scott C. Truver, Correspondence with author, April 2006.

194   International Court of Justice, 'Corfu Channel case (Merits)', Judgement of 9 April 1949.

195   Truver, 'Mines and underwater IEDs in US ports and waterways', p. 119.

196   Thomas R. Bernitt and Sam J. Tangredi, 'Mine warfare and globalization: Low-tech warfare in a high-tech world' in Sam J. Tangredi (ed.), *Globalization and Maritime Power*, Washington DC: National Defence UP, 2002, p. 396; Truver, 'Mines and underwater IEDs in US ports and waterways', p. 119.

attacked more publicly by small boats or stand-off weapons. Partly because of these delays, the US Navy in particular is looking to incorporate a mine-clearing capability on a wider range of ships and eliminate the necessity for a specialised force.[197]

Mines can also impose substantial economic costs. In 1984, for example, just 39 mines laid in three Nicaraguan ports had a significant effect on the Nicaraguan economy. It is conceivable that mines could be deployed surreptitiously from ships visiting American and European ports, a technique the *Ghat* demonstrated to considerable effect, with the intention of inflicting economic damage or to limit naval movements, expeditionary deployments and ferry operations even though[198] the large oil and cargo ships now in service would not necessarily sink. In 1987, for example, a tanker, the *Bridgeton,* struck a mine during the Iran-Iraq "Tanker War";[199] four of its 31 compartments flooded but it did not founder and, because of its bulk, was used to sweep mines for a convoy of other ships, including US Navy surface combatants, as it moved northwards. Insurgents, however, would not need to sink ships. The presence of mines—or even the suspicion that they were there[200]—would force ports to close until they had been cleared.[201] According to Rear Admiral Thomas Atkin, the commander of the US Coast Guard's Deployable Operations Group (DOG), a single World War II-style mine could shut down the oil port of Houston, Texas.[202] In order to deter terrorists from using mines, an MCM force capable of deploying nationally or regionally and equipped with up-to-date

197   See, for example, Melissa Nelson, 'Robots clear waterways of deadly mines', *AP,* 27 July 2007.

198   Stables, 'Mines, small boats may pose threat to US ports'.

199   David B. Crist, 'Joint special operations in support of Earnest Will', *Joint Forces Quarterly,* Autumn/Winter 2001-2, pp. 15-22; Navias and Hooton, *Tanker Wars,* pp. 143-4; Nadia El-Sayed El-Shazly, *The Gulf Tanker War: Iran and Iraq's Maritime Swordplay,* London: Macmillan, 1998, pp. 293-4.

200   The mine crisis of Jan. 1980 on the Sacramento River in California demonstrated that the threat of mines could be sufficient to close down a waterway. A self-styled 'patriotic scuba diver' telephoned a warning that the river had been mined to protest against the sale of wheat to Russia. All river traffic was stopped for four days until the US Navy was able to declare that no mines had been laid and the river was safe for navigation. Truver, 'Mines and underwater IEDs in US ports and waterways', pp. 110-11.

201   *Ibid.,* pp. 107-8.

202   Jean, 'Improvised explosive devices: Could they threaten US ports?'

surveys would need to be kept on stand-by.[203] Experience gained when the port of Umm Qasr in Iraq was cleared in 2003, an operation which took an international force nine days to clear 900 square miles (2,331 sq km), showed that prior knowledge of the river bottom is vital if such a course of action is to be accomplished without having to investigate every item of suspicious debris.[204]

There are, however, three weaknesses with naval mines based on older designs: if planted on the bottom they sink gradually into the mud or silt, sometimes to a depth which can degrade their effectiveness, unlike some modern mines that are designed to be buried in silt and remain operational; they can drift out of position, meaning they do not maintain a persistent threat; and they tend to be indiscriminate although, as the *Samuel B. Roberts* incident illustrated, some sort of discrimination is possible if sea traffic is moving slowly enough for mines to be laid between the passage of one ship and the next. These weaknesses mean that naval minefields generally need to be re-laid regularly, although none of these disadvantages is as great a problem for terrorists as for regular navies. One successful attack on a major target, or simply re-laying on an irregular basis, could achieve the terrorists' aim of inducing fear and insecurity.

Terrorists are unlikely to lay mines in deep water because at depths greater than 300 feet (90 metres) moored mines are largely impracticable and bottom mines largely ineffective. The position would change, however, if terrorists could obtain rising mines: mines that sit on the bottom but release an explosive charge to the surface when activated by sound or pressure changes. If terrorists are restricted to moored or bottom mines they are therefore likely to be seeded in shallower water in the vicinity of ports, harbours and chokepoints of which the southern end of the Malacca Straits, the Singapore Straits and the Phillips Channel are amongst the most vulnerable.[205] They could also be simply cast upon the waters and allowed to

203   On the difficulties that are likely to be encountered in establishing and deploy-
       ing such as force see Michael C. Sparks, 'A critical vulnerability, a valid threat:
       US ports and terrorist mining', Norfolk, VA: Joint Forces Staff College Masters
       Thesis, 2005, pp. 29-30; Truver, 'Mines and underwater IEDs in US ports and
       waterways', pp. 117-23 and Jean, 'Improvised explosive devices: Could they
       threaten US ports?'

204   Sparks, 'A critical vulnerability, a valid threat: US ports and terrorist mining',
       pp. 29-57; Truver, 'Mines and underwater IEDs in US ports and waterways', p.
       121.

205   Peter Lewis Young, 'Mining the Straits of Southeast Asia', *Jane's IR*, Feb. 1996,
       pp. 91-2.

drift, a tactic employed by both the North Vietnamese and the Viet Cong who used mines disguised as garbage and baskets.[206] It is interesting to note the FBI warning about bombs or mines disguised as ordinary flotsam such as old car tyres, a tactic that is also hauntingly reminiscent of the special weapons and booby traps used by both sides in the Second World War but associated especially with Britain's Special Operations Executive (SOE).[207] In the autumn of 2006 a mine disguised as flotsam was found drifting in the northern Gulf off Iraq.[208] The final option for use only in very shallow water—between a depth of about 50 feet (15 metres) and the surf zone—is the remotely controlled mine, the line-of-sight equivalent of the roadside IED. It involves an explosive charge, which is attached to a command wire that stretches back over the beach or riverbank to a hidden operator who triggers it when a suitable target craft is in range. A remotely-controlled IED was used on the Shatt al-Arab waterway in 2006 to kill members of a British patrol.[209]

Despite their advantages, mines do not appear to have attracted widespread interest from terrorist groups. Only the LTTE have utilised them, including a remote control design that they deployed first off the Jaffna peninsula around Kilali in the early 1990s. They have subsequently developed an impressive variety of fairly simple mines, almost all improvised from a range of materials including, in one variant, a domestic rice cooker, in order to pursue what could be better described as an irregular war at sea.[210]

Undersea warfare: swimmers and "human torpedoes". If, in most instances, mines represent the passive form of undersea warfare, the active form can be mounted either by submarines or by swimmers (also referred to as divers or frogmen). The use of swimmers by terrorists came to public attention early in 2003, again perhaps as a result of the interrogation of al-Nashiri or Omar al-Faruq, and resurfaced in 2005 following reports from the Philip-

---

206   Even though floating mines are outlawed by the 1907 Hague Convention.

207   'FBI warns that terrorists may use floating bombs', *Washington Post,* 29 June 2004.

208   Private information, Sept. 2006.

209   Michael Evans, 'Four servicemen killed in Basra river patrol blast', *The Times,* 13 Nov. 2006.

210   Murphy, 'Maritime threat: Tactics and technologies of the Sea Tigers', pp. 9-10; Gunaratna, 'Sea Tiger success threatens the spread of copycat tactics', p. 14 and Peter Chalk, 'Training the Tigers: The strategy of separatist success in Sri Lanka', *Jane's IR,* Jan. 2007, p. 25.

pines.[211] But terrorist groups had used swimmers long before this. In 1976, for example, the Cuban anti-Castro group Omega-7 used a swimmer to attach a limpet mine to a Soviet cargo ship docked at Port Elizabeth, New Jersey.[212] However, as with mine warfare, it was the LTTE Sea Tigers and the anti-Israeli groups that assembled the most comprehensive capacity, the latter benefiting from considerable state support (see below). Menefee suggests, for example, that in 1970 swimmers were used to plant underwater mines during an attack on the Israeli port of Eilat (or Elath).[213]

The LTTE swimmers were equipped at first with regular, open-circuit diving equipment, but a number were killed in 1986 because kit of this type releases air bubbles which rise to the surface, betraying the swimmer's position. As a result the Sea Tigers bought "re-breather" kits enabling swimmers to use recirculated air, which were reported to have been used successfully in an operation to reconnoitre the hull of a berthed SLN vessel in 1993.[214] In 2006 Sea Tiger swimmers were arrested when they came ashore on the western side of Sri Lanka, close to Colombo. The Sri Lankan government claimed they had been attempting to attach limpet mines to Sri Lankan Navy (SLN) vessels.[215] Like Al Qaeda, the Sea Tigers have also shown an interest in acquiring Swimmer Delivery Vehicles (SDVs).[216] Where they have proved more successful is in the development of a semi-submersible "human torpedo" or "suicide scooter". Guided to the target by

211 On the possibility that the information was obtained through interrogation see Mintz, '15 freighters believed to be linked to Al Qaeda'. Omar al-Faruq was variously named as al-Qaeda's chief of operations or chief organiser and liaison in Southeast Asia: 'Officials identify al-Qaida plotters', *Michigan Daily*, 17 Sept. 2002 and Dan Murphy, 'Southeast Asia easy source of Al Qaeda recruits', *Christian Science Monitor*, 9 Oct. 2002.

212 MIPT Incident Profile: Anti-Castro Cubans attacked maritime target, 16 Sept. 1976. Anti-Castro Cuban swimmers could also have planted the explosives that damaged the *Caribbean Venture* in Miami in 1968: MIPT Incident Profile: Anti-Castro Cubans attacked maritime target, 8 Aug. 1968. They may have made a similar attack on a Cuban fishing boat moored in Lima: MIPT Incident Profile: Anti-Castro Cubans attacked maritime target, 22 July 1977. Other reports mention 'bombs' or 'bombings' without specifying their locations.

213 Menefee, *TMV*, p. 32.

214 According to Rohan Gunaratna, the Sea Tigers purchased more 're-breather' kits in 2001. Gunaratna, 'The asymmetric threat from maritime terrorism', p. 25.

215 Peter Apps, 'Sri Lanka, Tigers claim victory in naval clash', *Reuters AlertNet*, 17 June 2006.

216 On Al Qaeda's interest see Mintz, '15 freighters believed to be linked to Al Qaeda'.

a single operative equipped with diving gear who might stay with the craft all the way to the target or drop away prior to detonation, it is designed to deliver an explosive charge of between 25 and 50 kilograms (55 to 110 lbs). They are believed to have been used in several attacks, at least two of which were known to be successful.[217]

In 2003, the CIA Director George Tenet told the US Senate Select Committee on Intelligence that Al Qaeda was "developing or refining new means of attack, including...underwater methods to attack maritime targets", at the same time as the *Los Angeles Times* published a detailed report of suspicious activity at a diving school in Eindhoven in the Netherlands.[218] A local mosque in Eindhoven had acquired something of a reputation for Islamist activism and it was reported that a number of students at the school were Islamist extremists. There were also press reports of a link between the diving students and the Al Qaeda cell in Morocco that had planned attacks on ships passing through the Straits of Gibraltar. Most of the suspicion, however, settled on one instructor in particular who had arrived in the Netherlands some time in 1993 and claimed political asylum. Despite this, he was able to afford expensive lessons and equipment including, midway through 2001, a bulk order for suits and equipment worth $7,000 that was allegedly paid for by a money transfer from India. He also displayed impressive dedication and completed his diving instructor's course in record time. From the late 1990s through to 2001 somewhere between 50 and 150 Muslim men attended courses in Eindhoven, many of them travelling from the Middle East for that express purpose. The alleged chief instructor was never charged with any offence and protested his innocence throughout, including one very public protestation on television, which is not a known Al Qaeda tactic. Dutch police, however, believed his pupils were an Al Qaeda recruitment cell and twelve of them were charged. Because Dutch anti-terrorism laws at the time were weak they were arraigned under offences that ranged from assisting an enemy in wartime to the possession of illegal drugs. All of them were acquitted when the case came to court apart from two who were convicted of possessing fraudulent documents. Some of them left the country and one at least moved to the UK.[219]

217   Murphy, 'Maritime threat: Tactics and technologies of the Sea Tigers', p. 9.

218   'DCI's worldwide threat briefing–The threat in 2003', as prepared for delivery to the US Senate Select Committee on Intelligence, 11 Feb. 2003; Sebastian Rotella, 'Fears persist of al-Qaeda link to dive centre', *LA Times*, 15 Feb. 2003.

219   Mark Hosenball, 'Look out below–The terror threat from the sea', *Newsweek*,

Later, in August 2003, the US Department of Homeland Security issued a bulletin entitled "Swimmer Attack Indicators and Protective Measures" which advised anyone connected to the maritime industry to look out for suspicious activity. Although the DHS made it clear that it had no information relating to a specific threat, it made a number of specific recommendations regarding suspicious behaviour and possible preventive measures and said that the warning was consistent with known Al-Qaeda objectives.[220] A diving manual, for example, was among the possessions recovered from the Afghan home of Al Qaeda's military commander, Mohammed Atef (who was killed in 2001). Other documents also recovered in Afghanistan indicated that Al Qaeda was interested in diving, diving medicine and swimmer technology.[221]

The possibility that terrorists in Southeast Asia might have a scuba capability was first suspected when it was revealed that Ruland Ullah, one of the Abu Sayyaf Group (ASG) members who had kidnapped tourists from the Malaysian resort of Sipadan in 2000, worked there as a diving instructor prior to the attack and admitted subsequently that he had trained other ASG members in scuba techniques.[222] His testimony runs parallel with that of a scuba diving instructor who was kidnapped from a holiday resort in Sabah in 2000, also by the ASG: he claimed, upon his release in 2003, that the group had known he was an instructor and had wanted his expertise in order to mount an underwater attack.[223] These accounts may not be as contradictory as they first appear because the ASG was at that time divided between a number of poorly coordinated gangs. In 2005 there was a further report indicating the ASG's continuing interest in sub-surface attacks,

---

28 March 2005.

220 Charles R. Smith, 'Al Qaeda plans scuba diver, one man submarine attack', *Cyber Diver News Network,* 26 Aug. 2003; also Greg Hardesty, 'US seaports warned to beware of terrorist divers', *Cyber Diver News Network,* 31 Aug. 2003. For access to the DHS advisory bulletin to which these reports refer go to: http://www.esisac.com/publicdocs/Other_Advisories/Swimmer%20Attack%20Indicators%20and%20Protective%20Measures%20IB1.doc

221 Gunaratna, 'The threat to the maritime domain: How real is the terrorist threat?' p. 87.

222 Rommel C. Banlaoi, 'The Abu Sayyaf group: Threat of maritime piracy and terrorism' in Lehr, *Violence at Sea,* p. 128. According to Anthony Davis, Ullah escaped in June 2002 during a firefight between the ASG and Philippine Marines. Anthony Davis, 'Resilient Abu Sayyaf resists military pressure', *Jane's IR,* 1 Sept. 2003.

223 'Peril on the sea'; 'Sipidan instructor to testify against Abu Sayyaf–linked rebels', *Cyber Diver News Network,* 24 Sept. 2004.

this time in cooperation with the Indonesian-based Jemaah Islamiyah (JI) group. A group that included an operative who was already suspected of involvement in a bus bombing early in 2005, was sent for scuba training in Palawan province in preparation for a JI-planned attack either somewhere outside the Philippines or alternatively against oil and gas pipelines off the coast of Mindanao.[224] Other incidents in the region include a report from Indonesia that the Al Qaeda operative Omar al-Faruq had told interrogators in 2002 that he had planned attacks on US warships while on a port visit.[225] In 2003 the owner of a diving school in Malaysia reported that a group of ethnic Malays had asked for diving instruction but had appeared to lack any interest in learning how to resurface.[226] Just how reliable these reports are, particularly the Malaysian report, Baharan's statement and some others from the Philippines, is however open to some doubt.[227]

These attempts might sound amateurish but underwater threats need to be treated with respect. Skilled and highly-trained swimmers, those that have completed special forces training, are highly capable as wartime experience has demonstrated. Although no evidence has emerged to indicate that any terrorist group has swimmers who have attained this level of proficiency, it has been reported that Palestinian swimmers were trained by Yugoslavia (see below) and LTTE swimmers by Norwegian mercenaries over a number of months on an island in the Andaman Sea.[228] Hizbollah is also said to have a swimmer unit, the capability of which is unknown.

Swimmers who are selected for suicide missions appear to receive only the most rudimentary scuba training. Compared with almost any other diver— naval, commercial or recreational—they would be regarded as novices on this basis. While a suicide swimmer is likely to be unconcerned about the problem of the "bends", there are other problems that could critically affect his mission and which can be overcome only through skilled training, regu-

224 Jim Gomez, 'Terrorists push scuba training, guerrilla says', *The San Diego Union-Tribune*, 18 March 2005. On the possibility that oil and gas pipelines were the targets see Michael Greenberg, *et al.*, *Maritime Terrorism*, p. 13.

225 Mintz, '15 freighters believed to be linked to Al Qaeda'; Vijay Sakhuja, 'Terrorist's underwater strategy', Institute of Peace and Conflict Studies, *Article no. 1679*, 22 March 2005.

226 'Peril on the sea'; Mansoor Ijaz, 'The maritime threat from al-Qaeda', *Financial Times*, 19 Oct. 2003.

227 Chalk, 'Maritime terrorism in the contemporary era', p. 37.

228 Davis, 'Tiger International'; Bharadwaj, 'Maritime aspects of Sri Lankan conflict', p. 246.

lar practice and familiarity with high quality equipment. The most serious is oxygen toxicity, or hyperoxia, brought on by breathing compressed air. Without proper monitoring, attacks can occur without warning and result in death if, as usually happens, the swimmer is unable to retain the mouthpiece of the regulator. The second is depth restriction: the very maximum a novice swimmer can descend to safely is 130 feet (40 metres). There is, furthermore, a linear relationship between depth and duration; the deeper the dive the shorter the swimmer can remained submerged. Admittedly, however, zeal can overcome a great deal and if a swimmer has no intention of returning it might be possible to exceed these limits.

Swimmers are also slow: even the fittest diver using the most sophisticated fins cannot exceed two and a half miles per hour (4kph), while tides and currents could slow this to zero or even push them backwards. Moreover, speed under water cannot be increased by superior fitness alone; it requires the proper application of technique, something that is not acquired easily. Speed will also decrease with distance. The 5,000 metres is regarded as the swimming equivalent of the Marathon. On the rare occasions it is attempted it is swum unencumbered by "skin" swimmers in a pool. Attack or suicide swimmers would be carrying loads. They would also certainly need to wear suits, a wet suit in the tropics and a dry suit everywhere else. Both types would have a serious "drag" effect. With these factors in mind, the maximum practical distance between a target and a launch point is unlikely to be more than two kilometres (1.25 miles).[229]

However, even extreme physical fitness would only be useful if the swimmer could find the target: disorientation is a common problem. To navigate from a start point to a target depends on the ability to master vector geometry, compass variation, tidal flow and currents. Novice divers are, for the most part, incapable of navigating successfully without experienced support. Outside the tropics, sea water is usually cold and dark even at short distances from the shore. The environment in ports is not only dark but turbulent and extremely noisy, which adds significantly to the disorientation problem. The owner of the Eindhoven diving school where several men trained with colleagues to simulate a clandestine approach to a ship in Rotterdam harbour reported that the dark waters and the deafening noise made it difficult for even experienced divers to find what they were look-

---

229   However, it is worth noting that in May 1992 PLF swimmers reportedly swum about 2.7 nautical miles (5 km) from a departure point in Jordan to Eilat pulling water-proof containers or rafts. The reports do not indicate how long they took. Lorenz, 'The threat of maritime terrorism to Israel', p. 16. (See below)

ing for. In his view, a comparative amateur strapped with heavy explosives, probably battling stress and fear, would quickly get into trouble.[230]

Many of these problems could be overcome with mechanical assistance. The range and load-carrying capacity of swimmers could be increased by the use of Swimmer Delivery Vehicles (SDVs). The simplest are a type of tug or sledge that pulls the swimmer along. They do not, however, solve the problems of navigation or disorientation. The most sophisticated versions, used by military units such as the US Navy SEALS and the British Special Boat Squadron (SBS), are fully or partially enclosed and can carry small groups of swimmers up to about 50 miles (80 km). They are not submarines; the swimmers depend on their own air supply and are therefore constricted by the same physical limitations regarding depth and air use. Like all diving equipment they require extensive and specialised training if they are to be used effectively and safely. In 2005 a very experienced SBS officer, Lieutenant-Colonel Richard van der Horst, was killed during a training exercise off Norway while exiting such a vehicle.[231]

The US has taken the swimmer threat to homeland targets seriously. In 2005 the US Coast Guard launched a programme to train the members of its law enforcement teams based in 13 ports around the US in how to deal with swimmer threats.[232] The teams were reportedly trained to use shore-based sonar for general surveillance and boat-based imaging sonar to investigate suspicious returns, and practiced using nets and other "non-lethal" means to incapacitate and capture their targets.[233] In 2007 the FBI issued an advisory notice asking diving instructors to be on the alert for requests for specialised training that might indicate "nefarious activity".[234]

Undersea warfare: submarines and submersibles. A submarine would present the greater threat to shipping. The current assessment, however, is that the technical and operational demands of submarine operations are too great

230 Rotella, 'Fears persist of al-Qaeda link to dive centre'.

231 'SBS commander killed in accident', *BBC News*, 16 March 2005; Michael Smith, 'SBS commander killed on assault exercise', *Daily Telegraph*, 16 March 2005; and Sean Rayment, 'SBS commander's widow to sue MOD over diving death', *Daily Telegraph*, 27 Nov. 2005.

232 Hosenball, 'Look out below'.

233 Eric Lipton, 'Coast Guard turns its eyes underwater', *New York Times*, 2 Feb. 2005.

234 'FBI issues scuba industry alert over requests for specialized training, 'nefarious activity", *UnderwaterTimes.com*, 22 June 2007; 'Scuba warning issued for instructors', *AP*, 27 June 2007; also Mimi Hall, 'Uncle Sam to scuba divers: I want you', *USA Today*, 9 July 2007.

for the majority of states and beyond the capabilities of all known non-state actors unless they received substantial assistance from a state with a submarine service.

This does not mean that non-state actors are not trying to obtain such a capability and, given that many navies currently assign ASW a relatively low priority, this is a risk that needs to be kept under review. Governments around the world are disposing of submarines and on the basis that anything that can be sold will be sold, the expectation must be that at some stage one may end up being bought by insurgents or criminals. In 1997, for example, a Russian immigrant to the United States was indicted for attempting to procure a Russian submarine on behalf of unspecified Colombian drug traffickers. The plan was to base the submarine in Panama, or another Central American country, pretending it was to be used for oceanographic research. Instead it was to have rendezvoused with cocaine-smuggling ships in the Pacific and then run in to drop-off points along the US West Coast. According to the indictment, discussions were also held regarding the provision of a party of 18-20 Russian submariners to crew the vessels for two years.[235]

The main axes of development, however, are semi-submersible craft, mini-submarines and the exploitation of commercially available sport and autonomous research submarines. The IRGCN are believed to operate a fleet of semi-submersibles with attack capabilities, a technology they might be willing to transfer to their proxies Hizbollah and possibly Hamas. Although they would be an option for a number of other terrorist groups it is criminal organisations that have shown the most interest in this type of craft. Drug cartels used, and continue to use, 'go-fast' boats capable of speeds up to 60 knots but because they leave a long tell-tale wake can be spotted easily from the air. Semi-submersibles, although slow, appeared to offer a cost-effective alternative but if powered by battery this would have meant they could only travel underwater for relatively short periods. To overcome this problem, Colombian drug gangs first employed large tubes that were towed behind cargo ships or fishing vessels. Once this method was recognised the gangs turned their attention to the development of self-propelled, semi-submersibles (SPSS) using diesel engines for power.

---

235   Mireya Navarro, 'Russian submarine drifts into center of a brazen drug plot', *New York Times*, 7 March 1997. Also Douglas Farah, 'Russian mob, drug cartels joining forces', *The Washington Post*, 29 Sept. 1997. Chris Kraul, 'Drug traffickers dive in', *LA Times*, 6 Nov. 2007 also reports that the Cali cartel planned to buy a Russian submarine in 1993.

The first semi-submersible was discovered in 1993 and their use has grown steadily since then.[236] Although no one design solution has emerged, the common features are a hull, which can be made of metal or wood but more usually fiberglass, the bulk of which is below the surface, and a crude "conning tower" protruding above the surface, through which fresh air for the crew and the diesel engine can be drawn. Although the "conning tower" enables the crew to navigate the vessel more easily they remain, in many cases, little more than extremely low-profile boats because, lacking buoyancy tanks, they cannot submerge.[237] Such craft have a small enough radar signature to generally avoid detection and are often able to reach the coast of Central America from the Pacific coast of Colombia, although they might take two weeks to do so.[238] In 2006, for example, a submersible reportedly capable of travelling about six feet (1.8m) below the surface was intercepted in the Pacific off Costa Rica.[239] A second report released within days of the discovery appeared to contradict the original report when it suggested the boat was a cigarette-style fast boat that rode low in the water because of the weight of the drugs it was carrying. It suggested that the three pipes that had been reported as projecting above the surface were exhaust pipes, not breathing tubes. Moreover, according to the Costa Rican coast guard, the boat had a lead laminate covering to "conceal it from radar".[240] This description, however, matches some of the designs based on 'go-fast' speedboats with sealed decks.[241] Of possibly greater interest in this case was the fact that a Sri Lankan Tamil was on board; whether or not he had a connection with the LTTE was never explained.

Construction standards appear to be as variable as the designs. According to Colombian Navy engineers some have GPS navigation devices and satellite phones, are built almost entirely from fiberglass which would make them almost impossible to detect using radar and, when equipped with

---

236   Contrary to a 2001 State Department assessment. See Joshua Sinai, 'Future trends in worldwide maritime terrorism', *The Quarterly Journal*, vol. III, no. 1, March 2004, p. 53, Note 21.

237   'Drug gangs expand their fleet', *Strategy Page*, 2 Nov. 2007; 'Insurgent submersibles'. *Jane's Terrorism & Security Monitor*, June 2008, pp. 6–7..

238   'Cocaine smugglers threatening submarine'. *The Star*, 27th June 2008.

239   'Submarine with cocaine seized off Costa Rica', *Reuters*, 20 Nov. 2006; 'Submarine carrying 3 tons of cocaine seized off Costa Rica', *USA Today*, 21 Nov. 2006.

240   'Drug 'submarine' off Costa Rica was disguised boat', *Reuters*, 22 Nov. 2006.

241   'Insurgent submersibles'. *Jane's T&SM*, p. 7.

ballast tanks, would be able to cut through water almost seamlessly.[242] Development is continuing: Carbon fiber hulls have appeared and speeds have increased from generally around eight knots (15kph) to in some cases 12 to 14 knots (22-26kph).[243] On the other hand, the crew of a semi-submersible that sank off Tumaco in 2007 described their craft as a "death trap" while others have been described as "floating coffins" without sanitary facilities or adequate ventilation.[244]

Two small drug-running submersibles were seized in 1997 and in 2005 another was discovered close to the Pacific port of Tumaco that was eight meters (26 feet) in length and described as capable of carrying around ten tons of cocaine, worth about $200 million.[245] Also in 2005 the US Coast Guard intercepted a "submarine-like vessel" off the Galapagos Islands with more than two tons of cocaine aboard.[246] At least two submersibles were discovered during the first part of 2007, followed by two more in October, each of which were described as 55 feet (17 meters) in length, powered by a 350-horsepower Cummins diesel engine and capable of transporting five tons of cocaine.[247]

The usage rate appears to be increasing rapidly: Reports from Colombia suggest 18 were discovered between 2005 and the beginning of 2007;[248] ac-

---

242   Juan Forero, 'Drug traffic beneath the waves', *Washington Post*, 6 Feb. 2008. In Feb. 2008, the Bogotá newspaper *El Tiempo* reported that Humberto Cuevas, who designed submersibles for the cartel boss Wilber Varela, had been arrested. His designs were apparently prized especially because they rode more completely underwater than others and were consequently harder to detect: 'Drug lord's sub designer in custody', *El Tiempo* (Bogotá), 6 Feb. 2008.

243   Elaine Silvestrini. 'Authorities want to torpedo use of drug-smuggling subs'. *Tampa Bay Online*, 26th June 2008; 'Cocaine smugglers threatening submarine'.

244   Kraul, 'Drug traffickers dive in'; Silvestrini. 'Authorities want to torpedo use of drug-smuggling subs'

245   'Colombian police find drug sub', *BBC News*, 26 March 2005.

246   'Submarine-like vessel transporting cocaine seized in Pacific', *News from Russia. com*, 15 Sept. 2005.

247   On the craft discovered in the first half of 2007 see 'Colombian Navy seizes sub in coke probe'; Jack Date and Theresa Cook, 'Feds nab suspected cocaine smugglers in Pacific', *AP*, 22 Aug. 2007. On the discoveries in the second half of the year see Kraul, 'Drug traffickers dive in'.

248   Forero, 'Drug traffic beneath the waves'; 'Another cocaine-laden submarine sinks off Colombia', *Reuters*, 3 Jan. 2008; also 'Colombia Navy seizes sub in coke probe', *AP*, 7 Aug. 2007; Kraul, 'Drug traffickers dive in'; 'Drug gangs expand their fleet' and 'Drug sub war intensifies', *Strategy Page*, 11 Jan. 2008. 'Insurgent submersibles'. *Jane's T&SM*, p. 7 reports that the bulk of the increase

cording to US Southern Command (SOUTHCOM), 30 were discovered during the first two months of 2008, the same number observed during the whole of 2007. The craft seized in 2008 ranged in size from 45 feet (14m) to 82 feet (25m) in length and although described as being "garage-level technology" some apparently had a range of 2,000 miles at six knots (11kph).[249] Even the range of the smaller boats could probably be extended by in-transit refueling from pre-positioned bowsers.[250]

In contrast insurgent groups appear to be more interested in acquiring or building mini-submarines.[251] Whether criminals are also interested is not clear. Although the costs and technical challenges would probably deter them two "submarines" and a semi-submersible were discovered close to Colombia at the beginning of 2008, each reportedly capable of carrying over ten tons of cocaine. The semi-submersible was captured off Buenaventura but the two "submarines" were scuttled before they could be examined.[252] Outside the Pacific region, a 33-foot (10m) "submarine" was discovered in the estuary of the River Vigo in the north-west coast of Spain in 2006. Its purpose appeared to be to ferry drugs from ships in international waters to the Spanish coast.[253] The report issued by the Guardia Civil indicated that it had a submersible capability but that the buoyancy system, which needed to balance the weight of the fuel as it was consumed against the weight of the cargo, was adjusted manually which would have been difficult to judge. The supposition is that the operator probably panicked and abandoned the craft which was sinking when it was apprehended.[254]

In 2000, however, a craft that appeared to be a true submarine was found under construction in a suburb of Bogotá. It was steel-hulled, 100

---

came in 2007 when nine vessels were discovered, eight of them in the Pacific.

249   Jason Sherman, 'SOUTHCOM detects sharp boost in narco submarine fleet size', *Inside the Navy*, 10 March 2008, p. 13. A subsequent report from SOUTHCOM put the number of semi-submersibles discovered in 2007 at 40. Mark D. Faram, 'War on drugs goes underwater', *Navy Times*, 28 April 2008.

250   'Insurgent submersibles'. *Jane's T&SM*, p. 8.

251   For an introduction to this category of weapons and related SDVs and midget submarines see Joris Janssen Lok. 'Mini-submarines and special forces pose maximum threat'. *Jane's International Defence Review*, 1st June 1998, pp. 63-8.

252   'Another cocaine-laden submarine sinks off Colombia'; 'Operación conjunta detecta semisumergible en aguas del Pacífico Colombiano', Armada Nacional de Colombia, 3 Jan. 2008.

253   'Spanish police find 'drugs' sub', *BBC News*, 14 Aug. 2006; Forero, 'Drug traffic beneath the waves'.

254   'Insurgent submersibles'. *Jane's T&SM*, p. 8.

feet (30m) long, and probably cost in the region of $20 million. It was completed to a high engineering standard and the Spanish translations of Russian manuals found in the building where it was being built suggested a possible Russian organised crime connection.[255] Some estimates suggested it would have been capable of transporting up to 200 tons of cocaine at snorkel depth to rendezvous sites around the Caribbean and, perhaps, off the American coast. Another report has suggested it might have been capable of diving much deeper, perhaps to as much as 330 feet (100 meters),[256] but to operate it as a submarine the cartel involved, which has never been identified, would still have needed to draw on at least a nucleus of trained, experienced personnel from a submarine-operating navy.

The Sea Tigers have long sought a fully submersible capability and, along with some anti-Israel insurgent groups, have pioneered the use of sub-surface equipment by non-state actors. Reports circulated that the organisation was planning to buy mini-submarines from the DPRK and a submarine from South Africa, but no evidence emerged to indicate that these purchases were made.[257] In 2003 there was a report that the group had obtained 34 underwater scooters in Denmark and smuggled them into Sri Lanka via Colombo's main airport without the knowledge of the Sri

---

255 Sinai, 'Future trends in worldwide maritime terrorism', p. 53; 'Drug submarine found in Colombia', *BBC News*, 7 Sept. 2000; 'Colombia: The Submarine Door', *Semitronic*, ND.

256 Forero, 'Drug traffic beneath the waves'.

257 Private information, Dec. 2005. However one website, which in other respects appears accurate, does claim that the Tigers have a midget-submarine in their inventory, of what is described as 'unconventional indigenous design and construction with sonar': 'LTTE's Military Capability', *TamilTigers.net*, ND (but no later than 2005). Also Gunaratna, 'Sea Tiger success threatens the spread of copycat tactics', p. 14. That the Tigers attempted to purchase a submarine in South Africa is not perhaps as surprising as it appears. In the late 1990s the country was emerging from the apartheid era and there was widespread sympathy for fellow 'liberation' movements amongst the country's new ruling elite. This sympathy extended to the LTTE who were able to set up at least two training camps and purchase arms. See Rohan Gunaratna, 'LTTE in South Africa', *Frontline*, vol. 15, no. 25, 5-18 Dec. 1998 and 'LTTE in South Africa II', *Frontline*, vol. 15, no. 24, 21 Nov.-4 Dec. 1998; also Nirupama Subramanian, 'SA takes stand on LTTE: Lanka rests easy', *Indian Express*, 19 Nov. 1998, who mentions Sri Lankan concern that the LTTE might have purchased 'at least one South African helicopter'. On continuing concerns about LTTE connections in South Africa and possible contact there between the LTTE and Hizbollah see B. Raman, 'Action against LTTE's gun-running', International Terrorism Monitor: Paper no. 190. South Asia Analysis Group *Paper No. 2138*, 16 Feb. 2007.

Lankan authorities.[258] Most famously they attempted to build a submarine in Phuket, Thailand, but their efforts were discovered.[259] Three more mini-submarines were then discovered under construction in a village south of the town.[260] According to Gunaratna, when the Phuket boatyard was closed the LTTE moved their boat-building operations to New Zealand where they constructed craft to be used in suicide operations.[261] Reports emanating from India in 2007 suggested that the Sea Tigers were renewing their efforts to develop some sort of sub-surface capability, probably in order to transport supplies safely across the increasingly patrolled Palk Strait but also, allegedly, to attack shipping in the Indian Ocean.[262] The larger LTTE submarine discovered in Phuket might have been used to transport divers but in all probability was being built to transport supplies.[263]

Operating and building mini-submarines, however, might be within the compass of a wider range of terrorist groups. In 1999 there was a report that the Moro Islamic Liberation Front (MILF) had made enquiries about buying a mini-sub from North Korea.[264] In 2002 a conference in Singapore

258 'LTTE use talks to obtain underwater scooters'. *The Island,* 17 March 2003. See also the discussion about the use of such equipment by the LTTE in R.S. Vasan. 'Incident Analysis: Sinking of SLN Dvora Craft on 22nd March 2008'. South Asia Analysis Group *Paper No. 2652,* 28th March 2008.

259 On the submarine find in Thailand see 'The LTTE in South East Asia: With special focus on Thailand', *Svik.org,* 2005, p. 7; Anthony Davis, 'Tracking Tigers in Phuket: A secret Tamil guerrilla base embarrasses Bangkok', *Asiaweek. com,* vol. 29, no. 23, 16 June 2003; Gunaratna, 'The asymmetric threat from maritime terrorism', p. 26, and Vijay Sakhuja, 'Mini submarine–A vessel of choice with drug cartels and terrorists', South Asia Analysis Group, *Paper no. 1313,* 30 March 2005. Gunaratna also reports that the Sea Tigers attempted to build a submarine in India but their efforts there were also disrupted. Gunaratna: 'The asymmetric threat from maritime terrorism', pp. 26 & 28.

260 Sakhuja, 'Mini submarine'; 'Three more mini-subs found in Rawai', *The Nation* (Bangkok), 5 June 2000.

261 Gunaratna, 'The threat to the maritime domain: How real is the terrorist threat?' pp. 83-4.

262 Walter Jayawardhana, 'Tamil Tigers are also developing a mini submarine for gun running, drug smuggling and piracy', *LankaWeb,* 30 March 2007; 'LTTE might be trying to acquire submarine: Report', *Zee News,* 30 March 2007.

263 Tanner Campbell and Rohan Gunaratna, 'Maritime terrorism, piracy and crime' in Rohan Gunaratna (ed), *Terrorism in Asia Pacific: Threat and Response,* Singapore: Eastern UP, 2003, p. 84. The then Sri Lankan ambassador to Thailand believed the reverse to be true; that the vessel was intended primarily for offensive operations. 'Insurgent submersibles'. *Jane's T&SM,* p. 9

264 Sakhuja, 'Mini submarine'. The attempt, which was apparently recorded in documents discovered when AFP troops overran the MILF's 'Buliok' camp in

was briefed about what was described as a non-pressurised "mini-submarine" capable of carrying six swimmers that had been captured from Al-Qaeda or an associated group in Southeast Asia.[265] There was no information as to whether this vessel was the only one the group or groups involved had in their possession. The same report indicated the Al-Qaeda had also developed an explosive-packed "human torpedo" that, like the Sea Tiger's semi-submersible equivalent, was designed to explode on impact with a target. It was not made clear if the group or groups had acquired more such vessels and undertaken additional development work. In Colombia it has been suggested that FARC might have colluded in the construction of some submersibles that have been used to transport cocaine.[266]

Finally, anti-Israel groups are know to have adapted small submersible leisure craft and it appears eminently possible that insurgents groups might similarly adapt autonomous submarines, remotely controlled devices designed for scientific research, which are coming onto the market in increasing numbers.[267] Given their limited budgets, however, such groups are unlikely to be tempted to splash out on the exclusive, luxury submarines designed only for the extremely wealthy as an act of 'martyrdom' conducted using such a craft might be seen as one of sybaritic immolation rather noble sacrifice.[268]

Stand-off weapons. As warships push out their defensive perimeters, first through the use of small arms and floating booms, and perhaps later with the installation of sophisticated weapons such as the *Mini-Typhoon* electro-optical guided chain gun and small, fast-reaction missiles, and as small craft are increasingly kept away from high value targets such as oil tankers, gas carriers and cruise ships in ports and harbour approaches, so terrorists will need the capability of inflicting unacceptable levels of damage from a greater distance. The threat from aerial or more sophisticated stand-off weapons may therefore increase.

2003, involved the planned purchase of a vessel 45 feet (14m) in length capable of carrying six people including two divers: 'Mini-subs: the next terrorist threat?' *Journal of Electronic Defense,* July 2003 and 'Philippines: New concerns arise with rebel submarine plan'. *Stratfor,* 14th March 2003.

265   Newman, 'Terrorists feared to be planning sub-surface naval attacks'.

266   'Cocaine smugglers threatening submarine'; 'Insurgent submersibles'. *Jane's T&SM,* pp. 6 & 8.

267   'Insurgent submersibles'. *Jane's T&SM,* p. 9

268   Jessica Dicker. 'Private subs plumb deep pockets, deeper waters'. *CNNMoney.com,* 3 August 2007.

Small single engined private planes could conceivably be used as flying bombs in a manner similar to the way the 9/11 attackers used large airliners. Al Nashiri is believed to have considered this option.[269] It is unlikely that one small, single-engined plane on its own not augmented by explosives, or even several small planes, could do great damage to a building, as incidents in Tampa, Milan and New York demonstrated.[270] The effect they might have on a ship could be more worrying. Although a plane of this type is usually smaller and lighter than a medium-sized car, the heavy engine block could be forced through two or three bulkheads if it was driven into the side or deck of a ship, even at the relatively modest speeds of which such aircraft are capable. This purely kinetic effect would be increased if it was carrying explosives. The suggestion that a plane of this size might be capable of delivering a charge weighting hundreds of pounds seems far-fetched, but a charge measured in tens of pounds would appear to be achievable.[271] The end result would be the equivalent of a small car bomb which, if unleashed against any cargo ship that lacked the reinforcement that is usual on gas and nuclear carriers, could cause considerable damage. If employed against a passenger ferry or cruise ship the psychological effect would be terrifying, although the actual numbers of killed and injured would depend on the depth to which the aircraft penetrated the interior spaces. However, loading the explosive onto a small aircraft would present problems given the size of the airframe and the layout of most cabins, while the pilot would need to be highly skilled in order to locate and take accurate aim at the target even if it was stationary.

Terrorists have already used missiles against ships. On 14 July 2006 an Israeli Navy corvette, the *INS Hanit*, patrolling off the coast of Lebanon, was badly damaged by a device fired from an area under the control of the

---

269   There is a report that al-Nashiri was undertaking flight training in a small Gulf emirate prior to his arrest; the suggestion is that this could have been a prelude to a maritime attack. Blanche, 'Tanker terror: Gulf's oil routes under threat'.

270   'Small plane crashes into Florida building', *BBC News*, 6 Jan. 2002; 'Plane hits Milan skyscraper', *BBC News*, 18 April 2002; 'Aircraft hits New York building', *BBC News*, 12 Oct. 2006.

271   Richard A. Clarke in his report on LNG risks suggests that small planes should be capable of delivering 700 pounds (318kg) of explosive: Clarke, 'LNG facilities in urban areas', p. 80. He nonetheless rates the likelihood of success against an LNG carrier using this method as low. The obvious comparison is with Japanese World War II *kamikaze* attacks. These used a variety of aircraft capable of carrying a variety of bombs; most however were armed with 500kg (1,100lbs) bombs while a few could carry 750kg (1,650 lbs) devices.

Iranian-backed Hizbollah group. First reports suggested it was some sort of light aircraft or drone packed with explosives.[272] Later reports made it clear that the vessel had been hit by a missile, probably a C-802, a specialised, subsonic, Iranian anti-ship weapon based on a Chinese design which carries a 165 kilogram (383 lb) warhead.[273] A second ship, the *Moon Light*, a Cambodian freighter with an Egyptian crew, that was sailing nearby was hit by another missile at about the same time.[274] The evidence suggests that the attack was a two-missile salvo. Why the second missile missed the *Hanit* is unclear but could be explained on the basis of a simultaneous "high/low" attack: the first, high-level missile could have been intended as bait to distract the *Hanit's* defence systems away from the second, sea-skimming, missile. Both would have been guided to their targets using the missiles' own guidance systems; the high flying missile could have overflown the *Hanit* and then "locked on" to the *Moon Light* 36 kilometers (22 miles) away as its next visible target. If this scenario is correct, then the missile that actually struck the *Hanit* could either have been another C-802 or a C-701 TV-guided missile.[275] Initial reports suggested that the strikes occurred roughly 50 miles (80 km) off the coast but, given the Israeli ship's mission, 12-15 miles (20-25 km) seems more realistic and it could have been as close as eight to ten miles (around 16 km).[276]

Finding and targeting the ships would have been a sophisticated operation.[277] The assumption until now has been that only states are capable of buying, maintaining and operating such sophisticated weapons and that they would not allow them to be used even by their proxies. While this remains the assumption, the evidence in this case is equivocal. There was

---

272   'Israel confirms 4 sailors missing from naval ship', *Reuters*, 15 July 2006.

273   Mark Mazzetti and Thom Shanker, 'Hizbollah's unexpected firepower', *International Herald Tribune*, 19 July 2006; Ramit Plushnick-Masti, 'Israel: Iran aided Hizbollah attack', *The Mercury News*, 15 July 2006; 'Hizbollah brings out Iranian Silkworm to hit Israel corvette', *DEBKA-file*, 15 July 2006.

274   ONI, WWTTS Report, 26 July 2006.

275   'INS Hanit suffers Iranian missile attack', *Defense Update News Commentary*, 17 July 2006; Jonathan Howland, 'Iran, China intent on countering navies', *Jewish Institute for National Security Affairs Online*, 18 Jan. 2007. For a detailed analysis see Kirk Spencer and Trent Telenko, 'An analysis of the Hizbollah anti-ship missile strike: The attack on the INS Ani–Hanit', *Israel Resource Review*, 25 July 2006.

276   'INS Hanit suffers Iranian missile attack'.

277   Spencer and Telenko, 'An analysis of the Hizbollah anti-ship missile strike'; Matt Hilburn, 'Hizbollah's surprise', *Sea Power*, Sept. 2006.

no confirmation that Iranian forces, which in this case meant operatives from the Al Quds section of the Iranian Revolutionary Guards Corps, were in Lebanon when the attack took place, but the fact that they could not be found does not mean they were not there. If they were not, then these firings represent either a substantial increase in terrorist fire power or an effective merger between a state and an organisation that uses terror. Hizbollah has penetrated many Lebanese institutions, including Beirut airport, and it is perhaps significant that the missiles were fired from within its perimeter and the airport's radar was used to track the Israeli ship.[278] Another report suggested the radar was operated either by rogue elements within the Lebanese armed forces or with the full knowledge of the Lebanese high command.[279] The missiles could have been delivered directly from Iran (or Syria) by air. Any firing team could have quickly exited the same way. The Israeli view is that, with the exception of the long-range Shihab missile, "Hizbollah has everything Iran has."[280] Furthermore, that the group tripled its stock of C-802 ASCM's once the war was over.[281]

The other anti-ship weapons available and favoured by terrorists are in most cases widely available, relatively cheap and simple to operate, but puny in comparison with C-802s:

Anti-tank guided weapons: Although these are not ideal for the task they could be converted for marine use. They could easily penetrate the relatively thin hulls of most ships and cause a great deal of damage and even achieve a "mission kill" if they disabled the ship's engine, but, because their warheads are designed to penetrate heavy armour, it is just as likely they would pass through the hulls and out the other side without exploding. They are relatively easy to use but would be difficult to control from a small boat. Nor would obtaining these weapons be straightforward as they are not commonly available, unlike RPGs and automatic weapons.

Rocket-propelled grenades (RPGs): These were used extensively against maritime targets during the Iran-Iraq "Tanker War" (and have also been used by pirates, off Somalia in particular). They have a limited effective

---

278   Confidential information.

279   Toby Harnden, 'Lebanese forces accused of helping Hizbollah rocket attack in Israeli ship', *Sunday Telegraph*, 6 Aug. 2006.

280   Harry de Quetteville, 'Terrorists' missiles are from Teheran armoury', *Daily Telegraph*, 17 July 2006; Toby Harnden, 'Iran admits it gave Hizbollah missiles to hit all Israel', *Sunday Telegraph*, 6 Aug. 2006.

281   Barak Ravid, 'Israel to UN: Hezbollah has tripled its land-to-sea missile arsenal', *Haaretz*, 31 Oct. 2007.

range, no more than 300-400 metres, and although they are of limited use against ships, could possibly halt a vessel if the grenades were fired at the engine spaces, or force the crew to abandon ship if they were aimed at the accommodation block, in both cases causing a fire, or at the bridge to disable it.

Machine guns: These could achieve a result similar to RPGs if fired at the same areas. Heavy weapons such as 0.5 calibre belt-fed guns would be particularly effective but lighter weapons, if they could be aimed accurately, might inflict sufficient damage by causing fires, or death or injury to people, to force a crew to abandon ship.

Mortars: Against a moving target mortars would be largely ineffective.[282] They could, however, inflict damage to ships tied up alongside in a port.[283] The Portuguese FP-25 group claimed credit for an unsuccessful attack in 1985 when a 60mm mortar was used to attack NATO warships in Lisbon harbour.[284] There are, however, some warhead types that could cause problems.

"Katyusha"-style rockets: When fired from multiple launch tubes these unguided rockets are primarily an area bombardment weapon for use against static targets or concentrations of ground troops. Singly or in small numbers they are far less effective, although they can engender great fear in a civilian population as the attacks on northern Israeli towns by Hizbollah demonstrated in 2006. They can be used against ships in port: they were used to attack the US Navy ships visiting Aqaba in 2005. But, as that attack demonstrated, because they lack any form of guidance they are inaccurate and therefore of limited utility even though each 122mm rocket is capable of delivering a warhead weighting around 33 pounds (15 kilos). They can also be fitted with non-conventional warheads, including RDDs, although it is unlikely that any terrorist groups has such a capacity.

Man-portable Air Defence Systems (MANPADS): These shoulder-launched anti-aircraft weapons are widely available. The most common are

---

282   Coffen-Smout, 'Pirates, warlords and rogue fishing vessels in Somalia's unruly seas', p. 4 cites a March 1995 report of Somali pirates firing a mortar at the *Long Barda*, a British racing yacht in the Gulf of Aden.

283   However, Khalid Sheik Mohammed apparently planned to use mortars to hit a plane as it took off from London's Heathrow Airport: David Leppard, 'Al-Qaeda's Heathrow jet plot revealed', *The Sunday Times*, 9 Oct. 2005.

284   MIPT Terrorism Knowledge Base Incident Profile: Popular Forces of April 25 attack Military Target, 28 Jan. 1985.

the Russian-made Strela (SA-7 and SA-14) and Igla (SA-16 and SA-18) and the American "Stinger". Homing on an object's infra-red emissions, MANPADS could be fired against ships from shore locations or even small boats in the hope of picking up the heat from the ships' stacks. While insurgent and terrorist groups clearly have access to these weapons and have used them against air targets, there has been no recorded incident of their use against ships.[285]

Without exception, terrorists would have a much higher chance of success with any of these weapons if they were fired from the shore against ships stationary in port or moving only very slowly through a narrow channel. They could be mounted on small craft but achieving a successful hit is problematic without a stabilised mounting.

Ships as delivery systems for weapons

The bigger the bang, the bigger the effect: The threat that has attracted the most attention is the use of a freight container to deliver a bomb.[286] The idea is that, theoretically at least, terrorists could pack a bomb into a container in Karachi and explode it on arrival in Kansas.[287]

The headline threat envisages two types of device. The first is a nuclearweapon. If a terrorist group was able to steal an already assembled device in working order or, alternatively, if it was able to obtain the necessary technology and components and if it was then able to assemble them; if the terrorists were able to deliver either device to the target; and if they were able to detonate it successfully, then we would no longer be worrying about maritime security. The rules of the game would have changed.[288] However, it is important not to overstate the threat by equat-

285   For more details on the widespread availability of MANPADS see 'MANPADS proliferation', Federation of American Scientists Arms Sales Monitoring Project *ISSUE Brief no. 1,* 13 Jan. 2004.

286   On the history of the container and its fundamental role in the globalisation phenomenon see Marc Levinson, *The Box: How the Shipping Container made the World Smaller and the World Economy Bigger,* Princeton UP, 2006.

287   OECD, *Security in Maritime Transport,* pp. 8-9.

288   For a comprehensive review of the issues see Michael Levi, *On Nuclear Terrorism,* Cambridge and London: Harvard UP, 2007. This does not mean that al-Qaeda is not necessarily trying despite the difficulties. See David Ignattius. 'Portents of a nuclear al-Qaeda'. *Washington Post,* 18 October 2007; Michael Posner, 'Intelligence officers call al Qaeda nuclear threat real', *GovernmentExecutive.com,* 2 April 2008.

ing the destructive power of a crude device with the sophisticated weapons possessed by major states.[289]

The second is a "dirty bomb", that is, a high explosive device wrapped in radiological material, which is designed to spread contamination and is known, more precisely, as a Radiological Dispersion Device or RDD. It is important that this threat is also not exaggerated.[290] First, terrorists would have considerable difficulty in obtaining the components and then assembling a working device. Secondly, while contamination would undoubtedly cause serious problems, a radiological weapon is not a nuclear weapon. It is possible that the explosion (not radiation) could kill people close to the detonation,[291] but how many would die from subsequent radiation poisoning is questionable. It is the prevailing weather conditions and terrain that will determine the extent of the contamination, and the amount and type of the radioactive material that will determine the number of casualties. Tests have demonstrated that up to 100 times more radioactive material is need to contaminate an urban than a rural area.[292] Most analysts believe no more than ten people would die from radiation poisoning; other analysts suggest that the only people likely to receive a lethal dose would die in the blast.[293] The expectation is that fear of radiation will lead to panic and that more people will be killed trying to escape than from the radiation itself.[294]

289 Colin S. Gray. *Another Bloody Century: Future Warfare.* London: Weidenfeld & Nicholson, 2005, p. 257. See also Clarke C. Apt, 'The economic impact of nuclear terrorist attacks on freight transport systems in an age of seaport vulnerability', Cambridge, MA: Apt Associates, Inc. 30 April 2003. Executive Summary. For a wider perspective see Jonathan Medalia. *Terrorist Nuclear Attacks on Seaports: Threat and Response.* Congressional Research Service, RS21293; updated 13 Aug. 2003.

290 For a through examination of the issues see Peter D. Zimmerman with Cheryl Loeb, 'Dirty bombs: The threat revisited', *Defence Horizons no. 38,* Jan. 2004 and James L. Ford. 'Radiological dispersal devices: Assessing the transnational threat', *Strategic Forum no. 136,* March 1998. Rosoff and van Winterfeldt in their analysis of possible 'dirty bomb' attack scenarios on the ports of Los Angeles and Long Beach concluded that 'the health impacts will be relatively small': H. Rosoff and D. von Winterfeldt, 'A risk and economic analysis of dirty bomb attacks on the ports of Los Angeles and Long Beach', *Risk Analysis,* vol. 27, no. 3, June 2007, p. 541.

291 Peter D. Zimmerman and James M. Acton, 'Radiological lessons: Radiation weapons beyond 'dirty bombs', *Jane's IR,* June 2007, p. 19.

292 Ford, 'Radiological dispersal devices'.

293 Peter D. Zimmerman, *et al.,* 'Seize the Cesium', *New York Times,* 1 Aug. 2007.

294 Graham Allison, *Nuclear Terrorism: The Risks and Consequences of the Ultimate Disaster,* London: Constable and Robinson, 2006, pp. 57 & 59.

Nonetheless, the incident in November 1995 when Chechen rebels placed a 30 pound (14 kg) container of Caesium in an Moscow park show that such groups are prepared to use such material to achieve their ends.[295]

The fear that the radiation from a "dirty bomb" would be sufficient to cause a rise in long-term cancer deaths, or render the contaminated area uninhabitable for years—thus justifying the designation "weapons of mass disruption"—is based on what could be unjustified assumptions. Research on the after-effects of the Hiroshima and Nagasaki bombs led to the formulation of the Linear No Threshold (LNT) model in 1958 that related radiation exposure to long-term cancer deaths. However, the Hiroshima and Nagasaki victims received doses of radiation that were far higher than anything that had been experienced before. More recent research, based largely on the effects of the Chernobyl disaster, which led to 56 attributable cancer deaths rather than the 100,000 predicted by Greenpeace on the basis of the LNT model, has raised questions about whether low doses of radiation have the same effect as higher doses; it suggests that contrary to the prevailing theory, there is a threshold and low doses—certainly below 100 millisieverts (mSv) and probably below 200 mSv—will not cause any rise in long-term cancer-related fatalities.[296] Providing these results have not been distorted by under-reporting or misdiagnosis, it is likely that irradiated areas could be brought back into productive use much more quickly than previously thought.[297] Nonetheless, jihadist terrorists clearly have the ambition to use unconventional weapons to cause catastrophic numbers of deaths (which a "dirty bomb" would not do) and incite unprecedented levels of fear (which a "dirty bomb" might engender, unless members of the public are better informed about the potential consequences), and there are indications of this interest continuing despite the technical difficulties.[298] However, although Zimmerman and his colleagues are dismissive of many of the fears surrounding the direct effects of a "dirty bomb" attack they do

295   Ford, 'Radiological dispersal devices'.

296   A sievert, like a rad, is a measure of radiation dose or dose equivalent. A rad (which used to be called a roentgen) represents 0.01 joules of energy deposited per kg of body tissue. A sievert is equal to 100 rads. Zimmerman and Acton 'Radiological lessons: Radiation weapons beyond 'dirty bombs'', p. 20.

297   For a summary of this research see Nick Davidson, 'Chernobyl's 'nuclear nightmares'', BBC News, 13 July 2006.

298   Brian Michael Jenkins, Unconquerable Nation: Knowing Our Enemy, Strengthening Ourselves, Santa Monica: RAND, 2006, p. 81; Tom Harper, 'Dirty bomb threat high and rising', Sunday Telegraph, 17 June 2007. Also Josh Meyer, 'Al Qaeda said to focus on WMDs', LA Times, 3 Feb. 2008.

point to the risks associated with what they call "I-cubed" attacks, involving the ingestion, inhalation or immersion of radioactive material.[299]

The risk is therefore there.[300] Even so, the idea that terrorists would attempt to deliver either type of weapon in a shipping container is inherently implausible for two reasons. First, the point has already been made that terrorists have an aversion to failure, seek to minimise risk and are wary of anything other than incremental innovation. They plan, they practice, and they do all they can to ensure things will not go wrong. To steal or to assemble either type of device, but especially a nuclear device, would require any terrorist group to invest a substantial amount of time and money. It truly would be a one-shot deal. The risk of detection would be substantially higher than with other operations because the group would have to interact with actors outside its normal range of the experience in order to obtain either a weapon or the requisite skills and components.

Secondly, terrorist groups always want to be in control.[301] Given the investment necessary to build or obtain a nuclear or radiological device it is hard to imagine that they would entrust anything so valuable to the vagaries of the international, inter-modal transport system. Containers get lost, they are stolen, delayed, dropped, broken open, left out in the sun, drenched with seawater, lost overboard and set on fire. Sophisticated weapons are often sensitive to changes in temperature and humidity, vibration and the natural pitch and roll of ships at sea. In many cases their mission readiness declines if they are not maintained frequently.[302] Obviously most containers are delivered without serious mishap, but that cannot be guaranteed. Consequently, it is hard to know for certain when or even if a container will be delivered to where it is supposed to go. If a terrorist group wants to detonate a container remotely while it is still in the system it has no way of knowing where precisely it will be; if, for instance, it is in the middle of a stack of thousands of containers which would mask an electronic signal. All in all there are simply too many things that can go wrong.

---

299   Peter D. Zimmerman, 'The smoky bomb threat', *New York Times*, 19 Dec. 2006 and Zimmerman, *et al.*, 'Seize the Cesium'. For a fuller discussion see Zimmerman and Acton 'Radiological lessons: Radiation weapons beyond 'dirty bombs', pp. 21-2.

300   This discussion has been informed, in part, by the author's interviews with Bruce Stubbs, June 2004 and Aug. 2006.

301   Jenkins, *Unconquerable Nation*, p. 82.

302   James Jay Carafano, 'Missing the real missile threat', *Washington Post*, 26 July 2006.

A state actor might be able to engineer a greater degree of control by using a state-owned shipping line but, as James Jay Carafano has suggested, a more realistic threat would be to use a ship, which could be less than 300 gross tons, as a launch platform for a short range ballistic missile such as a Scud, position it close to the coast, fire the missile and scuttle the ship. If this were done over very deep water, proving who was responsible might be almost impossible.[303] Alternatively a ballistic missile could be fired "from a ship by peeling back the top, erecting it, launching it at good distance, covering back up and moving away", a procedure which the ballistic missile proliferation report commissioned by the US Secretary of Defense Donald Rumsfield stated that a rogue state had already accomplished.[304]

If a terrorist group did want to use such devices and did not have access to a missile the alternative, and much more likely, scenarios are that they would be assembled inside the target country using as many locally available components as possible,[305] or that they would be brought in using smaller craft. The use of a car or panel van, a small aircraft, or a small boat such as a fishing smack or private yacht sailed into a small port or beached on an isolated stretch of coast, is a cheaper and more reliable method than using the container system.[306] As the head of the US Domestic Nuclear

---

303   *Ibid.* The US Coast Guard has also acknowledged this possibility: Wagner, 'Government lacks clear plans to ID small vessels used as terrorist weapons' as has the US. Department of Homeland Security: 'Small vessel security strategy', April 2008, p. 14 which refers to a vessel as small as 200 tons being suitable as a launch platform although substantial cooperation between the ship's crew and the launch team would be required if the launch was to be achieved successfully..

304   David A. Kier, 'Cruising for trouble', *The Washington Times*, 24 Nov. 2005.

305   Randall J. Larsen, 'Rethinking border security', *The Institute of Homeland Security* White Paper, 1 Nov. 2005, pp. 3-5; also 'US port security unlikely to stop nukes: experts', *Reuters*, 7 Nov. 2006.

306   Larsen, 'Rethinking border security', p. 6; also Randall J. Larsen, Statement before the Homeland Security Subcommittee on the Prevention of Nuclear and Biological Attack, US House of Representatives, 19 April 2005; James Jay Carafano, 'Port security and foreign-owned maritime infrastructure: Statement before the House Committee on Transportation and Infrastructure, Subcommittee on Coast Guard and Maritime Transportation', *The Heritage Foundation*, 9 March 2006, p. 4. The USCG's technology adviser, Guy Thomas, also agrees with this assessment: 'Most of us believe it will come in a small boat.' Stew Magnuson, 'Maritime domain roadmap seeks to ID all vessels', *National Defense*, Jan. 2007; also Wagner, 'Government lacks clear plans to ID small vessels used as terrorist weapons'. Karl Schultz, the head of US Coast Guard's Miami sector, admitted in 2007 that the 'small boat threat...continues to present technology and policy challenges and remains a primary maritime security concern': Alice

Detection Office remarked in 2007: "giving up a nuclear device, putting it in a container and letting it float around the world for a couple of weeks is probably folly". He, too, observed that more attention should be devoted to the threat from what he termed "non-port of entry venues" such as unguarded stretches of coastline or land border.[307] Terrorists might, and probably do, use containers to smuggle equipment, components, money and even personnel, but they are unlikely to use them to move anything as valuable or as sensitive as a nuclear or radiological device.

The global shipping network: a vulnerable system

Despite all the security precautions implemented since 2001 the global shipping network is a relatively "soft" target. Although the difficulties involved make delivery of a WMD device using the international container system and "spectacular" attacks on ports or chokepoints unlikely, the system itself is vulnerable to disruption with multiple entry points, many of them in weak states.[308] (It is also, in theory, vulnerable to disruption from blockages of vital waterways caused unintentionally by pirate action.) The system is also vulnerable because of its complexity. Barnes and Oloruntoba point out that security incidents can occur at any time in large, highly complex systems such as supply or shipping networks—either suddenly, or slowly in ways that are unrecognisable until the disruption occurs. They identify two types of vulnerability: the first emerging from the operational complexity within a port and the second as an attribute of maritime movements with ports as nodes which, when taken together, form a system of systems that can generate considerable uncertainty, as well as operational sequences that can cause or contribute to errors or losses.[309] Similarly the Cranfield School

---

Lipowicz, 'Maritime security: Better tracking of small craft needed', *Washington Technology*, 29 Nov. 2007. See the responses proposed in US. Department of Homeland Security, 'Small vessel security strategy'.

307   Jon Fox, 'US nuclear detection official doubts threat by sea', NTI *Global Security Newswire*, 25 May 2007; also Stables, 'DHS to increase focus on threat poised by small watercraft'.

308   For a description of the system see OECD, *Security in Maritime Transport*, pp. 25-9. Also Maarten Van de Voort and Kevin A. O'Brien, "Seacurity': Improving the security of the global sea-container shipping system', RAND Europe, MR-1695-JRC, 2003.

309   Paul Barnes and Richard Oloruntoba, 'Assurance of security in maritime supply chains: Conceptual issues of vulnerability and crisis management', *Journal of International Management*, vol. 11, 2005, pp. 527-8. Also Cranfield School of Management, 'Supply chain vulnerability: Executive report', Jan. 2002, p. 6.

of Management in its study also identified dual vulnerabilities: internal, caused by sub-optimal interaction and cooperation between entities within the supply chain; and external, caused by natural causes or events such as terrorism.[310] The economic effects of any serious disruption could be felt globally and the psychological effects of incidents triggered by terrorist activity could reach into people's everyday lives.

Superficially this appears to be little different from the observation made by Alfred Thayer Mahan over a hundred years ago when he called the sea the "great highway",[311] and warned that the global maritime transport system that used it was delicate. Greater volumes, however, are being carried with greater efficiency than ever before. According to the World Bank, global maritime trade amounted to 21,480 billion ton-miles in 1999 and was expected to grow to 35,000 billion ton-miles in 2010 and 41,800 billion ton-miles by 2014.[312] Greater efficiency is being achieved through greater concentration. To achieve this ships have had to get bigger. By way of comparison, the average size of the ships sunk by U-boats in the North Atlantic between 1942 and 1944 was around 5,500 gross tons; the average size of the ships in the UK managed fleet now is around 26,000 gross tons.[313] Redundancy, reserves, buffer stocks, have all been stripped away because they cost money and security no longer appeared to be an issue. The drive for efficiency, predicated on never-ending, low-cost security, means that in many ways the global shipping system is more delicate now than it was then Mahan was writing.[314]

That shipping system consists of key points joined together by well-trodden pathways across the oceans. In modern parlance these pathways are known as SLOCs—Sea Lines of Communication. Most of the key points are ports. Some, however, are narrow passages—"chokepoints"—

---

310   Cranfield School of Management, 'Supply chain vulnerability', p. 2.

311   Alfred Thayer Mahan, *The Influence of Sea Power upon History, 1660-1783*, New York: Dover, 1987, p. 25.

312   Sakhuja, 'Indian Ocean and the safety of sea lines of communication'.

313   The North Atlantic figure is calculated from the tables in John Terraine, *Business in Great Waters*, London: Leo Cooper, 1989, pp. 767-9. The current UK figure was calculated based on the figures in UK Department of Transport (UK), *Transport Statistics Report: Maritime Statistics 2002*, London: The Stationery Office, 2003, p. 10.

314   Anna Bernasek, 'The friction economy', *Fortune*, vol. 145, no. 4, 18 Feb. 2002, pp. 104-10; Stephen E. Flynn, 'Port security is still a house of cards', *FEER*, Jan./Feb. 2006; Cranfield School of Management, 'Supply chain vulnerability', p. 1.

that geography imposes on maritime movement, forcing the pathways together.[315] They are not getting any wider but more and bigger ships are passing through them; the volume of oil passing through the Malacca Straits is
expected to double to 20 million bbl per day by 2020, for example. Even
in this age of services the world depends upon trade, that is, the safe and
reliable exchange of raw materials and manufactured goods. Anything that
threatens the points or the pathways is, axiomatically, a threat to international security.[316] Of the 80 per cent of the world's trade that moves by sea,
75 per cent needs to transit one of the world's five major chokepoints: the
Panama Canal, the Suez Canal, the Straits of Gibraltar, the Straits of Hormuz or the Straits of Singapore and Malacca. A significant and prolonged
disruption of any of these points would have a serious effect on world
trade.[317] As discussed earlier, blocking any of these chokepoints would not
be easy.[318] Nonetheless, harassing activity involving, for example, heavy
machine gun and RPG fire on ships, suicide boat attacks and the random
use of mines, if used individually, is unlikely to block a major waterway
but could encourage some shipping to divert and the remainder to demand
additional protection, including possibly convoy, all of which would add
substantially to insurance and transport costs. If such attacks were 'layered',
each weapon reinforcing the effect of another, and particularly if they were
mounted in straits where the littoral states were unwilling or inadequately

315   'Chokepoints' need not be at sea. Piracy is an increasing problem on the River
       Danube and occurs particularly at Cernavoda where ships queue to enter the
       channel to the Romanian Black Sea resort of Constanta: Bojan Pancevski, 'Pi-
       rates of the Danube give shipping owners the blues', *Sunday Telegraph,* 23 July
       2006.

316   Amongst a wide literature see, for example, OECD, *Security in Maritime Trans-
       port,* p. 14 & pp. 19-21; Burnett, *Dangerous Waters,* pp. 11 & 147-8; Chalk,
       'Threats to the maritime environment', p. 11; Henry J. Kenny, *An Analysis of
       Possible Threats to Shipping in Key Southeast Asian Sea Lanes,* Alexandria, Va.:
       Centre for Naval Analyses, Feb. 1996; Donna J. Nincic, 'Sea lane security and
       US maritime trade: Chokepoints as scare resources' in Tangredi, *Globalization
       and Maritime Power,* pp. 143-69; John H. Noer, 'Southeast Asian chokepoints:
       Keeping sea lines of communication open', *Strategic Forum,* no. 98, Dec. 1996;
       Reynolds B. Peele, 'The importance of maritime chokepoints', *Parameters,*
       Summer 1997, pp. 61-74; Jeremy Stoker, 'Nonintervention: Littoral operations
       in the littoral environment', *NWCR,* Autumn 1998; Vego, *Naval Strategy and
       Operations on Narrow Seas,* pp. 42-3, 51 & 88-90.

317   Ijaz, 'The maritime threat from Al-Qaeda'. Also Jerry Frank, 'Big business gets
       political over rising global risks', *Lloyd's List,* 24 Jan. 2008.

318   Blair and Lieberthal, 'Smooth sailing: The world's shipping lanes are safe', pp.
       8-11.

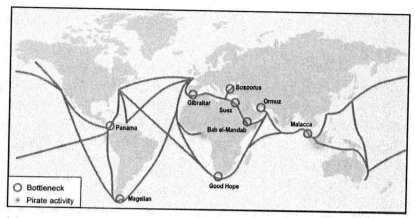

Map 1. SLOCs, chokepoints and areas of pirate activity *Source: OECD 2003,* http://www.oecd.org/dataoecd/63/13/4375896.pdf

prepared to take counter action, or resisted offers of outside assistance, then the disruption could be prolonged unnecessarily.[319]

Major ports are potentially more vulnerable. They, too, are effectively chokepoints.[320] The trend has been to concentrate trans-oceanic trade in bigger and bigger ships of all types—oil tankers, gas carriers, bulk cargo vessels and container ships—that can only dock in a small number of giant "hub" ports from which goods are then shipped in smaller vessels to surrounding satellite ports. Although the terrorist threat is largely hypothetical at the moment, ports do present terrorists with the opportunity to inflict the combination of physically inspired but psychologically destructive violence that they look to achieve.[321] The "hub" ports would be the obvious targets and whatever the extent of the physical damage, the press would be close at hand to magnify the psychological impact.

---

319   Eric Watkins, 'Obstacles to closer counter-terrorism cooperation in the Malacca Straits', The Jamestown Foundation *Terrorism Monitor,* vol. V, Issue 13, 6 July 2007, pp. 10-12.

320   A 'hub port' is a port capable of handling the new generation of large container ships that are now entering service. Because they 'collect' numerous trades at a single concentrated point they possess similar attributes to a chokepoint. See Daniel Y. Coulter, 'Globalization of maritime commerce: The rise of hub ports' in Tangredi, *Globalization and Maritime Power,* pp. 133-41.

321   In order to achieve their enormous throughputs these ports are dependent on information technology. A 'cyber-attack', while offering less dramatic pictures, could potentially be more disruptive than a bomb: *ibid.,* p. 139 and Cordner, 'Maritime terrorism: the next 'soft target".

This greater concentration on larger ships and "hub" ports gives rise to what the insurance industry calls "accumulation risk". To give one example: when the 5,500 TEU *Hyundai Fortune* caught fire off Yemen in March 2006, 850 out of 3,100 containers were affected, giving rise to a potential claim of $200 million for just one third of its load. In the next five to ten years, container ships will be built that are capable of carrying between 12,000 and 18,000 TEU. This accumulation risk at ports will rise commensurately. Hong Kong, the world's second busiest container port, can accommodate more than 250,000 TEU, meaning that goods valued in excess of $5 billion could be sitting on its wharfs at any one time.[322]

What the direct and contingent economic costs of port shutdowns might be as a result of an attack is the subject of lively debate. The practical example that is cited most often is the 2002 shutdown of US West Coast ports as a result of an employers' lock-out. The Pacific Maritime Association (PMA), which represented the port employers, commissioned an economic consultancy firm, Martin Associates, to undertake an impact study. This concluded that a 10-day shutdown would cost the US economy $1.94 billion per day, a figure that has been quoted widely.[323] Yet almost as soon as the dispute was settled, other commentators were suggesting that the figure was an overestimate. The Martin study suggested that if a shutdown continued for 20 days, the cost to the US economy would be $48.6 billion. Anderson, however, suggested a figure of $4.669 billion for a four-week shutdown, commenting that figure of $1-2 billion per day would be closer to the economic impact of "*sinking* the ships rather than delaying them".[324] The Anderson report also contended that the effect was not constant but would grow geometrically over time: only about ten per cent of the impact would be felt over the first ten days but the effects would become progressively more serious until after 30 days this growth

---

322   Gordon Fry and Michael Thompson, 'The bigger the ship, the greater the risk', *Lloyd's List,* 9 June 2006.

323   Martin Associates, 'An assessment of the impact of West Coast container operations and the potential impacts of an interruption of port operations, 2000', Lancaster, PA: Martin Associates, 23 Oct. 2001. The PMA also commissioned a report focusing on the effects of the trans-Pacific trade which also made use of the Martin Associates figures. Stephen S. Cohen, 'Economic impact of a West Coast dock shutdown', University of California at Berkeley, Jan. 2002.

324   Patrick L. Anderson, 'Lost earnings due to the West Coast port shutdown–Preliminary estimate', Lansing MI: Anderson Economic Group Working Paper 2002-10, 7 Oct. 2002, pp. 1-2.

could tail off as shippers found alternative routes. Substitution, in other words, would begin to take place.

The idea of substitution is central to the argument of another critic, Peter Hall.[325] After making clear that he shares the criticisms of others with regard to the problems associated with impact studies—their inability to deal with long-term changes in industrial organisation, demand, macroeconomic conditions, production and transportation technologies[326]—he argues with regard to substitution, first, that one of the reasons why the Martin study figure was so high was the *lack* of substitution options available to shippers moving goods through West Coast ports. The impact study assumed that all West Coast ports would be closed because the relevant labour contract covered all the ports from Seattle to San Diego and was designed precisely to prevent shippers playing one port off against another. Secondly, Hall argues that while the Martin methodology, based on a continuous monotonic function, accurately reflected job and other impacts in the vicinity of the ports it became less reliable beyond that because it worked on the incorrect assumption "that existing spatial-organisational production structures are fixed...(and did) not adequately address the possibilities for substitution within and between sectors even in the short run".[327] He continues:

structural changes in the transportation system mean that port impact studies are more accurate in estimating the relatively unimportant and declining direct employment and other benefits of cargo-handling activities, but are increasingly unreliable at estimating the much more significant and growing economic contributions that are represented by the cargo itself...The only way to get an amount of $1.94 billion per day is to turn to the port-dependent impacts of the shutdown, but this is precisely where port impact studies are least reliable.[328]

The conclusion Hall reached, based on the reasoning that most economic value is not lost as the Martin study assumes but is substituted or

---

325   Peter V. Hall, "'We'd have to sink the ships': Impact Studies and the 2002 West Coast Port Lockout', *Economic Development Quarterly*, vol. 18, no. 4, Nov. 2004, pp. 354-67.

326   Hall, "We'd have to sink the ships", p. 360.

327   *Ibid.*, p. 355. The CBO in its study (see below) also points out that if Martin Associates had used the more reliable ratio of GDP to wages and salaries rather than business revenues to wages and salaries the impact of the shutdown using their methodology would have gone down to $470 million per day.

328   Hall, "We'd have to sink the ships", p. 359.

delayed, is that the cost of shutdown should be no more than $390 million per day, about one fifth of the Martin estimate.[329]

Hall and the Martin study both assumed that shippers would be in a position to anticipate a shutdown and take at least some diversionary action or arrange some degree of substitution at a relatively early stage. The Congressional Budget Office (CBO) for its 2006 study was asked specifically to evaluate unexpected disruptions, an approach that more accurately reflects the circumstances that would pertain after a terrorist incident.[330] In the two scenarios they examined only the ports of Los Angeles and Long Beach were affected directly. All other West Coast ports remained open as did ports elsewhere in the United States. The first scenario posited a one week closure and assumed the backlog of shipments would take one month to clear. Using the LIFT (Long-Term Interindustry Forecasting Tool) model, the CBO researchers concluded that such a shutdown would reduce GDP by $150 million per day but that once the problem had been resolved GDP would return to where it would have been.[331] In the three-year scenario the pattern of losses would vary over time as shippers found alternative routes and customers adopted substitutes but GDP losses would not be recouped. The net effect would be a reduction in real GDP of between 0.35 and 0.55 per cent, that is to say between $45 billion and $70 billion per year, which translates to between $125 million and $200 million per day. Real GDP, however, reflects only domestic production and consumer and business expenditure would fall more substantially because less would be spent on both domestic and imported goods. Inflation would increase by two per cent in the first year and might trigger an increase in interest rates. Available jobs would be about one million fewer on average over the three-year period.[332]

The CBO also attempted to put these figures in perspective. It pointed out that according to the Federal Reserve Bank of New York, the 9/11 attacks cost New York City an estimated $33-36 billion but whereas GDP was forecast to drop sharply in 2002 from 2.7 per cent just prior to the attacks to one per cent, it actually grew by 1.6 per cent. Hurricanes Katrina

---

329   *Ibid.*, p. 363.

330   Congressional Budget Office (CBO), 'The economic coasts of disruptions in container shipments', Washington, DC: The Congress of the United States, Congressional Budget Office, 29 March 2006.

331   CBO, 'The economic costs of disruptions in container shipments', p. 14. CBO also cite a report prepared by the economic forecasting firm DRI-WEFA (now Global Insight) which suggests a lower figure of $65 million per day.

332   *Ibid.*, pp. 18-21.

and Rita led to the loss of physical capital of between $70 and $130 billion. The storms slowed GDP growth by about 0.5 per cent in the second half of 2005 but CBO estimates suggested that growth in 2006 would have been boosted by a similar amount as oil production resumed and reconstruction work began.[333]

Nonetheless, large figures continue to be discussed: "Recent analysis of a coordinated terrorist attack against four major US economic ports indicates that there would be in the order of $400 to $800 billion in long-term direct and indirect economic impacts to the United States."[334] Figures of these magnitudes suggest that WMD attacks are being contemplated or ports with hard-to-replace infrastructure are being assessed.

While the temptation to exaggerate must be resisted, no one is suggesting that the effects of port shutdowns would be anything less than serious. Looking beyond the ports to the modern global shipping system as a whole, its success is based on four attributes: speed, integrity (i.e. goods will not be lost through damage or pilferage), reliability and low cost. To work efficiently as a system each attribute depends on the other and they all, in turn, depend upon ready access and minimal in-transit security. The erosion of any one of these attributes could degrade the system's performance. The system would slow and costs would rise, which in turn would undermine customers' confidence and affect how they used it.

Security is not necessarily a numbers game, nor is strategy. A low number of attacks does not necessarily signal a low-level threat. Terrorism is predicated on generating a disproportionate effect from minimal resources. The physical security of key points in the system is, of course, essential as these are the places where attacks will take place. However, such point attacks do not need to be either numerous nor spectacular in order to degrade the performance of the system as a system with its reliance on strict timetables, short turnaround times, maximum utilisation, narrow financial margins, widespread dependence on information technology on ships to minimise crew sizes and in ports to maximise cargo flow, and sensitivity to fluctuations in shareholder and customer confidence, all of which make it vulnerable to disruption.[335] Attacks on the global maritime

---

333   *Ibid.*, pp. 12-13.

334   Scott Truver, correspondence with author, Jan. 2008.

335   A point illustrated by the nervousness in the oil markets following the attacks Al Qaeda carried out in 2004 on oil installations in Saudi Arabia. The first attack on the Red Sea port of Yanbu (which took place one week after the suicide boat attack on the Iraqi oil terminal at Basra) elicited relatively little response.

transport network would fit Robert Bunker's concept of "bond relationship targeting", which he describes as an end state that rather than being characterised by "gross physical destruction or injury...is a tailored disruption within a thing, between it and other things or between it and its environment by degrading, severing or altering the bonds and relationships which define its existence".[336]

Loss of confidence in the system would most likely be expressed through the price mechanism, particularly through increases in commodity prices and rates for insurance and shipping, which would affect productivity.[337] [338] The global maritime transport system's sensitivity to attack is untested but aspects of it, such as the "just-in-time" (JIT) inventory system, appear potentially vulnerable to shocks such as terrorist assaults. Around 90 per cent of the world's maritime trade now moves in containers.[339] While the proportion that are carrying JIT goods is unknown, it is nonetheless evident that a significant number of international manufacturers and retailers now use JIT because it enables components to be delivered to a production line, and products to stores, just at the time they are needed, rather than being held in stock. Its economic benefits led buyers and sellers to demand more from the transportation system that links them. Improvements in that system increased confidence in the system's ability to deliver goods safely

---

However, the price of oil increased sharply after the second attack in Khobar, as did the level of rhetoric about the likelihood that Al Qaeda was pursing a policy of 'oil terrorism'. On the Yanbu attack see, for example, 'Al Qaeda strikes at US-Saudi oil', *DEBKAfile Special Report*, 4 May 2004. On the Khobar attack and the subsequent oil price rise see, for example, Robin Gedye, 'Al Qaeda rampage ends in bloody gunfight', *Daily Telegraph*, 31 May 2004 and David Litterick, 'Petrol soars to £1 a litre amid fears of oil terrorism', *Daily Telegraph*, 2 June 2004.

336   Robert J. Bunker, 'Battlespace dynamics, information warfare to netwar, and bond-relationship targeting' in Robert J. Bunker (ed.), *Non-State Threats and Future Wars*, London and Portland, OR: Frank Cass, 2003, p. 104.

337   The terror threat already places burdens on industry. Yonah Alexander and Tyler Richardson in 'He who commands the sea...', *Jerusalem Post*, 19 Dec. 2002 comment that 'the added costs placed on oil companies and insurance brokers reduces the flow of oil into the global market, far outweighing the cost accrued from (any) physical damage to the vessels'.

338   Historically, routes which showed the most marked decline in piracy and privateering prior to 1800 showed the highest increases in ship ton per man, with insurance rates dropping by two thirds between 1675 and 1770 and continuing to drop during the nineteenth century: Douglass C. North, 'Sources of productivity change in ocean shipping, 1600-1850', *Journal of Political Economy*, vol. 76, no. 5, Sept.-Oct. 1968, pp. 959-60.

339   Van de Voort and O'Brien, "Seacurity", p. 1.

and cost-effectively, which meant that more companies in more countries adopted JIT. As confidence spread, so did increased trade. As confidence increased, companies were prepared to rely on the security of their goods in transit; ships, in effect, became warehouses. Stockholdings throughout the system fell dramatically, releasing working capital, which, in turn, led to sharp rises in productivity. But JIT systems work most effectively when markets are stable and less so when they are volatile.[340] If exogenous activity were to exacerbate known vulnerabilities in the international trading system for any reason, it could mean that stockholdings throughout the system could rise again as buyers responded to the increased uncertainty, tying up working capital, space and labour. Productivity would fall. Economic performance would decline which would erode that elusive economic driver, confidence.[341]

A study by David Closs of Michigan State University in 2002 revealed that large US manufacturers held an average of 1.57 months of stock in the early 1990s. By 2001 this had fallen to 1.36 months. Closs expected this to increase to 1.43 months in 2002 in response to the events of 9/11, as what has come to be called "just-in-case" inventory was raised. In other words, in just one year, the fear of terrorist disruption might have *halved* the logistic chain productivity gains made over the previous decade and could have added between $50 and $80 billion to business costs in the US alone. Sensitivity to this issue meant that, although immediately following 9/11 the United States closed its ports, it opened them again two days later, not because the authorities had a better understanding of the real level of the threat, but because the absence of components would have forced manufacturers at all levels of the economy to close production lines and lay off workers. These costs would have been in addition to the new supply-chain security measures put in place since 9/11, which, estimates suggest, cost the US $65 billion annually.[342] That this scenario did not in fact come about is attributable to other, benign, economic factors including lower demand

---

340   Cranfield School of Management, 'Supply chain vulnerability', p. 5.

341   Damian Reece, the City Editor of the *Daily Telegraph,* has written that confidence 'is like oxygen...You only really appreciate its importance when it is not there. Business is all about confidence. When its there in abundance economies grow, wealth is created and employment expands. When confidence dissipates so does growth, economies go into reverse and people lose their jobs': 'Business comment', *Daily Telegraph,* 10 Aug. 2007.

342   P. Damas, 'Supply chains at war', *American Shipper,* 1 Nov. 2001.

for fuel.[343] The OECD when making its calculation admitted that working out what level of "just-in-case" inventory companies would be comfortable with would be difficult. For purely illustrative purposes, it pointed out that returning inventories to 1990 levels in relation to GDP would consume approximately $300 billion of OECD working capital and increase inventory carrying costs by about $75 billion per year (0.7 per cent of GDP).[344]

In other words, the *fear* of attack has already meant that some of the bonds that hold the system together are no longer trusted wholeheartedly and have been supplemented by a range of regulatory and operational measures, including an attempt to build a surveillance scheme to track international ship movements, that have added a substantial layer of direct and indirect cost.[345] While the chances of multiple attacks (or even a single attack) of sufficient magnitude to inflict tangible damage on the system are remote, the concern must be that if these were to be successful, and therefore the current arrangements were to be found wanting, the cost of additional security measures, perhaps driven by demands for levels of security that are unattainable, might prove to be so prohibitive that businesses would start to repatriate their operations. This could trigger a gradual decline in worldwide trade which could, in turn, have ramifications for interstate relations and global security.

Multiple targets and multiple problems

It has been argued that the sheer expanse of the oceans, which amounts to almost two and half times the land surface of the planet, coupled with the anarchic state that prevails over the high seas (and, as argued earlier, can

---

343 Bernasek, 'The friction economy', pp. 104-10. See also OECD, *Security in Maritime Transport*, p. 20 and Richardson, *A Time Bomb for Global Trade*, p. 67. In Aug. 2004, Closs pointed to the figures collated by Robert Delaney for the Logistics Institute's annual 'State of logistics' report, which showed an increase in stockholding, but added the clarification that while 'his numbers don't reflect increases to the degree that we expected, a major source of the differences are due to lower demand for fuel (reduced transportation expense) and his assumptions regarding inventory carrying cost. The actual interest rates turned out to be much lower than most of us expected.' David Closs, correspondence with author.

344 OECD, 'The economic consequences of terrorism', Economics Department *Working Papers* no. 334, 17 July 2002, p. 26.

345 See, for example, Alan Erera, *et al*, 'Cost of security for sea cargo transport', The Logistics Institute–Asia Pacific, 26 May 2003, which describes real and potential costs without attributing values to them.

extend right up to the coast in the case of weak or failed states), "offers terrorists virtually unparalleled opportunity for "strategic reach" and "geographical flexibility" in terms of range of targets, the freedom to manoeuvre and the ability to disperse and deploy assets.[346] Moreover, that "given the sheer volume and vitality of global seaborne trade…the large number of crucial ports, transhipment nodes and…trading links, the maritime environment offers an almost limitless range of tempting, high pay-off targets, many of which are fringed by densely populated urban conurbations."[347] Theoretically, this is the case. When such thinking, which is essentially navalist, is overlain with the observation that "contemporary warfare is indeed non-spatial and multidimensional…where geographic, legalistic and jurisdictional fields of operation lose their meaning",[348] then the potential and the suitability of the sea as a medium for insurgent and terrorist operations appears to be all too plain. However, while it is sensible to remain alive to possibilities, this approach runs the risk of over-emphasising the combative aspect of the threat and downplaying insurgents use of the sea for mundane logistical purposes, in much the same way that the naval missions of trade protection and blockade have taken something of a back seat in the era of expeditionary war and power projection.

Therefore, the caveat that these combative opportunities in the maritime domain are open only to those groups with the necessary and relevant skills and motivation is crucial,[349] because these opportunities have been matched, in many cases, by countervailing obstacles. On the other hand, while law enforcement agencies have recorded some resounding successes, terrorist or insurgent use of the sea for logistical operations has probably proceeded with little hindrance.

The purpose of this chapter has been to illustrate the range of operational opportunities that have been engaged or considered by waterborne terrorists and insurgents. The next chapter will examine how terrorists and insurgents have actually made use of the sea. While terrorism is a phenomenon with shared characteristics, the threat is not from terrorism as a concept, or the sea as a theoretically anarchic space, but from the aims and capabilities of specific terrorist groups (and even sub-groups) as far as these

---

346   Herbert-Burns, 'Terrorism in the early 21st century maritime domain', p. 157.

347   *Ibid.*

348   Stephen Sloan, 'Responding to the threat' in Bunker, *Networks, Terrorism and Global Insurgency,* p. xxiii.

349   Herbert-Burns, 'Terrorism in the early 21st century maritime domain', p. 157.

are known and understood, and their ability to exploit the freedom that that anarchy provides.

5

MARITIME TERRORISTS

Terrorists at sea

It is because few terrorist groups have mounted operations at sea and on waterways that the number of incidents has been so small. Some of the groups that have mounted maritime operations have done so occasionally or opportunistically (the "opportunists"). Others have tried and withdrawn (the "defeated"). Only a handful have developed what could be described as an effective maritime capability with a coherent concept of operations and, as a result, have mounted sustained maritime campaigns or made regular use of maritime assets to support their activities on land, or both (the "coherent").

The "opportunists". The first set—the opportunists—include groups as diverse as the Provisional IRA, ETA and a group whose activities have been touched upon already, the Chechens.[1] The Provisional IRA planted bombs on two ferries, the *Duke of Argyll* in 1972 and the *Ulster Queen* in 1974. In 1976, when a cell was caught planning to plant explosives on the cruise liner *Queen Elizabeth II*, it looked as if the group might be taking maritime terrorism seriously. Lord Mountbatten was brutally assassinated in 1979 when his boat was bombed in Mullaghmore harbour. In 1981 the group bombed and partially scuttled a coaler, the *Nellie M*, announcing that British ships should stay out of Irish waters if they wanted to avoid the same fate. However, this attack, and another on the *St Bedan* in 1982, attracted little publicity and

---

1   See Menefee, *TMV*; Gunaratna, 'The asymmetric threat from maritime terrorism', p. 26.

SMALL BOATS, WEAK STATES, DIRTY MONEY

apart from occasional forays against Royal Navy vessels, the IRA did not mount attacks at sea again.[2]

The Basque separatist group ETA had a similar history. In 1981 it bombed a Spanish naval vessel; some sources claimed frogmen had attached a limpet mine to the hull. In 1984 a fishing vessel had its propeller blown off by a bomb that might have been placed there by frogmen, but if this was true it was the last time ETA ever used them.[3] Finally, it planned—some would argue only contemplated—attacks on three passenger ferries (detailed in Chapter Four), because it always regarded the Spanish tourist industry as a target.

The "defeated". In most cases it is inaccurate to suggest that the groups that have withdrawn from the sea have done so because they have been defeated. Defeat and victory can be a difficult to define or sometimes even to identify in inter-state war, let alone in irregular war and insurgency where the actors drift in and out of engagement. Groups may withdraw from the maritime sphere because the defenders have made it too difficult to operate, because they are no longer achieving their objectives, because a vital resource such as a leader or base area has been eliminated, or because the group as a whole has changed direction or collapsed.

Perhaps the Cuban anti-Castro groups provide the clearest example of withdrawal in the face of a hostile environment. Following the Revolution anti-Castro groups, by then largely exiled from Cuba itself, stepped up their efforts to unseat him and his government. In 1960 a Belgian ship delivering explosives was blown up in Havana harbour. After 1961 and the abortive Bay of Pigs invasion, the groups' options were reduced severely. They continued to try and infiltrate men and arms but with little success. In perhaps the most spectacular action the Cuban Liberation Front attacked and held the northern fishing village of Boca de Samua for an hour in 1971, machine gunning buildings and sabotaging the local electricity supply before escaping in two boats. A few further attacks were mounted until momentum was lost in the late-1970s. In parallel with these raids groups attacked Cuban fishermen, often in Bahamian waters, and mounted attacks on Cuban, Soviet and, eventually, neutral shipping trading with Cuba. However, once the FBI arrested one of the principal anti-Castro leaders in Miami in 1968 the campaign was

---

2   Menefee, *TMV,* pp. 17 & 19. Discussion with Steven Haines, Feb. 2008. The Real IRA also displayed an apparent interest in maritime attacks. Its leader attempted to purchase marine magnets: see Thomas Harding, 'Terrorist leader told MI5 agent that Real IRA made Omagh bomb', *Daily Telegraph,* 19 June 2003.

3   Menefee, *TMV,* pp. 19-22.

effectively over although, like the raids, desultory attacks continued until the late 1970s.[4]

The second example, Al-Gama'a al-Islamiyya, ceased its operations in the face of public criticism. It was formed in 1970, after the Muslim Brotherhood renounced the use of violence. Its spiritual leader, Omar Abdel-Rahman, also known as the "blind sheikh", was arrested and sentenced in the United States for his involvement in the first attack on the World Trade Center in 1993. As part of the group's wider campaign against foreign tourists in Egypt, it mounted seven attacks on cruise ships on the Nile between 1992 and 1996, firing at passengers from positions on the river bank.[5] However, its attack on tourists visiting the Luxor temple of Hatshepsut in 1997, which left 58 foreigners and four Egyptians dead, caused such widespread revulsion within Egypt that the group lost support and reluctantly called a ceasefire.[6] After 9/11 the Egyptian government took advantage of the public's newfound hostility to terrorism to arrest large numbers of the group's remaining supporters.[7]

The "coherent". Although there is much to be learnt from groups that have failed, nonetheless it is the third group—the handful of organisations that have made coherent and effective use of the sea—that deserves more detailed examination.

The principal actors

Estimates vary as to the number of terrorist or insurgent groups that have conducted maritime attacks over the past twenty years or so. Gunaratna listed 24, nine of which he regarded as active and eight which he suggested had an unused capability.[8] Herbert-Burns suggested there were 36 groups that had attacked maritime targets, had the capacity to do so or had used the sea regularly for logistical operations.[9] Six groups or clusters of groups (clusters because they operate in the same area and use almost identical operating methods) are worth looking at closely:

---

4   *Ibid.*, pp. 92-3.

5   For details of the attacks see MIPT Terrorism Knowledge Base 'Al-Gama'a al-Islamiyya'. Also Anthony Foster, 'An emerging threat shapes up as terrorists take to the high seas', *Jane's IR,* July 1998, pp. 43 & 45.

6   Foreign Terrorist Organizations, Gama'a al-Islamiyya (IG), p. 194.

7   'Chance for a clampdown', *Economist.com,* 25 Oct. 2001.

8   Gunaratna, 'The asymmetric threat from maritime terrorism', p. 26.

9   Herbert-Burns, 'Terrorism in the early 21st century maritime domain', p. 157.

1. Al Qaeda and its affiliates
2. Anti-Israel Groups
3. Gerakan Aceh Merdeka (GAM)
4. Liberation Tigers of Tamil Eelam (LTTE)
5. Nicaraguan "Contras"
6. Philippine "Moro" groups.

Al Qaeda and its affiliates. Al Qaeda was not the first terrorist grou͟ tempt a mass casualty attack but it was the first to execute one succes. when it attacked two US embassies in East Africa in 1998. When it cͻ bined mass casualty terrorism with an attack on the US homeland in 2001 ͺ changed how many people, and the US government in particular, thought of terrorism. Without 9/11 to give them context, the attacks on the USS *Cole* and the *Limburg* might have been largely forgotten. But they were not. Consequently, the thoughts and actions of one man, Abd al-Rahim al-Nashiri, have had a dramatic impact on the way people think of terrorism in the maritime domain. While he denied the role attributed to him in his evidence to the Combatant Status Review Tribunal at Guantanamo Bay in March 2007, most commentators still regard him as Al Qaeda's principal maritime strategist.[10]

The details of Al Qaeda's attacks have been recounted already. It is therefore worth looking instead at what al-Nashiri believed were the most effective ways a terrorist group could use its limited resources. He was not an original thinker but, like KSM and their boss, bin Laden, he was a big thinker. Outside the Middle East Al Qaeda's *modus operandi* against land-based, iconic targets has generally been characterised by the use of multiple, simultaneous attacks aimed at killing and harming as many people as possible. This was the hallmark of the attacks in East Africa in 1998, the US in 2001, Spain in 2004 and the UK in 2005. Al-Nashiri clearly subscribed to this strategy;

10   Walid Muhammad bin Attash, also known as Tawfiq bin Attash and as 'Khallad', who had once been head of bin Laden's bodyguard detail, and is known to have had a role in the *Cole* bombing, claimed in his testimony to the Combatant Status Review Tribunal (for ISN 10014) that it was he who had planned the attack on the USS *Cole*, bought the explosives, procured the false documents to buy the boat and recruited the bombers. See also Josh White, 'Al-Qaeda Suspect Says He Planned *Cole* Attack', *The Washington Post*, 20 March 2007, Toby Harnden, 'Detainee 'Admits USS *Cole* Bombing", *Daily Telegraph*, 20 March 2007 and 'USS Cole attack "plotter" charged'. *BBC News*, 30 June 2008.. Al-Nashiri's own testimony is Combatant Status Review Tribunal Hearing for ISN 10015. That he was known colloquially within Al Qaeda as *Ameer al Bahr* or 'Prince of the Sea' would appear to confirm his status. Gunaratna, 'The threat to the maritime domain: How real is the terrorist threat?' p. 84.

The planned Hormuz attack was much re... tive the link with JI was almost certainly the
... have been its undoing. Al Qaeda was ... was formed in Indonesia in the 1960s when
...ighter with a crane that was capable of liftin... for the establishment of *sharia* law in that
...was to equip the small boats with IEDs and pa... differences in aims and methods between the
with the aim of assembling "the biggest conve... ...vertheless formed what has been described
... the Straits the speedboats were to have b... ...ship. There is some overlap of perso... ...em
...attack one or more warships. If the... ...mps including one, Camp Abu... ...our ele-
...was to have been manoe... ...ich was operated b...
...resulting explosio... ...cility know... ...attack warships and other
...included men... ...hat w...[20] H...
... up in the vicinity of other vessels ... ...apparently, to attack ports but to
ships. ... including, possibly, cruise

3. The use of small private planes loaded with explosives as "flying bombs".
4. Underwater attacks using swimmers.[13]

When it came to actual operations he favoured suicide attacks against stationary or near-stationary targets and, like all Al Qaeda commanders, laid great stress on extensive pre-attack surveillance.[14] He appeared to recognise the importance of chokepoints—he planned to attack ships in the Straits of Hormuz and Gibraltar—although the suspicion must be that the visual impact of a ship or several ships burning and disabled in a narrow waterway was the primary result he was looking for. It is extremely unlikely that either waterway would have been blocked, although an attack in the Straits of Hormuz would have caused useful turbulence in the world's oil markets.

Both of these plans also demonstrate that he was prepared to undertake simultaneous attacks. The Gibraltar plan apparently would have involved several explosive-laden boats slamming into a number of US and British war-

---

11   'Who's who in al-Qaeda', *BBC News*, 27 April 2007; US Department of Justice, 'Al Qaeda associates charged in attack on USS Cole, attempted attack on another U.S. naval vessel', 15 May 2003.

12   Philip Shenon, 'Threats and responses: Terror network; a major suspect in Qaeda attacks is in US custody', *New York Times*, 22 Nov. 2002.

13   Christopher Dickey, 'High sea terrorism', *Newsweek*, 27 Jan. 2003; Chalk, 'Maritime terrorism in the contemporary era', p. 30, note 45.

14   Chalk, 'Maritime terrorism in the contemporary era', pp. 34-5. The suggestion has been made that the stress on long-term surveillance emerges not from Al Qaeda operational doctrine but from Arab cultural preferences and reveals a deep-rooted rigidity of thought in contrast to Western flexibility and risk-taking.

parently Tawfiq bin Attash[24] was also present and suggested that a similar operation should be attempted against US Navy ships at Port Klang, Malaysia. During his later interrogation, Omar al-Faruq revealed that at about the same time a Somali member of Al Qaeda named Ghalib was plotting to attack US Navy ships in the Indonesian port of Surabaya but was unable to carry it through because he could not recruit enough personnel.[25]

JI first attracted Western attention in December 2001 when the Singapore government uncovered a plot to attack a variety of Western targets (see below).[26] US forces in Afghanistan later found a videotape linking Al Qaeda with the plot.[27] In 2002 the Singapore authorities uncovered a second plot involving members of JI and the MILF.[28] In fact there was almost certainly multiple plots, many of which were not taken forward, but for which the driving force was Hambali, who among the leaders of JI was perhaps the one most in sympathy with Al Qaeda's aim of striking at Western targets.[29] It was he who provided the link with al-Qaeda and actively encouraged the Singapore plotters to proceed.[30]

Since the two Bali bombings in 2003 and 2005 and the bombing of the Australian embassy in Jakarta in 2004, the last two perpetrated by what was virtually a breakaway group led by Noordin Top, the Indonesian authorities, with American and Australian assistance, have successfully put JI under great pressure.[31] In 2007 the group's military leader, Abu Dujana,

24   *The 9/11 Commission Report*, p. 151.

25   Abuza, 'Terrorism in Southeast Asia', p. 4 and *Militant Islam in Southeast Asia*, p. 162..

26   Republic of Singapore, 'The Jemaah Islamiyah arrests and the threat of terrorism', p. 2; Abuza, *Militant Islam in Southeast Asia*, pp. 154-7.

27   Vaughn *et al.*, 'Terrorism in Southeast Asia', p. 11; Republic of Singapore, *ibid.*, p. 9 & note 9 p. 29; Abuza, *Militant Islam in Southeast Asia*, p. 157..

28   Republic of Singapore. *ibid*, p. 2. See also Jeremy Zakis and Steven Macko, 'Major terrorist plot in Singapore discovered: Al-Qaeda believed well established in the Asian region', EmergencyNet News *Special Report*, 12 Jan. 2002.

29   Ressa. *Seeds of Terror*, p. 155..

30   Republic of Singapore. *ibid*, p. 2; Vaughn *et al. ibid*, p. 10.

31   For detail on the group since Hambali's arrest see International Crisis Group. 'Indonesia: Jemaah Islamiyah's current status', Update Briefing *Asia Briefing no. 63*, 3 May 2007, and Zachary Abuza, 'Jemaah Islamiya still a potent force for violence in Southeast Asia', The Jamestown Foundation *Terrorism Focus*, vol. 4, no. 19, 27 March 2007. On Noordin Top and his group in particular see International Crisis Group, 'Terrorism in Indonesia: Noordin's networks', *Asia Report no. 114*, 5 May 2006 and Zachary Abuza, 'JI's moneyman and top recruiter: A profile of Noordin Mohammed top', The Jamestown Foundation

the US linked him to the East African bombings, indicting him as conspirator.[11] However, he did not attempt mass casualty attacks at, or from, the sea, although given his record there is no reason to believe he would not have attempted to fuse his maritime and mass-casualty experience had he had not been captured.[12] Nonetheless, while he was free to do so he adopted and adapted the tactics and methods that had been developed and used by other groups, particularly the Sea Tigers, as mentioned already, and directed them against iconic targets. According to reports of his interrogation, the four elements of his strategy were:

1. The use of small boats loaded with explosives to attack warships and other targets.
2. The use of *medium-sized* ships not, apparently, to attack ports but to be blown up in the vicinity of other vessels including, possibly, cruise ships.
3. The use of small private planes loaded with explosives as "flying bombs".
4. Underwater attacks using swimmers.[13]

When it came to actual operations he favoured suicide attacks against stationary or near-stationary targets and, like all Al Qaeda commanders, laid great stress on extensive pre-attack surveillance.[14] He appeared to recognise the importance of chokepoints—he planned to attack ships in the Straits of Hormuz and Gibraltar—although the suspicion must be that the visual impact of a ship or several ships burning and disabled in a narrow waterway was the primary result he was looking for. It is extremely unlikely that either waterway would have been blocked, although an attack in the Straits of Hormuz would have caused useful turbulence in the world's oil markets.

Both of these plans also demonstrate that he was prepared to undertake simultaneous attacks. The Gibraltar plan apparently would have involved several explosive-laden boats slamming into a number of US and British war-

---

11   'Who's who in al-Qaeda', *BBC News*, 27 April 2007; US Department of Justice, 'Al Qaeda associates charged in attack on USS Cole, attempted attack on another U.S. naval vessel', 15 May 2003.

12   Philip Shenon, 'Threats and responses: Terror network; a major suspect in Qaeda attacks is in US custody', *New York Times*, 22 Nov. 2002.

13   Christopher Dickey, 'High sea terrorism', *Newsweek*, 27 Jan. 2003; Chalk, 'Maritime terrorism in the contemporary era', p. 30, note 45.

14   Chalk, 'Maritime terrorism in the contemporary era', pp. 34-5. The suggestion has been made that the stress on long-term surveillance emerges not from Al Qaeda operational doctrine but from Arab cultural preferences and reveals a deep-rooted rigidity of thought in contrast to Western flexibility and risk-taking.

The planned Hormuz attack was much more complicated and this
ht have been its undoing. Al Qaeda was reported to have purchased a
ighter with a crane that was capable of lifting small speedboats. The plan
was to equip the small boats with IEDs and pack the freighter with explosives
with the aim of assembling "the biggest conventional bomb" ever built. Once
in the Straits the speedboats were to have been lowered into the water and
used to attack one or more warships. If they were intercepted and destroyed
then the freighter was to have been manoeuvred sufficiently close to the target to destroy it in the resulting explosion. The reports suggest that most of
the freighter's crew, who included men from India and Pakistan, some of
them Christians, had no idea what was intended. Three suggestions have
been put forward to explain why the plan was cancelled: first, that owing to
its complexity, so many people knew about it that its security was compromised; secondly, that al-Nashiri had difficulty obtaining the huge quantity of
explosives required (although other sources deny this); thirdly, that the plot
was due to be executed to coincide with the 9/11 hijackings in the US and,
because of the security concerns, the Hormuz attack was cancelled to avoid a
risk of jeopardising the "planes operation".[15]

While al-Nashiri appears to have been the guiding hand behind much of
Al Qaeda's maritime strategy he was not behind all the attacks. Before 9/11
several Southeast Asian groups had sent members to help the *Mujahidin* fight
the Soviets in Afghanistan. As a result of the contacts with Al Qaeda made
there they became radicalised and subsequently formed a loose cooperative
"brotherhood". Groups that have generally regarded as members include
Jemaah Islamiyah (JI), Laskar Jihad, the Indonesian Islamic Liberation Front
and the Majelis Mujahidin Indonesia (MMI) in Indonesia, and the ASG and
to a degree the MILF in the Philippines, both of which received support from
Al Qaeda from the late 1980s.[16] Al Qaeda introduced Omar al-Faruq into
the region to facilitate this cooperation.[17]

15   Christopher Dickey, 'Evil genius', *Newsweek Web Exclusive*, 20 Feb. 2003.

16   On the development of Al Qaeda's Southeast Asian network see Zachary Abuza.
Militant Islam in Southeast Asia: Crucible of Terror. Boulder & London: Lynne
Rienner, 2003, pp. 128-75. On Al Qaeda support for the MILF and ASG
specifically see *ibid*, pp. 136-8 and David M. Jones, *et al.*, 'Looking for the pat-
tern: al-Qaeda in Southeast Asia–The genealogy of a terror network', *Studies in
Conflict and Terrorism*, vol. 26, 2003, p. 446.

17   Republic of Singapore, 'The Jemaah Islamiyah arrests and the threat of terrorism', *White Paper*, 7 Jan. 2003, pp. 4-5; Dana R. Dillon,, 'Southeast Asia and
the brotherhood of terrorism', The Heritage Foundation *Heritage Lectures*, 20
Dec. 2004. Al-Faruq escaped from detention at Bagram Air Base in Afghani-

From Al Qaeda's perspective the link with JI was almost certainly the most important. This group was formed in Indonesia in the 1960s when its founders started agitating for the establishment of *sharia* law in that country.[18] Although there are differences in aims and methods between the two organisations they have nevertheless formed what has been described as a highly symbiotic relationship. There is some overlap of personnel and they have shared training camps including one, Camp Abu Bakar on Mindanao in the Philippines, which was operated by the MILF but within which JI maintained their own facility known as Camp Hodeibia.[19] GAM also trained in Camp Abu Bakar.[20] Hambali, the pseudonym of Riduan Isamuddin, was the key link between the two organisations and since his arrest in 2003 cooperation may have declined.[21]

Before his arrest, he was reported to have hosted a meeting in Kuala Lumpur in January 2000 where Al-Qaeda representatives sketched out the 9/11 operation and initiated the mission that culminated in the bombing of the *USS Cole*.[22] These representatives then reassembled in Bangkok, where they reviewed why the attack on the USS *The Sullivans* in January 2000 had failed and amended the plan to prepare for the successful attack the USS *Cole* in October.[23] Ap-

stan in 2005 and was subsequently killed by British troops in a raid on a house in Basra in Iraq in 2006: Francis Harris, 'Top terrorist escapes US custody', *Daily Telegraph*, 3 Nov. 2005; Damian McElroy, 'British troops track and kill al-Qa'eda escaper who taunted Americans', *Daily Telegraph*, 26 Sept. 2006.

18 For a brief overview of the group see Council of Foreign Relations Backgrounder, 'Jemaah Islamiah', 13 June 2007. For a more comprehensive review of the group's history and activities up until the arrest of Hambali see International Crisis Group, 'Indonesian backgrounder: How the Jemaah Islamiyah terrorist network operates', *Asia Report no. 43*, 11 Dec. 2002; and International Crisis Group, 'Jemaah Islamiyah in South East Asia: Damaged but still dangerous', *Asia Report no. 63*, 26 Aug. 2003

19 Bruce Vaughn et al., 'Terrorism in Southeast Asia', *Congressional Research Service*, 7 Feb. 2005 (RL31672), pp. 6-7; Republic of Singapore, 'The Jemaah Islamiyah arrests and the threat of terrorism', p. 4; Ressa. *Seeds of Terror*, p. 134.

20 Republic of Singapore, 'The Jemaah Islamiyah arrests and the threat of terrorism', p. 4.

21 *The 9/11 Commission Report* pp. 150-2; Vaughn et al., 'Terrorism in Southeast Asia', p. 8; For a full account of Hambali's role and importance see Ressa. *Seeds of Terror*, pp. 71-75.

22 *The 9/11 Commission Report*, p. 150; Ressa. *Seeds of Terror*, pp. 78-79; 'Hambali: 'Asia's bin Laden", *BBC News*, 10 Feb. 2006.

23 *The 9/11 Commission Report*, pp. 158-9; Jack Kelley, 'Malaysia site of 9/11 plotting, FBI says', *USA Today*, 30 Jan. 2002.

parently Tawfiq bin Attash[24] was also present and suggested that a similar operation should be attempted against US Navy ships at Port Klang, Malaysia. During his later interrogation, Omar al-Faruq revealed that at about the same time a Somali member of Al Qaeda named Ghalib was plotting to attack US Navy ships in the Indonesian port of Surabaya but was unable to carry it through because he could not recruit enough personnel.[25]

JI first attracted Western attention in December 2001 when the Singapore government uncovered a plot to attack a variety of Western targets (see below).[26] US forces in Afghanistan later found a videotape linking Al Qaeda with the plot.[27] In 2002 the Singapore authorities uncovered a second plot involving members of JI and the MILF.[28] In fact there was almost certainly multiple plots, many of which were not taken forward, but for which the driving force was Hambali, who among the leaders of JI was perhaps the one most in sympathy with Al Qaeda's aim of striking at Western targets.[29] It was he who provided the link with al-Qaeda and actively encouraged the Singapore plotters to proceed.[30]

Since the two Bali bombings in 2003 and 2005 and the bombing of the Australian embassy in Jakarta in 2004, the last two perpetrated by what was virtually a breakaway group led by Noordin Top, the Indonesian authorities, with American and Australian assistance, have successfully put JI under great pressure.[31] In 2007 the group's military leader, Abu Dujana,

---

24   *The 9/11 Commission Report*, p. 151.

25   Abuza, 'Terrorism in Southeast Asia', p. 4 and *Militant Islam in Southeast Asia*, p. 162..

26   Republic of Singapore, 'The Jemaah Islamiyah arrests and the threat of terrorism', p. 2; Abuza, *Militant Islam in Southeast Asia*, pp. 154-7.

27   Vaughn *et al.*, 'Terrorism in Southeast Asia', p. 11; Republic of Singapore, *ibid.*, p. 9 & note 9 p. 29; Abuza, *Militant Islam in Southeast Asia*, p. 157..

28   Republic of Singapore. *ibid*, p. 2. See also Jeremy Zakis and Steven Macko, 'Major terrorist plot in Singapore discovered: Al-Qaeda believed well established in the Asian region', EmergencyNet News *Special Report*, 12 Jan. 2002.

29   Ressa. *Seeds of Terror*, p. 155..

30   Republic of Singapore. *ibid*, p. 2; Vaughn *et al. ibid*, p. 10.

31   For detail on the group since Hambali's arrest see International Crisis Group. 'Indonesia: Jemaah Islamiyah's current status', Update Briefing *Asia Briefing no. 63*, 3 May 2007, and Zachary Abuza, 'Jemaah Islamiya still a potent force for violence in Southeast Asia', The Jamestown Foundation *Terrorism Focus*, vol. 4, no. 19, 27 March 2007. On Noordin Top and his group in particular see International Crisis Group, 'Terrorism in Indonesia: Noordin's networks', *Asia Report no. 114*, 5 May 2006 and Zachary Abuza, 'JI's moneyman and top recruiter: A profile of Noordin Mohammed top', The Jamestown Foundation

who was regarded as the most dangerous operative still at large following the arrest of Hambali in 2003, was captured. However, there was little evidence to link him to major bomb attacks and some reason to believe that he opposed Noordin Top's attacks on foreigners.[32] Most commentators, including Sidney Jones of the International Crisis Group, regarded the arrest as a major blow for JI but one that was far from fatal: "…this is not the end", Jones was reported as saying, "the group will rebuild itself".[33] In the past JI has exploited the sectarian conflicts that have arisen on Indonesia's outer islands, in central Sulawesi in particular, between Muslim "immigrants" from Java and Madura and "native" Christian and Hindu groups, and Abuza suggests that it might well return to this activity, posing as "protectors" of Muslim communities and concentrating on welfare provision in order to rebuild its organisation and replenish its ranks.[34] Jones believes that JI is no longer a regional organisation, that it is wrong to call it "al-Qaeda affiliated" because that link was always limited, and that as it rebuilds it will concentrate on internal Indonesian issues—but that splinter groups, impatient with such a long-term view, could present a terrorist risk.[35] Chalk and Ungerer agree essentially with Jones but add that the group's re-building task could be made easier by complacency among Indonesian authorities who appear to believe that further counter-terrorist activity against JI is unwarranted.[36]

Although other Al Qaeda affiliated groups in Southeast Asia, including Laskar Jihad and Kumpulan Militan Malaysia (KMM), both regional affiliates of JI, have been suspected of planning or even executing maritime

Terrorism Focus, vol. 3, no. 29, 19 June 2006.

32   'Jemaah Islamiyah's Abu Dujana', *Jane's TSM*, 11 July 2007.

33   Ian MacKinnon, 'Indonesian police arrest Islamist leader', *The Guardian*, 14 June 2007; Tom McCawley, 'Indonesia's terrorist hunt bears fruit', *Christian Science Monitor*, 15 June 2007; Zachary Abuza, 'Indonesia neutralizes JI as immediate threat', The Jamestown Foundation *Terrorism Focus*, vol. 4, no. 19, 19 June 2007; 'Wounded but still dangerous', *Economist.com*, 14 June 2007; Noor Huda Ismail, 'JI weakened, yet potential for violence remains', The Jamestown Foundation *Terrorism Focus*, vol. IV, Issue 21, 3 July 2007.

34   Zachary Abuza, 'Shifting focus: Jamaah Islamiyah's long-term agenda towards Islamism', *Jane's IR*, vol. 19, no. 7, July 2007, pp. 22-6.

35   Sidney Jones, 'Arrested development: Jemaah Islamiyah down but not out', *Jane's IR*, Aug. 2007, pp. 22-5.

36   Peter Chalk and Carl Ungerer. 'Neighbourhood Watch: The Evolving Terrorist Threat in Southeast Asia'. Australian Strategic Policy Institute Strategy Report, June 2008, pp. 15 & 40.

attacks, it is the JI plot uncovered in Singapore in 2001 that stands out.[37] It consisted of three plans that were well developed, although they had originated at different times over a number of years. The first plan was to attack a shuttle bus that transported US military personnel and their families from their quarters to an underground railway station. The second involved the use of truck bombs against high-value diplomatic and commercial targets. Only the third was strictly maritime.[38] It was a suicide mission that involved the use of IED-equipped small craft to attack a slow-moving US Navy ship. The planners had identified a "kill zone" in the narrowest part of the channel where a ship would have had the least chance of avoiding its attacker. The group's reconnaissance had clearly been thorough; it had planned to make use of the topography to hide the boat from visual and radar detection until the last minute. The plan was devised in the mid-1990s but at the time the group felt that it lacked the expertise to carry it out. Two unidentified Middle-Easterners revisited it in early 2001 and it was being taken forward when it was uncovered in the December of that year.[39] According to other reports, Al Qaeda worked with JI to acquire the necessary bomb making materials and false documents.[40]

There is also evidence of Hizbollah involvement in a similar plot. In 2002 the Singapore government accused it of recruiting five Singaporeans in 1995. Their mission would have been to acquire a small craft, fill it with explosives and ram it into either an American or an Israeli ship in either Singapore harbour or the Straits of Malacca. The plan had obvious similarities with the subsequent Al Qaeda attack on the USS *Cole*.[41] This similarity has led to some speculation that Hizbollah, which appears willing to cooperate with Al Qaeda, might have assisted with or helped to plan the attack on the *Cole*.[42]

---

37   With regard to other groups see Bradford, 'The growing prospects for maritime security cooperation in Southeast Asia', p. 70.

38   Republic of Singapore, 'The Jemaah Islamiyah arrests and the threat of terrorism', pp. 12-13; Ressa. *Seeds of Terror*, pp. 157-158.

39   Republic of Singapore, 'The Jemaah Islamiyah arrests and the threat of terrorism',pp. 29-30.

40   Vaughn *et al.*, 'Terrorism in Southeast Asia', p. 11.

41   Council of Foreign Relations Backgrounder 'Hizbollah', updated 17 July 2006; Zachary Abuza, 'Activating Hizbollah cells 'to make no place safe for Israelis': The implications for Southeast Asia', *The Counterterrorism Blog*, 25 July 2006; 'Hizbollah planned to attack US and Israeli ships in Singapore', Institute for counter-terrorism *Spotlight*, 9 June 2002.

42   Chalk, 'Maritime terrorism in the contemporary era', p. 35; a UPI report in

Anti-Israel groups. Since the attacks of 9/11, maritime analysts have tended to focus on the possibility of more attacks like those on the *Cole* and the *Limburg*, plus the potential for terrorist attacks on shipping in the Malacca Straits and on major international ports—thus neglecting the maritime aspect of the long-running conflict between Israel and various, primarily Palestinian, insurgent groups such at Fatah, the Palestine Liberation Front (PLF), the Popular Front for the Liberation of Palestine-General Command (PFLP-GC) and, latterly, the Islamist-influence groups such as Hamas, Palestinian Islamic Jihad and Hizbollah. This is unjustified. Like the conflict in Sri Lanka, the maritime conflict between Israel and these groups displays many of the defining characteristics of irregular warfare at sea.

To bring them together as a collective and compare them with a single group such as the Sea Tigers runs the risk of not comparing like with like. The risk, however, is small because, whatever their ultimate ideological and strategic differences, each group has used the maritime domain for the same reason and employed largely the same tactics.[43] Their aims were to exploit Israel's one porous border, its maritime flank, where most of its

2001 suggested a link on the basis that the sophisticated shaped charge used in the attack was characteristic of Iranian bomb making: 'USS Cole update: Hizbollah built bomb', 21 May 2001. On possible wider links between the two groups see Jessica Stern, 'The protean enemy', *Foreign Affairs*, vol. 82, no. 4, 2003, p. 32, where she writes that Hizbollah gave Al Qaeda logistical support for the East African embassy bombings and that the relationship between the groups then deepened after Al Qaeda was driven from its sanctuaries in Afghanistan. Also Maria Ressa, 'Bin Laden forges tactical alliance between al Qaeda and Hizbollah', *ABS-CBN Interactive*, 18 Aug. 2006. Ressa suggests that al-Qaeda and Hizbollah use the same people interchangeably in much the same way that fighters in the Philippines appear to move freely between the ASG, MILF and MNLF. Ressa. *Seeds of Terror*, pp. 130-131.There are also suggestions that Al Qaeda has received support from Iran directly, including the use of its territory as a logistical hub: Stephen Fidler, 'Al Qaeda linked to operations from Iran', *Financial Times*, 6 July 2007. A terrorist logistical hub is generally regarded as a clandestine operating environment where extremists can establish and operate safe houses, command posts, financial networks, logistical and training bases. There is also some suspicion that Al Qaeda might have assisted Iran in the 1996 Khobar Towers attack. See *The 9/11 Commission Report*, p. 60 and Dan Eggan, '9/11 panel links Al Qaeda, Iran: Bin Laden might have part in Khobar Towers, report says', *The Washington Post*, 26 June 2004.

43   The Palestinian groups that have undertaken maritime missions are the PLO (known since 1993 as the Palestinian Authority) and its constituent organisations Fatah, PLF and the PFLP; PFLP-GC, PIJ, Hamas and Hizbollah: Lorenz, 'The threat of maritime terrorism to Israel', pp. 26-30.

cities are located, to land raiding parties, often to grab hostages that they could exchange for prisoners held by Israel, and to land arms.

The Palestinian naval threat was born in 1967 with the creation, at a pan-Arab summit immediately before the Six Day War, of a "Palestinian Arab Navy".[44] Following the Arab defeat the naval effort was expanded. In September 1970 ("Black September" in the annals of Palestinian history), King Hussein drove the Palestinians out of their bases in Jordan. They relocated to southern Lebanon. From this position the prospect of mounting attacks against Israel's exposed coastline presented a more available option. Katz, in fact, argues that although the first water-borne raid into Israel came across the Dead Sea in 1969, by the early 1970s, with most of the Jordan valley sealed, the Syrian and Lebanese borders well protected and Sinai occupied, the sea was virtually the Palestinians' only option.[45] Although this is broadly correct, it was only once the land border between Israel and Lebanon was closed completely that the Palestinian groups turned to maritime operations in earnest. The necessary capability took time to materialise but once it was in place three of the four major Palestinian attacks on Israel during the 1970s came from the sea,[46] and by the end of the 1980s most observers believed that the Palestinians possessed the most capable and best-equipped maritime arms of any insurgent groups.

The concentration at first was on collecting intelligence on Israeli ship movements in harbours around the Mediterranean, and on developing tactics such as attaching limpet mines to ships vital to Israel's economy. Fishermen and smugglers were recruited and a small body of combat swimmers and commandos established. Most of the attacks that were undertaken appeared to be small operations designed to test Israel's response.[47] George Habash, the leader and founder of the PFLP, likened Israel to an island surrounded by enemies that could only survive because of its air and sea links which, if severed, could bring it to its knees.[48] Although this was far

---

44   Katz, *Guards Without Frontiers*, p. 154; Lorenz, 'The threat of maritime terrorism to Israel', p. 8.

45   Katz, *Guards Without Frontiers*, pp. 154-5.

46   Lorenz, 'The threat of maritime terrorism to Israel', p. 6. The three maritime attacks are the Savoy and Coastal Road incidents and the Haran family murders. The exception is the May 1974 attack on Ma'alot, a town six miles south of the Lebanon border, when children were taken hostage in a school, of whom 22 died and 50 were wounded in the subsequent rescue..

47   *Ibid.*, p. 7.

48   George Habash interview in LIFE magazine, 12 June 1970, cited in Lorenz, 'The threat of maritime terrorism to Israel', p. 7.

from an original insight—it is a concern that has animated Israeli naval thinking since independence[49]—it appears to have inspired two attacks: the 1973 attack on the *Sanya* (mentioned above) and, in 1971, the attack on the SS *Coral Sea*, an Israeli-owned but Liberian-registered oil tanker, which was struck by ten rocket propelled grenades as it transited the Bab el-Mandeb. The PFLP's intention was to discourage ships from using the Israeli Red Sea port of Eilat.[50] The attack was mounted from a small motor launch that had been lowered from a large trawler off Perim Island. A fire started in one of the cargo tanks but was quickly extinguished.[51] Other groups focused on establishing a regular clandestine ferry route between Cyprus and Beirut and between Beirut and Gaza.[52] Fatah was reported to possess a small "navy" of vessels ranging in size from 150 tons up to 500-ton *markabs* based in Cyprus and the Lebanese port of Tripoli largely for this purpose.[53]

Also during the early 1970s, Fatah created a specialised protection group for Yasser Arafat and other members of the organisation's high command. Given the name Force 17, it developed into an elite commando operation while continuing to answer to Arafat personally.[54] Within Force 17 the elite of the elite were the naval swimmers who eventually led Fatah military displays on many occasions when the group was headquartered in Beirut.[55]

Intriguingly, Force 17 could be viewed as the counterpart of the IDF/Navy's own naval commando unit, Flotilla 13 (Shayetet 13).[56] This unit, which grew out of the Palyam, a small elite force that was part of the Hagana (the original Jewish resistance movement), was formed in 1949, shortly after the end of the first Arab-Israel War. Tzalel argues that what he calls

---

49   Moshe Tzalel, *From Ice-Breaker to Missile Boat: The Evolution of Israel's Naval Strategy*, Westport, CT & London: Greenwood Press, 2000, p. 5.

50   On the *Coral Sea* incident see MIPT Incident Profile: Popular Front for the Liberation of Palestine (PFLP) attacked Maritime Target, Israel, 4 June 1971; Katz, *Guards Without Frontiers*, p. 155 where he attributes the attack to Fatah.

51   Tzalel, *From Ice-Breaker to Missile Boat*, p. 45.

52   Katz, *Guards Without Frontiers*, p. 155

53   Menefee, *TMV*, p. 33; Brian M Jenkins, *et al.*, 'A chronology of terrorist attacks and other criminal actions against maritime targets' in Parritt, *Violence at Sea*, p. 66.

54   For a brief background note on this organisation see Aaron Mannes, 'The end of Force 17?' *Counterterrorism Blog*, 9 Oct. 2007.

55   Katz, *Guards Without Frontiers*, p. 161.

56   'Shayetet 13', The Israel Special Forces Database.

the "Palyam-school" has always had an important influence on Israeli naval thought and force structure.[57]

As the Israel-Lebanon border was made progressively more secure and difficult to penetrate, interest in the maritime domain as an attack medium increased. In 1974 three terrorists attacked Israel's most northerly city, Nahariya, situated only five and a half miles (9 km) from the border, with the aim of kidnapping hostages. The attack failed and the attackers were killed but the event caused consternation within Israel, which responded by introducing the maritime control zones, barred to civilian use and monitored by radar and lookouts, that have prevented most subsequent incursion attempts against the city.[58]

Within a year Fatah had begun to circumvent these zones by employing its larger vessels as mother ships to support small craft, usually Zodiacs, to land supplies of weapons, saboteurs and raiding parties, sailing them far out to sea before turning towards the Israeli coast.[59] In 1975, Force 17 used this method to mount its most significant raid to date. A 150-ton mother ship sailed from Sidon and landed a terrorist team on a beach south of Tel Aviv. As soon as the group arrived its members began firing and throwing grenades. When fire was returned they ran into the Savoy Hotel and took hostages. When Israeli police and IDF forces stormed the hotel, the terrorists blew it up killing themselves, their hostages and several of the rescuers. The mother ship was apprehended and escorted into Haifa.[60]

The operation had been planned by Fatah's military leader Khalil al-Wazir, otherwise known as Abu Jihad, who was a very talented operational commander.[61] His stated maritime objectives were, first, to open a new front against Israel and thereby divert troops from the land borders; secondly, to undermine Israeli morale; and, thirdly, to infiltrate commanders,

---

57   Tzalel, *From Ice-Breaker to Missile Boat*, pp. 7 & 9-10.

58   Lorenz, 'The threat of maritime terrorism to Israel', p. 8 and Samuel Pyeatt Menefee, 'Piracy and maritime crimes of violence', unpublished MS, p. 206 are clear that the assault craft travelled directly from Lebanon. Katz, *Guards Without Frontiers*, p. 156, on the other hand, writes about the assault being mounted from a mother ship.

59   Menefee, *TMV*, p. 33; Lorenz, 'The threat of maritime terrorism to Israel', p. 8.

60   Katz, *Guards Without Frontiers*, pp. 157-8; Lorenz, 'The threat of maritime terrorism to Israel', pp. 9-10; Menefee, 'Piracy and maritime crimes of violence', p. 206.

61   Katz, *Guards Without Frontiers*, p. 158; Lorenz, 'The threat of maritime terrorism to Israel', p. 9.

messages and supplies into the Occupied Territories. On the strength of his ability as demonstrated by the Savoy Hotel operation, Fatah's naval arm attracted expert training from Egypt, Syria, the Soviet Union and, quite possibly, Cuba and North Korea. The Syrians, in particular, were reported as having provided advanced underwater combat and sabotage training.[62] Fatah was not alone in receiving support: Yugoslavia helped the Popular Front for the Liberation of Palestine-General Command (PFLP-GC) and the Palestine National Front (PNF) to assemble teams of frogmen equipped, according to the same reports, with re-breather apparatus.[63]

On 11 March 1978, Abu Jihad executed an operation to grab hostages from a hotel in Bat Yam, near Tel Aviv, and demand the release of Palestinians held by Israel. The mother ship sailed from Dabur, a port just south of Tyre, but the captain dropped the raiding party too far from the coast, an error which, when compounded by rough seas and the team's poor navigation, meant that the group landed half way between Tel Aviv and Haifa, on the other side of the city from their objective. In an attempt to redeem the situation they hijacked a bus. A gun battle ensued, now known as the Coastal Road or Country Club Massacre, in which all the terrorists and their 36 hostages were killed.[64]

The Coastal Road raid had been mounted shortly after Operation "Joy of Ages" when Israeli commandoes had struck Tyre and destroyed significant numbers of Palestinian boats and quantities of equipment. Previously, when Israeli naval commandos had mounted assaults on Palestinian maritime bases in Lebanon, a mission regarded as being of crucial importance for Flotilla 13 ever since the bases had first been established,[65] they had succeeded in inhibited Palestinian operations. The fact that the "Joy of Ages" incursion did not disrupt the Coastal Road attack indicated that single raids were unlikely to be sufficient to combat the Palestinian maritime threat and more substantial action was required. The Coastal Road raid, therefore, even if it was not the sole reason why Israel decided on 14 March 1978 to launch Operation Litani, a limited invasion of southern

---

62   Katz, *Guards Without Frontiers*, p. 158.

63   Jenkins, *et al.*, 'A chronology of terrorist attacks and other criminal actions', pp. 66-7. The Yugoslavs were also reported to be responsible for training ETA frogmen.

64   Jenkins, *et al.*, 'A chronology of terrorist attacks and other criminal actions', p. 66; Katz, *Guards Without Frontiers*, pp. 159-60; Lorenz, 'The threat of maritime terrorism to Israel', p. 10; 'Coastal road massacre', *Wikipedia*.

65   Tzalel, *From Ice-Breaker to Missile Boat*, p. 74.

Lebanon (excluding the city of Tyre), was a significant contributory factor.[66] The ground operation exposed an extensive naval infrastructure of workshops and weapons stores. It also uncovered equipment, including one-man mini-submarines (bought from sporting goods suppliers but ideal for solo suicide missions), small reconnaissance boats apparently supplied by Libya, fibreglass speed boats equipped with machine guns, Zodiacs, diving gear, navigational devices and rafts fitted with multiple Katyusha-122 rocket launchers. Documents seized revealed that Fatah was trying to buy small warships and coastal radars of their own from the Soviet Union, from Arab navies or on the black market.[67]

Although the Israelis regarded the invasion as a success, Palestinian maritime bases were forced only a relatively short distance north beyond the Litani River. Fatah and other groups were therefore still in a position to mount significant maritime operations. On 30 September 1978 Fatah attacked the port of Eilat using a Greek-registered freighter, the *Agaeus Dimitrius*. The intention was to use it first, as a platform to fire 42 Katyusha-122 rockets at the port's oil installations, secondly as a floating bomb to be rammed, loaded with three tons of explosives, onto a beach crowded with holiday-makers (who presumably were expected to stand around, watch and wait). The ship, however, was intercepted as it approached the resort and when it failed to stop was fired on and the terrorists on board captured.[68] Also on 30 September two mother ships, the *Ginan* and the *Stephanie,* were intercepted; the second was following a regular sea lane between Cyprus and Egypt from where it would have launched a fast boat with a raiding party while still in international waters.[69]

Further raids were launched the following year. On the night of 22 April 1979 the Abu Abbas Group was once again successful in penetrating the city of Nahariya. The raiding party stormed into the apartment of the Haran family. The mother was able to hide with her infant son but in the process smothered him. The terrorists meanwhile dragged the father and daughter to the beach where they had left their boats. Cornered by po-

---

66 Katz, *Guards Without Frontiers,* p. 160; Lorenz. 'The threat of maritime terrorism to Israel', p. 11.

67 Katz, *Guards Without Frontiers,* p. 163.

68 Menefee, *TMV,* p. 32; Katz, *Guards Without Frontiers,* pp. 160-1; Lorenz, 'The threat of maritime terrorism to Israel', p. 11; 'Islamic terrorism timeline', Entry for 3 Oct. 1978.

69 Katz, *Guards Without Frontiers,* p. 161; Lorenz, 'The threat of maritime terrorism to Israel', p. 10.

lice and the IAF, the terrorists' leader, Samir Quntar, then aged 17, first crushed the girl's head with a rock before shooting the father.[70] In 2006 the leader of Hizbollah, Hassan Nasrallah, named the freeing of Quntar as the principal, public reason why his organisation had kidnapped two Israeli soldiers, the event that triggered Operation Change of Direction, the massive 2006 Israeli assault on southern Lebanon.[71]

The Haran murders marked the beginning of an interval which lasted until 1986, during which no Palestinian raiders eluded the IDF/Navy. For much of the time it also coincided with an Israeli troop presence in Lebanon which was reinforced in 1982, under the auspices of Operation "Peace in Galilee", because UNIFIL, the United Nations peace-keeping force that had been made responsible for southern Lebanon after the 1978 invasion, was demonstrably incapable of preventing rocket attacks on Israel's northern settlements. The presence of these troops, on ground that was favourable to guerrilla operations, meant that the main focus of Palestinian efforts moved away from maritime raids towards attacks on exposed Israeli military targets in Lebanon. This trend was reinforced by the forcible removal of the anti-Israel groups from their naval bases in Beirut and Tripoli (although they retained a presence in Sidon) and their relocation to Tunisia—the new home of the PLO headquarters—Algeria, Yemen and Libya.

Despite the greater distances the raiding parties needed to travel from their new bases, and the continuing effectiveness of the IDF/Navy, which severely hampered their operations, the PLO and other groups nevertheless did not give up maritime raiding. Details of these incidents are not readily available but Katz reports that, in the period between 1979 and 1984, the IDF/Navy intercepted 30 "major terrorist attempts to infiltrate men and material into Israel", the interceptions taking place in Lebanese territorial waters in several cases,[72] and that between April 1985 and early 1987, 20 more planned "attacks" were disrupted.[73] Neither was the search for advanced naval equipment abandoned;[74] in 1982, for example, there

---

70   Katz, *Guards Without Frontiers*, pp. 153-4; Lorenz, 'The threat of maritime terrorism to Israel', p. 8.

71   Harry de Quetteville, 'No, I hope these men rot in jail', *Sunday Telegraph*, 23 July 2006; 'Nasrallah: Hostages in secure location, far away', *YNetNews.com*, 12 July 2006.

72   Katz, *Guards Without Frontiers*, p. 161.

73   *Ibid.*, p. 174.

74   *Ibid.*, pp. 163, 168 & 176.

were reports that Fatah had received four World War II-type one-man "submarines" from Yugoslavia.[75]

The two most significant events of the 1980s occurred in 1985, of which the most famous was the hijacking of the *Achille Lauro* by the PLF in October. Before that, in April, Abu Jihad launched an operation that was to have culminated in a seaborne suicide assault on the compound housing the Israeli Ministry of Defence and IDF General Staff. However, the boat carrying the terrorists to their target from Algeria, the 1,000-ton *Attaviros*, was intercepted and sunk.[76] Because the Israeli government believed that the real target of the raid was the Israeli Defence Minister, Yitzhak Rabin, Abu Jihad was later assassinated.[77] The Israeli maritime defensive perimeter was finally breached in July 1986, when the target once again was Nahariya. Four heavily armed PFLP terrorists in a Zodiac eluded an Israeli patrol craft, landed on the outskirts of the city and set up a defensive position from where they held off a heavy Israeli assault for three hours before being killed. From the plans found in their possession it was clear that their objective was to mount a murderous attack on holiday-makers on the city's seafront.[78]

During the 1980s yachts became favoured for both transport and raiding. In most cases they were foreign-owned in order to divert suspicion. Force 17 tried this tactic twice in 1985 but in both cases the IDF/Navy mounted interceptions.[79] Perhaps more damaging was the seizure of the SS *Anton* in 1986 and of the *Maria R* in 1987, both of which yielded hauls of Fatah commanders in transit.[80] Suspecting that their operations were being compromised by the presence of Israeli agents in Larnaca in Cyprus, Fatah members seized an Israeli yacht, the *First*, in 1985, killing one member of

---

75   Menefee, *TMV,* p. 33; Jenkins, *et al.,* 'A chronology of terrorist attacks and other criminal actions', p. 66. Just what sort of threat such equipment really presents, given the high level of skill required to operate it and the intensive maintenance needed to keep it operational, is questionable.

76   Katz, *Guards Without Frontiers,* pp. 164–6.

77   *Ibid.*

78   Katz, *Guards Without Frontiers,* pp. 173–4.

79   UNSC, Letter dated 4 Sept. 1985 from the Permanent Representative of Israel to the United Nations, addressed to the Secretary-General. In the letter the yachts involved are named as the *Ganda* and the *Kasilradi.* Katz, *Guards Without Frontiers,* pp. 166–7 in his account refers to them as the *Ganda* and the *Casselardit.* Menefee, *TMV,* 1996, p. 33 refers to them as the *Ganda* and the *Kasil Radis* (and places both incidents in 1978).

80   Katz, *Guards Without Frontiers,* p. 174.

the crew and abducting two others. Israel retaliated by bombing Fatah's headquarters in Tunis, killing 60 and wounding 100.[81]

The success of the IDF/Navy made it a target, a development that largely coincided with the emergence of more aggressive, Islamist-inspired groups such as Hamas and Palestinian Islamic Jihad, a group with particularly strong ties to Iran.[82] In fact, some of the tactics used resembled those developed by the Iranian Revolutionary Guards Corps. The IDF/Navy observed the deployment of four-man fast boats armed with RPGs against its vessels in what were likely to be suicide missions. In December 1987 a fast boat emerged from behind a fishing craft off Sidon. Its crew fired rocket propelled grenades at a *Dabur* patrol craft. Before they were killed they managed to inflict severe damage on the patrol craft and mortally wound the second in command. Hamas subsequently claimed responsibility for the incident.[83] However, the first avowed suicide attack at sea was carried out by the secular PFLP-GC in April 1988, when a bomber manoeuvred a fishing boat close to an Israeli naval vessel and detonated an explosive charge which, however, failed to inflict either casualities or damage.[84] Shaul Shai refers to five further suicide attacks against Israeli naval vessels between 1988 and 1997, all unsuccessful, that were conducted off the Lebanon coast by either the Palestinian groups such as Fatah, PFLP and PFLP-GC or the Shi'ite Muslim organisation Amal.[85]

Attempts to infiltrate Israel by sea continued. The most elaborate was a PLF mission that sailed from Benghazi in Libya in 1990 with the aim of inserting two teams on the Israeli coast near Gaash and Nitzanim. The plan was to shell houses and hotels along the shore with Katyusha rockets, cannon and machine gun fire, and then to land, capture the Sheraton hotel and kill everyone they encountered. The mother ship launched six speedboats, which according to reports had been painted with radar absorbent material. One sank immediately. The remainder headed for the Israeli coast. One

---

81   Menefee, *TMV,* p. 33; Katz, *Guards Without Frontiers,* p. 167; Lorenz, 'The threat of maritime terrorism to Israel', p. 13; MIPT Terrorism Knowledge Base. Incident Profile: Al-Fatah Attacked Maritime Target, 25 Sept. 1985, Cyprus.

82   MIPT, Group Profile: 'Palestinian Islamic jihad'.

83   Katz, *Guards Without Frontiers,* pp. 174-5. Hamas was formed in 1987.

84   Lorenz, 'The threat of maritime terrorism to Israel', p. 14. It is worth noting that the LTTE's first maritime suicide attack occurred two years later, on 12 July 1990, when six Sri Lankan personnel were killed in an explosive boat attack in Trincomalee harbour. See 'Suicide attacks by the LTTE' at http://www.satp.org/satporgtp/countries/shrilanka/database/data_suicide_killings.htm

85   Cited in Lorenz, 'The threat of maritime terrorism to Israel', p. 15.

was a dedicated tanker which returned to Port Said as scheduled. Two of the four remaining craft experienced mechanical failure, forcing 16 raiders to cram into the two serviceable boats. One was intercepted 22 miles (40 km) off Gaash. The other made landfall at Nitzanim but had already been detected by Israeli security forces; four of the raiders were killed on the beach and seven captured. According to the PLF leader, Abu Abbas, the raid had taken nearly three years to prepare and cost about $3 million (equivalent to $4.7 million in 2006).[86]

Other infiltration attempts included a raid on Coral Beach at Eilat in 1992, in which four swimmers from the PLF swam over two and a half miles (5km) from the coast of Jordan towing their weapons in water-proof containers. One leaked, pulling a swimmer to his death. Once ashore, the remainder of the team killed an unarmed security guard but were then killed in turn before they could open fire on holiday-makers.[87] In 1993 a Fatah faction bombed an Israeli ship, the *Jrush Salom*, also in Eilat.[88]

Palestinian coastal raiding effectively came to an end with the signing of the Oslo Accords and the formation of the Palestinian Authority in 1993. This agreement did not include the new Islamist-inspired groupings which continued to attack IDF/Navy craft. Three incidents took place off Gaza early in the new century. On 7 November 2000, the same year that saw the *Cole* attack, Hamas used a fishing boat in an attempted suicide attack on an Israeli naval vessel off Rafah at the northern end of the Gaza Strip. When the Israeli navy ordered the boat to stop it changed course towards the IDF/Navy vessel and exploded about 100 metres away without causing any damage.[89] Palestinian Islamic Jihad used the same tactic in November 2002, causing injuries to four Israeli sailors.[90] In January 2003, Hamas

---

86   Lorenz, *Ibid.*, pp. 15-16; Howland, 'Israel's navy steps up to security challenge in wake of Gaza pull-out'. A brief video of the events at Nitzanim beach can be viewed at http://www.youtube.com/watch?v=JuejlGFtD5s. In Bohn's account the mother ship is named the *Tiny Star* and the first boat to fail is the tanker craft: Bohn, *The Achille Lauro Hijacking*, pp. 121-3.

87   Lorenz, 'The threat of maritime terrorism to Israel', p. 16; Aaron Mannes, 'A life of terror: Abu Abbas dies', *National Review Online*, 10 March 2004.

88   Lorenz, 'The threat of maritime terrorism to Israel', p. 16; MIPT Incident Profile: Al-Fatah Attacked Maritime Target, 25 Dec. 1993.

89   'Patterns of Terrorism in Israel in 2000'; Gunaratna, 'Sea Tiger success threatens the spread of copycat tactics', p. 12.

90   Lee Keath, 'Palestinians attack Israel navy boat', *AP*, 23 Nov. 2002; 'Palestinian suicide boat attacks Israeli navy boat', *Reuters*, 23 Nov. 2002; 'Fishing boat explodes near Israeli vessel', *CNN.com*, 22 Nov. 2002; Ellis Shuman, 'IDF block-

positioned a booby-trapped life raft such that it drifted into an area patrolled by Israeli naval vessels. It exploded when fired on without causing any injury.[91]

Raids were also attempted. In August 2002, Jordanian security services disrupted a plan before it could be put into effect to use swimmers in an attack that mirrored the 1992 attack on Coral Beach.[92] In a plan uncovered in October 2002, Hamas intended to smuggle a bomb aboard an Eilat-based tourist ship.[93] In 2003 Israeli security forces arrested a fisherman who had been asked to help Palestinian Islamic Jihad prepare maritime assaults: it was reported that he had been given $500,000 to buy the necessary equipment.[94] Swimmers have been used frequently to transport arms from Egypt into Gaza and to infiltrate coastal areas.[95] Three attempts were made to infiltrate the Dugit settlement between 2002 and 2004,[96] and Hamas mounted a substantial raid at Tel Fatifa in March 2004 to avenge the assassination of its founder and spiritual leader, Sheik Ahmed Yassin, earlier in the month.[97] Playing a variation on a theme, the Israeli port of Ashdod was attacked from the landward side in March 2004 by terrorists who were infiltrated hidden inside a container.[98]

---

ades Gaza coast after encounter with terror fishing boat', *Israel Insider*, 24 Nov. 2002; Lorenz, 'The threat of maritime terrorism to Israel', p. 18 suggests the life raft was steered by a suicide swimmer.

91 'Seizing of the Abu Hasan, May 22, 2003', Israel Ministry of Foreign Affairs *Press Release*, 22 May 2003; Jonathan Howland, 'Israel's navy steps up to security challenge in wake of Gaza pull-out', *JINSA Online*, 31 May 2006. Also Howland correspondence with the author.

92 Lorenz, 'The threat of maritime terrorism to Israel', p. 22.

93 *Ibid.*

94 Arieh O'Sullivan, 'Security forces uncover Islamic Jihad maritime unit', *Israel Ministry of Foreign Affairs* report, 5 Feb. 2004.

95 Arieh O'Sullivan, 'On guard off Gaza's coast', *Jerusalem Post*, 5 July 2002; Howland, 'Israel's navy steps up to security challenge in wake of Gaza pull-out'.

96 'Seizing of the Abu Hasan, May 22, 2003'; 'Israeli soldiers kill two Palestinian frogmen', *AP*, 27 March 2004; 'Attempted terror attack via the sea thwarted', Israel Ministry of Foreign Affairs *Press Release*, 10 Nov. 2004.

97 'Hamas attack on Israeli beach settlement repelled', *Irish Examiner*, 27 March 2004; 'Israeli soldiers kill two Palestinian frogmen'; Lorenz, 'The threat of maritime terrorism to Israel', p. 18.

98 See '10 killed in Ashdod port 'suicide attack'', *Jerusalem Newswire*, 15 March 2004; Christopher Slaney, 'How they bombed Ashdod', *Fairplay*, 8 April 2004, pp. 20-1. It is also worth noting that the Ashdod bombers evaded port security measures that were much stricter than those required under the International Ship and Port Facility Security (ISPS) code. See Bill Watson, 'In search of the

Among the institutions authorised under the Oslo Accords was a Palestinian Coast Guard, based in Gaza, with a mandate to prevent drug and arms smuggling from Egypt.[99] Fatah naval units amounting to about 1,500 men were absorbed into the new service. Arms smuggling, however, did not stop. It appears to have been undertaken by all the groups operating in the Gaza Strip, including Fatah. Hamas won power in the Palestinian legislative elections of 2006. Although it had not previously demonstrated a serious interest in the maritime dimension, in 2007 it announced the creation of its own coast guard unit to protect Gaza's fishermen and prevent drug smuggling.[100]

The extent to which anti-Israeli groups have used the sea for arms smuggling has been suggested by a number of significant interceptions. In May 2001 IDF/Navy forces intercepted a ship named the *Santorini* in the Mediterranean. It had sailed from Tripoli in Lebanon and was stopped 150 miles (240km) off Tyre. The PFLP-GC and Hizbollah had arranged the arms shipment found on board with Syrian help.[101] The arms were loaded into large barrels and the intention was to drop them off the Gaza coast where they would have been collected by unspecified Palestinian groups.[102] The munitions included Strela man-portable anti-aircraft missiles (MANPADS), Katyusha rockets and mortars. During their interrogation the crew declared that theirs was the fourth shipment—that three previous shipments, which also involved a second vessel, the *Calypso-2*, had slipped through.[103] The PFLP-GC leader, Ahmed Jibril, also asserted that this ship-

---

Trojan Horse', *Fairplay,* 8 April 2004, pp. 17-19; 'Palestinians and al-Qaeda bond through ship container', *DEBKAfile,* 17 March 2004; Lorenz, 'The threat of maritime terrorism to Israel', pp. 22-3.

99   See, for example, Council of Foreign Relations, Backgrounder, 'Reorganizing the Palestinian security forces', 4 Oct. 2005; Gal Luft, 'The Palestinian Security Services–Between police and army', The Institute for Counter Terrorism, 19 July 1999.

100 'Hamas announces formation of its new coast guard unit', *AP,* 11 Aug. 2007; Ali Waked, 'Hamas confirms establishment of 'navy", *YnetNews.com,* 11 Aug. 2007; Hanan Greenberg, 'IDF says ready to battle Hamas at sea', *YnetNews. com,* 9 Aug. 2007.

101 'Iran and Syria as strategic support for Palestinian terrorism', Israel Ministry of Foreign Affairs, 30 Sept. 2002, Paragraphs 67-71.

102 Ellis Shuman, 'Gaza-bound weapons arsenal seized by Israeli Navy', *Israel Insider,* 9 May 2001.

103 'Hezbollah', Intelligence and Terrorism Information Centre at the Centre for Special Studies *Special Bulletin,* June 2003.

ment had not been the first and would not be the last.[104] The PFLP-GC received substantial support from Iran and it is likely that the *Santorini* was operated in cooperation with Hizbollah, a conclusion reinforced by the presence of Hizbollah guards who closed nearby roads during the loading operation prior to the vessel's third run.[105]

In 2002 Israeli forces seized the *Karine A* in the Red Sea 300 miles (550 km) off Eilat before it could enter the Suez Canal. The operation, which was organised from Lebanon, almost certainly by Hizbollah, but was financed and directed by Iran, involved the transfer of 50 tons of weapons including Katyusha rockets, anti-tank missiles, and anti-tank and anti-personnel mines from Iran to Fatah, Fatah's al-Aqsa Martyrs Brigade and, quite possibly, Hamas and Palestinian Islamic Jihad as well.[106] On board the ship, which was loaded at the Iranian island of Kish in the Persian Gulf, were around 80 Iranian-manufactured submersible containers with compressed air ballast tanks that would have allowed them to float just below the surface.[107] The apparent intention was to load the munitions into three smaller boats off the Egyptian coast. The smaller boats would then have moved closer to Gaza where they would have dropped the containers into the sea. Sympathetic fishermen would then have collected them as they drifted towards the shore.[108]

In May 2003, Israeli commandos seized the trawler *Abu Hassan* off Rosh Hanikra, close to Haifa. It was loaded with a sophisticated cargo of fuses, timers and training materials. The Egyptian owner had been recruited and trained by Hizbollah to carry out maritime support missions and might well have had a role in recruiting crew members for the *Karine-A* opera-

---

104   Shuman, 'Gaza-bound weapons arsenal seized by Israeli Navy'.

105   'Iran as a state sponsoring and operating terror', Intelligence and Terrorism Information Centre at the Centre for Special Studies *Special Bulletin,* April 2003, p. 34; 'Iran and Syria as strategic support for Palestinian terrorism', particularly paragraphs 70(c) and 71. Confidential information, Sept. 2006.

106   'Hezbollah'; 'Iran and Syria as strategic support for Palestinian terrorism', paragraphs 63-66.

107   Graham Usher and Julian Borger, 'Israel halts Palestinian arms ship', *The Guardian,* 5 Jan. 2002; Yoni Talmer, 'IDF naval commandoes seize PA-bound weapons ship', *Israel Insider,* 6 Jan. 2002. For more details on the *Karine A* and the *Santorini* see 'Weapons found on the 'Karine-A' and 'Santorini', *WarOnLine,* 20 July 2002.

108   Howland, 'Israel's navy steps up to security challenge in wake of Gaza pull-out'.

tion. Most importantly Abu Amra, an explosives expert, was on board.[109] The ship had sailed from Egypt to a rendezvous off the Lebanese coast where it had picked up Abu Amra and another Hizbollah operative. It had then turned south, the intention being to land the men on the Egyptian coast close to Gaza, where they would then have been smuggled across the border. One of the likely organisers of the mission was Fathi Razam, the deputy chief of the PA's coast guard.[110]

Whilst these might have been the largest hauls, numerous other attempts have been made to bring in smaller quantities of arms.[111] The assumption is that many of these have been successful. Even though Israel surrendered control of the Gaza-Egypt border in September 2005, the sea apparently retained its importance as a smuggling route for some time because the land crossings were unreliable and the tunnels that riddle the border area had limited capacity. Kalashnikov rifles could be passed through without difficulty but boats were able to transport much larger quantities of arms and bulkier items such as explosives more easily.[112] According to the IDF/ Navy, the smugglers received large sums of money and worked closely with the terrorist organisations. A single vessel carrying half a ton of explosives, for example, could be missed among the 400-600 Palestinian fishing boats that operate off the Gaza Strip on most nights.[113] From the time Hamas

---

109 Greg Myre, 'Israel says explosives expert on fishing boat it seized', *New York Times*, 23 May 2003; 'Navy seizes Hizbollah bomb expert and explosives-making materials on boat', *Israel Insider*, 23 May 2003.

110 Herbert-Burns, 'Terrorism in the early 21st century maritime domain', pp. 165-7; 'IDF seizes bomb making supply ship heading for Gaza', *JINSA Online*, 26 May 2003; 'Seizing of the Abu Hasan, May 22, 2003'.

111 Ellis Shuman, 'IDF operates against Palestinian arms smuggling attempt on Gaza coast', *Israel Insider*, 28 Aug. 2002; Yaakov Katz, 'Lebanese nab terrorists heading for Gaza', *The Jerusalem Post*, 12 Jan. 2006; Hanan Greenberg, 'Navy seizes explosives off Gaza shore', *YnetNews.com*, 14 May 2006; 'IDF Naval craft seized several hundred kg of explosives', Israel Ministry of Foreign Affairs *Press Release*, 14 May 2006; 'Navy foils arms-smuggling attempt', *Arutz Sheva– IsrealNationalNews.com*, 22 June 2006; 'Israeli navy fires on Palestinian boats suspected of smuggling', *Israel Insider*, 11 March 2007.

112 Hanan Greenberg. 'Navy: easier for terrorists to smuggle arms by sea', *Ynet-News.com*, 15 May 2006; Lorenz, 'The threat of maritime terrorism to Israel', p. 19. Jonathan Howland, private correspondence with the author, 2006. On the small arms influx when Israel surrendered control of the border strip see 'Dealers smuggle weapons into Gaza from Egypt'. *Associated Press*, 15 September 2005.

113 Howland, 'Israel's navy steps up to security challenge in wake of Gaza pull-out'. On the numbers of boats involved see also Alan Johnston, 'Gaza fishermen risk Israeli fire', *BBC News*, 13 Oct. 2006 and Shuman, 'IDF operates against Pal-

gained control Gaza, and certainly since January 2008 when Hamas pulled down the border fence, most arms have moved across the land frontier.[114]

Since 2000 a new element has entered the conflict: the close connection between Hizbollah and Iran.[115] Hizbollah has at least four faces: political, including an elected representative presence in Lebanon's parliament; humanitarian, through the provision of educational, medical and welfare services; military, which is made up of a well-equipped, irregular armed force known as the Islamic Resistance that is targeted at Israel but also has the resources to defend itself against any attempt by Lebanon's indigenous army to disarm it; and terrorist, through its External Security Organisation (ESO) which conducts international terrorist attacks, of which the two in Buenos Aires, the first on the Israeli embassy in 1992 and the second on a Jewish centre in 1994, are examples.[116]

Although it is capable of mounting some operations on its own initiative, in many respects Hizbollah appears to be an arm of Iranian foreign policy and a proxy for its armed forces.[117] Reports suggested that two senior figures within the ESO, both named as its "head", had senior roles within the Iranian apparatus: the first, Imad Mugniyah, who was one of the hijackers of TWA Flight 847, during which the US Navy diver Robert Stetem was murdered, was reported to have been chosen by the Iranian President, Mahmoud Ahmadinejad, to oversee Iranian retaliation in the case of a Western or Israeli strike on Iran's nuclear programme; the other senior figure was Qassem Suleimani, whose membership of Iran's Revolutionary Guard Corps reinforced the suspicion that all ESO attacks required Iranian

---

estinian arms smuggling attempt on Gaza coast' where he quotes Israeli naval sources suggesting that the total fleet is around 1,000 boats.

114   'Arms smuggling through the Gaza-Egypt border – Background'. Israel Ministry of Foreign Affairs, 20 February 2008.

115   Hizbollah is an abbreviation of the group's full name in Arabic, which is 'Hizb Allah-Al-thawra Al-Islamiya fi Lubnan'. Hezbollah is the normal American spelling.

116   'Buenos Aires bomber 'identified'', *BBC News*, 10 Nov. 2005.

117   'Hezbollah is a strategic arm of Iran', *Intelligence and Terrorism Information Centre at the Centre for Special Studies*, 8 Sept. 2006. See also 'Hizballah / Hizbollah / Hizbullah / Hezbollah', *GlobalSecurity.org*, ND; Matthew Levitt, 'Hezbollah finances: Funding the party of God', *The Washington Institute for Near East Policy*, Feb. 2005; and Lara Deeb, 'Hizbollah: A Primer', *Middle East Report Online*, 31 July 2006. Thom Shanker. 'A new enemy gains on the US'. *New York Times*, 30th July 2006.

authorisation.[118] The ESO is also known as the Islamic Jihad Organisation (IJO—not to be confused with Palestinian Islamic Jihad[119]), which perhaps coincidentally is also a designation that has been used by Iran's Revolutionary Guard Corps as a cover name for state-sanctioned overseas operations.[120] In 2007, US forces in Iraq captured a Lebanese member of Hizbollah, Ali Mussa Dardouk. He had been a member of the group that had mounted the Karbala attack in which five US servicemen died. According to Brigadier General Kevin J. Bergner, Dardouk worked with the Iranian Revolutionary Guard Corps' Quds Force and had the task of organising special groups "in ways that mirrored how Hezbollah was organised in Lebanon", and although there was no indication that Hizbollah had an organisation in Iraq, Dakdouk, who had received training in Iran, was judged to be a "proxy...to do things (the Iranians) didn't want to have to do themselves.[121] In 2007 the US government moved to declare the Iranian Revolutionary Guard Corps a "specially designated global terrorist" body, the first branch of a national military organisation to be so listed, as reports also emerged of the Corps' involvement in smuggling and other corrupt activity.[122]

In the maritime domain Iran has developed a significant irregular warfare capability. This first came to prominence during the Iran-Iraq "Tanker War", during which "swarms" of three or four Swedish-built Boghammer fast boats or Boston Whaler-type craft were used to attack tankers and other targets. Each boat was equipped with a mix that included 107mm rockets,

118 'Ahmadinejad recruits Hezbollah terror chief', *WorldNetDaily,* 23 April 2006; 'Hezbollah is a strategic arm of Iran', p. 10. For an account of the Iranian link to the Buenos Aires bombing see Ze'ev Schiff, 'How Iran planned the Buenos Aires blast', *Haaretz,* ND. Also 'Hezbollah (Part Two)', *Intelligence and Terrorism Information Centre at the Centre for Special Studies,* June 2003: Appendix 5, 'The bombing of the Jewish community centre in Argentina (1994)–an example of the modus operandi of Hezbollah's overseas terrorist apparatus'.

119 'Who are Islamic jihad?' *BBC News,* 9 Aug. 2001; 'Palestinian Islamic jihad', Institute for Counter-Terrorism; MIPT Terrorism Knowledge Base, Group Profile: 'Palestinian Islamic jihad'.

120 'Islamic jihad' was the name of the organisation that claimed responsibility for the 1984-85 Red Sea mining operation. In Aug. 1984 the organisation was praised on Tehran Radio, although this praise was followed quickly by a denunciation: Truver, 'Mines of Aug.', p. 110.

121 Lee Keath, 'US: Iranian force carried out attack', *AP,* 2 July 2007 and Lee Keath, 'General: Iran was behind deadly Karbala attack', *AP,* 2 July 2007.

122 Robin Wright, 'Iranian unit to be labelled 'terrorist', *The Washington Post,* 15 Aug. 2007; Philip Sherwell, 'Iranian Guards amass secret fortunes', *Sunday Telegraph,* 19 Aug. 2007; Toby Harnden, 'Iran's Revolutionary Guards a 'terror group", *Daily Telegraph,* 20 Aug. 2007.

RPGs and machine guns that were used to rake a ship's superstructure with fire.[123] The expectation amongst naval experts now is they would mount similar attacks only this time in "swarms" of between 30 and 50 boats at a time. Attacks of this magnitude could quite possibly overwhelm the defences even of ships that can put up helicopters. While most of these Iranian craft are still armed with light automatic weapons, rockets and RPGs it is known that Iranian engineers, probably with Chinese or North Korean assistance, have managed to stabilise heavier stand-off weapons. Such "swarm" attacks might also be used to distract attention from the approach of more heavily armed missile or torpedo boats or semi-submersibles, or an aerial attack using explosive-laden UAVs or light aircraft, or land-based anti-ship missiles of the type used against the Israeli corvette patrolling off Lebanon.[124]

There is evidence that, from late 2000, Iran began to reinforce Hizbollah's existing maritime area denial capability. While it is difficult to determine whether these maritime elements fall under the command of Islamic Resistance or the ESO (or whether each wing maintains its own maritime capability), it is understood that the main operating base is located south of Beirut, but that elements are also present in the many small ports and harbours along the Lebanese coast.[125] It appears that the primary roles for this force are, first, to prevent the IAF/Navy from operating close enough to the Lebanese coast to interfere with supply operations and, secondly, to facilitate coastal raids. This suspicion has been reinforced by the comments of an Iranian officer that Hizbollah has a submarine unit and a "naval commando unit that operates Chinese-manufactured speed boats, capable of targeting the Israeli navy."[126] Reports also suggest that the group has acquired a Soviet-era patrol boat, although for what reason is unclear.[127] The belief is that most of this equipment reaches Hizbollah from Iran overland through Syria but that some comes by sea. In the latter case shipments

---

123   Crist, 'Joint special operations in support of Earnest Will', p. 16.

124   Since the attack Israel has expressed concern that a more advanced Russian-built sea-skimming missile, the SSN-X-26 Yakhont, which Iran has acquired, might be transferred to Syria and thus to Hizbollah. With a range of over 160 miles (300 km) and a warhead in excess of 440 lbs (200 kg) this weapon represents an even more potent threat than the C-802. Yaakov Katz, 'J'lem worried by Iranian owned anti-ship missile', *The Jerusalem Post*, 28 Aug. 2007.

125   Ali M. Koknar, 'Corsairs at starboard: Jihad at sea', *Journal of International Security Affairs*, no. 7, Summer 2004, p. 63. Private information, Sept. 2006.

126   Ali Nouri Zadeh, 'Iranian officer: Hizbollah has commando naval unit', *Asharq Alawsat*, 29 July 2006.

127   Chalk, 'Maritime terrorism in the contemporary era', p. 29, note 42.

might move up the Red Sea and through the Suez Canal following a route similar to that of the *Karine A,* and then onward to Lebanon. Alternatively, they could be transshipped to fishing boats off the Gaza coast before they are moved northwards using, in reverse, some of the same smuggling networks that supply Hamas and the other Palestinian groups.[128]

Equipment, however, is not enough. Training is essential. Small boat combat demands experience and practice; lack of either leads to losses.[129] Swarm tactics in particular require intense practice, high standards of seamanship, and close command and control if collisions between fast moving craft are to be avoided and attacks pressed successfully. Against a sophisticated enemy such as a Western navy, rather than slow moving merchantman as in the "Tanker War", attackers would need to limit electro-magnetic emissions and be able to operate at night in order to optimise the inherent "stealthiness" of small boats.[130] Iranian experience and training could enable Hizbollah to quickly minimise these limitations. Although Iranian naval tactics have been developed to exploit the particular geography of the Persian Gulf, nonetheless a number of IRGCN attack methodologies and equipment developments – particularly the use of dispersed swarming whereby fast attack craft deploy from separate locations and only concentrate briefly to attack a target thus maximising surprise and denying the defender the opportunity to counter-attack a mass formation, the use of mini-submarines for reconnaissance purposes, low-observable and low-signature technologies, and the integrated use of land-based weapons such as anti-ship cruise missiles and coastal-based torpedoes – are capable of being transferred to Hizbollah.[131] Furthermore it is likely that Hizbollah units have trained alongside IRGCN units because the sophistication of modern technical intelligence gathering methods makes it difficult to develop and practice small boat tactics unobserved.[132] Given its access to this capability, given that it has considered maritime attacks in the past, and given its

---

128 'Shin Bet chief accuses Egypt of closing its eyes to Palestinian arms smuggling to Gaza. But DEBKA*file* reports its volume is dwarfed by Hizballah's illegal imports', DEBKA*file*, 2 Oct. 2006.

129 Benjamin S. Yates, 'David vs. Goliath: Small boat challenges to naval operations in coastal warfare', Thesis, United States Marine Corps, Command and Staff College, Marine Corps University, 1998, p. 25.

130 *Ibid.,* p. 24.

131 For a useful description of Iran's asymmetric naval capability see Fariborz Haghshenass, 'Iran's doctrine of asymmetric naval warfare', The Washington Institute for Near East Policy *Policy Watch no. 1179,* 21 Dec. 2006.

132 Confidential information, June 2008.

demonstrable global reach, Hizbollah is possibly in a position to become a more formidable maritime adversary than the Sea Tigers, Al Qaeda or any other group.[133]

The question that remains, however, is why is Iran reinforcing Hizbollah's maritime capability? The answer is not immediately clear. None of it has been deployed. What is does do, however, is add another element to the strategic mix and further complicate the tactical picture that Western navies and the Israeli navy must confront when operating off the Levantine coast. This aim accords with Iran's objective in supporting Hizbollah generally.[134]

Gerakan Aceh Merdeka (GAM). Aceh is the Indonesian province located at the northernmost tip of Sumatra. It came to wide public attention because the epicentre of the 2004 Indian Ocean tsunami was in the seabed off its western coast and, consequently, the area suffered widespread devastation. The province has a long history of resistance to external rule dating back at least to the colonial period. GAM, or the Free Aceh Movement, began fighting for independence from Indonesia in 1976. However, on 15 August 2005, in a move almost certainly influenced by the effects of the tsunami, it signed a peace agreement with the Indonesian government that fell short of its stated aim of full independence.[135] The Indonesian armed forces had often used brutal methods to suppress the insurgency.[136] As part of the agreement the Indonesian government agreed to withdraw all non-indigenous units. In return the movement announced in December 2005 that it had disbanded

---

133   Matthew Levitt, 'Hizbollah: A case study of global reach', The Washington Institute for Near East Policy *Policy Watch*; remarks to a conference on 'Post-modern terrorism: Trends, scenarios, and future trends', International Institute for Counter-Terrorism, Herzliya, Israel, 8 Sept. 2003; Barak Ben-Zur and Christopher Hamilton, 'Hizbollah's global terror option', The Washington Institute for Near East Policy, *Policy Watch no. 1129*, 21 July 2006.

134   See Daniel Byman, *Deadly Connections: States that Sponsor Terrorism*, Cambridge UP, 2005, pp. 94-6; Kathryn Haahr-Escolano, 'Iran's changing relationship with Hizbollah', The Jamestown Foundation *Terrorism Monitor*, vol. II, no. 19, 7 Oct. 2004, pp. 6-8.

135   For a history of GAM until 2003 see Kirsten E. Schulz, 'The Free Aceh movement (GAM): Anatomy of a separatist organization', Washington, DC: East-West Centre, 2004. On the peace agreement see 'Indonesia agrees Aceh peace deal', *BBC News*, 17 July 2005.

136   Erich Marquardt, 'Examining the threats to Indonesia's national tnterests', *PINR*, 2 March 2005.

its military wing.[137] The belief, however, is that it retained at least some of its maritime capability.[138]

GAM has been referred to as an Islamist group.[139] The population of Aceh are Muslim and GAM did appear to have established links with Islamist insurgent groups across Southeast Asia.[140] Suggestions were made that the group had established relations with Al Qaeda. There are grounds for believing that two of bin Laden's lieutenants, Ayman al-Zawahiri and Mohammed Atef, visited Aceh in 2000 in the hope they could establish a base area and training facilities but that, because the rebellion was always more ethno-nationalist than Islamist in character, GAM rejected their suggestion.[141] Although GAM recruits trained at MILF camps in the Philippines, the group was not generally regarded as part of the post-Afghan terrorist "brotherhood" that coalesced around Al Qaeda.[142] GAM does, however, have other international connections including, possibly, with the Tamil Tigers. It reportedly received arms from Iran and Libya, and sent large numbers of fighters to Libya for training.[143]

---

137   Gareth Evans, 'Aceh is building peace from its ruins', *International Herald Tribune,* 23 Dec. 2005. However, as with all such accords, difficulties emerged. See International Crisis Group, 'Aceh: Now for the hard part', Asia Briefing no. 48, 29 March 2006.

138   Confidential information, Sept. 2006.

139   For example John C.K. Daly, 'Al Qaeda and maritime terrorism (Part II)', The Jamestown Foundation *Terrorism Monitor,* vol. 1, no. 5, 7 Nov. 2003.

140   Yang Razali Kassim, 'GAM, Islam and the future of Aceh', IDSS *Commentaries,* 8 Feb. 2005; GlobalSecurity.org suggest GAM have links with separatist groups in southern Thailand such as the Pattani United Liberation Organization (PULO), Bersatu and Gerakan Mujahideen Islam Pattani (GMIP), and the Malaysian Islamist group Kumpulan Mujahiden Malaysia (KMM) that has known links with JI: 'Thailand Islamic insurgency', *GlobalSecurity.org,* ND.

141   Abuza, *Militant Islam in Southeast Asia,* p. 176; Koknar, 'Corsairs at Starboard: Jihad at Sea', p. 58; Andrew Tan, 'The threat of terrorism in Southeast Asia: Threats and responses', paper delivered to the Council of Asian Liberals and Democrats, 10th Anniversary Conference, 9-10 Dec. 2003. Tan makes it clear that GAM distanced itself from Al Qaeda. Also Dillon, 'Southeast Asia and the brotherhood of terrorism'.

142   On GAM's use of MILF camps see Dillon, 'Southeast Asia and the brotherhood of terrorism'; Anthony Davis, 'MILF links to external terrorist groups', *Jane's IR,* 1 April 2002, pp. 22-3; Amitav Acharya, 'Terrorism and security in Asia: Redefining regional order?' Murdoch University Asia Research Centre *Working Paper no. 113,* Oct. 2004, p. 5.

143   Schulze, 'The Free Aceh movement', pp. 30-1; MIPT Terrorism Knowledge Base, Group Profile: 'Free Aceh movement'; Dillon, 'Southeast Asia and the brotherhood of terrorism'; Abuza, *Militant Islam in Southeast Asia,* p. 176.

GAM's maritime arm was developed as a matter of necessity rather than choice given Aceh's location. Developing it, however, presented no difficulty as the group could draw on the strong Acehese maritime tradition and the cultural and trading links that extended across the Malacca Straits to Malaysia and Thailand.[144] When it was operational it had, unlike the Sea Tigers, only a narrow and specialised capability. Its primary focus was gun running.[145] It appears that GAM, unlike the LTTE or the MILF, preferred to use criminal suppliers rather than establish its own arms purchasing network.[146] According to Mark Valencia most of the suppliers were Chinese syndicates based in Malaysia and Thailand who brought the arms into Malaysia and then transferred them to Aceh in small boats.[147] The direct route through Thailand appeared to focus on Adang about 50 miles (75 km) off the Thai-Malaysian coast and other small islands off the Thai provinces of Satun and Trang from which fishing boats would transfer the arms across the Malacca Strait.[148] The Indonesian military made several seizures, and tried to prevent the trade by banning fishing off Aceh's southeast coast.[149]

Its second focus appeared to be raising money by capturing and ransoming ship's crews. Although these are not the actions of a group seeking international recognition and respectability, and the organisation consequently disclaimed responsibility repeatedly, kidnap-and-ransom did become a feature of maritime predation in the Straits from 2001 through to the conclusion of the peace accord.[150] The suspicion to which this gives rise is reinforced by the knowledge that GAM (or people claiming to be

---

144 Jeffrey Chen, 'The emerging nexus between piracy and maritime Terrorism in Southeast Asia Waters: A Case Study of the Gerakan Aceh Merdeka (GAM)' in Lehr, *Violence at Sea*, 2007, p. 145.

145 'GAM relies on...gun-runners operating along the rugged coastline to fuel their rebellion': Paul Dillon, 'Piracy disappears in tsunami's wake', *AlJazeera. net*, 31 Jan. 2005.

146 Anthony Davis, 'Police interdict arms traffic to Aceh', *Jane's IR*, 1 April 2004.

147 According to Zachary Abuza GAM buys most of its arms in bazaars in Cambodia, Thailand and the Philippines: Abuza, *Militant Islam in Southeast Asia*, p. 176.

148 Davis, 'Police interdict arms traffic to Aceh'.

149 Mark J. Valencia,'Security issues in the malacca strait: Whose security and why it matters', paper presented at the MIMA Conference on the Straits of Malacca held at the Prince Hotel, Kuala Lumper, 11-12 Oct. 2004, pp. 3-4; also Schulze, 'The Free Aceh movement', p. 33.

150 Catherine Zara Raymond, 'The Malacca Straits and the threat of maritime terrorism', *PINR*, 24 Aug. 2005.

GAM) kidnapped people on land for ransom. In fact, kidnappings became so frequent in 2001 and 2002 that concerns were raised that GAM was undergoing a process of criminalisation similar to that of the ASG.[151] It was, moreover, no stranger to criminality; it was unquestionably involved in drug cultivation and dealing to pay for arms. An unknown but reputedly substantial portion of the world's supply of marijuana was believed to come from Aceh and a number of players in addition to GAM, such as the TNI, the police and local criminal syndicates, were not only involved in this trade but to a degree cooperated with each other.[152]

Despite this the GAM leadership, exiled in Sweden, rejected the accusation that such acts were sanctioned centrally. Schulze suggests it is likely that they were the product of "warlordism and the result of local decision making" driven perhaps by what he calls the "economically driven recruits" who joined GAM in 1999.[153] Schulze believes this explains the sudden surge of piracy in Malacca Strait, an activity that he maintains does not fit GAM's way of working.[154] Whether some of the acts of piracy and kidnapping that took place around the Aceh coast were those of the group centrally, or of a splinter group or groups, or common criminals or members of TNI posing as GAM, has never been clear. In August 2003, for example, two vessels described as "disguised" oil service craft or tugs attacked a large, Taiwanese-registered fishing vessel, the *Dong Yih*. The 'disguised' craft chased the fishing vessel for two hours, hitting it with over 200 rounds one of which wounded the vessel's captain.[155] The IMB suggested this was another GAM attack but ONI took the view that the craft were Indonesian, possibly even naval patrol boats enforcing Indonesia's recently declared ban on vessels approaching Acehese waters "without proper permits".[156] In another example the Indonesian authorities reported in 2007, that Rusli bin Abdulgani, the "long sought and feared pirate of tankers, merchant vessels as well as fishing boats in the Malacca Strait", had been captured. Reputedly he used his network, which was alleged to cover Medan and Aceh, to extort protection money from ship owners. He claimed that he did this

---

151   Schulze, 'The Free Aceh movement', pp. 17 & 28.

152   *Ibid.*, pp. 27-8.

153   *Ibid.*, p. 28.

154   *Ibid.*, p. 29.

155   Bradsher, 'Problems with pirates continue in sea lanes of South Asia'.

156   NGA ASAM. 2003-275, 9 Aug. 2003; Herbert-Burns and Zucker, 'Drawing the line between piracy and maritime terrorism', p. 33.

on behalf of GAM, but "judging from his fancy way of living" he retained much if not all of the proceeds of his activities himself.[157]

On the other hand, in September 2001, a GAM spokesman, while denying that the group was involved in piracy, went on to issue a warning to ships using the Malacca Straits that they would need to "seek permission" if they were to pass without hindrance—a demand very similar to the one made by the LTTE in the case of the MV *Princess Kash* for example —and pointed to the attack on a 348 DWT coal carrier, the *Ocean Silver*, that had been captured and which was freed only after the payment of a $34,000 ransom, as an indication of what would happen.[158] The spokesman's denial that GAM was involved in any act of piracy rang even hollower when the hostages reported that they had been held in a GAM camp in Aceh where their kidnappers admitted they were GAM members. Again, although the group denied it, the suspicion persists that GAM or GAM members also undertook the attacks on the *Trimanggada*—assaulted by 50 men in three boats—in April 2003, the *Penrider* in August 2003, possibly the *Cherry 201* in January 2004, and the *Tri Samurda* in March 2005. The attack on the *Tri Samurda* raised particular alarm because it was a methane gas carrier and the raiders were armed with RPGs.[159] The *Penrider* was boarded close to the entrance to Port Klang in Malaysia by men equipped with grenade launchers and automatic weapons, and sailed across the Strait to Indonesia where the ship was released but the officers were retained and a ransom of $100,000 was demanded (although only $52,000 was actually paid, according to the Royal Malaysian Maritime Police).[160] The crew of the *Cherry 201* were less fortunate: when the owners tried to bargain, the kidnappers shot four of the crew, although eight managed to escape when the firing began.[161] There are also grounds for believing GAM was involved

157 'Pirate ring leader caught in Cirebon', *Antara News*, 30 Sept. 2007; 'Former GAM members 'high sea robbers', *Jakarta Post*, 2 Oct. 2007.

158 'Aceh rebels warn ships to seek permission to use Malacca Straits', US Department of Transportation, *Transportation and Security Review*, vol. 2, no. 14, 5 Sept. 2001; NGA ASAM 2001-266, 25 Aug. 2001. Also Herbert-Burns and Zucker, 'Drawing the line between piracy and maritime terrorism', p. 32.

159 ONI WWTTS Report, 6 April 2005, Paragraph K.2; 'Pirates storm Indonesian tanker', *BBC News* report, 14 March 2005.

160 IMO, Reports on Acts of Piracy and Armed Robbery Against Ships', MSC.4/Circ.40, 4 Sept. 2003, Annex One; Keith Bradsher, 'Problems with pirates continue in sea lanes of South Asia', *New York Times*, 15 Aug. 2003. Also Herbert-Burns, 'Terrorism in the early 21st century maritime domain', pp. 167-8.

161 NGA ASAM 2004-37, 5 Feb. 2004 on the *Cherry 201* and 2003-274, 10 Aug.

in kidnapping fishing boats and their crews. A headman from the village of Hutan Merlintang in Malaysia told Liss that victims who had returned said they had been taken by men who claimed to be GAM and who in the earliest years had held them hostage in GAM territory.[162]

Liberation Tigers of Tamil Eelam (LTTE). The LTTE's aim has been to gain independence for the Tamil-populated northern and eastern areas of Sri Lanka. The conflict traces its origins back to the 1950s, when the Sinhalese-dominated government attempted to reverse what the Sinhalese majority on the island saw as the undue influence of the Tamil minority. It was given added impetus by the anti-Tamil riots of 1983, which led to many Tamils fleeing Colombo and the southern parts of the island and re-settling in the Tamil north or even in the Tamil areas of India.[163] Founded in 1972, the LTTE had by 1987 emerged as the dominant Tamil militant group with effective control over the Jaffna peninsula and much of the east coast.[164] The group married terrorism, including suicide terrorism, to the operational techniques of classic guerrilla warfare. From the very beginning it recognised that a maritime arm was essential. The group's founder, Velu-pillai Prabhakaran, made this clear when he said that, "(g)eographically the security of Tamil Eelam is interlinked with that of its seas. It is only when we are strong on the seas and break the dominance the enemy now has that we will be able to retain the land areas we liberated and drive our enemies from our homeland."[165]

When the insurgency started the group's rear base area was across the Palk Strait in the Indian state of Tamil Nadu.[166] Its existence was vital early on, although by the mid-1980s it had become a divisive issue.[167] Contact

2003 on the *Penrider.*

162 Liss, 'The roots of piracy in Southeast Asia'.

163 For useful background on the conflict see Jeremy Barnicle, *et al.*, 'Securing the peace: An action strategy for Sri Lanka', Woodrow Wilson School for Public and International Affairs, Princeton University and Centre for Strategic and International Studies, Draft, Jan. 2004.

164 Bharadwaj, 'Maritime aspects of Sri Lankan conflict', p. 239. For background on the rise of Tamil militant groups see Gamini Samaranayake, 'Patterns of political violence and responses of the government in Sri Lanka, 1971-1996', *Terrorism and Political Violence,* vol. 11, no. 1, Spring 1999, pp. 110-22.

165 Quoted in R. Hariharan, 'Sri Lanka: How strong are the Tigers?' South East Asia Analysis Group *Note no. 297,* 28 Feb. 2006.

166 For details on these base areas see Sakhuja, 'The dynamics of LTTE's commercial maritime infrastructure', pp. 1-2.

167 On the reasons why the rear base became a divisive issue see Dharmeratnam

between the base area and the front was first maintained by use of a mixture of fast dinghies for personnel transport and slower fishing vessels for logistical movements, both equipped only with small arms and grenades. The Sri Lankan Navy (SLN) recognised that it needed to sever this link. Once it had been re-equipped with faster and more heavily armed patrol craft, particularly the Israeli-built Dvora and Super Dvora, it inflicted heavy losses on both types of Tamil craft.[168] To counter this threat the Tigers reorganised their naval resources and formed the Sea Tigers, the Kadal Puli, in 1984. As it developed from an essentially defensive force to one that conducted sea control, supply and amphibious support operations in an area from the Strait around the north of Sri Lanka and down the coast as far as Trincomalee, it became the most capable and tactically astute of all the seaborne insurgency groups.[169] It played a vital role in the Sri Lankan forces' surrender of the Elephant Pass base complex in 2000 by fighting its way through an SLN covering force to land nearly 1,500 Tiger troops and their supplies at Kudarappu-Maamunai. The capture of the base was key to control of the Jaffna peninsula. The subsequent withdrawal of the Sri Lankan forces altered the strategic situation in the north of the country and led to the subsequent cease-fire.[170]

The pivotal role of the Sea Tigers in the LTTE's overall order of battle, and the importance the group attached to the sea, has never diminished.[171] Because the land areas held by the LTTE have never been contiguous, the

---

Sivaram, 'The importance of 'Rearbase': Taraki, 1989', *TamilNet.com*, 17 Feb. 2006.

168   'SL Naval History from 1984'; Rafik Jalaldeen, 'Navy's pivotal role in battle against terrorism', *Daily News* (Colombo), 10 Dec. 2007.

169   In Peter Chalk's estimation, LTTE 'set the benchmark' for maritime terrorism. Interview with author, 2004. For a brief review of some of the earliest Sea Tiger attacks see Menefee, *TMV*, pp. 49-50. For a list of its bases and installations see 'LTTE bides time to win Eelam', *Sunday Observer* (Colombo), 30 Oct. 2005.

170   Suryanarayan, 'Sea Tigers–threat to Indian security'; R. Hariharan. 'Sri Lanka: taking stock of LTTE', *PINR*, 29 July 2005; N. Manoharan, 'Tigers with fins: Naval wing of the LTTE', Institute of Peace and Conflict Studies *Article no. 1757*, 31 May 2005. The other side of the coin, of course, is that 'the Sri Lankan army which has a major force advantage over the LTTE in the peninsula, is handicapped by the inadequacy of air support and the inability of the navy to control the seas': N. Ram cited in Bharadwaj, 'Maritime aspects of Sri Lankan conflict', p. 238.

171   The Sea Tigers are reportedly the most expensive arm of the LTTE organisation: Bharadwaj, 'Maritime aspects of Sri Lankan conflict', p. 245.

group's ability to move its cadres freely by sea has been vital.[172] During the LTTE's negotiations with the Sri Lankan government in 2003 the LTTE demanded *de facto* naval status for the Sea Tigers, equal to that of the SLN, and control of over contiguous marine resources.[173] If this demand had been conceded—and the Norwegian-led mediation team did propose an exclusive sea area for the Sea Tigers—it would have given the LTTE control over some two-thirds of the Sri Lankan coastline.[174] It would also have established a "third navy" in the region, which would have had implications for Indian as well as Sri Lankan security and set a disturbing international precedent.[175] Naturally enough, the proposal was not acceptable to either country's government.

In the time since the group was formed in 1984 it has destroyed between a third and a half of the Sri Lankan navy's coastal fleet.[176] Its equipment has included patrol boasts captured from the SLN and others that it adapted, such as armed trawlers. It has built its own boats and its own suicide boats. It has acquired its own fleet of ocean-going freighters to carry weapons and equipment in addition to legitimate cargo. As mentioned earlier it has built its own mines, most of which were improvised, and attempted to buy submersibles and build its own.

172   Sudha Ramachandran, 'The Sea Tigers of Tamil Eelam', *Asia Times Online,* 31 Aug. 2006.

173   V. Suryanarayan, 'Prabhakaran: Back to the old game', *The Hindu,* 1 Dec. 2003 and V. Suryanarayan, 'Sea Tigers and Indian security', *Journal of Indian Ocean Studies,* vol. 12, no. 3, Dec. 2004, p. 409; on the LTTE's demand that the ceasefire monitors grant the Sea Tigers equal status with the Sri Lankan Navy see P.K. Balachandran, 'LTTE wants monitors to protect Sea Tiger vessels also', *Hindustan Times.com,* 13 May 2006 and 'Soosai reiterates sovereign right to seas bordering Tamil Homeland', *TamilNet,* 13 May 2006. The LTTE also strongly deny the assertion by the Sri Lankan Monitoring Mission (SLMM), responsible for monitoring the ceasefire agreement, that non-state actors have no rights over contiguous sea space. See S. Muthucumaran, 'The sea rights of states in formation', *SiberNews,* 15 May 2006. For a Sri Lankan perspective see Rohan Joshap, 'Sri Lankan Navy...LTTE Sea Tigers and the right to territorial seas', Sri Lankan Ministry of Defence: The Media Centre for National Security, 21 July 2006.

174   Ramachandran, 'The Sea Tigers of Tamil Eelam'.

175   V.S. Sambandan, 'SLMM head, Sea Tigers meet', *The Hindu,* 17 July 2003; V. Suryanarayan, 'Sri Lanka and India's security', *The Hindu,* 25 April 2003; B. Raman, 'Maritime terrorism: An Indian perspective', South Asia Analysis Group *Paper no. 1154,* 29 Oct. 2004, p. 8.

176   Barnicle, *et al.,* 'Securing the peace: An action strategy for Sri Lanka', pp. 5-6; Suryanarayan. 'Sea Tigers–threat to Indian security'; Sakhuja, 'The dynamics of LTTE's commercial maritime infrastructure', p. 7.

The two most important categories of boats operated by the Sea Tigers are attack and logistics craft. The logistics craft are fast but lightly armed. Their role is to collect the weapons and equipment from the Sea Tigers' freighters in international waters and run them to beach pick-up points. Naturally the SLN has attempted to intercept this activity. Consequently, the logistics craft are shielded by the attack craft that are heavily armed with a combination of 23mm cannon, machine guns and RPGs. They tend to operate in packs of three. Their aim is to draw the SLN away from the logistics craft. These operations generally take place at night to nullify Sri Lankan air superiority. The Sea Tigers break off any engagement at first light. They land their craft on beaches where they are pulled out of the water and hidden under jungle cover during the day.

For suicide missions a mixture of modified craft including fishing trawlers and racing style boats has been used supplemented by specialised, indigenously manufactured vessels. The specialised vessels are difficult to detect because most attacks take place under cover of darkness and the boats lie low in the water. As with the attack boats the suicide craft generally operate in groups of two or three with two, and latterly three, suicide bombers on each boat to ensure that if one is killed during the attack run the mission will still be completed.[177] Suicide attacks are a vital part of LTTE operations on land and at sea. They have been designed, in Peter Chalk's words, to "engender chronic operational paralysis in the enemy", and he reports that one retired member of the SLN has admitted that the "fear of being caught in a martyr strike has been one of the main factors contributing to decreases in recruitment to the (Sri Lankan) navy over the past several years."[178]

Sea Tiger numbers grew throughout the period of the ceasefire; in 2001 the force reportedly consisted of between 3,000 and 4,000 men. When the tsunami struck the Sri Lankan coast in late 2004 reports, which the group itself denied, suggested that the force had lost a substantial number of men and boats as a result.[179] Despite these denials, estimates made in 2006 suggested Sea Tiger numbers had dropped to 1,500-2,000 and an unknown

---

177   Murphy, 'Maritime threat: tactics and technologies of the Sea Tigers', pp. 8-9. For an earlier report on the indigenously manufactured suicide craft see Roger Davies, 'Sea tigers, stealth technology and the North Korean connection', *Jane's IR*, vol. 13, no. 3, March 2001, pp. 2-3.

178   Chalk, 'Maritime terrorism in the contemporary era', pp. 38-9.

179   P.K. Balachandran, 'Tsunami did not wreck our navy: LTTE', *Hindustan Times* 1 Jan. 2005.

number of boats had been lost.[180] There is possibility that a surprisingly large proportion of the Tigers' fleet may have survived because, as mentioned, their standard procedure was to store the key attack and logistics craft away from the sea in jungle hideouts when not in use.[181]

It is believed, nonetheless, that the need to replace naval assets lost in the tsunami became one of the principal motives behind fund-raising activity amongst the Tamil diaspora around the world.[182] Fund-raising was pursued with vigour from 2005 onwards and raised substantial funds for the organisation. In 2006 Human Rights Watch issued a report detailing the methods the LTTE used amongst diapora communities.[183] To indicate the scale of the LTTE's income from their rackets and "taxes", they were estimated to have squeezed $120 million from the 70,000-strong expatriate Tamil community in France alone. On top of the general levy extracted from individual expatriates each week they were reported to have demanded a €2,000 "loan" from each family specifically to replace lost naval equipment. Reluctance to pay was met by intimidation and threats often accompanied by further threats to kill family members still living in Sri Lanka.[184]

180   Hariharan, 'Sri Lanka: How strong are the Tigers?'

181   Davis, 'Tamil Tigers seek to rebuild naval force'; Confidential interview, Aug. 2005.

182   Murphy, 'Maritime threat: Tactics and technology of the Sea Tigers', p. 6; Private information, Dec. 2005.

183   Human Rights Watch, 'Funding the 'final war': LTTE intimidation and extortion in the Tamil diaspora', vol. 18, no. 1(c), March 2007.

184   Murphy, 'Maritime threat: Tactics and technology of the Sea Tigers', p. 6; Private information, Dec. 2005. Also Christophe Cornevin, 'Tigers demanding money in Mafia style...', Le Figaro, 2 Dec. 2005 and V.S. Sambandan, 'LTTE raising funds for 'final war'', The Hindu, 16 March 2006; Roht William Wadhwaney, 'Lankan expats 'forced to fund LTTE'', Gulf Times, 11 May 2006. For a broader view of LTTE fund raising and other external operations see Byman, et al., Trends in Outside Support for Insurgency Movements, Santa Monica: RAND, 2001, pp. 42-59; Peiris, 'Secessionist war and terrorism in Sri Lanka: Transnational impulses', pp. 86-8; Peter Chalk, 'Liberation Tigers of Tamil Eelam's International Organisation and Operations–A Preliminary Analysis', Canadian Security Intelligence Service: Commentary no. 77, Winter 1999; and John Solomon and B.C. Tan, 'Feeding the Tiger: How Sri Lankan insurgents fund their war', Jane's IR, Aug. 2007. More recently the LTTE have come under sustained air attack and this appears to have resulted in a greater push for money from Tamils living in North America to pay for anti-aircraft weapons: Shaun Waterman, 'Tamil moves in N America cause concern', ISN Security Watch, 29 Aug. 2006; also Solomon and Tan, 'Feeding the Tiger'. Finally see 'LTTE linchpin KP free', Peace Lanka, 18 Dec. 2007 which provides further details on LTTE fund raising operations. The author of this blog does not reveal his or her

The Sri Lankan Ministry of Defence has suggested that the Tamil Tigers' total annual income from its worldwide fund-raising operations (including their criminal income) amounted to $300 million annually in the decade between 1997 and 2007, up from around $40 million annually in the mid-1980s.[185] In 2006 an Indian-based research group, the Strategic Foresight Group (SFG), estimated the LTTE's total annual income to be between $175 million and $385 million.[186] In 2007 Solomon and Tan and the Associated Press both put the figure at between $200 and $300 million.[187]

The LTTE have also been accused of piracy.[188] The first alleged incident took place off Vettilaikerni in October 1994 when the MV *Ocean Trader* was attacked. Attacks continued at the rate of about two a year until 2001, after which they became less frequent. Of the known cases several, like the first, occurred in the 50 mile (93 km) wide strip of coastal water that the LTTE asserts as its own. However questionable this assertion may be it nonetheless blurs the distinction between piracy and insurgent attack.[189] The MV *Princes Wave*, attacked in 1996, and the MV *Cordiality*, attacked in 1997 (NGA ASAM 1997-76), were loading cargoes of valuable ilmenite (titanium ore) in what the LTTE claimed was a government attempt to

---

identity, which must mean the information should be treated circumspectly, although internal evidence suggests they may be connected to the Indian police or security services.

185 'LTTE terrorists have annual profit margin of US $300million', *The Media Centre for National Security*, Ministry of Defence, Public Security, Law and Order (Sri Lanka), 27 July 2007.

186 Of that $100 million to $250 million was believed to come from drug trafficking although, as the study acknowledged, there was no direct evidence of LTTE involvement. Local taxation and extortion were estimated to contribute about $30 million; human smuggling and funds siphoned off from NGOs were believed to generate a further $3 to 5 million; the contribution from the Tamil expatriate community was believed to bring in $40 to 50 million, while the group's business ventures were thought to yield profits of between $35 and $50 million: P.K. Balachandran, 'Lanka most militarised in South Asia: study', *Hindustan Times*, 21 Sept. 2006.

187 Solomon and Tan, 'Feeding the Tiger'; 'AP IMPACT: An investigation into fundraising and weapons smuggling by Sri Lanka's Tamil Tigers', *AP*, 5 Nov. 2007.

188 For example, Gunaratna,'The asymmetric threat from maritime terrorism', p. 28 and 'Sri Lanka's perspective on maritime security in the region and its relevance to the world–Sri Lanka Foreign Minister Rohitha B', *Asian Tribune*, 4 June 2007. In respect of individual incidents, reference has been made whenever possible to NGA ASAMs.

189 On the 50-mile claim see Nirupama Subramanian, 'Disguised message by Sea Tigers might have led to ship's highjack', *Indian Express*, 21 Aug. 1998.

strip assets from Tamil areas.[190] The group claimed that MV *Princess Kash*, hijacked in 1998 (NGA ASAM 1998-50), was brought in for inspection because it had entered the LTTE-claimed area without permission, and the same is possibly true of the *Yu Jia* (NGA ASAM 1999-103).[191] All the ferries that the group has attacked have been empty of civilian passengers except the *Irish Mona* (NGA ASAM 1999-103), which in 1995 was used to lure two SLN patrol boats into a kill zone using distress messages. Several ships, such as the MV *Mercs Uhana* in 2000, have been attacked or hijacked off Point Pedro and might have been delivering supplies to the SLA garrisons on the Jaffna Peninsula. The reports about the grounding of the MV *Farah III* in December 2006 (NGA ASAM 2007-7) are (as usual) contradictory, although on balance an armed attack by the Sea Tigers would appear to be the most likely explanation, given that the rebels removed the ship's cargo of 14,000 tons of rice.[192] Details on the attack on the MV *City of Liverpool* (NGA ASAM 2007-23) suggest that the SLN knew it was an LTTE ship and attacked it to draw the Sea Tigers into an engagement.[193]

There was also a strong suspicion that the group pirated vessels and transformed them into "phantom ships".[194] Although no firm evidence of this alleged activity has come to light,[195] Sakhuja suggests that the MV *Sik Yang*, a small cargo ship that went missing en route from Tuticorin in India to Malacca in 1999, might be an example.[196] The group's most audacious act of piracy, one that was certainly reminiscent of a "phantom ship" cargo fraud, was the hijacking of 32,000 mortar shells intended for the SLA. The manufacturer arranged for the consignment to be loaded on board a

190   'Sri Lanka's perspective on maritime security in the region and its relevance to the world–Sri Lanka Foreign Minister Rohitha B'; 'LTTE allays shipping fears', *TamilNet*, 12 Sept. 1997.

191   Subramanian, 'Disguised message by Sea Tigers might have led to ship's high-jack'; 'Tiger tricks', *Shiptalk*, 29 May 2007.

192   'Cargo boat 'looted off Sri Lanka'', *BBC News*, 1 May 2007.

193   The ship was reportedly part of the LTTE fleet that operated in the Indian Ocean: Sakhuja, 'The dynamics of LTTE's commercial maritime infrastructure', p. 5.

194   Chalk, 'Training the Tigers', p. 26.

195   Gunaratna, 'The asymmetric threat from maritime terrorism', p. 29.

196   Vijay Sakhuja, 'Sea piracy in South Asia', South Asia analysis group *Paper no. 1259*, 18 Feb. 2005. The NGA ASAM 1999-54, 25 May 1999 also suggests this might have been an LTTE 'phantom ship' hijack.

freighter, the *Stillus Limassol*, which because it was never seen again suggests it was probably one from the LTTE's own fleet.[197]

The LTTE's cease-fire with the Sri Lankan government, negotiated in 2002, crumbled in 2006.[198] The ferocity of the group's attacks on Sri Lankan naval units and facilities in 2006 demonstrated the continuing importance it attached to maintaining its ability to operate freely at sea and preventing the Sri Lankan forces from doing the same.[199] However, the SLN had greater success in disrupting or neutralising Sea Tiger operations. Furthermore the fact that some of these operations were disrupted before they were launched raised questions about the LTTE's operational security and, possibly, their continuing tactical competence.[200] In May 2006 the Sea Tigers used 15 boats to attack a single Sri Lankan troop ship, the *Pearl Cruise II*, carrying over 700 Sri Lankan soldiers to the crucial Jaffna sector. Seventeen Sri Lankan sailors and an estimated 50 Tamil Tigers were killed in what *The Times* described as one of the "bloodiest naval engagements in modern times". Although a Sea Tiger suicide craft apparently hit the troop ship it did not sink and after a two and a half hour battle the Sea Tigers were forced to withdraw. The SLN reportedly lost one Dvora patrol boat in the encounter.[201] In June the Sea Tigers used 20 boats to attack SLN patrol craft in a lagoon 100 miles (160km) north of Colombo. They approached

---

197 Sakhuja, 'Sea piracy in South Asia'.

198 'Sri Lanka's Tigers on the loose', *The Economist* Global Agenda, 28 Dec. 2005; Peter Foster, 'Revenge attacks on Tigers as army chief is hurt in blast', *Daily Telegraph*, 26 April 2006; Rahul Bedi, 'Refugees facing bleak future as Tigers hit back', *Sunday Telegraph*, 1 May 2006; Rahul Bedi, 'Sri Lanka falls into spiral of death', *Daily Telegraph*, 3 Aug. 2006; Rüdiger Falksohn and Padma Rao, 'Old animosities, new pain: Civil war returns to Sri Lanka', *Spiegel Online*, 23 Aug. 2006.

199 The attack on a 'Jetliner' ferry carrying over 800 Sri Lankan soldiers in Aug. 2006 is an example of the Sea Tigers' attempt to prevent the Sri Lankan forces moving freely. See 'Sri Lankan Navy repulses LTTE attempt to destroy troop carrier, heavy fighting continues in East', *Colombo Page*, 1 Aug. 2006.

200 R. Hariharan, 'Sri Lanka 2006: LTTE's unbalanced score card', *Asian Tribune*, 12 Jan. 2007; B Raman. LTTE: Diminishing Options and Assets – International Terrorism Monitor – Paper No. 354'. South Asia Analysis Group *Paper No. 2557*, 18 January 2008.

201 Richard Beeston, 'Tamil Tigers sink peace hopes with suicide raid at sea', *The Times*, 13 May 2006; Peter Foster, 'Tamil Tiger naval raid brings war closer to Sri Lanka', *Daily Telegraph*, 12 May 2006; 'Air strikes on Sri Lanka rebels after sea battle leaves 45 dead', *Channel NewsAsia.com*, 11 May 2006. For a Tamil report of the attack see D.B.S. Jeyaraj, 'The marine battle over 'MV Pearl Cruise II': An overview', *Tamil week*, 14 May 2006.

their targets by hiding amongst fishing boats.[202] In September the SLN claimed to have sunk twelve of the 20 Sea Tiger vessels that attacked its base at Kasnkasanthurai on the Jaffna peninsula.[203] In October the Sea Tigers attacked again, this time targeting the naval base at Dakshina close to the southern port of Galle. Once again the attack craft hid among fishing boats in order to get closer to their targets.[204] Fearing attacks on the country's main port the Sri Lankan Navy banned all small boats from around Colombo, allowing trawlers to enter and leave the zone only during the hours of daylight.[205] A few days later the Sri Lankan Navy intercepted a 15-boat Sea Tiger convoy off the Jaffna peninsula and claimed to have destroyed two of them in a prolonged engagement.[206]

Engagements between the Sea Tigers and the SLN continued in 2007, and although reports were characterised by the usual claim and counter-claim from either side as to the losses suffered, it appeared that the Sea Tigers (and the Tigers generally) suffered some serious reverses.[207] Nonethe-

---

202   Peter Foster, '17 killed in sea battle as Tamils attack navy', *Daily Telegraph*, 29 June 2006.

203   Michael Hirst, "100 Tigers killed' in sea battle with Sri Lankan navy', *Daily Telegraph*, 3 Sept. 2006.

204   Peter Foster, 'Sri Lankan rebels attack southern port popular with tourists', *Daily Telegraph*, 18 Oct. 2006; Shimali Senanayake, 'Bombs rock Sri Lankan port town', *International Herald Tribune*, 18 Oct. 2006; 'Suspected Tamil Tiger suicide bombers attack Sri Lankan port', *Channel NewsAsia*, 18 Oct. 2006; 'Security stepped up after bombing of Sri Lankan port', *Channel NewsAsia*, 19 Oct. 2006; Ranil Wijayapala and Rajmi Manatunga,'Navy foils LTTE suicide bid on Dakshina base', *Daily News* (Colombo), 19 Oct. 2006; Leigh Murray, 'Sri Lankan Navy destroys 2 rebel boats', *ABC News International*, 21 Oct. 2006.

205   'Sri Lanka bans small boats totally in Colombo harbour area', *Colombo Page*, 24 Oct. 2006.

206   'S Lankan navy 'sinks rebel boats", *BBC News*, 20 Oct. 2006.

207   Simon Gardner, 'Sri Lankan navy battles rebels at sea, troops ambushed', *Reuters*, 18 Nov. 2006; 'Tamil Tigers sea HQ 'destroyed", *BBC News*, 4 April 2007; Tony Birtley, 'Sri Lanka battles Tigers at sea', *Aljazeera.net*, 11 June 2007; Sunil Jayasiri, 'LTTE boats destroyed, Sea Tigers killed', *Daily Mirror* (Sri Lanka), 21 June 2007. In July 2007 ONI reported that the Sea Tigers' leader, Colonel Soosai, was critically injured when a suicide craft in which he was travelling exploded on 19 June: ONI, WWTTS report, 18 July 2007, Paragraph H. 10. At the end of the month the Sri Lankan air force claimed to have destroyed the Sea Tigers' principal training base at Alampil near Mullaittivu: Paul Tighe, 'Sri Lanka says military destroyed Tamil rebel training base', *Bloomberg.com*, 30 July 2007; Paul Tighe, 'Sri Lanka destroys rebel flotilla, raids financial center', *Bloomberg.com*, 14 Sept. 2007; Paul Tighe, 'Sri Lanka says leader of Tamil rebel

less, the Sea Tigers remained capable of offensive activity.[208] In May 2007 a commando raid was launched against the SLN facility on the strategically important Delft Island at the northern end of the Jaffna peninsula, while in June the Sri Lankan authorities uncovered a plan to mount seaborne attacks against Colombo.[209] When the SLN captured a "locally-modified 'giant' boat" off Point Pedro in June 2007 it was discovered to be armed with a Chinese-manufactured 14.5mm twin barrelled cannon and Japanese-manufactured radar and outboard motors that were not usually sold "without proper permission from a government".[210] In March 2008, 14 SLN sailors were killed when their Super Dvora craft was hit by what was described initially as a sea mine but which the Sea Tigers later claimed was a suicide attack.[211] In May 2008 the SLN supply ship *Invincible* was sunk

sea unit killed', *Bloomberg.com*, 3 Oct. 2007; 'Sri Lanka says 40 rebels killed in sea battle', *Agence France-Presse*, 26 Dec. 2007. By early 2008 it was suggested that the Sea Tigers might have been affected by the SLN's interdiction of its supply vessels as a result of which the Tigers' naval arm might have been suffering from a shortage of fuel: 'Tigers suffer setbacks', *Jane's TSM*, Jan. 2008, pp. 12-13. For background on the policy of the government of President Mahinda Rajapakse to increase the level of violence see 'Sri Lanka: Bloody mindsets', ISN *Security Watch*, 24 July 2007. On the 'information war' see Roland Buerk, 'Who is winning Sri Lanka's War?', *BBC News*, 25 May 2007 and 'Sri Lanka lashes out at war reporting'. *Agence France-Presse*, 5 June 2008.

208   Iqbal Athas, 'Battles highlight Sea Tigers' capabilities', *Jane's DW*, 4 Oct. 2006; 'Six Lankan naval personnel killed by LTTE', *The Times of India*, 6 Feb. 2008. More generally see Peter Foster, 'Tamil Tiger suicide squad in audacious strike', *Daily Telegraph*, 24 Oct. 2007.

209   On the significance of the attack see R. Hariharan, 'Sri Lanka: Implications of the LTTE's Delft Attack', *India Defence*, 14 June 2007. On the attack itself see 'Tamil rebels launch naval attack', *BBC News*, 24 May 2007 and Chen Zhanjie, 'Sri Lanka's security situation worsens further', *Xinhua News Agency*, 24 May 2007; 'Sri Lanka navy sinks three LTTE boats, top Tiger commander killed', *Colombo Page*, 28 Sept. 2007. On the planned attack on Colombo see 'Sri Lankan rebels planning attack on Colombo port: report', *Agence France-Presse*, 14 June 2007.

210   Jayasiri, 'LTTE boats destroyed, Sea Tigers killed', and Sunil Jayasiri, 'LTTE gets equipment from Japan', *Daily Mirror* (Sri Lanka), 26 June 2007. It also appears to have moved the focus of its maritime operations from the east to the west coast of India to avoid the close surveillance off Tamil Nadu: 'LTTE shifting operations to Kerala coast: Top Navy official', *Zee News*, 26 Nov. 2007.

211   'Tigers sink Sri Lanka Craft, heavy land battles erupt', *Agence France-Presse*, 22 March 2008; 'LTTE attack destroys navy craft: ten missing', *The Sunday Times* (Colombo), 23 March 2008; Ranga Sirilal, 'Sri Lanka navy, air force strike at Tiger rebels', *Reuters AlertNet*, 25 March 2008. See also the analysis in R.S. Vasan. 'Incident Analysis: Sinking of SLN Dvora Craft on 22nd March 2008'. South Asia Analysis Group *Paper No. 2652*, 28 March 2008.

in Trincomalee harbour probably as the result of an attack by a suicide diver.[212]

In parallel with its assaults at sea the Tigers have repeatedly killed Sri Lankan navy sailors on land. The series of land mine attacks on buses carrying SLN personnel in December 2005 and January, April and May 2006, each one of which left around ten dead, culminated when a convoy of buses carrying sailors on leave was attacked in October by a suicide bomber, leaving 98 dead and another 100 injured.[213]

Although some Indian commentators voiced concerns about the Sea Tigers' ability to affect Indian national security as early as 2004, the international impact of the LTTE's maritime campaign has been muted. For much of the insurgency India been reluctant to take sides in the struggle, conscious of its own substantial Tamil minority concentrated in Tamil Nadu state.[214] Sea Tiger activity in 2007, however, appeared to trigger a re-think in Indian defence circles spurred perhaps by the discovery of an LTTE boat laden with explosives off the southern Indian coast in February,[215] and the domestic political reaction to the capture and killing of Indian fishermen by Sea Tiger cadres in March, even though similar incidents had occurred in the past.[216]

---

212   R S Vasan. 'Sri Lanka: Sinking of A 520/MV Invincible in Trincomalee'. South Asia Analysis Group *Paper No. 2700*, 13 May 2008.

213   'Blasts kill 13 Lanka sailors', *BBC News*, 23 Dec. 2005; 'Sailors killed in Sri Lanka blast', *BBC News*, 12 Jan. 2006; 'Sailors killed in Sri Lanka blast', *BBC News*, 11 April 2006; Frances Harrison, 'Sailors killed in Sri Lanka blast', *BBC News*, 23 May 2006; 'Sri Lanka attack causes carnage', *BBC News*, 16 Oct. 2006; Ranil Wijayapala, 'Global community condemns LTTE suicide attack on unarmed sailors', *Daily News*, 18 Oct. 2006.

214   Suryanarayan, 'Sea Tigers–threat to Indian security' and 'India must neutralise 'Sea Tigers''; 'India worried by LTTE air, sea power: Narayanan', *Newkerala. com*, 29 May 2007.

215   'Deadly weapons, suicide belt seized off Kodiakarai', *The Hindu*, 15 Feb. 2007; Animesh Roul, 'LTTE infiltration in south India', *The Counterterrorism Blog*, 11 March 2007; Raman, 'Action Against LTTE's Gun-Running'.

216   'Indian fishermen seek safety against SL Navy', *Hindustan Times*, 5 March 2007; 'Tamil Tigers humiliate India by killing Indians; Karunanidhi forced to act against pro-Tiger Vaiko', *Asia Tribune*, 30 April 2007; M.R. Narayan Swamy, 'LTTE sympathy to erode over fishermen abductions', *Indo-Asian News Service (IANS)*, 20 May 2007. On previous incidents and subsequent calls for Indian action see, for example, 'World, South Asia: Tamil fishermen attacked', *BBC Online Network*, 29 Sept. 1998; 'Jayalalithaa for joint naval exercises to check LTTE', *The Hindu*, 7 Dec. 2003. To put these clashes into perspective, it is important to note that fishermen from both sides of the Palk Strait have poached in each others' waters for years, and because the richer fishing grounds are on the Sri Lankan side this gave the LTTE an opportunity to pose as the

The result was increased Indian naval activity in the Palk Strait and the Bay of Bengal.[217]

The Sea Tigers have shown repeatedly what maritime insurgents can achieve if they pursue their goals with determination, innovation and, in their case, suicidal intent. Even as Sri Lanka's strategic location draws the renewed attention of external powers, it would be foolish to assume that the Tigers will not continue to present a potent threat.[218]

Furthermore, if one seeks to understand maritime insurgency, then the LTTE's Sea Tiger organisation is the group that needs to be studied most closely. Evidence exists that this is exactly what some other insurgency groups have done, in some cases directly. For example, one report suggests that the LTTE were twice part of an Al Qaeda team in the Philippines training the Moro Islamic Liberation Front (MILF) and the Abu Sayyaf Group (ASG), and it is suspected that they may have transferred some of their technology to the ASG.[219]

The Nicaraguan "Contras". The word "contras" was a collective term for a number of groups opposed to the Sandinista government in Nicaragua although there was often no formal connection between them. The United States, which tried to unify the movement, was their main backer, although

---

protectors of Sri Lankan fishermen. V. Suryanarayan, 'Fishing in choppy waters', *The Hindu*, 25 Feb. 2004.

217   Ministry of Defence (Sri Lanka), 'Tiger air, sea power worries India', 30 May 2007; 'Indian navy heightens vigil to check Sri Lanka Tamil Tiger clout', *Lankaeverything.com*, 5 June 2007; The Media Centre for National Security (Sri Lanka), 'Indian Navy boosts its presence in the Bay of Bengal to curb LTTE', 7 June 2007; 'Indian Navy tightens surveillance along Tamil Nadu-Sri Lankan coast line', *Indian Defence*, 14 June 2007 and 'India's support helped weaken LTTE: Sri Lanka', *Rediff.com*, 15 Jan. 2008.

218   'Sri Lanka: Exercises with US send a message to China', STRATFOR *Global Intelligence Brief*, 19 Oct. 2006; Rahul Bedi, 'US Marines to train Sri Lankan navy', *India e News.com*, 25 Oct. 2006. This exercise was subsequently deferred. 'Sri Lanka: 20 rebels killed in sea battle', *Rediff News*, 20 Oct. 2006. As the Associated Press commented: 'Sri Lanka's resources are limited, as is the interest of the West'. While LTTE operatives will be arrested if they are discovered breaking the law in Western countries, it is likely that the LTTE will escape serious investigation because Al Qaeda and its affiliates will remain the focus of attention for some time: 'AP IMPACT: An investigation into fundraising and weapons smuggling by Sri Lanka's Tamil Tigers'.

219   Confidential interview, June 2004. Graham Gerard Ong. 'Next wave of terror targets: Will they be at sea?' *The Straits Times*, 15 Sept. 2003, suggests the LTTE might have trained al-Gamaya al-Islamiya and Egyptian Islamic Jihad (the groups led by al-Zawahiri which merged with Al Qaeda).

not the only one. Starting in 1983 these groups, responding to US pressure and acting in many instances under US guidance, launched a maritime campaign directed at the Nicaraguan economy. Ports on both the Caribbean and Pacific coasts were attacked; oil supplies and oil infrastructure in particular were struck in a series of coordinated commando and air raids. One of the groups, the Nicaraguan Democratic Force (FDN), announced in October 1983 that the waters of Puerto Sandino had been mined, although it is questionable whether any mines were actually laid. In 1984 the various groups increased pressure on the Nicaraguan government by mining all of the country's ports, ostensibly to prevent the arrivals of arms shipments from Cuba and the Soviet Union. This time mines were deployed. A number of ships were hit, including a Soviet and a Liberian tanker, a Japanese cargo ship and fishing vessels. Mining was supplemented by machine gun attacks mounted from high-speed boats supported by helicopters. These attacks forced various ships to divert away from Nicaraguan ports just at the time when the country's primary agricultural exports needed to be shipped overseas. As Menefee comments: "Similar in nature to Russian activity during the Korean War and to the mining of the Red Sea…the Contra mining campaign and related harbour attacks show what is possible for an insurrectionary force to accomplish with assistance from an involved state."[220]

Philippine "Moro" groups.[221] If it is safe to assume that people have a very general understanding of the Israel-Palestinian conflict but are almost certainly unaware of its maritime dimension, then the reverse is probably true about what people know of the long-running insurgency in the Philippines. The high profile attacks on *Superferry 14* and the abductions of foreigners from

---

220   Menefee, *TMV,* p. 97. In fact, that assistance amounted to the actual conduct of operations. According to Todd Greentree, the mining operation was undertaken by CIA clandestine operatives and US Navy SEALS and the first the Contras knew about it was when their CIA handlers told them to claim responsibility. Todd Greentree. 'Irregular Maritime Strategy'. (In My View), *NWCR,* Vol. 61, No. 1, Winter 2008, pp. 140-1.

221   In addition to Muslim-based insurgency the Philippine government has, since the late 1960s, also had to counter an insurgent challenge from the Maoist Communist Party of the Philippines and its military arm the New People's Army (NPA). Despite their political and philosophical differences the NPA and the MILF have been known to cooperate, particularly in areas where they overlap such as central Mindanao. Abuza, *Militant Islam in Southeast Asia,* p. 41. For background on the NPA and a brief description of the other Communist splinter groups see Anthony Davis, 'NPA rebels complicate Manila's counterinsurgency strategy', *Jane's IR,* 1 June 2003.

seemingly idyllic and luxurious resorts have made people aware that terrorists in the Philippines attack maritime targets, but any understanding of who those terrorists are and what inspires them is almost certainly vague.

The word "Moro" denotes the Muslim inhabitants of the Philippines, who are concentrated mainly on the southern islands of Mindanao and the Sulu archipelago; the word is believed to derive from the Spanish *Moro* ("Moor"), the name given to the Muslim inhabitants of southern Iberia between 711 and 1492 and, more generally, the Arab-Berber inhabitants of North Africa. The Spanish occupation of the Philippines began in 1565 within living memory of the *reconquista*.[222] The history of Moro resistance has been a long one, against first Spanish domination (although Spain barely penetrated the southern islands) and then American. The specific reason why the unrest continued after Philippine independence was the influx of immigrants from the more crowded northern islands, Luzon in particular, to the less populated southern islands, which started during the 1950s with the central government's encouragement.[223] The vast majority of the migrants were Christian and by the late 1960s constituted a majority in areas previously considered Muslim. The influx, which coincided with a new self-awareness amongst the Muslim communities of the south—bolstered by new international ties—sparked inter-communal violence, which by 1972 had reached the point that the government under Ferdinand Marcos declared martial law.[224]

The first uprisings were isolated but one group, the Moro National Liberation Front, led (but not founded) by Nur Misuari, brought them together. It attracted funds from Libya and from Muslim backers in Malaysia.[225] It quickly recruited tens of thousands of members and controlled large

---

222   International Crisis Group, 'Southern Philippines backgrounder: Terrorism and the peace process', *Asia Report no. 80*, 13 July 2004, p. 3.

223   For two summaries of the origins of the Muslim unrest see Abuza, *Militant Islam in Southeast Asia*, pp. 33-38 and Marco Garrido, 'The evolution of Muslim insurgency', *Asiaweek*, 6 March 2003.

224   'Moro National Liberation Front', ICG, 'Southern Philippines backgrounder', pp. 3-4. Interestingly this is almost a mirror image of the migration that took place in Indonesia, whereby under the Suharto regime between 1965 and 1985 when Muslims were forcefully relocated from the overcrowded central islands of Java and Madura to the outer islands, which were predominantly Christian and Hindu. This movement sparked inter-communal violence and separatist demands: Abuza, 'Shifting focus: Jamaah Islamiyah's long-term agenda towards Islamism', p. 23.

225   'Moro National Liberation Front'; Abuza, *Militant Islam in Southeast Asia*, pp. 38-39.

areas of the southern island of Mindanao in support of its aim to create an independent Muslim state on Mindanao and in the neighbouring Sulu archipelago. The government responded militarily. The fighting reached its height in 1973-74 but by 1976 the government was able to subdue the rebellion by deploying the bulk of the Philippine Army in the southern islands and using non-military tactics designed to encourage internal division. In that year the Tripoli Agreement, brokered by the Organisation of the Islamic Conference (OIC), was signed. The Marcos government, however, proceeded to implement it according to its own interpretation, principally by dividing the proposed autonomous region into two. The talks consequently broke down and the MNLF declared a resumption of hostilities in 1977.[226]

The Agreement nonetheless achieved what the government wanted. The MNLF was demoralised and never regained its former vigour, much of which drained away in factionalism and traditional tribal rivalry. The first defection was by the group that became the MNLF/Reformist Movement led by Dimad Undato.[227] However, the most serious was that of the Moro Islamic Liberation Front (MILF) under the leadership of Salamat Hashim. The leadership of the MNLF was predominantly Tausug from the Sulu islands; the largest Moro population was concentrated in western and central Mindanao; the MILF drew much of its support from the Maguindanao people of Mindanao. Although the final break only occurred in 1984 it developed from 1977 when Hashim, who was at that point Misuari's deputy, organised the "New Leadership" faction in dissatisfaction with the MNLF's attempt at a negotiated settlement and the highly unfavourable outcome.[228] The MILF advocated a more pronounced Islamic agenda and rejected negotiation in favour of renewed insurgent war, a determination perhaps driven by the greater influx of Christian immigrants on Mindanao than in the Sulu islands.[229]

226   Thomas M. McKenna, 'Muslim separatism in the Philippines: Meaningful autonomy or endless war? The Tripoli Agreement–A charter for Philippine Muslim autonomy.' *Asian Social Issues Program*, 2000.

227   'Moro National Liberation Front'.

228   ICG, 'Southern Philippines backgrounder', p. 4; Ressa. *Seeds of Terror*, pp. 125-6; Abuza, *Militant Islam in Southeast Asia*, pp. 39-41.

229   Angel M. Rabasa, *Political Islam in Southeast Asia: Moderates, Radicals and Terrorists*, Adelphi Paper 358, Oxford UP for IISS, 2003, p. 51; David Wright-Neville, 'Dangerous dynamics: Activists, militants and terrorists in Southeast Asia', *The Pacific Review*, vol. 17, no. 1, March 2004, p. 36. The Christian proportion of the Mindanao population had possibly reached 80 per cent by 1983.

After Marcos was overthrown in 1986, the Philippine government, led by President Corazon Aquino, signed ceasefire agreements with the MILF and the MNLF/Reformist Movement, and later in the year reached agreement (the "Sulu Agreement") with Nur Misuari of the rump MNLF to open formal discussions on a political solution.[230] In 1987 the MNLF signed the "Jeddah Agreement" in which it agreed to relinquish its goal of full independence in return for a new government offer of full autonomy.[231] Talks continued sporadically during 1987 but led nowhere and in 1988 the MNLF returned once again to armed conflict, although few incidents took place.[232] The bulk of the membership, however, rejected the proposed agreement and defected to the MILF, which became the largest Moro resistance grouping with an armed wing, named the Bangsamoro Islamic Armed Forces (BIAF), of 10-15,000 men.[233] It is the only group that retains the capacity to maintain a sustained insurgency against the Philippine government.[234] However, although a clash between the AFP and MILF in July 2007 demonstrated that the latter remained a deadly opponent, its military capability has declined considerably since its peak in 1999-2001. Only a fraction of its total force are full time combatants and

---

Peter Chalk, 'Militant Islamic extremism in Southeast Asia' in Paul J. Smith (ed.), *Terrorism and Violence in Southeast Asia: Transnational Challenges to States and Regional Stability*, Armonk, NY: M.E. Sharpe, 2005, Note 12, p. 33.

230 Bernardo M. Villegas, 'The Philippines in 1986: Democratic reconstruction in the post-Marcos era', *Asian Survey*, vol. 27, no. 2, Feb. 1987, p. 197; also Fidel V. Ramos, 'Break not the OIC-brokered peace', *Manila Times*, 5 Sept. 2006.

231 For a summary of the main agreements between the GRP and the various 'Moro' movements see ICG, 'Southern Philippines backgrounder', Appendix C, pp. 29-32.

232 'Moro National Liberation Front'.

233 Vaughn *et al.*, 'Terrorism in Southeast Asia', p. 21 estimate 10,000; Abuza, in *Balik Terrorism*, p. 37 estimates 12,000 and in *Militant Islam in Southeast Asia*, p. 46 suggests between 12 and 15,000 men. A former MILF central committee member told the ICG that the armed force was between 10 and 15,000 strong and that between 1987 and 1990 122,000 MILF members had undergone basic training and could be used to back up the regular force if necessary: ICG, 'Southern Philippines backgrounder', pp. 4-5. Anthony Davis quotes AFP sources suggesting the MILF had around 12,600 fighters in 2000, whereas Western intelligence sources usually suggest the figure should be closer to 15,000: Anthony Davis, 'Attention shifts to Moro Islamic Liberation Front', *Jane's IR*, 1 April 2002, p. 21.

234 McKenna, 'Muslim separatism in the Philippines', The 1996 peace agreement.' *Asian Social Issues Program*, 2000.

the prolonged peace process has led to declines in combat readiness, training and weapons acquisition.[235]

In 1996 a new Philippine President, Fidel Ramos, who had been armed forces Chief of Staff at the time of Marcos' overthrow, reached a new agreement with the MNLF alone. The government ignored the MILF and the more violent ASG, which had been formed in 1992. It did this possibly for two reasons: firstly the MNLF retained OIC recognition as the representative of the Moro people and Misuari retained strong personal links with international leaders, while secondly, the MILF powerbase was on the now predominantly Christian Mindanao and the government came under strong local pressure not to negotiate with what was regarded as a Muslim terrorist group.[236] The MILF initially drew strength from Misuari's compromise but in 1997 it also agreed a cessation of hostiles.[237] Negotiations proceeded slowly, however, and it resumed hostilities in 1999. In February 2000 bombs exploded on the ferry *Our Lady Mediatrix* off Ozamis City; in July the group withdrew from the talks altogether in the face of President Joseph Estrada's reluctance to agree to its demands.[238] In 2001, following Estrada's overthrow, the group signed another ceasefire agreement with another Philippine President, Gloria Macapagal-Arroyo, but sporadic violence continued and became worse in 2003, first in February when the Philippine military accused the group of harbouring other terrorist groups, and then in March when a bomb exploded at Davao City airport killing over 20 people and injuring 150.[239] This was followed by another bomb in April, on a ferry as it drew away from Sasa Wharf near Davao City, which killed 16 and wounded 30 more.[240] The MILF denied both attacks but the results none-

---

235   Zachary Abuza, 'The Philippine peace process: Too soon to claim a settlement with the Moro Islamic Liberation Front?' The Jebsen Center for Counter-terrorism Studies *Research Briefing Series*. vol. 3, no. 3, Feb. 2008, p. 7.

236   ICG, 'Southern Philippines backgrounder', p. 4; Thomas M. McKenna, 'Muslim separatism in the Philippines: meaningful autonomy or endless war? Impediments to peace and the current crisis.' *Asian Social Issues Program*, 2000.

237   Davis, 'Attention shifts to Moro Islamic Liberation Front', p. 20.

238   ICG, 'Southern Philippines backgrounder', p. 6; McKenna, 'Muslim separatism in the Philippines: The 1996 peace agreement.'

239   Human Rights Watch, 'Lives destroyed: Attacks against civilians in the Philippines', pp. 6-7.

240   'Guide to the Philippines conflict', *BBC News*, 10 Feb. 2005; ICG, 'Southern Philippines backgrounder: Terrorism and the Peace Process', p. 22. The Davao bombings appear to have been in retaliation for the AFP's assault on the MILF's Buliok camp complex, one of the group's last remaining safe havens: Anthony

theless appeared to focus minds; shortly before his death in 2003, Salamat Hashim renounced terrorism and a new ceasefire was agreed.[241]

David Wright-Neville, who prior to becoming an academic researcher served in Australian intelligence, argues that the MILF has generally calibrated its use of violence carefully in support of clear political objectives.[242] Thomas McKenna suggests more broadly that the entire Moro insurgency was by no means inevitable; on the contrary, the Marcos government must shoulder much of the blame by militarising the conflict in 1972, as should successive administrations by their refusal to recognise that the conflict is not amenable to a military solution. Furthermore, he writes, "since 1987, the MILF has engaged in offensive action only to force the government to the negotiating table with a show of its armed capacity".[243] These views have merit—most MILF attacks have been against AFP targets—but they are hard to accept without reservation, given the manifest willingness of all the "Moro" insurgent groups, including the MILF, to target civilians. During every ceasefire violent incidents continued to occur.

The MILF's relations with other terrorist and insurgent groups have, on the other hand, shown less evidence of careful calibration. Between 1978 and 1987 Hashim worked hard to build an international support base, one element of which was a link to Osama bin Laden that probably came through Abu Sayyaf with whom he attended Al-Azhar University in Cairo during the early 1970s.[244] Accounts from former MILF members suggest that the "New Leadership" faction under Hashim's direction sent 500 men to the Afghan border camps for training in 1980 and that many smaller groups followed intermittently after that. Hashim himself was based in Pakistan from 1982 to 1987.[245] This traffic reached a peak in 1988; very

---

Davis, 'MILF turns to terrorism', *Jane's IR,* 1 April 2003. Also Ressa. *Seeds of Terror,* p. 142.

241   'Lethal blast hits Philippines', *BBC News,* 2 April 2003; 'Guide to the Philippines conflict'; 'Philippines signs ceasefire with guerrilla group', *ABC NewsOnline,* 18 July 2003.

242   Wright-Neville, 'Dangerous dynamics: Activists, militants and terrorists in Southeast Asia', 2004, p. 36.

243   McKenna, 'Muslim separatism in the Philippines: meaningful autonomy or endless war? Impediments to peace and the current crisis'.

244   ICG, 'Southern Philippines backgrounder', p. 4.

245   Ressa, who discusses this traffic in some detail, suggests only 360 MILF trainees reached Afghanistan of which a smaller number, 180, actually fought there and of these only 70 survived and returned to the Philippines. Ressa. *Seeds of Terror,* pp. 126-128.

few made the journey after 1991. Nonetheless, the inclusion of such well-trained fighters in the MILF regular force gave the organisation impetus when it emerged more publicly after the MNLF's 1996 agreement with the Philippine government.[246] Its network of 46 major and minor camps became the backbone of its strength; they were not simply military camps but large guerrilla base areas with civilian populations, within which the group attempted to implement Islamic-style government under *sharia* law. The MILF made every effort to induce the Philippines government to recognise the camps' boundaries and make them essentially no-go areas for the AFP.[247] The AFP, well aware of the safe havens the camps provided, assaulted them in 2000. The campaign lasted four months and culminated in the occupation of the largest and most important, Abu Bakar, located on the borders of Maguindanao and Lanao del Sur, with its mix of schools, religious seminaries, Islamic courts and a military academy where jihadist fighters from the Middle East and Southeast Asia had been trained.[248] The "Buliok" complex located in the Liguasan Marsh, North Cotabato, that replaced Abu Bakar was overrun in 2003 in an action the AFP justified as a clearing operation against the "Pentagon" kidnap gang.[249] Whatever its short-term success, the "war on the camps" was undermined by its political and financial cost.[250] Although the MILF was no longer able to mount battalion-size operations it could mount smaller assaults and, because it was forced to disperse, became harder to track.[251]

The links between the MILF and the Jemaah Islamiyah (JI) were forged in Afghanistan in the 1980s. They were based on personal relationships between Salamat Hashim and JI leaders such as Abdullah Sungkar and Zulkarnean to whom he gave permission to set up the JI Hudaibiyah sub-

---

246   ICG, 'Southern Philippines backgrounder', p. 4.

247   *Ibid.*, p. 6.

248   Davis, 'Attention shifts to Moro Islamic Liberation Front', pp. 20-1; Anthony Davis, 'Insurgent stronghold overrun by Philippine forces', *Jane's IR,* 21 Aug. 2000. According to Ressa, Abu Bakar covered 10,000 hectares (over 38 square miles). Ressa. *Seeds of Terror,* p. 124. On the military academy see *Seeds of Terror,* p. 129. She suggests that after Abu Bakar was overrun, JI gave the MILF its own training base inside one of its Indonesia camps. *Seeds of Terror,* p. 139.

249   Ressa. *Seeds of Terror,* pp. 140-141

250   ICG, 'Southern Philippines backgrounder', pp. 6-7; Davis, 'Attention shifts to Moro Islamic Liberation Front', p. 21; ; Inday Espina-Varona and Johnna Villaviray. 'Capture of MILF camps has downside for govt'. *The Manila Times* Special Feature, 19 June 2002.

251   Davis, 'Attention shifts to Moro Islamic Liberation Front', p. 21.

camp within the boundaries of the MILF's larger Abu Bakar compound in 1994. This was followed by another agreement that sanctioned the establishment of the more advanced "military academy" within the same compound in 1998.[252] The arrangement appears to have been mutually beneficial with JI operatives such as Hambali furnishing funds, Fathur Rahman al-Ghozi providing the skills to make bombs and Zulkifli overseeing the Davao City bombings in March and April 2003.[253] There also appears to have been direct contact with Al Qaeda, although whether or not that was sustained is unknown.[254]

JI operatives, including Zulkifli, were also instrumental in building the relationship with the ASG. Compared with the MILF the ASG was tiny: estimates suggest its numbers have usually been in the hundreds and never more than 1,000.[255] Despite its size it has been responsible for the deaths of over 400 people since 2000, which is not only more than the other "Moro" groups combined but, apart from Al Qaeda and JI, is probably more than almost any other terrorist group in the world.[256] Its recruits were drawn primarily from the Tausug ethnic group whereas the MILF, because it was based on Mindanao, had developed a broader ethnic appeal. The group had

---

252   ICG, 'Southern Philippines backgrounder', p. i, p. 6 & p. 13. According to JI documents seized by Indonesian police some 3,000 JI operatives passed through the camp between the mid-1990s and 2003: Simon Elegant,'Still going strong', *TIME*, 15 Dec. 2003. See also Ressa. *Seeds of Terror*, pp. 134-135.

253   ICG, 'Southern Philippines backgrounder', pp. i & 13-17; Davis, 'MILF links to external terrorist organisations', p. 23 and Anthony Davis, 'Blasts suggest MILF-JI links', *Jane's IR*, 1 May 2003.

254   Davis, 'MILF links to external terrorist organisations', p. 23. Abuza, *Militant Islam in Southeast Asia*', pp. 95-9; in his view the links between the MILF and Al Qaeda 'are well established'. For Ressa the links between al-Qaeda, the MILF and Jemaah Islamiyah in Southeast Asia 'remain uncertain' (*Seeds of Terror*, p.130), although she points to several direct personal contacts between the three groups. *Seeds of Terror*, pp. 133-136. Her view is that al-Ghozi was an operative for JI *and* al-Qaeda. *Seeds of Terror*, p 135. She points out that Omar al-Faruq, Bin Laden's so-called 'envoy' in Southeast Asia, helped the MILF as well as the ASG and, based on US and Philippine intelligence reports, names him as the 'emir' of an Arab training camp within the Abu Bakar complex. *Seeds of Terror*, pp. 7-8 & 134.

255   MIPT Terrorism Knowledge Base, Group Profile: Abu Sayyaf Group. Abuza suggests the group had around 600 members from the mid-1990s to 2000 and used the money from ransom payments to increase this to 1,000 after 2000. However, the joint Philippine-US 'Balikatan' exercise in 2002 reduced its numbers to between 200 and 400: Abuza, *Balik Terrorism*, pp. 8 & 10.

256   Human Rights Watch, 'Lives destroyed: Attacks against civilians in the Philippines', p. 3.

an important supporting role in Ramzi Yousef's "Bojinka" plot to bring down airliners over the Pacific.[257] As a consequence it received Al Qaeda money. When the plot was discovered, and most of Yousef's cell arrested, the funding stopped. There are grounds for believing that the MILF, like the ASG, received funds from Al Qaeda through an Islamic charity,[258] but attempts by the senior Al Qaeda operative Omar al-Faruq to persuade the ASG to combine with the MILF were rejected by the ASG founder, Abdurajak Janjalani, in 1994 or 1995, on the grounds that at that time the MILF was more interested in money than *jihad* (which was ironic, given the course that his own group was to follow after his death).[259] However, according to Abuza the real reason for the rejection was that the MILF refused to share Al Qaeda funding with it.[260] The group's situation worsened after Abdurajak Janjalani was killed in 1998 and his deputy turned police informer in 1999.[261] The group that had started life as a zealous Islamist terrorist group broke into two or three violent gangs, each with its own leader, which in their search for funds quickly began to pursue criminal rather than political ends, primarily through kidnapping and extortion but also through drug cultivation.[262] The income from these activities appeared to reinforce the group's criminal direction. It enabled what was now a loose affiliation of sub-groups to become a significant player in the region's arms market as both buyers and dealers. It also attracted recruits who were more interested in the prospect of violent action and easy money.[263]

257 See Chapter 4 above.

258 Rabasa, *Political Islam in Southeast Asia*, p. 51; ICG, 'Southern Philippines backgrounder', p. 22. Wright-Neville is sceptical about this. He points to an interview Hashim gave in 2000 where he said that bin Laden channelled money to the Moro community generally for mosque building but that the MILF was not a direct recipient. Wright-Neville: 'Dangerous dynamics: Activists, militants and terrorists in Southeast Asia', p. 38.

259 ICG, 'Southern Philippines backgrounder:', p. 22 suggests this took place in 1994 as does Ressa, *Seeds of Terror,* p. 134; Abuza, *Militant Islam in Southeast Asia*, p. 110 suggests 1995.

260 Abuza, *Militant Islam in Southeast Asia*, p. 110.

261 *Ibid.*, p. 111. Ressa, *Seeds of Terror,* p. 109.

262 Abuza, *Militant Islam in Southeast Asia*, pp. 111-12; Abuza, *Balik Terrorism*, pp. 12-13. As one of the ASG's kidnap victims, Gracia Burnham, put it: 'The bottom line was money': quoted in Ressa, *Seeds of Terror*, pp. 110-111.

263 Angel M. Rabasa, *et al.*, *Beyond al-Qaeda: Part 2 – The Outer Rings of the Terrorist Universe.* Santa Monica: RAND 2006, pp. 117-21. Also the description in Ressa, *Seeds of Terror,* p. 26.

Starting in 2000, however, most of the leaders of the various factions were killed or captured, but Abdurajak Janjalani's younger brother Kadaffy, based on Basilan, remained at large.[264] Kadaffy had long wanted to train with the MILF but they had refused. In 2001, however, Zulkifli agreed to provide training in the Hudaibiyah sub-camp provided the ASG was prepared to offer JI operatives "practical experience" in its camps on Tawi-Tawi and Basilan.[265] In 2002 the only other remaining faction commander, Abu Sabaya, was killed. Kadaffy assumed overall command and worked "very hard to get the ASG back to its roots", helped possibly by his close relationship with JI and an actual or anticipated influx of volunteers from the MILF who had become frustrated by the larger group's accommodation with the Philippine government.[266] Even during the period when the group was broken into several small criminal gangs, links between these groups and international terrorist organisations had never been severed entirely.[267] In 2002 the ASG, with support from JI, bombed targets in Zamboanga City. Among the dead was a US Special Forces officer.[268] It was possibly this incident, coupled with Zulkifli's intervention on their behalf, which encouraged the MILF to offer the ASG access to their training facili-

---

264   For further background on the Janjalani brothers, one the founder and the other his successor, and the changing status of the ASG's Islamist priorities, see Rommel C. Banlaoi, 'Leadership dynamics in terrorist organizations in Southeast Asia: The Abu Sayyaf case', paper presented at the symposium 'The dynamics and structures of terrorist threats in Southeast Asia' organised by the Institute of Defense Analyses, Kuala Lumpur, 18-20 April 2005, pp. 2, 4-5 & 7-8. See also Abuza, *Balik Terrorism*, pp. 2-20 and pp. 27-8 where he disagrees with Banlaoi on the details of the group's internal structure. On the various factions or gangs and the fate of their various leaders see Abuza, *Militant Islam in Southeast Asia*, p. 111. According to the journalist Jade Verde, Kadaffy was apparently a 'reluctant successor' whose leadership was resisted by many of the ASG faction leaders such as Nadzmi (Global), Andang (Robot) and Susukan because he had not proved his worth: Jade Verde, 'Abu Sayyaf's Khadaffy Montaño Abubakar Janjalani', *American Chronicle*, 13 June 2007.

265   ICG, 'Southern Philippines backgrounder', p. 22; Abuza, *Balik Terrorism*, p. 22.

266   On the influx from the MILF see Banlaoi, 'Leadership dynamics in terrorist organizations in Southeast Asia: The Abu Sayyaf case', p. 10. On Kadaffy's determination see Abuza, *Balik Terrorism*, p. 13 and Jade Verde, 'Abu Sayyaf's Khadaffy Montaño Abubakar Janjalani'.

267   Abuza, *Militant Islam in Southeast Asia*, pp. 110-13 and *Balik Terrorism*, p. 21; Peter Chalk, 'Separatism and Southeast Asia: The Islamic factor in Southern Thailand, Mindanao, and Aceh', *Studies in Conflict and Terrorism*, vol. 24, no. 4, 1 July 2001, p. 249.

268   Abuza, *Militant Islam in Southeast Asia*, p. 113.

ties.[269] It is also possible that several operations could have been conducted jointly: the bombings in Manila later in 2002 and the Davao bombings in 2003 might have been joint MILF-ASG and JI-MILF-ASG operations respectively; in March 2003 the MILF might have been involved in an ASG attack in Lamitan, and in May 2003 the ASG might have returned the favour by supporting the MILF's major assault on Siocon.[270] It is clear from Gracia Burnham's account of her ordeal that after her kidnap from the Dos Palmas resort in May 2001 by the ASG, her captors and her companions were hidden on an MILF camp for several weeks.[271] Eduardo Santos of the Philippine Navy holds the view that many of the most violent operatives move freely between the different organisations.[272]

The ASG's status subsequently has been less clear. As a direct consequence of its high profile kidnappings of Westerners, the group came under sustained pressure from the Philippines Army, supported by US Special Forces and intelligence, starting with the first Balikatan exercise in 2002, through Operation Endgame from late 2003 through to 2006, and particularly during Operation OPLAN Ultimatum, which began in August 2006.[273] Reports suggest that in 2005 the ASG was driven out of Mindanao and forced to re-establish itself on the island of Jolo following a dispute with the MILF that had badly strained their relationship.[274] The AFP tightened the noose around the group, restricting its area of operations on the island.

269   ICG, 'Southern Philippines backgrounder', p. 22.

270   Abuza, *Militant Islam in Southeast Asia*, p. 113 on Manila; ICG, 'Southern Philippines backgrounder', pp. 23-4 on Davao; Anthony Davis, 'Philippines fears new wave of attacks by Abu Sayyaf group', *Jane's IR*, vol. 17, no. 5, May 2005, p. 12 and Davis, 'Resilient Abu Sayyaf resists military pressure' on the other incidents.

271   Gracia Burnham with Dean Merrill, *In the Presence of My Enemies*, Wheatin, IL: Tyndale House Publishers, 2003, p. 139; Davis, 'Resilient Abu Sayyaf resists military pressure'.

272   Eduardo Ma R. Santos comment to Stefan Eklöf, Singapore 2004. See also Abuza, *Balik Terrorism*, pp. 22-3.

273   Davis, 'Resilient Abu Sayyaf resists military pressure', on Baliktan; Zachary Abuza, 'On the defensive: Rebels lose ground in Southern Philippines', *Jane's IR*, April 2007, pp. 12-14 on Operations Endgame and Ultimatum; Kate McGeown, 'Is this the end for Abu Sayyaf?' *BBC News*, 23 Jan. 2007 also on Operation Ultimatum.

274   Confidential information, Feb. 2005. Zachary Abuza suggests they were driven out after the MILF came under intense pressure from the Philippine government and armed forces: Abuza, 'On the defensive: Rebels lose ground in Southern Philippines', p. 13.

In July 2006 the Philippines police and intelligence services uncovered a joint ASG and JI plan to attack US troops supporting the counter-terrorism operation and to hijack a cargo ship in order to hold its crew hostage in exchange for terrorists jailed in the Philippines, Indonesia and Malaysia.[275] In December 2006 the body of Kadaffy Janjalani was found buried in a garden.[276] His death alone would not be enough to spell the end of the organisation, partly because of the links to JI, the MNLF and the MILF, but particularly because clan and family ties in the region are regarded as so important.[277] As Abuza has pointed out the ASG is amorphous and works in small bands; in 2000-1 there were 10 identified on Basilan and 16 on Jolo.[278] Even after Janjalani's death, several important operatives remained at large although Abu Sulaiman, who was thought to have been the mastermind behind the bombing of the *Superferry 14* and was regarded by some commentators as more significant than Janjalani, was reported dead early in 2007.[279] In June 2007 Yasser Igasan, the group's financier, was reportedly elected its new leader, although other reports suggest the leader is now Albader Pared.[280] In the meanwhile the AFP shifted its emphasis away from

---

275   'Philippine chief says terror plot foiled against US troops', *AP,* 5 July 2007.

276   Zachary Abuza, 'Abu Sayyaf chieftain Khadaffi Janjalani reported killed', *The Counterterrorism Blog,* 28 Dec. 2006; Jim Gomez, 'DNA tests confirm death terror group leader in the Philippines', *AP,* 20 Jan. 2007.

277   McGeown, 'Is this the end for Abu Sayyaf?' Noor Huda Ismail, 'Retracing the steps of JI's Abdullah Sunata', The Jamestown Foundation *Terrorism Monitor,* vol. 5, Issue 4, 1 March 2007, pp. 9-11; Simon Roughneen, 'Philippine escalation may speak wider war', ISN *Security Watch,* 21 Aug. 2007.

278   Banlaoi, 'Leadership dynamics in terrorist organizations in Southeast Asia: The Abu Sayyaf case', p. 5. For more details on Kadaffy Janjalani's death, which other ASG leaders are believed to have been killed and which ones are believed to have survived see Abuza, 'On the defensive: Rebels lose ground in Southern Philippines' pp. 13-14.

279   Richard Weitz, 'Death of a terrorist: Abu Sayyaf's Abu Sulaiman', *WorldPoliticsReview,* 5 Feb. 2007; McGeown, 'Is this the end for Abu Sayyaf?' Other commentators suggested that these deaths were unlikely to have a serious affect on the group as it enjoyed widespread support in the area and the leaders could be replaced: 'A weakened Abu Sayyaf looking for a new leader', CSIS *Transnational Threats Update,* vol. 4, no. 12, Jan. 2007, p. 6.

280   'Army: Janjalani successor is ASG's bag man', *GMA News TV,* 27 June 2007; Taharudin Piang Ampatuan, 'Aby Sayaf's New Leader: Yasser Igasan the religious scholar', Rajaratnam School of International Studies *Commentaries,* 9 July 2007; Human Rights Watch, 'Lives destroyed: Attacks against civilians in the Philippines', p. 25.

hunting and killing the group's leaders and towards civil-military tasks,[281] despite the ASG's continuing use of violence: in April 2007 six Christian hostages were beheaded and local villagers were forced to deliver their severed heads to a local Army camp.[282] In November 2007 a spokesman for US Special Operations Command-Pacific, which had supported the AFP in their campaign, told reporters that although the ASG had not been defeated it had been weakened significantly.[283] Yet, roughly six months later, reports emerged that the group was attracting new recruits as young as 13 with offers of money and guns and, although still effectively leaderless, was regarded by some military sources as more dangerous than before.[284]

According to the International Crisis Group the MILF has always been a loose-knit organisation but became more so after the AFP's assault on its camps in 2000, which decentralised it still further, and the lack of leadership in the period between Hashim's death and 2005 when the new chairman, Ebraham el Haj Murad, felt secure enough to assert some measure of authority.[285] Some units became so detached as to be regarded as "lost commands" by the MILF leadership.[286] In 2002 the Philippines government and the MILF announced they were setting up a Joint Ad Hoc Ac-

281   Julie Alipala, 'New Oplan to bring dev't to Sulu, says Esperon', *Inquirer.net*, 26 April 2007.

282   'Abu Sayyaf Group beheads hostages', *Keesing's World News Archive*, 2 May 2007; also Human Rights Watch, 'Lives destroyed: Attacks against civilians in the Philippines', pp. 22-3.

283   Bill Gertz, 'Inside the Ring: Pacific terrorism', *Washington Times*, 2 Nov. 2007. However, in Nov. 2007 a bomb exploded in Manila which killed a Congressman who supported government efforts to eradicate the ASG. Doubts surrounded the ASG's denial of responsibility: Zachary Abuza, 'Manila bombing highlights possible shift in ASG strategy', The Jamestown Foundation *Terrorism Focus*, vol. 4, no. 38, 20 Nov. 2007. For some further details on the Special Operations Command unit in the area, the Joint Special Operations Task Force-Philippines (JSOTF-P), and its similarity in terms of profile and mission to the Combined Joint Task Force-Horn of Africa (CJTF-HOF) see Herbert Docena, 'How the US got its Philippine bases back', *Asia Times*, 28 Nov. 2007.

284   'Abu Sayyaf actively recruiting young blood – police'. *GMANEWS.TV*, 17 June 2008.

285   ICG, 'Southern Philippines backgrounder', p. i; Zachary Abuza, 'MILF's stalled peace process and its impact on terrorism in Southeast Asia', The Jamestown Foundation *Terrorism Monitor*, vol. IV, Issue 14, 13 July 2006, p. 9.

286   John McBeth, 'Terrorism–Across Borders', *FEER*, 22 July 2004, p. 27; Davis, 'Attention shifts to Moro Islamic Liberation Front', p. 23.

tion Group to hunt down criminals and JI and ASG terrorists. Not one was arrested. The agreement terminated in June 2007.[287]

The risk for the MILF is that its organisational structure makes it prone to fragmentation, like the MNLF before it.[288] It appears that it is divided over the issue of JI: some see it as a brother organisation made up of *mujahideen* whom they have a religious duty to support; others see it as an insurance policy should negotiations with the government collapse. Although contacts between the two groups might have become more discrete, it appears that JI still has access to MILF training facilities in the Taragona base camp in eastern Mindanao.[289] Moreover, the relationship between the MILF and the ASG appeared to continue for some time after Hashim's death, contrary to the MILF's repeated denials. The evidence was too strong to be ignored and was confirmed by an Indonesian JI member.[290] Kadaffy Janjalani, for example, might well have been given sanctuary between mid-2004 and late-2005.[291] These arrangements were of benefit to all sides: the ASG could act as a deniable proxy while the hunt for ASG operatives ensured the AFP was unable to concentrate its forces against the MILF; the ASG had access to safe areas where it could train and rest; JI also had access to safe areas and had a reliable ally in the ASG which shared its Islamist ideology.[292] Nor did the MILF suffer for this support:

---

287   Joint Communiqué between the Government of the Republic of the Philippines and the Moro Islamic Liberation Front, 6 May 2002; ICG, 'Southern Philippines backgrounder', p. 8; Abuza, 'MILF's stalled peace process and its impact on terrorism in Southeast Asia', p. 9; Anthony Vargas, 'Liaison team disbands, Bossi rescue snagged', *Manila Times,* 22 June 2007.

288   ICG, 'Southern Philippines backgrounder', p. 4; 'Philippines grapples with guerrillas', *Jane's TSM,* Jan. 2008, p. 15.

289   Abuza, 'The Philippine peace process: Too soon to claim a settlement with the Moro Islamic Liberation Front?', p. 7.

290   Vaughn *et al.,* 'Terrorism in Southeast Asia', p. 21; ICG, 'Southern Philippines backgrounder', p. 25; Zachary Abuza, 'MILF and GRP served notice', *The Counterterrorism Blog,* 31 March 2005 and Zachary Abuza, 'Dulmatin, JI's Top technician trains a new generation of fighters', The Jamestown Foundation *Terrorism Focus,* vol. 3, no. 26, 5 July 2006; 'US envoy in Philippines calls southern island 'Mecca of terror'', *Xinhua.net,* 10 April 2005; Dillon, 'Southeast Asia and the brotherhood of terrorism'; Davis, 'Philippines fears new wave of attacks by Abu Sayyaf group', p. 11. Even Dulmatin's wife allegedly confirmed this help under interrogation: Anthony Vargas, 'JI terrorist's wife says MILF helps Abu', *Manila Times,* 10 Oct. 2006.

291   Abuza, 'On the defensive: Rebels lose ground in Southern Philippines', p. 14.

292   Abuza, *Balik Terrorism,* pp. 16-17; Human Rights Watch, 'Lives destroyed: Attacks against civilians in the Philippines', pp. 24-5 on the suspected links

the Philippine government pleaded repeatedly for the US not to designate it a Foreign Terrorist Organisation.[293]

Questions therefore continue to be asked about whether or not the MILF leadership sanctioned contacts with JI, the ASG and the criminal Pentagon gang.[294] This might be a convenient fiction; it could be part of a deliberate strategy that allows local commanders wide discretion; or it could mean that the leadership's hold over its often physically isolated provincial commands is in reality almost non-existent.[295] The group certainly does suffer from strains amounting to factionalism as the talks with the government drag on.[296] Wright-Neville, who argues that the objectives of the MILF and the wider jihadist movement are not congruent, and that most of the Front's fighters would find the jihadist ideology irrelevant to their cause and even alien, nonetheless expressed concern that this frustration might lead the movement's younger members to seek more radical alternatives and even, perhaps, to argue that any Moro insurgency would only succeed if allied to the larger Muslim fight against Western globalism.[297] To move closer, in other words, to the viewpoint of the ASG.

The Philippines: a maritime theatre. The geography of the Philippines, particularly the southern Philippines, means that any insurgent group, if it is to be successful, has to have a maritime arm. During the guerrilla phase of the Philippines War of 1899-1902 the US blockade effectively cut off Aguinaldo, the rebel leader, from foreign support and prevented him from moving men and supplies.[298] The MNLF, in contrast, appears to have benefited from external arms supplies, said to come from China and a number of Arab states, particularly Libya, and from the use of bases in the Malay-

---

between MILF 'lost commands' and the ASG.

293   Abuza, 'MILF's stalled peace process and its impact on terrorism in Southeast Asia', p. 9. Ressa, *Seeds of Terror*, p. 13.

294   Zachary Abuza, Comments as part of USIP Current Issue Briefing 'Crunchtime for Mindanao peace process?' 8 Feb. 2005.

295   ICG, 'Southern Philippines backgrounder', pp. ii & 9-12.

296   Abuza, 'MILF's stalled peace process and its impact on terrorism in Southeast Asia', p. 9; Zachary Abuza, 'MILF seeks leverage as fighting against Abu Sayyaf and MNLF escalates', The Jamestown Foundation *Terrorism Focus*, vol. 4, Issue 27, 14 Aug. 2007; Manny Mogato and Carmel Crimmins. 'Manila sees risk of split in Muslim rebel group'. *Reuters AlertNet*, 17 June 2008.

297   Wright-Neville, 'Dangerous dynamics: Activists, militants and terrorists in Southeast Asia', pp. 38 & 39.

298   Max Boot, *The Savage Wars of Peace: Small Wars and the Rise of American Power*, New York: Basic Books, 2002, p. 128.

sian state of Sabah. The long history of piracy, coastal raiding and smuggling, particularly in the waters between Mindanao and northern Borneo, means that the use of the sea by insurgents and terrorists is almost indistinguishable from—and in practical terms interchangeable with—piracy. Eduardo Santos takes the view that some elements of the MNLF and the MILF "are constantly involved in armed robberies at sea in Southern and Southeastern Mindanao and extortion as their regular sources of funds and income", while in Banlaoi's view there is no doubt that "maritime piracy is becoming a preferred method of funding for some terrorist groups with strong maritime traditions. This makes the threat of maritime piracy and terrorism overlapping."[299]

The Moro National Liberation Front (MNLF), in the period immediately before and then following the signing of the 1976 accord, and as foreign assistance began to evaporate, took to hijacking ships to gain publicity and also to earn money from ransom payments. In 1975 the *Suehiro Maru* was hijacked in Zamboanga. After 1977, when the group began to suffer defections, inter-island ferries became a favourite target: MNLF members would board as passengers and then seize the ship much in the manner of Chinese pirates in the years between the First and Second World Wars.[300] In contrast an external attack was mounted on the *Don Carlos* in 1978 using four speedboats. In 1982 two ferries, the *Santa Lucia* and the *Lady Ruth,* were bombed at the quayside in Pagadian, with a total of six dead and 120 injured, apparently to extort money from the owners.[301] The ASG bombed the *Superferry 14* for the same reason 22 years later. The MNLF extorted money from local fishing cooperatives; if the money was not forthcoming a boat would be hijacked and the crew forced to jump overboard, a practice that Santos links to the Ambak Pare group.[302] "We're paying up

---

299   Santos, 'Piracy and armed robbery against ships in the Philippines', p. 42; Banlaoi, 'The Abu Sayyaf Group: Threat of Maritime Piracy and Terrorism', p. 122.

300   The attack on the SS *Sunning* noted above was carried out this way. A.G. Course in his book includes several other examples. See also 'Outrage. Conference', *TIME,* 6 Dec. 1926 report about similar attack in 1926 on the *Waihoi* which also had parallels with the attacks on the Vietnamese 'boat people' during the 1980s in that in the two days following the original hijack, 21 groups of pirates raided the vessel for further plunder.

301   Menefee, *TMV,* p. 82.

302   Santos, 'Piracy and armed robbery against ships in the Philippines', p. 44; Hyslop, 'Contemporary piracy', pp. 16-17. '*Ambak pare*' translates as 'Jump buddy!'

to 40,000 pesos (about $3,500 in 2007 US dollars) monthly in protection money," the lawyer for the Zamboanga fishermen's cooperative told a reporter in 1988. "When we're late with the money because of a poor catch the *ambak pare* aren't always understanding."[303]

As with piracy, ascribing responsibility for coastal raids has not been easy, although the ferocity of the attacks and the weight of arms the raiders generally carried would suggest insurgents rather than purely criminal pirates were usually responsible. An MNLF source was reported as saying the group had mounted 487 raids on the Malaysian coast between 1974 and 1978.[304] Menefee believes the MNLF was responsible for the violent attack on Lahad Datu in Sabah in 1985. Banks and airline offices throughout the town were looted, leaving 21 people dead and injured.[305] Ten years later the ASG mounted an almost identical but even more violent attack on the Philippines town of Ipil.

The ASG adopted a violent maritime strategy that brought it international notoriety. The Moro Islamic Liberation Front, although no less active, appears to have been much more circumspect. It can be linked to six incidents, four of which were clearly deliberate attacks on maritime targets. In 1997 two ships, the *Miguel Lujan,* a cargo ship and the *Leonara,* an inter-island ferry, were sprayed with machine-gun fire whilst in the harbour at Isabela. Five people were injured and the passengers on board the ferry were reduced to panic.[306] In 2000 bombs linked to the MILF went off on two more inter-island ferries.[307] The first exploded on a bus driven on board the *Our Lady Mediatrix* which exploded off Ozamis City in February, killing over 40 people and injuring a further 30.[308] The explosion appeared

---

303   'A tide of pirates', p. 28.

304   Menefee, *TMV,* p. 83.

305   *Ibid,* pp. 82-3.

306   Eklöf, *Pirates in Paradise,* p. 112; IMB, 'Piracy and armed robbery against ships: A special report', p. 17.

307   Rommel C. Banlaoi, 'Maritime terrorism in Southeast Asia: The Abu Sayyaf threat', *NWCR,* Winter 2005, p. 71; Bradford, 'The growing prospects for maritime security cooperation in Southeast Asia', p. 67 and Antonio Lopez, 'Meeting force with force', *AsiaWeek.com,* 10 March 2000.

308   Banlaoi, 'Maritime terrorism in Southeast Asia: The Abu Sayyaf Threat', p. 71; Chalk, 'Separatism and Southeast Asia: The Islamic factor in Southern Thailand, Mindanao, and Aceh', p. 249; 'Death toll rises in Philippine blasts' *BBC News,* 26 Feb. 2000; 'At least 16 die of burns in Philippines bus bombing', *CNN.com,* 25 Feb. 2000 and Lopez, 'Meeting force with force'. Herbert-Burns and Zucker, 'Drawing the line between piracy and maritime terrorism', p. 34

to be timed to coincide with the detonation of a number of other bombs planted on other buses owned by the same company that killed a further 10 people in what looked like an extortion attempt. The only small reason to pause in blaming the MILF was that the bomb on the ferry bus was constructed differently from those used against the other buses.[309] The MILF strenuously denied responsibility for the attacks. The second incident, in September 2000, on a ferry arriving in Zamboanga killed one person but was caused almost certainly by the accidental detonation of a bomb that was being delivered to a land target.[310]

The fourth deliberate attack took place at Sasa Wharf in Davao City in 2003 when a bomb was detonated amongst market stalls close to where the ferries *Filipina Princess* and *Superferry 15* were moored.[311] Sixteen people died and 55 were injured in an attack that mimicked MNLF attacks in 1982; these attacks appeared to be designed, as detailed above, to reinforce the political message conveyed by the bombing of Davao City airport the month before. Finally, in 2005 two people died when an explosion occurred on board the *Dona Ramona* as it docked in the port of Lamitan. The MILF was blamed but suspicion settled subsequently on an apparently disgruntled employee as the more likely perpetrator.[312]

When it comes to the use of piracy to raise funds, the MILF does not appear to be any different from the other "Moro" groups. Santos accuses it of being particularly active around northern and southwestern Mindanao.[313]

ascribe the attack to the ASG.

309 'Toll rises to 45 on Philippines bus bombings', The Institute for Counter-Terrorism *Spotlight*, 28 Feb. 2000.

310 'Philippine ferry blast kills one', *BBC News*, 20 Sept. 2000.

311 MIPT Terrorism Knowledge Base Incident Profile: MILF attacks Transportation Target, 2 April 2003; Human Rights Watch, 'Lives destroyed: Attacks against civilians in the Philippines', pp. 8-9; Jaime Burnell, 'Securing the Seas in Southeast Asia', International Centre for Political Violence and Terrorism Research, ND.

312 'At least 30 wounded in Philippine terror blast', *Channel NewsAsia*, 28 Aug. 2005; 'Bomb blast hits Philippines ferry', *BBC News*, 28 Aug. 2005; 'Ferry blast injures 30 in southern Philippines', *New York Times*, 28 Aug. 2005; 'Philippine, Indonesia govts warn of possible terrorist attacks', *Bloomberg.com*, 29 Aug. 2005; Dona Z. Pazzibugan, *et al.*, 'Bomb designed to burn, police say', *The Nation*, 31 Aug. available 2005; 'Death toll from Basilan ferry blast rises to 3', *The Nation*, 7 Sept. 2005; Lino dela Cruz, 'Moro rebel: 'Unseen hand' seen in Abu revival', *SunStarNetworkOnline*, 30 Aug. 2005.

313 Santos, 'Piracy and armed robbery against ships in the Philippines', pp. 44-5.

The Abu Sayyaf Group (ASG), even when it is under pressure, remains highly dangerous. Its operations on the water, like its operations on land, have exhibited no real differences from those of other "Moro" groups except for greater violence and ruthlessness.

First, almost from its inception, it attacked passenger vessels. The group's first recorded attack, on a military checkpoint on the outskirts of the Basilan town of Isabela, took place in 1991.[314] Later in August it bombed the MV *Doulous,* a Christian missionary ship and floating library when it was docked in Zamboanga harbour, leaving two missionaries dead.[315] In 2003 the group threatened to hijack ferries operated by both the WG&A and Sulpicio companies. As mentioned above, the attack on WG&A's 10,000-ton ferry *Superferry 14* on 27 February 2004 was the deadliest attack so far on any passenger vessel. A bomb made of 7.7 lbs (3.5 kg) of TNT caused an explosion and subsequent fire as the ferry left Manila Bay. The bomb, which was hidden inside a portable television set, was deliberately placed amongst the cheapest seating in the depths of the ship in order to induce the maximum panic and greatest loss of life.[316] Although the ferry was the newest in the company's fleet and had only just been introduced into service, the death toll would probably not have been as high if the ship had been operating to the highest fire and safety standards.[317] Although the attack is generally regarded as marking the ASG's return to politically motivated activity after a long period when it was considered to be largely a criminally motivated organisation, it was reportedly mounted because the ferry's owners refused to pay a ransom demand.[318]

---

314   Rabasa, *Political Islam in Southeast Asia,* p. 53.

315   Banlaoi, 'Maritime terrorism in Southeast Asia: The Abu Sayyaf Threat', pp. 68-9; Abuza, *Balik Terrorism,* p. 4; Chalk, 'Separatism and Southeast Asia', p. 249; Eklöf, *Pirates in Paradise,* p. 113.

316   Simon Elegant, 'The Return of Abu Sayyaf', *TIME Asia,* 23 Aug. 2004; Banlaoi, 'Maritime Terrorism in Southeast Asia: The Abu Sayyaf Threat', pp. 71-2; Abuza, *Balik Terrorism,* p. 1; Eklöf, *Pirates in Paradise,* p. 116. 'Abu Sayyaf claims responsibility for ferry blast', *Fox News,* 29 Feb. 2004 and 'We bombed ferry claims Abu Sayyaf', *The Nation,* 29 Feb. 2004. See also 'Terrorist links to *Superferry 14* probed', *Fairplay,* vol. 350, Issue 6271, 8 April 2004, p. 12 and 'Bomb caused Philippine ferry fire', *BBC News,* 11 Oct. 2004. The ASG collaborated with the tiny Rajah Solaiman Movement (RSM) made up of Christian converts to Islam known as 'reverts'. See Banlaoi, 'Maritime terrorism in Southeast Asia: The Abu Sayyaf threat', p. 70 and Rommel C. Banlaoi, 'The rise of the Rajah Solaiman movement (RSM)', IDSS *Commentaries,* 9 Oct. 2006.

317   Rohan Gunaratna, interview with author, 2006.

318   Republic of the Philippines, Office of the Press Secretary, '2 Abu Sayyaf ban-

Shortly after the *Superferry 14* bombing the ASG abducted three people from a sailing boat.[319] Later in the year there were indications that the group was planning a further round of attacks on inter-island "Superferries".[320] In 2006 evidence was uncovered of a plan to hijack *Superferry* vessels sailing between Manila and Mindanao.[321] The group also attacked tugs, holding their crews for ransom: the reported incidents concerned the *East Ocean 2* hijacked in the Sulu Sea in 2004 and the *Bonggaya 91* off Sabah in 2005, two of whose crew died in captivity but, to judge from the experience of kidnap-and ransom cases in the Malacca Straits, there were probably many more that went unreported.[322] In the case of the *TB SM 88*, hijacked near Jolo in 2002, it appears that the hijack was perpetrated by criminal pirates who, once they realised they could not raise a ransom for the master and three officers they had kidnapped, handed them over to the ASG, providing further evidence of the close connections between criminal and ostensibly political piracy in the region. All the hostages are believed to be have been killed.

Secondly, over-the-beach assaults were a feature of ASG activities from the mid-1990s through to 2000. Jolo is one of the Sulu island chain. For centuries the Sulu pirates, with fearful savagery, raided coastal villages in search of slaves.[323] Like the inheritors of a tradition, the ASG mounted over-the-beach assaults for the twofold purpose of killing people and grabbing kidnap victims, a combination that, when Western victims were taken, attracted immense media attention.

---

dits in Super Ferry bombing presented to GMA', 11 Oct. 2004; Eklöf, *Pirates in Paradise*, p. 116 reports that Kadaffy Janjalani had written demanding $1 million to allow the company to make unimpeded use of Mindanao waters. Extortion continues to be the reason for at least some ASG bombings. See, for example, 'Philippines blast 'extortion bid", *BBC News,* 28 March 2006.

319   Banlaoi, 'Maritime terrorism in Southeast Asia: The Abu Sayyaf threat', p. 73.

320   On the 2003 threats see Banlaoi, *Ibid.,* p. 73; on the 2004 indications see Abuza, *Balik Terrorism,* p. 10. In 2006 three ASG or MILF operatives were intercepted carrying two homemade bombs before they could board another ferry, this time the *Superferry 3,* although they were probably being transported for use in Manila: 'Philippines arrest 3 people carrying bombs', Joyo Indonesia News Service, 29 Aug. 2006.

321   Al Jacinto, 'Plot to hijack ships in Mindanao uncovered', *ABS-CBN Interactive,* 3 April 2006.

322   Eklöf, *Pirates in Paradise,* p. 115.

323   Warren, 'A tale of two centuries', pp. 3-5; also Owen Rutter, *The Pirate Wind: Tales of the Sea-Robbers of Malaya,* Singapore and Oxford: Oxford UP 1986, pp. 31-55.

The assault on the predominantly Christian town of Ipil in Zamboanga del Sur on Mindanao in 1995 involved raids on seven banks, and, because it left about 100 people dead, became known as the Ipil massacre.[324] In fact, although the ASG was blamed, it was not solely responsible. The raid had been planned and mounted by a group headed by Melham Alam, Misuari's rival within the MNLF. Nonetheless, it brought the ASG the notoriety it welcomed primarily because it was singled out for blame by the Philippine military.[325] After Abdurajak Janjalani's death and during the period when the group split into semi-criminal gangs, the faction based on Sulu and led by Commander Robot, the pseudonym of Galib Andang, struck the Malaysian diving resort of Pulau Sipadan in April 2000. The gang seized ten tourists and 11 resort workers and took them to Jolo for ransom.[326] The fact their ransom demand of $1 million per Westerner was paid taught the ASG they could obtain more money for Western hostages. The Philippines government refused to pay ransom but allowed the government of Libya, which was interested in rehabilitating its international reputation, to negotiate with the kidnappers. It put together a $25 million fund for 'development projects', all of which was reportedly reimbursed later by Western governments.[327] In September three Malaysians were kidnapped from the

324   'Ipil massacre', ND; Ressa. *Seeds of Terror*, pp. 41-43; Eklöf, *Pirates in Paradise*, pp. 113-14, who reports that only 40 died. For photographs of the town after the attack visit http://www.lazamboangatimes.com/victoria.html. Carolina Hernandez reports that 'foreigners' (a category that usually refers to operatives linked to al-Qaeda or JI) also took part: Carolina G. Hernandez, 'Fighting terrorism in Southeast Asia: A view from the Philippines', The Woodrow Wilson Center for Scholars *Asia Program Special Report no. 112*, 'Fighting terrorism on the Southeast Asian front', June 2004, p. 28.

325   Paul A. Rodell, 'The Philippines and the challenge of international terrorism' in Smith (ed.), *Terrorism and Violence in Southeast Asia*, 2005, p. 132.

326   MIPT Terrorism Knowledge Base Incident Profile: ASG attacking Private Citizens and Property Target, 23 April 2000; also Banlaoi, 'Leadership dynamics in terrorist organizations in Southeast Asia: The Abu Sayyaf case', p. 6; Terry McCarthy, 'An invasion of paradise', *TIME*, 8 May 2000; Penny Crisp, 'A religious war comes to paradise', *Asia week*, vol. 26, no. 17, 5 May 2000; Sangwon Suh and Antonio Lopez, 'Getting tough', *Asiaweek*, vol. 26, no. 38, 29 Sept. 2000; and 'Timeline: The Jolo hostage drama', *BBC News report*, 12 Sept. 2000. Andang apparently acquired the name 'robot' because of his stiff gait: Davis, 'Resilient Abu Sayyaf resists military pressure'.

327   Ressa. *Seeds of Terror*, p. 112. Banlaoi, 'Maritime terrorism in Southeast Asia: The Abu Sayyaf threat', p. 72 contradicts this account suggesting that the group received a $15 million ransom from the Philippine government to end the crisis. Reports that circulated after the event suggest that several parties in addition to the ASG benefited including members of the security forces, local

Pasir Beach Resort in Sabah.[328] On 22 May 2001 ASG members raided the Pearl Farm beach resort on Samal Island in Mindanao.[329] No hostages were taken but two resort workers were killed and three injured. On 28 May 2001 the group abducted three Americans, included two missionaries, Gracia and Martin Burnham, and 17 Filipinos from the Dos Palmas resort in Palawan in the Philippines.[330] In a similar manner to the *TB SM 88* hijack and crew kidnap mentioned above, criminal pirates kidnapped three Indonesian and three Filipino workers from the Borneo Paradise Resort in October 2003 in a raid that mimicked the ASG. The one survivor later testified that the pirates handed them over or sold them to the ASG in Tawi-Tawi province, where the remainder were killed in a shoot-out with Philippine government forces.[331]

Commander Global, Nadzmi Sabdullah, who was captured in 2001, planned both the Pulau Sipadan and Dos Palmas raids.[332] Andang was captured during the combined US-Philippine exercise Balikatan 02-1 in 2002 and died in a subsequent jailbreak in 2005.[333] It is possible that the ransom payments were used to "buy" local support, the loyalty of competing factions and even protection from local police and military authorities, not only in the Philippines but also in Malaysia.[334] The group, together with

and national government officials. A subsequent FBI report also suggested that al-Qaeda had received funds from Muslim terrorist groups in the Philippines. Ressa. *Seeds of Terror*, pp. 115-116.

328 Banlaoi, 'Maritime terrorism in Southeast Asia: The Abu Sayyaf threat', p. 72.

329 Banlaoi, 'The Abu Sayyaf Group: Threat of maritime piracy and terrorism', p. 129

330 MIPT Terrorism Knowledge Base Incident Profile: ASG attacking Tourist Target, 27 May 2001; Alex Spillius, 'Americans amongst 20 hostages in resort raid', *Daily Telegraph*, 5 June 2001. Martin Burnham was killed when the AFP caught the gang. Gracia Burnham recounted their ordeal in Burnham with Dean Merrill, *In the Presence of My Enemies*.

331 Davis, 'The Sulu Triangle'.

332 'Rebel leader caught in Philippines', *BBC News*, 9 July 2001.

333 Banlaoi, 'Maritime terrorism in Southeast Asia: The Abu Sayyaf threat', pp. 69 & 73. Those who remained were sentenced in 2007. Manny Mogato, 'Philippine Muslim rebels jailed for kidnap, beheading', *Reuters*, 6 Dec. 2007. For more detail on the US military involvement in the area and details about all the various US-RP joint exercises undertaken between 1992 and 2006 see 'Unconventional warfare: Are US forces engaged in an 'offensive war' in the Philippines?' Focus on the Philippines *Special Reports* no. 1, Jan. 2007, pp. 12-18 & 20-1.

334 Banlaoi, 'Leadership dynamics in terrorist organizations in Southeast Asia: The Abu Sayyaf case', pp. 12 & 17; Rabasa, *et al.*, *Beyond al-Qaeda: Part 2*, p. 116;

operatives from its Indonesian ally JI, appeared to be able to move between Sabah in Malaysia and the southern Philippines with relative ease and often with the connivance of local law enforcement agencies.[335] The group's notoriety meant that following 9/11 concerns were expressed that the ASG could be in a position to threaten international shipping; Jolo lies astride a north-south shipping lane that is important for the Australia-Japan ore and gas trades, and is a route which would become even more important if the Malacca Straits were to be blocked and east-west traffic forced to divert via the Lombok Strait.[336] It might well have been these concerns that inspired US and Australian interest in the region.

There is no question that the ASG possessed a skilled and well-equipped maritime capability that gave it the capacity to strike a range of targets over a wide area by day or night.[337] Although the Balikatan exercises had, by 2003, restricted the group's land-based operations to Jolo it retained the ability to move freely at sea, particularly at night, using fast "*bancas*" that could outrun almost anything in the Philippine naval inventory.[338] Although the sheer number of interceptions mounted by the Philippine Navy from 2002 onwards restricted this freedom the group was nonetheless able to conduct tactical withdrawals from one island to the next as it came under pressure.[339] In 2006 there were suggestions that the group had even bolstered its raiding capacity by developing a swimmer capability, possibly with JI.[340] JI, in turn, similarly exploited free movement at sea: in February 2005 JI gunmen attacked a beachside café in Ambon in Indonesia, killing two customers in what was seen as a practice run for what followed: attacks

Davis, 'Resilient Abu Sayyaf resists military pressure'.

335   'Southeast Asia's tri-border black spot', *Jane's TSM,* May 2007, pp. 10-11; 'Jihardist alliances in Southeast Asia', *Jane's TSM,* 15 March 2006; Ian Storey, 'The Triborder Sea Area: Maritime Southeast Asia's ungoverned space', The Jamestown Foundation *Terrorism Monitor,* vol. V, Issue 19, 11 Oct. 2007, p. 2.

336   For an analysis of the threats to the various Southeast Asian shipping routes see Kenny, *An Analysis of Possible Threats to Shipping in Key Southeast Asian Sea Lanes.*

337   Banlaoi, 'Maritime terrorism in Southeast Asia: The Abu Sayyaf threat', pp. 71 & 73.

338   Davis, 'Resilient Abu Sayyaf resists military pressure'.

339   Abuza, 'On the defensive: Rebels lose ground in Southern Philippines', pp. 12 & 16.

340   Davis, 'Philippines fears new wave of attacks by Abu Sayyaf group', p. 12; Anthony Vargas, 'Seaborne bombers may strike in Cebu', *ABS-CBN Interactive,* 21 Nov. 2006.

on isolated police and army posts. One on Seram Island in May 2005 left five policemen dead.[341]

Like the other "Moro" groups, however, the ASG used maritime insurgency primarily to raise funds, although how much was for the cause and how much was for personal gain, a leftover from the days when common criminality was its driving force, was hard to know.[342] In terms of maritime insurgency practice, the group is of interest because it demonstrated how maritime mobility can enable a group to retain freedom of manoeuvre; its attack on the *Superferry 14* focused worldwide attention on the vulnerability of open-access maritime transport and its raids on coastal resorts showed the difficulty any counter-insurgency force can experience when tasked to defend isolated towns and beaches from what can be described fairly as "Viking-style" or, more accurately, "Sulu-style" raiding.

The main reasons to go to sea: movement and supply

Around 90 per cent of the world's trade moves by sea during some portion of its journey. Arguably 90 per cent of insurgent or terrorist supplies also move by sea at some stage, though there is no way of telling. Whatever the true figure, the sea is likely to be of most use to insurgent or terrorist groups as a transport medium. The Provisional IRA took delivery of arms from its American supporters and from Libya by sea: in addition to the *Eksund*, which has been mentioned already, Libya made two shipments in 1972 and a third, using a vessel named the *Claudia*, in 1973; in 1985 and 1986 it made two further shipments on board the *Casamara* and the *Villa* respectively; American arms were received in 1984, involving a transfer from a trawler named the *Valhalla* that sailed from Boston to another trawler, the *Marita Ann*, at a point off the coast of County Kerry.[343] The Iranians sent the Palestinians arms for the *intifada* the same way.[344] Al Qaeda is be-

---

341   Abuza, 'Shifting focus: Jamaah Islamiyah's long-term agenda towards Islamism', p. 24.

342   See the comment on mixed motives in 'Kidnappers make ransom demand after hostage grab on Malaysian resort', *CNN.com*, 27 April 2000.

343   'The IRA's store of weaponry', *BBC News*, 14 Aug. 2001; Stewart. *The Brutal Seas*, pp. 322-4; also Sean Boyne, 'Uncovering the Irish Republican Army', *Jane's IR*, 1 Aug. 1996.,

344   Usher and Borger. 'Israel halts Palestinian arms ship'. For more details on this and a previous incident see 'Weapons found on the 'Karine-A' and 'Santorini''. Despite these setbacks Palestinian groups have continued to try and bring in arms by sea: see 'Israel intercepts Hizballah shipment to Palestinians', ICT *News & Commentary*, 24 May 2003 and, more recently, 'Israeli navy intercepts TNT

lieved to have transported the explosives it used in the East African embassy bombings by sea.[345] Coalition Task Force (CTF) 150 was established in the Arabian Sea because of fears that Al Qaeda operatives would attempt to escape by ship. Equally, Operation Active Endeavour was established in the eastern Mediterranean to deter insurgents from using ships to move men and materiel.

The assumption in the past was that insurgents could live off the population and steal from their opponents. This is what Mao taught. This assertion might always have been somewhat questionable, particularly given the support rendered by states such as the Soviet Union for many years, and while some insurgencies are low cost operations, many of the most resilient clearly depend on external assistance. Terrorists and insurgents, particularly if they come from outside the theatre of operations, as has been witnessed in Iraq, are usually wealthy compared to the people amongst whom they mix. They therefore depend on external supply for the sophisticated arms and explosives they now use, for the skilled operatives they need to build bombs and direct operations, for suicide volunteers, and for the money that they spread around to encourage silence, cooperation and a flow of basic recruits.[346] Evidence for this trend comes from a declassified US intelligence report cited by Senator Jo Lieberman:

al Qaeda in Iraq is dependent for its survival on the support it receives from the broader, global Al Qaeda network...(it is) sustained by a transportation network of facilitators and smugglers...(and) although small in number, these foreign fighters are a vital strategic asset, providing it with the essential human ammunition it needs to conduct high-visibility, mass-casualty suicide bombings.[347]

Why support networks are important from a counter-terrorist perspective, and therefore why maritime security operations are important, is because they might constitute what Clausewitz termed a 'centre of gravity',

---

on way to Gaza', *The Washington Times*, 9 May 2006.

345   Richardson, *A Time Bomb for Global Trade*, pp. 14-15. Speculation focused in particular on the *Jennifer* which was subsequently renamed the *Sky-1* and was reported sunk off the coast of Somalia sometime in 2001, although no wreck has been found. Andrea Felstead and Mark Odell, 'Agencies fear extent of al-Qaeda's sea network', *FT.com Special Reports*, 21 Feb. 2002; also Gunaratna, 'The threat to the maritime domain: How real is the terrorist threat?' p. 85.

346   David Kilcullen, 'Counterinsurgency *Redux*', *Survival*, vol. 48, no. 4, Winter 2006, p. 119; also Michael Knights and Zack Snyder, 'The role played by funding in the Iraq insurgency', *Jane's IR*, Aug. 2005, pp. 8-15.

347   Joseph Lieberman, 'Al Qaeda's travel agent', *Wall Street Journal*, 20 Aug. 2007.

which he describes as "the hub of all power and movement, on which everything depends". His advice is that this is "the point against which all... energies should be directed".[348] As Gray points out, this concept "retains its utility even if one rejects Clausewitz's preference for applying strength against strength" and therefore, as US Assistant Secretary of Defence for Special Operations Michael Vickers argued, "if we can deter the support network...then we can start achieving a deterrent effect on the whole terrorist network" and constrain their ability to operate.[349]

The 9/11 attacks caused such consternation that many previous assumptions about terrorist motivations, tactics and capabilities were challenged. One of the areas that came under the microscope was ship ownership. This is a tangled subject. Many owners are concerned to hide their beneficial interest in a ship in order to avoid their regulatory or tax obligations. The use of bearer shares, nominee shareholders and various business intermediaries such as agents or lawyers is the method most commonly used to disguise who ownes what.[350] During the period when these concerns were being raised and investigated, reports began to appear in the press of an "Al Qaeda navy".[351]

The Al Qaeda "navy". From the end of 2001 through to 2004 there were several press reports, all of them apparently well informed, about the existence of what came to be called an "Al Qaeda navy".[352] Although the concern grew in the post-9/11 climate it appeared to be based on earlier reports that bin Laden operated a very small number of ships when he was based in the Sudan, which were disposed of some time before 2001—that is, before

---

348   Carl von Clausewitz. (ed. and tr. Michael Howard and Peter Paret). *On War.* Princeton: Princeton UP, 1976, pp. 595-6.

349   Colin S. Gray. *Modern Strategy.* Oxford: Oxford UP, 1999, p. 96. For Michael Vickers comment see Eric Schmitt and Thom Shanker, 'US adapts Cold-War idea to fight terrorists', *New York Times,* 18 March 2008.

350   For a useful description of these evasive practices see Herbert-Burns, 'Terrorism in the early 21st century maritime domain', pp. 158-61; also Felstead and Odell, 'Agencies fear extent of al-Qaeda's sea network'.

351   For example, Felstead and Odell, 'Agencies fear extent of al-Qaeda's sea network'; Martin Bright, *et al.,* 'Hunt for 20 terror ships', *The Observer,* 23 Dec. 2001, and Mintz, '15 freighters believed to be linked to Al Qaeda'; 'Al-Qaeda's 'Navy'–How Much of a Threat?' *Centre for Defence Information,* 20 Aug. 2003.

352   John Mackinlay, *Globalisation and Insurgency,* Adelphi Paper 352, Oxford: OUP for the IISS, 2002, p. 88; David Osler, 'Nato unmasks al-Qa'eda fleet', *Lloyd's List,* 29 Nov. 2001.

the later speculation arose.[353] Opinion in the intelligence community appears to be divided over whether bin Laden controlled any ships directly.[354] Officials talked of up to 15 ships, although some estimates talked of 30 and even 50 ships, engaged mostly in legitimate trade. They were reputed to have acted as transports but the principal fear was that they could be used to attack ports or shipping.[355] A Syrian businessman reportedly bought the first ship, the *Jennifer*, on Al Qaeda's behalf in 1993 or 1994.[356] The continuing reports and rumours appeared to be given some substance in 2002 when Tonga announced it would close its international ship register at the request of the US authorities who had noticed a significant correlation between Tongan-flagged vessels and those involved in people and arms smuggling. In particular, they were interested in the operations of a company called Nova, registered in Delaware, which appeared to have links with Al Qaeda.[357] In February 2002 eight Pakistanis jumped off the *Twillinger*, one of the company's ships in Trieste; they claimed to be crew members but their papers were false.[358] A similar incident happened in Casablanca in August 2002, this time involving 15 Pakistanis and a ship named the

---

353   Michael Scheuer suggests that during the period when bin Laden was based in the Sudan (1991-96) he established what Scheuer describes as a 'naval bridge' between Sudan and Yemen to supply Hasan al-Turabi's Islamist regime in Khartoum with guns and fighters in one direction and to infiltrate Al Qaeda fighters into Saudi Arabia via Yemen in the other: Michael Scheuer, 'Yemen's role in al-Qaeda's strategy', The Jamestown Foundation *Terrorism Focus*, vol. V, Issue 5, 5 Feb. 2008.

354   Confidential information, Sept. and Oct. 2006; 'Dispute over al-Qaida's terrorist navy", *WorldNetDaily,* 19 Feb. 2004.

355   Probably the most influential article was Mintz. '15 freighters believed to be linked to Al Qaeda'. Also see Paul Harris and Martin Bright. 'How the armada of terror menaces Britain', *The Observer,* 23 Dec. 2001. On the higher estimate see Newman, 'Terrorists feared to be planning sub-surface naval attacks'; 'Al-Qaeda's 'Navy'–How much of a threat?' and Daly, 'Al Qaeda and maritime terrorism (Part I)'.

356   'Bin Laden bought ship 'for terror", *The Times,* 17 Oct. 2004; Osler, 'Nato unmasks al-Qa'eda fleet'; Richardson, *A Time Bomb for Global Trade,* p. 15. Another suggestion was that the fleet had been bought from 'a Greek shipping agent suspected of having a direct relationship with Osama bin Laden': 'What al-Qaida could do with 'terror navy", *WorldNetDaily,* 20 Oct. 2003.

357   Vijay Sakhuja, 'Who steers Al Qaeda's fleet?' Institute of Peace and Conflict Studies, *Article no. 975,* 28 Feb. 2003.

358   'Al-Qaeda's 'navy'–How much of a threat?'; Mintz, '15 freighters believed to be linked to Al Qaeda'.

Sara.[359] The Tongan flag had also proved useful to other terrorists and their associates. The *Karine A*, which was intercepted off the Sinai coast in January 2002 carrying Iranian arms destined for Palestinian terrorists, was also registered in Tonga.[360] Later, in November 2002, US intelligence sources told reporters that, following his capture, al-Nashiri had revealed the identities of 15 small- to medium-sized cargo vessels that had been operating under various flags of convenience, and that more might be identified in the future.[361] Despite all this detail the story is now largely discounted; maritime expert Charles Dragonette is convinced the reports had "little foundation in reality".[362] In all probability it was a misconception based on concerns over the ownership of ships by "front" companies.[363] Nonetheless, there is no disputing that Al Qaeda and its affiliates have ready access to shipping through associates, sympathisers and the charter market (as does any adequately funded terrorist organisation).[364]

LTTE maritime support operations. The LTTE, on the other hand, unquestionably do have their own fleet known, informally and rather quaintly, as the "Sea Pigeons", which while often crewed by Sea Tigers is managed and controlled separately.[365] As mentioned the group had, from its inception, a need to move men and supplies across the strait dividing Sri Lanka

359 Mintz, '15 freighters believed to be linked to Al Qaeda'.

360 See Richardson, *A Time Bomb for Global Trade*, pp. 95-6; 'The ships that died of shame', *Sydney Morning Herald*, 14 Jan. 2003 and 'New al-Qaeda threat: 15-ship mystery navy', *WorldNetDaily*, 29 Sept. 2003. Also 'What al-Qaeda could do with 'terror navy'' for a discussion on the possible links between the organiser of the *Karine A* operation and Al Qaeda. Sakhuja claims the *Karine-A* and the *Twillinger* were sister ships: Sakhuja, 'Who steers Al Qaeda's fleet?' On the continuing interest this fleet provokes, and the links between terrorism and drug smuggling, see Philip Sherwell, 'The Royal Navy closes one of al-Qaeda's last escape routes', *Sunday Telegraph*, 21 March 2004.

361 'The ships that died of shame'; Julian Borger and Brian Whitaker, 'US watching al-Qaida's fleet', *The Guardian*, 1 Jan. 2003.

362 Dragonette, 'Lost at Sea', p. 175 and Catherine Meldrum, 'Murky waters–Financing maritime terrorism and crime', *Jane's IR*, 1 June 2007.

363 Osler, 'Nato unmasks al-Qa'eda fleet'; 'Terrorism probe extends to shipping', *American Maritime Officer*, Oct. 2001.

364 Private interviews, April and Sept. 2005. Its use of the sea continues: in Dec. 2003, for example, the US Navy intercepted three Al Qaeda-linked boats in the Persian Gulf with two tons of hashish on board; other seizures followed: A. Brownfeld, 'Al-Qaeda's drug-running network', *Jane's TSM*, 1 Feb. 2004.

365 Byman *et al.*, *Trends in Outside Support for Insurgency Movements*, p. 119; Sakhuja, 'The dynamics of LTTE's commercial maritime infrastructure', p. 3 on the separate command and control arrangements.

from its base areas in India.[366] It was India's foreign intelligence service, the Research and Analysis Wing (RAW), that enabled the LTTE to build its maritime capability by training LTTE operatives at Vishakapatnam in Andhra Pradesh and facilitating the construction of the group's first deep-water boats.[367] In 1987 the Indian government withdrew its support for the insurgency. The southern part of the subcontinent was being forced to absorb increasing numbers of refugees and the crisis was fuelling separatist tendencies there as well.[368] Without Indian support the group had to look for alternative sources of finance and supplies. Angered by what it saw as Indian betrayal, it assassinated Rajiv Gandhi in 1991, a blunder that only made its position worse. Its base areas in Tamil Nadu were closed, forcing it to move all its facilities to Sri Lanka.[369] Nonetheless, the area which houses approximately 65,000 Tamil refugees spread across 113 camps continued to be an important area for LTTE support and procurement operations.[370] The

---

366 Mackinlay, *Globalisation and Insurgency*, pp. 71-2. For further details on the LTTE fleet including how it was started in the mid-1980s, ship numbers and how they are employed see Rohan Gunaratna, 'International and regional implications of the Sri Lankan Tamil insurgency', *Tamilnation.org*, 2 Dec. 1998; Davis, 'Tiger International'; Sakhuja, 'The dynamics of LTTE's commercial maritime infrastructure", and Chalk, 'Liberation Tigers of Tamil Eelam's international organisation and operations–A preliminary analysis', pp. 2 & 7-9.

367 Gunaratna, 'The threat to the maritime domain: How real is the terrorist threat?', p. 83; Edward Cody, 'Roots of Gandhi slaying lie in India's role in Sri Lanka', *The Washington Post,* 30 May 1991.

368 Byman *et al., Trends in Outside Support for Insurgency Movements*, p. 118; Rohan Gunaratna, 'International and regional implications of the Sri Lankan Tamil insurgency', *Tamilnation.org*, 2 Dec. 1998.

369 Sakhuja, 'The dynamics of LTTE's commercial maritime infrastructure", p. 2; Rohan Gunaratna, 'The transformation of terror?' *Asia Times Online*, 25 Sept. 2002. There are indications that the links were not severed entirely or have been revived subsequently: 'LTTE may get arms from S Indian hideouts–Report', *Rediff.com*, 24 Sept. 2007; 'LTTE has arms stores in India: Report', *Zee News*, 12 Oct. 2007. Also Robert Karniol, 'Tamil Tigers' hangout: S-E Asia', *The Straits Times*, 22 Oct. 2007. In 2008, in an attempt to restrict supply movements and to prevent LTTE cadres from fleeing to Tamil Nadu, the SLN laid sea mines along the sea border with India, provoking protests from Indian fishermen who have traditionally fished in Sri Lankan waters: 'Sri Lankan Navy plants mines along maritime border with India', *The Times of India*, 23 Jan. 2008; K. Praveen Kumar, 'Lanka mines sea borders to block Tamil Tigers', *Newindpress*, 23 Jan. 2008; Jaya Menon, 'Fishermen up in arms against Lankan Navy's move to lay sea mines', *Indian Express*, 25 Jan. 2008.

370 Solomon and Tan, 'Feeding the Tiger'.

group also appeared to have moved some of its support and boat building operations to India's Kerala coast in an attempt to avoid surveillance.[371]

The group's most pressing requirement was for arms. Although it quickly established an indigenous armaments industry that was capable of manufacturing weapons of remarkable sophistication, it still needed to buy many of the weapons and explosives it needed, plus other supplies. Without Indian support these needed to be paid for. The group began to raise money from two sources: donations from the large Tamil diaspora community, and crime.[372] The supplies could only be delivered to Sri Lanka by sea.

The group's development of an ocean-going maritime capability was not a response born out of panic. On the contrary, the LTTE maritime shipping network was established well before Indian support was withdrawn. It turned from chartering vessels to owning its own in 1984 after purchasing its first freighter, the MV *Cholan,* from a Bombay businessman.[373] At about the same time it placed its first construction order for a second freighter, the *Kadalpura,* and established a connection with the military regime in Burma.[374] Although its first choice for an operating base was apparently Singapore, the LTTE's connection with the Burmese regime meant that from 1987 it was allowed to use bases on several small islands off the Burmese coast, the most important of which was Twante.[375] These bases were eventually closed in 1995 following intense diplomatic pressure by the Sri Lankan government.[376] The Tigers then switched their operations to

---

371 'LTTE spreading its wings in Kerala?' *The Times of India,* 6 March 2008.

372 Rabasa, *et al., Beyond al-Qaeda: Part 2,* 2006, pp. 108-9.

373 Sakhuja, 'The dynamics of LTTE's commercial maritime infrastructure", p. 2; Gunaratna, 'International and regional implications of the Sri Lankan Tamil insurgency'; Bharadwaj, 'Maritime aspects of Sri Lankan conflict', p. 245; Peiris, 'Secessionist war and terrorism in Sri Lanka: transnational impulses', p. 98; 'LTTE linchpin KP free'.

374 'Kadalpura' translates as 'sea pigeons'. It was captured by the SLN in 1987. Gunaratna, 'International and regional implications of the Sri Lankan Tamil insurgency'; Bharadwaj, 'Maritime aspects of Sri Lankan conflict', p. 245; Sakhuja, 'The dynamics of LTTE's commercial maritime infrastructure", p. 2.

375 Sakhuja, 'The dynamics of LTTE's commercial maritime infrastructure", p. 2; Daniel Byman *et al., Trends in Outside Support for Insurgency Movements,* pp. 121-2, note 14; Davis, 'Tiger International'; Gunaratna, 'International and regional implications of the Sri Lankan Tamil insurgency'; Bharadwaj, 'Maritime aspects of Sri Lankan conflict', p. 245. On Singapore see V. Jayanth. 'LTTE's flourishing shipping network'. *The Hindu,* 29 March 2000; Davis, 'Tamil tiger international'..

376 According to Peiris, LTTE ships continued to use Burmese ports even after

Phuket in Thailand, and a number of offshore islands, whence they operated for much of the 1990s.[377]

The LTTE has bought arms around the world and transported them to Sri Lanka, in most cases in its own ships, as the *Swene* and *Stillus Limassol* cases mentioned earlier demonstrate. Weapons became widely available in Southeast Asia in the 1980s and into the 1990s as a consequence of the war between Vietnam and the Khmers Rouges. While the war was being fought Thai Army sources estimate that between 20 and 30 per cent of all Chinese arms intended for the conflict were taken and sold by corrupt members of the Thai military. As the fighting wound down even larger volumes of weapons became available. Many were sold initially to Burmese groups but by the early 1990s several new purchasers had emerged, of which the largest and best organised was the LTTE. They recruited members of the Tamil diaspora and opened front companies in Phuket and Trang province on the Andaman Sea and in Bangkok. By 1995 its network had spread to Phnom Penh and then to Saigon, Sihanoukville and Cheng Mai. As well as buying arms the network moved people and traded documents. Movement by sea has been crucial to the arms trade; according to the Thai military, by the end of the 1990s 80 per cent of the arms leaving Cambodia left by ship. Arms destined for the LTTE appear to have been moved from Sihanoukville across the Gulf of Thailand to the long established smuggling centre of Rayong on Thailand's eastern coast and then to Ranong on the Andaman Sea.[378] Some arms flowed north to feed the northeast Indian insurgent groups via the Bangladeshi ports of Chittagong and Cox's Bazaar. Some of the consignments were moved by the Arakanese smugglers who developed out of the insurgent Arakan Liberation Party (ALP), but others have been moved by the LTTE for themselves and for others.[379]

Twente and its other bases were closed: Peiris, 'Secessionist war and terrorism in Sri Lanka: transnational impulses', p. 107.

377   Davis, 'Tracking Tigers in Phuket'; Gunaratna, 'The transformation of terror?'; Jayanth. 'LTTE's flourishing shipping network'; Peiris, 'Secessionist war and terrorism in Sri Lanka: transnational impulses', p. 107; Bertil Lintner, 'Arms Trade: The Phuket Connection', *The Week*, 30 April 2000.

378   Other ports reported to be used were Krabi, Sattoship, Haadyal and Songahla: 'LTTE bides time to win Eelam'.

379   Bertil Lintner, 'LTTE purchases: A link with Cambodia', *Jane's IR*, Dec. 1996, p. 9; Anthony Davis, 'Tamil Tiger International', *Jane's IR*, vol. 8, no. 10, 1 Oct. 1996; Anthony Davis, 'Thailand cracks down on illicit arms trade', *Jane's IR*, 1 Dec. 2003, p. 34; also Sakhuja, 'The dynamics of LTTE's commercial maritime infrastructure", p. 6; "Floating market' in illicit weapons arms terrorists', *Jane's*

Various suggestions have been made as to how many ocean-going cargo ships the group has operated at any one time. The numbers appear to fluctuate between nine and 15, although a figure of 11 is mentioned most frequently.[380] In truth, no one outside the organisation probably knows how many ships are involved, although in 2007 the SLN claimed that the LTTE had owned ten ships of which it had destroyed nine.[381] The owned fleet is probably supplemented by chartered vessels, which operate not merely in the Indian Ocean but also in the Mediterranean and the Pacific.[382]

When supplying the LTTE units in Sri Lanka, the ships transfer their loads to high-speed logistics craft about 120 miles off the northeast coast. For most of the period of the conflict the SLN was reluctant to attack the ships directly in international waters for fear of sparking an international incident if it acted on incorrect information.[383] Despite this the group suffered a number of significant losses amongst the ocean-going fleet; the loss of one, the MV *Yahata*, transformed into the MV *Ahat* by the simple expedient of painting out the first and last letters in 1993, revealed that the group wires its ships with explosives to prevent whatever they are carrying from falling into Sri Lankan hands. In this case the senior LTTE commander, Krishnakumar Sathasivam, better known as "Kittu", who was on board ordered the captain and his civilian crew to jump over the side before blowing up the ship along with himself and the other LTTE personnel on

TSM, 17 May 2006; and Solomon and Tan, 'Feeding the Tiger'. The author of the blog 'LTTE linchpin KP free' alleges a close relationship between senior Thai army officers and the LTTE procurement wing. Because the author is anonymous this information needs to be treated with circumspection,

380   Sakhuja, 'The dynamics of LTTE's commercial maritime infrastructure", pp. 3-4; Daniel Byman *et al.*, *Trends in Outside Support for Insurgency Movements*, p. 119. For a useful summary of known LTTE ships up until 2002, including registrations, see Rohan Gunaratna, 'Asia Pacific: Organised crime and international terrorist networks' in A.P.S. Gill and Ajai Sahni, *The Global Threat of Terror: Ideological, Material and Political Linkages*, New Delhi: Bulwark Books for The Institute of Conflict Management, 2002, p. 260.

381   'Sri Lankan Navy completely destroy three LTTE ships and demolish their arms shipment capabilities', Sri Lankan Navy *Security News*, 11 Sept. 2007; B. Muralidhar Reddy, 'Three LTTE ships destroyed: Navy', *The Hindu*, 12 Sept. 2007.

382   Sakhuja, 'The Dynamics of LTTE's Commercial Maritime Infrastructure', p. 2; P.K. Ghosh, 'Maritime Security Challenges in South Asia and the Indian Ocean: Response Strategies', Paper prepared for the CSIS American-Pacific Sealanes Security Institute Conference on Maritime Security in Asia held in Honolulu, Hawaii, 18-20 Jan. 2004, p. 6. Also 'LTTE linchpin KP free'.

383   Murphy, 'Maritime Threat: Tactics and Technology of the Sea Tigers', p. 6.

board.[384] Malaysia seized the MV *Sun Bird* in 1990, India interdicted or impounded three ships between 1991 and 1999, and in February 1996 the Sri Lankan Air force sank the MV *Horizon* and the MV *Comex Jules*.[385] Since 2000 the SLN has shown itself more prepared to intercept LTTE ships in international waters. In 2003 two oilers, the MV *Shoskin* and the MV *Koimar*, were both engaged over 200 miles (370 km) off Sri Lanka's eastern seaboard.[386] In 2007 the SLN intercepted the MV *Kyoi* 200 nautical miles off Dondra Head in February and the MV *Seiyoo* at roughly the same range but further to the east in March. It sank three more vessels over 600 nautical miles (1,100 km) southeast of the island in September and the 3,000 ton MV *Matsushima* 920 nautical miles (1,700 km) south of Dondra Head on 7 October.[387] It appears that these successes might have been the result of foreign intelligence support.[388] Reports emanating from Sri Lanka

---

384 Davis, 'Tamil Tiger International'; Sakhuja, 'The dynamics of LTTE's commercial maritime infrastructure", p. 3; Bharadwaj, 'Maritime aspects of Sri Lankan conflict', p. 243; B. Raman, 'Action Against LTTE's Maritime Terrorism - International Terrorism Monitor: Paper no. 58', South Asia Analysis Group *Paper no. 1802*, 18 May 2006. For further details of LTTE loses see *ibid.*, pp. 3-5. Also Peiris, 'Secessionist war and terrorism in Sri Lanka: transnational impulses', p. 112 and Daniel Byman *et al.*, *Trends in Outside Support for Insurgency Movements*, p. 120, note 7.

385 Davis, 'Tamil Tiger International'; Gunaratna, 'The asymmetric threat from maritime terrorism', p. 29.

386 Sakhuja, 'The dynamics of LTTE's commercial maritime infrastructure", p. 4.

387 For the details see Sri Lanka Navy, 'Destruction of 'Matsushima'", 7 Oct. 2007 and Asif Fuard. 'Is the tide turning against the LTTE?' *The Sunday Times* (Colombo), 14 Oct. 2007. The ships sunk in Sept. were named as the *Koshia*, the *Seishin* and the *Manyoshi*. See also 'Sri Lankan Navy completely destroy three LTTE ships and demolish their arms shipment capabilities'; Reddy, 'Three LTTE ships destroyed: Navy'. It certainly appears to be the case that at the very least the ships destroyed in Sept. and Oct. were located as the result of an intelligence-driven operation. For a broad-brush account of the background from an SLN perspective see Jalaldeen, 'Navy's pivotal role in battle against terrorism' and Ravin Edirisinghe, 'SL navy's role in eradicating international maritime terrorism: Year 2007 and challenges ahead', *Asian Tribune*, 10 Jan. 2008. Whether this intelligence was related to the reported (but unconfirmed) arrest of the LTTE's principal arms procurement agent, Kumaran Pathmanathan ('KP') is unclear: B. Muralidhar Reddy, 'Top LTTE man held in Bangkok', *The Hindu*, 12 Sept. 2007. For doubts about the arrest see Karniol, 'Tamil Tigers' hangout: S-E Asia'. For background on KP see 'Who is KP?', *Lanka Guardian*, 10 Sept. 2007. The blog 'LTTE linchpin KP free' alleges that KP was arrested but subsequently freed in late 2007 on the orders of senior Thai army officers after payment of a million dollar bribe.

388 'Tigers suffer setbacks'; P.S Suryanarayana. 'India's naval surveillance a big help

---

suggest that the LTTE supply fleet, or at least that part of it that was attacked successfully by the SLN, used Indonesia as its "home base". Goods were brought out from Indonesian ports and transferred to ships that were described as "floating warehouses" in international waters. These ships then loitered just west of Java before moving closer to the Sri Lankan coast when needed.[389] The general assumption is that the LTTE will recover from this setback by first resorting to more indigenous supply sources on Sri Lanka or in the Tamil areas of southern India and, secondly, perhaps by initiating more effective deception measures and positioning its ships further out to sea in future, beyond the range of land-based aerial surveillance.

Not all the ocean going vessels carry Tamil Tiger supplies exclusively. On the contrary they probably transport legitimate cargo at least 95 per cent of the time, earning the group additional income.[390] When they are carrying supplies for the Tigers these will be hidden amongst innocent goods. They have shown, in other words, how an insurgent group with a maritime capability can use it, in parallel with insurgent activity, to generate funds perfectly legally.

They have also shown, however, that the same ships can also be used to move criminal cargoes. In the case of the Tigers this usually means smuggling arms, illegal migrants and drugs, either on their own account or for criminal gangs.[391] According to a report prepared for the US Federal Research Service in 2003, the LTTE use narcotics to fund their opera-

---

to Sri Lanka'. *The Hindu*, 4 June 2008.

389 'Sri Lankan Tamil Tiger ships used Indonesia as 'home base'–sources', *The Island* (Colombo), 21 Oct. 2007. Also Bharatha Mallawarachi, 'Sri Lankan military investigates Indonesian ship on suspected involvement with Tamil rebels', *AP*, 26 Dec. 2007. For the report on 'floating warehouses' see 'Countering LTTE: India admits helping Lanka', *NDTV.com*, 16 Jan. 2008 and 'Global concern over maritime security cripples LTTE', *News Post India*, 21 Jan. 2008.

390 Daniel Byman *et al., Trends in Outside Support for Insurgency Movements*, p. 120; Gunaratna, 'International and regional implications of the Sri Lankan Tamil insurgency'; Sakhuja, 'The dynamics of LTTE's commercial maritime infrastructure", p. 3; Peiris, 'Secessionist war and terrorism in Sri Lanka: transnational impulses', p. 98; 'AP IMPACT: An investigation into fundraising and weapons smuggling by Sri Lanka's Tamil Tigers'; Solomon and Tan report that 'much hearsay exists about the LTTE's telecommunications and shipping ventures in Southeast Asia, but there is no definite proof': Solomon and Tan, 'Feeding the Tiger'.

391 Chalk, 'Liberation Tigers of Tamil Eelam's international organisation and operations–A preliminary analysis', pp. 5-6; Bharadwaj, 'Maritime aspects of Sri Lankan conflict', p. 239. Also Gunaratna, 'The asymmetric threat from maritime terrorism', p. 29.

tions.[392] The President of Canada's Mackenzie Institute, John Thompson, has argued that following their formation in the 1970s the LTTE financed themselves through extortion rackets but that this changed following the 1979 Iranian Revolution and the subsequent Soviet invasion of Afghanistan, which disrupted the established opium and heroin smuggling routes through south-central Asia. The LTTE's familiarity with smuggling, a product of their origins in long-established Tamil smuggling communities, meant that they were in a position to offer an alternative.[393] Sri Lanka's strategic location meant that it could serve as a transhipment point between the Golden Triangle and the Golden Crescent and Europe,[394] a position which in turn might have stimulated the LTTE to form a relationship with the Burmese regime.[395] On at least two occasions, in 1999 and 2000, vessels sailing between Sri Lanka and India and vice versa were seized with drugs on board.[396] Tamil networks in Europe and Canada have been involved directly in drug distribution and human trafficking.[397] In Pakistan

392   LaVerle Berry, et al., 'Nations hospitable to organized crime and terrorism', report prepared for the Federal Research Division, Library of Congress, Washington, DC, Oct. 2003, p. 105. See also Frank Cilluffo, 'The threat posed from convergence of organized crime, drug trafficking, and terrorism', testimony before the US House Committee on the Judiciary, Subcommittee on Crime, CSIS on the Hill, 13 Dec. 2000, and Daja Wijesekera, 'The Liberation Tigers of Tamil Eelam (LTTE): The Asian mafia', Low Intensity Conflict and Law Enforcement, vol. 2, no. 2, Autumn 1993, pp. 312 & 316-17. Wijesekera also suggests (p. 311) that the LTTE worked with the Medellin cartel in the 1980s, but in the absence of further evidence this seems far-fetched.

393   John Thompson, 'Terrorism and transnational crime: The case of the LTTE', Paper for the Centre for Conflict Studies, Fall Seminar, 3-4 Oct. 2003.

394   Berry, et al., 'Nations hospitable to organized crime and terrorism', p. 105; Solomon and Tan, 'Feeding the Tiger'.

395   Sakhuja, 'The dynamics of LTTE's commercial maritime infrastructure", p. 3, 5, 6 & 11; Davis, 'Tiger International'; Peiris, 'Secessionist war and terrorism in Sri Lanka: transnational impulses', p. 98-9.

396   Berry, et al., 'Nations hospitable to organized crime and terrorism', pp. 106-7; 'The heroin trail through India', Indian Express, 3 Nov. 1999.

397   Berry, et al., 'Nations hospitable to organized crime and terrorism', p. 105; John Thompson, 'Terrorism and transnational crime: The Case of the LTTE'; Peiris, 'Secessionist war and terrorism in Sri Lanka: transnational impulses', pp. 90-3; Lakshman Hulugalle, 'LTTE and drug smuggling', LankaLibrary Forum, 8 Nov. 2006; Hulugalle is head of the Sri Lankan military's Media Centre for National Security and therefore his account should be treated with appropriate care. Peter Chalk makes the point that definitive proof is lacking in Canada despite two intensive police investigations: Rabasa, et al., Beyond al-Qaeda: Part 2, p. 105. Also Solomon and Tan, 'Feeding the Tiger'.

the LTTE have been linked to a "drug lord" and in India to a New Delhi-based gangster who was also reportedly involved in LTTE extortion rackets before he was arrested in 2000.[398] In France, the LTTE have reportedly "sub-contracted" their extortion operations to two Tamil gangs, presumably to insert a degree of "deniability".[399]

The LTTE's role in human trafficking from Sri Lanka and India to Western countries, Australia, Canada and Great Britain in particular, is more widely recognised. It earns the group a substantial income from charges that are estimated to range from $18,000 to $32,000 per migrant.[400] In 2000 the Sri Lankan authorities broke up an LTTE operation that was moving up to 700 people per month into Europe using forged visas.[401] It is suspected, but unproven, that the LTTE have been involved in the movement of migrants from Pakistan across the Indian Ocean to north, east and even southern Africa where they are handed over to other gangs for onward movement to Europe.[402] Thailand served as an important centre for these operations.[403] Gunaratna mentions the *Rud Pink Fow*, which sailed from Phuket in Thailand in 1992 bound for Mossel Bay in South Africa.[404] In July 2003 a North Korean-flagged ship operated by a Sri Lankan company was seized with 254 migrants on board. In November 2005 a ship named the *Kosmo* was seized in Thai waters. Evidence found on the ship and in Pattaya revealed the LTTE's pivotal role in an operation to smuggle migrants to Australia.[405]

It is at the point where needs and capabilities can be matched for mutual benefit without compromising each group's core mission that arm's-length relationships between politically motivated gangs and their criminally moti-

---

398 Berry, *et al.*, 'Nations hospitable to organized crime and terrorism', p. 107. Also 'Swiss papers accuse Tamil Tigers of using drug money for fund raising activities', *The Sunday Times* (Sri Lanka), 20 Aug. 2000.

399 Solomon and Tan, 'Feeding the Tiger'.

400 Rabasa, *Beyond al-Qaeda: Part 2*, p. 103.

401 'LTTE human smuggling operation in Sri Lanka said foiled', *Kyodo World News Service*, 17 May 2000; and 'LTTE human smuggling operation busted', 18 May 2000.

402 Private information, Dec. 2005. R. Ramasubramanian, 'Human Smuggling in Sri Lanka', Institute of Peace and Conflict Studies *Article no. 1383*, 6 May 2004. More broadly see Gunaratna, 'The asymmetric threat from maritime terrorism', p. 29.

403 Rabasa, *Beyond al-Qaeda: Part 2*, pp. 103-4.

404 Gunaratna, 'The asymmetric threat from maritime terrorism', p. 29.

405 'Australia target in human smuggling scam', *The Age*, 19 Nov. 2005.

vated look-alikes become possible. Each is looking for money. Neither cares greatly how they make it. Business is business: in the LTTE's case that can extend to moving supplies for other groups—the ASG, MILF and the United Liberation Front of Assam (ULFA) have all been mentioned in this context.[406] The LTTE, the ULFA and several other insurgent groups operating in India's northeatern states are believed to share a common interest in the narcotics trade.[407] There can also be collaboration with known criminal groups such as the Arakanese smugglers who move drugs as well as arms, and insurgent groups in northeast India and Burma.[408] In 2007 the Sri Lankan Foreign Minister, Rohitha Bogollagama, claimed that "LTTE ships have been used to provide alternate supply channels to other groups and crime syndicates for their arms, human smuggling and drug trafficking activities".[409]

What makes some groups successful?

Insurgent groups use terrorism as a tactic and some employ that tactic more often than others. Several such groups have pursued targets of opportunity at sea. Others, such as the PIRA, have attempted to launch coherent campaigns. However, the groups that have exploited the sea most successfully are, in the main, those that have had no option. Groups that have lacked this imperative have generally abandoned it. Terrorist groups that have gone to sea out of necessity and waged successful campaigns have landed forces on exposed flanks, moved supplies and protected their supply lines, they have, moreover, acted like pirates by stealing money and grabbing hostages. Occasionally they have attacked maritime targets.

Necessity is the primary motivation, the maritime terrorists' equivalent of the pirates' opportunity. As with opportunity it is not unalloyed and is

---

406   Raman, 'Maritime terrorism: An Indian perspective'; Animesh Roul, 'Is there any linkage between ULFA and LTTE?' *The Counterterrorism Blog,* 3 Dec. 2006. Peiris suggests that in 1994, the LTTE transferred 'at least' two shiploads of weapons to the MILF on behalf of the Harkut-ul-Mujahideen (HUM), a terrorist organisation supported by Pakistan's Inter-Service Intelligence (ISI) agency: Peiris, 'Secessionist war and terrorism in Sri Lanka: transnational impulses', pp. 110-11 and Raman, 'Action Against LTTE's Maritime Terrorism'.

407   Peiris, 'Secessionist war and terrorism in Sri Lanka: transnational impulses', pp. 101-2.

408   Sakhuja, 'The dynamics of LTTE's commercial maritime infrastructure", p. 6; Anthony Davis, 'Tamil Tiger arms intercepted', *Jane's IR,* vol. 16, no. 2, Feb. 2004, p. 6.

409   'Sri Lanka's perspective on maritime security in the region and its relevance to the world–Sri Lanka Foreign Minister Rohitha B'.

insufficient to ensure success. Experience has shown there are eight major factors that influence how effectively a terrorist group operates at sea:

1. Legal and jurisdictional opportunities.
2. Geographical necessity.
3. Inadequate security.
4. Secure base areas.
5. Maritime tradition.
6. Charismatic and effective leadership.
7. State support.
8. Promise of reward.

There is considerable overlap with the factors that influence piracy. Like them, these factors interact with each other and, while circumstances determine which predominates, it is usual to find most are present in some degree whenever groups that use terrorism are active at sea.

Legal and jurisdiction opportunities. International law is a political construct. States abide by it for a number of reasons. Although respect for the rule of law is certainly a motive for some states, reasons of state and the calculus of advantage ultimately drive actual observance. It is not the purpose of this book to explore why some states support insurgents. It is enough to recognise that some do. Insurgents need cover. States can give them sanctuary; obviously they can be given base areas on land but they can also find shelter in the territorial waters of states that lack the means, will or desire to pursue them. There is little cover on the ocean but ships are islands of territoriality that can be used to mask nefarious activity. States, especially the USA, are aware of this and initiatives such as the Proliferation Security Initiative (PSI), the amendments to the SUA Convention and the somewhat ill-starred Regional Maritime Security Initiative (RMSI) have been designed to limit this freedom. The problem is that this freedom can only be limited to a degree before it compromises the essential freedom of the sea, which is fundamental to trade and the unhindered movement of naval forces. Flag state sovereignty therefore has to be maintained and as an unavoidable consequence international law will continue to provide terrorists with a place where they can hide whether they choose the protection of a strong state or the shelter of a weak one.

Geographical necessity. In most cases, but not always, geography determines whether terrorists need to go to sea or not. The Nicaraguan "contras" did not have to use the sea, nor did Al Qaeda. In most cases geography shapes the why and the how of what terrorists do on the water. Two campaigns illustrate this.

Sri Lanka and Ireland are divided islands. Sri Lanka is divided between the rebel north and east and the remainder, which is government held. Ireland is divided between the United Kingdom and the Republic of Ireland. For much of their history the Tamil Tigers have had access to safe areas overseas, first in Tamil Nadu and then later in small islands off Burma and Thailand. Their principal bases, however, have always been "in theatre", divided by sea from their rear areas. The Provisional IRA (PIRA) was able to maintain secure base areas across the porous land border with the Irish Republic, immune from British attack. It was the British base areas that were across water on the mainland; even there they were not immune from PIRA assaults. Both the LTTE and the PIRA needed to bring in supplies by sea. Because the Tamil Tigers have to bring their supplies directly into the areas they control, the Sri Lankan Navy could limit or extinguish the rebellion by imposing a blockade.[410] The Tigers need to prevent this and have therefore invested in a naval capability that is strong enough to neutralise the SLN close to the Sri Lankan coast, although never strong enough to defeat it. The PIRA did not have to bring its supplies into Northern Ireland directly. It could land them in the Republic. The Royal Navy could not blockade the Republic; instead the British depended on intelligence, which they could then feed to Irish or other allied countries in the hope that they would agree to make an interception. Even then the PIRA, unlike the LTTE, was never dependent on sea shipments alone. It could also bring in weapons by air or hidden in regular cargo moved through the international transport system.[411] Consequently, while both groups have extensive international arms buying networks, the Tamil Tigers needed to invest in a maritime capability to prevent their supplies being intercepted during the final stage of their journey, while the PIRA had to become adept at using various methods of transport, hiding arms amongst consignments of other goods and disguising the true nature of the shipments from British intelligence.

---

410   Bharadwaj, 'Maritime aspects of Sri Lankan conflict', pp. 237 & 238-9.

411   This was the method used by the Loyalist paramilitary units who, for obvious reasons, had to ship their arms into Ulster directly. Although the Royal Navy operated the 'Granada Patrol' in the North Channel that separates Ulster from Scotland, to deter the use of trawlers and other small vessels for arms smuggling, guns and explosives were almost certainly shipped into Northern Ireland hidden in normal container cargo, although no consignments were ever discovered. Discussion with Steven Haines, Feb. 2008.

Similarly, Israel's tightly controlled land borders meant that insurgents such as the PLO had to develop maritime capabilities and exploit the proximity of Lebanese bases if they were to be able to exploit Israel's sea flank. All three Philippine groups, which in addition extorted money from coastal settlements by using methods indistinguishable from those of organised criminals, also needed to bring supplies in by sea. GAM was similarly dependent on overseas supply sources and probably preyed piratically on local seafarers. Once they had been driven out of Cuba the anti-Castro groups had little option but to engage in coastal raiding and attacks on shipping if they were to continue their fight.

Inadequate security. Inadequate security is a given for any insurgency to succeed. In the maritime domain the clearest contrast has been between what the two most determined and resourceful maritime insurgencies have been able to achieve. The Sea Tigers have fought the Sri Lankan Navy to a virtual stalemate for long periods. Neither has been able to overcome the other. Both can achieve local sea superiority to carry out specific operations; this is of greater benefit to the Tamil Tigers because they depend on maritime re-supply. In contrast, although the Palestinian groups achieved success initially, particularly in their ability to land raiding parties, the IDF/Navy achieved almost complete control over the sea areas it regarded as vital to its interests, reduced coastal raiding to negligible levels and imposed severe (although by no means total) restrictions on Palestinian maritime logistical activity. In Southeast Asia GAM, ASG, MNLF and groups such as JI, which needed to move personnel and supplies by sea, benefited from underinvestment in maritime security by Indonesia and the Philippines and poor international security cooperation between all the states in the region.

Secure base areas. All insurgent groups need secure base areas for planning, rest, logistical support and training, but the fact that people cannot live permanently at sea and depend upon reliable boats makes those who operate at sea arguably more dependent on bases than their land-orientated counterparts. Piracy has usually been eliminated only once pirate base areas have been overrun rather than through maritime interdiction. The same appears to be case for maritime terrorism. Two clear examples are the Palestinian groups and GAM. The Palestinian groups operated a string of small workshops and bases along the Lebanese coast with a particular concentration around Tripoli in the north. When Israel invaded Lebanon in 1982 and dispersed the PLO, Libya became the nearest maritime base area and others were as far away as Tunisia and Algeria. This move seriously restricted the Palestinians' maritime options and operational tempo.

However, an organisation's determination affects how it copes with the destruction of its bases. Although GAM's maritime operations were conducted mainly in the Malacca Straits and not off Aceh's Indian Ocean coast, they were nonetheless affected badly by the 2004 tsunami. It appears that the scale of the losses GAM suffered (along with the criminal pirates in the same area) was sufficient to close down their maritime operations. By contrast the LTTE's Sea Tigers, despite losing some 2,000 personnel plus unspecified numbers of boats and other equipment, including four coastal radars in the vicinity of Mullaittivu,[412] replaced its loses quickly and resumed operations.[413] As far as Al Qaeda is concerned, Gunaratna suggests that a significant reason why it was unable to build on the success of the *Cole* and *Limburg* attacks and develop a sustainable maritime attack capability was that its resources were scattered and it was unable to secure a safe base area from which to operate.[414]

Maritime tradition. The sea is an alien environment. To operate anywhere outside a port or harbour a terrorist group needs to be trained or be in a position to draw on the support and skills of a maritime community. Two groups exemplify this: the ASG and the Sea Tigers.

The ASG are primarily a Tausug group. The Tausugs are the predominant ethnic group of the Sulu islands (with minorities on Mindanao in Zamboanga and Tawi-Tawi provinces and on the island of Basilan, and a substantial presence in Sabah).[415] They are Muslims and the ASG draws its members from "Muslim families with strong, centuries-old seafaring traditions. Their deep knowledge of the maritime domain gives them ample capability to conduct maritime terrorism."[416] The Sulu archipelago was, as mentioned earlier, the home of the Sulu pirates who were notorious for raiding coastal towns and villages in search of slaves. It may or may not be a coincidence that the ASG has a similar reputation for coastal raiding and hostage taking.

---

412 Davis, 'Tamil Tigers seek to rebuild naval force'.

413 R.S. Vasan, 'Sea control and the LTTE', Observer Research Foundation *Strategic Trends*, vol. IV. Issue 27, 7 Aug. 2006.

414 Gunaratna,'The asymmetric threat from maritime terrorism', p. 87.

415 Tausug people, *Wikipedia*; for a description of the various ASG factions based in these locations see Banlaoi, 'Maritime terrorism in Southeast Asia: The Abu Sayyaf threat', p. 69.

416 *Ibid.*, p. 71.

The Sea Tigers' maritime capability is equally well rooted in local sea-faring communities, particularly Valvettiturai, which has a long-standing reputation as a smuggling centre and as the home of the "audacious" Karai-yar fishing caste.[417] V. Suryanarayan describes the existence of "a close nexus among fishermen, smugglers and Tamil militants" and points out that the group's founder, Velupillai Prabhakaran, and other leaders all hailed from the town.[418] Sakhuja writes about a "…cohesive community held together by ties of kinship and caste. There were links between its smugglers, fisher folk and ordinary tradesmen",[419] who have done business all across south and Southeast Asia for centuries.[420]

Similarly Palestinian groups have worked with smugglers ever since the inception of their maritime capability in 1966. More recently they have sought to hide amongst the Gaza fishing fleet, something that would be impossible without the fishermen's connivance.

Charismatic and effective leadership. Visionary leadership exercised with de-termination can overcome many obstacles. Al Qaeda emerged from the deserts and mountains of Saudi Arabia and Afghanistan. It had no appar-ent affinity with the sea. It had no pressing need to use the sea to mount attacks, lacked maritime experience and had no obvious maritime tradition upon which to draw. Yet it mounted two of the most effective maritime terrorist attacks in history and planned several more. Reports suggest that one man, al-Nashiri, drove Al Qaeda's maritime strategy and operations. A Saudi of Yemeni extraction, he apparently observed shipping off the Yemen coast and recognised what could be achieved.[421] He assembled a specialised group with the requisite skills. He probably drew on the experience of local seafarers for the boat-handling skills that he needed, which would explain the concern, expressed when members of this gang escaped from jail in 2006, that Al Qaeda would seek to exploit these skills—or, given that the

---

417 Suryanarayan, 'Sea Tigers–threat to Indian security'; Sakhuja, 'The dynamics of LTTE's commercial maritime infrastructure", p. 7; Manoharan, 'Tigers with fins: Naval wing of the LTTE'; Wijesekera, 'The Liberation Tigers of Tamil Eelam (LTTE): The Asian Mafia', p. 309 and Peiris, 'Secessionist war and ter-rorism in Sri Lanka: transnational impulses', pp. 88-9.

418 Suryanarayan, 'Sea Tigers–threat to Indian security'; Wijesekera, 'The Libera-tion Tigers of Tamil Eelam (LTTE): The Asian Mafia', p. 310.

419 Sakhuja, 'The dynamics of LTTE's commercial maritime infrastructure", p. 7.

420 Davis, 'Tiger International'.

421 *The 9/11 Commission Report*, p. 15

breakout had outside help, that it already had a plan in mind.[422] Al Qaeda, however, unlike the LTTE did not build an infrastructure to capture and exploit this expertise. The momentum went out of its maritime operations once al-Nashiri was caught. To say that this loss was attributable solely to his capture would be going too far: he was captured along with other leaders in the international campaign that drove the group out of its base areas in Afghanistan and placed serious restrictions on its operational freedom.[423] Nonetheless, it has not so far been able to replace his vision, drive and organisational ability.

Leaders can also, of course, share a vision. Velupillai Prabhakaran might be a "plump, baby-faced, small time smuggler turned guerrilla",[424] but there is no doubt that he dominates the LTTE and has successfully instilled it with the belief that a powerful maritme arm together with innovatitive thinking are vital for success. In addition to being the only insurgent organisation that effectively has its own navy and air force, it was also able to hijack the *Intelsat-12* satellite between 2005 and 2007 to transmit its own news programmes. When its access was discovered it was said to have regarded the loss as merely a temporary setback.[425] Maritime mastery is a key element in the success of the insurgency as a whole. Raman rates the LTTE as the "most intelligent and futuristic-thinking terrorist organisation in the world". For Chalk the LTTE "remains at the cutting edge of terrorist-insurgent sophistication and innovation".[426] Bharadwaj writes that the "LTTE has introduced a different way of conducting the war at sea";[427] while according to Sakhuja, the LTTE's leaders have "tremendous capacity and vision…" and are "convinced that maritime infrastructure is crucial and (that they) must…develop a navy…"[428]

---

422 Christine Seib, 'Lloyd's flags risks to ships in Sri Lankan and Yemeni waters', *The Times*, 22 May 2006.

423 Chalk, 'Maritime terrorism in the contemporary era', p. 35; Matthew Pennington and Paul Haven, 'Experts: Mohammed arrest slowed al-Qaida', *Washington Post*, 16 March 2007.

424 Cited in Jerrold M. Post. *The Mind of the Terrorist*. New York: Palgrave Macmillan, 2007, p. 98.

425 On its air capability see Animesh Roul, 'Sri Lanka: Rebels with an air force', ISN *Security Watch*, 2 May 2007. On the satellite hijack see Roland Buerk, 'Tamil Tigers unveil latest tactic', *BBC News*, 26 March 2007; John C.K. Daly, 'LTTE: Technologically innovative rebels', ISN *Security Watch*, 5 June 2007.

426 Chalk, 'Training the Tigers', p. 28.

427 Bharadwaj, 'Maritime aspects of Sri Lankan conflict', p. 238.

428 B. Raman, 'The Omens from Katunayake', South Asia Analysis Group *Paper*

State support. State support for insurgencies with a significant maritime dimension has taken several forms. According to Kamarulnizam Abdullah, for example, a regional security expert at the National University of Malaysia, the "Sabah government under Tun Mustapha Harun (who was chief minister from 1967 to 1975) supported the MNLF. He provided logistical support. The federal government knew but kept silent."[429]

Similarly the LTTE benefited from Indian support. Although the group had established some training camps in Tamil Nadu in 1982, official Indian support did not begin until 1983 and was terminated in 1987. The rationale for the Indian support was that Sri Lanka had moved away from non-aligned status and become too close to the West, and also to Pakistan and China with which India had fought border wars since independence. This support, which was channelled through the Research and Analysis Wing (RAW), enabled the LTTE to build an extensive network of base camps and to establish a supply route across the Palk Strait. According to Gunaratna some 20,000 LTTE operatives passed through these camps up to mid-1987 when the Indo-Lanka accord signed in July brought this central government support to a close and the group into conflict with the Indian Peace Keeping Force (IPKF). Wijesekera reports that there were 35 bases where training was carried out by retired Indian army officers. Nonetheless, until the assassination of Rajiv Gandhi in 1991, the central government's position was ignored by the Tamil Nadu's state government under its Chief Ministers M.G. Ramachandran and then Muthuvel Karunanidhi (who was dismissed in 1991), which allowed the LTTE to continue much of its activity.[430] As mentioned earlier, Burma allowed the Tamil Tigers to use islands off its coast between 1987 and 1995, possibly in exchange for payment or because of a common interest in drug smuggling.[431] Yugoslavia apparently trained ETA and Palestinian swimmers.

---

no. 285, 26 July 2001; Sakhuja, 'The dynamics of LTTE's commercial maritime infrastructure", p. 12.

429   Suh and Lopez, 'Getting tough'.

430   Gunaratna, 'International and regional implications of the Sri Lankan Tamil insurgency'; Sakhuja, 'The dynamics of LTTE's commercial maritime infrastructure", pp. 1-2; Wijesekera, 'The Liberation Tigers of Tamil Eelam (LTTE): The Asian Mafia', pp. 312 & 315; Peiris, 'Secessionist war and terrorism in Sri Lanka: transnational impulses', p. 106.

431   Gunaratna, 'International and regional implications of the Sri Lankan Tamil insurgency'; Sakhuja, 'The dynamics of LTTE's commercial maritime infrastructure", p. 2; Davis, 'Tiger International'.

State support can, however, do more than compensate for weakness or gaps in capability; it can provide operatives with the skill and experience needed to identify unrecognised opportunities and the resources to enable groups to undertake larger operations than they would be able to do on their own. The resistance mounted by the Nicaraguan "contras" might or might not have been successful overall without US assistance but it is questionable, if this support had not been available, whether any of the constituent groups would have been able to mount maritime operations. They certainly depended on that support to mine Nicaragua's most important ports. While the mines were actually laid by Central American commandos (possibly from El Salvador), Americans employed by the CIA supervised the operation from a ship located outside Nicaragua's territorial waters.[432]

The creation of the Palestinian "navy" was announced at a pan-Arab summit in 1967. From then on it received substantial support from a range of sources including the Soviet Union, countries in Eastern Europe and Arab states. Although the Palestinians had talented maritime commanders of whom Khalil al-Wazir (Abu Jihad) was possibly the most prominent, to what extent their maritime operations would have been successful without that extensive and continuing support is unclear. As it was, Palestinian naval operations pushed Israel hard until it invaded Lebanon in 1982 and closed down the Palestinians' bases south of Beirut. Such support continues. In the case of Hizbollah it entails today, as is now known, the provision of sophisticated anti-ship missiles and, quite possibly, the technicians needed to maintain and fire them.

The promise of reward. Terrorists, like pirates, would not put to sea without the promise of reward. As Louise Richardson points out, terrorist movements have two types of goal: long term goals that can only be realised through political change and short term goals such as wreaking revenge, causing disorder, forcing concessions or reinforcing internal cohesion.[433] The maritime contribution to achieving long term goals will always be one of supporting the campaign on land or linking various campaigns in different theatres; revolutions, like wars, are not won at sea.[434] The focus, there-

---

432 Menefee, *TMV*, p. 97. According to Greentree, 'Irregular maritime strategy', US Navy SEALS were also involved directly.

433 Richardson, *What Terrorists Want*, pp. 75-80.

434 The relationship between maritime strategy and terrorist 'strategy' is tenuous at best. Nonetheless, Julian Corbett's famous observation, that however profound the influence of the maritime dimension might be all conflicts ('except in the rarest cases') have been decided on land, loses none of its force even when one

fore, must be on identifying what secondary motivations can be fulfilled at sea—a focus, moreover, that is reinforced by the recognition that terrorists' long term goals are often unattainable or poorly defined. Whatever success terrorism can achieve can come about only as part of a broader political strategy. Successful strategic effect requires a clear and realisable political objective. Terrorism generally fails because the policy question has not been answered with sufficient clarity.[435] It can also fail because the link between the political direction and the terrorist application lacks a shared understanding. As Colin Gray has put it: "As for the political vision that should propel the entire process, it may lack practical connection to behaviour in the field (for example, in the case of a united Ireland for the IRA)".[436] Given most terrorist groups' lack of experience and poor understanding of the maritime domain, this link is likely to be particularly weak when it comes to maritime operations, which helps to explain why so few groups have operated successfully in that environment. Nonetheless, it is possible that short term objectives, which Richardson groups under three headings—revenge, renown and reaction—can be achieved at sea.[437]

The desire for revenge is ubiquitous amongst terrorists.[438] They want their victims to experience in a physical way the pain and hurt that they, in their own judgement, have suffered symbolically, politically or economically.[439] Revenge is achieved most completely through killing or such acts of humiliation as making kidnap victims beg publicly for their lives. The targets certainly exist. There are warships of oppressor states such as the USS *Cole*, and passengers on cruise ships and ferries such as the *Achille Lauro* and *Superferry 14*. The modern equivalents of the German industrialist Hans-Martin Schleyer, who was abducted and murdered by the Baader-Meinhof gang in 1977, or the politician Aldo Moro,

or both protagonists adopt 'irregular' methods: Julian S. Corbett, *Some Principles of Maritime Strategy*, Annapolis, MD: Naval Institute Press, 1988; orig. pub. 1911, p. 16.

435 Martin N. Murphy, 'Terrorism and political effect', Unpublished Paper, 2003, p. 21; Richardson, *What Terrorists Want*, p. 85.

436 Colin S. Gray, 'On strategic performance', *Joint Force Quarterly*, Winter 1995-96, p. 32

437 Richardson, *What Terrorists Want*, p. 80.

438 *Ibid.*, p. 88; Martha Crenshaw makes the point that if there is a single common emotion that sparks terrorism it is revenge, for which there are numerous historical examples: Martha Crenshaw, 'The causes of terrorism', *Comparative Politics*, vol. 13, no. 4, July 1981, p. 394.

439 Murphy, 'Terrorism and political effect', p. 24.

who met a similar fate at the hands of the Italian Red Brigades in 1978, exist on yachts or in coastal mansions, and while such attacks have not happened as yet (and the potential targets are reported to have taken elaborate precautions to ensure they do not) yachts have been attacked and the Abu Sayyaf Group has snatched Westerners from coastal resorts. Renown comes through publicity but in Richardson's view it also involves glory, the regard that is given to a terrorist group by its supporters or peers as a consequence of a successful attack; the more audacious the attack or the more symbolic the target, the greater the glory.[440] Attaining this regard at sea is arguably harder. Mounting seaborne attacks demands special skills. Attracting publicity can be difficult, as the *Limburg* incident demonstrated, either for practical reasons such as distance from shore or because such incidents have limited resonance with audiences for whom the sea is an alien environment. Lastly reaction, any reaction, is welcomed by terrorists. It demonstrates that their enemy takes them seriously, and if it is oppressive can sometimes encourage a population to take their side. An attack at sea, however, is unlikely to provoke a reaction at sea because terrorists have little or no presence there. Yet a counter-attack on land is also hard to provoke, as the *Cole* and *Limburg* attacks showed, as both terrorists and counter-terrorists have difficulty in establishing a justifiable link between the two mediums and placing the reaction in context.

As David Kilcullen has pointed out, groups such as Al Qaeda and Hizbollah use physical operations such as bombings and beheadings as support material for their integrated "armed propaganda" campaigns. In other words it is the "information" side of their operations that has primacy, while the physical destruction and death are merely the means to achieve a propaganda result.[441] The one noteworthy reaction to a maritime assault, the forcing down of the aircraft carrying the *Achille Lauro* hijackers, ended unsatisfactorily for all concerned. Consequently, because terrorists have not yet found a way of realising sufficient psychological effect from the sea to achieve political consequences on land, and because the obstacles that inhibit success make reward more readily achievable on land, terrorists' reward at sea must derive in the main from other sources.

---

440   Richardson, *What Terrorists Want,* pp. 94 & 95.

441   David Kilcullen, 'New paradigms for 21st century conflict', *E-Journal USA*, May 2007.

The obstacles confronting the maritime terrorist

When the phrase "maritime terrorism" is used three scenarios probably spring to mind for most people: attacks on ports using large ships such as LNG carriers, the use of containers to deliver weapons of mass destruction (the "bomb-in-a-box" threat), and the use of small boats with bombs on board to attack warships and tankers. The previous chapter discussed the difficulties and obstacles that terrorists would need to overcome to fulfil the first two scenarios. It is worthwhile now considering what obstacles they would need to overcome if they were to employ what is believed to be the most likely method they will use, a small boat to deliver an explosive charge (the WBIED), and coastal raids, a method that has perhaps attracted less attention than it should.

Put very simply, terrorists have two broad categories of targets to choose between: people and property. The value of any particular target from either category increases if it has symbolic currency. Brian Michael Jenkins asserted, some years ago, that terrorists want more people watching than they want dead.[442] Except for the small but growing number of what have already been described as "annihilation terrorists" who are prepared to contemplate the man-made equivalent of mass-extermination events, this remains true today.[443]

Achieving theatrical death on land is clearly within the terrorist compass. At sea it is more difficult. Death and injury to ships' crews is hardly newsworthy, as press and official indifference to the fate of crew members

---

442 Brian Michael Jenkins made this assertion more than once. See, for example, 'International terrorism: A new mode of conflict' in David Carlton and Carlo Schaerf, eds, *International Terrorism and World Security*, London: Croom Helm, 1975, p. 15. However, Jenkins has now reconsidered his position in the light of new terrorist attitudes and the possibility that they could acquire WMD. See Brian Michael Jenkins, 'Will terrorists go nuclear? A reappraisal,' in Harvey W. Kushner, *The Future of Terrorism: Violence in the New Millennium*, Thousand Oaks, CA: Sage Publications, 1998, p. 249, also *Terrorism: Current and Long Term Threats*, RAND Testimony CT-187, Nov. 2001. Jenkins returned to this notion more recently when he wrote that 'weapons of mass destruction have entered the terrorists' imagination, if not yet their arsenal': Brain Michael Jenkins, 'Redefining the enemy: The world has changed but our mindset has not', RAND *Review*, Spring 2004, p. 20.

443 Who has any doubt what Iran's President Ahmadinejad, a wholehearted supporter of terrorism, meant when he said that 'Islamic countries' must 'mobilise...to remove...the fake Zionist regime' and warning that 'an intense fury will lead to a huge explosion'? 'Iran's Ahmadinejad calls for 'removal of Zionist regime", *Agence France-Presse*, 8 July 2006.

at the hands of pirates has shown. In order to kill large numbers of people they need to be concentrated in one place. At sea such concentrations are only to found on board cruise liners and ferries. Given the security measures that have been implemented in most major cruise terminals to prevent internal seizure, a terrorist group's most realistic current alternative is the suicide boat crashed into the ship's side.

The alternatives to attacks against people are attacks against economic targets, which in the maritime environment means ships, ports, or fixed seabed installations such as oil or gas platforms, oil or gas terminals, pipelines or cables. Compared to aircraft, ships are strong and hard to blow up. Fixed installations—oil platforms and terminals, especially because of the material they handle—are more vulnerable simply because they cannot move.

However, driving a boat into even a fixed target is not the same as driving a car into a building. Roads are static; the surface of the sea is not. If the maritime target is also moving the "relative motion calculus" becomes substantially harder to compute.[444] Outside a harbour the problems grow exponentially. Most terrorists are landlubbers; the sea is not what they are used to. Training in navigation, coastal piloting and ship handling takes time even if terrorists are able to draw on a maritime tradition. Training needs to be supplemented by experience. Any operation has to take account of tidal movement, currents, wind, sea state, visibility, proximity to land, underwater obstacles and the often unpredictable course changes of other boats.[445] This knowledge, while applicable to all areas of the sea, is also particular to the target environment. Knowledge of local sea conditions and shipping patterns is critical. Terrorists like to place targets under intense, long-term surveillance. They also like to practice their attack patterns. Both are particularly sensible preparatory steps in the unpredictable maritime environment, but there are fewer places at sea where it is possible to loiter discreetly than there are on land. Whilst it would be perfectly possible for terrorists to survey a target from a boat hidden in the middle of a fishing fleet they would be conspicuous if the remainder of the fleet left to follow the fish and they stayed behind. They would be exposed equally if they posed as sun-seekers on days without sun. Testing weapons and practicing the actual attack run could be equally problematic.

---

444   Pelkofski, 'Before the storm', p. 22.

445   *Ibid.*, p. 22. Although, as Herbert-Burns points out, this unpredictability (for which fishing boats in particular are notorious) could serve terrorists well when they move to the attack phase of their operation: Herbert-Burns, 'Compound piracy at sea in the early twenty-first century', p. 105.

The obstacles do not end there. Most terrorists are tactically conservative; they stick to what they know works.[446] Experience has shown that grandiose plans have often had to be scaled back.[447] Bruce Hoffman has noted that terrorists shy away from attacks that are complex and demand sophistication in their planning and execution.[448] Operating at sea generally requires both; attacking ships requires specialist knowledge, skills and equipment.

Yet it is the third obstacle that is likely to give terrorist planners the most pause for thought. In degrees that vary according to their objectives, terrorists need an audience whatever star might be guiding them; otherwise, as Benjamin Netanyahu memorably put it: "Unreported, terrorist acts would be like the proverbial tree falling in the silent forest."[449] Jihadist attacks in particular must, in Jenkins' words, "offer good visuals, demonstrate organisational reach and skills, cause heavy casualties, create terror, and provide opportunities for individual heroism and sacrifice. Iconic targets are desirable…"[450] For any attack where press coverage is the predominant requirement, positioning the ship or timing the attack such that the media can observe the event or readily cover its aftermath would certainly present a problem. It would mean, almost inevitably, that the attack would need to be carried out close to land, perhaps in a port or harbour. Some experts would disagree: they assert that the increased resources of the international media coupled with satellite communications mean that even if a cruise ship, for example, were to be attacked in mid-ocean news teams would be on site within hours.[451] This is possible but aircraft have only limited endurance. Even those groups, such as Al Qaeda, that like to record events for subsequent distribution would not find filming from a moving boat as straightforward as filming on land. Consequently, for range of choice and

---

446   For a discussion of this see, for example, Bruce Hoffman, 'Change and conti-
       nuity in terrorism', *Studies in Conflict and Terrorism*, vol. 24, 2001, pp. 417 &
       423-4 and Ehud Sprinzak, 'The great superterrorism scare', *Foreign Policy*, Fall
       1998, p. 113. On the other hand Hoffman sees the *Achille Lauro* hijacking as
       evidence of innovation (though presumably inadvertent): Hoffman, *Inside Ter-
       rorism*, p. 198

447   Jenkins, *Unconquerable Nation*, pp. 82-4.

448   Bruce Hoffman, *Responding to Terrorism across the Technological Spectrum*, Carlisle
       Barracks, PA: US Army War College, Strategic Studies Institute, 1994, p. 2.

449   Benjamin Netanyahu, 'Terrorism and the media' in Benjamin Netanyahu (ed.),
       Terrorism: How The West Can Win, New York: Avon Books, 1986, p. 109. Also
       Chalk, 'Maritime terrorism in the contemporary era', p. 21.

450   Jenkins, *Unconquerable Nation*, pp. 80-1.

451   Chalk, 'Maritime terrorism in the contemporary era', p. 23.

ease of access if nothing else, fixed targets on land have—and will remain—the terrorists' preference.[452]

There is, however, the halfway house option of raiding fixed land targets from the sea. The Sea Tigers have conducted what are, in effect, full-scale amphibious assaults but a number of other groups, the Palestinians, the MNLF and the ASG have launched raids to kill people and capture hostages. As there are so many economic and infrastructure targets such as power stations, oil terminals and refineries, and mass casualty targets that are readily accessible from the sea such as shopping malls, hotels and exposed beaches, there must be some surprise that the tactic has not been used more frequently. Raiders in most cases could launch their boats, spend anywhere from 30 minutes and to several hours assaulting a target and then make their escape before most of the world's law enforcement organisations could mount an effective response.

When he was Britain's First Sea Lord, Sir Alan West never wavered in warning that maritime terrorism was "a clear and present danger" that could "potentially cripple global trade and have grave knock-on effects on developed economies".[453] He was not alone in issuing such a warning. While there is no doubt that there are some potentially very worrying scenarios, that is what they are: potential scenarios. The threat maritime terrorism presents to international security, to the free flow of people and goods, as opposed to threats in a specific and usually local context, remains, to date at least, a low level problem. The public debate, the academic debate and even the intelligence debate all suffer from "circularity": we discuss possible scenarios, they listen, we pick up their chatter which reflects what we have been saying and we regard that as proof that our suspicions were correct. It is important, in other words, not to exaggerate the threat.[454]

452   For a fuller discussion of the pros and cons, and the reluctance of terrorists to take to the water, see Chalk, 'Threats to the maritime environment', p. 9; Jenkins *et al.*, 'A chronology of terrorist attacks and other criminal actions', pp. 63-85; Thomas S. Schiller, 'Maritime terrorism: The threat' in Parritt, *Violence at Sea*, pp. 87-92 and Pelkofski, 'Before the storm', pp. 21-2.

453   Michael Smith, 'Navy steps up al-Qaeda anti-terror patrols', *Daily Telegraph*, 26 Nov. 2002; Gordon Thomas, 'Al-Qaeda's suicide bomber navy poses real and present WMD threat says Britain's navy chief', *bushcountry.org*, 25 Sept. 2003; 'First sea lord warns of al-Qaeda plot to target merchant ships', *Lloyd's List*, 6 Aug. 2004; Sean Rayment, 'Navy chief has 'too few ships to guard sea lanes from terrorists'', *Sunday Telegraph*, 7 Sept. 2003.

454   Mark J. Valencia is very clear that a few sensationalists have overblown the threat. In his view the will might be there but the experience is lacking: interview with author, 2004. Although the situations are not analogous, it is perhaps

Why do terrorists use the sea?

Nonetheless, a small number of terrorist groups practice maritime terrorism and another equally small group have shown interest in maritime operations. Certainly terrorist targeting has demonstrated a displacement pattern: as one target set is hardened they move on to another that is soft. It has been suggested that as so many maritime targets are poorly secured this would attract the terrorists' attention. There certainly are plenty of soft targets at sea, but whether they are sufficiently accessible to displace land targets in the hierarchy of terrorist preferences is questionable.

It is also important to draw a distinction between maritime terrorism and maritime operations by insurgent groups more generally. From the position that this wider perspective affords, groups can be seen to use the sea for three purposes: terrorism, naval or proto-naval activity, and support operations.

Maritime terrorism has been a threat to a very limited number of countries: Israel, Sri Lanka, the Philippines, Yemen, Nicaragua and what was once the Spanish Sahara. Until Al Qaeda attacked the *Cole* and the *Limburg* no one else was greatly interested. Except in the case of Sri Lanka, the threat was peripheral. It was the Al Qaeda attacks that briefly caught people's attention and, rather more enduringly, the attention of governments and the maritime industry. When an attack on land is successful it captures the headlines, which is what it is designed to do. When attacks have been mounted at sea the results have been muted. Only those on the *Achille Lauro* and the *Cole* have attracted significant international attention. That terrorists themselves recognise this is reflected in the fact that so few have taken place. Barring the sinking of a large cruise ship with thousands of Westerners dead, another successful attack on a warship, the successful delivery of a nuclear or RDD device to a major port, or the execution of multiple and harmful attacks on the world's transport system, this is likely to remain the position.

Timing, admittedly, can be everything and a successful attack on an oil tanker when supplies are tight would send tremors through the market. Putting it bluntly, however, terrorist groups are not Nazi Germany, able to deploy submarines on a scale that almost brought Britain to the verge of starvation. Terrorists want to instil fear, not just be a nuisance. Unless they

---

worth recalling that the strong concerns expressed in the early 1980s about the potential terrorist threat to offshore oil installations have so far not been realised. See, for example, Jan S. Breemer, 'Offshore energy terrorism: Perspectives on a problem', *Terrorism*, vol. 6, no. 3, 1983, pp. 455-68.

take the strategic decision to cripple the global international shipping network and commit the requisite resources, ingenuity and political acumen to achieve that goal, given the relatively limited means at their disposal it is not they who will defeat us, it is we who will defeat ourselves.

All political violence, war included, is concerned to achieve psychological effect through the medium of physical force. In the case of terrorism the balance is merely exaggerated because of the resource disequilibrium between the protagonists. When the resources are more balanced and psychological effect can be achieved only through substantial and sustained physical destruction, then force needs to be concentrated. In such circumstances the insurgent group will begin to approximate more closely in terms of strategy, tactics, technology and organisation to its regular opponent. Concentration need not be about field formations; it can also extend, for example, to the creation and utilisation of fixed base areas. If the insurgent group is defeated because it has concentrated prematurely, then it will, if it is still organisationally coherent, revert to irregular tactics and its previously dispersed organisational form. When forces concentrate they have assets to protect and therefore devote more of their resources to defence. On the sea only the Sea Tigers have evolved in this way. Because they have assets to protect and need to guard the maritime flank of the territory they hold, their current operational patterns are closer to those of a regular navy than of a hit-and-run guerrilla group. In Sakhuja's view the LTTE have "all the attributes of a sea power" and amount to a "major non-state maritime force."[455] The Palestinian groups in Lebanon were also moving in this direction. Before the Israeli invasion of 1982 they were looking to buy warships and coastal radars from the Soviet Union and other states.[456] Their ambitions were thwarted and they were forced to disperse.

The question then arises: if all these groups have found it difficult to achieve the equivalent psychological effect from the sea that they can on land and, except in the case of the LTTE, the risks of concentrating their forces outweighs the potential gains, why are they still interested in maritime operations? The answer is that insurgents and other disaffected groups need to move munitions and materiel and often men and money, in some cases over long distances and in large quantities to support their land campaigns. Almost by definition they have to move these things discreetly.

455   Sakhuja, 'The dynamics of LTTE's commercial maritime infrastructure", pp. 8 & 12.

456   Katz, *Guards Without Frontiers*, p. 163.

Ships and boats can do both. The sea remains a vast space, but because maritime traffic tends to follow predictable patterns this can mean the vessel population in narrow waters can become almost innumerable. Finding rogue vessels or, worse, rogue cargo amongst otherwise legitimate cargo remains a formidable task. Any realistic assessment must conclude that the advantage lies with the terrorist and insurgent (as it still does with smugglers) rather than with navies or law enforcement agencies. Even if a state suspects that the ship of another flag state is carrying illegal cargo, while it arguably has the right to board that ship with the master's consent the master does not necessarily have the right, depending upon the domestic legislation of the flag state, to give permission for the ship to be searched. If that permission is withheld, discretion is virtually guaranteed. States that conduct searches without flag state consent or the authority of a UN Security Council resolution leave themselves open to claims for compensation and the risk of retaliation.

All insurgent and terrorist groups that use the sea share it with a wide variety of criminals including smugglers, human traffickers, illegal fishermen and pirates. Terrorists and pirates might or might not cooperate, but if they share common interests they revolve around small boats, weak states and dirty money. Terrorists and other criminals might or might not cooperate, but if they share a common interest it revolves around discretion.

6

ASSESSING THE THREAT

So where is the threat or risk?

This book set out to answer three questions:

1. What form does piracy take in the contemporary world and does it present a threat to international security?
2. What is maritime terrorism and does it, too, present a threat to international security?
3. Are piracy and maritime terrorism similar or linked and, if they are, does this present a threat to international security?

What form does piracy take in the contemporary world and does it present a threat to international security? The phenomenon of piracy occurs locally around the globe in what Samuel Pyeatt Menefee has called "piracy clusters". The occurrence and survival of "common piracy" are determined by a number of factors, the balance between which varies from location to location. International shipping passing the Somali coast or calling at specific ports in Indonesia, the Philippines, Vietnam, Bangladesh, Tanzania, Peru, Santos in Brazil and Kingston in Jamaica are at some risk. However, the shipping routes between the world's major economies, which carry the bulk of the world's trade, are largely unaffected. Even where these routes traverse areas where pirates are active, such as the Malacca Straits, the Gulf of Aden or the Sulu Sea, ships are rarely attacked, particularly if they take adequate precautions, unless they slow down, anchor or stop.[1] Pirates have

---

1   Marcus Hand, 'Anti-piracy lookouts credited with foiling Somali hijack gangs', *Lloyd's List*, 20 Aug. 2007; Bateman, 'Assessing the threat of maritime terrorism: Issues for the Asia-Pacific region', p. 81. However, it must be recognised that taking adequate precautions is easy to say but harder to do. Attention is difficult to sustain and declines naturally as the watch becomes fatigued. Standards

a negligible effect on world trade. As Steve Carmel, a Senior Vice President of the Maersk Line, has put it: "Piracy is a large issue for regional, coastwise trade in some parts of the world, like Africa ... but for international trade and the ships that facilitate it – not so much".[2]

However, while the precise number is unlikely to exceed the numbers killed or injured on the roads of most major countries, many mariners are killed, wounded, kidnapped or traumatised in some way every year.[3] Traumatic memories can often stay with victims long after the event. Therefore, whatever the effect might be on trade, the potential danger piracy presents to all seafarers, and the fear it induces, which extends to those on large ships and yachts, cannot be ignored. Its affect on crews is much more serious than many in the shipping industry, and in flag and littoral states, are prepared to admit.

Furthermore, any reservation that the threats to international shipping have been overstated cannot be extended to the threat piracy presents to coastal communities, fishermen and local shipping. This threat has generally been underestimated, if not ignored, as have the consequential links between piracy and overfishing (often by corruptly accredited foreign boats that in some cases are associated with organised crime).[4]

Piracy could threaten the international trade and shipping system (as opposed to individual ships) if a maritime or environmental disaster caused by pirate activity, direct or inadvertent, were to disrupt tightly programmed shipping schedules. Some states are more sensitive to this threat than others, particularly those such as Japan, Korea, Taiwan and China whose supply routes pass through Southeast Asian waters. The potential consequences that significant disruption might have on economic stability

---

of watch-keeping slip and precautions such as locking accommodation doors (itself a contravention of safety procedure) can be forgotten. Pirates tend to attack at twilight when visibility is curtailed or at night when watch-keepers have already been on duty for several hours.

2   Steve Carmel. 'Commercial Shipping and the Maritime Strategy'. *NWCR*, Vol. 61, No. 2, Spring 2008 p. 43.

3   The IMB recorded 317 violent incidents against seafarers in 2006, but given the scale of under-reporting this must be regarded as a partial figure: ICC-IMB Piracy Report 2006, Table 8, p. 10. Numbers of road deaths (in 2001) have been compared with *terrorism* fatalities by N. Wilson and G. Thompson: 'Deaths from international terrorism compared with road crash deaths in OECD countries', *Injury Prevention*, vol. 12, no. 4, 1 Aug. 2006, pp. 332-3.

4   And not merely between overfishing and piracy but between overfishing and illegal migration. See, for example, Sharon LaFraniere, 'Europe takes Africa's fish, and boatloads of migrants follow', *New York Times*, 14 Jan. 2008.

in the region has attracted the attention of the United States and also India, which is concerned that the presence of additional naval forces engaged in SLOC protection might affect security in the Indian Ocean.

Piracy is an organised activity. More organised gangs can affect international security more severely. It is when piracy is linked to national or transnational organised crime that it presents the greatest threat. This is the point at which piracy's connections to wider criminal activity, such as the illicit movement of drugs, counterfeit goods and trafficked people, mean that it can help to fuel the corruption that protects such activity, which in turn limits economic opportunity by imposing the unproductive burden of high security costs on what are generally already fragile economies. Alongside other maritime crimes, such as arms and drug smuggling, people-trafficking, illegal oil bunkering and illegal fishing, piracy can weaken and destabilise states, a process with security implications that extend beyond the crime itself.

What is maritime terrorism and does it, too, present a threat to international security? Maritime terrorism is, quite simply, terrorism at or from the sea. It became a subject of great concern after the 9/11 attacks because security officials and public commentators, fearful of another attack on the same scale, drew a false analogy between the inherent features of aircraft, as used by terrorists, and those of ships, despite the fact that very few terrorist attacks at sea had occurred. Notwithstanding plentiful theoretical opportunities such attacks have remained rare, so rare that this category does not even merit a separate mention in the US State Department's *Patterns of Global Terrorism* and *Country Reports on Terrorism*.[5] The reasons why have been discussed: the need for specific maritime skills; the need for specialised equipment; the fact that most terrorists are land-centric, even urban, have no affinity with the maritime environment and no incentive to change because the land is target rich and their operational outlooks are generally conservative; the fact that terrorist groups have limited resources to invest in new theatres while at the same time innovating and investing in the technology they need to stay ahead in their chosen terrestrial target spectrum; and finally the more restricted publicity potential of maritime targets towards which land-based audiences, for the most part, feel little empathy. Should attacks take place in the future the targets that appear

---

5   The US Department of State published *Patterns of Global Terrorism* until 2003, after which they were replaced by *Country Reports on Terrorism*. See http://www. state.gov/s/ct/rls/crt/

most at risk are warships because of their supreme iconic status, cruise ships and ferries for their mass casualty potential, and coastal or offshore oil and gas infrastructure to create supply shortages.

Terrorism, however, is a tactic, not an end in itself. The speculative focus on large-scale attacks has tended to obscure the fact that none of the groups that have mounted terrorist attacks at sea have taken to the water for that reason alone. Details are understandably hard to come by but it is reasonable to assume that, compared with logistical support, terrorism has played an insignificant part in most groups' maritime activity. Groups need to move men and equipment to support their land campaigns and earn money to support these operations. One group alone, the LTTE's Sea Tigers, has gone further by combining terrorist attacks, logistical support and limited sea control activity to the point where it can be regarded as a "non-state navy".

Are piracy and maritime terrorism similar or linked and, if they are, does this present a threat to international security? Since the events of 9/11, a strain in security discourse has yoked piracy and maritime terrorism together; has viewed them as complementary to the point where some commentators have suggested that a "piracy-terrorism" nexus exists or might exist in the future.[6] The impetus behind this can again be traced back to the false analogy between aircraft and ships which led to the suggestion that pirates could help terrorists learn how to steal and control ships for attack purposes. 'Nexus' is an evocative word that needs to be used with care because, in this context, it can gloss over the motivational and operational reasons that generally keep criminals and terrorists apart and imply an instrumentality that does not exist.

Nevertheless, because the factors that encourage and sustain pirates and terrorist groups' use of the sea are broadly similar, their activities and operating areas can overlap and, if not shared currently, might provide one or the other with opportunities in the future. These similarities are most apparent when terrorist groups steal or extort money from seafarers and coastal villages, the clearest examples of which have occurred in the Malaysian-Philippine-Indonesian maritime tri-border region and on the rivers and coastal waters of Nigeria. Despite these commonalities, no concrete links between pirates and terrorists have so far been uncovered.

---

6   Andrew Holt, 'Plugging the holes in maritime security', The Jamestown Foundation *Terrorism Monitor*, vol. 2, no. 9, 6 May 2004, p. 7. See also the fuller discussion in Chalk. *The Maritime Dimension of International Security*, pp. 31-3.

Disorder and the sea: out of sight, out of mind

If, when looked at in isolation from other varieties of maritime disorder and from any links it might have to organised crime, piracy is a localised problem, and if, when looked at similarly in isolation, maritime terrorism does not present a major challenge, why should either be regarded as threat to international security? Should they instead be seen as two aspects of a more generalised problem of maritime disorder?

Throughout history the sea has been an anarchic province. The real extent of that anarchy has varied according to the interest and determination of the predominant maritime power of each age to protect shipping and suppress lawlessness. In our own era, when the idea of national self-determination has become the deciding principle of international relations, conferences have replaced corvettes. At conferences, lines have been drawn on the surface of the oceans, designating this part territorial waters and that part an economic zone, but like the lines drawn on maps of Africa by European imperialists, they can bear little relation to reality. Of course, they can help facilitate economic exploitation. Nations can more easily carve up the seabed for oil or mineral extraction, for example (although this is far from certain as disputes over the South China Sea between China, Vietnam, the Philippines and Indonesia have demonstrated[7]). But seafarers know that once over the horizon they are on their own and that their problems are all too often out of sight and out of mind. It is as it always was: to paraphrase J.C. Wylie, the ultimate determinant is the man in a boat with a gun.[8] If that man is a pirate or a terrorist he almost certainly gets what he wants. If that man is on board a navy or coast guard vessel he should win but there is a good chance he will not, as initial contact between the USS *Carter*

---

7   See, for example, Henry J. Kenny, 'The South China Sea: A Dangerous Ground', *NWCR*, Summer 1996 and Michael Studeman, 'Calculating China's advances in the South China Sea: Identifying the triggers of 'expansionism'', *NWCR*, Spring 1998. The dispute lessened greatly after 1995 when China adopted a diplomatic strategy which emphasised that the country was pursuing economic not territorial goals, and that every state in the region could benefit from its economic expansion. Ralf Emmers, 'What explains the de-escalation of the Spratly's Dispute?' IDSS *Commentary*, 5 Dec. 2006. Nonetheless, all the disputes and claims in the South China Sea remain latent and vulnerable to renewed Chinese assertiveness. See Barry Wain, 'All at sea over resources in East Asia', *Yale Global*, 14 Aug. 2007.

8   Wylie wrote: 'The ultimate determinant in war is the man on the scene with a gun': J.C. Wylie, *Military Strategy: A General Theory of Power Control*, New Brunswick: Rutgers UP, 1967, p. 85.

Hall and pirates off Somalia and the *Alondra Rainbow* case involving India both demonstrated in their separate ways. If international law is the most concrete expression of international society, the idea of nations working together often expressing that cooperation through law, then piracy specifically, but maritime disorder generally, demonstrates it has a profound and humbling limit. Law that cannot or will not be implemented is no law at all.[9] Disputes over boundaries, arguments over what these boundaries mean, ambiguity over the status of ships operating within these boundaries, the willingness or unwillingness of states to exercise their responsibilities under international law or under their own laws, all contribute to the perpetuation of maritime anarchy.

Maritime disorder and initiatives for tackling it

Where order has been present it has been kept by a maritime hegemon; it has depended on the self-interest of an imperial or global power or powers to enforce it, whether alone or with the help of regional allies. In the absence of such a power or powers, seafarers have generally been subject to the depredations of criminal pirates or state-sponsored privateers.

An anarchic state obtains on the high seas in particular. In the case of failed states (such as Somalia) or weak states (such as Sierra Leone and Guinea-Bissau), the absence of regulation and law enforcement may extend right up to the coast.[10] Even in the case of slightly stronger states (such as Indonesia, the Philippines and Bangladesh), it may extend to the coast in areas away from major population centres and, because of inadequate law enforcement or corruption, can effectively include major ports such as Chittagong in Bangladesh and Lagos in Nigeria.

Confronted by this comparatively unregulated realm, and in order to erode the advantages this confers on criminals and terrorists, some states have devised strategies designed to gain greater understanding of the threats, criminal and political, which thrive there. The US strategy to achieve "maritime domain awareness" is one example. The scheme is complex. Definitions of its purpose, and expectations about what can be achieved cost-effectively, change regularly. To succeed in its broad aim of building an

---

9   Law with order: The sad irony is that the law of piracy was 'a traditional monument to the policy of peace and protected uses of the seas', but this monument is a tombstone if no state is prepared to enforce it. See Thomas J. Clingan, Jr. 'The law of piracy' in Ellen, *Piracy at Sea*, pp. 171-2.

10   Foreign Policy and the Fund for Peace, 'The failed states index 2007', *Foreign Policy,* July/Aug. 2007.

intelligible picture of threats at sea that is clear and accurate enough for action to be taken demands that several substantial technical and procedural problems are overcome. The peculiarly American temptation to place too much emphasis on technical solutions, which in this case would translate into an over-dependence on surveillance unsupported by the necessary intelligence, needs to be checked. Nonetheless, the scale of the project and the difficulties that it faces illustrate the immensity of the challenges posed by the ever changing and multiple character of illicit maritime activity.

The recognition that no one state can hope to control this activity came when Admiral Mike Mullen, when he was the US Navy's Chief of Naval Operations, called for the creation of a "thousand-ship navy" (TSN) in 2006. The idea was that navies and other users of the sea, commercial as well as state, should, regardless of their capabilities or technical sophistication, work to promote global maritime security by cooperating to confront common problems such as terrorism and arms smuggling.[11] The concept, which is now referred to more frequently as the "Global Maritime Partnership" (GMP), had first been outlined a year before in the article by John Morgan and Charles W. Martoglio published in the US Naval Institute's *Proceedings* in which pirates, human traffickers, drug smugglers and other criminals were identified—alongside political non-state actors, and other concerns such as environmental degradation and what has been termed Illegal, Unreported and Unregulated (IUU) fishing—as being amongst the transnational threats that the power of the world's maritime organisations should be harnessed to confront.[12] The attempts by some navies to lay undue stress on the threats of piracy and maritime terrorism, or the two threats together, are misplaced as they can lay their proponents open to charges of exaggeration. Piracy and maritime terrorism are only two crimes amongst several that contribute to, or feed on, maritime disorder. The real challenge, as Morgan and Martoglio identified, lies in the control and suppression of a cat's cradle of interrelated threats, which because they can challenge free navigation and undermine the manageable exploitation of the world's seas, have the potential to affect relations between states.

What exactly GMP might mean in practice has been difficult to determine, in part because the US Navy has been at pains to stress the voluntary

11   Admiral Mike Mullen, 'Remarks to the 17ᵗʰ International Seapower Symposium, Naval War College, Newport, RI', 21 Sept. 2005.

12   John G. Morgan and Charles W. Martoglio, 'The 1,000-ship navy: Global maritime network', US Naval Institute *Proceedings*, vol. 131, no. 11, Nov. 2005, pp. 14-17.

nature of any association, and has consequently avoided explicit prescriptions about what should be included. Whilst, in broad terms, the aim is to encourage information sharing to achieve a common awareness of the types and quantity of illicit maritime activity, the additional capabilities needed in order to place the necessary ships and aircraft in positions where they can intercept or deter criminals and terrorists, are daunting.[13] Consequently, as most navies currently lack the capacity to act on such information effectively, the concept also extends to capacity building, and it has been suggested that major navies, the US Navy in particular, should provide support and assistance to enable this to happen. Despite the US Navy's attempts to minimise its own role, such suggestions have nonetheless provoked accusations that it was attempting to play what one commentator called "globo-cop" in the maritime arena.[14]

MDA and GMP are both attempts at security arrangements that, while not compromising irreparably the principle of free navigation, grapple with a problem of maritime disorder that is growing with apparent rapidity as all forms of maritime exploitation intensify and illicit activity keeps pace. In this context, those who argue that maritime security can be ensured though multilateral treaties or regimes in anything other than a limited or temporary sense, without the leadership of a hegemonic power, have scant evidence upon which to base their faith.

The restless sea

Pressures on the sea have been mounting steadily since 1945. Since the end of the Cold War the incidence of piracy has risen. The volume of both legitimate goods and smuggled goods such as drugs, arms, natural resources, slaves and other illegal migrants transported by sea have both increased substantially while fish stocks have been depleted, in some areas almost to exhaustion. Exploitation of the sea has now reached unprecedented levels driven by the rapidly rising demand for resources and living space on land due to population growth and environmental degradation.[15] In a move-

---

13   See, for example, George Galdorisi and Darren Sutton, 'Achieving the global maritime partnership: Operational needs and technical realities', *RUSI Defence Systems*, June 2007, pp. 68-71.

14   Gurpreet S. Kuranar, "Thousand-ship Navy': A reincarnation of controversial PSI?', Institute for Defence Studies and Analysis (New Delhi), *Strategic Comments*, 28 Dec. 2006.

15   With regard to pollution see, for example, Mike Henderson, 'No ocean is untainted by the polluting hand of Man', *The Times*, 15 Feb. 2008 and Magnus

ment that could be described as a "migration", and which one astute observer has described as a "scramble" to evoke parallels with the nineteenth-century scramble for Africa,[16] states, people and corporations are turning to the sea more than ever before for energy, in the form of offshore oil and gas and structures that capture wind or tidal power, minerals, drinking water distilled from the sea, and waste disposal, and are exploiting it more than ever for food, both from increasingly depleted fish stocks and from fish farmed in sheltered waters. Added to these pressures is the exploitation of coastal areas by the wealthy portion of the world's population for tourism and leisure, including the building of structures on the sea itself, such as those seen currently in South Pacific island lagoons and the "palm island" developments in Dubai. This is a trend that is likely to continue, as the proportion of the world's population able to afford such privileges grows. Greater economic activity will create more targets for maritime crime and terrorism.

Pressure will also be felt on Mahan's "great highway". As the trend for using fewer, and larger, cargo ships in a smaller number of giant ports continues (while the number of narrow chokepoints remains constant), and the quantity of goods in transit grows, opportunities for damaging criminal interdiction will increase.[17]

As seaward movements intensify, and coastal activity increases, climate change is likely simultaneously to cause the sea to encroach upon the land. These opposing pressures mean that the sea will become more contested in the future.[18] Resource depletion and the loss of productive land to environmental damage will increase the economic and political pressure on the littorals and may well make conflict more likely. Currently international law, in the form of UNCLOS, sets the limits of territorial seas and determines the rights of states within their "exclusive economic zones", that is, within the portion of the sea (up to a limit not exceeding 200 nm from the coast)

Linklater, 'Sea's treasures may no longer be with us from here to eternity', *The Times*, 15 Feb. 2008.

16   Rear Admiral Chris Parry, RN, 'The future maritime strategic context', RUSI Future Maritime Operations Conference, London, 22-3 Nov. 2006.

17   Martin N. Murphy, 'Disorder in the littorals: The irrelevance of expeditionary warfare', Presentation delivered to the Netherlands Defence Academy Symposium, 'Expeditionary operations–Effects and challenges', Breda, 13-14 Dec. 2006.

18   'Realistic' (pseudonym), 'The route to irrelevance–or a Wake-Up Call', *The Naval Review*, vol. 94, no. 4, 2006, pp. 311-16; Justin Stares, 'EU seeks to extend territorial powers', *Lloyd's List*, 19 July 2006.

over which a state has special rights over marine resources, thereby imposing some degree of order on coastal regions. UNCLOS was the product of a compromise between the often conflicting interests of coastal states and maritime powers, and there is a danger that in the future political pressures exerted by seaward migration and rising sea levels, and the attendant environmental and security concerns, could create rifts between states as differences of interpretation give rise to disputes to the point where UNCLOS is able to exert less and less force in practice, or even fractures.

What might change?

Piracy and maritime terrorism have to date been localised problems that have had little significant effect on international order. Against a background of an increasingly pressured environment that is not just theoretically anarchic but practically chaotic, there is no guarantee that this relatively benign situation will continue. Furthermore, if change does happen it could occur relatively quickly. While the scale of the increase can be disputed, there is no doubt that the number of piracy incidents in traditional areas has grown over the last thirty years. In the cases of Somalia and Nigeria it has grown from almost nothing in much less time. The number of terrorist incidents might have increased from none to a few but they have nonetheless changed in character from the chaos of the *Achille Lauro* attack to the professionalism of the *Cole*, *Limburg* and *Superferry 14* assaults. Over the same period the LTTE's Sea Tigers grew from nothing to a serious force that has fought the Sri Lankan navy to a virtual standstill, instilled concern in the Indian Navy and provided an inspiration for other insurgent groups. Possible developments in maritime criminality and terror must be assessed in the context of rapid information and technological transfer, coupled with upward trends in population and economic activity, and the concomitant rising demand for marine resources. These could aggravate three kinds of threat and vulnerability in particular: criminality and criminal-terrorist cooperation; weaknesses in the international maritime transport system; and the threat of maritime insurgency.[19]

Criminality and Criminal-Terrorist Cooperation. The speculation that pirates and criminals might help terrorists to mount attacks at sea has not been ful-

---

19   Martin N. Murphy, *Contemporary Piracy and Maritime Terrorism*, Adelphi Paper no. 388. Abingdon and New York: Routledge for the International Institute of Strategic Studies, 2007, p. 76.

filled.[20] It is possible, but remains unlikely.[21] Four reasons are usually advanced to explain how criminals are distinct from terrorists: motivation, legitimacy, publicity, and the use of violence. Nonetheless, there are examples that indicate they have helped each other on land and that the inhibitions felt generally by both might, under certain circumstances, be set aside.

First, motivation: criminals are interested in money. Terrorists are interested in righting what they see as social wrongs and achieving political power; they are driven supposedly by ideals, however warped they might be.[22] Criminals want to exploit the world; terrorists want to change it. Some criminals do, however, appear to want to effect political change. In India Dawood Ibrahim, the leader of the gang known as the "D Company" become so involved in political conflicts that he, along with another Muslim gangster, Ibrahim Memon, is generally believed to have been behind the bombs that destroyed financial centres in Mumbai (Bombay) in 1993.[23] He is also believed to have links with the group that attacked the Indian Parliament building in 2001, with Lashkar-e-Taiba, a group that India suspects was behind a series of bombings in New Delhi in October 2005, and with Al Qaeda with which it is alleged he has made a deal to share smuggling routes.[24] Furthermore, it is suspected that he has enjoyed the protection of

---

20   Richard Halloran, 'What if Asia's pirates and terrorists joined hands?' *South China Morning Post*, 17 May 2003; 'Maritime piracy and terrorism are converging', CSIS *Transnational Threats Update*, vol. 1, no. 9, June 2003, p. 1 and Koknar, 'Piracy and terrorism are joining forces'.

21   P. Mukundan, interview with author.

22   As James H. Anderson writes: 'This distinction remains a useful starting point for analysis, even though it is sometimes difficult to ascertain the dominant motivation in practice': James H. Anderson, *International Terrorism and Crime: Trends and Linkages*, Conclusions, ND.

23   See Gilbert King, *The Most Dangerous Man in the World: Dawood Ibrahim*, New York: Chamberlain Bros, 2004, pp. 25-31. Also B. Raman. 'Dawood Ibrahim: The Global Terrorist', South Asia Analysis Group Paper no. 818, 19 Oct. 2003 and David E. Kaplan, 'Paying for terror', *US News & World Report*, 5 Dec. 2005. On Menon see Edward A. Gargan, 'India bombings: Gangs involved, but who else?' *New York Times*, 16 May 1993. Moreover Ibrahim was apparently not the only Muslim gangster so motivated. Police in Calcutta blamed the 1993 bombings there on Rashid Khan. See Subir Bhaumik, 'Calcutta mafia boss convicted over blast', *BBC News*, 30 Aug. 2001.

24   David E. Kaplan, 'A Godfather's lethal mix of business and politics', *US News & World Report*, 5 Dec. 2005. For more on the links between 'D Company' and Al Qaeda see King, *The Most Dangerous Man in the World*, pp. 73-88 and Gunaratna, *Inside Al-Qaeda*, pp. 206-7. On the Oct. 2005 bombings see 'Bomb blasts in New Delhi, scores killed', *The Jawa Report*, 29 Oct. 2005. On the at-

Pakistan's Inter-Services Intelligence agency which guaranteed him the use of Pakistan's coastal smuggling routes in exchange for his cooperation.[25] In Brazil many *favela* dwellers believe the PCC and other drug traffickers fight for them against a government that they regard as their oppressor and which have, in Williams words, "developed alternative forms of governance based on rudimentary but effective forms of paternalism, the provision of welfare services, a degree of protection against violence, and career opportunities for young men who would otherwise be unemployed".[26]

Second, legitimacy: previously the relationships most terrorist groups had with criminals were restricted because they hoped to be in government some day. They therefore wanted neither to compromise their future authority nor to alienate their supporters. Extremist groups, such as Al Qaeda and FARC, have changed this assumption.[27]

Third, publicity: for the most part terrorists want as many people as possible to know what they have done and why they have done it. Publicity is their friend. Criminals, including pirates, prefer discretion. Publicity is their enemy, largely because the level of publicity often determines the level of the state's response. Even though some mafia leaders, such as John Gotti in the US and the Kray twins in the UK, revelled in their notoriety they were generally much more reticent about the details of their crimes. In a break with that tradition, Central American gangs actively court publicity as a way of demonstrating their power to the police and recruiting new members.[28] While the Mexican cartels do not seek publicity in the same way, the sheer scale of the attacks on the police, which prompted the columnist Jesus Silva-Herzog to compare the level of violence to that of the

---

tack on the Indian Parliament see 'Parliament suicide attack stuns India', *BBC News*, 13 Dec. 2001.

25   Kaplan, 'A Godfather's lethal mix of business and politics'.

26   Logan, 'Brazil's P.C.C.: The True Power Behind the Violence'. Phil Williams. *From the New Middle Ages to a New Dark Age: The Decline of the State and US Strategy.* Carlisle, PA: US Army War College, Strategic Studies Institute, 2008, pp. 23-4.

27   Barry R. McCaffrey and John A. Basso, 'Narcotics, Terrorism, and International Crime: The Convergence Phenomenon' in Russell D. Howard and Reid L. Sawyer, eds, *Terrorism and Counterterrorism: Understanding the New Security Environment,* Guildford, CT: McGraw-Hill/Dushkin, 2003, p. 210.

28   Gilmore, 'Gang Warfare', p. 49.

Iraq war, had, according to polls published in June 2008, seriously eroded confidence in the Calderón government.[29]

Fourth, the use and purpose of violence: most criminals have traditionally avoided violence where they can. Although a minority have used it excessively and some have combined it with gratuitous cruelty, most criminals who employ violence use it in a controlled way.[30] Both criminals and terrorists use violence in self-defence. They both use it offensively to attack rival groups or government forces. The crucial difference is that while both use violence to *communicate* they do so to different audiences and on a different scale. Organised criminal gangs have traditionally assassinated rival individuals or killed members of opposing gangs. Terrorists generally, unlike most criminals, use what is called "triangular" violence: they threaten to kill one person or group in order to influence another.[31] Historically criminals have seen few advantages in killing large numbers of people. Perhaps the best known exception was the mid-flight bombing of a passenger aircraft over Colombia in 1989 by the "Extraditables", a group of cocaine smugglers led by Pablo Escobar who wanted to avoid extradition to the US.[32] Now, however, criminal groups in Central America, such as MS-13 and M-18, and others in Mexico—such as Los Zetas (which drew many of its original personnel from the US-trained Special Air Mobile Force Groups), linked closely to the Gulf cartel, and the Arellano Felix Organisation (AFO) that employed well-trained, almost paramilitary forces—and in Brazil, such as the "Comando Vermelho" (CV) and the PCC, and even in Europe, have become demonstrably more willing to use what amounts to terrorism to influence government policy, mainly to deter the authorities

---

29   Laurence Iliff and Alfredo Corchado. 'Mexico drug wars'. *Dallas Morning News*, 7 June 2008.

30   Godson and Olson, 'International Organized Crime', p. 21.

31   UN Commission on Crime Prevention and Criminal Justice, 'Differences and Similarities between Transnational Organized Crime and Terrorist Crimes', Fifth Session, Vienna, 21-31 May 1996.

32   MIPT Terrorism Knowledge Base, Group Profile: 'The Extraditables'; Stan Yarbro, 'Colombian jet crashes, killing 107', *Washington Post*, 28 Nov. 1989; Xavier Raufer, 'Gray Areas: A New Security Threat', Institute for International Studies *Political Warfare: Intelligence, Active Measures and Terrorism Report*, no. 20, Spring 1992, p. 6, who also reports that the group were responsible for the assassination of three Colombian presidential candidates, a minister of justice, a public prosecutor, the editor of a major newspaper and the leader of M-19, a rival narco-terrorist group.

from interfering in their activities.[33] In 2002 a PCC gang was intercepted with a 65 lb (30 kg) bomb it intended to use to blow up the São Paulo stock exchange.[34] In December 2004, members of MS-13 killed all 28 passengers on a bus in Honduras to deter the government from continuing with its "*mano dura*" ("strong hand") crackdown.[35] The fighting in Mexico between the Sinaloa and Gulf drug cartels and the government has been described as having moved from "the domain of law enforcement into that of low level conflict".[36] In 2006 five severed heads were thrown onto a nightclub dance floor in Uruapan, and in 2007 the tactic was repeated when a severed head was thrown into a military camp shortly after the Mexican army was drafted in to reinforce the government's anti-drug clampdown.[37]

---

33   Jerrold Post refers to this activity as "criminal terrorism': Post, *The Mind of the Terrorist*, p. 5. On the Central American gangs see Ana Arana, 'How the Street Gangs Took Central America', *Foreign Affairs*, vol. 84, no. 3, May/June 2005, pp. 98 & 103. On the Mexican cartels see Gordon James Knowles, 'Threat Analysis: Organized Crime and Narco-Terrorism in Northern Mexico', *Military Review*, Jan.-Feb. 2008, p. 79; Grayson, 'Mexico and the Drug Cartels'; Alfredo Corchado, 'Cartel's enforcers outpower their boss', *Dallas Morning News*, 11 June 2007; 'Drug Cartels: Arellano-Felix Organization', DEA Background Information, Feb. 1997; Graham H. Turbiville, Jr., 'Mexico's Evolving Security Posture', *Military Review*, May-June 2001, p. 45; Héctor Tobar, 'New phase seen in Mexico's drug war', *LA Times*, 18 May 2008; and for background on the origins of the Zetas see Brendan M. Case, *et al*, 'Officials develop clearer picture of Zetas', *El Universal*, 21 March 2005 and Héctor Tobar, 'A Mexican cartel army's war within', *LA Times*, 20 May 2007. On the Brazilian gangs see Logan, 'Brazil's P.C.C.: The True Power Behind the Violence'; Michael Day, 'Crime Groups Turn to Terrorism in Rio de Janeiro', *Jane's IR*, 1 Aug. 2003; Andrew Downie, 'Brazil gang takes on state', *Christian Science Monitor*, 16 May 2006; Monte Reel, 'Brazilian city wakes to prison gang's power', *Washington Post*, 21 May 2006 and Jonathan Wheatley, 'Gang leaders take Brazil hostage from inside jail', *Financial Times*, 17 May 2006. On the incidents in Europe see Gorka, 'The 'New' Threat of Organised Crime and Terrorism'.

34   Anthony Faiola, 'Brazilian gangs take turf wars out of slums', *Washington Post*, 15 Dec. 2002

35   Gilmore, 'Gang Warfare', p. 50.

36   'Mexico's three reasons to be fearful', *Jane's FR*, no. 2936, 12 July 2007, p. 2. Also Oscar Becerra, 'Fighting Back: Mexico Declares War on Drug Cartels', *Jane's IR*, April 2007, pp. 6-11; Laurence Iliff, 'Cartels go on offensive against Mexican army', *Dallas Morning News*, 12 May 2007; Ioan Grillo, 'Drug cartels target military in Mexico', *AP*, 14 May 2007 and 'Can the army out-gun the drug lords?' *The Economist*, 15 May 2008.

37   'Severed head greets new troops in Mexico drug war', *Reuters*, 12 May 2007; on the nightclub incident see Grayson, 'Mexico and the Drug Cartels'; on both of these incidents and others see James C. McKinley, Jr., 'With beheadings and attacks, drug gangs terrorize Mexico', *New York Times*, 26 Oct. 2006 and Becerra,

These developments should not be exaggerated. Differences still out-weigh similarities.[38] Nonetheless, terrorists and criminals in general, if not usually pirates in particular, have on occasion found reason to work to-gether, although pirates and terrorists have separately made money at sea by attacking ships and kidnapping seafarers. However, as criminals and terrorists quite naturally have many more interests on land, most maritime operations are undertaken to support those interests by facilitating the ter-rorist and criminal equivalent of "trade"—that is, the movement of sup-plies between different parts of a single criminal or terrorist enterprise or the exchange of goods such as arms, drugs or migrants between enterprises. As Rohan Gunaratna has noted, for terrorists "the maritime domain is pri-marily a medium to support operations not to mount attacks".[39]

Terrorists and insurgents have always needed money to support their cause and have rarely had qualms about using criminal methods to get it. In the past, however, terrorists rarely sought out direct or regular contact with criminals; in fact, increasing criminality was often regarded as a sign of senescence. This has changed. Terrorists and insurgents, faced with re-duced state sponsorship following the end of the Cold War and the incep-tion of the "global war on terror", both of which made it far more difficult for them to raise funds and transfer money by legal or quasi-legal means, turned to crime, and criminal accomplices, more readily and at an earlier stage in the normal evolutionary cycle in order to survive.

Although individual attacks can be mounted relatively cheaply, main-taining a terrorist network is an expensive undertaking. Ronald Noble, the Secretary-General of Interpol, estimated that only ten per cent of Al Qae-da's estimated 2001 expenditure of $30-$50 million went on attacks; the rest was used to run the organisation.[40] State sponsorship of terrorist groups

---

'Fighting Back: Mexico Declares War on Drug Cartels', p. 9, who suggests they might have been the work of 'Maras' gangs, hired by the Mexican cartels, who are known to use dismemberment to intimidate their rivals and the authorities. Also Chris Dishman, 'Transnational Organized Crime, Terrorism, and Terror-ism Funding', 10 Jan. 2007.

38   R.T. Naylor, *Wages of Crime: Black Markets, Illegal Finance and the Underworld Economy,* Cornell UP, 2002, pp. 44-87; Godson and Olson, 'International Or-ganized Crime', p. 19; also Hoffman, *Inside Terrorism,* p. 42.

39   Gunaratna, 'The threat to the maritime domain: How real is the terrorist threat?' p. 82, note 3.

40   Mark Huband, 'Extremists in Europe find fraud pays', *Financial Times,* 15 June 2004. Interestingly the report goes on to quote unnamed US officials who esti-mated that in 2004 Al Qaeda's annual expenditure was closer to $10 million.

declined, partly because of the demise of the Soviet Union, which acted as quartermaster and guardian to many of the states that sponsored terrorism directly, and partly because those states began to see that terrorism was a less easily deniable form of covert warfare. Terrorist groups that wanted to survive had to finance their activities by turning to private benefactors, by siphoning off funds from legitimate businesses, by illicit funding through charity organisations, or by resorting to such criminal activities as credit card fraud, counterfeiting of goods, drug and human trafficking, kidnapping, extortion and bank robbery.[41] The groups that survived the shakeout were the ones that learned how to launder money.[42] This remains vitally important but has come under enormous pressure from law enforcements agencies around the world. One of the successes of the "war on terrorism" has been the tracing, disruption and in some cases freezing of terrorist funds. Al Qaeda was believed to have lost $130 million as a result. As the transfer of money from legitimate businesses, charities and benefactors through the formal banking system became increasingly difficult, ever larger quantities had to be moved via the informal *hawala* system or by courier.[43] These pressures have forced terrorist groups more and more into crime. Local groups, for example, have had to become self-supporting.[44] As Holden-Rhodes and

41   See US National Strategy for Combating Terrorism, pp. 7-8; Ian O. Lesser, 'Countering the New Terrorism: Implications for Strategy', in Ian O. Lesser *et al.*, *Countering the New Terrorism,* Santa Monica: RAND, 1999, pp. 106 & 137; Kimberley L. Thackuk, 'Terrorism's Financial Lifeline: Can It Be Severed?' *Strategic Forum no. 191,* May 2002, pp. 1 & 3; Kaplan, 'Paying for terror'.

42   David Veness, 'Terrorism and Counterterrorism: An International Perspective', *Studies in Conflict and Terrorism,* vol. 24, 2001, p. 410.

43   One of the hardest knocks Al Qaeda sustained was the failure of BCCI (Bank of Credit and Commerce International). See Richard Sale, 'Collapse of BCCI shorts Bin Laden', *United Press International,* 1 March 2001. The bank was also involved in laundering money for Abu Nidal, the Medellin cartel and Manuel Noriega. See Chalk, *Grey-Area Phenomena in Southeast Asia,* p. 50. Ironically it is alleged that BCCI was the main channel the CIA used to pass funds to the Afghan *Mujahideen.*

44   There is evidence that the Islamic group responsible for the Madrid train bombings financed its activities through drug trafficking (and possibly arms deals). Jamal Ahmidan, who was responsible for the group's money, had an extensive criminal record but was not regarded as a terrorist: 'March 11 attackers trade drugs for explosives', CSIS *Transnational Threats Update,* vol. 2, no. 7, April 2004, p. 5. See also 'Madrid bombings: 3 Moroccans held', *CNN.com,* 24 May 2005. According to Kaplan, Ahmidan was the brother of one of Morocco's most successful hashish smugglers, and when his home was raided over $2 million in drugs and cash was recovered. Kaplan also reports that the planned 2002 attacks on warships transiting the Gibraltar Straits were financed using drug money: Kaplan,

Lupsha wrote in 1993: "If you want to make a revolution…you need hard cash to do it…Bank robberies and kidnappings are still useful, but drug trafficking can generate the cash to pay the bills."[45] Ineluctably, therefore, terrorist groups have come to look and behave even more like criminal groups than they did in the past, and although it would be unreasonable and unrealistic to argue that terrorism and criminality have merged, they clearly share much common ground and generate many of the same effects. Speaking in 2006 Jean-Paul Laborde, the Chief of the Terrorism Prevention Branch of UNODC, said: "The threat posed by transnational and non-state actors involved in drugs and crime was one of the greatest challenges to international security and peace…Networks involved in drugs, crime and terrorism were exploiting globalization, threatening State sovereignty and endangering security."[46]

Designation	Definition
Transformation	Terrorist group "transforms" itself so it can carry out criminal activities without outside support
Convergence	Terrorist and criminal groups come together (form partnerships) to exploit long- to medium-term criminal opportunities for their mutual benefit (without loosing their separate identities)
Cooperation	Terrorist-criminal cooperation covers a range of mutually beneficial contacts ranging from the provision of arms, documents and "safe houses" through to the exchange of skills, intelligence and other specific services

Table 8. Terrorists and criminals: Transformation, convergence and cooperation[47]

'Paying for terror'.

45   J.F. Holden-Rhodes and Peter A. Lupsha, 'Horsemen of the Apocalypse: Gray Area Phenomena and the New World Disorder', *Low Intensity Conflict and Law Enforcement*, Autumn, vol. 2, no. 2, 1993, p. 220.

46   UN General Assembly, Department of Public Information, 'Criminal involvement by transnational, non-state actors poses major threat to international security, third committee told', 4 Oct. 2006.

47   Typology based on Chris Dishman, 'Terrorism, Crime and Transformation', *Studies in Conflict and Terrorism*, vol. 24, 2001, pp. 43-58; Thomas M. Sanderson, 'Transnational Terror and Organized Crime: Blurring the Lines', *SAIS Review*, vol. 24, no. 1, Winter-Spring, 2004, pp. 49–61; Phil Williams, 'Terrorism and Organized Crime: Convergence, Nexus or Transformation?' in G. Jervas (ed.), *Report on Terrorism*, Swedish Defence Research Establishment, 1998, pp. 69-92 where he suggests a similar three-level model from full integration to arm's-length association; and Tamara Makarenko, 'A Model of Terrorist-Criminal Relations', *Jane's IR*, Aug. 2003, pp. 6-11, who puts forward the idea of alliances into which both criminals and terrorists can enter and a linear model of convergence where criminals and terrorists can effectively become a single entity.

Given these developments, criminals and terrorists might now be coming together in any of three ways that can be summarised as transformation, convergence or cooperation.

Some analysts are unsure about the idea of cooperation. Chris Dishman points out that there is little evidence that either major transnational criminal organisations (TCOs) or terrorists are interested in co-operating. If they do it is only for short periods because the risks outweigh the benefits.[48] Picarelli picks up this point, noting that terrorism and organised crime are high-risk endeavours and that because terrorists and organised criminals are risk averse, they are reluctant to add to that risk by engaging in long-term collaboration.[49] Cooperation need not be intentional, however; criminals might be unaware of the real identity of the people with whom they are dealing or, in the case of smugglers, the goods they are transporting.[50]

As far as terrorists are concerned, Dishman saw the major challenge for the future as the emergence of groups where the aim of "financial well-being co-exists or over-rides traditional political motivations".[51] He envisaged that criminal groups—although they were traditionally reluctant to draw attention to themselves unnecessarily—could also undergo a transformation and use terror (almost certainly tactically) "to force government leniency and negotiation".[52] Finally, he pointed out that "both TCOs and terrorists already maintain organisations that are capable, to some extent, of engaging in terrorism and organised criminal activities" and that this "'in-house' capability obviates the need for terrorists to appeal to criminal organisations to foster profit-minded relationships. In essence, a political or criminal organisation would…*mutate* (its) own structure and organisation…rather than co-operate with (other) groups".[53] All these developments appear to have come about. FARC and the Turkish PKK have demonstrated that mutation does take place. Both groups have become deeply

---

48 Dishman, 'Terrorism, Crime and Transformation', pp. 45-6 & 56.

49 John T. Picarelli, 'The Turbulent Nexus of TOC and Terrorism: A Theory of Malevolent International Relations', *Global Crime*, vol. 7, no. 1, Feb. 2006, p. 4.

50 Inday Espina-Varona, 'Terror groups to use crime to raise funds', *The Manila Times*, 7 Jan. 2007; Sara A. Carter, 'Terrorists teaming with drug cartels', *Washington Times*, 8 Aug. 2007. Also Sara A. Carter, 'Drug cartel-terrorist ties known in 2001', *Washington Times*, 14 Aug. 2007.

51 Dishman, 'Terrorism, Crime and Transformation', p. 44.

52 *Ibid.*, p. 47. See also pp. 50-1, where he cites the activities of the Medellin cartel as an example.

53 *Ibid.*, p. 48.

involved in the drugs business and epitomise the phenomenon known as "narco-terrorism". Makarenko essentially agrees, pointing out that the problems inherent in alliances mean that most terrorist and criminal groups have developed the capacity to engage in criminal and terrorist acts on their own.[54] Hizbollah, for example, has developed an extensive international criminal network that is involved in intellectual property crime, drug and cigarette smuggling, and the African illegal diamond trade to support its insurgency.[55] For Williams, too, the transformation hypothesis is the most compelling, and he points to the anti-Castro groups as a clear example of terrorists who abandoned their substantive political agenda, probably in the early 1980s, to concentrate on traditional mob rackets.[56]

On the other hand, there is also evidence that points towards examples of convergence or cooperation taking place for specific reasons at specific times.[57] Antonio Maria Costa, the Executive Director of the UN Office of Drugs and Crime (UNODC), is quoted as saying: "The world is seeing the birth of a new hybrid of organised crime-terrorist organisations".[58] Williams, who is sceptical about cooperation, does acknowledge that cases of collaboration limited to customer-supplier and occasional service contract relationships have occurred even though they have not been common.[59] Nonetheless, Al Qaeda, the LTTE and many TCOs operate like modern business organisations;[60] ONI/USCG have commented that "organised crime...will continue to develop business strategies similar to those used

54   Makarenko, 'A Model of Terrorist-Criminal Relations', p. 7.

55   Michael P. Arena, 'Hizbollah's Global Criminal Operations', *Global Crime*, vol. 7, Nos. 3-4, Aug.-Nov. 2006, pp. 454-70.

56   Williams, 'Terrorism and Organized Crime: Convergence, Nexus or Transformation?' p. 89.

57   See several CSIS *Transnational Threats Update* reports, for example, 'Islamic terrorists linked to Camorra', vol. 2, no. 7, April 2004, p. 4; 'Italian mobsters linked to Islamic terrorists', vol. 2, no. 9, June 2004, p. 4; 'Could organised crime in Russia's eastern regions aid terrorists?', vol. 1, no. 11, Aug. 2003, pp. 1-2.

58   'UN Warns About Nexus Between Drugs, Crime and Terrorism', UN Press Release SOC/CP/311, 1 Oct. 2004. Also Kaplan, 'Paying for terror'.

59   Williams, 'Terrorism and Organized Crime: Convergence, Nexus or Transformation?' p. 89.

60   One Tamil militant reported that 'the LTTE functions like a multinational corporation...(LTTE leader) Prabhakaran's acumen is as much that of a CEO as of a military commander': Davis, 'Tiger International'.

by legitimate corporations".[61] Modern business theory stresses the importance of flexibility and finding partners when a capability is lacking, rather
than forcing the organisation to do something it is not capable of doing
well or which would place excessive demands on scarce resources. Modern
terrorist groups and modern criminals also appear to be following this paradigm as they are apparently willing to seek out partners as and when they
need them. As Bruce Hoffman points out, Al Qaeda encourages "creative
approaches and out-of-box thinking" and "actively encourages subsidiary
groups fighting under the corporate banner to mix and match approaches".
Terrorist organisations have a history of imitating each other and therefore
this cooperative model is likely to spread.[62]

In the first instance terrorists are likely to turn to other terrorists for help.
Terrorists are not fools; they recognise that cooperating with criminals exposes them to security risks. Compared with terrorist groups, most criminal gangs are easier to track and penetrate, while their individual members
are more likely to become informers in exchange for money or immunity.[63]
Nonetheless, there will be situations where other terrorist groups lack essential skills or resources.

In these cases turning to criminals may be the next best option. In his report for the Congressional Research Service on the links between terrorism
and drugs, Mark Kleiman lists four reasons why criminals and terrorists
might cooperate: first and foremost, for money; secondly, for creation of
chaos and instability in the source and transit countries; thirdly, to encourage a climate where corruption is acceptable and intimidation is unop-
posed; and fourthly, to provide cover and a common infrastructure for their

---

61   ONI/USCG, *Threats and Challenges to Maritime Security 2020*, 1999, p. 15.

62   McCaffrey and Busso, 'Narcotics, Terrorism, and International Crime: The
      Convergence Phenomenon', p. 211; Bergen, *Holy War, Inc*, pp. 33-4; Bruce
      Hoffman, 'Redefining Counterterrorism: The Terrorist Leader as CEO', *RAND
      Review*, Spring 2004, p. 14. Brad McAllister, on the other hand, argues that Al
      Qaeda's network structure, which it had been forced to adopt because it was
      without a safe haven, lacks the flexibility of business networks and severely
      inhibits its offensive capability: Brad McAllister, 'Al Qaeda and the Innovative
      Firm: Demythologizing the Network', *Studies in Conflict and Terrorism*, vol. 27,
      2004, pp. 297-319.

63   According to US investigators 'some of the most useful intelligence they are
      now receiving on terrorists linked to al-Qaeda has been given by informers or
      infiltrators of criminal gangs': Mark Huband, 'Al-Qaeda forms drug links as
      anti-terror war bites', *Financial Times*, 15 June 2004. Also Kaplan, 'Paying for
      terror'.

joint and separate activities.[64] Concrete examples of this cooperation can be found. For instance, terrorist groups have shown they are well suited to creating the climate of instability that enables drug cultivation and production to proceed without interruption. Groups such as FARC in Colombia, the United Wa State Army in Burma and the Taliban in Afghanistan have all demonstrated they can create and then control zones where they can exercise power on their terms. They can then sell the narcotic product to criminal gangs that have the assets and experience to transport and distribute it. Central American gangs are working to destabilise parts of the region to facilitate the transit of drugs and migrants. Possible insurgent-criminal cooperation has also been observed in Brazil. Some members of the Brazilian military and national police believe that the FARC has provided military training to some of the gangs in Rio and São Paulo.[65] The LTTE's Sea Tigers worked with Arakanese smugglers in Burma and northeast India and almost certainly facilitated the movement of drugs between Asia and Europe and migrants to Europe, North America and Australia. Unspecified criminal groups have acted as "cut-outs" between major international arms dealers and terrorists,[66] while unspecified terrorist groups have in the past couple of decades made increasing use of the human smuggling routes across the Mediterranean to bring operatives into Europe, and bought arms and documents from smugglers and forgers.[67] In the Philippines the MILF and the ASG have connections with the "Pentagon" gang of kidnappers.

However, the issues of flexibility and partnership, and Hoffman's point that Al Qaeda and other groups encourage "out-of-box" creative thinking, suggest that an analytical approach that focuses on group motivations at the expense of the those of individual actors might be out of touch. Picarelli has suggested that the emergence of a new criminal sub-culture prepared to supply anyone with specific, illicit goods and services, such as documents or smuggling across specific sections of border, has meant that criminals

---

64   Mark A. R. Kleiman, *Illicit Drugs and the Terrorist Threat: Causal Links and Implications for Domestic Drug Control Policy*, Congressional Research Service, RL32334; updated 20 April 2004, pp. 2-7.

65   Day, 'Crime Groups Turn to Terrorism in Rio de Janeiro'.

66   "Floating market' in illicit weapons arms terrorists'.

67   Italian authorities suspect that one Islamist gang was responsible for landing over 30 groups of migrants on an island off Sicily and that the trade brought them into contact with several organised groups including the Neapolitan 'Camorra' as early as 1998: Kaplan, 'Paying for terror'; also 'Islamic terrorists linked to the Camorra', p. 4.

and terrorists have found it easier to deal with each other.[68] The increasing pace of change, and the need to respond quickly to both opportunities and reverses, has placed a higher premium on individual skills and meant that criminals and terrorists have, like businesses but unlike governments, become more adaptive. He points to the business example of Wal-Mart, which was able to resume its operations hours after Hurricane Katrina had swept through the US Gulf states in 2005 while the state and federal governments were still struggling to respond; the criminal example of smugglers who, when the Albanian authorities closed the port of Vlore to disrupt their activities, switched their operations to a Greek port in a matter of days; and terrorist groups in Iraq which have demonstrated a fearsome ability to adapt IED technology and tactics to changing circumstances. In his view this adaptability has profound implications for the future of criminal-terrorist interaction.[69]

This flexibility and adaptability extend also to loyalty. Louise Shelley drew a distinction between "traditional" and "new" criminal organisations, which Picarelli builds upon to separate "sovereign-bound" from "sovereign-free" criminal and terrorist groups.[70] "Sovereign-bound" groups respect sovereign power and when they seek to control certain localities, regions or even countries are seeking to supplant specific states; "sovereign-bound" terrorist groups tend to be ethno-nationalist while their criminal counterparts can make some form of "investment" in their societies, such as the cooperative links between the *yakuza* and the police in Japan.[71] Neither "sovereign-free" terrorist groups, such as Al Qaeda and its affiliates and Aum Shinrikyo, which generally have religious or millenarian goals, nor "sovereign-free" criminals, who have short-term goals driven by market

---

68 See in this regard the report that Islamist terrorists paid a Mexican drug cartel to smuggle Afghan and Iraqi operatives through Laredo, TX and their weapons, which reportedly included Milan anti-tank missiles, RPGs and other firearms through tunnels under the border, in order to attack the intelligence training facility at Fort Huachuca, AZ: Sara A. Carter, 'Islamists target Arizona base', *Washington Times*, 26 Nov. 2007.

69 Picarelli, 'The Turbulent Nexus of TOC and Terrorism', pp. 7-9. Also Galeotti, 'The New World of Organised Crime', p. 47 and Godson and Olson, 'International Organized Crime', p. 23 where they note the 'inherent flexibility' of narcotic traffickers..

70 Picarelli, 'The Turbulent Nexus of TOC and Terrorism', pp. 14-15.

71 Louise I. Shelley, 'The Unholy Trinity: Transnational Crime, Corruption, and Terrorism', *Brown Journal of World Affairs*, vol. XI, Issue 2, Winter/Spring 2005, p. 108.

forces and whose allegiance is solely to the money they make, are concerned about the damage they inflict on states. For such criminals working with terrorists presents no sort of problem. The Indian gangster Aftab Ansari, for example, who had close connections to Al Qaeda, "was trying to use the militants' network for underworld operations" while at the same time the "leaders of different militant outfits in Pakistan were trying to use his".[72]

"Traditional" and "new" criminal groups also differ in the way they use corruption: "traditional" groups tend to use it as a tool to gain long-term influence; the "new" groups depend on "high levels of systemic and institutionalised corruption" to secure deals and "buy-off" interference.[73] While "traditional" criminal groups such as Colombian drug cartels are willing to undermine weak states—as appears to be happening in West Africa including, for example, Ivory Coast and Guinea-Bissau[74]— "new" groups thrive in the absence of government.[75] Terrorists can also thrive in such situations. Where such groups converge in weak states they can form "black holes" (defined as areas where politically interested criminals or criminally inspired terrorists can "effectively challenge the legitimacy of a state, and ultimately replace the state in many, if not all, of its functions"[76]) that serve as safe havens for their continued operations, as has occurred in Pakistan's Federally Administered Tribal Area (FATA) and the "tri-border" region centred on Cuidad del Este in Paraguay, where terrorist groups such as Hizbollah and Hamas freely do business with criminals including Brazilian gangsters and Japanese *yakuza*.[77] They need not be remote; they can be

---

72   Stern, 'The Protean Enemy', pp. 35-6.

73   Shelley, 'The Unholy Trinity', p. 106. Also Phil Williams, 'Transnational Criminal Networks' in John Arquilla and David Ronfeldt, *Networks and Netwars*, Santa Monica: RAND, 2001, pp. 78-80.

74   Nico Colombant, 'West Africa's drug circulation increases, worrying officials', *NewsVOA.com*, 18 June 2007; Stephanie Hanson, 'In West Africa, Threat of Narco-States', Council of Foreign Relations *Daily Analysis*, 10 July 2007; Mario de Queiroz, 'Guinea-Bissau: African paradise for South American traffickers', *Inter Press Services News Agency*, 10 Aug. 2007; 'Drug cartels begin cracking West Africa', *Jane's FR*, 23 Aug. 2007; 'UN: Cocaine influx could destabilise Guinea-Bissau', *AP*, 1 Nov. 2007; Kevin Sullivan. 'Route of evil'. *Washington Post*, 25 May 2008; Mbachu, 'The West Africa-South America Drug Route'.

75   Shelley, 'The Unholy Trinity', p. 106.

76   Tamara Makarenko, 'The Crime-Terror Continuum: Tracing the Interplay between TOC and Terrorism', *Global Crime*, vol. 6, no. 1, Feb. 2004, pp. 139-40; Shelley, 'The Unholy Trinity', p. 107; Godson and Olson, 'International Organized Crime', p. 26..

77   Sullivan, 'Terrorism, Crime and Private Armies', p. 73. On the FATA see Griff

found in the midst of cities.[78] The ultimate in "black holes" are failed states, which because they can become in Max Manwaring's words, "breeding grounds for instability and terrorism", represent the most "dangerous long-term security challenge facing the global community today".[79] A vital fact is that these are not "ungoverned" or "lawless" spaces; they are governed by insurgents, criminals or warlords for their own ends.[80] The concern must be that as so many weak states are coastal states, and as organised criminal groups or even individuals with special skills associated with such groups are displaying a greater willingness to work with terrorists, this cooperation or convergence will manifest itself in increased use of the maritime domain.[81]

Threats to international shipping networks. Half a century of peace, the cargo integrity that came with containerisation, bigger ships, global communications and weather forecasting, the decline in piracy during the twentieth century compared to the eighteenth and nineteenth, all combined to encourage people to assess threats in terms of the risk of accidents, not attack, and left the international shipping network unprepared for deliberate, perhaps multiple, disruptions. Although, as described earlier, no group has the resources to seriously threaten the economy of a major state directly, the huge investment in the system, in both money and confidence, means there is a temptation to play down threats and brush aside their implications which could leave terrorists with an opportunity they could exploit.

The target would be confidence in the system. Though the sensitivity of markets varies—attacks on oil installations, for instance, have not to date had lasting effects on prices—sensitivity could become vulnerability to the point where terrorists could achieve disproportionate gains from apparently random attacks, provided these were persistent and amplified by a determined information campaign. The cumulative loss of confidence in the ability of the system or its constituent parts to deliver goods and raw materials reliably that might result from extensive terrorist disruption would be re-

---

Witte, 'Pakistan seen losing fight against Taliban and al-Qaeda', *Washington Post*, 3 Oct. 2007.

78   John P. Sullivan, 'Maras Morphing: Revisiting Third Generation Gangs', *Global Crime*, vol. 7, Nos. 3-4, Aug.-Nov. 2006, pp. 488 & 501.

79   Max Manwaring. 'The New Global Security Landscape: The Road Ahead' in Bunker, *Networks, Terrorism and Global Insurgency*, p. 24.

80   Manwaring, *A Contemporary Challenge to State Sovereignty*, p. 9

81   Mark J. Valencia sees a correlation between 'weak' states and piracy, especially if the issue of the economy is taken into account: interview with author.

flected in rising prices, particularly energy and commodity prices and rates for insurance and shipping, which would affect productivity. The economic effects of any serious disturbance could be felt globally and states, particularly weaker states, might be faced with instability if food and fuel supplies were severely affected or prices rose dramatically.

The terrorism-related risks that most concern marine insurers currently are pollution, the blockage of a chokepoint forcing shipping to make a time-consuming diversion, and the closure of a port with significant numbers of ships trapped inside. Other, remoter threats might also be realised. A material like LNG may not be an attractive tool for terrorists on its own, but a supply chain consisting of ships dispersed across the oceans, 200-300 miles apart, departing and arriving at terminals and transiting chokepoints on predictable schedules that are set contractually years in advance, could be severely damaged by an attack on an LNG carrier and the threat of more. The prospect of achieving a level of disruption that would send tremors not only throughout the target economy but also through all economies dependent on similar supply chains, could excite a terrorist's interest in LNG or another similar resource, despite the practical challenges it presents. Likewise, while the detonation of explosive devices in ports or on board ships, or on ships rammed into offshore or coastal terminals where oil was loaded or discharged—all very difficult to achieve—might not individually be especially disruptive, cumulatively they could, if successful, reach a level that would weaken the maritime transport system sufficiently to shake confidence in the security of the world's supply chains for energy, raw materials and finished goods.

Such potential weaknesses in the commercial maritime transport system demand serious attention, but there will always be limits to what can be achieved if the system is to remain efficient. Given these limitations, the industry, its customers and the public at large need to recognise that terrorists may well succeed and that if they do, strategies, plans and resources needs to be in place to minimise the damage and disruption. The attractiveness of "confidence" as a target needs to be reduced. Resilience needs to replace fragility by managing the shock and controlling the fear upon which terrorists depend. The alternative is that as the volume of trade transported by sea increases, and the sea's resources are exploited with greater intensity, the system's vulnerabilities to disruption, including disruption by terror attacks, will have correspondingly greater implications for the world's economy and security.

Maritime insurgency. Prognoses of the future of maritime terrorism have usually been "more of the same", but with larger explosions and more deaths. These could prove to be accurate but begs the question: what would induce insurgent or terrorist groups to invest their limited resources in trying to overcome the manifest functional difficulties of operating at sea?

David Kilcullen is one writer who has talked about complex irregular warfare and the way in which its practitioners can exploit the sort of cluttered physical, human and informational environment found in the littorals that can degrade Western target acquisition systems.[82] He wrote with the growing size and number of undifferentiated cityscapes in mind. Other environments have the same effect. Coastal waters and the contiguous littorals offer good cover: a combination of the wild terrain associated traditionally with guerrilla operations and crowded environments more akin to the habitat of urban terrorists.[83] As Commodore Simon Williams of the Royal Navy put it, maritime patrol operations are "...really no different than civil-military contacts in Baghdad or Ramadi...At sea, the houses are fishing grounds. The streets are traditional sea lanes..."[84] Rough coasts and rough water can hide movement as well as rough country, particularly as both can frustrate and distort radar, sonar and communications signals. Beaches crowded with people, and offshore waters crowded with pleasure craft and fishing boats, can offer insurgents cover similar to city streets. In the past irregular fighters put distance between themselves and their enemies by mounting raids from bases in mountains and jungles. Now they prefer to hide in densely populated cities close to their targets. Density, not distance, is now the key to irregular war fighting.[85]

If—and only if—circumstances changed on land, terrorists might wish or need to operate more at sea. Two scenarios—an increased use of "sea bases" by US and possibly other forces, and a major political shift taking place in a coastal region that fortifies terrorist, particularly jihadist, pres-

---

82   'Complex Irregular Warfare: The Face of Contemporary Conflict, *The Military Balance, 2005-2006.* London: Routledge for the IISS, 2005, p. 414; Frank.G. Hoffman, 'Complex Irregular Warfare: The Next Revolution in Military Affairs', *Orbis,* vol. 50, no. 3, Summer 2006, pp. 395-411.

83   Martin N. Murphy, 'Suppression of Piracy and Maritime Terrorism: A Suitable Role for a Navy?' *NWCR,* vol. 60, no. 3, 2007, pp. 35.

84   Quoted in Jim Garamone, 'Maritime ops in Middle East have deterrent effect', *American Forces Information Service News Articles,* 27 April 2006.

85   Frank G. Hoffman, 'Small Wars Revisited: The United States and Nontraditional Wars', *The Journal of Strategic Studies,* vol. 28, no. 6, Dec. 2005, pp. 923 & 931.

sures—exemplify the kinds of development that might lead to an increase in the incidence of maritime insurgency.[86]

All military forces need rear areas where they can rest, repair and recuperate. In expeditionary war such areas can be difficult to secure. They present the defender with large, static and valuable targets either for air and missile strikes or for Special Forces and insurgent raids. The solution which has been proposed and is being developed enthusiastically by maritime powers is the concept of the "sea base".[87] In essence the "rear area" will operate at sea out of sight of land. It will consist of a collection of vessels that are capable of sustaining the land operation. Carriers, surface vessels and submarines will provide air and fire support. Supplies and reinforcements will be ferried into the theatre using landing craft and vertical lift aircraft which on the return run will bring back casualties for treatment and troops on rotation. The "sea base" will in turn be the focus of the supply lines from secure homeland or out of theatre base areas. The sea base will be mobile. It will move close to shore when needed and retire deeper into the ocean if threatened. If will be protected by the full panoply of naval force: carrier-borne air power, surface AAW and ASW, and submarines. The size of the base will be tailored to the demands of the mission.[88] Some sense of how it will operate was provided by the collection of naval vessels including a Carrier Strike Group, an Expeditionary Strike Group, maritime pre-positioning ships and a hospital ship that assembled off Aceh in 2005 to provide post-tsunami relief.[89]

The origins of the concept might have lain in concerns over the vulnerability of "in theatre" base areas to nuclear bombardment, but its development has also been coloured by the experience of Hizbollah's attack on the US Marine base in Beirut in 1983, when two truck bombs killed 241 American and 58 French servicemen, prompting the peacekeeping force to

---

86   This section has been shaped by a valuable discussion with David Kilcullen, Sept. 2006.

87   Jason Sherman, 'Pentagon group details Sea Base concept', *Defense News*, 13 Aug. 2001.

88   For a history of the concept see Robert O. Work,'On Sea Basing' in Carnes Lord (ed),, *Reposturing the Force: US Overseas Presence in the Twenty-first Century*, Naval War College *Newport Papers 26*, Feb. 2006, pp. 95-101; Geoffrey Till, *Naval Transformation, Ground Forces, and the Expeditionary Impulse: The Sea-Basing Debate*, The Letort Papers. Carlisle, PA: US Army War College, Dec. 2006.

89   'US 7th Fleet to provide naval support for Aceh province', *Navy Newsstand*, 1 Jan. 2005.

withdraw. The belief is that if such headquarters and supply facilities are positioned at sea this vulnerability will be avoided.

As conceived originally, sea bases were not intended for long term deployments; however, it is possible that the US might have no option but to use them in this way. If the "long war" against global jihad is to be waged then the main theatres are likely to be in Central Asia, the Caucasus, the Middle East, parts of South and Southeast Asia, Northeast Africa including the Horn, the North African littoral and the Gulf of Guinea. Given not only the vulnerability of land bases but also the political hostility to which they can give rise, positioning bases offshore to support the various sub-conflicts would be an attractive option.

It has been suggested, for example, that US forces could continue to support indigenous Iraqi security forces following a Coalition withdrawal by operating from a sea base. Such a base would need to be positioned either in the northern Persian Gulf or in the eastern Mediterranean. Both, however, are narrow seas already well frequented by insurgent maritime activity. It is possible that such a transfer of key American assets from the land to the sea would give insurgents and terrorists in these regions the incentive to develop a greater maritime attack capability in order to be able to harass or disrupt the operation of the sea base, possibly with state support. Nevertheless, the difficulties of operating at sea that are typically experienced by non-state actors would remain, and the target would have very sophisticated defences. A sea base is less vulnerable than a base on land and it is likely that terrorists would take a long time to amass the maritime expertise necessary to effectively confront one directly, if they were able to do so; but as experience with land bases has shown, the expense and the fatigue induced by uninterruptedly high alert levels reduce military efficiency and discourage reenlistment. The sea base's natural response, which would be to retire to deeper water, would increase transit times and costs and possibly impair its effectiveness.

While the maritime terror threat is at present minor, there are indications that insurgent activity is increasing in some coastal regions: the Indian Navy, for example, is concerned about the threat of "seaborne terrorist strikes against its vast coastline, including [against] strategic offshore and onshore installations". According to Chief Admiral Sureesh Mehta, the security situation across the entire Indian Ocean has become "complex, fluid and significantly challenging", with a "dramatic increase in asymmetric threats".[90] This is a view with which the US concurs.[91] When maritime terrorism is seen through a wider lens, the most significant challenge may well come in the future from jihadist groups. One of the distinguishing features of jihadist terrorism is its global outlook. Jihadist organisations such as Al Qaeda are skilled at opening new fronts in their war where they detect opportunity, observe weakness or are able to build local alliances.[92] Sheik Abu-Bakar Naji, reputedly Al-Qaeda's chief theoretician, has written about the need to extend the jihadist conflict to anywhere in the world with a significant Muslim presence and to create parallel societies alongside existing ones, a formulation that echoes Williams' discussion of "formal" and "informal" states co-existing within a single border.[93] New instability in a given state, or other kinds of political change as in Somalia or in the Malaysian-Philippine-Indonesian maritime "tri-border" region, might allow jihadists to operate with greater freedom than they do at present.[94] If such changes took place in regions where the sea offered significant strategic opportunities, such groups might be inclined to invest in developing a maritime capability to supplement and support their strengthened presence on land, perhaps looking to the LTTE's Sea Tigers as a model.[95] 'Chatter'

---

90   'Navy gears up for sea-borne terrorist attack', *Rediff.com,* 29 May 2007; also Neelesh Misra and Rahul Singh, 'Terror alarm along India's coastline', *Hindustan Times,* 12 March 2007; 'Terror threat from the seas real: Antony', *Zee News,* 11 March 2008 and 'Maritime terrorism gains roots in Indian Ocean'. *The Times of India,* 9 August 2008.

91   'India's fears of terrorists using sea routes well-grounded: US', *The Times of India,* 24 Aug. 2007.

92   Bruce Hoffman, 'Remember Al Qaeda? They're baaack', *LA Times,* 20 Feb. 2007; Josh Meyer, 'Al Qaeda 'co-opts' new affiliates', *LA Times,* 16 Sept. 2007; Coughlin, 'Al Qaeda 'as strong today as it was on 9/11''.

93   Amir Taheri. 'Al Qaeda's plan B'. *New York Post,* 1 July 2008; Williams. *From the New Middle Ages to a New Dark Age,* p. 13.

94   See the comment on this area as a safe haven in US Department of State, Country Reports on Terrorism, 2006 available at http://www.state.gov/s/ct/rls/crt/2006/82728.htm. Also the relevant chapters by Rabasa and Chalk in Rabasa, *et al. Ungoverned Territories.* For more specific comments on the 'tri-border' region see Kim Cragin, *et al. Sharing the Dragon's Teeth: Terrorist Groups and the Exchange of New Technologies.* Santa Monica: RAND, 2007, pp. 23-46; 'Southeast Asia's tri-border black spot' and Storey, 'The Triborder Sea Area: Maritime Southeast Asia's Ungovered Space'.

95   See, for example, the remarks of the head of the Canadian navy, Vice Admiral Drew Robertson: 'Navy will have to learn to fight terrorists and pirates: admiral', *The Canadian Press,* 16 Sept. 2007.

on jihadist websites indicates they are not blind to these possibilities.[96] Naji writes about attacking seaports while the al-Qaeda strategist Al-Suri writes about attacking chokepoints such as the Straits of Hormuz and the Bab el Mandeb specifically, about targeting ships and of blocking passages using "mines and sinking ships in them, or by threatening the movement there by piracy, martyrdom operations and by the power of weapons".[97]

To begin with, the focus would be on developing greater capacity to move cadres, equipment and funds. Though the possibility of jihadist insurgents developing anything more substantial than an enhanced logistical ability at sea might seem remote, time and again terrorist and insurgent organisations have been able to depend on the scepticism of military and other analysts about their capabilities and determination to spring successful surprises. The attacks of 9/11 should have undermined this tendency to underestimate terrorist capabilities; so too should the IDF's experience at the hands of Hizbullah in 2006, when it encountered a sophisticated and elaborate layered defensive system that it had never known existed.[98]

With this experience in mind, we might expect terrorists and insurgents in maritime theatres, emboldened by major successes on land, to build on existing maritime expertise to become able eventually to harass commercial and naval traffic to a degree that hindered its free movement and made certain coastal regions high-risk areas for all kinds of vessel.[99] Such an elaboration of insurgent capability at sea could take place in the eastern Mediterranean, off the Horn of Africa (including Yemen),[100] or in South-

---

96   'Jihadist website commentary argues 'maritime terrorism' strategic necessity', *Biyokulule Online*, 29 April 2008. This website is a known venue for supporters rather than operatives but similar rhetoric has been noted on extremist sites that are associated more closely with Al Qaeda. A summary of the contents of this posting can also be found at 'Al-Qaeda Affiliated E-Journal: 'The Sea is The Next Strategic Step Towards Controlling The World And Restoring The Islamic Caliphate", MEMRI, 1 May 2008.

97   Lia. *Architect of Global Jihad,* p. 401.

98   Andrew Exum, 'Hizballah at War: A Military Assessment', *The Washington Institute for Near East Policy,* Policy Focus, no. 63, 12 Dec. 2006; 'Hizbullah's Islamic Resistance', *Jane's TSM,* 13 Sept. 2006.

99   In Rohan Gunaratna's view 'most threat groups with access to water move (over time) from conducting support operations to guiding surface and underwater attack capabilities': Gunaratna, 'The asymmetric threat from maritime terrorism', p. 88. This book argues that this progression is possible under certain political circumstances but is neither as automatic nor as straightforward as this statement implies.

100   Yemen appears to be particularly vulnerable. See Michael Knights, 'Jihadist par-

east Asia, anywhere from Mindanao in the Philippines through the Indonesian archipelago to Sumatra, and across to southern Thailand.[101] With regard to the Arabian Peninsula, the contributor to the jihadist website mentioned above makes the point that Yemen and the Horn of Africa "represents a strategic point to expel the enemy from the most important pillars of its battle." The success that Somali pirates had achieved in hijacking vessels is noted and the implication that is drawn is that "the area is beyond the control of the arsenal of the Crusader Zionist campaign."[102] Southeast Asia is an area of porous borders where operatives and contraband can be moved with relative ease and where it has been demonstrated that "black holes" can be created within which non-state groups can operate, as was the case with the MILF camps on Mindanao which were "no-go" areas for RP forces.[103] The region's annual population growth rate is the highest in

---

dise–Yemen's terrorist threat re-emerges', *Jane's IR*, May 2008; Brian O'Neill, 'Yemen's three rebellions', The Jamestown Foundation *Terrorism Monitor*, Vol, VI, Issue 10, 15 May 2008, pp. 7-9 and two articles from the *Arab Reform Bulletin*, Vol. 6, Issue 6, July 2008: Jeremy M. Sharp 'Yemen: where is the stability tipping point?' and Intissar Fakir. 'Yemen: economic and regional challenges'. For further background see Andrew McGregor, 'Shi'ite insurgency in Yemen: Iranian intervention of mountain revolt?' The Jamestown Foundation *Terrorism Monitor*, vol. II, Issue 16, 12 Aug. 2004, pp. 4-6; Gregory D. Johnsen, 'Is al-Qaeda in Yemen re-grouping?' The Jamestown Foundation *Terrorism Focus*, vol. IV, Issue 15, 22 May 2007, p. 1; Kathy Gannon, 'Yemen employs new terror approach', *Washington Post*, 4 July 2007; Dominic Moran, 'Yemen violence raises nuclear questions', ISN *Security Watch*, 9 July 2007; Gregory D. Johnsen and Brian O'Neill, 'Yemen attack reveals struggle among al-Qaeda's ranks', The Jamestown Foundation *Terrorism Focus*, vol. IV, Issue 22, 10 July 2007, p. 2; Gregory D. Johnsen, 'Yemen faces second generation of islamist militants', The Jamestown Foundation *Terrorism Focus*, vol. IV, Issue 27, 14 Aug. 2007; Dominic Moran, 'Yemeni unity questioned', ISN *Security Watch*, 12 Sept. 2007; Gregory D. Johnsen, 'Al-Qaeda in Yemen reorganizes under Nasir al-Wahayshi', The Jamestown Foundation *Terrorism Monitor*, vol. V, Issue 11, 18 March 2008; Brian O'Neill, 'Al-Qaeda new hardliners in Yemen strike western interests', The Janestown Foundation *Terrorism Focus*, Vol, 5, Issue 15, 16 April 2008 and Scheuer, 'Yemen's role in al-Qaeda's strategy'. For a wider geographical focus see Theodore W. Karasik and Kim Cragin, 'Case Study: The Arabian Peninsula' in Rabasa. *Ungoverned Territories*, pp. 77-110.

101   John C.K. Daly, 'Courting Sharia in Indonesia', ISN *Security Watch*, 9 July 2007.

102   'Jihadist website commentary argues 'maritime terrorism' strategic necessity'.

103   'The Southeast Asian nations of Indonesia, Malaysia, the Philippines and Thailand...have functioned as safe havens, training grounds, meeting places, money-laundering centres, and centres for the trafficking of arms, humans and narcotics. The area is ripe for this kind of activity because of its large population of Muslim minorities (excepting predominantly Muslim Indonesia), poor

the world. While economic expansion will ameliorate some of the effects of that growth and bring huge benefits for millions of people, it is also likely to trigger economic dislocation, shifts in population from rural to urban areas and painful social changes, each one of which could provide Salafist Islamism with opportunities to grow.[104] If maritime insurgency was to arise it could represent a serious threat to security beyond whatever region within which it took place.

Conclusion: assessing the threat

Terrorism at sea, while currently a minor threat to international order, has the potential to develop. If current trends continue it is likely that the sea will become a more contested space, one in which terrorists are likely to be presented with more potential targets and more opportunities to mount attacks. In addition, the continuing and in many cases unavoidable vulnerabilities of the global maritime transport system could magnify the consequences of any attacks, with effects throughout the system as a whole. Ports in almost all countries are poorly protected with little or no security either on the quayside or on ships. They are weak links in the system, which give terrorists (and pirates) relatively easy access to vessels.

There may be no proven links between pirates and terrorists, but in some contexts pirates (and criminals generally) can nonetheless assist terrorists by sustaining a *milieu* that deflects intelligence and law enforcement attention from terrorist activity. Criminals such as pirates and smugglers do not have to cooperate with terrorists to achieve this affect; they can help them inadvertently by simply going about their normal business. By doing so in a context in which multiple layers of criminal activity are in operation simultaneously in a mephitic environment that is difficult for an outsider to penetrate, the intelligence picture can become confused and terrorist activities can be made harder to discern. Their motives might dif-

---

banking transparency, weak border controls, and geographic proximity to the Golden Triangle...': Berry, *et al.*, 'Nations hospitable to organized crime and terrorism', p. 107. Also International Crisis Group, 'Southern Philippines backgrounder', p. 2 on the importance of the Philippine insurgencies to the continuing viability of trans-national terrorism in Southeast Asia. Nonetheless the situation is not static and success does not flow only in one direction. See Joe Cochrane, *et al.*, 'Asia is winning the fight on terror', *Newsweek*, 20 Aug. 2007 and Eric Schmitt. 'Experts see gains against Asian terror networks'. *New York Times*, 9 June 2008.

104   Brian Nichiporuk, *et al.*, 'Demographics and Security in Maritime Southeast Asia', *Georgetown JIA*, Winter/Spring 2006, pp. 83-91.

fer but their methods can be similar.[105] As Joshua Ho has written, piracy can form "the background noise from which maritime terrorist attacks may materialise".[106]

However, it is the highly organised form of criminal piracy and its links to national or transnational organised and "professionalised" crime that demand the closest attention. Admiral Mullen takes a similar view: "Piracy...is a global threat to security because of its deepening ties to international criminal networks, smuggling of hazardous cargoes, and disruption of vital commerce".[107]

Both piracy and terrorism are "grey-area" threats. Peter Chalk defines these as "threats to the stability of sovereign states [from] non-state actors and non-governmental processes and organisations".[108] The security threat that confronts most governments today is dynamic, multi-faceted and amorphous. Criminals and terrorists do not have the same objectives and even now, as a rule, they do not collude.[109] Increasingly, however, as their inhibitions against cooperation fade, their means and the effects of their activities overlap—effects including deepened corruption, increased drug addiction, and organised gang violence (that more and more involves

---

105   Louise I. Shelley and John Picarelli, 'Methods not Motives: Implications of the Convergenece of International Organized Crime and Terrorism', *Police Practice and Research,* vol. 3, no. 4, 2002, p. 308.

106   Ho, 'The security of sea lanes in Southeast Asia', p. 562.

107   Mullen, 'Remarks as delivered for the 17th International Seapower Symposium'.

108   See Chalk, *Grey-Area Phenomena in Southeast Asia,* p. 5, where he notes that this definition is based on ideas developed by Holden-Rhodes and Lupsha in 'Horsemen of the Apocalypse: Gray Area Phenomena and the New World Disorder', pp. 212–26, which possibly emerged first out of the work of Xavier Raufer. See Raufer, 'Gray Areas: A New Security Threat', pp. 1, 4-7 & 18. Also Alison Jamieson, 'An Italian Example: Gray Areas in a Western Democracy', pp. 5 & 15 in the same issue of *Political Warfare* and the essays in Max G. Manwaring (ed.) *Gray Area Phenemena: Confronting the New World Disorder.* Boulder & Oxford: Westview Press, 1993. For further discussion of the new kinds of security threats facing the world, see Moisés Naím, 'Five Wars We're Losing', *Foreign Policy,* Jan.-Feb. 2003, pp. 28-37, and Paul J. Smith, 'Transnational Security Threats and State Survival: A Role for the Military?' *Parameters,* Aug. 2000, pp. 77-91 for a review of a broader range of threats.

109   For more on the relationship between criminals and terrorists, see Canadian Centre for Intelligence and Security Studies, 'Actual and Potential Links Between Terrorism and Criminality', ITAC Presents: Trends in Terrorism Series, Volume 2006–5, 2006, p. 2.

the murder of law enforcement officials), such as has been seen in Mexico, Brazil and some Central American states.[110]

The opportunity for pirates and maritime terrorists to operate is created largely by the failure of weak states to deny them safe havens and free movement at sea, and the accessibility of potential targets in their waters.[111] Much of this activity is determined by geography. It is geography that distinguishes piracy from other crime and maritime terrorism from other terrorism. But the weak points are not, in the first instance, vulnerable ports and straits but vulnerable states. As the political scientist Martha Crenshaw has observed in relation to terrorism, "the most salient political factor in the category of permissive causes is a government's inability or unwillingness to prevent terrorism … The absence of effective security measures is a necessary cause."[112]

Piracy might be a second-order problem on its own, but it is a symptom of state weakness, which in the context of wider criminal networks helps to perpetuate that weakness which in its turn helps terrorism and organised crime to flourish. Terrorism expert Brian Michael Jenkins remarks that "while we should not take piracy as a marker for terrorism, it is a useful indication of the level of security…whatever means [are used] to suppress piracy will have a "knock-on" effect of making the operating environment more difficult for terrorists."[113] The failure to confront piracy effectively has its consequences. As with any crime, incidents of piracy are likely to increase and become more serious if they are not suppressed. As the "broken windows" theory of policing suggests, serious crime can take root in areas where the small things go unpunished.[114]

In 1857 the British Attorney-General FitzRoy Kelly wrote: "Pirates are always the enemy of every state".[115] What piracy and maritime terrorism

---

110 Manuel Roig-Franzia, 'Drug trade tyranny on the border', *Washington Post*, 16 March 2008. and Manuel Roig-Franzia 'Mexico's police chief is killed in brazen attack by gunmen', *Washington Post*, 9 May 2008.

111 I am indebted to Sam Bateman for crystallising this notion for me.

112 Crenshaw, 'The Causes of Terrorism', pp. 382-3.

113 Quoted in Nathaniel Xavier, 'No terrorism threat in Straits', *The Star On-line*, 5 July 2004.

114 James Q. Wilson and George L. Kelling put forward the theory originally in 1982 in an *Atlantic Monthly* article entitled 'Broken Windows' which is available at http://www.manhattan-institute.org/pdf/_atlantic_monthly-broken_windows.pdf. In the maritime context see Martin N. Murphy, 'Maritime Terrorism: The Threat in Context', *Jane's IR*, vol. 18, no. 2, Feb. 2006, p. 25.

115 Menefee, 'Piracy, Terrorism, and the Insurgent Passenger', p. 46.

reveal—perhaps even more clearly than do organised crime and terrorism on land—is that the divergences between states' responses to common problems are as wide as they have ever been and common cause is difficult to achieve. So long as vulnerable states operate behind inviolable borders, treating their external responsibilities as largely theoretical, then their problems, whether they involve piracy, smuggling or terrorism, will affect their neighbours and the ships that pass their coasts. Furthermore, as the sea comes under increasing pressure in the coming century, the problem of maritime disorder unfettered by strong authority could extend well beyond the waters of weak states.

SELECT BIBLIOGRAPHY

Books and Monographs

Abuza, Zachary. *Balik Terrorism: The Return of the Abu Sayyaf.* Carlisle, PA: US Army War College, Strategic Studies Institute, Sept., 2005.

————. *Militant Islam in Southeast Asia: Crucible of Terror.* Boulder & London: Lynne Rienner, 2003.

Adams, Neal. *Terrorism and Oil.* Tulsa: PennWell, 2003.

Allison, Graham. *Nuclear Terrorism: The Risks and Consequences of the Ultimate Disaster.* London: Constable and Robinson, 2006 (orig. pub, 2004).

August, Oliver. *Inside the Red Mansion: On the Trail of China's Most Wanted Man.* New York: Houghton Mifflin Company, 2007.

Benjamin, Daniel; and Simon, Steven. *The Age of Sacred Terror.* New York: Random House Trade Paperback, 2003.

Bergen, Peter L. *Holy War, Inc: Inside the Secret World of Osama bin Laden.* London: Weidenfeld & Nicholson, 2001.

Black, Jeremy. *The Dotted Red Line: Britain's Defence Policy in the Modern World.* London: The Social Affairs Unit, 2006.

Blyth, Ken (with Peter Corris). *Petro Pirates: The Hijacking of the* Petro Ranger. St Leonards, NSW: Allen & Unwin, 2000.

Bohn, Michael K. *The Achille Lauro Hijacking: Lessons in the Politics and Prejudices of Terrorism.* Washington, DC: Potomac Books, 2004.

Boot, Max. *The Savage Wars of Peace: Small Wars and the Rise of American Power.* New York: Basic Books, 2002.

Bunker, Robert J., ed. *Networks, Terrorism and Global Insurgency.* Abingdon & New York: Routledge, 2005.

————. ed. *Non-State Threats and Future Wars.* London & Portland, OR: Frank Cass, 2003.

Burnett, John S. *Dangerous Waters: Modern Piracy and Terror on the High Seas.* New York: Dutton, 2002.

Burnham, Gracia (with Merrill, Dean). *In The Presence Of My Enemies.* Wheaton, IL: Tyndale House Publishers, 2003.

Buzan, Barry; Wæver, Ole; and de Wilde, Jaap. *Security: A New Framework for Analysis.* Boulder & London: Lynne Rienner Publishers, 1998.

Byman, Daniel. *Deadly Connections: States that Sponsor Terrorism.* Cambridge: Cambridge UP, 2005.

———. Chalk, Peter; Hoffman, Bruce; Rosenau, William; and Brannan, David. *Trends in Outside Support for Insurgency Movements,* Santa Monica: RAND, 2001.

Cable, James. *Gunboat Diplomacy 1919-1991,* Third Edition. New York: St.Martin's Press, 1994.

———. *Navies in Violent Peace.* London: Macmillan, 1989.

Cann, John P. *Brown Waters of Africa: Portuguese Riverine Warfare, 1961-1974.* St. Petersburg, FL: Hailer Publishing, 2007.

Chalk, Peter. *Grey-Area Phenomena in Southeast Asia: Piracy, Drug Trafficking and Political Terrorism.* Canberra: Strategic and Defence Studies Centre, The Australian National University, 1997.

———. *The Maritime Dimension of International Security: Terrorism, Piracy, and Challenges for the United States.* Santa Monica: RAND, 2008.

———. *Non-Military Security and Global Order: The Impact of Extremism, Violence and Chaos on National and International Security.* London: Macmillan, 2000.

Churchill, R.R.; and Lowe, A.V. *The Law of the Sea.* Thi Edition. Manchester: Manchester UP, 1999.

Clarke, Richa A. *Against All Enemies: Inside America's War on Terror.* London: The Free Press, 2004.

Clausewitz, Carl von. (ed. and tr. Howard, Michael and Paret, Peter). *On War.* Princeton: Princeton UP, 1976.

Conway, Barbara. *Maritime Fraud.* London: Lloyd's of London Press, 1990.

———. *The Piracy Business.* London: Hamlyn Paperbacks, 1981.

Corbett, Julian S. *Some Principles of Maritime Strategy.* Annapolis, MD: Naval Institute Press, 1988; orig. pub 1911.

Course, A.G. *Pirates of the Eastern Seas.* London: Frederick Muller, 1966.

Cragin, Kim; Chalk, Peter; Daly, Sara A.; Jackson, Brian A. *Sharing the Dragon's Teeth: Terrorist Groups and the Exchange of New Technologies.* Santa Monica: RAND, 2007.

Dubner, Barry H. *The Law of International Sea Piracy.* The Hague: Martinus Nijhoff Publishers, 1980.

Earle, Peter. *The Pirate Wars.* London: Methuen, 2003.

Eklöf, Stefan. *Pirates in Paradise.* Copenhagen: NIAS Press, 2006.

Ellen, Eric, ed. *Piracy at Sea.* Paris: ICC Publishing 1989.

———. *Shipping at Risk.* Paris: ICC Publishing, 1997.

El-Shazly, Nadia El-Sayed. *The Gulf Tanker War: Iran and Iraq's Maritime Swordplay.* London: Macmillan, 1998.

Fitzhugh, Thomas C., III, ed. *International Perspectives on Maritime Security.* Charlotte, NC: Maritime Security Council, 1996.

Flynn, Stephen. *America the Vulnerable.* New York: HarperCollins, 2004.

———. *The Edge of Disaster.* New York: Random House, 2007.

Forbes, Andrew. *The Strategic Importance of Seaborne Trade and Shipping.* Papers in Australian Maritime Affairs, no. 10. Canberra: RAN Sea Power Centre, 2003.

Frécon, Eric. *Pavillon noir sur l'Asie du Sud-Est: Histoire d'une résurgence de la piraterie maritime en Asie du Sud-Est.* Bangkok: IRASEC and Paris: L'Harmattan, 2002.

———. *The Resurgence of Sea Piracy in Southeast Asia.* IRASEC Occasional Paper No. 5, June 2008 at http://irasec.com/fr/publications_detail.php?hId=92 (3 July 2008).

Freedman, Lawrence, ed. *Superterrorism: Policy Responses.* Oxford: Blackwell, 2002.

Galdorisi, George V.; and Vienna, Kevin R. *Beyond the Law of the Sea: New Directions for U.S. Oceans Policy.* Westport, CT & London: Praeger, 1997.

Gill, A.P.S. and Sahni, Ajai. *The Global Threat of Terror: Ideological, Material and Political Linkages.* New Delhi: Bulwark Books for The Institute of Conflict Management, 2002.

Gill, Martin, ed. *Issues in Maritime Crime: Mayhem at Sea.* Leicester: Perpetuity Press, 1995.

Godson, Roy, ed. *Menace to Society: Political-Criminal Collaboration Around the World.* New Brunswick & London: Transaction Publishers, 2003.

Gosse, Philip. *The History of Piracy.* New York: Tudor Publishing, 1946 (orig. pub, 1932).

Gottschalk, Jack A.; and Flanagan, Brian P. *Jolly Roger with an Uzi: The Rise and Threat of Modern Piracy.* Annapolis: Naval Institute Press, 2000.

Grant, Bruce. *The Boat People: An 'Age' Investigation.* Harmondsworth: Penguin, 1979.

Gray, Colin S. *Another Bloody Century: Future Warfare.* London: Weidenfeld & Nicholson, 2005.

———. *Modern Strategy.* Oxford: Oxford UP, 1999.

Gray, Jim; Monday, Mark; Stubblefield, Gary. *Maritime Terror: Protecting Yourself, Your Vessel and Your Crew against Piracy.* Boulder: Sycamore Island Books, 1999.

Greenberg, Michael D; Chalk, Peter; Willis, Henry H.; Khilko, Ivan; Ortiz, David S. *Maritime Terrorism: Risk and Liability.* Santa Monica: RAND, 2006.

Gunaratna, Rohan. *Inside Al-Qaeda: Global Network of Terror.* London: Hurst, 2002.

Hepburn, James. *The Black Flag.* London: Headline, 1995.

Herr, R.A., ed. *Sovereignty at Sea: From Westphalia to Madrid.* Wollongong Papers in Maritime Policy no. 11. University of Wollongong: Centre for Maritime Policy, 2000.

Ho, Joshua; and Raymond, Catherine Zara. *The Best of Times, The Worst of Times: Maritime Security in the Asia-Pacific.* Singapore: World Scientific Publishing/Institute of Defence and Strategic Studies, 2005.

Hoffman, Bruce. *Inside Terrorism.* London: Gollancz, 1998.

———. *Responding to Terrorism across the Technological Spectrum.* Carlisle Barracks PA: US Army War College, Strategic Studies Institute, 1994.

Huxley, Tim. *Disintegrating Indonesia? Implications for Regional Security,* Adelphi Paper 349. Oxford: OUP for the International Institute of Strategic Studies, 2002.

Hympendahl, Klaus (tr. Sokolinsky, Martin). *Pirates Aboard!* Dobbs Ferry: Sheridan House, 2005.

Jenkins, Brian Michael. *Unconquerable Nation: Knowing Our Enemy, Strengthening Ourselves.* Santa Monica: RAND, 2006.

Johnson, Derek; and Valencia, Mark. *Piracy in Southeast Asia: Status, Issues and Responsibilities.* Singapore: ISEAS Publications, 2005.

Jones, Stephen. *Maritime Security: A Practical Guide.* London: The Nautical Institute, 2006.

Juergensmeyer, Mark, *Terror in the Mind of God,* Third Edition, Berkeley and London: University of California Press, 2003.

Katz, Samuel. M. *Guards Without Frontiers.* London: Arms and Armour Press, 1990.

King. Gilbert. *The Most Dangerous Man in the World: Dawood Ibrahim.* New York: Chamberlain Bros, 2004.

Lacquer, Walter. *No End To War: Terrorism in the Twenty-First Century.* New York & London: Continuum, 2003.

Langewiesche, William. *The Outlaw Sea.* New York: North Point Press, 2004.

Lehr, Peter, ed. *Violence at Sea: Piracy in the Age of Global Terrorism.* New York: Routledge, 2007.

Lesser, Ian O. et. al., eds. *Countering the New Terrorism.* Santa Monica: RAND, 1999.

Levi, Michael. *On Nuclear Terrorism.* Cambridge & London: Harvard UP, 2007.

Levinson, Marc. *The Box: How the Shipping Container made the World Smaller and the World Economy Bigger.* Princeton: Princeton UP, 2006.

Lintner, Bertil. *Blood Brothers: The Criminal Underworld of Asia.* New York: Palgrave Macmillan, 2003.

MacDonald, Laura M. *Curse of the Narrows.* New York: Walker & Company, 2005.

Mackinlay, John. *Globalisation and Insurgency,* Adelphi Paper 352. Oxford: OUP for the International Institute of Strategic Studies, 2002.

McRaven, William H. *Spec Ops: Case Studies in Special Operations Warfare, Theory and Practice.* Novato CA: Presidio Press, 1996.

Mahan, Alfred Thayer. *The Influence of Sea Power upon History, 1660-1783.* New York: Dover, 1987 (orig. pub, 1890).

Manwaring, Max G. *A Contemporary Challenge to State Sovereignty: Gangs and Other Illicit Transnational Criminal Organizations in Central America, El Salvador, Mexico, Jamaica and Brazil.* US Army War College, Strategic Studies Institute, Dec. 2007.

———. ed. *Gray Area Phenemena: Confronting the New World Disoer.* Boulder & Oxford: Westview Press, 1993.

———. *Street Gangs: The New Urban Insurgency.* Carlisle, PA: US Army War College, Strategic Studies Institute, 2005.

Mattingley, Garrett. *The Defeat of the Spanish Armada.* London: Pimlico, 2000 (orig pub. 1959).

Menefee, Samuel Pyeatt. *Trends in Maritime Violence.* Jane's Special Report. Coulsdon: Jane's Information Group, 1996.

Miller, Harry. *Pirates of the Far East.* London: Robert, Hale & Co, 1970.

Mueller, G.O.W; and Adler, Freda. *Outlaws of the Ocean.* New York: Heart Marine Books, 1985.

Murphy, Martin N. *Contemporary Piracy and Maritime Terrorism.* Adelphi Paper no. 388. Abingdon & New York: Routledge for the International Institute of Strategic Studies, 2007.

Murray, Dian H. *Pirates of the South China Coast,* Palo Alto: Stanford UP, 1987.

National Commission on Terrorist Attacks upon the United States, The. *The 9/11 Commission Report: Final Report of the National Commission on Terrorist Attacks upon the United States.* Authorized Edition. 2004. New York and London: W.W.Norton & Company, 2004.

Navias, Martin S.; and Hooton, E.R. *Tanker Wars: The Assault on Merchant Shipping during the Iran-Iraq Crisis, 1980-1988.* London: I.B. Tauris, 1996.

Naylor, R.T. *Wages of Crime: Black Markets, Illegal Finance and the Underworld Economy.* Cornell UP 2002.

Noer, John H; with Gregory, David. *Chokepoints: Maritime Economic Concerns in Southeast Asia.* Washington, DC: National Defence UP, 1996.

Ong-Webb, Graham Gerald, ed. *Piracy, Terrorism and Securing the Malacca Straits.* Singapore: Institute for Southeast Asian Studies, 2006.

Parritt, B A H. *Security at Sea: A Practical Guide.* London: The Nautical Institute, 1991.

———. ed. *Violence at Sea.* Paris: ICC Publishing, 1986.

Pennell, C.R., ed. *Bandits at Sea: A Pirates Reader.* New York: New York UP, 2001.

Post, Jerrold M. *The Mind of the Terrorist.* New York: Palgrave Macmillan, 2007.

Rabasa, Angel M. *Political Islam in Southeast Asia: Moderates, Radicals and Terrorists.* Adelphi Paper 358. Oxford: OUP for International Institute of Strategic Studies, 2003.

———; Boraz, Steven; Chalk, Peter; Cragin, Kim; Karasik, Theodore W.; Moroney, Jennifer D.P.; O'Brien, Kevin A.; Peters, John E. *Ungoverned Territories: Understanding and Reducing Terrorism Risks.* Santa Monica: RAND, 2007

———; *et al. Beyond al-Qaeda: Part 2 – The Outer Rings of the Terrorist Universe.* Santa Monica: RAND, 2006.

Reeve, Simon. *The New Jackals: Ramzi Yousef, Osama bin Laden and the Future of Terrorism.* London: André Deutsch, 1999.

Ressa, Maria A. *Seeds of Terror.* New York: Free Press, 2003.

Richason, Louise. *What Terrorists Want: Understanding the Enemy, Containing the Threat.* New York: Random House, 2006.

Richason, Michael. *A Time Bomb for Global Trade: Maritime-related Terrorism in an Age of Weapons of Mass Destruction.* Singapore: Institute of Southeast Asian Studies, 2004.

Roger, N A M. *The Safegua of the Sea: A Naval History of Britain, Volume One 660-1649.* London: HarperCollins, 1997.

Ronzitti, Natalino, ed. *Maritime Terrorism and International Law.* Dordrecht, Boston and London: Martinus Nijhoff Publishers, 1990.

Rubin, Alfred P. *The Law of Piracy.* Second Edition. Irvington-on-Hudson: Transnational Publishers, 1998.

Rutter, Owen. *The Pirate Wind: Tales of the Sea-Robbers of Malaya.* Singapore & Oxford: Oxford UP, 1986; orig. pub, 1930.

Shay, Shaul. *The Red Sea Terror Triangle.* New Brunswick & London: Transaction Publishers, 2007 (orig. pub 2005).

Smith, Paul J., ed. *Terrorism and Violence in Southeast Asia: Transnational Challenges to States and Regional Stability.* Armonk, NY: M.E. Sharpe, 2005.

Stewart, Douglas. *The Brutal Seas: Organised Crime at Work.* Bloomington, IN & Milton Keynes, UK: Author House, 2006.

Stille, Alexander. *Excellent Cadavers: Mafia and the Death of the First Italian Republic,* New York: Vintage Books, 1996.

Stuart, Robert. *In Search of Pirates: A Modern-Day Odyssey in the South China Sea.* Edinburgh and London: Mainstream Publishing, 2002.

Tangredi, Sam J. ed. *Globalization and Maritime Power.* Washington DC: National Defence UP, 2002.

Terraine, John. *Business in Great Waters: The U-Boat Wars, 1916-1945.* London: Leo Cooper, 1989.

Thompson, Janice E. *Mercenaries, Pirates and Sovereigns: State-building and Extraterritorial Violence in Early Modern Europe.* Princeton: Princeton UP, 1994.

418

Tien, Nhat; Phuc, Duong; and Thuy, Vu Thanh. *Pirates on the Gulf of Siam: Report from the Vietnamese Boat People Living in the Refugee Camp in Songkhla, Thailand.* San Diego: Boat People SOS Committee, 1981.

Till, Geoffrey. *Naval Transformation, Ground Forces, and the Expeditionary Impulse: The Sea-Basing Debate.* Carlisle, PA: US Army War College, The Letort Papers, Dec., 2006.

Tzalel, Moshe. *From Ice-Breaker to Missile Boat: The Evolution of Israel's Naval Strategy.* Westport, CT & London: Greenwood Press, 2000.

Vego, Milan N. *Naval Strategy and Operations on Narrow Seas.* London & Portland: Frank Cass, 1999.

Villar, Roger. *Piracy Today: Robbery and Violence at Sea since 1980.* London: Conway Maritime Press, 1985.

Vo, Nghia M. *The Vietnamese Boat People, 1954 and 1975-1992.* Jefferson, NC & London: McFarland & Co, 2006.

Ward, Ralph T. *Pirates in History.* Baltimore: York Press, 1974.

Wardlaw, Grant. *Political Terrorism: Theory, Tactics, and Counter-Measures.* Second Edition. Cambridge: Cambridge UP, 1989 (orig. pub. 1982).

Warren, James Francis. *Iranun and Balangingi: Globalization, Maritime Raiding and the Birth of Ethnicity.* Quezon City: New Day Publishers, 2002.

White, Terry. *Swords of Lighting: Special Forces and the Changing Face of Warfare.* London: Brassey's, 1992.

Williams, Phil. *From the New Middle Ages to a New Dark Age: The Decline of the State and US Strategy.* Carlisle, PA: US Army War College, Strategic Studies Institute, 2008.

———; and Vlassis, Dimitri, eds. *Combating Transnational Crime: Concepts, Activities and Responses.* Abingdon & New York: Frank Cass, 2001.

Wylie, J.C. *Military Strategy: A General Theory of Power Control,* New Brunswick: Rutgers UP, 1967.

Young, Adam J. *Contemporary Maritime Piracy in Southeast Asia: History, Causes and Remedies.* Singapore & Lieden: Institute of Southeast Asian Studies/ International Institute for Asian Studies, 2007.

Articles and Book Chapters

Abbott, Jason; and Renwick, Neil. 'Pirates? Maritime piracy and societal security in Southeast Asia'. *Pacifica Review,* vol. 11, no. 1, Feb. 1999, pp. 7-24.

Abhyankar, Jayant. 'The case of the Anna Sierra' in Ellen, Eric, ed. 1997. *Shipping at Risk.* London: ICC-International Maritime Bureau, pp. 274-279

———. 'Maritime fraud and piracy'. *Transnational Organised Crime,* vol. 4, no. 3-4, Autumn/Winter 1998, pp. 157-194.

———. 'Phantom ships' in Ellen, Eric, ed. 1997. *Shipping at Risk.* London: ICC-International Maritime Bureau, pp.58-74.

Abuza, Zachary. 'On the defensive: Rebels lose ground in southern Philippines'. *Jane's Intelligence Review* (hereafter *JIR*), April 2007, pp. 12-16.
———. 'Shifting Focus: Jamaah Islamiyah's Long-Term Agenda Towas Islamism'. *JIR*, vol. 19, no. 7, July, 2007, pp. 22-26.
Anderson, J.L. 'Piracy and world history: An economic perspective on maritime predation'. *Journal of World History*, vol. 6, no. 2, 1995, pp. 175-199. Reprinted in Pennell, C.R., ed. *Bandits at Sea: A Pirates Reader*. New York: New York UP, 2001, pp. 82-106. [All references to Pennell]
Arana, Ana. 'How the street gangs took Central America'. *Foreign Affairs*, vol. 84, no. 3, May/June, 2005, pp. 98-110.
Arena, Michael P. 'Hizbollah's global criminal operations'. *Global Crime*, vol. 7, Nos. 3-4, Aug.-Nov. 2006, pp. 454-470.
Arlacchi, Pino. 'The dynamics of illegal markets' in Williams, Phil; and Vlassis, Dimitri, eds. *Combating Transnational Crime: Concepts, Activities and Responses*. Abingdon & New York: Frank Cass, 2001, pp. 5-12.
Ball, Wayne S. 'The old grey *Mare*, national enclosure of the oceans'. *Ocean Development and International Law*, vol. 27, 1996, pp. 97-124.
Banlaoi, Rommel C. 'The Abu Sayyaf group: Threat of maritime piracy and terrorism' in Lehr, Peter, ed. *Violence at Sea: Piracy in the Age of Global Terrorism*. New York: Routledge, 2007, pp. 121-137.
———. 'Maritime terrorism in Southeast Asia: The Abu Sayyaf threat'. *Naval War College Review*, Winter 2005, pp. 63-80.
Barnes, Paul; and Oloruntoba, Richa. 'Assurance of security in maritime supply chains: Conceptual issues of vulnerability and crisis management'. *Journal of International Management*, vol. 11, 2005, pp. 519-540.
Bateman, Sam. 'Assessing the threat of maritime terrorism: Issues for the Asia-Pacific region'. *Security Challenges*, vol. 2, no. 3, Oct., 2006, pp. 77-91 at http://www.kokodafoundation.org/journal/SC%20Vol%202%20No%203/vol%202%20no%203%20Bateman.pdf (26 June 2007).
———. 'Piracy and the challenge of cooperative security and enforcement policy'. *Maritime Studies*. March/April, no. 117, 2001, pp. 11-22.
———. 'The regime of straits transit passage in the Asia Pacific: political and strategic issues' in Rothwell, Donald R.; and Bateman, Sam., ed. *Navigational Rights and Freedoms and the New Law of the Sea*. The Hague, Boston and London: Martinus Nijhoff Publishers, 2000, pp. 94-109.
Becerra, Oscar. 'Fighting back: Mexico declares war on drug cartels'. *JIR*, April 2007, pp. 6-11.
Beckman, Robert C. 'Combatting piracy and armed robbery against ships in Southeast Asia: The way forwa'. *Ocean Development and International Law*, vol. 33, 2002, pp. 317-341.
Bernasek, Anna. 'The friction economy'. *Fortune*, vol. 145, no. 4, 18 Feb. 2002, pp. 104-110.

Bernitt, Thomas R.; and Tangredi, Sam J. 'Mine warfare and globalization: Low-tech warfare in a high-tech world' in Tangredi, Sam J., ed. *Globalization and Maritime Power.* Washington DC: National Defence UP, 2002, pp. 389-404.

Berry, N. O. 'Theories on the efficacy of terrorism' in Wilkinson, Paul; and Stewart, Alasdair M. *Contemporary Research on Terrorism.* Abeeen: Abeeen UP, 1987, pp. 293-306.

Betts, Richa K. 'The soft underbelly of American primacy: Tactical advantages of terror', *Political Science Quarterly,* vol. 117, no. 1, 2002, pp. 19-36.

Bharadwaj, Atul. 'Maritime aspects of Sri Lankan conflict'. *Journal of Indian Ocean Studies,* vol. 8, no. 3, Dec. 2000, pp. 237-247.

Birnie, P W. 'Piracy, past, present and future'. *Marine Policy,* vol.II, no. 3, July 1987, pp. 163-183.

Blair, Dennis; and Lieberthal, Kenneth. 'Smooth sailing: The world's shipping lanes are safe'. *Foreign Affairs,* vol. 86, no. 3, May/June 2007, pp. 7-13.

Blanche, Ed. 'Terror attacks threaten Gulf's oil routes'. *JIR,* vol. 14, no. 12, Dec. 2002, pp. 6-11.

Boyne, Sean. 'Uncovering the Irish Republican Army'. *JIR,* 1 Aug. 1996 at http://www.pbs.org/wgbh/pages/frontline/shows/ira/inside/weapons.html (7 Sept. 2007).

Bradford, John F. 'The growing prospects for maritime security cooperation in Southeast Asia'. *Naval War College Review,* vol. 58, no. 3, Summer 2005, pp. 63-86.

————. 'Japanese anti-piracy initiatives in Southeast Asia: Policy formulations and the coastal state responses'. *Contemporary Southeast Asia.* vol. 26, no. 3, 2004, pp. 480-505.

————. 'Shifting the Tides against Piracy in Southeast Asian Waters'. *Asian Survey,* Vol. XLVIII, No. 3, May/June 2008, pp. 473-491.

Breemer, Jan S. 'Offshore energy terrorism: Perspectives on a problem'. *Terrorism,* vol. 6, no. 3, 1983, pp. 455-468.

Brevé, Federico. 'The maras: A menace to the americas'. *Military Review,* July-Aug. 2007, pp. 88-95 at http://usacac.army.mil/CAC/milreview/English/JulAug07/Breve.pdf (9 Aug. 2007).

Brittin, Burdick H. 'The law of piracy: Does it meet the present and potential challenges?' in Ellen, Eric, ed. *Piracy at Sea,* Paris: ICC Publishing, 1989, pp. 159-167.

Bunker, Robert J. 'Battlespace dynamics, information warfare to netwar, and bond-relationship targeting' in Bunker, Robert J. ed. *Non-State Threats and Future Wars.* London & Portland, OR: Frank Cass, 2003, pp. 97-108.

Campbell, Tanner; and Gunaratna, Rohan. 'Maritime terrorism, piracy and crime' in Gunaratna, Rohan. *Terrorism in Asia Pacific: Threat and Response.* Singapore: Eastern UP, 2003, pp. 70-88.

Carmel. Steve. 'Commercial Shipping and the Maritime Strategy'. *Naval War College Review*, Vol. 61, No. 2, Spring 2008 pp. 39-46 at http://www.nwc.navy.mil/press/review/documents/NWCRSP08.pdf (12 July 2008).

Carpenter, William M; and Wiencek, David. G. 'Maritime piracy: A growing threat in the post-Cold War world' in Fitzhugh, Thomas C., III, ed. *International Perspectives on Maritime Security*. Charlotte, NC: Maritime Security Council, 1996, pp. 225-236.

———. 'Maritime piracy in asia' in Carpenter, William M; and Wiencek, David. G. *Asian Security Handbook: An Assessment of Political-Security Issues in the Asia-Pacific Region*. Armonk, NY and London: M.E.Sharpe, 1996.

Chalk, Peter. 'Case study: The East African corridor' in Rabasa, Angel M. *Ungoverned Territories: Understanding and Reducing Terrorism Risks*. Santa Monica: RAND, 2007, pp. 147-172.

———. 'Contemporary maritime piracy in Southeast Asia'. *Studies in Conflict and Terrorism*, vol. 21, no. 1, 1998, pp.87-112.

———. 'Maritime piracy: A global overview'. *JIR*, Aug., vol. 12, no. 8, 2000, pp.47-50.

———. 'Maritime terrorism in the contemporary era: Threat and potential future contingencies' in *The MIPT Terrorism Annual, 2006*. Oklahoma City: National Memorial Institute for the Prevention of Terrorism 2006.

———. 'Militant Islamic extremism in Southeast Asia' in Smith, Paul J., ed. *Terrorism and Violence in Southeast Asia: Transnational Challenges to States and Regional Stability*. Armonk, NY: M.E. Sharpe, 2005, pp. 19-37.

———. 'Past experience of maritime terrorism'. *JIR*, vol. 14, no. 12, Dec. 2002, pp. 8-9.

———. 'Piracy re-emerges as a modern-day threat'. *Jane's Navy International*, May, 2002, pp. 12-17.

———. 'Separatism and Southeast Asia: The Islamic factor in Southern Thailand, Mindanao, and Aceh'. *Studies in Conflict and Terrorism*, vol. 24, no. 4, 1 July 2001, pp. 241-269.

———. 'Training the Tigers: The strategy of separatist success in Sri Lanka'. *JIR*, Jan. 2007, pp. 24-28.

Chanda, Nayan. 'Foot in the water'. *FEER* (hereafter *FEER*), 9 March 2000 at http://www.feer.com/articles/2000/0003_09/p28security.html (23 Aug. 2003).

Chen, Jeffrey. 'The emerging nexus between piracy and maritime terrorism in Southeast Asia waters: A case study of the Gerakan Aceh Meeka (GAM)' in Lehr, Peter, ed. *Violence at Sea: Piracy in the Age of Global Terrorism*. New York: Routledge, 2007, pp. 139-154.

Chenevier, Justin. 'Piracy under the law of the sea convention: Conceptual basis and practical limitations'. *MLAANZ Journal*, vol. 15, Part 2, 1997, pp. 21-61.

Clingan, Thomas J., Jr. 'The law of piracy' in Ellen, Eric, ed. *Piracy at Sea*, Paris: ICC Publishing, 1989, pp. 168-172.

Collett, Nigel A. 'Firearms and piracy: The case for a change in practice'. *Seaways*, Jan., 2007, pp. 15-17.

'Complex irregular warfare: The face of contemporary conflict'. *The Military Balance, 2005-2006*. London: Routledge for the IISS, 2005, pp. 412-420.

Coner, Lee. 'Maritime terrorism: The next 'soft target'?' *Defence and Foreign Affairs Daily*, 9 Dec. 2003.

Coulter, Daniel J. 'Globalization of maritime commerce: The rise of hub ports' in Tangredi, Sam J. *Globalization and Maritime Power*, Washington DC: National Defence UP, 2002, pp. 133-141.

Crenshaw, Martha. 'The causes of terrorism'. *Comparative Politics*. vol. 13, no.4, July 1981, pp. 379-399.

———. 'Theories of terrorism: Instrumental and organisational approaches' in Rapoport, David C., ed. *Inside Terrorist Organisations*, Second Edition. London & Portland, OR: Frank Cass, 2001, pp. 13-31.

Crist, David B. 'Joint special operations in support of Ernest Will'. *Joint Forces Quarterly*, Autumn/Winter 2001-2, pp. 15-22.

Davey, Richa. 'Maritime security overview'. *RUSI Security Monitor*, vol. 1, no. 5, Dec./Jan. 2002-3, pp. 17-19.

Davies, Roger. 'Sea Tigers, stealth technology and the North Korean connection'. *JIR*, vol. 13, no. 3, March 2001, pp. 2-3.

Davis, Anthony. 'Attention shifts to Moro Islamic Liberation Front'. *JIR*, 1 April 2002, pp. 20-23.

———. 'MILF links to external terrorist groups'. *JIR*, 1 April 2002, pp. 22-23

———. 'NPA rebels complicate Manila's counterinsurgency strategy'. *JIR*, 1 June 2002.

———. 'Philippines fears new wave of attacks by Abu Sayyaf Group'. *JIR*. vol. 17, no. 5, May 2005, pp. 10-12.

———. 'Piracy in Southeast Asia shows signs of increased organisation'. *JIR*. vol. 16, no. 6, June 2004, pp. 37-41.

———. 'Resilient Abu Sayyaf resists military pressure'. *JIR*, 1 Sept. 2003.

———. 'Sulu Triangle, The'. *JIR*. vol. 16, no. 6, June 2004, p. 40.

———. 'Tamil Tiger International'. *JIR*, vol. 8, no. 10, 1 Oct. 1996.

———. 'Thailand cracks down on illicit arms trade'. *JIR*, 1 Dec. 2003, pp. 30-35

Day, Michael. 'Crime groups turn to terrorism in Rio de Janeiro'. *JIR*, 1 Aug. 2003.

Dishman, Chris. 'Terrorism, crime and transformation'. *Studies in Conflict and Terrorism*, vol. 24, 2001, pp. 43-58.

Doolin, Joel A. 'The proliferation security initiative: Cornerstone of a new international Norm'. *Naval War College Review*, vol. 59, no. 2, Spring 2006, pp. 29-57.

Dragonette. Charles H. 'Maritime Legends'. *Bulletin of the Atomic Scientists.* vol. 62, no. 5, Sept./Oct. 2006, pp. 18-19.

———. 'Maritime Terrorism: Underway as Before?' in Fitzhugh, Thomas C., III, ed. *International Perspectives on Maritime Security.* Charlotte, NC: Maritime Security Council, 1996, pp. 159-172.

Dzurek, Daniel J. 'Piracy in Southeast Asia'. *Oceanus,* vol. 32, Part 4, 1989-90, pp. 65-70.

Dubner, Barry H. 'Human Rights and Environmental Disaster – Two Problems that defy the 'Norms' of the International Law of Sea Piracy'. *Syracuse Journal of International Law,* vol. 23, no.1, 1997, pp. 1-65.

Ebbe, Obi N.I. 'Slicing Nigeria's "National Cake"' in Godson, Roy, ed. *Menace to Society: Political-Criminal Collaboration Around the World.* New Brunswick & London: Transaction Publishers, 2003, pp. 137-174.

Ellen, Eric. 'Bringing Piracy to Account'. *Jane's Navy International,* April 1997, pp. 29-35.

———. 'The Dimensions of International Maritime Crime', in Gill, Martin, ed. *Issues in Maritime Crime: Mayhem at Sea.* Leicester: Perpetuity Press, 1995.

Eppright, Charles T. "'Counterterrorism' and Conventional Military Force: The Relationship between Political Effect and Utility'. *Studies in Conflict and Terrorism,* vol. 20, no. 4, 1997, pp. 333-344.

Fay, James A. 'Risks of LNG and LPG'. *Annual Review Energy,* vol. 5, 1980, pp. 89-105 at http://arjournals.annualreviews.org/doi/pdf/10.1146/annurev.eg.05.110180.000513?cookieSet=1 (8 Oct. 2007).

Finch, Stephen B., Jr. 'Pueblo and Mayaguez: A Legal Analysis'. *Case Western Reserve Journal of International Law,* vol. 9, 1997, pp. 79-116.

Flynn, Stephen. 'Port Security Is Still A House of Cas'. *FEER,* Jan./Feb. 2006 at http://www.feer.com/articles1/2006/0601/free/p005.html (23 Jan. 2006).

———. 'The Unguaed Homeland' in Hoge, Jr, James F.; and Rose, Gideon Rose. *How Did This Happen? Terrorism and the New War.* Oxfo: PublicAffairs, 2001, pp. 183-198.

Foster, Anthony. 'An Emerging Threat Shapes Up As Terrorists Take To The High Seas'. *JIR,* July 1998, pp. 42-45.

Frécon, Eric. 'Piracy and Armed Robbery at Sea along the Malacca Straits: Initial Impression from Fieldwork in the Riau Islands' in Graham Gerald Ong-Webb, ed. *Piracy, Terrorism and Securing the Malacca Straits.* Singapore: Institute for Southeast Asian Studies, 2006, pp. 68-83.

Fursdon, Edwa. 'Sea Piracy – or Maritime Mugging?' *INTERSEC,* vol. 5, no. 5, May 1995, pp. 166-169.

Galdorisi, George. 'The United States and the Law of the Sea: Changing Interests and New Imperatives'. *Naval War College Review,* Autumn, 1996.

—— and Kaufman, Alan G. 'Military Activities in the Exclusive Economic Zone: Preventing Uncertainty and Defusing Conflict'. *California Western International Law Journal*, vol. 32, 2002, pp. 253-301.

—— and Sutton, Darren. 'Achieving the Global Maritime Partnership: Operational Needs and Technical Realities'. *RUSI Defence Systems*, June 2007, pp. 68-71 at http://www.rusi.org/downloads/assets/Galdorisi_and_Sutton,_Achieving_the_Global_Maritime_Partnership.pdf

Galeotti, Mark. 'The New World of Organised Crime'. *JIR*, vol. 12, no. 9, Sept. 2000, pp. 47-52.

Gehman Jr., Harold W. *Lost Patrol: The Attack on the* USS Cole', US Naval Institute *Proceedings*, vol. 127, no. 4, April 2001, pp. 34-37.

Gearson, John. 'The Nature of Modern Terrorism' in Lawrence Freedman, ed. *Superterrorism: Policy Responses*. Oxfo: Blackwell, 2002, pp. 7-24.

Gilmore, Anna. 'Gang warfare'. *JIR*, vol. 19, no. 7, July 2007, pp. 48-53.

Godson, Roy. 'The Political-Criminal Nexus and Global Security' in Godson, Roy, ed. *Menace to Society: Political-Criminal Collaboration Around the World*. New Brunswick & London: Transaction Publishers, 2003, pp. 1-26.

—— and Olson, William J. 'International Organized Crime'. *Society*, vol. 32, 1995, pp. 18-29.

Goodman, Timothy H. "Leaving the Corsair's Name To Other Times': How to Enforce the Law of Sea Piracy in the 21ˢᵗ Century through Regional International Agreements'. *Case Western Reserve Journal of International Law*, vol. 31, no.1, 1999, pp. 139-168.

Gorka, Sebastyen. 'The 'New' Threat of Organised Crime and Terrorism'. *Jane's Intelligence & Security Monitor*. June 2000.

Gray, Colin S. 'On Strategic Performance', *Joint Force Quarterly*, Winter 1995-6, pp. 30-36.

——. 'Thinking Asymmetrically in Times of Terror'. *Parameters*, Spring 2002, pp. 5-14

Grazebrook, A W. 'Naval Forces and the Control of Piracy in Southeast Asia'. *Naval Forces*, vol. 6, no. 1, 1995, pp. 58-60.

Gunaratna, Rohan. 'Asia Pacific: Organised Crime and International Terrorist Networks' in Gill, A.P.S.; and Sahni, Ajai. *The Global Threat of Terror: Ideological, Material and Political Linkages*. New Delhi: Bulwark Books for The Institute of Conflict Management, 2002, pp. 241-268.

——. 'The Asymmetric Threat from Maritime Terrorism'. *Jane's Navy International*, Oct., 2001, pp. 24-29

——. 'Sea Tiger Success Threatens the Spread of Copycat Tactics'. *JIR*, vol. 13, no. 3, March 2001, pp. 12-16.

——. 'Terror from the Sky'. *JIR*, Oct., 2001, pp. 6-9.

——. 'The Threat to the Maritime Domain: How Real is the Terrorist Threat?' in Lloyd, Richmond M., ed. *Economics and Maritime Strategy: Implica-*

SMALL BOATS, WEAK STATES, DIRTY MONEY

tions for the 21ˢᵗ Century. Proceedings of a Workshop sponsored by the William B. Ruger Chair at the Naval War College, Newport, RI, 6-8 Nov. 2006, pp. 81-89.

Haines, Steven W. 'Criminal Violence at Sea: Observations on the Threat and Appropriate Responses' in Parritt, B.A.H., ed. 1986. *Violence at Sea.* Paris: ICC Publishing, pp. 93-108.

Halberstam, Malvina. 'Terrorism on the High Seas: The Achille Lauro, Piracy and the IMO Convention on Maritime Safety'. *The American Journal of International Law.* vol. 82, no. 2, April 1988, pp. 269-310.

Hall, Peter V. "'We'd Have to Sink the Ships': Impact Studies and the 2002 West Coast Port Lockout'. *Economic Development Quarterly,* vol. 18, no. 4, Nov. 2004, pp. 354-367.

Harva Research in International Law. 'Draft Convention on Piracy with Comments'. *The American Journal of International Law.* vol. 26, Supplement, 1932, pp. 739-885.

Hathaway, Jeffrey J.; and McGee, Terry R. McGee. 'MDA Support to the Drug War'. US Coast Gua *Proceedings,* Fall 2006, pp.17-19.

Havens, Jerry. 'Terrorism: Ready to Blow?' *Bulletin of the Atomic Scientists,* vol. 59, no. 4, 2003, pp. 16-18.

Heitman, Helmoed-Römer. 'Forgotten 'Wars''. *Jane's Defence Weekly,* vol. 41, no. 38, 22 Sept. 2005, pp. 24-29.

Herbert-Burns, Rupert. 'Compound Piracy at Sea in the Early Twenty-first Century: A Tactical to Operational-Level Perspective on Contemporary, Multiphase Piratical Methodology' in Lehr, Peter, ed. *Violence at Sea: Piracy in the Age of Terrorism.* New York: Routledge, 2007, pp. 95-120.

———. 'Terrorism in the Early 21ˢᵗ Century Maritime Domain' in Ho, Joshua; and Raymond, Catherine Zara. *The Best of Times, The Worst of Times: Maritime Security in the Asia-Pacific.* Singapore: World Scientific Publishing/Institute of Defence and Strategic Studies, 2005, pp. 155-177.

———; and Zucker, Lauren. 'Drawing the line between piracy and maritime terrorism'. *JIR.* vol. 16, no. 9, Sept. 2004, pp. 30-35.

Hilburn, Matt. 'Hezbollah's Surprise'. *Sea Power,* Sept. 2006 at http://www.navyleague.org/sea_power/sep06-10.php (23 Sept. 2006).

Ho, Joshua. 'The Security of Sea Lanes in Southeast Asia'. *Asian Survey,* vol. XLVI, no. 4, July/Aug. 2006, pp. 558-574.

Hoffman, Bruce. 'Change and Continuity in Terrorism'. *Studies in Conflict and Terrorism,* vol. 24, 2001, pp.417-428.

Hoffman, Frank. 'Complex Irregular Warfare: The Next Revolution in Military Affairs'. *Orbis,* vol. 50, no. 3, Summer 2005, pp. 395-411 at http://www.fpri.org/orbis/5003/hoffman.complexirregularwarfare.pdf

———. 'Small Wars Revisited: The United States and Nontraditional Wars'. *The Journal of Strategic Studies,* vol. 28, no. 6, Dec. 2005, pp. 913-940.

Holden-Rhodes, J F; and Lupsha, Peter A. 'Horsemen of the Apocalypse: Gray Area Phenomena and the New World Disoer'. *Low Intensity Conflict and Law Enforcement*, vol. 2, no. 2, Autumn 1993, pp. 212-226.

Hunt, Matthew. 'Bleed to Bankruptcy: Economic Targeting Tactics in the Global Jihad'. *JIR*, Jan. 2007 pp. 14-17.

Hunter, Thomas B. 'The Growing Threat of Modern Piracy'. US Naval Institute *Proceedings*, vol. 125, no. 7, July 1999, pp. 72-75.

Hyslop, I. R. 'Contemporary Piracy', in Ellen, Eric, ed. *Piracy at Sea*, Paris: ICC Publishing, 1989, pp. 3-40.

Ignarski, Jonathan. 'Piracy, Law and Marine Insurance' in Eric Ellen, ed. *Piracy at Sea*, Paris: ICC Publishing, 1989, pp. 181-187.

Jenkins, Brian Michael. 'Redefining the Enemy: The World Has Changed But Our Mindset Has Not'. RAND *Review*, Spring 2004, pp. 16-23

———. *et al.* 'A chronology of terrorist attacks and other criminal actions against Maritime Targets', in Parritt, B.A.H., ed. *Violence at Sea*. Paris: ICC Publishing, 1986, pp. 63-68.

Johnson, D.H.N. 'Piracy in Modern International Law'. *Grotius Society Transactions*. vol. 63, 1957, pp. 63-85.

Johnson, Stewart S. 'Territorial Issues and Conflict Potential in the South China Sea'. *Conflict Quarterley*, vol. IV, no. 4, Fall, 1994, pp. 26-44 at http://www.lib.unb.ca/Texts/JCS/CQ/vol014_4fall1994/PDF/johnson.pdf (24 Jan. 2008).

Jones, David M.; and Smith, Mike L.; and Weeding, Mark. 'Looking for the Pattern: al-Qaeda in Southeast Asia – The Genealogy of a Terror Network'. *Studies in Conflict and Terrorism*. vol. 26, 2003, pp. 443-457.

Jones, Sidney. 'Arrested Development: Jemaah Islamiyah Down But Not Out'. *JIR*, Aug. 2007, pp. 22-25.

Karasik, Theodore W.; and Cragin, Kim. 'Case Study: The Arabian Peninsula' in Rabasa, Angel M. *Ungoverned Territories: Understanding and Reducing Terrorism Risks*. Santa Monica: RAND, 2007, pp. 77-110.

Kenny, Henry J. 'The South China Sea: A Dangerous Ground'. *Naval War College Review*, Summer 1996.

Kilcullen, David J. 'Countering Global Insurgency'. *The Journal of Strategic Studies*, vol. 28, no. 4, Aug., 2005, pp. 597-617.

———. 'Counterinsurgency *Redux*'. *Survival.* vol. 48, no. 4, Winter 2006, p. 111-130 at http://www.smallwarsjournal.com/documents/kilcullen1. pdf (5 Feb. 2007).

———. 'New Paradigms for 21st Century Conflict'. *E-Journal USA*, May 2007 at http://usinfo.state.gov/journals/itps/0507/ijpe/kilcullen.htm (3 Sept. 2007).

Knights, Michael. 'Jihadist paise – Yemen's terrorist threat re-emerges'. *JIR*, May 2008.

————; and Snyder, Zach. 'The role played by funding in the Iraq insurgency'. *JIR,* Aug. 2005, pp. 8-15.

Knowles, Goon James. 'Threat Analysis: Organized Crime and Narco-Terrorism in Northern Mexico'. *Military Review,* Jan.-Feb. 2008, pp. 73-84 at http://usacac.leavenworth.army.mil/CAC/milreview/English/JanFeb08/ KnowlesEngJanFeb08.pdf (20th Feb. 2008).

Koknar, Ali M. 'Corsairs at Starboa: Jihad at Sea'. *Journal of International Security Affairs,* no. 7, Summer 2004, pp. 57-66 at http://www.securityaffairs.org/ issues/2004/07/No_7_Summer_2004_Full_Issue.pdf (29 July 2006).

Kontorovich, Eugene. 'The Piracy Analogy: Modern Universal Jurisdiction's Hollow Foundation'. *Harva International Law Review,* vol. 45, no.1, Winter 2004, pp. 183-237.

Kubarych, Roger. 'How Oil Shocks Affect Markets: Consider the Five Most Recent Scenarios'. *The International Economy Magazine,* Summer 2005 at http://findarticles.com/p/articles/mi_m2633/is_3_19/ai_n15787119 (14 Sept. 2007).

League of Nations. Committee of Experts for the Progressive Codification of International Law. 'Questionnaire no. 6: Piracy'. *The American Journal of International Law.* vol. 20, no. 3, Supplement, April 1926, pp. 222-229

Lesser, Ian O. 'Countering the New Terrorism: Implications for Strategy', in Lesser, Ian O. *et. al. Countering the New Terrorism.* Santa Monica: RAND, 1999, pp. 85-144.

Lindquist Johan. 'Modern Spaces, Wild Places and International Hinterlands: The Cultural Economy of Decoupling and Misrecognition'. *Anthropology Today,* vol. 16, no. 3, June 2000.

Lok. Joris Janssen. 'Mini-submarines and special forces pose maximum threat'. *Jane's International Defence Review,* 1st June 1998, pp. 63-8.

Luft, Gal; and Korin, Anne. 'Terrorism Goes to Sea'. *Foreign Affairs,* vol. 83, no. 6, Nov./Dec. 2004, pp. 61-71

Luis Jesus, H.E. José. 'Protection of Foreign Ships against Piracy and Terrorism at Sea: Legal Aspects'. *The International Journal of Marine and Coastal Law,* vol. 18, no. 3, 2003, pp. 363-400.

Lupsha, Peter. 'Organized Crime' in Bailey, William G., ed. *The Encyclopedia of Police Science.* New York & London: Garland Publishing, 1995, pp. 492-497.

Lutz, James M. and Lutz, Brenda J. 'Terrorism as Economic Warfare'. *Global Economy Journal,* Vol. 6 No. 2, 2006.

McAllister, Brad. 'Al Qaeda and the Innovative Firm: Demythologizing the Network'. *Studies in Conflict and Terrorism,* vol. 27, 2004, pp. 297-319.

McCaffrey, Barry R.; and Busso, John A. 'Narcotics, Terrorism, and International Crime: The Convergence Phenomenon' in Howa, Russell D.; and Sawyer, Reid L., eds. *Terrorism and Counterterrorism: Understanding the New*

Security Environment. Guildfo, CT: McGraw-Hill/Dushkin, 2003, pp. 206-211.

McKenna, James J., Jr. 'Organized Crime in the former Royal Colony of Hong Kong' in Ryan, Patrick J.; and Rush, George E., eds. *Understanding Organized Crime in Global Perspective: A Reader.* Thousand Oaks CA and London: SAGE Publications, 1997, pp.205-213.

Makarenko, Tamara. 'Countering the Terror-Crime Nexus'. *JIR,* April 2002.

———. 'The Crime-Terror Continuum: Tracing the Interplay between Transnational Organised Crime and Terrorism'. *Global Crime,* vol. 6, no. 1, Feb. 2004, pp. 129-145.

———. 'A Model of Terrorist-Criminal Relations'. *JIR,* Aug. 2003, pp. 6-11.

———. 'Transnational Crime and its Evolving Links to Terrorism and Instability'. *JIR,* Nov. 2001, pp. 22-24.

Manwaring. Max. 'New Global Security Landscape, The: The Road Ahead' in Bunker, Robert J., ed. *Networks, Terrorism and Global Insurgency.* Abingdon & New York: Routledge, 2005, pp. 20-39.

Meldrum, Catherine. 'Murky Waters: Financing Maritime Terrorism and Crime'. *JIR.* June 2007.

Menefee, Samuel Pyeatt. 'Piracy, Terrorism, and the Insurgent Passenger: A Historical and Legal Perspective' in Ronzitti, Natalino, ed. *Maritime Terrorism and International Law.* Dorecht, Boston and London: Martinus Nijhoff Publishers, 1990, pp. 43-68.

———. 'Scourges of the Sea: Piracy and Violent Maritime Crime', 1 *Marine Policy Reports,* vol. 13, Spring 1989, pp. 13-35.

———. 'Terrorism at Sea: The Historical Development of an International Legal Response' in B.A.H. Parritt, ed. *Violence at Sea.* Paris: ICC Publishing, 1986, pp. 191-220.

———. 'Under-Reporting of the Problems of Maritime Piracy and Terrorism: Are we Viewing the Tip of the Iceberg?' in Mejia, Maximo Q., Jr, (ed). *Contemporary Issues in Maritime Security.* Malmö: WMU Publications, 2005, pp. 245-263.

Morgan, John G.; and Martoglio, Charles W. '1,000-ship Navy: Global Maritime Network, The'. US Naval Institute *Proceedings,* vol. 131, no. 11, Nov. 2005, pp. 14-17.

Morris, Michael F. 'Al Qaeda as an Insurgency'. *Joint Forces Quarterly,* no. 39, Fourth Quarter, 2005, pp. 41-50 at http://www.dtic.mil/doctrine/jel/jfq_pubs/1039.pdf 26 Feb. 2007.

Mukherjee, P.K. 'Piracy, Unlawful Acts and Maritime Violence'. *The Journal of International Maritime Law'.* vol. 10, no. 4, Aug.-Sept. 2004, pp. 301-302.

Murphy, Martin N. 'The Blue, Green and Brown: Insurgency and Counter-insurgency on the Water'. *Contemporary Security Policy*, vol. 28, no. 1, April 2007, pp. 63-79.

———. 'Maritime Terrorism: The Threat in Context'. *JIR*, vol. 18, no. 2, Feb. 2006, pp. 20-25.

———. 'Maritime Threat: Tactics and Technology of the Sea Tigers'. *JIR*, vol. 18, no. 6, June 2006, pp. 6-10.

———. 'Piracy and UNCLOS: Does International Law Help Regional States Combat Piracy?' in Lehr, Peter (ed.). *Violence at Sea: Piracy in the Age of Terrorism*. New York: Routledge, 2007, pp. 155-182.

———. 'Slow Alarm: The Response of the Marine Insurance Industry to the Threat of Piracy and Maritime Terrorism'. *Maritime Studies*, no. 148, May/June 2006, pp. 1-14.

———. 'Suppression of Piracy and Maritime Terrorism: A Suitable Role for a Navy?' *Naval War College Review*, vol. 60, no. 3, Summer 2007, pp. 23-45.

———. 'Tanker Terror: The Unfounded Fear of Liquefied Gas Ships'. *JIR*, vol. 19, no. 12, Dec. 2007, pp. 20-24.

Naím, Moisés. 'Five Wars We're Losing'. *Foreign Policy*, Jan./Feb. 2003, pp. 28-37.

Netanyahu, Benjamin. 'Terrorism and the Media' in Benjamin Netanyahu, ed. *Terrorism: How The West Can Win*. New York: Avon Books, 1986, pp. 109-110.

Nichiporuk, Brian; Grammich, Cliffo; Rabasa, Angel; and DaVanzo, Julie. 'Demographics and Security in Maritime Southeast Asia'. *Georgetown Journal of International Affairs*, Winter/Spring 2006, pp. 83-91 at http://www.rand.org/pubs/reprints/2006/RAND_RP1219.pdf (1 Nov. 2007).

Nincic, Donna J. 'The Challenge of Maritime Terrorism: Threat Identification, WMD and Regime Response'. *The Journal of Strategic Studies*, vol. 28, no. 4, Aug. 2006, pp. 619-644.

———. 'Sea Lane Security and US Maritime Trade: Chokepoints as Scare Resources' in Tangredi, Sam J. *Globalization and Maritime Power*, Washington DC: National Defence UP, 2002, pp. 143-169.

Noer, John H. 'Southeast Asian Chokepoints: Keeping Sea Lines of Communication Open'. *Strategic Forum*, no. 98, Dec. 1996.

North, Douglass C. 'Sources of Productivity Change in Ocean Shipping, 1600-1850'. *Journal of Political Economy*, vol. 76, no. 5, Sept.-Oct. 1968, pp. 953-970.

O'Brien, Kevin A.; and Karasik, Theodore W. 'Case Study: West Africa' in Rabasa, Angel M. *Ungoverned Territories: Understanding and Reducing Terrorism Risks*. Santa Monica: RAND, 2007, pp. 173-205.

Office of the Defence Attaché, Permanent Mission of Nigeria to the United Nations. 'Piracy Control in Nigeria's Territorial Seas' in Ellen, Eric, ed. *Piracy at Sea*. Paris: ICC Publishing, 1989, pp. 219-223.

Oxman, Berna H. 'The Territorial Temptation: A Siren Song at Sea'. *The American Journal of International Law*, vol. 100, no. 4, Oct. 2006, pp. 830-851.

Patrick, Stewart. 'Weak States and Global Threats: Fact or Fiction?' *The Washington Quarterly*, Spring 2006, pp. 27-53 at http://www.twq.com/06spring/docs/06spring_patrick.pdf (26 May 2006).

Pearl, David. 'ONI and Combating Piracy'. *ONI Quarterly*, April 2008, pp. 4-8.

———. 'Safan Al Bisarat Hijacking: A MOTR Case Study'. *ONI Quarterly*, April 2008, pp. 9-11.

Peele, Reynolds B. 'The Importance of Maritime Chokepoints'. *Parameters*, Summer 1997, pp. 61-74.

Peiris, G.H. 'Secessionist War and Terrorism in Sri Lanka: Transnational Impulses' in Gill, A.P.S.; and Sahni, Ajai. *The Global Threat of Terror: Ideological, Material and Political Linkages*. New Delhi: Bulwark Books for The Institute of Conflict Management, 2002, pp. 85-126.

Pelkofski, James. 'Before the Storm: Al Qaeda's Coming Maritime Campaign'. US Naval Institute *Proceedings*, vol. 131, no. 12, Dec. 2005, pp. 20-24.

Peterson, M. J. 'An Historical Perspective on the Incidence of Piracy', in Eric Ellen, ed. *Piracy at Sea*. Paris: ICC Publishing, 1989, pp. 41-60.

Picarelli, John T. 'The Turbulent Nexus of Transnational Organised Crime and Terrorism: A Theory of Malevolent International Relations'. *Global Crime*, vol. 7, no. 1, Feb. 2006, pp. 1-24.

Pugh, Michael. 'Is Mahan Still Alive? State Naval Power in the International System'. *Journal of Conflict Studies*, vol. 17, no. 2, Fall 1996, pp. 109-124.

———. 'Piracy and Armed Robbery at Sea: Problems and Remedies'. *Issues of Low Intensity Conflict*, vol. 2, no. 1, Summer 1993, pp. 1-18.

Quentin, Sophia. 2003. 'Shipping Activities: Targets of Maritime Terrorism'. *MIRMAL*, vol. 2, 20 Jan. 2003 at http://www.derechomaritimo.info/pagina/mater.htm (12th June 2007).

Rabasa, Angel. 'Case Study: The Sulawesi-Mindanao Arc' in Rabasa, Angel M. *Ungoverned Territories: Understanding and Reducing Terrorism Risks*. Santa Monica: RAND, 2007, pp. 111-145.

Rapoport, David C. 'Messianic Sanctions for Terror'. *Comparative Politics*, vol. 20, no. 2, 1988, pp. 195-213.

Raymond, Catherine Zara. 'Piracy in Southeast Asia: New Trends, Issues and Responses'. *Harva Asia Quarterly*, 9 Feb. 2006 at http://www.asiaquarterly.com/index.php?option=com_content&task=view&id=30&Itemid=1 (9 Feb. 2006).

'Realistic'. 'The Route to Irrelevance – or a Wake-Up Call'. *The Naval Review*, vol. 94, no. 4, 2006, pp. 311-16.

Renwick, Neil; and Abbott, Jason. 'Piratical Violence and Maritime Security in South East Asia'. *Security Dialogue*, vol. 30, no. 2, June 1999, pp. 183-196.

Richason, Michael. 'Crimes Under Flags of Convenience'. *Maritime Studies*, no. 127, Nov./Oct. 2002, pp. 22-24.

Roach, J. Ashley. 'Enhancing Maritime Security in the Straits of Malacca and Singapore'. *Journal of International Affairs*, vol. 59, no. 1, Fall/Winter 2005, pp. 97-116.

Rodell, Paul A. 'The Philippines and the Challenge of International Terrorism' in Smith, Paul J., ed. *Terrorism and Violence in Southeast Asia: Transnational Challenges to States and Regional Stability*. Armonk, NY: M.E. Sharpe, 2005, pp. 122-142.

Ronzitti, Natalino. 'The Law of the Sea and the Use of Force Against Terrorist Activities' in Ronzitti, Natalino, ed. *Maritime Terrorism and International Law*. Dorecht, Boston and London: Martinus Nijhoff Publishers, 1990, pp 1-14.

Rosamond, Jon. 'Boaing Party: Pursuing Pirates to the World's End'. *Jane's Navy International*, vol. 112, no. 6, July/Aug. 2007, pp. 14-21.

Rosoff, H.; and von Winterfeldt, D. 'A Risk and Economic Analysis of Dirty Bomb Attacks on the Ports of Los Angeles and Long Beach'. *Risk Analysis*, vol. 27, no. 3, June 2007, pp. 533-546.

Roy, Mihir. 'The Sea Lines of Communication: An Indian Ocean Perspective' in Forbes, Andrew, ed. *The Strategic Importance of Seaborne Trade and Shipping*, Papers in Australian Maritime Affairs, no. 10, RAN Sea Power Centre, 2003, pp. 85-96.

Samaranayake, Gamini. 'Patterns of Political Violence and Responses of the Government in Sri Lanka, 1971-1996'. *Terrorism and Political Violence*, vol. 11, no. 1, Spring 1999, pp. 110-122.

Sanderson, Thomas M. 'Transnational Terror and Organized Crime: Blurring the Lines'. *SAIS Review*, vol. XXIV, no. 1, Winter-Spring 2004, pp. 49-61.

Santos, Eduao Ma R. 'Piracy and Armed Robbery against Ships in the Philippines' in Ong-Webb, Graham Gerald, ed. *Piracy, Terrorism and Securing the Malacca Straits*. Singapore: Institute for Southeast Asian Studies, 2006, pp. 37-51.

Schiller, Thomas S. 'Maritime Terrorism: The Threat' in B.A.H Parritt, ed. *Violence at Sea*. Paris: ICC Publishing, 1986, pp. 87-92.

Schmid, Alex P. 'The Links between Transnational Organized Crime and Terrorist Crime'. *Transnational Organized Crime*, vol. 2, no. 4, Winter 1996, pp. 40-82.

Sekimizu, Koji; Sainlos, Jean-Claude; and Paw, James N. 'The Marine Electronic Highway in the Straits of Malacca and Singapore – An Innovative Project for the Management of Highly Congested and Confined Waters'. *Tropi-*

cal Coasts, July 2001 at http://www.imo.org/includes/blastDataOnly.asp/
data_id%3D3670/marineelectronichighwatarticle.pdf (2 July 2007).

Shelley, Louise I. 'The Unholy Trinity: Transnational Crime, Corruption, and
Terrorism'. *Brown Journal of World Affairs,* vol. XI, Issue 2, Winter/
Spring 2005, pp. 101-111 at http://www.american.edu/traccc/resources/
publications/shelle79.pdf (10th July 2007).

———. 'Unravelling the New Criminal Nexus'. *Georgetown Journal of International Affairs,* Winter/Spring 2005, pp.5-13 at http://www.american.
edu/traccc/resources/publications/shelle64.pdf (11 July 2007).

———; and Picarelli, John. 'Methods not Motives: Implications of the Convergenece of International Organized Crime and Terrorism'. *Police Practice
and Research,* vol. 3, no. 4, 2002, pp. 305-318

———; Picarelli, John; and Corpora, Chris. 'Global Crime Inc' in Love, Maryann
Cusimano. *Beyond Sovereignty: Issues for a Global Agenda.* Second Edition. Belmont: Wadsworth Publishing, 2003, pp. 143-166 (at http://
www.american.edu/traccc/resources/publications/shelle72.pdf 8 July
2007).

Shuntian Yao. 'Privilege and Corruption: The Problems of China's Socialist Market Economy'. *American Journal of Economics and Sociology,* vol. 61, no.
1, Jan. 2002, pp. 279-299..

Silvamani, P.P. 'The LIMOs are here to stay'. *Navy Despatch,* Dec., 2005, p. 11 at
http://indiannavy.nic.in/NavDespatch05/Chapter%202.pdf

Sinai, Joshua. 'Future Trends in Worldwide Maritime Terrorism'. *The Quarterly
Journal,* vol. III, no. 1, March 2004, pp. 49-66.

Sloan, Stephen. 'Responding to the Threat' in Bunker, Robert J., ed. *Networks,
Terrorism and Global Insurgency.* Abingdon & New York: Routledge,
2005, pp. xx-xxvi.

Smith, Paul J. 'Transnational Security Threats and State Survival: A Role for the
Military?' *Parameters,* Aug. 2000, pp. 77-91.

———. 'Transnational Terrorism and the Al-Qaeda Model: Confronting New
Realities'. *Parameters,* Summer 2002, pp. 33-46.

Solomon, John; and Tan, B.C. 'Feeding the Tiger: How Sri Lakan Insurgents
Fund Their War'. *JIR,* Aug. 2007.

'Southeast Asia's Tri-boer Black Spot'. *Jane's Terrorism & Security Monitor,* May
2007, pp. 10-11.

Sprinzak Ehud. 'The Great Superterrorism Scare'. *Foreign Policy,* Fall 1998, pp.
110-134.

Steel, D G. 'Piracy – Can the Oer of the Oceans be Safeguaed?' *RUSI Journal,* vol.
140, no. 5, Oct. 1995, pp. 17-25.

Stern, Jessica. 'The Protean Enemy'. *Foreign Affairs,* vol. 82, no. 4, 2003, pp.
27-40.

Stewart, Douglas. 'Perils of the Sea – Baltimar Zephyr' in Eric Ellen, ed. *Shipping at Risk*. Paris: ICC Publishing, 1997, pp. 9-15.

Stoker, Jeremy. 'Nonintervention: Littoral Operations in the Littoral Environment', *Naval War College Review*, Autumn 1998.

Storey, Ian. 'Securing Southeast Asia's Sea Lanes: A Work in Progress'. *Asia Policy*, No. 6, July 2008, pp. 95-127 at http://nbr.org/publications/asia_policy/AP6/AP6_E_Storey.pdf (4 July 2008)

Suárez de Vivero, Juan Luis; and Mateos, Juan Carlos Rodríguez. 'New Factors in Ocean Governance: From Economic to Security-based Boundaries'. *Marine Policy*, vol. 28, Issue 2, March 2004, pp. 185-188.

Sullivan, John P. 'Maras Morphing: Revisiting Thi Generation Gangs'. *Global Crime*, vol. 7, Nos. 3-4, Aug.-Nov. 2006, pp. 487-504.

———. 'Terrorism, Crime and Private Armies' in Bunker, Robert J., ed. 2005. *Networks, Terrorism and Global Insurgency*. Abingdon & New York: Routledge, 2005, pp. 69-83.

Suryanarayan, V. 'Sea Tigers and Indian Security'. *Journal of Indian Ocean Studies*, vol. 12, no. 3, Dec., 2004, pp. 404-411.

Teitler, Ger. 'Piracy in Southeast Asia: A Historical Comparison'. *MAST*, vol. 1, no. 1, 2002, pp. 67-83.

Thackuk, Kimberley L.; and Tangredi, Sam J. 'Transnational Threats and Maritime Responses' in Tangredi, Sam J. ed.. *Globalization and Maritime Power*. Washington DC: National Defence UP, 2002, pp. 57-78.

Till, Geoffrey. 'Coastal Focus for Maritime Security'. *Jane's Navy International*, May 1996, pp. 10-19.

Treves, Tullio. 'The Rome Convention for the Suppression of Unlawful Acts Against the Safety of Maritime Navigation' in Ronzitti, Natalino, ed. *Maritime Terrorism and International Law*. Dorecht, Boston and London: Martinus Nijhoff Publishers, 1990, pp 69-90.

Truver, Scott C. 'Maritime Terrorism 1985'. US Naval Institute *Proceedings*, vol. 112, no. 5, May 1986, pp. 160-173.

———. 'Mines and Underwater IEDs in US Ports and Waterways: Context, Threats, Challenges and Solutions'. *Naval War College Review*, Winter 2007, pp. 106-127.

———. 'Mines of August: An International Whodunit'. US Naval Institute *Proceedings*, Vol. 111, No. 5, May 1985, pp. 95-117.

Turbiville, Graham H., Jr. 'Mexico's Evolving Security Posture'. *Military Review*, May-June 2001, pp. 39-46 at http://usacac.army.mil/CAC/milreview/English/MayJun01/MayJun01/turb.pdf (4 Sept. 2007).

Vagg, Jon. 'Rough Seas? Contemporary Piracy in South East Asia'. *British Journal of Criminology*, vol. 35, no. 1, 1995, pp. 63-80.

Valencia, Mark J. 'Piracy and Terrorism in Southeast Asia: Similarities, Differences and their Implications' in Johnson, Derk; and Valencia, Mark. *Piracy in*

Southeast Asia: Status, Issues and Responsibilities. Singapore: ISEAS Publications, 2005, pp. 77-102.

Veness, David. 'Terrorism and Counterterrorism: An International Perspective'. *Studies in Conflict and Terrorism,* vol. 24, 2001, pp. 407-416.

Villegas, Bernao M. 'The Philippines in 1986: Democratic Reconstruction in the post-Marcos Era'. *Asian Survey,* vol. 27, no. 2, A Survey of Asia in 1986: Part II, Feb. 1987, pp. 194-205.

Walsh, Don. 'Tourism and Terrorism: A Difficult Journey Ahead for the Cruise Ship Industry'. *Sea Power,* Dec. 2002 at http://www.navyleague.org/sea_power/dec_02_51.php (13th May 2004).

Wijesekera, Daya. 'The Liberation Tigers of Tamil Eelam (LTTE): The Asian Mafia'. *Low Intensity Conflict and Law Enforcement,* vol. 2, no. 2, Autumn 1993, pp. 308-317.

Wilkinson, Paul. 1987. 'Navies in a Terrorist World'. *Jane's Naval Review,* 1987, pp. 166-176.

———. 'Technology and Terrorism'. *Terrorism and Political Violence,* vol. 5, no. 2, Summer 1993, pp. 1-11.

———. 'Terrorism and the Maritime Environment' in Parritt, B.A.H., ed. 1986. *Violence at Sea.* Paris: ICC Publishing, 1986, pp. 27-40.

Williams, Phil. 'Combating Transnational Organized Crime' in Pumphrey, Carolyn W., ed. *Transnational Threats: Blending Law Enforcement and Military Strategies.* Carlisle, PA: US Army Wall College, Strategic Studies Institute, 2000, pp. 185-202.

———. 'Terrorism and Organized Crime: Convergence, Nexus, or Transformation?' in Jervas, Gunnar, ed. *FOA Report on Terrorism.* Stockholm: National Defence Research Establishment, (FOA-R-98-00788-170-SE), 1998, pp. 69-92.

———. 'Transnational Criminal Networks' in Arquilla, John; and Ronfeldt, David. *Networks and Netwars.* Santa Monica: RAND, 2001, pp. 61-97.

———. 'Transnational Criminal Organisations and International Security' in Arquilla, John; and Ronfeldt, David. *In Athena's Camp: Preparing for Conflict in the Information Age.* Santa Monica, RAND, 1997, pp. 315-337 at http://www.rand.org/pubs/monograph_reports/MR880/MR880.ch14.pdf (9 July 2007).

Wilson, H; and Thompson, G. 'Deaths from International Terrorism Compared with Road Crash Deaths in OECD Countries'. *Injury Prevention,* vol. 12, no. 4, 1 Aug. 2006, pp. 332-333 at http://injuryprevention.bmj.com/cgi/reprint/11/6/332 (7 Sept. 2007).

Wood, I D H. 'Piracy is Deadlier than Ever'. US Naval Institute *Proceedings, vol.* 126, no. 1, 2000, pp. 60-64.

Work, Robert O. 'On Sea Basing' in Lo, Carnes (ed.). *Reposturing the Force: US Overseas Presence in the Twenty-first Century*. Naval War College *Newport Papers 26*, Feb. 2006, pp. 95-101.

Worrall, John L. 'The Routine Activities of Maritime Piracy'. *Security Journal*, vol. 13, no. 4, Oct. 2000, pp. 35-52.

Wright, Leigh R. 'Piracy in the Southeast Asian Archipelago'. *Journal of Oriental Studies*, vol. 14, 1976, pp. 23-33.

Wright-Neville, David. 'Dangerous Dynamics: Activists, Militants and Terrorists in Southeast Asia'. *The Pacific Review*, vol. 17, no. 1, March 2004, pp. 27-46.

Young, Adam J.; and Valencia, Mark J. 'Conflation of Piracy and Terrorism in Southeast Asia: Rectitude and Utility', *Contemporary Southeast Asia*, vol. 25, no. 2, Aug. 2003, pp. 269-283.

Young, Peter Lewis. 'Mining the Straits of Southeast Asia'. *JIR*, Feb. 1996, pp. 91-94.

Zha, Daojiong; and Valencia, Mark. 'Mischief Reef: Geopolitics and Implications'. *Journal of Contemporary Asia*. 1 March 2001 at http://www.highbeam. com/library/doc3.asp?DOCID=1G1:70637976&num=2&ctrlInfo=Ro und5b%3AProd%3ASR%3AResult&ao= (11 Aug. 2004).

Zimmerman, Peter D.; and Acton, James M. 'Radiological Lessons: Radiation Weapons Beyond 'Dirty Bombs'. *JIR*, June 2007, pp. 18-22.

Zou Keyuan. 'Seeking Effectiveness for the Crackdown of Piracy at Sea'. *Journal of International Affairs*, vol. 59, no. 1, Fall/Winter, 2005, pp. 117-134.

Reports and Working Papers

Acharya, Amitav. 'Terrorism and Security in Asia: Redefining Regional Oer?' Muoch University Asia Research Centre *Working Paper no. 113*, Oct. 2004 at http://wwwarc.muoch.edu.au/wp/wp113.pdf (7 Sept. 2007).

Anderson, Patrick L. 'Lost Earnings Due to the West Coast Port Shutdown – Preliminary Estimate'. Lansing MI: Anderson Economic Group Working Paper 2002-10, 7 Oct. 2002 at http://www.andersoneconomicgroup. com/modules.php?name=Content&pa=display_aeg&doc_ID=859 (6 Sept. 2007).

Apt, Clarke C. 'The Economic Impact of Nuclear Terrorist Attacks on Freight Transport Systems in an Age of Seaport Vulnerability'. Cambridge, MA: Apt Associates, Inc. 30 April 2003. Executive Summary at http://www. abtassociates.com/reports/ES-Economic_Impact_of_Nuclear_Terrorist_Attacks.pdf (20 May 2008).

Bateman, Sam.; Raymond, Catherine Zara; and Ho, Joshua. 'Safety and Security in the Malacca and Singapore Straits'. Policy Paper. Singapore: Institute of Defence and Strategic Studies, May 2006 at http://www.rsis.edu.sg/publications/policy_papers/IDSS%20S&S%20book.pdf (7 Sept. 2007).

Berry, LaVerle; Curtis, Glenn E.; Gibbs, John N.; Hudson, Rexfo S.; Karacan, Tara; Kollars, Nina A; and Miró, Ramón. 'Nations Hospitable to Organized Crime and Terrorism'. A Report prepared for the Federal Research Division, Library of Congress, Washington, DC, Oct. 2003, at http://www.loc.gov/rr/f/pdf-files/Nats_Hospitable.pdf (22 June 2007).

Blancha, Christopher M. 'Al Qaeda: Statements and Evolving Ideology'. Washington, DC: Congressional Research Service, 20 June 2005.

Canadian Centre for Intelligence and Security Studies. 'Actual and Potential Links between Terrorism and Criminality'. *ITAC Presents: Trends in Terrorism Series,* Volume 2006-5, 2006 at http://www.csis-scrs.gc.ca/en/itac/itacdocs/2006-5.pdf (15 March 2007).

Chalk, Peter. 'Liberation Tigers of Tamil Eelam's International Organisation and Operations – A Preliminary Analysis'. Canadian Security Intelligence Service: Commentary no. 77, Winter, 1999 at http://www.fas.org/irp/world/para/docs/com77e.htm (8 March 2007).

————; and Ungerer, Carl. 'Neighbourhood Watch: The Evolving Terrorist Threat in Southeast Asia'. Australian Strategic Policy Institute Strategy Report, June 2008 at http://www.aspi.org.au/publications/publication_details.aspx?ContentID=172 (7 July 2008).

Chan, Jane. 'Southeast Asia Maritime Security Review, 2nd Quarter 2008'. S. Rajaratnam School of International Studies, Maritime Security Programme, ND, at http://www.rsis.edu.sg/research/PDF/Southeast_Asia_Maritime_Security_Review-2ndQtr08.pdf (22 July 2008).

————; and Joshua Ho. Report on Armed Robbery and Piracy in Southeast Asia 2007'. S. Rajaratnam School of International Studies, Maritime Security Programme, 31 Jan. 2008 at http://www.ntu.edu.sg/rsis/research/PDF/Armed_Robbery_and_Piracy_in_SEA-2007.pdf (14 May 2008).

————. 'Report on Armed Robbery and Piracy in Southeast Asia, 1st Quarter 2007. S. Rajaratnam School of International Studies, Maritime Security Programme, ND, at http://www.ntu.edu.sg/RSIS/research/PDF/Armed_Robbery_and_Piracy_in_SEA-1stQtr07.pdf (7 Sept. 2007).

————. 'Report on Armed Robbery and Piracy in Southeast Asia, 2nd Quarter 2007'. S. Rajaratnam School of International Studies, Maritime Security Programme, ND, at http://www.ntu.edu.sg/RSIS/research/PDF/Armed_Robbery_and_Piracy_in_SEA-2ndQtr07.pdf (7 Sept. 2007).

————. 'Report on Armed Robbery and Piracy in Southeast Asia, 1st Quarter 2008'. S. Rajaratnam School of International Studies, Maritime Security Programme, ND, at http://www.ntu.edu.sg/rsis/research/PDF/Armed_Robbery_and_Piracy_in_SEA-1stQtr08.pdf (14 May 2008).

Clarke, Richa A. 2005. 'LNG Facilities in Urban Areas: A Security Risk Management Analysis for Attorney-General Patrick Lynch, Rhode Island'. Good Harbor Consulting, May 2005, Ref: GHC-RI-0505A at http://www.projo.com/extra/2005/lng/clarkereport.pdf (3 Dec. 2005).

Cohen, Stephen S. 'Economic Impact of a West Coast Dock Shutdown'. University of California at Berkeley, Jan. 2002 at http://brie.berkeley.edu/publications/ships%202002%20final.pdf (2 Jan. 2008).

Congressional Budget Office. 'The Economic Costs of Disruptions in Container Shipments'. Washington, DC: The Congress of the United States, Congressional Budget Office, 29 March 2006 at http://www.cbo.gov/ftpdocs/71xx/doc7106/03-29-Container_Shipments.pdf (3 Jan. 2008).

Coesman, Anthony H.; and Wagner, Abraham. 'The Tanker War and the Lessons of Naval Conflict'. CSIS *Working Paper*, 26 Sept. 1993 at http://www.csis.org/media/csis/pubs/9005lessonsiraniraqii-chap14.pdf (7 Sept. 2007).

Cranfield School of Management. 'Supply Chain Vulnerability: Executive Report'. Jan. 2002 at http://www.som.cranfield.ac.uk/som/research/centres/lscm/downloads/Vulnerability_report.pdf (5 Jan. 2008).

Curtis, Glenn E.; Elan, Seth L.; Hudson, Rexfo S.; and Kollars, Nina A. 'Transnational Activities of Chinese Crime Organizations'. A Report prepared for the Federal Research Division, Library of Congress, April. Washington, DC: Federal Research Division, Library of Congress 2003 at http://www.loc.gov/rr/f/pdf-files/ChineseOrgCrime.pdf (21 June 2007).

Department of Transport (UK). *Transport Statistics Report: Maritime Statistics 2002*. London: The Stationery Office, 2003.

Eklof, Stefan.. 'The Return of Piracy: Decolonization and International Relations in a Maritime Boer Region (the Sulu Sea), 1959-63'. Lund University Centre for East and South-East Asian Studies *Working Paper no. 15*, 2005 at http://www.ace.lu.se/images/Syd_och_sydostasienstudier/working_papers/Eklof.pdf (6 Sept. 2007).

Erera, Alan; Kwek, Keng-Huat; Goswani, Nanadini; White, Chip; and Zhang, Huiwen. 'Cost of Security for Sea Cargo Transport'. The Logistics Institute – Asia Pacific. 26 May 2003 at http://www2.isye.gatech.edu/setra/reports/Security_Cost_Report_May2003.pdf (5 Jan. 2008).

Exum, Andrew. 'Hizballah at War: A Military Assessment'. *The Washington Institute for Near East Policy*, Policy Focus, no. 63, 12 Dec. 2006 at http://www.washingtoninstitute.org/templateC04.php?CID=260 (12 Aug. 2007).

Fay, James A. 'Spills and Fires from LNG and Oil Tankers in Boston Harbour', 26 March 2003 at http://www.wildcalifornia.org/cgi-files/0/pdfs/1076793808_Humboldt_Bay_LNG_Boston_Spills_Fay.pdf (3

July 2004). Also at http://www.boerpowerplants.org/pdf_docs/boston_
LNG_tanker_fire_impact.pdf

F.E.R.I.T Report. ND.

Gilmore, William. 'Agreement Concerning Co-operation in Suppressing Illicit
Maritime and Air Trafficking in Narcotic Drugs and Psychotropic Substances in the Caribbean Area, 2003.' London: The Stationary Office,
2005.

'Global Extent of Illegal Fishing, The'. A report prepared by MRAG and Fisheries Center, University of British Columbia, April 2008 at http://www.
illegal-fishing.info/uploads/MRAGExtentGlobalIllegalFishing.pdf   (9
May 2008).

Hernandez, Carolina G. 'Fighting Terrorism in Southeast Asia: A View from
the Philippines'. The Woodrow Wilson Center for Scholars. *Asia Program Special Report no. 112,*'Fighting Terrorism on the Southeast Asian
Front', June 2003, pp. 25-30 at http://www.wilsoncenter.org/topics/
pubs/Asia%20Report%20112.pdf (7 Sept. 2007).

Ho, Joshua. The Security of Regional Sea Lanes'. Singapore: Institute of Defence
and Strategic Studies, *Working Paper no. 81,* June 2005 at http://www.
rsis.edu.sg/publications/WorkingPapers/WP81.pdf (6 Sept. 2007)..

House of Commons Transport Committee. *Piracy.* HC 1026. London: The Stationery Office, 2006.

Human Rights Watch. 'Funding the 'Final War': LTTE Intimidation and Extortion in the Tamil Diaspora'. vol. 18, no. 1(c), March 2007 at http://hrw.
org/reports/2006/ltte0306/ (15 June 2007).

———. 'Lives Destroyed: Attacks Against Civilians in the Philippines'. July 2007
at   http://hrw.org/reports/2007/philippines0707/philippines_lives_de-
stroyed.pdf (22 Aug. 2007).

———. 'Rivers of Blood: Guns, Oil and Power in Nigeria's Rivers State'. Briefing
Paper, Feb. 2005 at http://hrw.org/backgrounder/africa/nigeria0205/
index.htm

———. 'Too High a Price: The Human Rights Cost of the Indonesian Military's
Economic Activities'. vol. 18, no. 5 (c), June 2006 at http://hrw.org/
reports/2006/indonesia0606/indonesia0606text.pdf (18 Jan. 2007).

———. 'Organised Maritime Crime in the Far East'. Jan. 1991.

———. 'Phantom Ships'. July 1994.

———. 'Piracy and Armed Robbery Against Ships: A Special Report'. July 1997.

———. 'Special Piracy Report'. June 1992.

———. 'Solving the Problems of Piracy and Phantom Ships'. Oct. 1997.

International Crisis Group. ' Aceh: Now for the ha part'. Asia Briefing no. 48,
29 March 2006 at http://www.crisisgroup.org/library/documents/asia/
indonesia/b48_aceh_now_for_the_ha_part.pdf (7 Sept. 2007).

———. 'Indonesia: Jemaah Islamiyah's Current Status'. Update Briefing *Asia Briefing no. 63*, 3 May 2007 at http://www.crisisgroup.org/library/documents/asia/indonesia/b63_indonesia_jemaah_islamiyah_s_current_status.pdf (15 June 2007).

———. 'Indonesian Backgrounder: How the Jemaah Islamiyah Terrorist Network Operates'. *Asia Report no. 43*, 11 Dec. 2002 at http://www.crisisgroup.org/library/documents/report_archive/A400845_11122002.pdf (15 June 2007).

———. 'Jemaah Islamiyah in South East Asia: Damaged But Still Dangerous'. *Asia Report no. 63*, 26 Aug. 2003 at http://www.crisisgroup.org/library/documents/report_archive/A401104_26082003.pdf (15 June 2007).

———. 'Nigeria: Failed Elections Failing State?' *Africa Report no. 126*, 30 May 2007 at http://www.crisisgroup.org/library/documents/africa/west_africa/126_nigeria_failed_elections.pdf (1 June 2007).

———. 'Southern Philippines Backgrounder: Terrorism and the Peace Process'. *Asia Report no. 80*, 13 July 2004 at http://www.crisisgroup.org/library/documents/asia/south_east_asia/080_southern_philippines_backgrounder_terrorism_n_peace_process.pdf (23 June 2007).

———. 'The Swamps of Insurgency: Nigeria's Delta Unrest'. *Africa Report no. 115*, 3 Aug. 2006 at http://www.crisisgroup.org/library/documents/africa/west_africa/115_the_swamps_of_insurgency_nigeria_s_delta_unrest.pdf (31 March 2008).

———. 'Terrorism in Indonesia: Nooin's Networks'. *Asia Report no. 114*, 5 May 2006 at http://www.crisisgroup.org/library/documents/asia/indonesia/114_terrorism_in_indonesia_nooin_s_networks.pdf (15 June 2007).

Kenny, Henry J. 'An Analysis of Possible Threats to Shipping in Key Southeast Asian Sea Lanes'. Alexandria Va.: Centre for Naval Analyses, Feb., 1996.

Kleiman, Mark A. R. 'Illicit Drugs and the Terrorist Threat: Causal Links and Implications for Domestic Drug Control Policy'. Congressional Research Service, RL32334; updated 20 April 2004.

Levitt, Matthew. 'Hezbollah finances: Funding the party of God'. *The Washington Institute for Near East Policy*, Feb. 2005 at http://www.washingtoninstitute.org/templateC06.php?CID=772 (17 Oct. 2006).

Liss, Carolin. 'Maritime Security in Southeast Asia: Between a Rock and a Ha Place?' Muoch University, Asia Research Centre *Working Paper no. 141*, Feb. 2007 at http://wwwarc.muoch.edu.au/wp/wp141.pdf (2 July 2007).

———. 2005. 'Private Security Companies in the Fight against Piracy in Asia'. Perth, Western Australia: Muoch University *Working Paper, no. 120*,

June 2005 at http://wwwarc.muoch.edu.au/wp/wp120.pdf (3 Aug. 2005).

Lorenz, Akiva J. 'The threat of maritime terrorism to Israel'. *Intelligence and Terrorism Information Centre at the Israel Intelligence Heritage and Commemoration Centre*, 1 Oct. 2007 at http://www.ict.org.il/apage/16357.php (24 Oct. 2007).

'MANPADS Proliferation'. Federation of American Scientists Arms Sales Monitoring Project *ISSUE Brief no. 1*, 13 Jan. 2004 at http://www.fas.org/asmp/campaigns/MANPADS/MANPADS.html (7 Sept. 2007).

Martin Associates. 'An Assessment of the Impact of West Coast Container Operations and the Potential Impacts of an Interruption of Port Operations, 2000'. Lancaster, PA: Martin Associates, 23 Oct. 2001.

Medalia, Jonathan. *Terrorist Nuclear Attacks on Seaports: Threat and Response*. Congressional Research Service, RS21293; updated 13 Aug. 2003 at http://www.fas.org/irp/crs/RS21293.pdf

Melham, G.A.; Kalelkar, A.S.; Saraf, S.; and Ozog, Henry. 'Managing LNG Risks: Separating the Facts from the Myths'. IoMosaic Corporation *White Paper*, Aug. 2006 at http://archives1.iomosaic.com/whitepapers/Managing%20LNG%20Risks.pdf (22 Aug. 2007).

OECD. 'The Economic Consequences of Terrorism'. Economics Department Working Papers no. 334, 17 July 2002 at http://www.olis.oecd.org/olis/2002doc.nsf/43bb6130e5e86e5fc12569fa005d004c/a332bc19d6f8 6f13c1256bf9005749dd/$FILE/JT00129726.PDF (1 Sept. 2007)

———. 'Security in Maritime Transport: Risk Factors and Economic Impact'. Directorate for Science, Technology and Industry, July 2003, http://www.oecd.org/dataoecd/63/13/4375896.pdf (1 Sept. 2007).

Parfomak, Paul. 'Liquefied Natural Gas (LNG) Infrastructure Security: Background and Issues for Congress'. Congressional Research Service RL32073, 16 March 2005 at http://ncseonline.org/nle/crsreports/05mar/RL32073.pdf (15 July 2006).

Perl, Raphael F. 'Trends in Terrorism'. Congressional Research Service RL33555, 21 July 2006 at http://fpc.state.gov/documents/organization/69479.pdf (31 July 2006).

———; and O'Rourke, Ronald. 'Terrorist Attack on the USS Cole: Background and Issues for Congress'. Congressional Research Service RS20721, 30 Jan. 2001 at http://www.gwu.edu/~nsarchiv/NSAEBB/NSAEBB55/crs20010130.pdf (2 Dec. 2005).

Piracy and Armed Robbery Against Ships Annual Report 2002. Barking: ICC International Maritime Bureau, 2003.

——— *and Armed Robbery Against Ships Annual Report 2003*. Barking: ICC International Maritime Bureau, 2004.

SMALL BOATS, WEAK STATES, DIRTY MONEY

——— and Armed Robbery Against Ships Annual Report 2004. Barking: ICC
   International Maritime Bureau, 2005
——— and Armed Robbery Against Ships Annual Report 2005. Barking: ICC
   International Maritime Bureau, 2006.
——— and Armed Robbery Against Ships Annual Report 2006. Barking: ICC
   International Maritime Bureau, 2007.
——— and Armed Robbery Against Ships Report for the Period 1 Jan.-31 March
   2007. Barking: ICC International Maritime Bureau, 2007.
——— and Armed Robbery Against Ships Annual Report 2007. London: ICC
   International Maritime Bureau, 2008
'Piracy-Threat at Sea: A Risk Analysis'. Munich Re Group *Knowledge Series*, 22
   Sept. 2006.
Raymond, Catherine Zara. 'Piracy in Southeast Asia: New Trends, Issues and Responses'. Institute of Defence and Strategic Studies, Working Paper no.
   89, Oct. 2005 at http://www.rsis.edu.sg/publications/WorkingPapers/
   WP89.pdf (6 Sept. 2007)..
Ribano, Clare M. 2007. 'Gangs in Central America'. Congressional Research Serv-
   ice, RL34112, 2 Aug. 2007.
Sandia National Laboratories. 'Guidance on Risk Analysis and Safety Implications
   of a Large Liquefied Natural Gas (LNG) Spill Over Water'. *Sandia Report*, Dec. 2004 (SAND2004-6258) at http://www.energy.ca.gov/lng/
   documents/2004-12_SANDIA-DOE_RISK_ANALYSIS.PDF (2 Dec.
   2005).
Schulze, Kirsten E. 'Free Aceh Movement (GAM), The: Anatomy of a Separatist
   Movement'. Policy Studies no. 2. Washington, DC: East-West Centre,
   2004 at http://www.eastwestcenter.org/fileadmin/stored/pdfs/PS002.
   pdf (6 Sept. 2007).
Singapore, Republic of. 'The Jemaah Islamiyah Arrests and the Threat of Terrorism'. *White Paper*, 7 Jan. 2003 via http://www.channelnewsasia.com/
   cna/arrests/ (29 July 2006).
Society of International Gas Tanker & Terminal Operators (SIGTTO). 'Safe Havens for Disabled Gas Carriers'. Thi Edition, 2003..
Takai, Susumu. 'Suppression of Modern Piracy and the Role of the Navy'. *NIDS
   Security Reports no.4*, National Institute for Defence Studies, Tokyo,
   March 2003, pp.38-58. at www.nids.go.jp/english/dissemination/kiyo/
   pdf/bulletin_e2002_2.pdf (9 Jan. 2005).
'Unconventional Warfare: Are US forces engaged in an 'offensive war' in the Philip-
   pines?' Focus on the Philippines *Special Reports* no. 1, Jan. 2007 at http://
   www.focusweb.org/pdf/unconventionalwarfare.pdf (28 Nov. 2007).
US Department of Energy; Office of Intelligence, Office of Threat Assessment.
   'Piracy: The Threat to Tanker Traffic'. Number 2, March 1993.

Van de Voort, Maarten; and O'Brien, Kevin A. "Seacurity': Improving the Security of the Global Sea-Container Shipping System'. RAND Europe, MR-1695-JRC, 2003 at http://www.rand.org/pubs/monograph_reports/MR1695/MR1695.pdf (23 May 2005).

Vaughn, Bruce; Chanlett-Avery, Emma; Cronin, Richa; Manyin, Mark; Niksch, Larry. 2005. 'Terrorism in Southeast Asia'. Congressional Research Service, RL31672, 7 Feb. 2005 at http://www.fas.org/sgp/crs/terror/RL31672.pdf (31 July 2006).

Warren, James F. 'A Tale of Two Centuries: The Globalisation of Maritime Raiding and Piracy in Southeast Asia at the end of the Eighteenth and Twentieth Centuries'. National University of Singapore, Asia Research Institute *Working Paper Series*, no. 2, June 2003 at http://www.ari.nus.edu.sg/docs/wps/wps03_002.pdf (6 Aug. 2006).

Commentaries and Issue Papers

Abuza, Zachary. 'Dulmatin, JI's Top Technician Trains A New Generation of Fighters'. The Jamestown Foundation *Terrorism Focus*, vol. 3, no. 26, 5 July 2006 at http://jamestown.org/terrorism/news/article.php?articleid=2370051 (19 June 2007).

———. 'Indonesia neutralizes JI as immediate threat'. The Jamestown Foundation *Terrorism Focus*, vol. 4, no. 7, 25 July 2007 at http://www.jamestown.org/terrorism/news/article.php?articleid=2373479 (19 June 2007).

———. 'Jemaah Islamiya Still a Potent Force for Violence in Southeast Asia'. The Jamestown Foundation *Terrorism Focus*, vol. 4, no. 19, 27 March 2007 at http://jamestown.org/terrorism/news/article.php?articleid=2370287 (19 June 2007).

———. 'JI's Moneyman and Top Recruiter: A Profile of Nooin Mohammed Top'. The Jamestown Foundation *Terrorism Focus*, vol. 3, no. 29, 19 June 2006 at http://www.jamestown.org/terrorism/news/article.php?articleid=2370080 (19 June 2007).

———. 'Manila Bombing Highlights Possible Shift in ASG Strategy'. The Jamestown Foundation *Terrorism Focus*, vol. 4, no. 38, 20 Nov. 2007 at http://www.jamestown.org/terrorism/news/article.php?articleid=2373800 (21 Nov. 2007).

———. 'MILF seeks leverage as fighting against Abu Sayyaf and MNLF escalates'. The Jamestown Foundation *Terrorism Focus*, vol. 4, Issue 27, 14 Aug. 2007 at http://www.jamestown.org/terrorism/news/article.php?articleid=2373617 (29 Aug. 2007).

———. 'MILF's Stalled Peace Process and its Impact on Terrorism in Southeast Asia'. The Jamestown Foundation *Terrorism Monitor*, vol. IV, Issue 14,

13 July 2006 pp. 8-10 at http://jamestown.org/terrorism/news/uploads/ TM_004_014.pdf (26 June 2007).

————. 'The Philippine Peace Process: Too Soon to Claim a Settlement with the Moro Islamic Liberation Front?' The Jebsen Center for Counter-terrorism Studies *Research Briefing Series.* vol. 3, no. 3, Feb. 2008 at http:// fletcher.tufts.edu/jebsencenter/pdfs/JCCTS_ResearchSeries_3.3_Abuza_02-2008_FINAL.pdf (10th May 2008).

————. 'Terrorism in Southeast Asia: Keeping Al-Qaeda at Bay'. The Jamestown Foundation *Terrorism Monitor,* vol. II, Issue 9, 6 May 2004, pp. 4-6 at http://www.jamestown.org/images/pdf/ter_002_009.pdf (28 Aug. 2006).

'Al Qaeda's 'Navy'—How Much of a Threat?' *Centre for Defence Information,* 20 Aug. 2003 at http://www.cdi.org/friendlyversion/printversion. cfm?documentID=1644 (2 June 2004).

Ampatuan, Taharudin Piang. 'Abu Sayyaf's New Leader: Yasser Igasan The Religious Scholar'. Rajaratnam School of International Studies *Commentaries,* 9 July 2007 at http://www.rsis.edu.sg/publications/Perspective/ RSIS0712007.pdf (4 Sept. 2007).

"Asymmetric Warfare', the USS Cole and the Intifada'. *The Estimate,* vol. XII, no. 22, 2000.

Atkin, Rupert. 'Role of insurers key to beating piracy' (Letter to the Editor). *Lloyd's List,* 18 July 2007.

Banlaoi, Rommel C. 'The Rise of the Rajah Solaiman Movement (RSM)'. Institute of Defence and Strategic Studies *Commentaries,* 9 Oct. 2006 at http:// www.rsis.edu.sg/publications/Perspective/IDSS1092006.pdf (7 Sept. 2007).

Barnicle, Jeremy, *et al.* 'Securing the Peace: An Action Strategy for Sri Lanka'. Woodrow Wilson School for Public and International Affairs, Princeton University and Centre for Strategic and International Studies, Draft, Jan. 2004 at http://www.wws.princeton.edu/research/PWReports/F03/ wws591c.pdf (22 Aug. 2007).

Ben-Zur, Barak; and Hamilton, Christopher. 'Hizbollah's Global Terror Option'. The Washington Institute for Near East Policy, Policy Watch no. 1129, 21 July 2006 at http://www.washingtoninstitute.org/templateC05. php?CID=2494 (7 Sept. 2007).

Boonaro, Federico. 'The Importance of the Spratly Islands'. *Power and Interest News Report,* 28 Nov. 2006 at http://www.pinr.com/report.php?ac=view_ printable&report_id=589&language_id=1 (28 Nov. 2006).

Brownfeld, A. 'Al-Qaeda's Drug-running Network'. *Jane's Terrorism & Security Monitor,* 1 Feb. 2004.

Chalecki, Elizabeth L. 'A New Vigilance: Identifying and Reducing the Risks of Environmental Terrorism'. *Pacific Institute for Studies in Development,*

Environment, and Security. Sept. 2001 at http://www.pacinst.org/reports/environment_and_terrorism/environmental_terrorism_final.pdf (1 Sept. 2006).

Chalk, Peter. 'Africa suffers wave of maritime violence'. RAND *Commentary*, 2001 at http://www.rand.org/commentary/040101JIR.html (22 July 2004).

Council of Foreign Relations. Backgrounder. 'Hizbollah'. Updated 17 July 2006 at http://www.cfr.org/publication/9155/ (7 Sept. 2007).

———. Backgrounder, 'Jemaah Islamiah', 13 June 2007 at http://www.cfr.org/publication/8948/jemaah_islamiyah.html?breadcrumb=%2Fissue%2F135%2Fterrorism (7 Sept. 2007).

———. Backgrounder. 'Reorganizing the Palestinian security forces', 4 Oct. 2005 at http://www.cfr.org/publication/8081/#2 (7 Sept. 2007).

Daly, John C. K. 'Al Qaeda and Maritime Terrorism (Part I)'. The Jamestown Foundation *Terrorism Monitor*, vol. 1, no. 4, 24 Oct. 2003 at http://www.jamestown.org/publications_details.php?volume_id=391&&issue_id=2873 (7 Sept. 2007).

———. 'Al Qaeda and Maritime Terrorism (Part II)'. The Jamestown Foundation *Terrorism Monitor*, vol. 1, no. 5, 7 Nov. 2003 at http://www.jamestown.org/publications_details.php?volume_id=391&issue_id=2872&article_id=23400 (7 Sept. 2007).

———. 'Courting Sharia in Indonesia'. ISN *Security Watch*, 9 July 2007 at http://www.isn.ethz.ch/news/sw/details_print.cfm?id=17837 (9 July 2007).

———. 'LTTE: Technologically Innovative Rebels'. ISN *Security Watch*, 5 June 2007 at http://www.isn.ethz.ch/news/sw/details.cfm?id=17696 (7 Sept. 2007)..

———. 'Nigeria Continues to Slide Towas Instability'. The Jamestown Foundation *Terrorism Monitor*, vol. 4, no. 24, 14 Dec. 2006 at http://www.jamestown.org/terrorism/news/uploads/TM_004_024.pdf (15 Dec. 2006).

———. 'Nigeria's Navy Struggles with Attacks on Offshore Oil Facilities'. The Jamestown Foundation *Terrorism Monitor*, Vol. 6, No. 14, 10 July 2008, pp. 6-9 at http://jamestown.org/terrorism/news/uploads/TM_006_014.pdf (11 July 2008).

———. 'The Threat to Iraqi oil'. The Jamestown Foundation *Terrorism Monitor*, vol. 2, no. 12, 17 June 2004 at http://www.jamestown.org/publications_details.php?volume_id=400&issue_id=2990&article_id=2368122 (7 Sept. 2007).

Deeb, Lara. 'Hizbollah: A Primer'. *Middle East Report Online*, 31 July 2006 at http://www.merip.org/mero/mero073106.html (7 Sept. 2007).

Dillon, Dana R. 'Piracy in Asia: A Growing Barrier to International Trade'. The Heritage Foundation *Backgrounder*, no. 1379, 22 June 2000 at http://www.heritage.org/Research/AsiaandthePacific/BG1379.cfm

Dragonette. Charles H. 'Lost at Sea' (Letter to the Editor). *Foreign Affairs*, vol. 84, no. 2, March/April, 2005, pp. 174-175.

Eklof, Stefan. 'Piracy: A Critical Perspective'. International Institute for Asian Studies. *Newsletter*. Number 36, March 2005 at http://www.iias.nl/nl/36/IIAS_NL36_12.pdf (7 Sept. 2007).

Emmers, Ralf. 'What Explains the De-escalation of the Spratly's Dispute?' Institute of Defence and Strategic Studies *Commentary*, 5 Dec. 2006 at http://www.rsis.edu.sg/publications/Perspective/IDSS1242006.pdf (7 Sept. 2007).

Fakir, Intissar. 'Yemen: Economic and Regional Challenges'. *Arab Reform Bulletin*, Vol. 6, Issue 6, July 2008 at http://www.carnegieendowment.org/publications/index.cfm?fa=view&id=20288&prog=zgp&proj=zdrl,zme#fakir (12 July 2008).

"Floating market' in illicit weapons arms terrorists'. *Jane's Terrorism & Security Monitor*, 17 May 2006.

Fo, James L. 'Radiological Dispersal Devices: Assessing the Transnational Threat'. *Strategic Forum no. 136*, March 1998 at http://www.ndu.edu/inss/strforum/SF136/forum136.html (9 Sept. 2004)

Frécon, Eric. 'Piracy in the Malacca Straits: Notes from the Field'. International Institute for Asian Studies. *Newsletter*. Number 36, March 2005 at http://www.iias.nl/nl/36/IIAS_NL36_10.pdf (7 Sept. 2007).

Greentree, Todd. 'Irregular Maritime Strategy'. (In My View), *Naval War College Review*, Vol. 61, No. 1, Winter 2008, pp. 140-1 at http://www.nwc.navy.mil/press/review/documents/NWCRW08.pdf (11 July 2008).

Gunaratna, Rohan. 'International and Regional Implications of the Sri Lankan Tamil Insurgency'. *Tamilnation.org*, 2 Dec. 1998 at http://www.tamilnation.org/ltte/98rohan.htm (8 Aug. 2005).

———. 'Trends in Maritime Terrorism – the Sri Lankan case'. *Lanka Outlook*, Autumn 1998.

Haahr-Escolano, Kathryn. 'Iran's Changing Relationship with Hizbollah'. The Jamestown Foundation *Terrorism Monitor*. vol. II, no. 19, 7 Oct. 2004, pp. 6-8 at http://jamestown.org/terrorism/news/uploads/ter_002_019.pdf (7 Sept. 2007).

Haghshenass, Fariborz. 'Iran's doctrine of asymmetric naval warfare'. The Washington Institute for Near East Policy *Policy Watch no. 1179*, 21 December 2006 at http://www.washingtoninstitute.org/templateC05.php?CID=2548 (12 May 2008).

Hansen, Morten. 'Security in Maritime Southeast Asia: Private Solutions to Public Problems'. Institute of Defence and Strategic Studies *Commentaries*, 4 May 2005 at http://www.rsis.edu.sg/publications/Perspective/IDSS222005.pdf (7 Sept. 2007).

Hanson, Stephanie. 'In West Africa, Threat of Narco-States'. Council of Foreign Relations *Daily Analysis*, 10 July 2007 at http://www.cfr.org/publication/13750/in_west_africa_threat_of_narcostates.html (7 Sept. 2007)

Hariharan. R.. 'Sri Lanka: How Strong Are The Tigers?' South East Asia Analysis Group *Note no. 297*, 28 Feb. 2006 at http://www.saag.org/%5Cnotes3%5Cnote297.html (29 Feb. 2006).

————. 'Sri Lanka: Implications of the LTTE's Delft Attack'. *India Defence*, 14 June 2007 at http://www.india-defence.com/reports-3310 (7 Sept. 2007).

————. 2005. 'Sri Lanka: Taking Stock of LTTE'. *Power and Interest News Report*, 29 July 2005 at http://www.pinr.com/report.php?ac=view_printable&report_id=336&language_id=1 (30 Aug. 2005).

Heffelfinger, Chris. 'Al-Qaeda Oil Attack Thwarted in Yemen'. The Jamestown Foundation *Terrorism Focus*, vol. III, no. 37, 26 Sept. 2006, pp. 3-4 at http://jamestown.org/terrorism/news/uploads/tf_003_037.pdf (7 Sept. 2007).

Henderson, Simon. 2006. 'Al-Qaeda Attack on Abqaiq: The Vulnerability of Saudi Oil'. The Washington Institute for Near East Policy *PolicyWatch no. 1082*, 28 Feb. 2006 at http://www.washingtoninstitute.org/templateC05.php?CID=2446 (11 March 2007).

'Hizbullah's Islamic Resistance'. *Jane's Terrorism & Security Monitor*, 13 Sept. 2006.

Ho, Joshua. 'The IMO-KL Meeting on the Straits of Malacca and Singapore'. Institute of Defence and Strategic Studies *Commentaries*, 5 Oct. 2006 at http://www.rsis.edu.sg/publications/Perspective/IDSS1072006.pdf (7 Sept. 2007).

————. 'Managing the Peace-Conflict Continuum: A Coast Gua for Singapore?' Institute of Defence and Strategic Studies *Commentaries*, 28 Nov. 2005 at http://www.ntu.edu.sg/RSIS/publications/Perspective/IDSS862005.pdf (7 March 2008).

Holt, Andrew. 'Plugging the Holes in Maritime Security'. The Jamestown Foundation *Terrorism Monitor*, vol. 2, no. 9, 6 May 2004, pp. 6-8 at http://www.jamestown.org/images/pdf/ter_002_009.pdf (7 May 2005).

Howland, Jonathan. 'Counter Maritime Terror, US Thwarts Attacks, Builds Up Foreign Navies'. *Jewish Institute for National Security Affairs Online*, 17 June 2004 at http://www.jinsa.org/articles/articles.html/function/view/categoryid/1701/documentid/2567/history/3,2360,655,1701,2567 (20 July 2004).

————. 'Hazaous Seas: Maritime Sector Vulnerable to Devastating Terrorist Attacks'. *Jewish Institute for National Security Affairs Online*, 1 April 2004 at http://www.jinsa.org/articles/articles.html/function/view/categoryid/1701/documentid/2426 (21 June 2004).

————. 'Iran, China Intent on Countering Navies'. *Jewish Institute for National Security Affairs Online,* 18 Jan. 2007 at http://www.jinsa.org/articles/articles.html/function/view/categoryid/164/documentid/3652/history/3,2360,656,164,3652 (20 Jan. 2007).

————. 'Israel's Navy Steps Up to Security Challenge in Wake of Gaza Pull-Out'. *Jewish Institute for National Security Affairs Online,* 31 May 2006 at http://www.jinsa.org/articles/articles.html/function/view/categoryid/154/documentid/3417/history/3,2360,654,154,3417 (25 July 2006).

Husick, Lawrence A.; and Gale, Stephen. 'Planning a Sea-borne Terrorist Attack'. *Foreign Policy Research Institute,* 21 March 2005 at http://www.fpri.org/enotes/20050321.americawar.husickgale.seaborneterroristattack.html (31 March 2005).

'Insurgent submersibles'. *Janes's Terrorism and Security Monitor,* June 2008, pp. 6-9..

'Intelligence Brief: M.E.N.D. Escalates Instability in Nigeria'. *Power and Interest News Report,* 27 April 2006 at http://www.pinr.com/report.php?ac=view_printable&report_id=480&language_id=1 (27 April 2006).

Ismail, Noor Huda. 'JI weakened, yet potential for violence remains'. The Jamestown Foundation *Terrorism Focus,* vol. IV, Issue 21, 3 July 2007 at http://www.jamestown.org/terrorism/news/article.php?articleid=2373515 (3 Sept. 2007).

————. 'Retracing the Steps of JI's Abdullah Sunata'. The Jamestown Foundation *Terrorism Monitor,* vol. V, Issue 4, 1 March, 2007 pp. 9-11 at http://jamestown.org/terrorism/news/uploads/TM_005_004.pdf (13th March 2007).

'Jemaah Islamiyah's Abu Dujana'. *Jane's Terrorism and Security Monitor,* 11 July 2007.

Ji Guoxing. 'SLOC Security in the Asia Pacific'. Asia-Pacific Centre for Security Studies: *Centre Occasional Paper,* Feb. 2000 at http://www.apcss.org/Publications/Ocasional%20Papers/OPSloc.htm (2 April 2004).

'Jihadist alliances in Southeast Asia'. *Jane's Terrorism & Security Monitor,* 15 March 2006.

Johnsen, Gregory D. 'Al-Qaeda in Yemen Reorganizes under Nasir al-Wahayshi'. The Jamestown Foundation *Terrorism Monitor,* vol. V, Issue 11, 18 March 2008 at http://www.jamestown.org/terrorism/news/article.php?articleid=2374041 (18 March 2008).

————. 'Is al-Qaeda in Yemen re-grouping?' The Jamestown Foundation *Terrorism Focus,* vol. IV, Issue 15, 22 May 2007, p. 1 at http://jamestown.org/terrorism/news/uploads/tf_004_015.pdf (10th July 2007).

————. 'Tracking Yemen's 23 Escaped Jihai Operatives – Part 1'. The Jamestown Foundation *Terrorism Monitor,* vol. V, Issue 18, 27 Sept. 2007, pp. 5-7

at http://www.jamestown.org/terrorism/news/uploads/TM_005_018.
pdf (28 Sept. 2007).

———. 'Yemen Faces Second Generation of Islamist Militants'. The Jamestown
Foundation *Terrorism Focus,* vol. IV, Issue 27, 14 Aug. 2007 at http://
www.jamestown.org/terrorism/news/article.php?articleid=2373616

———; and O'Neill, Brian. 'Yemen Attack Reveals Struggle Among Al-Qaeda's
Ranks'. The Jamestown Foundation *Terrorism Focus,* vol. IV, Issue 22,
10 July 2007, p. 2 at http://jamestown.org/terrorism/news/uploads/
tf_004_022.pdf (10th July 2007).

Joshap, Rohan. 'Sri Lankan Navy...LTTE Sea Tigers and the Right to Territorial Seas'. Sri Lankan Ministry of Defence: The Media Centre for National Security, 21 July 2006 at http://www.nationalsecurity.lk/fullnews.
php?id=299 (7 Sept. 2007)

Kassim, Yang Razali. 'GAM, Islam and the Future of Aceh'. Institute of Defence
and Strategic Studies *Commentaries,* 8 Feb. 2005 at http://www.rsis.edu.
sg/publications/Perspective/IDSS072005.pdf (7 Sept. 2007).

Kuranar, Gurpreet S. "'Thousand-Ship Navy': A Reincarnation of Controversial
PSI?' Institute for Defence Studies and Analysis (New Delhi), *Strategic
Comments,* 28 Dec. 2006 at http://www.idsa.in/publications/stratcom-
ments/GurpreetKhurana281206.htm (7 Sept. 2007).

Larsen, Randall J. 'Rethinking Boer Security'. *The Institute of Homeland Security
White Paper,* 1 Nov. 2005 at http://tihls.org/White_Paper__Rethink-
ing_Boer_Security_1_Nov_05.pdf (1 Dec. 2005).

Lauer, Martha. 'Mexican Drug Policy: Internal Corruption in an Externalized
War'. Council on Hemispheric Relations *Press Release,* 26 June 2007
at http://www.coha.org/2007/06/26/mexican-drug-policy-internal-cor-
ruption-in-an-externalized-war/ (25 Aug. 2007).

'Liquid Natural Gas Terrorism'. *Jane's Terrorism and Security Monitor,* 12 Sept.
2007.

Liss, Carolin. 'The Roots of Piracy in Southeast Asia'. *Austral Policy Forum,*
07-18A, 22 Oct. 2007 at http://www.globalcollab.org/Nautilus/aus-
tralia/apsnet/policy-forum/2007/the-roots-of-piracy-in-southeast-
asia/?searchterm=carolin%20Liss (6 Jan. 2008).

Logan, Samuel. 2006. 'Brazil's P.C.C.: The True Power Behind the Violence'.
Power and Interest News Report, 24 May 2006 at http://www.pinr.com/
report.php?ac=view_printable&report_id=495&language_id=1 (7 Sept.
2007).

———. 'Governance in Guatemala Increasingly Threatened by Organized Crime'.
Power and Interest News Report, 19 Oct. 2007 at http://www.pinr.com/
report.php?ac=view_printable&report_id=703&language_id=1 (24 Oct.
2007).

————; and McCarty, M. Casey. 'Violence on the US-Mexico Boer'. ISN *Security Watch*, 29 Jan. 2008 at http://www.isn.ethz.ch/news/sw/details_print. cfm?id=18581 (29 Jan. 2008).

McGregor, Andrew. 'Al-Qaeda's Great Escape in Yemen'. The Jamestown Foundation *Terrorism Focus*, vol. III, Issue 5, 7 Feb. 2006 at http://www.jamestown.org/terrorism/news/article.php?issue_id=3611 (27 Jan. 2007).

————. 'Shi'ite Insurgency in Yemen: Iranian Intervention of Mountain Revolt?' The Jamestown Foundation *Terrorism Monitor*, vol. II, Issue 16, 12 Aug. 2004, pp. 4-6 at http://jamestown.org/terrorism/news/uploads/ter_002_016.pdf (9 July 2007).

Mannes, Aaron. 'A life of terror: Abu Abbas dies'. *National Review Online*, 10 March 2004 at http://www.nationalreview.com/comment/mannes200403101409.asp (8 Dec. 2007).

Manoharan, N. 'Tigers with Fins: Naval Wing of the LTTE'. Institute of Peace and Conflict Studies *Article no. 1757*, 31 May 2005 at http://www.ipcs.org/whatsNewArticle11.jsp?action=showView&kValue=1770&status=article&mod=b (21 Oct. 2006).

Marquardt, Erich. 'Examining the Threats to Indonesia's National Interests'. *Power and Interest News Report*, 2 March 2005 at http://www.pinr.com/report.php?ac=view_printable&report_id=274&language_id=1 (9 Aug. 2005).

————. 'Mujahid Dokubo-Asari: The Niger Delta's Ijaw Leader'. The Jamestown Foundation *Terrorism Monitor*, vol. V, Issue 15, 2 Aug. 2007, pp. 1-4 at http://www.jamestown.org/terrorism/news/uploads/TM_005_015.pdf (2 Aug. 2007).

Mbachu, Dulue. 'Niger Delta: Nowhere to Hide'. ISN *Security Watch*, 27 June 2008 at http://www.isn.ethz.ch/news/sw/details.cfm?id=19131 (30 June 2008).

————. 'Niger Delta: 'Robin Hood' has a face'. ISN *Security Watch*, 26 March 2008 at http://www.isn.ethz.ch/news/sw/details.cfm?id=18787 (31 March 2008).

————. 'Nigeria: Tensions over Bakassi Peninsula'. ISN Security Watch, 21 July 2008 at http://www.isn.ethz.ch/news/sw/details.cfm?id=19216 (21 July 2008).

————. 'The Poverty of Oil Wealth in Nigeria's Delta'. ISN *Security Watch*, 3 Feb. 2006 at http://www.isn.ethz.ch/news/sw/details.cfm?ID=14670 (3 Feb. 2006).

————. 'The West Africa-South America Drug Route'. ISN *Security Watch*, 28 Feb. 2008 at http://www.isn.ethz.ch/news/sw/details.cfm?id=18702 (28 Feb. 2008).

'Mexico's three reasons to be fearful'. *Jane's Foreign Report*, no. 2936, 12 July 2007, pp. 1-3.

Moran, Dominic. "Al-Qaida' hits back in Yemen'. ISN *Security Watch,* 17 Nov. 2006 at http://www.isn.ethz.ch/news/sw/details_print.cfm?id=16930 (17 Nov. 2006).

———. 'Yemeni unity questioned'. ISN *Security Watch,* 12 Sept. 2007 at http://www.isn.ethz.ch/news/sw/details.cfm?id=18109 (13 Sept. 2007).

———. 'Yemen violence raises nuclear questions'. ISN *Security Watch,* 9 July 2007 at http://www.isn.ethz.ch/news/sw/details.cfm?id=17841 (9 July 2007).

Muthucumaran, S. 'The Sea Rights of States in Formation'. *SiberNews,* 15 May 2006 at http://www.sibernews.com/the-news/featured-articles/the-sea-rights-of-states-in-formation-200605154303/ (7 Sept. 2007).

'New People's Army'. *Jane's Terrorism & Security Monitor,* 6 June 2006.

Okonta, Ike. 'MEND: Anatomy of a People's Militia'. *Pambazuka News,* 2 Nov. 2006 at http://www.pambazuka.org/en/category/features/38119 and at http://www.dawodu.com/okonta2.htm (7 Aug. 2007).

———. 'Niger Delta: Behind the Mask'. *Pambazuka News,* 26 Oct. 2006 at http://www.pambazuka.org/en/category/features/38005 (7 Aug. 2007).

O'Neill, Brian. 'Al-Qaeda New Haliners in Yemen Strike Western Interests'. The Janestown Foundation *Terrorism Focus,* Vol, 5, Issue 15, 16 April 2008 at http://www.jamestown.org/terrorism/news/article.php?articleid=2374103 (16 April 2008).

———. 'Yemen's Three Rebellions'. The Jamestown Foundation *Terrorism Monitor,* Vol, VI, Issue 10, 15 May 2008, pp. 7-9 at http://jamestown.org/terrorism/news/uploads/TM_006_010.pdf (16 May 2008).

Ong, Graham Gera; and Ho, Joshua. 2005. 'Maritime Air Patrols: The New Weapon against Piracy in the Malacca Straits'. Institute of Defence and Strategic Studies *Commentaries,* no. 70, 13 Oct. 2005 at http://www.rsis.edu.sg/publications/Perspective/IDSS702005.pdf (7 Sept. 2007).

'Philippines grapples with guerrillas'. *Jane's Terrorism and Security Monitor,* Jan. 2008, pp. 14-16.

Raman, B. 'Action Against LTTE's Gun-Running - International Terrorism Monitor: Paper no. 190. South Asia Analysis Group *Paper no. 2138,* 16 Feb. 2007 at http://www.saag.org/%5Cpapers22%5Cpaper2138.html (29 Feb. 2007).

———. 'Action Against LTTE's Maritime Terrorism - International Terrorism Monitor: Paper no. 58'. South Asia Analysis Group *Paper no. 1802,* 18 May 2006 at http://www.saag.org/papers19/paper1802.html (19 May 2006).

———. 'Dawood Ibrahim: The Global Terrorist'. South Asia Analysis Group *Paper no. 818,* 19 Oct. 2003 at http://www.saag.org/papers9/paper818.html (22 June 2004).

———. LTTE: Diminishing Options and Assets – International Terrorism Monitor – Paper No. 354'. South Asia Analysis Group *Paper No. 2557,* 18

January 2008 at http://www.southasiaanalysis.org/papers26/paper2557. html (26 May 2008).

———. 'Maritime Terrorism: An Indian Perspective'. South Asia Analysis Group *Paper no. 1154*, 29 Oct. 2004 at http://www.saag. org/%5Cpapers12%5Cpaper1154.html (9 Aug. 2006).

———. 'The Omens from Katunayake'. South Asia Analysis Group *Paper no. 285*, 26 July 2001 at http://www.saag.org/%5Cpapers3%5Cpaper285.html (7 Sept. 2007).

Ramasubramanian, R. 'Human Smuggling in Sri Lanka'. Institute of Peace and Conflict Studies *Article no. 1383*, 6 May 2004 at http://www.ipcs.org/ printArticle.jsp?kValue=1383 (4 July 2007).

Raufer, Xavier. 'Gray Areas: A New Security Threat'. Institute for International Studies *Political Warfare: Intelligence, Active Measures and Terrorism Report*, no. 20, Spring 1992, pp. 1, 4-7 & 18.

Raymond, Catherine Zara. 'The Malacca Straits and the Threat of Maritime Terrorism,'. *Power and Interest News Report*, 24 Aug. 2005 at http://www. pinr.com/report.php?ac=view_printable&report_id=352&language_ id=1 (24 Aug. 2005). Also available as 'Storm over the Malacca Strait'. 2005. *Asia Times Online* 25 Aug. at http://www.atimes.com/atimes/ Southeast_Asia/GH25Ae03.html.

Roughneen, Simon. 'Philippine Escalation May Speak Wider War'. ISN *Security Watch*, 21 Aug. 2007 at http://www.isn.ethz.ch/news/sw/details. cfm?id=18019 (22 Aug. 2007).

Roul, Animesh. 'Sri Lanka: Rebels with an Air Force'. ISN *Security Watch*, 2 May 2007 at http://www.isn.ethz.ch/news/sw/details.cfm?id=17559 (7 Sept. 2007).

Sakhuja, Vijay. 'Casablanca: Al Qaeda's Maritime Node'. Institute of Peace and Conflict Studies. *Article no. 1039*, 21 May 2003.

———. 'The Dynamics of LTTE's Commercial Maritime Infrastructure'. Observer Research Foundation *Occasional Paper*, April 2006 at http://www. observerindia.com/cms/export/orfonline/modules/occasionalpaper/at-tachments/ltte_1163397851109.pdf (12th Aug. 2008).

———. 'Indian Ocean and the Safety of Sea Lines of Communication'. *Strategic Analysis*, Aug., vol. XXV, no. 5, 2001, pp. 688-689.

———. 'Malacca: Who's To Pay For Smooth Sailing?' *Asia Times*, 16 May 2007.

———. 'Maritime Legal Conundrum'. Institute of Peace and Conflict Studies *Paper no. 1778*, 29 June 2005 at http://www.ipcs.org/India_articles2.j sp?action=showView&kValue=1791&country=1016&status=article&m od=a (9 July 2006).

———. 'Maritime Oer and Piracy'. *Strategic Analysis*, vol. XXIV, no. 5, Aug. 2000, pp. 923-938.

————. 'Mini Submarine – A Vessel of Choice with Drug Cartels and Terrorists'. South Asia Analysis Group, *Paper no. 1313*, 30 March 2005 at http://www.saag.org/papers14/paper1312.html (23 April 2005).

————. 'Sea Muggers Back in the Malacca Straits, The'. South Asia Analysis Group, *Paper no. 1300*, 23 March 2005 at http://www.saag.org/papers13/paper1300.html (23 April 2005).

————. 'Sea Piracy: India Boosts Countermeasures'. Institute of Peace and Conflict Studies. *Article no. 987*, 14 March 2003.

————. 'Sea Piracy in South Asia'. South Asia Analysis Group *Paper no. 1259*, 18 Feb. 2005 at http://www.saag.org/papers13/paper1259.html (15 March 2007).

————. 'Terrorist's Underwater Strategy'. Institute of Peace and Conflict Studies. *Article no. 1679*, 22 March 2005.

————. 'Who Steer's Al Qaeda's Fleet?' Institute of Peace and Conflict Studies. *Article no. 975*, 28 Feb. 2003 at http://www.ipcs.org/printArticle.jsp?kValue=975 (4 July 2007).

Sawhney, Rajeev. 'Redefining the Limits of the Straits: A Composite Malacca Straits Security System'. Institute of Defence and Strategic Studies *Commentaries*, 18 May 2006 at http://www.rsis.edu.sg/publications/Perspective/IDSS0372006.pdf (7 Sept. 2007).

Scheuer, Michael. 'Abu Yahya al-Libi: Al Qaeda's Theological Enforcer – Part 1'. The Jamestown Foundation *Terrorism Focus*, vol. IV, Issue 25, 31 July 2007 at http://www.jamestown.org/terrorism/news/article.php?articleid=2373586 (7 Sept. 2007).

————. 'Aby Yahya al-Libi: Al Qaeda's Theological Enforcer – Part 2'. The Jamestown Foundation *Terrorism Focus*, vol. IV, Issue 27, 14 Aug. 2007 at http://www.jamestown.org/terrorism/news/article.php?articleid=2373619 (14 May 2008).

————. 'Yemen's Role in al-Qaeda's Strategy'. The Jamestown Foundation *Terrorism Focus*, vol. V, Issue 5, 5 Feb. 2008 at http://www.jamestown.org/terrorism/news/article.php?articleid=2373951 (10 Feb. 2008).

Shiiq, Said. 'Puntland: The Epicenter of Somalia's Piracy and Human Trafficking'. *Garowe Online*, 28 Dec. 2007 at http://www.garoweonline.com/artman2/publish/Opinion_20/Puntland_The_Epicenter_of_Somalia_s_Piracy_and_Human_Trafficking.shtml (29 Dec. 2007).

Silvamani, P.P.. 'The LIMOs are here to stay'. *Navy Despatch*, Dec. 2005 at http://indiannavy.nic.in/NavDespatch05/Chapter%202.pdf (7 Sept. 2007).

Smith, Daniel V. 'Terrorist attack on the *USS Cole*'. Jewish Institute of National Security Affairs *Online*, 13 Oct. 2000 at http://www.jinsa.org/articles/articles.html/function/view/categoryid/164/documentid/1047/history/3,2360,656,164,1047 (20 July 2004).

Sharp, Jeremy M. 'Yemen: Where is the Stability Tipping Point?'. *Arab Reform Bulletin*, Vol. 6, Issue 6, July 2008 at http://www.carnegieendowment. org/publications/index.cfm?fa=view&id=20288&prog=zgp&proj=zdrl,z me#sharp (12 July 2008).

'Southeast Asia's tri-boer black spot'. *Jane's Terrorism & Security Monitor*, May 2007, pp. 10-11.

Spencer, Kirk; and Telenko, Trent. 'An Analysis of the Hizbollah Anti-ship Missile Strike: The Attack on the INS Ani –Hanit'. *Israel Resource Review*, 25 July 2006 at http://israelbehindthenews.com/Archives/Jul-25-06. htm#OnTheMark (7 Sept. 2007).

'Sri Lanka: Bloody Mindsets'. ISN *Security Watch*, 24 July 2007 at http://www.isn. ethz.ch/news/sw/details_print.cfm?id=17901 (24 July 2007).

Storey, Ian. 'The Triboer Sea Area: Maritime Southeast Asia's Ungoverned Space'. The Jamestown Foundation *Terrorism Monitor*, vol. V, Issue 19, 11 Oct. 2007, pp. 1-4 at http://www.jamestown.org/terrorism/news/uploads/ TM_005_019.pdf (11 Oct. 2007) also available at "Triboer sea' is SE Asian danger zone'. *Asia Times Online*, 18 Oct. 2007 at http://www. atimes.com/atimes/Southeast_Asia/IJ18Ae01.html.

Thackuk, Kimberley L. 'Terrorism's Financial Lifeline: Can It Be Severed?' *Strategic Forum no. 191*, May 2002 at http://www.ndu.edu/inss/strforum/ SF191/SF191.pdf

Thomas, Bobby. 'Malacca Straits a 'war risk zone'? Lloyd's should review its assessment'. Institute of Defence and Strategic Studies *Commentaries*, 19 Aug. 2005 at http://www.rsis.edu.sg/publications/Perspective/IDSS572005. pdf(7 Sept. 2007).

'Tigers suffer setbacks'. *Jane's Terrorism and Security Monitor*, Jan. 2008, pp. 12-13.

Vasan, R.S. 'Alondra Rainbow Revisited: A Study of Related Issues in the Light of the Recent Judgement of Mumbai High Court'. South Asia Analysis Group *Paper no. 1379*, 13 May 2005 at http://saag.org/papers14/ paper1379.html (9 July 2006).

———. 'Incident Analysis: Sinking of SLN Dvora Craft on 22nd March 2008'. South Asia Analysis Group *Paper No. 2652*, 28 March 2008 at http:// www.southasiaanalysis.org/papers27/paper2652.html (25 May 2008).

———. 'Sea Control and the LTTE'. Observer Research Foundation *Strategic Trends*. vol. IV. Issue 27. 7 Aug. 2006.

———. 'Sri Lanka: Sinking of A 520/MV Invincible in Trincomalee'. South Asia Analysis Group *Paper No. 2700*, 13 May 2008 at http://www.southasiaanalysis.org/papers27/paper2700.html (26 May 2008).

Waterman, Shaun. 'Tamil Moves in N America Cause Concern'. ISN *Security Watch*, 29 Aug. 2006 at http://www.isn.ethz.ch/news/sw/details. cfm?ID=16587 (30 Aug. 2007).

Watkins, Eric. 'Facing the Terrorist Threat in the Malacca Strait'. The Jamestown Foundation *Terrorism Monitor*, vol. 2, no. 9. 6 May 2004 at http://www.jamestown.org/images/pdf/ter_002_009.pdf

Wellington, Bestman. 'Nigeria's Cults and their Role in the Niger Delta Insurgency'. The Jamestown Foundation *Terrorism Monitor*, vol. V, Issue 13, 6 July 2007, pp. 8-10 at http://www.jamestown.org/terrorism/news/uploads/TM_005_013.pdf (7 Aug. 2007).

———. 'Origin of the Niger Delta's Deewell and Deebarn Militias'. The Jamestown Foundation *Terrorism Monitor,* vol. V, Issue 18, 27 Sept. 2007, pp. 10-12 at http://www.jamestown.org/terrorism/news/uploads/TM_005_018.pdf (accessed 28 Sept. 2007).

West, Sungata. 'Piracy Revenues Financing Warlos in Somali Insurgency'. The Jamestown Foundation *Terrorism Focus*, vol. IV, Issue 42, 19 Dec. 2007 at http://www.jamestown.org/terrorism/news/article.php?articleid=2373863 (20 Dec. 2007).

Wu, Friedrich. 'China's Losing Battle against Corruption'. Institute of Defence and Strategic Studies *Commentaries,* 17 Oct. 2006 at http://www.rsis.edu.sg/publications/Perspective/IDSS1132006.pdf (18 Jan. 2007).

Yamada, Yoshihikio. 'Defending Asian Seas from Marauding by Pirates'. The Tokyo Foundation *Japanese Dynamism no. 6,* March 2004.

Zimmerman, Peter D; with Loeb, Cheryl. 'Dirty Bombs: The Threat Revisited'. *Defence Horizons no. 38,* Jan. 2004 at http://www.ndu.edu/ctnsp/DH38.pdf (6 July 2004).

Blogs, Conference Papers, Dissertations, Interviews, Presentations,Recommendations, Testimony and Theses

Abhyankar, Jayant. 'Piracy – A Growing Menace'. Paper presented at the Okazaki Institute conference, 'Combating Piracy and Armed Robbery at Sea: Charting the Future in Asia-Pacific Waters', Bangkok, 24-25 March 2001.

Abuza, Zachary. 'Abu Sayyaf Chieftain Khadaffi Janjalani Reported Killed'. *The Counterterrorism Blog,* 28 Dec. 2006 at http://counterterrorismblog.org/2006/12/abu_sayyaf_chieftain_khadaffy.php (26 June 2007).

———. 'Activating Hizbollah cells 'to make no place safe for Israelis': The Implications for Southeast Asia'. *The Counterterrorism Blog,* 25 July 2006 at http://counterterrorismblog.org/2006/07/activating_Hizbollah_cells_to.php (7 Sept. 2007).

———. 'Comments as part of USIP Current Issue Briefing 'Crunchtime for Mindanao Peace Process?' 8 Feb. 2005 at http://www.usip.org/philippines/reports/mindanao_abuza.html (4 Aug. 2006).

————. 'MILF and GRP served notice'. *The Counterterrorism Blog*, 31 March 2005 at http://counterterror.typepad.com/the_counterterrorism_blog/2005/03/milf_grp_served.html (7 Sept. 2007).

'Aden-Abyan Islamic Army' *GlobalSecurity.org*. ND at http://www.globalsecurity.org/military/world/para/aden-abyan.htm (14 Sept. 2007).

Agbakoba, Edwa G. 'The Fight against Piracy and Armed Robbery against Ships', International Maritime Organisation, ND at http://home.wanadoo.nl/m.bruyneel/archive/modern/imopirac.htm (3 May 2004).

'Al-Qaeda Affiliated E-Journal: 'The Sea is The Next Strategic Step Towas Controlling The World And Restoring The Islamic Caliphate''. MEMRI, 1 May 2008 at http://memriiwmp.org/content/en/blog_personal.htm?id=378 (9 May 2008).

Amaechi, Chibuike Rotimi. 'Fundamental Causes of Maritime Insecurity'. A lecture delivered to a workshop on combating piracy and armed robbery at sea organised by the Joint Standing Committee of the Nigerian Maritime Administration and Safety Agency (NIMSA) and the Nigerian Navy at Abuja, and published by *The Tide Online*, 6 May 2008 at http://www.thetidenews.com/article.aspx?qate=05/06/2008&qrTitle=Fundamenta l%20causes%20of%20maritime%20insecurity&qrColumn=FOR%20THE%20RECOS (7 May 2008).

Anderson, James H. 'International Terrorism and Crime: Trends and Linkages', ND.

Banlaoi, Rommel C. 'Leadership Dynamics in Terrorist Organizations in Southeast Asia: The Abu Sayyaf Case'. A Paper presented at the international symposium, 'The Dynamics and Structures of Terrorist Threats in Southeast Asia' organized by the Institute of Defense Analyses in cooperation with the Southeast Asia Regional Centre for Counter-Terrorism and US Pacific Command held at the Palace of Golden Horses Hotel, Kuala Lumper, Malaysia, 18-20 April 2005.

Bateman, Sam. 'Maritime Transnational Violence - Problems of Control and Jurisdiction', Paper for Seminar on 'Transnational Crime' at the APCSS Biennial Conference, Honolulu, 16-18 July 2002.

————. 'Sea Lane Security'. A paper presented at the APEC High-Level Meeting on Maritime Security Cooperation held in Manila, 8 ̄9 Sept. 2003.

Bruyneel, Mark. 'Current reports on piracy by the IMO and IMB – a comparison', Paper prepared for the People and the Sea II Conference organised by the Centre for Maritime Research (MARE) and the International Institute for Asian Studies (IIAS), Amsteam, 4 - 6 Sept., 2003 at http://home.wanadoo.nl/m.bruyneel/archive/modern/CurrentreportsonpiracybytheIMOandtheIMB.pdf (7 Sept. 2007).

———. 'Modern-day Piracy Statistics'. 7 Feb. 2001 (updated 28 Nov. 2001) available at http://home.wanadoo.nl/m.bruyneel/archive/modern/figures.htm (7 Sept. 2007).

———. 'MT Global Mars attack, The'. April 2000 at http://home.wanadoo.nl/m.bruyneel/archive/modern/global.htm (7 Sept. 2007).

———. 'Tale of a Modern Pirate Gang', 21 Nov. 2000 at http://home.wanadoo.nl/m.bruyneel/archive/modern/gang.htm (3 May 2004).

Burnell, Jamie. 'Securing the Seas in Southeast Asia'. International Centre for Political Violence and Terrorism Research, ND, at http://www.intertanko.com/pubupload/jamie.ppt (7 Sept. 2007).

Carafano, James Jay. 'Port Security and Foreign-owned Maritime Infrastructure: Statement before the House Committee on Transportation and Infrastructure, Subcommittee on Coast Gua and Maritime Transportation'. *The Heritage Foundation*, 9 March 2006 at http://www.heritage.org/Research/HomelandDefense/tst030606a.cfm (13 March 2006).

Chalk, Peter. 'Threats to the Maritime Environment: Piracy and Terrorism', *Presentation to RAND Stakeholder Consultation*, 28-30 Oct. 2002.

Chong Chee Kin. 'Attack is no surprise for Semporna folk'. Unpublished communication, 29 April 2000 at http://www.malaysia.net/lists/sangkancil/2000-04/msg01132.html (3 July 2007).

Cilluffo, Frank. 'The Threat Posed from Convergence of Organized Crime, Drug Trafficking, and Terrorism'. Testimony before the US House Committee on the Judiciary, Subcommittee on Crime. *CSIS on the Hill*, 13 Dec. 2000.

Coffen-Smout, Scott. 'Pirates, Warlos and Rogue Fishing Vessels in Somalia's Unruly Seas'. ND at http://www.chebucto.ns.ca/~ar120/somalia.html (6 July 2006).

Combatant Status Review Tribunal. Hearing for ISN 10014, Walid Muhammad bin Attash, 12 March 2007 at http://www.defenselink.mil/news/transcript_ISN10014.pdf (7 Sept. 2007).

——— Status Review Tribunal. Hearing for ISN 10015, Abd al Rahim al Nashiri, 14 March 2007 at http://www.globalsecurity.org/security/library/report/2007/al-nashiri_csrt-hearing070314.htm (7 Sept. 2007).

Crenshaw, Martha. 'The Strategic Development of Terrorism'. A paper delivered at the Annual Meeting of the American Political Science Association, New Orleans, Aug./Sept. 1985.

'DCI's Worldwide Threat Briefing – The Threat in 2003'. As prepared for delivery to the US Senate Select Committee on Intelligence, 11 Feb. 2003 at http://www.fas.org/irp/congress/2003_hr/021103tenet.html (7 Sept. 2007).

457

Dillon, Dana R. 'Southeast Asia and the brotherhood of terrorism'. The Heritage Foundation *Heritage Lectures*, 20 Dec. 2004 at http://www.heritage.org/Research/AsiaandthePacific/hl860.cfm (7 Sept. 2007).

Dishman, Chris. 'Transnational Organized Crime, Terrorism, and Terrorism Funding', 10 Jan. 2007.

'Drug Cartels: Arellano-Felix Organization'. DEA Background Information, Feb. 1997 at http://www.pbs.org/wgbh/pages/frontline/shows/mexico/etc/arellano.html (24 Aug. 2007).

Ebersold, William B. 'Cruise Industry in Figures'. *Business Briefing: Global Cruise 2004*, pp. 15-16 available at http://www.touchbriefings.com/pdf/858/ebersold.pdf (7 Sept. 2007).

European Fertiliser Manufacturers Association. 'Guidance for Sea Transport of Ammonium Nitrate Based Fertilisers'. 2004 at http://www.efma.org/publications/Sea%20Transport/Sea%20Transport.pdf (7 Sept. 2007).

'Factsheet on the Regional Cooperation Agreement on Combating Piracy and Armed Robbery Against Ships in Asia (RECAAP)'. ND.

Farley, Mark C. 'International and Regional Trends in Maritime Piracy, 1989-1993'. Monterey: Naval Postgraduate School. Masters Thesis. 1993.

Foreign Policy and the Fund for Peace. 'The Failed States Index 2007'. *Foreign Policy*, July/Aug. 2007 at http://www.foreignpolicy.com/story/cms.php?story_id=3865 (7 Sept. 2007).

Foreign Terrorist Organizations. Gama's al-Islamiyya (IG) at http://www.state.gov/documents/organization/65479.pdf (7 Sept. 2007).

Frécon, Eric. 'Belakang Padang and Jemaja: Two Indonesian Islands Plagued by Piracy'. Paper presented at the International Institute for Asian Studies (IIAS) Conference on 'Ports, Pirates and Hinterlands in East and Southeast Asia: Historical and Contemporary Perspectives' held in Shanghai, 10-12 Nov. 2005.

———. 'Jolly Roger over Southeast Asia: History of the Resurgence of the Sea Piracy'. Unpublished English translation, 2005.

———. 'Pirates Set the Straits on Fire: Causes and Contexts of the Pirate Arsons in the Malay Archipelagos since the Nineties'. Paper prepared for the Conference on 'Maritime Piracy in Southeast Asia' hosted by the Konrad Adenauer Foundation, Kuala Lumpur, 13-15 July 2006 at http://www.kas.de/db_files/dokumente/veranstaltungsbeitraege/7_dokument_dok_pdf_10478_2.pdf (17 Nov. 2007).

General Accountability Office. 'Port Security in the Caribbean Basin'. Presented to the Cognizant Committee as required by the SAFE Port Act of 2006, 13 April 2007.

Ghosh, P K. 2004. 'Maritime Security Challenges in South Asia and the Indian Ocean: Response Strategies'. Paper prepared for the CSIS American-Pacific Sealanes Security Institute Conference on Maritime Security in Asia held in Honolulu, Hawaii, 18-20 Jan. 2004 at http://community.middlebury.edu/~scs/docs/ghosh,%20maritime%20security%20challenges%20in%20SAsia%20&%20Indian%20Ocean.pdf (22 June 2007).

Grayson, George W. 'Mexico and the Drug Cartels'. Foreign Policy Research Institute *E-Notes*, Aug. 2007 at http://www.fpri.org/enotes/200708.grayson.mexicodrugcartels.html (25 Aug. 2007).

Hall, Kim. 'Consensus and Cooperation between Littoral States and User Nations in Combating Maritime Piracy and Violence in the Malacca Straits'. University of Cambridge. M.Phil Thesis, 2006.

Harsono, Andreas. 'Nationalism and Sea Piracy in the Malacca Strait'. Keynote speech for the Conference on 'Maritime Piracy in Southeast Asia' hosted by the Konrad Adenauer Foundation, Kuala Lumpur, 13-15 July 2006 at http://andreasharsono.blogspot.com/2006/07/nationalism-and-sea-piracy.html (16 June 2007) and http://www.kas.de/db_files/dokumente/veranstaltungsbeitraege/7_dokument_dok_pdf_10478_2.pdf (17 Nov. 2007)..

'Hezbollah'. Intelligence and Terrorism Information Centre at the Centre for Special Studies *Special Bulletin*, June 2003 at http://www.terrorism-info.org.il/malam_multimedia/English/eng_n/html/hezbollah.htm#E (7 Sept. 2007).

'Hezbollah is a strategic arm of Iran'. *Intelligence and Terrorism Information Centre at the Centre for Special Studies*, 8 Sept. 2006 at http://www.terrorism-info.org.il/malam_multimedia/English/eng_n/pdf/iran_hezbollah_e1.pdf (7 Sept. 2007).

'Hezbollah (Part Two)'. *Intelligence and Terrorism Information Centre at the Centre for Special Studies*, June 2003: Appendix 5, 'The bombing of the Jewish community centre in Argentina (1994) – an example of the modus operandi of Hezbollah's overseas terrorist apparatus' at http://www.intelligence.org.il/eng/bu/hizbullah/pb/app5.htm (7 Sept. 2007).

Ho, Joshua. 2004. 'Maritime Counter-Terrorism: A Singapore Perspective'. Paper Presented at the Observer Research Foundation Maritime Counter-Terrorism Workshop, 29-30 Nov. 2004.

Hulugalle, Lakshman. 'LTTE and drug smuggling'. *LankaLibrary Forum*, 8 Nov. 2006 at http://www.lankalibrary.com/phpBB/viewtopic.php?t=3006 (7 Sept. 2007).

Hussin, Abd Rahim. 'The Management of the Straits of Malacca: Buen Sharing as the Basis for Co-operation'. Paper presented at the LIMA International Maritime Conference, Awana Porto Malai, Langkawi, Malaysia, 4-5 Dec. 2005 at http://www.mima.gov.my/mima/htmls/conferences/LIMA05/Rahim%20-%20The%20management%20of%20Straits%20of%20Malacca%20-%20buen%20sharing%20as%20the%20basis%20for%20co-operation.pdf (9 July 2006).

International Court of Justice. 'Corfu Channel Case (Merits)'. Judgement of 9 April 1949 at http://www.icj-cij.org/docket/files/1/1645.pdf (15 Sept. 2007).

International Maritime Organisation 'Piracy and Armed Robbery against Ships: Recommendations to Governments for preventing and suppressing piracy and armed robbery against ships'. MSC/Circ.622/Rev.1, 16 June 1999 at http://www.imo.org/includes/blast_bindoc.asp?doc_id=940&format=PDF (28 March 2005).

————. Reports on Acts of Piracy and Armed Robbery Against Ships'. MSC.4/Circ.40, 4 Sept. 2003. Annex One. Available at http://www.imo.org/includes/blastDataOnly.asp/data_id%3D8084/40.pdf (7 Sept. 2007).

'Ipil Massacre', ND, at http://www.mahk.com/sc1522.htm (7 Sept. 2007).

'Iran as a state sponsoring and operating terror'. Intelligence and Terrorism Information Centre at the Centre for Special Studies *Special Bulletin,* April 2003 at http://www.terrorism-info.org.il/malam_multimedia/ENGLISH/IRAN/PDF/APR_03.PDF (7 Sept. 2007).

Islamic terrorism timeline'. Entry for 4 March 1973 at http://www.prophetofdoom.net/Islamic_Terrorism_Timeline_1973.Islam (7 Sept. 2007).

'Islamic terrorism timeline'. Entry for 3 Oct. 1978 at http://www.prophetofdoom.net/Islamic_Terrorism_Timeline_1978.Islam (6 Dec. 2007.

Jain, Rashmi. *Securing the Port of New York and New Jersey: Network-Centric Operations Applied to the Campaign Against Terrorism.* Appendix 1-4. Stevens Institute of Technology, 2004.

Jenkins, Brian Michael. 'Terrorism: Current and Long Term Threats'. RAND Testimony CT-187, Nov. 2001.

Kohlmann, Evan. 'Missed Opportunities: the December 1994 Air France Hijacking'. *Global Terror Alert* 2004 at http://www.globalterroralert.com/pdf/0105/airfrancehijack.pdf (3 Dec. 2005).

Larsen, Randall J. Statement before the Homeland Security Subcommittee on the Prevention of Nuclear and Biological Attack, US House of Representatives, 19 April 2005 at http://www.fas.org/irp/congress/2005_hr/041905larsen.pdf (3 Aug. 2006).

Levitt, Matthew. 2003. 'Hezbollah: A Case Study of Global Reach'. *The Washington Institute for Near East Policy.* Remarks to a conference on 'Post-Modern Terrorism: Trends, Scenarios, and Future Trends'. International Institute for Counter-Terrorism, Herzliya, Israel, 8 Sept. 2003 at http://www.washingtoninstitute.org/templateC07.php?CID=132 (4 Aug. 2006).

Lim Teck Ee. 'Straits of Malacca and Singapore: Past, Present and Future Co-operation'. Presentation to the Maritime Institute of Malaysia Conference, Kuala Lumpur, Malaysia, 12 Oct. 2004 at http://www.mima.gov.my/mima/htmls/conferences/som04/papers/lim.pdf (7 Jan. 2004).

'LTTE in South East Asia, The: With Special Focus on Thailand'. *Svik.org.* Report prepared 24 Nov. 2004; updated 28 July 2005 at http://www.svik.org/ PDF/ltteasia.pdf (4 Nov. 2005).

'LTTE linchpin KP free'. *Peace Lanka,* 18 Dec. 2007 at http://peacelanka.blogs- pot.com/2007/12/ltte-lynchpin-kp-free.html (21 Dec. 2007).

'LTTE's Military Capability'. *TamilTigers.net,* ND (although no later than 2005).

McDaniel, Michael S. 'Modern High Seas Piracy'. Presentation to the Propeller Club of the United States, 20 Nov. 2000 at http://www.cargolaw.com/ presentations_pirates.html (1 May 2004).

McKenna, Thomas M. 'Muslim Separatism in the Philippines: Meaningful Auton- omy or Endless War?' *Asian Social Issues Program* 2000 at http://www. asiasource.org/asip/mckenna.cfm#intro (25 June 2007).

———. The 1996 Peace Agreement.' at http://www.asiasource.org/asip/mcken- na_peace.cfm

———. Impediments to Peace and the Current Crisis'. at http://www.asiasource. org/asip/mckenna_crisis.cfm

MacKinnon, Doug. 'Transnational Dimensions of Maritime Crime'. Paper pre- sented at the Transnational Crime Conference, convened by the Aus- tralian Institute of Criminology, Canberra, 9-10 March 2000 at http:// www.aic.gov.au/conferences/transnational/mackinnon.pdf

Mannes, Aaron. 'The End of Force 17?' *Counterterrorism Blog,* 9 Oct. 2007 at http://counterterrorismblog.org/2007/10/the_end_of_force_17.php (17 Nov. 2007).

Marolda, Edwa J. 'Mine Warfare'. Naval Historical Center, 26 Aug. 2003 at http:// www.history.navy.mil/wars/korea/minewar.htm (7 Sept. 2007).

Martin-Clark, David. 'Case Notes: 'Bayswater Carriers Pte. Ltd. V. QBE Insur- ance (International) Pte. Ltd.' 2005 at http://www.onlinedmc.co.uk/ bayswater_carriers_v__qbe_insurance.htm (14 March 2006).

Menefee, Samuel Pyeatt. 'Delta Blues: Maritime and Riverine Crime in the Nige- rian Delta'. Paper delivered to the International Symposium on Coastal Zone Piracy, World Maritime University, Malmö, Sweden, 14 Nov. 2006.

———. 'Piracy and Maritime Crimes of Violence'. Unpublished MS. © S.P. Menefee. (This is an expanded version of *Trends in Maritime Violence*).

'Military Science in Western Europe in the Sixteenth Century', ND, at http:// www.drizzle.com/~celyn/jherek/16MilSci.pdf (7 Sept. 2007).

MIPT Terrorism Knowledge Base. Group Profile: Abu Sayyaf Group at http:// www.tkb.org/Group.jsp?groupID=204 (7 Sept. 2007).

———. Group Profile: 'Free Aceh Movement' at http://www.tkb.org/Group. jsp?groupID=3600 (7 Sept. 2007).

――――. Group Profile. 'Movement for the Emancipation of the Niger Delta' at http://www.tkb.org/Group.jsp?groupID=4692 (2 Jan. 2008).

――――. Group Profile: 'Who are Islamic jihad' at http://www.tkb.org/Group.jsp?groupID=82 (7 Sept. 2007).

――――. Group Profile: 'The Extraditables' at http://www.tkb.org/Group.jsp?groupID=4284 (7 Sept. 2007).

―――― Incident Profile: Al-Fatah Attacked Maritime Target, 25 Sept. 1985, Cyprus at http://www.tkb.org/Incident.jsp?incID=4371 (16 Sept. 2007).

―――― Incident Profile: Al-Fatah Attacked Maritime Target, 25 Dec. 1993, Israel at http://www.tkb.org/Incident.jsp?incID=7231 (8 Dec. 2007).

―――― Incident Profile: Anti-Castro Cubans attacked Maritime Target, 8 Aug. 1968 at http://www.tkb.org/Incident.jsp?incID=70 (6 Dec. 2007).

―――― Incident Profile: Anti-Castro Cubans attacked Maritime Target, 16 Sept. 1976 at http://www.tkb.org/Incident.jsp?incID=1836 (6 Dec. 2007).

―――― Incident Profile: Anti-Castro Cubans attacked Maritime Target, 22 July 1977 at http://www.tkb.org/Incident.jsp?incID=2004 (6 Dec. 2007).

―――― Incident Profile: ASG attacking Private Citizens and Property Target, 23 April 2000 available at http://www.tkb.org/Incident.jsp?incID=17575 (7 Sept. 2007).

―――― Incident Profile: ASG attacking Tourist Target, 27 May 2001 at http://www.tkb.org/Incident.jsp?incID=8432 (7 Sept. 2007).

―――― Incident Profile: Black Sept. attacked Maritime Target, 4 March 1973 at http://www.tkb.org/Incident.jsp?incID=1059 (6 Dec. 2007).

―――― Incident Profile: MILF attacks Transportation Target, 2 April 2003 at http://www.tkb.org/Incident.jsp?incID=15685 (7 Sept. 2007).

―――― Incident Profile: Popular Forces of April 25 attack Military Target, 28 Jan. 1985 at http://www.tkb.org/Incident.jsp?incID=4049 (7 Sept. 2007).

――――. Incident Profile: Popular Front for the Liberation of Palestine (PFLP) attacked Maritime Target, Israel, 4 June 1971 at http://www.tkb.org/Incident.jsp?incID=704 (3 Dec. 2007).

'Moro National Liberation Front'. 2001 at http://www.fas.org/irp/world/para/mnlf.htm (7 Sept. 2007).

Mukundan, Pottengal. 'Cargo Frauds'. Presentation to the International Union of Marine Insurers Annual Conference, London, 10-14 Sept. 2000.

Mullen, Admiral Mike Mullen. 'Remarks to the 17 International Seapower Symposium, Naval War College, Newport, RI', 21 Sept. 2005 at http://www.navy.mil/navydata/cno/mullen/speeches/mullen050921.txt (7 Sept. 2007).

Murphy, Martin N. 'Disoer in the Littorals: The Irrelevance of Expeditionary Warfare'. Presentation delivered to the Netherlands Defence Academy Symposium, 'Expeditionary Operations – Effects and Challenges', Breda, 13-14 Dec. 2006.

――――. 'Terrorism and Political Effect'. Unpublished Paper, 2003.

'Navy seizes 250,000 tons of fuel barges'. BNW News Blog, 11 Jan. 2006 at http://www.feedsfarm.com/article/3e9559ae4e7007686570b46ffa587511953 73c3b.html (15 May 2008).

'Operación conjunta detecta semisumergible en aguas del Pacífico Colombiano'. Armada Nacional de Colombia. 3 Jan. 2008 at http://www.armada.mil. co/?idcategoria=538934 (5 Jan. 2008).

'Palestinian Islamic jihad'. Institute for Counter-Terrorism, ND.

Parry, Rear Admiral Chris, RN. 'The Future Maritime Strategic Context'. RUSI Future Maritime Operations Conference, London, 22-23 Nov. 2006.

'Patterns of Terrorism in Israel in 2000'.

'Private Caste Armies in Bihar'. South Asia Terrorism Portal at http://www.satp. org/satporgtp/countries/india/terroristoutfits/private_armies.htm (7 Sept. 2007).

Republic of the Philippines Supreme Court, GR no. 111709, 30 Aug. 2001 at http://lawphil.net/judjuris/juri2001/aug2001/gr_111709_2001.html (7 Sept. 2007).

Roul, Animesh. 'LTTE infiltration in south India'. *Counterterrorism Blog,* 11 March 2007 at http://counterterrorismblog.org/2007/03/ltte_infiltration_in_south_ind.php (27 June 2007).

Ruijie He. 'Ganging up on the Jolly Roger in Asia: International Cooperation and Maritime Piracy'. Cambridge, MA: Massachusetts Institute of Technology. BS/MS thesis, June 2008.

Shachtman, Noah. 'Inside the *Brave New War,* Part 1', *Wired* Blog Network, 16 May 2007 at http://blog.wired.com/defense/2007/05/q_tell_me_a_lit. html (20 May 2007).

'Shayetet 13'. The Israel Special Forces Database at http://www.isayeret.com/services/freecontent/article.htm (1 Feb. 2008).

'SL Naval History from 1984'. ND.

Society of Gas Tanker and Terminal Operators (SIGTTO). 'Safe Havens for Disabled Gas Carriers'. Thi Edition, 2003.

Sondakh, Berna Kent. 'National Sovereignty and Security in the Strait of Malacca'. Presentation to the Maritime Institute of Malaysia Conference, Kuala Lumpur, Malaysia, 12 Oct. 2004 at http://www.mima.gov.my/mima/htmls/conferences/som04/papers/sondakh.pdf (7 Jan. 2004).

Sparks, Michael C. ' A Critical Vulnerability, A Valid Threat: US Ports and Terrorist Mining'. Norfolk, VA: Joint Forces Staff College Masters Thesis, 2005 at http://stinet.dtic.mil/cgi-bin/GetToc?AD=ADA436598&Location=U2&doc=GetToc.pdf (2 Jan. 2008).

'Sri Lanka: Exercises with US send a message to China'. STRATFOR *Global Intelligence Brief,* 19 Oct. 2006.

Sri Lanka Navy. 'Destruction of 'Matsushima'', 7 Oct. 2007' at http://www.navy. lk/index.php?id=482 (26 Feb. 2008).

Tan, Andrew. 'The Threat of Terrorism in Southeast Asia: Threats and Responses'. Paper delivered to the Council of Asian Liberals and Democrats, 10 Anniversary Conference, 9-10 Dec. 2003 at http://www.cald.org/website/10th%20Anniversary/presentations/tanonterrorism.htm (7 Sept. 2007).

'Texas City Disaster, The', ND, at http://www.texascity-library.org/History-TCDisaster.pdf and http://www.ezl.com/~fireball/Disaster20.htm (7 Sept. 2007).

'Thailand Islamic Insurgency'. GlobalSecurity.org, ND at http://www.globalsecurity.org/military/world/war/thailand2.htm (7 Sept. 2007).

Thompson, John. 'Terrorism and Transnational Crime: The Case of the LTTE'. Paper for the Centre for Conflict Studies, Fall Seminar, 3-4 Oct. 2003 at http://www.mackenzieinstitute.com/2003/terror100403.htm (22 June 2007).

UK P&I Club Issue 8. 'The carriage of liquefied gasses'. Available at http://www.ukpandi.com/UkPandi/Infopool.nsf/HTML/LPCtC8#a1 (7 Sept. 2007).

United Nations. 'Report of the Panel of Experts on Somalia pursuant to Security Council resolution 1474 (2003)', Oct. 2003.

────── Commission on Crime Prevention and Criminal Justice, 'Differences and Similarities between Transnational Organized Crime and Terrorist Crimes', Fifth Session, Vienna, 21-31 May 1996 at http://www.uncjin.org/Documents/5comm/7e.htm (22 June 2004).

────── General Assembly. 'Ninth United Nations Congress on the Prevention of Crime and the Treatment of Offenders. Discussion Guide'. Vienna: UN, A/Conf. 169/PM.1, 27 July 1993.

────── Security Council. Letter dated 4 Sept. 1985 from the Permanent Representative of Israel to the United Nations addressed to the Secretary-General. Available at http://domino.un.org/UNISPAL.nsf/9a798adbf322aff38525617b006d88d7/30b07d6f26ef9d6085256bdd006d2a73!OpenDocument (7 Sept. 2007).

────── Security Council. Resolution 1816 (2008). 2 June 2008 at http://daccessdds.un.org/doc/UNDOC/GEN/N08/361/77/PDF/N0836177.pdf?OpenElement (4 June 2008).

United States Department of Homeland Security. 'Small Vessel Security Strategy'. April 2008 at http://www.dhs.gov/xlibrary/assets/small-vessel-security-strategy.pdf (20 May 2008).

────── Department of Justice. 'Al Qaeda Associates Charged In Attack On USS Cole, Attempted Attack On Another U.S. Naval Vessel', 15 May 2003 at http://www.usdoj.gov/opa/pr/2003/May/03_crm_298.htm (7 Sept. 2007).

————. Energy Information Administration. 'World LNG shipping capacity expanding', 2004, at http://www.eia.doe.gov/oiaf/analysispaper/global/worldlng.html (7 Sept. 2007).

———— Office of Naval Intelligence and US Coast Gua Intelligence Cooination Centre. *Threats and Challenges to Maritime Security 2020.* 1 March 1999 at http://www.fas.org/irp/threat/maritime2020/ (26 Sept. 2003).

Valencia, Mark J. 'Security Issues in the Malacca Strait: Who's Security and Why it Matters'. Paper presented at the MIMA Conference on the Straits of Malacca held at the Prince Hotel, Kuala Lumper, 11-12 Oct. 2004 at http://www.mima.gov.my/mima/htmls/conferences/som04/papers/valencia.pdf (1 Dec. 2006).

Waryas, E. (Lloyd's Register America, Inc.). 'Major Disaster Planning: Understanding and Managing Your Risk'. Paper presented to the Fourth National Harbor Safety Committee Conference, Galveston, TX, 4 March 2002.

'Weapons found on the 'Karine-A' and 'Santorini'. *WarOnLine,* 20 July 2002 at http://www.waronline.org/en/analysis/pal_weapons.htm (7 Sept. 2007).

White House, The: Office of the Press Secretary. 'Fact Sheet: Plots, Casings, and Infiltrations Referenced in President Bush's Remarks on the War on Terror'. 6 Oct. 2005 at http://www.whitehouse.gov/news/releases/2005/10/20051006-7.html (7 Oct. 2005).

————. 'Policy for the Repression of Piracy and other Criminal Acts of Violence at Sea'. 13 June 2007.

Wikipedia. 'Coastal road massacre', at http://en.wikipedia.org/wiki/Coastal_Road_massacre (7 Sept. 2007).

————. 'Tausug people', at http://en.wikipedia.org/wiki/Tausug_people (7 Sept. 2007).

————. 'Texas City disaster', at http://en.wikipedia.org/wiki/Texas_City_disaster (7 Sept. 2007).

Winer, Jonathan. 'Nigerian Crime: Testimony before the House Sub-committee on Africa of the House International Relations Committee'. Washington, DC, 11 Sept. 1996 at http://www.fas.org/irp/congress/1996_hr/h960911w.htm (7 Sept. 2007).

Winters, Jeffrey A. 'Notes on B.J. Habibie', 1 March 1998 at http://gaya.scienza.de/INDON_0.HTM (7 Sept. 2007).

Wolfrum, Rüdiger. 'Fighting Terrorism at Sea: Options and Limitations under International Law'. Twenty-eighth Doherty Lecture organised by the Center for Oceans Law and Policy, University of Virginia School of Law, Charlottesville, Virginia delivered in Washington, DC, 13 April 2006 at http://www.virginia.edu/colp/pdf/Wolfrum-Doherty-Lecture-Terrorism-at-Sea.pdf (5 Nov. 2007).

Yates, Benjamin S. 'David vs. Goliath: Small boat challenges to naval operations in coastal warfare'. Thesis. United States Marine Corps, Command at Staff College, Marine Corps University, Masters Thesis, 1998.

Zhang Shouguo. 2004. 'China – Playing an Active Role in Fulfilling Maritime Security Obligations'. Presentation to OECD Workshop on Maritime Transport, Paris, 4-5 Nov. at http://www.oecd.org/dataoecd/19/61/33949707.pdf (2 Oct. 2006).

Journalism, News Reports and Press Releases

'3 Malacca Strait govts weigh allowing ships to carry arms'. *Straits Times,* 15 May 2005.

'10 killed in Ashdod port 'suicide attack''. *Jerusalem Newswire,* 15 March 2004.

'20 Cameroun soldiers die in Bakassi'. *Daily Trust* (Abuja), 14 Nov. 2007 at http://allafrica.com/stories/200711140122.html (25 March 2008).

'31 nations agree to make Malacca Strait safer for navigation'. *The Star Online,* 20 Sept. 2006 at http://thestaronline.com/news/story.asp?file=/2006/9/20/nation/20060920183727&sec=nation (23 Sept. 2006).

'71 boat people feared dead in pirate attack off Malaysia'. *New York Times,* 9 Aug. 1989 at http://query.nytimes.com/gst/fullpage.html?res=950DE0D9123BF93AA3575BC0A96F948260&sec=&pagewanted=print (7 Sept. 2007).

'1967: Bombs rain down on *Torrey Canyon*'. BBC News 'On This Day, 29 March at http://news.bbc.co.uk/onthisday/hi/dates/stories/march/29/newsid_2819000/2819369.stm (7 Sept. 2007).

'Abducted Cameroonians found dead'. *BBC News,* 14 June 2008 at http://news.bbc.co.uk/1/hi/world/africa/7455116.stm (18 June 2008).

'Abu Sayyaf actively recruiting young blood – police'. *GMANEWS.TV,* 17 June 2008 at http://www.gmanews.tv/story/101477/Abu-Sayyaf-actively-recruiting-young-blood---police# (18 June 2008).

'Abu Sayyaf claims responsibility for ferry blast'. *Fox News* report, 29 Feb. 2004 at http://www.foxnews.com/story/0,2933,112833,00.html (8 May 2004).

'Abu Sayyaf Group beheads hostages'. *Keesing's World News Archive,* 2 May 2007 at http://www.keesings.com/breaking_history/asia-pacific/philippines_abu_sayyaf_group_beheads_hostages_pub._2_may_2007/abu_sayyaf_group_beheads_hostages_full_text/ (7 Sept. 2007).

'Aceh rebels warn ships to seek permission to use Malacca Straits'. US Department of Transportation, *Transportation and Security Review.* vol. 2, no. 14, 5 Sept. 2001 at http://www.dot.state.al.us/TSTR/TSTR-9-5-01%20(2).doc (7 Sept. 2007).

'Ahmadinejad recruits Hezbollah terror chief'. *WorldNetDaily,* 23 April 2006 at http://www.wnd.com/news/article.asp?ARTICLE_ID=49866 (8 Jan. 2007).

Ahmed, Rashmee Z. 'Osama hand in glove with LTTE'. *The Times of India*, 22 Sept. 2001 at http://www1.timesofindia.indiatimes.com/cms.dll/articleshow?art_id=780319387 (28 June 2007).

'Air strikes on Sri Lanka rebels after sea battle leaves 45 dead'. *Channel NewsAsia.com*, 11 May 2006 at http://www.channelnewsasia.com/stories/afp_asia-pacific/view/207860/1/.html (12 May 2006).

'Aircraft hits New York building'. *BBC News*, 12 Oct. 2006 at http://news.bbc.co.uk/1/hi/world/americas/6042306.stm (7 Sept. 2007).

Albor, Teresa. 'Killers on the high seas'. *Sunday Morning Post*, 2 May 1993.

'Al Qaeda biggest threat to navy'. *BBC News* report, 10 March 2003 at http://news.bbc.co.uk/1/hi/uk/2837179.stm (23 April 2004).

"Al Qaeda Gulf chief' held by US'. *BBC News*, 22 Nov. 2002 at http://news.bbc.co.uk/1/hi/world/middle_east/2501121.stm (7 Sept. 2007).

'Al Qaeda new tactics, targets ocean liners'. CSIS *Transnational Threats Update*, vol. 2, no. 4, Jan. 2004 at http://csis.org/TNT/ttu/ttu_0401.pdf (20 July 2004).

'Al Qaeda operations are rather cheap'. *The Economist*. vol. 369, Issue, 8344, 10 April 2003, p. 45.

'Al Qaeda operative talking'. *CNN.com*, 23 Nov. 2002 at http://archives.cnn.com/2002/US/11/22/alqaeda.capture/ (13 March 2007).

'Al Qaeda says it hit Saudi oil facility'. *Aljazeera.net*, 25 Feb. 2006 at http://english.aljazeera.net/NR/exeres/A429E32C-D484-424E-9C58-D9E287580817.htm (7 Sept. 2007).

'Al Qaeda statement claims Iraq boat attack'. *Aljazeera.com*, 26 April 2004.

'Al Qaeda strikes at US-Saudi oil'. *DEBKAfile Special Report*, 4 May 2004 at http://www.debka.com/article.php?aid=837 (7 Sept. 2007).

'Al Qaeda suspect says Taliban financed failed plot on Israeli ship'. *Associated Press*, 21 Feb. 2006.

'Al Qaeda, tanker insurance rates, mines among key war concerns'. *Oil and Gas Journal*, 31 March 2003.

Alexander, Yonah; and Richason, Tyler. 'He who commands the sea...'. *Jerusalem Post*, 19 Dec. 2002.

Ali, Abdulsamad. 'Maritime body wants UN to move on piracy off the Horn of Africa'. *East African* (Nairobi), 31 July 2007 at http://allafrica.com/stories/200707310625.html (20 August 2007).

Ali, Sharidan M. 'Reducing risks posed by small vessels'. *The Star Online*, 9 Oct. 2006 at http://thestar.com.my/maritime/story.asp?file=/2006/10/9/maritime/15644443&sec=maritime (7 Sept. 2007).

———. 'Secure passage via Straits'. *The Star Online*, 21 Aug. 2006 at http://thestar.com.my/maritime/story.asp?file=/2006/8/21/maritime/15098461&sec=maritime (7 Sept. 2007).

————. 'Straits users should be taxed'. *The Star Online*, 7 Aug. 2006 at http://thestar.com.my/maritime/story.asp?file=/2006/8/7/maritime/2006080708193 4&sec=maritime (8 Aug. 2006).

Alipala, Julie. 'New Oplan to bring dev't to Sulu, says Esperon'. *Inquirer.net*, 26 April 2007 at http://newsinfo.inquirer.net/inquirerheadlines/regions/view_article.php?article_id=62724 (7 Sept. 2007).

'Alleged pirates freed after US declines to prosecute'. *Mail & Guaian Online*, 2 May 2006 at http://www.mg.co.za/articlePage.aspx?articleid=270541&area=/breaking_news/breaking_news__africa/# (27 Jan. 2007).

Ambrogi, Stefano. 'IMO asks Security Council to act on Somalia piracy'. *Reuters AlertNet*, 28 June 2007 at http://www.alertnet.org/thenews/newsdesk/L28830548.htm (29 June 2007).

————. 'Pirate attacks on the wane'. *Reuters*, 7 May 2005.

————. 'US Navy says al Qaeda poses major threat from sea'. *Reuters AlertNet*, 3 July 2006.

'Anger at Somali pirates' ransom'. *BBC News*, 18 March 2008 at http://news.bbc.co.uk/1/hi/world/africa/7302687.stm (19 March 2008).

'Another cocaine-laden submarine sinks off Colombia'. *Reuters*, 3 Jan. 2008 at http://abcnews.go.com/International/wireStory?id=4082359 (5 Jan. 2008).

'Anti-piracy agreement signed by 11 Asian countries'. 2006. *The Star Online*, 21 June 2006.

'Anti-piracy agreement wins approval'. *Fairplay*, 22 June 2006.

'AP IMPACT: An investigation into fundraising and weapons smuggling by Sri Lanka's Tamil Tigers'. *Associated Press*, 5 Nov. 2007 at http://www.iht.com/articles/ap/2007/11/06/asia/AS-FEA-GEN-Sri-Lanka-Tiger-Inc..php?page=1 (7 Nov. 2007).

Apps, Peter. 'Sri Lanka, Tigers claim victory in naval clash'. *Reuters AlertNet*, 17 June 2006.

'Armed escort boats to be detailed'. *Bernama.com*, 26 April 2005 at http://www.bernama.com.my/bernama/v3/printable.php?id=131289 (27 April 2005).

'Arms smuggling through the Gaza-Egypt boer – Background'. Israel Ministry of Foreign Affairs, 20 February 2008 at http://www.mfa.gov.il/MFA/Terrorism-+Obstacle+to+Peace/Terror+Groups/Arms+smuggling+through+the+Gaza-Egypt+boer+-+Background+20-Feb-2008.htm (7 July 2008).

'Army: Janjalani successor is ASG's bag man'. *GMA News TV*, 27 June 2007 at http://www.gmanews.tv/story/48554/Army-Janjalani-successor-is-ASGs-bag-man (27 June 2007).

'Asia unites against piracy'. *Strategypage.com*, 1 July 2006 at http://www.strategypage.com/htmw/htseamo/articles/20060701.aspx (7 Sept. 2007).

'At least 16 die of burns in Philippines bus bombing'. *CNN.com*, 25 Feb. 2000.

'At least 30 wounded in Philippine terror blast'. *Channel NewsAsia,* 28 Aug. 2005 at http://www.channelnewsasia.com/stories/afp_asiapacific/view/165344/1/. html (3 Dec. 2005).

Athas, Iqbal 'Battles highlight Sea Tigers' capabilities'. *Jane's Defence Weekly,* 4 Oct. 2006.

'Attack shuts down Shell Nigerian output'. *Lloyd's List,* 10 Oct. 2006.

'Attacks cripple Iraq oil exports' *BBC News,* 15 June 2004 at http://news.bbc. co.uk/1/hi/world/middle_east/3809587.stm (7 Sept. 2007).

'Attempted terror attack via the sea thwarted'. Israel Ministry of Foreign Affairs *Press Release,* 10 Nov. 2004 at http://www.mfa.gov.il/MFA/ Terrorism-+Obstacle+to+Peace/Terrorism+and+Islamic+Fundamenta lism-/Attempted+terror+attack+via+the+sea+thwarted+10-Nov-2004. htm?DisplayMode=print (8 Dec. 2007).

'Aussie crew 'fended off' Iranian gunboats'. *The Australian,* 22 June 2007 at http:// www.theaustralian.news.com.au/story/0,20867,21948930-601,00.html (7 Sept. 2007).

'Australia detains more Indonesian boats'. *ABC Radio Australia,* 17 July 2006 at http://www.radioaustralia.net.au/news/stories/s1688014.htm?Australia (18 July 2006).

'Australia links organized crime to illegal fishing'. *Reuters,* 26 May 2008 at http:// www.iht.com/articles/2008/05/26/asia/fish.php (27 May 2008).

'Australia target in human smuggling scam'. *The Age,* 19 Nov. 2005 at http:// www.theage.com.au/news/world/australia-target-in-human-smuggling-scam/2005/11/19/1132017016948.html# (18 March 2006).

Aziz, Noor Mohd. 'Boost for maritime security with launch of Information Sharing Centre in Singapore'. *Channel NewsAsia,* 29 Nov. 2006 at http:// www.channelnewsasia.com/stories/singaporelocalnews/view/244228/1/. html (30 Nov. 2006).

Baker, Peter; and Glasser, Susan B. 'Bush says 10 plots by al-Qaeda were foiled'. *The Washington Post,* 7 Oct. 2005 at http://www.washingtonpost.com/ wp-dyn/content/article/2005/10/06/AR2005100600455_pf.html (7 Sept. 2007).

Balachandran, P. K. 'Lanka most militarised in South Asia: study'. *Hindustan Times,* 21 Sept. 2006.

———. 'LTTE wants monitors to protect Sea Tiger vessels also'. *HindustanTimes,* 13 May 2006.

———. 'Tsunami did not wrick our navy: LTTE'. *HindustanTimes,* 1 Jan. 2005.

Banerjee, Neela; and Bradsher, Keith. 'A vulnerable time to be moving oil by sea'. *New York Times,* 19 Oct. 2002.

Barclay, Ian. 'Private sector helps ease piracy fears in Malacca Strait'. *Lloyd's List,* 4 July 2006.

Barrett, Ricky. 'Builders arm boats to chase off pirates'. *The Sun News*, 10 Aug. 2006.

Bedi, Rahul. 'Refugees facing bleak future as Tigers hit back'. *Sunday Telegraph*, 1 May 2006 at http://www.telegraph.co.uk/news/main.jhtml?xml=/news/2006/05/01/wsri01.xml (7 Sept. 2007).

———. 'Sri Lanka falls into spiral of death'. *Daily Telegraph*, 3 Aug. 2006 at http://www.telegraph.co.uk/news/main.jhtml?xml=/news/2006/08/03/wsri03.xml (7 Sept. 2007).

———. 'US Marines to train Sri Lankan navy'. 2006. *India e News.com*. 25 Oct. 2006 at http://www.indiaenews.com/srilanka/20061025/26189.htm (7 Sept. 2007).

Beech, Hannah. 'Smuggler's blues'. *TIMEAsia*, 7 Oct. 2002 at http://www.time.com/time/asia/covers/1101021014/story.html (9 Jan. 2008).

Beeston, Richa. 'Tamil Tigers sink peace hopes with suicide raid at sea'. *The Times*, 13 May 2006 at http://www.timesonline.co.uk/tol/news/world/asia/article717080.ece (12 Feb. 2008).

Bennhold, Katrin. 'Piracy, kidnapping and rescue off the Somali coast'. *International Herald Tribune*, 15 April 2008 at http://www.iht.com/articles/2008/04/15/europe/france.php (16 April 2008).

Bhaumik, Subir. 'Calcutta mafia boss convicted over blast'. *BBC News*, 30 Aug. 2001 at http://news.bbc.co.uk/1/hi/world/south_asia/1517154.stm (22 June 2004).

Bile, Mohamed Ali. 'Somalia's Islamists seize pirate strongholds'. *Reuters South Africa*, 13 Aug. 2006.

'Bin Laden bought ship 'for terror''. *The Times*, 17 Oct. 2004 at http://www.timesonline.co.uk/printFriendly/0,,2-524-1313688,00.html (22 Oct. 2004).

'Bin Laden: Goal is to bankrupt the US'. *CNN.com*, 1 Nov. 2004 at http://www.cnn.com/2004/WORLD/meast/11/01/binladen.tape/ (7 Sept. 2007).

'Bin Laden hails anti-Western attacks'. *BBC News*, 14 Oct. 2002 at http://news.bbc.co.uk/1/hi/world/middle_east/2327365.stm (23 April 2004).

Birtley, Tony. 'Sri Lanka battles Tigers at sea'. *Aljazeera.net*, 11 June 2007 at http://english.aljazeera.net/NR/exeres/F827D082-514A-42B8-BF43-03DA00F6FA7E.htm (12th June 2007).

Blanche, Ed. 'Tanker terror: Gulf's oil routes under threat'. *The Daily Star*, 22 April 2004 at http://www.dailystar.com.lb/article.asp?edition_id=10&categ_id=3&article_id=2597# (9 Aug. 2005).

'Blast holes US warship'. *BBC News* report, 12 Oct. 2000 at http://news.bbc.co.uk/1/hi/world/middle_east/968812.stm (25 April 2004).

'Blast tanker finally leaves Bonny River'. *Lloyd's List*, 13 March 2008.

'Blasts kill 13 Sri Lankan sailors'. *BBC News*, 23 Dec. 2005 at http://news.bbc.co.uk/1/hi/world/south_asia/4551892.stm (18 March 2006).

'Blast target Iraqi oil terminals'. *BBC News,* 25 April 2004 at http://news.bbc. co.uk/1/hi/world/middle_east/3656481.stm (15 July 2006).

Block, Robert. 'How terrorists' goals may be melding'. *Wall Street Journal,* 6 July 2007.

'Bloody cost of inaction, The'. *Fairplay,* 3 Sept. 1998, pp. 22-25.

Boey, David. '3 pirate attacks off Aceh in 2 days spark alarm'. *The Straits Times,* 5 July 2006.

————. 'Ship owners using hired guns'. *Straits Times,* 8 April 2005.

'Bomb blast hits Philippines ferry'. *BBC News,* 28 Aug. 2005 at http://news.bbc. co.uk/1/hi/world/asia-pacific/4192102.stm (14 July 2006).

'Bomb blasts in New Delhi, scores killed'. *The Jawa Report,* 29 Oct. 2005 at http:// mypetjawa.mu.nu/archives/129931.php (11 Dec. 2007).

'Bomb caused Philippine ferry fire'. *BBC News,* 11 Oct. 2004 at http://news.bbc. co.uk/2/hi/asia-pacific/3732356.stm (3 Dec. 2005).

Bonner, Raymond. 'Tamil guerrillas in Sri Lanka: Deadly and armed to the teeth'. *New York Times,* 7 March 1998 at http://query.nytimes.com/gst/fullpage. html?res=950DE3DD1630F934A35750C0A96E958260 (8 Feb. 2008).

Borger, Julian. 'Hijackers fly into Pentagon? No chance, said top brass'. *The Guaian,* 15 April 2004 at http://www.guaian.co.uk/international/story/0,,1192087,00.html (3 Dec. 2005).

————. 'Plot to sink warship on 9/11'. *The Guaian,* 21 Feb. 2003 at http://www. guaian.co.uk/alqaida/story/0,,900071,00.html (9 Oct. 2005).

Borger, Julian, and Whitaker, Brian. 'US watching al-Qaida's fleet'. *The Guaian,* 1 Jan. 2003 at http://www.guaian.co.uk/alqaida/story/0,,867245,00.html (9 Oct. 2005).

Borunda, Daniel. 'Drug cartels possess more firepower, technology'. *El Paso Times,* 2 June 2008 at http://www.elpasotimes.com/ci_9449210?source=most_emailed (3 June 2008).

Bousen, Corey. '*Tenyu* crew feared muered'. *Lloyd's List,* 30 December 1998.

Bradsher, Keith. 'Attacks on chemical ships in Southeast Asia seem to be piracy, not terror'. *New York Times,* 27 March 2003 at http://query.nytimes. com/search/restricted/article?res=F6071EFF35540C748EDDAA0894D B404482 (19 June 2004).

————. 'Problems with pirates continue in sea lanes of South Asia'. *New York Times,* 15 Aug. 2003 at http://www.nytimes.com/2003/08/15/business/worldbusiness/15PIRA.html?ex=1376366400&en=6eca93f6ef18c58b&ei=5007&partner=USERLAND (1 Nov. 2007).

Brant, Robin. 'Tackling rising threat of piracy'. *BBC News,* 23 May 2008 at http:// news.bbc.co.uk/1/hi/world/asia-pacific/7391004.stm (25 May 2008)

'Brazil's mighty prison gangs'. *BBC News,* 15 May 2006 at http://news.bbc. co.uk/1/hi/world/americas/4770097.stm (18 March 2008).

'Brazilian gangs attack police in three cities'. *Associated Press,* 13 May 2006 at http://www.ctv.ca/servlet/ArticleNews/story/CTVNews/20060513/brazil_gangsters_060513/20060513?hub=World (6 Aug. 2007).

Brewer, James. 'London Club tells members to be wary of Chinese legal system'. *Lloyd's List,* 10 July 2006.

Bright, Martin; Harris, Nick; and Walsh, Nick Paton. 'Hunt for 20 terror ships'. *The Observer,* 23 Dec. 2001 at http://observer.guaian.co.uk/international/story/0,6903,624196,00.html (11 June 2004).

Buchanan, Michael. 'London bombings cost just hundreds'. *BBC News,* 3 Jan. 2006 at http://news.bbc.co.uk/1/hi/uk/4576346.stm (7 Feb. 2007).

'Buenos Aires bomber 'identified''. *BBC News,* 10 Nov. 2005 at http://news.bbc.co.uk/1/hi/world/americas/4423612.stm (7 Sept. 2007).

Buerk, Roland. 'Tamil Tigers unveil latest tactic'. *BBC News,* 26 March 2007 at http://news.bbc.co.uk/1/hi/world/south_asia/6496381.stm (15 June 2007).

———. 'Who is winning Sri Lanka's War?' *BBC News,* 25 May 2007 at http://news.bbc.co.uk/1/hi/world/south_asia/6690633.stm (15 June 2007).

Burke, Michael 'Difficult decisions'. *Jamaica Observer,* 29 June 2006 at http://www.jamaicaobserver.com/columns/html/20060628T220000-0500_107982_OBS_DIFFICULT_DECISIONS_.asp (7 Sept. 2007).

Burkeman, Oliver. 'US captures key al-Qaeda suspect'. *Guaian Unlimited,* 22 Nov. 2002 at http://www.guaian.co.uk/alqaida/story/0,12469,845211,00.html (7 Sept. 2007).

Butcher, Tim. 'Missile attack on US ship in Joanian Red Sea port'. *Daily Telegraph,* 20 Aug. 2005 at http://www.telegraph.co.uk/news/main.jhtml?xml=/news/2005/08/20/wjoan20.xml (23 Dec. 2006).

'Calderon changes Mexico's drug war strategy'. *Associated Press,* 14 May 2007 at http://www.msnbc.msn.com/id/18662418/ (22 May 2007).

'Cambodia beefs up maritime security against terrorists, cross-boer criminals'. *People's Daily Online,* 28 Nov. 2007 at http://english.people.com.cn/90001/90777/6311041.html (29 Nov. 2007).

'Can the army out-gun the drug los?' *The Economist,* 15 May 2008 at http://www.economist.com/world/la/displayStory.cfm?story_id=11376335&fsrc=nwlgafree (17 May 2008).

'Captain tells of fear and loathing on the high sea'. *Lloyd's List,* 13 Oct. 2005.

'Carafano, James Jay 'Missing the real missile threat'. *Washington Post,* 26 July 2006 at http://www.washingtonpost.com/wp-dyn/content/article/2006/07/25/AR2006072500705.html (5 Aug. 2006).

'Cargo boat 'looted off Sri Lanka''. *BBC News,* 1 May 2007 at http://news.bbc.co.uk/1/hi/world/south_asia/6612663.stm (7 Sept. 2007).

Carnie, Tony. 'Oil piracy and gas dragons'. *Alexander's Gas & Oil Connections*, 27 May 2005 at http://www.gasandoil.com/goc/company/cna52313.htm (18 May 2006).

Carter, Sara A. 'Drug cartel-terrorist ties known in 2001'. *Washington Times*, 14 Aug. 2007 at http://www.washingtontimes.com/article/20070814/NAT ION/108140073&SearchID=73291731660332 (26 Aug. 2007).

———. 'Islamists target Arizona base'. *Washington Times*, 26 Nov. 2007 at http://www.washingtontimes.com/apps/pbcs.dll/article?AID=/20071126/NA-TION/111260034/1001 (26 Nov. 2007).

———. 'Terrorists teaming with drug cartels'. *Washington Times*, 8 Aug. 2007 at http://www.washingtontimes.com/apps/pbcs.dll/article?AID=/20070808/ NATION/108080088/1001 (8 Aug. 2007).

Case, Brendan M.; Corchado, Alfredo; and Iliff, Laurence. 'Officials develop clearer picture of Zetas'. *El Universal*, 21 March 2005 at http://www2.eluniversal.com.mx/pls/impreso/noticia.html?id_nota=9851&tabla=miami (1 Jan. 2008).

'Cement block, The'. *TIME*, 27 Oct. 1975 at http://www.time.com/time/magazine/article/0,9171,913575,00.html (31 Oct. 2006).

Chambers, Matt. 'Just in case'. *Wall Street Journal*, 27 Aug. 2007.

Chambon, Dominique. 'Once a terrorist, always a terrorist'. *International Review*, Winter 1993-4 at http://www.geocities.com/Paris/Rue/4637/terr5a.html (4 Oct. 2005).

'Chance for a clampdown'. *Economist.com*, 25 Oct. 2001 at http://www.economist.com/printedition/PrinterFriendly.cfm?Story_ID=836058 (7 Sept. 2007).

Chang, Andrew. 'Terror on the waves'. *ABC News.com*, 29 Jan. 2001. This article has been retitled. It is now called 'Seafarers note alarming rise in piracy' and is available at http://abcnews.go.com/International/ story?id=80020&page=1 (15 Nov. 2005).

Charoenpo, Anucha. 'Illegal Thai fishing robbed Indonesia off (sic) billions of catches and cash'. *South East Asian Press Alliance*, 2003 at http://www. seapabkk.org/fellowships/2002/anucha.html (18 Jan. 2007).

Chen, Melody. 'Captain tells pirate story'. *Taipei Times*, 12 Aug. 2003 at http:// www.taipeitimes.com/News/taiwan/archives/2003/08/12/2003063302 (7 Sept. 2007).

Chen Zhanjie. 'Sri Lanka's security situation worsens further'. *Xinhua News Agency*, 24 May 2007 at http://www.reliefweb.int/rw/RWB.NSF/db900SID/ SHES-73HK?OpenDocument (15 June 2007).

Chew Wai Yee. 'IMO calls on industry to fund Strait safety'. *Lloyd's List*, 5 Sept. 2007.

'China accused of piracy'. *Lloyd's List*, 11 March 1994, p. 11.

SMALL BOATS, WEAK STATES, DIRTY MONEY

'China executes 13 pirates'. *People's Daily Online,* 29 Jan. 2000 at http://english. people.com.cn/english/200001/29/eng20000129N103.html (7 Sept. 2007).

'China frees "Anna Sierra" hijackers.' *Lloyd's List,* 11 Feb. 1997.

'China: Miscellaneous; container confiscated from Singapore vessel by China'. *Lloyd's List,* 18 Nov. 1997.

'Choy, Linda, 'Official link to pirates rejected'. *South China Morning Post,* 19 Mar. 1994.

'Christmas shortage due to Suez blockage'. *I.T.Vibe,* 7 Dec. 2004 available at http://itvibe.com/news/3060/ (7 Sept. 2007).

Chuenniran, Achadtata. 'Pirates rob Thai tanker crew'. *Bangkok Post,* 28 April 2008 at http://www.bangkokpost.com/280408_News/28Apr2008_news13. php (29 April 2008).

'Claim that al-Qaeda team visited Gibraltar'. *Panorama* (Gibraltar). 6 June 2002 at http://www.panorama.gi/archive/020610/updates.htm (7 Sept. 2007).

Clarke, Jeremy. 'Danish ship and crew hijacked off Somalia – official'. *Reuters AlertNet,* 3 June 2007 at http://www.alertnet.org/thenews/newsdesk/ L03535763.htm (4 June 2007).

———. 'Two ships hijacked off Somali waters released'. *Reuters,* 7 April 2007 at http://www.reuters.com/article/homepageCrisis/idUSL07627880._ CH_.2400 (15 April 2008).

Clout, Laura. 'Somali pirates threaten to kill tanker crew'. *Daily Telegraph,* 11 Dec. 2007 at http://www.telegraph.co.uk/news/main.jhtml?xml=/ news/2007/12/11/wpirates111.xml (11 Dec. 2007).

'Clues destroyed as inferno rages'. *BBC News,* 12 Dec. 2005 at http://news.bbc. co.uk/1/hi/uk/4520148.stm (12th Dec. 2005).

'Coast Gua Chief: attack by small boats still possible'. *Philadelphia Inquirer.* 8 July 2004.

'Cocaine smugglers threatening submarine'. *The Star,* 27 June 2008 at http://www.int.iol.co.za/index.php?set_id=1&click_id=126&art_ id=vn20080627054829987C660615 (4 July 2008).

Cochrane, Joe; Yabes, Criselda; and Vitug, Marites D. 'Asia is winning the fight on terror'. *Newsweek,* 20 Aug. 2007 at http://www.msnbc.msn.com/ id/20226565/site/newsweek/ (17 Aug. 2007).

Cody, Edwa. 'Roots of Gandhi slaying lie in India's role in Sri Lanka'. *The Washington Post,* 30 May 1991.

Colombant, Nico. 'West Africa's drug circulation increases, worrying officials'. *NewsVOA.com,* 18 June 2007 at http://www.voanews.com/english/ archive/2007-06/2007-06-18-voa25.cfm (29 Aug. 2007).

'Colombia: The Submarine Door'. *Semitronic,* ND.

'Colombian Navy seizes sub in coke probe'. *Associated Press,* 7 Aug. 2007 at http:// abcnews.go.com/International/wireStory?id=3455526 (23 Aug. 2007).

'Columbian police find drugs sub'. *BBC News* report, 26 March 2005 at http://news.bbc.co.uk/1/hi/world/americas/4383707.stm (28 March 2005).

'Combating piracy and armed robbery against ships – call for an international code'. *IMO News*, no. 2, 1999, p. 11 at http://www.imo.org/includes/blastDataOnly.asp/data_id%3D697/99-2.pdf (28 March 2005).

Corchado, Alfredo. 'Cartel's enforcers outpower their boss'. *Dallas Morning News*, 11 June 2007 at http://www.dallasnews.com/sharedcontent/dws/news/world/stories/061107dnintzetas.3a36238.html# (25 Aug. 2007).

Cornevin, Christophe. 'Tigers demanding money in Mafia style...'. *Le Figaro*, 2 Dec. 2005 (in English at *Denunge.dk* 7 Dec. 2005).

Corrigan, R. 'Malaysia to allow armed escorts in Malacca Strait'. *Sea Watch*, May/June 2005, p. 14 at http://www.seasia.com.sg/base/newsletter/seawatch_mayjun05.pdf#search=%22Glenn%20Defense%20Marine%20malacca%20straits%22 (7 Sept. 2007).

'Corruption charges cheat Chittagong port sell-off'. *Fairplay*, 1 June 2006.

Cottrill, Ken. 'Modern Marauders: Pirates on the South China Seas use high-tec weapons'. *Popular Mechanics*, no. 12, 1997.

Coughlin, Con. 'Al Qaeda 'as strong today as it was on 9/11''. *Daily Telegraph*, 13 Oct. 2007 at http://www.telegraph.co.uk/news/main.jhtml;jsessionid=FKOPOMRWZQBJBQFIQMFSFF4AVCBQ0IV0?xml=/news/2007/09/13/wladen113.xml (14 Oct. 2007).

'Could organised crime in Russia's eastern region aid terrorists?' CSIS *Transnational Threats Update*, vol. 1, no. 11, Aug. 2003.

'Countering LTTE: India admits helping Lanka'. *NDTV.com*, 16 Jan. 2008 at http://www.ndtv.com/convergence/ndtv/story.aspx?id=NEWEN20080038643&ch=1/15/2008%205:55:00%20PM# (21 Jan. 2008).

'Craft 'rammed' Yemen oil tanker. *BBC News* report, 6 Oct. 2002 at http://news.bbc.co.uk/1/hi/world/middle_east/2303363.stm (23 April 2004).

Crisp, Penny. 'A religious war comes to paradise'. *Asiaweek*, vol. 26, no. 17, 5 May 2000 at http://www.asiaweek.com/asiaweek/magazine/2000/0505/nat.philippines1.html (23 June 2007).

'Cruise ship repels Somali pirates'. *BBC News*, 5 Nov. 2005 at http://news.bbc.co.uk/1/hi/world/africa/4409662.stm (5 Nov. 2005).

Cummins, Chris. 'US digs in to gua Iraq oil exports'. *Wall Street Journal*, 12 Nov. 2007.

'Cuna confirms indications of terrorist threat to QM2 but says security is adequate'. *Aon Counter-terrorism and Political Risk report*, 8 Jan. 2004.

Damas, P. 'Supply Chains at War'. *American Shipper*, 1 Nov. 2001.

Daly, Emma. 'ETA warns tourists of Spain risk'. *International Herald Tribune*, 31 March 2001 at http://www.iht.com/articles/2001/03/31/eta_ed3_.php (4 July 2007).

'Danish newspaper explains City of Poros slaughter'. *Washington Report on Middle Eastern Affairs*, Oct. 1988, p. 39 at http://www.washington-report.org/backissues/1088/8810039.htm (16 Aug. 2004).

'Dark alliance rules the high seas'. *Penguin Star*, ND at http://www.geocities.com/TheTropics/Cove/4232/9905/pirate-9905-01.html (1 May 2004). See also Andreas Harsono (q.v.)

Darnton, John. 'Pirates plying Nigerian Seas'. *New York Times*, 9 Jan. 1977.

Date, Jack; and Cook, Theresa. 'Feds nab suspected cocaine smugglers in Pacific'. *Associated Press*, 22 Aug. 2007 at http://abcnews.go.com/TheLaw/story?id=3512231&page=1 (23 Aug. 2007).

Davidson, Nick. 'Chernobyl's 'nuclear nightmares''. *BBC News*, 13 July 2006 at http://news.bbc.co.uk/1/hi/sci/tech/5173310.stm (7 Sept. 2007).

Davis, Anthony. 'Blasts suggest MILF-JI links'. *JIR*, 1 May 2003.

———. 'Insurgent stronghold overrun by Philippine forces'. *JIR*, 21 Aug. 2000.

———. 'MILF Turns to Terrorism'. *JIR*, 1 April 2003

———. 'Piracy and terrorism should not be conflated'. *JIR*, vol. 16, no. 8. Aug. 2004, p. 57.

———. 'Police inteict arms traffic to Aceh'. *JIR*, 1 April 2004.

———. 'Tamil Tiger arms intercepted'. *JIR*, vol. 16, no. 2, Feb. 2004, p. 6.

———. 'Tamil Tigers seek to rebuild naval force'. *JIR*, March 2005, p. 39.

———. 'Tiger International: How a secret global network keeps Sri Lanka's Tamil guerrilla organization up and killing'. *Asiaweek*, 26 July 1996 at http://www.asiaweek.com/asiaweek/96/0726/cs1.html (28 June 2004).

———. 'Tracking Tigers in Phuket: A secret Tamil guerrilla base embarrasses Bangkok'. *Asiaweek.com*, vol. 29, no. 23, 16 June 2000 at http://www.asiaweek.com/asiaweek/magazine/2000/0616/nat.security.html (4 April 2005).

Davies, Ed. 'Indonesia counts its islands before it's too late'. *Reuters*, 16 May 2007 at http://uk.reuters.com/article/environmentNews/idUK-JAK7973020070515 (4 June 2007).

Davies, Kathryn. 'Modern-day pirates use speedboats to raid Southeast Asian sea lanes'. *Christian Science Monitor*, 18 Sept. 1981 at http://www.csmonitor.com/1981/0918/091837.html (22 June 2007).

'Dead men tell no tales'. *The Economist*, 16 Dec. 1999.

'Deadly weapons, suicide belt seized off Kodiakarai'. *The Hindu*, 15 Feb. 2007 at http://www.hindu.com/2007/02/15/stories/2007021504860400.htm (7 Sept. 2007).

'Dealers smuggle weapons into Gaza from Egypt'. *Associated Press*, 15 September 2005 at http://www.nytimes.com/2005/09/15/international/middleeast/15GAZA.html (7 July 2008).

'Death toll from Basilan ferry blast rises to 3'. *The Nation*, 7 Sept. 2005.

'Death toll in Gulf of Aden migrant tragedy reaches 107, UN Refugee Agency reports'. *UN News Service*, 16 Feb. 2007 at http://allafrica.com/stories/200702160914.html (15 March 2007).

'Death toll rises in Philippine blasts' *BBC News*, 26 Feb. 2000 at http://news.bbc.co.uk/1/hi/world/asia-pacific/656800.stm (7 Sept. 2007).

Dela Cruz, Lino. 'Moro rebel: 'Unseen hand' seen in Abu revival'. *SunStarNetworkOnline*, 30 Aug. 2005 at http://www.sunstar.com.ph/static/net/2005/08/30/moro.rebel.unseen.hand.seen.in.abu.revival.html (7 Sept. 2007).

'Delta militants deny Bakassi raid'. *BBC News*, 15 November 2007 at http://news.bbc.co.uk/1/hi/world/africa/7096331.stm (17 June 2008).

De Queiroz, Mario. 'Guinea-Bissau: African paradise for South American traffickers'. *Inter Press Services News Agency*, 10 Aug. 2007 at http://www.ipsnews.net/news.asp?idnews=38857 (14 Aug. 2007).

De Quetteville, Harry. 'No, I hope these men rot in jail'. *Sunday Telegraph*, 23 July 2006 at http://www.telegraph.co.uk/news/main.jhtml?xml=/news/2006/07/23/wmid623.xml (7 Sept. 2007).

———. 'Terrorists' missiles are from Teheran armoury'. *Daily Telegraph*, 17 July 2006 at http://www.telegraph.co.uk/news/main.jhtml?xml=/news/2006/07/17/wmid317.xml (17 July 2006).

Dickey, Christopher. 'Evil Genius'. *Newsweek Web Exclusive*, 20 Feb. 2003.

———. 'High sea terrorism'. *Newsweek*, 27 Jan. 2003.

Dickler, Jessica. 'Private subs plumb deep pockets, deeper waters'. *CNNMoney.com*, 3 August 2007 at http://money.cnn.com/2007/08/02/lifestyle/luxury_submarines/index.htm (4 July 2008).

Dillon, Jo. 'UK leads attack on piracy'. *The Independent*, 27 Aug. 2000 at http://news.independent.co.uk/uk/this_britain/article271276.ece (1 Feb. 2007).

Dillon, Paul. 'Piracy disappears in tsunami's wake'. *AlJazeera.net*, 31 Jan. 2005 at http://english.aljazeera.net/NR/exeres/5F174A5E-0812-40C1-9CA4-3F09F7D4FFEE.htm (1 May 2006).

'Dispute over al-Qaida's 'terrorist navy''. *WorldNetDaily*, 19 Feb. 2004 at http://www.wnd.com/news/article.asp?ARTICLE_ID=37190 (8 Jan. 2007).

Docena, Herbert. 'How the US got its Philippine bases back'. *Asia Times*, 28 Nov. 2007 at http://www.atimes.com/atimes/Southeast_Asia/IK28Ae01.html (28 Nov. 2007).

Donville, Christopher. 'Yo-ho-ho and an M16'. *Bloomberg*, December 1997, pp. 30-42.

Downie, Andrew. 'Brazil gang takes on state'. *Christian Science Monitor*, 16 May 2006 at http://www.csmonitor.com/2006/0516/p06s01-woam.html (6 Aug. 2007).

————; and Tim, Jeffery. 'Blake's killers are jailed'. *Daily Telegraph*, 20 June 2002 at http://www.telegraph.co.uk/sport/main.jhtml?xml=/sport/2002/06/20/soyach21.xml (7 Sept. 2007)..

'Double vision on piracy'. *Fairplay*, 10 May 2007.

Drees, Caroline; and Ang, Edgar. 'US at risk from boats packed with explosives'. *Reuters*, 1 June 2006.

'Drug cartels begin cracking West Africa'. *Jane's Foreign Report*, 23 Aug. 2007.

'Drug gangs expand their fleet'. *Strategy Page*, 2 Nov. 2007 at http://www.strategypage.com/htmw/htsub/articles/20071102.aspx (6 Nov. 2007).

'Drug lo's sub designer in custody'. *El Tiempo* (Bogota), 6 Feb. 2008.

'Drug sub war intensifies'. *Strategy Page*, 11 Jan. 2008 at http://www.strategypage.com/htmw/htsub/articles/20080110.aspx (11 Jan. 2008).

'Drug submarine found in Colombia'. *BBC News*, 7 Sept. 2000 at http://news.bbc.co.uk/1/hi/world/americas/915059.stm (28 March 2005).

'Drug 'submarine' off Costa Rica was disguised boat'. *Reuters*, 22 Nov. 2006.

Duhul, Salad. 'GET SOME! Destroyer bombas militants'. *Associated Press*, 3 June 2007 at http://www.navytimes.com/news/2007/06/ap_somalia_070603/ (4 June 2007).

Ebiri, Kelvin. 'Explosion rocks ship in Port Harcourt'. *The Guaian* (Lagos), 12 Jan. 2008 at http://www.guaiannewsngr.com/news/article02//indexn2_h tml?pdate=120108&ptitle=Explosion%20Rocks%20Oil%20Ship%20 In%20Port%20Harcourt (19 March 2008).

Edem, Edem. 'Pirates kill 21 Camerounian soldiers'. *Leadership* (Abuja), 14 Nov. 2007 at http://allafrica.com/stories/200711140258.html (12 May 2008).

Eggan, Dan. '9/11 panel links Al Qaeda, Iran: Bin Laden might have part in Khobar Towers, report says'. *The Washington Post*, 26 June 2004 at http://www.washingtonpost.com/wp-dyn/articles/A6581-2004Jun25.html (7 September 2007).

'EIA cites importance of key world shipping routes'. *Oil and Gas Journal*, 9 March 1994.

'Eight dead in clash between fishermen and pirates off Mindanao waters'. *The Philippine Star*, 18 Oct. 2006.

Ekeinde, Austin. ''Rebels bomb tanker in Nigeria, exports spared'. *Reuters*, 11 Jan. 2008 at http://www.signonsandiego.com/news/world/20080111-0732-nigeria-fire-.html (19 March 2008).

Eklöf, Stefan. 'Piracy: Real Menace or Red Herring?' *Asia Times Online*, 4 Aug. 2005 at http://www.atimes.com/atimes/Southeast_Asia/GH04Ae01.html (5 Aug. 2005). Also at http://japanfocus.org/article.asp?id=351 (1 May 2006).

Elegant, Simon. 'The return of Abu Sayyaf'. *TIME Asia*, 23 Aug. 2004 at http://www.
time.com/time/asia/magazine/article/0,13673,501040830-686107,00.
html (14 July 2006).

————. 'Still going strong'. *TIME*, 15 Dec. 2003 at http://www.time.com/time/
magazine/article/0,9171,501031222-561532,00.html (26 June 2007).

'Elephant in the room, The'. *Fairplay*, 7 Sept. 2006.

Ellen, Eric. 'Is there an even darker side to China Sea piracy?' *Lloyd's List*, 18 December 1997.

————. 'Shipowners naïve to think that paying ransom will stop vessel seizures'.
ICC *Commercial Crime International*, March 1998, p. 4.

Ellis, Eric. 'Piracy on the high seas is on the rise in South-East Asia'. *Fortune*, 29
Sept. 2003 at http://www.singapore-window.org/sw03/030919fo.htm (2
Oct. 2006).

'Endangered Cargo'. *Shiptalk*, 29 May 2007 at http://www.shiptalk.com/index.asp
?ItemID=2112&rcid=191&pcid=178&cid=191'#anch (29 May 2007).

English, Ben; Gallagher, Ian; and Sommerfield, Jef. 'Al Qaeda targeting ocean
liners'. *FOX News report*, 30 Dec. 2003 at http://www.foxnews.com/
story/0%2C2933%2C106814%2C00.html (25 June 2004).

Espina-Varona, Inday. 'Terror groups to use crime to raise funds'. *The Manila
Times*, 7 Jan. 2007 at http://www.manilatimes.net/national/2007/jan/07/
yehey/top_stories/20070107top2.html (7 Jan. 2007).

————; and Villaviray, Johnna. 'Capture of MILF camps has downside for govt'.
The Manila Times Special Feature, 19 June 2002 at http://www.manila-
times.net/others/special/2002/jun/19/20020619spe1.html (11 July 2008).

Evans, Gareth. 'Aceh is building peace from its ruins'. *International Herald Tribune*, 23 Dec. 2005 at http://www.iht.com/articles/2005/12/23/news/
edevans.php (7 Sept. 2007).

Evans, Michael. 'Four servicemen killed in Basra river patrol blast'. *The Times*, 13
Nov. 2006 at http://www.timesonline.co.uk/article/0,,7374-2451706,00.
html (3 Jan. 2008).

'Explosive proof of gas safety'. *Fairplay*, 25 May 2006.

Fabey, Michael. 'Sitting ducks'. *Latin Trade*, Sept. 1999 at http://findarticles.
com/p/articles/mi_m0BEK/is_9_7/ai_55548157 (7 Sept. 2007).

'Facing a 'Liquid Auschwitz''. TIME, vol. 114, no. 1, 2 July 1979 at http://
www.time.com/time/magazine/article/0,9171,916830,00.html (7 Sept.
2007).

Faiola, Anthony. 'Brazilian gangs take turf wars out of slums'. *Washington Post*, 15
Dec. 2002.

Faison, Seth. 'Pirates, with speedboats, reign in China Sea port'. *New York Times*,
20 April 1997.

Falksohn, Rüdiger; and Rao, Padma. 'Old Animosities, New Pain: Civil War Returns to Sri Lanka'. *Spiegel Online,* 23 Aug. 2006 at http://service.spiegel. de/cache/international/spiegel/0,1518,433061,00.html (24 Aug. 2006).

Farah, Douglas. 'Russian mob, drug cartels joining forces'. *The Washington Post,* 29 Sept. 1997 at http://www.washingtonpost.com/wp-srv/inatl/longterm/ russiagov/stories/mafia092997.htm (4 April 2007).

Faram, Mark D. 'War on drugs goes underwater'. *Navy Times,* 28 April 2008.

'FBI issues scuba industry alert over requests for specialized training, 'nefarious activity''. *UnderwaterTimes.com,* 22 June 2007 at http://www.underwatertimes.com/news.php?article_id=64810251370 (26 June 2007).

'FBI warns that terrorists may use floating bombs'. *Washington Post,* 29 June 2004.

Felstead, Andrea; and Odell. Mark. 'Agencies fear extent of al-Qaeda's sea network'. *FT.com Special Reports,* 21 Feb. 2002 at http://specials.ft.com/attackonterrorism/FT3U47PPYXC.html (8 Oct. 2006).

Fegan, Brian. 'Plundering the sea'. *Inside Indonesia,* January-March 2003 at http:// www.insideindonesia.org/edit73/Fegan%20fishing.htm (3 July 2008).

Fernandez, Clarence. 'Malacca Strait users may have to pay fees – experts'. *Reuters,* 2 Aug. 2006.

———. 'Strait nations urged not to relax piracy vigil'. *Reuters,* 15 June 2007 at http://www.signonsandiego.com/news/business/20070615-0201-piracy-malacca-.html (16 June 2007).

———. 'World body opposes weapons on ships to fight piracy'. *Reuters AlertNet,* 19 Sept. 2006.

'Ferry blast injures 30 in southern Philippines'. *New York Times,* 28 Aug. 2005 at http://www.nytimes.com/aponline/international/AP-Philippines-Ferry-Blast.html?pagewanted=print (28 Aug. 2005).

Fidler, Stephen. 'Al Qaeda linked to operations from Iran'. *Financial Times,* 6 July 2007.

———; and Harris, Arlen. 'Attacks are raising security and insurance concerns'. *Financial Times,* 23 June 2005.

'First Sea Lo warns of al-Qaeda plot to target merchant ships'. *Lloyd's List.* 6 Aug. 2004.

'Fish trawlers decry pirate activities'. *The Vangua,* 5 May 2006 at http://www.illegal-fishing.info/item_single.php?item=news&item_id=225&approach_ id=13 (22 July 2007).

'Fishing boat explodes near Israeli vessel'. *CNN.com,* 22 Nov. 2002 at http://www. cnn.com/2002/WORLD/meast/11/22/mideast/ (14 July 2004).

Fleming, Nic. 'The cheap and easy recipe for bombs'. *Daily Telegraph,* 31 March 2004 at http://www.telegraph.co.uk/news/main.jhtml?xml=/ news/2004/03/31/nterr231.xml (1 July 2004).

Flynn, Matthew. 'China promises crackdown as it strives to escape image of a safe haven for pirates'. *Lloyd's List,* 24 February 1999.

Forero, Juan. 'Drug traffic beneath the waves'. *Washington Post,* 6 Feb. 2008 at http://www.washingtonpost.com/wp-dyn/content/article/2008/02/05/AR2008020503123.html (7 Feb. 2008).

'Former GAM members 'high sea robbers'. *Jakarta Post,* 2 Oct. 2007.

Foster, Peter. '17 killed in sea battle as Tamils attack navy'. *Daily Telegraph,* 29 June 2006 at http://www.telegraph.co.uk/news/main.jhtml?xml=/news/2006/06/29/wtamil29.xml (18 Oct. 2006).

————. 'Arms seized as terrorists are set free'. *Daily Telegraph,* 29 July 2000 at http://www.telegraph.co.uk/news/main.jhtml?xml=/news/2000/07/29/nira29.xml (1 July 2004).

————. 'Burgeoning lawlessness in India's Wild East. *Daily Telegraph,* 20 March 2007 at http://www.telegraph.co.uk/news/main.jhtml?xml=/news/2007/03/19/wganges19.xml (7 Sept. 2007).

————. 'Revenge attacks on Tigers as army chief is hurt in blast'. *Daily Telegraph,* 26 April 2006 at http://www.telegraph.co.uk/news/main.jhtml?xml=/news/2006/04/26/wtigers26.xml (7 Sept. 2007).

————. 'Secret arrest yielded 'treasure trove''. *Daily Telegraph,* 3 Aug. 2004 at http://www.telegraph.co.uk/news/main.jhtml?xml=/news/2004/08/03/wterr103.xml. (3 Aug. 2004).

————. 'Sri Lankan rebels attack southern port popular with tourists'. *Daily Telegraph,* 18 Oct. 2006 at http://www.telegraph.co.uk/news/main.jhtml?xml=/news/2006/10/18/ulanka.xml (18 Oct. 2006).

————. 'Tamil Tiger naval raid brings war closer to Sri Lanka'. *Daily Telegraph,* 12 May 2006 at http://www.telegraph.co.uk/news/main.jhtml?xml=/news/2006/05/12/wtamil12.xml (18 Oct. 2006).

————. 'Tamil Tiger suicide squad in audacious strike'. *Daily Telegraph,* 24 Oct. 2007 at http://www.telegraph.co.uk/news/main.jhtml?xml=/news/2007/10/23/wlanka123.xml (25 Oct. 2007).

Fox, Jon. 'US nuclear detection official doubts threat by sea'. NTI *Global Security Newswire,* 25 May 2007 at http://www.nti.org/d_newswire/issues/2007_5_25.html#30A5C1DB (6 June 2007).

Francis, David. 'As violence grows along boer, Congress debates funding for fighting Mexican drug cartels'. *World Politics Review,* 7 March 2008 at http://www.worldpoliticsreview.com/article.aspx?id=1735 (8 March 2008).

Frank, Jerry. 'Big business gets political over rising global risks'. *Lloyd's List,* 24 Jan. 2008.

Fraser, Niall. 'China: Mainland accussed of ship hijack.' *Lloyd's List,* 29 Nov. 1997.

'Freighter disappears off Africa'. *New York Times,* 21 Jan. 1978.

Fry, Goon; and Thompson, Michael. 'The bigger the ship, the greater the risk'.
   Lloyd's List, 9 June 2006.

Fua, Asif. 'Is the tide turning against the LTTE?' *The Sunday Times* (Colombo), 14
   October 2007 at http://sundaytimes.lk/071014/News/news00029.html
   (23 May 2008).

Gabriel, Omoh; Bivbere, Godfrey; and Ugwaudu, Ifeanyi. 'Renewed piracy attacks:
   fish scarcity looms, Nigeria may loose $600m export earnings'. *Vangua,* 2
   June 2008 at http://www.vanguangr.com/index.php?option=com_conte
   nt&task=view&id=9334&Itemid=0 (2 June 2008).

'GAM says it will not attack ships in Malacca Straights' (sic). *Islam Online,* 7 Sept.
   2001 at http://www.islam-online.net/English/News/2001-09/08/arti-
   cle5.shtml (7 Sept. 2007).

Ganesh, V. Shankar. 'Malaysian, Indonesian police to up anti-piracy operations in
   Straits of Malacca'. *New Straits Times,* 18 June 2007.

Gannon, Kathy. 'Yemen employs new terror approach'. *Washington Post,* 4
   July 2007 at http://www.washingtonpost.com/wp-dyn/content/arti-
   cle/2007/07/04/AR2007070400992.html (9 July 2007).

Garamone, Jim. 'Maritime ops in Middle East have deterrent effect'. *American
   Forces Information Service News Articles,* 27 April 2006 at http://www.
   defenselink.mil/news/Apr2006/20060427_4952.html (7 Sept. 2007).

———. '"Ring of steel" encircles Iraqi oil platforms'. Armed Forces Information
   Service *News Article,* 15 July 2006 at http://www.defenselink.mil/news/
   May2006/20060501_4986.html (15 July 2006).

Ganer, Simon. 'Sri Lankan navy battles rebels at sea, troops ambushed'. *Reuters,* 18
   Nov. 2006 at http://thestar.com.my/news/story.asp?file=/2006/11/18/
   worldupdates/2006-11-18T201751Z_01_NOOTR_RTRJONC_0_-
   276784-5&sec=Worldupdates (15 June 2007).

Gargan, Edwa A. 'India bombings: Gangs involved, but who else?' *New York Times,*
   16 May 1993 at http://query.nytimes.com/gst/fullpage.html?res=9F0CE
   5D81F3EF935A25756C0A965958260 (7 Sept. 2007).

'Gas fleet up 50% in two years'. *Fairplay,* 6 July 2006.

'Gasoline pipeline blast kills up to 200 in Nigeria'. *CNN.com,* 13 May 2006 at
   http://www.cnn.com/2006/WORLD/africa/05/12/nigeria.blast/index.
   html?section=cnn_topstories (15 May 2006).

Gatsiounis, Ioannis. 'Malaysia tweaks its terror compass'. *Asia Times.com,* 25 June
   2004 at http://www.atimes.com/atimes/Southeast_Asia/FF25Ae06.html
   (1 July 2007).

———. 'Pirates mock Malacca Straits security'. *AsiaTimes.com,* 9 April 2005 at http://
   www.atimes.com/atimes/Southeast_Asia/GD09Ae02.html (26 April 2005).

Gedye, Robin. 'Al Qaeda rampage ends in bloody gunfight', *Daily Telegraph,*
   31 May 2004 at http://www.telegraph.co.uk/news/main.jhtml?xml=/
   news/2004/05/31/wsaud31.xml (7 Sept. 2007).

Geibel, Adam. 'Cyclones, Firebolt and the Persian Gulf pirates'. *Strategy Page,* 22 Oct. 2003 at http://www.strategypage.com/dls/articles2003/20031022. asp (1 Nov. 2007).

Gertz, Bill. 'China enacts law extending its control'. *Washington Times,* 27 Jan. 2003.

———. 'Inside the Ring: Pacific terrorism'. *Washington Times,* 2 Nov. 2007.

Gettleman, Jeffrey. 'Somalia reconciliation conference opens, but soon stalls'. *New York Times,* 16 July 2007 at http://www.nytimes.com/2007/07/16/world/africa/16somalia.html?_r=1&ref=world&oref=slogin (17 July 2007).

Gillan, Audrey. 'Guns, grenades and GPS: the brutal reality of Somalia's pirates'. *The Guaian,* 12 June 2007 at http://www.guaian.co.uk/international/story/0,,2100605,00.html (13 June 2007).

Glanz, James. '15 miles offshore, safeguaing Iraq's oil lifeline', *New York Times,* 6 July 2004.

Glass, Charles. 'The New Piracy', *London Review of Books,* vol. 25, no. 24, 18 Dec. 2003 at http://www.lrb.co.uk/v25/n24/glas01_.html (4 July 2004).

Glenton, Bill. 'A sea change required on security risks'. *Financial Times,* 7 Sept. 2002.

Glionna, John M. 'A friendly voice, when pirates strike'. *Los Angeles Times,* 13 Nov. 2006 at http://www.latimes.com/news/nationworld/world/la-fg-pirates13nov13,0,260241.story?coll=la-home-headlines (13 Nov. 2006).

'Global concern over maritime security cripples LTTE'. *News Post India,* 21 Jan. 2008 at http://newspostindia.com/report-32426 (21 Jan. 2008).

Gomez, Jim. 'DNA tests confirm death terror group leader in the Philippines'. *Associated Press,* 20 Jan. 2007 at http://www.iht.com/articles/ap/2007/01/20/asia/AS-GEN-Philippines-Abu-Sayyaf.php (2 July 2007).

———. 'Terrorists push scuba training, guerrilla says'. *The San Diego Union-Tribune,* 18 March 2005 at http://www.signonsandiego.com/union-trib/20050318/news_1n18terror.html (22 July 2006) also available as 'Terror's New Frontier: Underwater'. *CBS News,* 18 March 2005 at http://www.cbsnews.com/stories/2005/03/18/terror/main681524.shtml?CMP=ILC-SearchStories (7 Sept. 2007)..

Goodenough, Patrick. 'Maritime security takes centre stage in SE Asia'. *CNSNews.com,* 29 June 2004 at http://www.cnsnews.com/ForeignBureaus/archive/200406/FOR20040629b.html (20 July 2004).

Goodspeed, Peter. 'Not since Captain Kidd has piracy been so rife'. *National Post,* 3 Aug. 2001.

Gorman, Christine. 'How gaen-variety fertilizer becomes killer bombs'. *TIME,* vol. 145, no. 18, 1 May 1995.

'Greece traces route of seized ship'. *CNN.com,* 24 June 2003 at http://edition.cnn.com/2003/WORLD/europe/06/23/greece.ship/ (1 July 2004).

Greenberg, Hanan. 'IDF says ready to battle Hamas at sea'. *YnetNews.com*, 9 Aug. 2007 at http://www.ynetnews.com/articles/0,7340,L-3435869,00.html (16 Sept. 2007).

———. 'Navy: easier for terrorists to smuggle arms by sea'. *YnetNews.com*, 15 May 2006 at http://www.ynetnews.com/articles/0,7340,L-3250947,00. html (28 July 2006).

———. 'Navy seizes explosives off Gaza shore'. *YnetNews.com*, 14 May 2006 at http://www.ynetnews.com/articles/0,7340,L-3250824,00.html (3 Sept. 2007).

Grey, Michael. 'Stevenson says victims of piracy must be offered structured support regime'. *Lloyd's List*, 25 May 2007.

Grier, Peter; and Bowers, Faye. 'How al-Qaeda might strike the US by sea'. *Christian Science Monitor*, 15 May 2003 at http://www.csmonitor. com/2003/0515/p02s02-usgn.htm (2 June 2004).

Grillo, Ioan. 'Drug cartels target military in Mexico'. *Associated Press*, 14 May 2007 at http://www.washingtonpost.com/wp-dyn/content/article/2007/05/14/ AR2007051400607.html (15 Feb. 2008).

———. 'Mexico's narco-insurgency'. *TIME*, 25 Jan. 2008 at http://www.time. com/time/world/article/0,8599,1707070,00.html (29 Jan. 2008).

Grissim, John. 'Pirates again stalking the seven seas'. *The World Paper*, May 1997.

———. 'The hijacking of the Anna Sierra'. *The World Paper*, May 1997.

'Group claims attack: Double suicide bombings'. *Associated Press*, 25 April 2007 at http://www.suburbanchicagonews.com/heraldnews/news/356058,4_1_ JO25_IRAQ_S1.article (22 May 2007).

'Guide to the Philippines conflict'. *BBC News*, 10 Feb. 2005 at http://news.bbc. co.uk/1/hi/world/asia-pacific/1695576.stm#milf (7 Sept. 2007).

Guidera, Anita. 'My private hell on the high sea'. *Irish Independent*, 29 March 2008 at http://www.independent.ie/national-news/my-private-hell-on-the-high-sea-1331733.html (19 April 2008).

Gunaratna, Rohan. 'LTTE in South Africa'. *Frontline*, vol. 15, no. 25, 5 Dec.-18 Dec. 1998 at http://www.hinduonnet.com/fline/fl1524/15240500.htm (17 Dec. 2007).

———. 'LTTE in South Africa II'. *Frontline*, vol. 15, no. 24, 21 Nov.-4 Dec. 1998 at http://www.hinduonnet.com/fline/fl1525/15250570.htm (17 Dec. 2007).

———. 'The transformation of terror?' *Asia Times Online*, 25 Sept. 2002 at http:// www.atimes.com/atimes/South_Asia/DI25Df05.html (8 Aug. 2005).

Gwin, Peter. 'Dark Passage'. *National Geographic*, vol. 212, no. 4, Oct. 2007, pp. 126-149.

Habibu, Sira; and Ibrahim, Nik Khusairi. 'Shocker over private armies patrolling straits'. *Lloyd's List*, 22 Dec. 2005 available in *Sea Watch*, Jan. 2006, p. 8

at http://www.seasia.com.sg/base/newsletter/seawatch_jan06.pdf (7 Sept. 2007).

Hall, Mimi. 'Uncle Sam to scuba divers: I want you'. *USA Today*, 9 July 2007 at http://www.usatoday.com/news/nation/2007-07-08-scuba_N.htm (7 Sept. 2007).

Halloran, Richa. 'What if Asia's pirates and terrorists joined hands?' *South China Morning Post*, 17 May 2003.

'Hamas announces formation of its new coast gua unit'. *Associated Press*, 11 Aug. 2007 at http://www.iht.com/articles/ap/2007/08/11/africa/ME-GEN-Palestinians-Navy.php (15 Aug. 2007).

'Hamas attack on Israeli beach settlement repelled'. *Irish Examiner*, 27 March 2004 at http://archives.tcm.ie/irishexaminer/2004/03/27/story77261633.asp (16 Sept. 2007).

'Hambali: 'Asia's bin Laden''. *BBC News*, 10 Feb. 2006 at http://news.bbc.co.uk/1/hi/world/asia-pacific/2346225.stm (7 Sept. 2007).

Hand, Marcus. 'Agencies deny rift over piracy reporting'. *Lloyd's List*, 3 May 2007.

———. 'Anti-piracy lookouts credited with foiling Somali hijack gangs'. *Lloyd's List*, 20 Aug. 2007.

———. 'Asian alliance to fight piracy goes ahead despite dissenters'. *Lloyd's List*, 22 June 2006.

———. 'Attacks hit bid to end Malacca war risk rating'. *Lloyd's List*, 5 July 2006.

———. 'Chemtanker feared hijacked'. *Lloyd's List*, 22 Dec. 2005.

———. 'Flags of convenience are 'assisting criminals''. *Lloyd's List*, 3 Nov. 2005.

———. 'Framework could be copied in other regions'. *Lloyd's List*, 7 Sept. 2007.

———. 'Funding sought for $1000m Malacca Strait safety projects'. *Lloyd's List*, 21 Sept. 2006.

———. 'IMB fights back over potential new Asian anti-piracy centre'. *Lloyd's List*, 26 May 2006.

———. 'IMB sounds red alert over Somalia piracy'. *Lloyds List*, 11 June 2007.

———. 'Indonesia detains pirates for tanker hijacking'. *Lloyd's List*, 26 Sept. 2007.

———. 'Indonesia holds 16 over vessel hijacks'. *Lloyd's List*, 30 June 2006.

———. 'Joint alert forces pirates to flee hijacked tanker'. *Lloyd's List*, 29 Dec. 2005.

———. 'Joint patrols cut Malacca attacks to 'zero per cent''. *Lloyd's List*, 14 April 2008.

———. 'Keep up pressure on pirates, urges IMB'. *Lloyd's List*, 12 May 2006.

———. 'Landmark deal for Malacca Strait safety'. *Lloyd's List*, 19 Sept. 2006.

———. 'Littoral states launch airborne pirate patrol over Malacca Strait'. *Lloyd's List*, 14 Sept. 2005.

———. 'Malaysian clampdown cuts attacks'. *Lloyd's List*, 20 March 2006.

———. 'Malaysian owners call for mandatory Malacca security funding'. *Lloyd's List*, 3 Oct. 2006.

———. 'Malaysian premier rejects private armed escorts in Malacca Strait'. *Lloyd's List*, 23 May 2005 available in *Sea Watch*, May/June 2005, p. 12 at http://www.seasia.com.sg/base/newsletter/seawatch_mayjun05. pdf#search=%22Glenn%20Defense%20Marine%20malacca%20 straits%22). (7 Sept. 2007).

———. 'Nippon Foundation calls for Malacca fund'. *Lloyd's List*, 15 March 2007.

———. 'No tolls in Malacca Strait for owners – Mitropoulos'. *Lloyd's List*, 20 Sept. 2006.

———. 'Pay-as-you-go safety scheme for Malacca Strait'. *Lloyd's List*, 2 June 2006.

———. 'Paying for passage: a new paradigm in maritime safety'. *Lloyd's List*, 14 June 2006.

———. 'Piracy alert wrangle leads to loss of life fears'. *Lloyd's List*, 25 April 2007.

———. 'Piracy attacks leave owners facing ransom cover dilemma'. *Lloyd's List*, 24 June 2005.

———. 'Piracy experts fear Malacca Strait attacks will set new kidnap agenda'. *Lloyd's List*, 12 July 2006.

———. 'Pirate attack warning at Anambas Islands'. *Lloyd's List*, 9 June 2008.

———. 'Pirates kidnap tug crew in Malacca Strait'. *Lloyd's List*, 14 Aug. 2007.

———. 'Poverty blamed for piracy'. *Lloyd's List*, 23 June 2006.

———. 'ReCAAP success in Asia prompts call for expansion'. *Lloyd's List*, 29 Feb. 2008.

———. 'Shipowners refuse to pay for Strait security'. *Lloyd's List*, 13 June 2007.

———. 'Somali pirates move even further from the coast'. *Lloyd's List*, 14 Nov. 2005.

———. 'Somalia pirates using 'mother vessel' tactics'. *Lloyd's List*, 18 May 2007.

———. 'Survey reveals human cost of piracy'. *Lloyd's List*, 14 June 2007.

———. 'UN Security Council comes down on Somali pirates'. *Lloyd's List*, 3 June 2008.

———. 'Users pledge to fund Malacca Strait safety'. *Lloyd's List*, 6 Sept. 2007.

———. and Brewer, James. 'Malacca Strait declared a high risk zone by Joint War Committee'. *Lloyd's List*, 1 July 2005.

Hansen, Louis; Wiltrout, Kate; and Eisman, Dale. 'US prowls Africa's coats to extinguish threat from pirates'. *The Virginian-Pilot*, 21 March 2006 at http://home.hamptonroads.com/stories/story.cfm?story=101775&ran=1 12450&tref=po (21 March 2006).

Hanson, Stephanie. 'In West Africa, Threat of Narco-States'. Council of Foreign Relations *Daily Analysis*, 10 July 2007 at http://www.cfr.org/publica-tion/13750/in_west_africa_threat_of_narcostates.html (29 Aug. 2007).

Haesty, Greg. 'US seaports warned to beware of terrorist divers'. *Cyber Diver News Network*, 31 Aug. 2003 at http://www.cdnn.info/industry/i030831/ i030831.html (23 July 2006).

Harding, Thomas. 'Terrorist leader told MI5 agent that Real IRA made Omagh bomb', *Daily Telegraph*, 19 June 2003 at http://www.telegraph.co.uk/ news/main.jhtml?xml=/news/2003/06/19/nmckev19.xml (7 Sept. 2007).

Hariharan, R. 'Sri Lanka 2006: LTTE's unbalanced score ca'. *Asian Tribune*, 12 Jan. 2007 at http://www.asiantribune.com/index.php?q=node/4100 (7 Sept. 2007).

Harnden, Toby. 'Detainee 'admits USS Cole bombing''. *Daily Telegraph*, 20 March 2007 at http://www.telegraph.co.uk/news/main.jhtml?xml=/ news/2007/03/20/wgitmo20.xml (20 March 2007).

———. 'Iran admits it gave Hizbollah missiles to hit all Israel'. *Sunday Telegraph*, 6 Aug. 2006 at http://www.telegraph.co.uk/news/main.jhtml?xml=/ news/2006/08/06/wmid206.xml (7 Sept. 2007).

———. 'Iran's Revolutionary Guards a 'terror group''. *Daily Telegraph*, 20 Aug. 2007 at http://www.telegraph.co.uk/news/main.jhtml?xml=/news/2007/08/16/ wiran116.xml (25 Oct. 2007).

———. 'Lebanese forces accused of helping Hezbollah rocket attack in Israeli ship'. *Sunday Telegraph*, 6 Aug. 2006 at http://www.telegraph.co.uk/ news/main.jhtml?xml=/news/2006/08/06/wmid306.xml (6 Aug. 2006).

Harper, Tom. 'Dirty bomb threat high and rising'. *Sunday Telegraph*, 17 June 2007 at http://www.telegraph.co.uk/news/main.jhtml?xml=/news/2007/06/17/ nterr117.xml (18 June 2007).

Harris, Francis. 'Top terrorist escapes US custody'. *Daily Telegraph*, 3 Nov. 2005 at http://www.telegraph.co.uk/news/main.jhtml?xml=/news/2005/11/03/ wescap03.xml (7 Sept. 2007).

———. 'Terrorist alert over Yemen jail breakout'. *Daily Telegraph*, 6 Feb. 2006 at http://www.telegraph.co.uk/news/main.jhtml?xml=/news/2006/02/06/ wyemen06.xml&sSheet=/news/2006/02/06/ixworld.html (15 July 2006).

Harrison, Frances. 'Sailors killed in Sri Lanka blast'. *BBC News*, 23 May 2006 at http://news.bbc.co.uk/1/hi/world/south_asia/1346409.stm (7 Sept. 2007).

Harsono, Andreas. 'Dark alliance rules the high seas'. *The Nation*, (Bangkok) 13 April 1999 at http://www.icij.org/investigate/harsono.html (1 May 2004) and at http://andreasharsono.blogspot.com/search?updated-min=1999-01-01T00%3A00%3A00%2B07%3A00&updated-max=2000-01-01T00%3A00%3A00%2B07%3A00&max-results=17 (16 June 2007). This article appears to be an edited version of a longer, unattributed article also entitled 'Dark alliance rules the high seas' (q.v.)

————. 'Mr Wong: Pirate or law-abiding citizen?' 13 April 1999 at http://andreasharsono.blogspot.com/1999/04/mr-wong-pirate-or-law-abiding-citizen.html (15 June 2007).

'Heavily-armed pirates attack, Thai, South Korea ships'. *Channel NewsAsia*, 30 April 2008 at http://www.channelnewsasia.com/stories/afp_asiapacific/view/344598/1/.html (4 May 2008).

Helmoed-Roemer, Heitman. 'Attacks underline escalation of Somali piracy threat'. *Jane's Defence Weekly*, 30 May 2007.

Henderson, Mike. 'No ocean is untainted by the polluting hand of Man'. *The Times*, 15 Feb. 2008 at http://www.timesonline.co.uk/tol/news/uk/science/article3369142.ece (16 Feb. 2008).

'Heroin trail through India, The'. *Indian Express*, 3 Nov. 1999 at http://www.indianexpress.com/res/web/pIe/ie/daily/19991103/ige03033.html (7 Sept. 2007).

Hiebert, Murray. 'Sink or swim?' *Far Eastern Economic Review*, 23 February 1989.

Hirshkorn, Phil. 'New York reduces 9/11death toll by 40'. *CNN.com*, 29 Oct. 2003 at http://www.cnn.com/2003/US/Northeast/10/29/wtc.deaths/ (7 Sept. 2007).

Hirst, Michael. "100 Tigers killed' in sea battle with Sri Lankan navy'. *Daily Telegraph*, 3 Sept. 2006 at http://www.telegraph.co.uk/news/main.jhtml?xml=/news/2006/09/03/wsri03.xml (18 Oct. 2006).

Hitt, Jack. 'Bandits in the global shipping lanes'. *The New York Times Magazine*, 20 Aug. 2000.

'Hizbollah brings out Iranian Silkworm to hit Israel corvette'. *DEBKA-file*, 15 July 2006 at http://www.debka.com/article.php?aid=1184 (7 Sept. 2007).

'Hizbollah planned to attack US and Israeli ships in Singapore'. 2002. Institute for Counter-Terrorism *Spotlight*, 9 June 2002 at http://www.ict.org.il/index.php?sid=119&lang=en&act=page&id=14136&str=singapore (7 Sept. 2007).

'HK gives Hainan piracy warning'. *Lloyd's List*, 18 March 1993.

Hoffman, Bruce. 'Remember Al Qaeda? They're baaack'. *Los Angeles Times*, 20 Feb. 2007 at http://www.latimes.com/news/opinion/commentary/la-oe-hoffman20feb20,0,7373740.story?coll=la-home-commentary (20 Feb. 2007).

Hosenball, Mark. 'Look Out Below – The terror threat from the sea'. *Newsweek*, 28 March 2005 at http://www.msnbc.msn.com/id/7244239/site/newsweek/ (23 March 2005).

Hotten, Russell. Nigerian militant's step up attack against Shell's oilfields'. *Daily Telegraph*, 19 June 2008 at http://www.telegraph.co.uk/money/main.jhtml?xml=/money/2008/06/19/bcnshell119.xml (19 June 2008).

Houreld, Katharine. 'Anti-piracy coalition turns their sights on elusive Somali mother ship'. *Associated Press*, 1 Dec. 2007 at http://www.signonsandiego.com/news/world/20071201-1251-huntingpirates.html (16 April 2008).

Huband, Mark. 'Al-Qaeda forms drug links as anti-terror war bites'. *Financial Times*, 15 June 2004.

———. 'Extremists in Europe find fraud pays'. *Financial Times*, 15 June 2004.

———. 'WMRC report blames Indonesian corruption for rise in piracy in Southeast Asian waters'. *Financial Times*, 14 Feb. 2004.

"Hundreds injured in cruise ship lurch'. *Daily Telegraph*, 20 July 2006 at http://www.telegraph.co.uk/news/main.jhtml;jsessionid=4SM15EDMSFZN BQFIQMFSFFOAVCBQ0IV0?xml=/news/2006/07/20/uship.xml (7 Sept. 2007).

'I beat pirates with a hose and a sonic cannon'. *BBC News*, 17 May 2007 at http://news.bbc.co.uk/1/hi/uk/6664677.stm (14 June 2007).

'IDF Naval craft seized several hundred kg of explosives'. Israel Ministry of Foreign Affairs *Press Release*, 14 May 2006 at http://www.mfa.gov.il/MFA/ Terrorism-+Obstacle+to+Peace/Terrorism+and+Islamic+Fundamental ism-/IDF+Naval+craft+seized+several+hundred+kg+of+explosives+14-May-2006.htm (8 Dec. 2007).

'IDF seizes bomb making supply ship heading for Gaza'. *Jewish Institute for National Security Affairs Online*, 26 May 2003 at http://www.jinsa.org/articles/articles.html/function/view/categoryid/852/documentid/2045/history/3,2360,654,852,2045 (2 Oct. 2006).

Ignattius, David. 'Portents of a nuclear al-Qaeda'. *Washington Post*, 18 October 2007 at http://www.washingtonpost.com/wp-dyn/content/article/2007/10/17/ AR2007101702114.html (27 May 2008).

Ijaz, Mansoor. 'The maritime threat from al-Qaeda'. *Financial Times*, 19 Oct. 2003.

Iliff, Laurence. 'Cartels go on offensive against Mexican army'. *Dallas Morning News*, 12 May 2007 at http://www.dallasnews.com/sharedcontent/dws/news/world/mexico/stories/DN-drugwar_12int.ART0.State. Edition2.42d2047.html# (22 May 2007).

———; and Corchado, Alfredo. 'Mexico drug wars'. *Dallas Morning News*, 7 June 2008 at http://www.dallasnews.com/sharedcontent/dws/news/world/ mexico/stories/DN-losing_07int.ART.State.Edition2.464c733.html (9 June 2008).

'In depth: Toronto Bomb Plot; Ammonium Nitrate'. *CBC News*, 5 June 2006 at http://www.cbc.ca/news/background/toronto-bomb-plot/ammonium-nitrate.html (7 Sept. 2007).

'India worried by LTTE air, sea power: Narayanan'. *Newkerala.com*, 29 May 2007.

'Indian fishermen seek safety against SL Navy'. *Hindustan Times,* 5 March 2007 at http://www.hindustantimes.com/news/181_1944877,0008.htm (6 March 2007).

'Indian navy heightens vigil to check Sri Lanka Tamil Tiger clout'. *Lankaeverything.com,* 5 June 2007 at http://www.lankaeverything.com/vinews/srilanka/20070605023901.php (6 June 2007).

'Indian Navy tightens surveillance along Tamil Nadu-Sri Lankan coast line'. *Indian Defence,* 14 June 2007 at http://www.india-defence.com/reports-3308 (7 Sept. 2007).

'India's fears of terrorists using sea routes well-grounded: US'. *The Times of India,* 24 Aug. 2007 at http://timesofindia.indiatimes.com/India/Indias_fears_of_terrorists_using_sea_routes_well-grounded_US/articleshow/2307380.cms (25 Aug. 2007).

'Indian support helped weaken LTTE: Sri Lanka'. *Rediff.com,* 15 Jan. 2008 at http://www.rediff.com/news/2008/jan/15lanka.htm (25 Jan. 2008).

'Indonesia agrees Aceh peace deal'. *BBC News,* 17 July at http://news.bbc.co.uk/1/hi/world/asia-pacific/4690293.stm (7 Sept. 2007).

'Indonesia determined to postpone ratification of Malacca Strait pact'. *Antara News Agency,* 25 Sept. 2006.

'Indonesia identifies three groups in sea crimes'. *Channel NewsAsia,* 31 May 2005 at http://www.channelnewsasia.com/stories/southeastasia/print/150342/1/.html (29 Sept. 2006).

'Indonesia rules out private armed escorts in Malacca Strait'. *Bloomberg.com,* 2 May 2005 at http://www.bloomberg.com/apps/news?pid=10000080&sid=aRlpGcMYBSME&refer=asia# (2 May 2005).

'Indonesia agrees Acch peace deal'. *BBC News,* 17 July at http://news.bbc.co.uk/1/hi/world/asia-pacific/4690293.stm (7 Set 2007).

'Indonesian rebels deny carrying out pirate attacks in Malacca Strait'. *Channel NewsAsia,* 17 March 2005 at http://www.channelnewsasia.com/stories/afp_asiapacific/view/137752/1/.html (9 Aug. 2005).

'Indonesians deported due to lack of evidence: China'. *Agence France-Presse,* 29 October 1998.

'Inquiry into Channel collision'. *CNN.com,* 2 Jan. 2003 at http://edition.cnn.com/2003/WORLD/europe/01/02/channel.collision/ (7 Sept. 2007).

'INS Hanit suffers Iranian missile attack'. *Defense Update News Commentary,* 17 July 2006 at http://www.defense-update.com/2006/07/ins-hanit-suffers-iranian-missile.html (29 Sept. 2006).

'Insurgent attacks on Iraq's oil sector'. *Reuters Foundation AlertNet,* 8 June 2006 at http://www.alertnet.org/thenews/newsdesk/L08531093.htm (15 July 2006).

'International cooperation beats modern-day pirates'. IMB. 24 Nov. 1999 at http://www.iccwbo.org/home/news_archives/1999/international_cooperation_beats_pirates.asp (7 Sept. 2007).

'Investigation discovers first phantom ships in the Mediterranean for 15 years'. ICC *Commercial Crime International,* vol. 16, no. 11, April 1999.

'IRA's store of weaponry, The'. *BBC News,* 14 Aug. 2001 at http://news.bbc.co.uk/1/hi/northern_ireland/1482426.stm (7 Sept. 2007).

'Iran and Syria as strategic support for Palestinian terrorism'. Israel Ministry of Foreign Affairs, 30 Sept. 2002 at http://www.mfa.gov.il/MFA/MFAArchive/2000_2009/2002/9/Iran%20and%20Syria%20as%20Strategic%20Support%20for%20Palestinia (8 Dec. 2007).

'Iran seizes UK vessels and crew'. *BBC News,* 21 June 2004 at http://news.bbc.co.uk/1/hi/world/middle_east/3826179.stm (7 Sept. 2007).

'Iran's Ahmadinejad calls for 'removal of Zionist regime''. *Agence France-Presse,* 8 July 2006.

Isaacs, Dan. 'The Nigerian Delta's troubled waters'. *BBC News,* 20 Feb. 2006 at http://news.bbc.co.uk/1/hi/world/africa/4732010.stm (10 March 2006).

Ishihara, Akihiro. 'JCG seeks foreign help in probe of pirate attack'. *Daily Yomiuri Online,* 20 June 2006.

'Islamic terrorists linked to the Camorra'. CSIS *Transnational Threats Update,* vol. 2, no. 7, April 2004, p. 4 at http://www.csis.org/media/csis/pubs/ttu_0404.pdf (3 Dec. 2007).

'Islamist terrorists linked to the Camorra'. *CSIS Transnational Threat Update,* vol. 2, no. 7, April 2004.

'Israel confirms 4 sailors missing from naval ship'. *Reuters,* 15 July 2006.

'Israel intercepts Hizballah shipment to Palestinians'. ICT *News & Commentary,* 24 May 2003.

'Israeli navy fires on Palestinian boats suspected of smuggling'. *Israel Insider,* 11 March 2007 at http://web.israelinsider.com/Articles/Briefs/10901.htm (8 Dec. 2007).

'Israeli navy intercepts TNT on way to Gaza'. *The Washington Times,* 9 May 2006.

'Israeli soldiers kill two Palestinian frogmen'. *Associated Press,* 27 March 2004 at http://www.taipeitimes.com/News/world/archives/2004/03/27/2003107961 (7 Dec. 2007).

'Istanbul bombing suspects charged'. *BBC News report,* 25 Feb. 2004 at http://news.bbc.co.uk/1/hi/world/europe/3486536.stm (14 Aug. 2005).

'Italian mobsters linked to Islamic terrorists'. *CSIS Transnational Threat Update,* vol. 2, no. 9, June 2004.

Jacinto, Al. 'Plot to hijack ships in Mindanao uncovered'. *ABS-CBN Interactive,* 3 April 2006 at http://www.abs-cbnnews.com/storypage.aspx?StoryId=34468 (26 April 2006).

'JakartaproposesStraits'safetyfund'. *TheStarOnline,*2Oct.2006athttp://thestar.com.my/maritime/story.asp?file=/2006/10/2/maritime/15577637&sec=maritime (7 Sept. 2007).

'Jakarta sees foreign plot behind piracy charges'. *The Business Time On-Line Edition,* 20 July 2004.

Jalaldeen, Rafik. 'Navy's pivotal role in battle against terrorism'. *Daily News* (Colombo), 10 Dec. 2007 at http://www.dailynews.lk/2007/12/10/fea06.asp (10 Dec. 2007).

'Jayalalithaa for joint naval exercises to check LTTE'. *The Hindu,* 7 Dec. 2003 at http://www.hindu.com/2003/12/08/stories/2003120805810100.htm (7 Sept. 2007).

Jayanth, V. 'LTTE's flourishing shipping network'. *The Hindu,* 29 March 2000 at http://www.ibiblio.org/obl/reg.burma/archives/200003/msg00066.html (29 June 2004).

Jayasiri, Sunil. 'LTTE boats destroyed, Sea Tigers killed'. *Daily Mirror* (Sri Lanka), 21 June 2007 at http://www.dailymirror.lk/2007/06/21/front/7.asp (22 June 2007).

———. 'LTTE gets equipment from Japan'. *Daily Mirror* (Sri Lanka), 26 June 2007 at http://www.dailymirror.lk/2007/06/26/front/04.asp (27 June 2007).

Jayawahana, Walter. 'Tamil Tiger leader says Osama bin Laden-led al Qaeda copied terrorist tactics from Liberation Tigers of Tamil Eelam'. *Go2lanka.com,* 12 Dec. 2002 at http://www.go2lanka.com/stories/021212.html (9 Aug. 2005).

———. 'Tamil Tigers are also developing a mini submarine for gun running, drug smuggling and piracy'. *LankaWeb,* 30 March 2007 at http://www.lankaweb.com/news/items07/300307-3.html (30 March 2007).

Jaynes, Gregory. 'Pirates of Lagos: Once an annoyance, now a major threat'. *New York Times,* 14 March 1981.

'JCG seeks foreign help in probe of pirate attack'. *Daily Yomiuri Online,* 20 June 2006.

Jean, Grace V. 'Improvised explosive devices: Could they threaten US ports?' *National Defense,* Jan. 2008 at http://www.nationaldefensemagazine.org/issues/2008/January/Improvised.htm (2 Jan. 2008).

Jenkins, Brian Michael,and Treverton, Gregory F. 'Misjudging the Jihad: Briefing Osama on all the war's wins and losses'. *San Francisco Chronicle,* 13 Nov. 2005 at http://www.sfgate.com/cgi-bin/article.cgi?f=/c/a/2005/11/13/INGUPFLGKH1.DTL&hw=brian+michael+jenkins&sn=003&sc=917 (26 Nov. 2005).

Jenkins, Cathy. 'US ships in Somali pirate clash'. *BBC News,* 18 March 2006 at http://news.bbc.co.uk/1/hi/world/africa/4821518.stm (19 March 2006).

Jeyaraj, D.B.S. 'The marine battle over 'MV Pearl Cruise II': An overview'. *Tamil week*, 14 May 2006 at http://tamilweek.com/news-features/archives/359 (16 May 2006).

'Jihadist website commentary argues 'maritime terrorism' strategic necessity'. *Biyokulule Online*, 29 April 2008 at http://www.biyokulule.com/view_content.php?articleid=1156 (2 May 2008).

Johnstone, Alan. 'Gaza fishermen risk Israeli fire'. *BBC News*, 13 Oct. 2006 at http://news.bbc.co.uk/1/hi/world/middle_east/6047764.stm (13 Oct. 2006).

Johnstone, Ralph. 'The Sea Gypsies: Ha Times for a Vanishing Philippine Tribe'. *Asiaweek*, 21 April 1993, pp. 46-55.

Joint Communiqué between the Government of the Republic of the Philippines and the Moro Islamic Liberation Front, 6 May 2002 at http://opapp.gov.ph/downloads/milf/GRP-MILF_Joint_Communique-May_6_2002.doc (7 Sept. 2007).

'Jolly Roger still flies, The'. *TIME*, 31 July 1978 at http://www.time.com/time/magazine/article/0,9171,946918,00.html (31 Oct. 2006).

'Jordanians find rocket launcher used in attack on US ships'. *New York Times*, 20 Aug. 2005.

'Jordanians hunt rocket suspects'. 2005. *BBC News*, 20 Aug. 2005 at http://news.bbc.co.uk/1/hi/world/middle_east/4168182.stm (7 Sept. 2007).

Kamm, Henry. 'Thai pirates kill 70 'boat people''. *New York Times*, 11 Jan. 1980.

Kane, Sean. 'Threat to safety rises on Nigeria piracy inaction'. *Lloyd's List*, 2 April 2008.

Kaplan, David E. 'Godfather's lethal mix of business and politics, A'. *US News & World Report*, 5 Dec. 2005 at http://www.usnews.com/usnews/news/articles/051205/5terror.b.htm (11 Dec. 2007).

———. 'Paying for terror'. *US News & World Report*, 5 Dec. 2005 at http://www.usnews.com/usnews/news/articles/051205/5terror.htm (28 Nov. 2005).

Karniol, Robert. 'Tamil Tigers' hangout: S-E Asia'. *The Straits Times*, 22 Oct. 2007.

Katz, Yaakov. 'J'lem worried by Iranian owned anti-ship missile'. *The Jerusalem Post*, 28 Aug. 2007 at http://www.jpost.com/servlet/Satellite?cid=118819 7171387&pagename=JPost%2FJPArticle%2FShowFull (8 Dec. 2007).

———. 'Lebanese nab terrorists heading for Gaza'. *The Jerusalem Post*, 12 Jan. 2006 at http://www.jpost.com/servlet/Satellite?cid=1136361069939&pagename=JPost%2FJPArticle%2FShowFull (12 Jan. 2006).

Keath, Lee. 'General: Iran was behind deadly Karbala attack'. *Associated Press*, 2 July 2007 at http://www.navytimes.com/news/2007/07/ap_iran_070702/ (3 July 2007).

————. 'Palestinians attack Israel navy boat'. *Associated Press,* 23 Nov. 2002 at http://nucnews.net/nucnews/2002nn/0211nn/021123nn.htm#331 (7 Dec. 2007).

————. 'US: Iranian force carried out attack'. *Associated Press,* 2 July 2007 at http://www.guaian.co.uk/worldlatest/story/0,,-6751689,00.html (2 July 2007).

Kelley, Jack. 'Malaysia site of 9/11 plotting, FBI says'. *USA Today,* 30 Jan. 2002 at http://www.usatoday.com/news/sept11/2002/01/29/usat-malaysia.htm (7 Sept. 2007).

Kennedy, Elizabeth A. 'Somali pirates find booming business'. *Associated Press,* 23 April 2008 at http://ap.google.com/article/ALeqM5ipMHyUWWbt-0DgJ6MbFCi3HeMrqFwD907Q7P80 (28 April 2008).

Khalif, Abdulkadir. 'How illegal fishing feeds Somali piracy'. *The East African* (Nairobi) 15 Nov. 2005 at http://allafrica.com/stories/200511150675. html (17 Nov. 2005). Also at http://www.ecc-platform.org/content/ view/357/173/.

'Kidnappers make ransom demand after hostage grab on Malaysian resort'. *CNN. com,* 27 April 2000 at http://archives.cnn.com/2000/ASIANOW/south-east/04/27/philippines.hostages/ (7 Sept. 2007).

Kier, David A. 'Cruising for trouble'. *The Washington Times,* 24 Nov. 2005 at http:// www.washtimes.com/op-ed/20051123-100554-6019r.htm (25 Nov. 2005).

'Killing by pirates on the rise'. *BBC News,* 26 July 2004 at http://news.bbc.co.uk/1/ hi/world/asia-pacific/3925277.stm (27 July 2004).

Koknar, Ali M. 'Piracy and terrorism are joining forces and creating troubled waters for the maritime industry'. *Security Management Online,* June 2004.

Kraul, Chris. 'Drug traffickers dive in'. *Los Angeles Time,* 6 Nov. 2007.

————. 'Ecuador's divided loyalties'. *Los Angeles Times,* 15 Jan. 2007.

Kumar, K Praveen. 'Lanka mines sea boers to block Tamil Tigers'. *Newindpress,* 23 Jan. 2008 at http://www.newindpress.com/NewsItems.asp?ID=IE92008 0122140818&Title=Chennai&Topic=0 (24 Jan. 2008).

Kupperman, Robert H,; and Kamen, Jeff. 'Greece, haven for terrorists'. *New York Times,* 16 Dec. 1988.

Lacey, Marc 'Somalis brave a sea of perils for $50-a-month jobs abroad'. *New York Times,* 29 May 2006 at http://select.nytimes.com/search/restricted/article ?res=F50F15FC345A0C7A8EDDAC0894DE404482 (3 July 2006).

LaFranchi, Howa. 'Mexico seeks anti-drug aid from US'. *Christian Science Monitor,* 8 Aug. 2007 at http://www.csmonitor.com/2007/0808/p01s01-usfp. html (8 Aug. 2007).

LaFraniere, Sharon. 'Europe takes Africa's fish, and boatloads of migrants follow'. *New York Times,* 14 Jan. 2008 at http://www.nytimes.com/2008/01/14/

world/africa/14fishing.html?_r=1&scp=1&sq=europe+takes+africa%27s
+fish&st=nyt&oref=slogin (24 Jan. 2008).
———. Pomfret, John; and Sun, Lena H. 'The Riady's persistent pursuit of influ-
    ence'. *Washington Post,* 27 May 1997 at http://www.washingtonpost.com/
    wp-srv/politics/special/campfin/stories/cf052797.htm (16 June 2007).
Lam, Tran Dinh Thanh. 'Pirates plague Vietnamese fishermen'. *Asia Times On-
    line,* 12 Nov. 2002 at http://www.atimes.com/atimes/Southeast_Asia/
    DK12Ae01.html (7 Sept. 2007).
Langit-Dursin, Richel. 'Indonesia key to end piracy in Malacca Straits'. *The Jakarta
    Post,* 6 Aug. 2006.
Last, Alex. 'Tempting riches of Nigeria oil crime'. *BBC News,* 30 Aug. 2006 at
    http://news.bbc.co.uk/1/hi/world/africa/5299296.stm (1 Sept. 2006).
Latitudes, vol. 33, Oct. 2003.
Lauriat, George. 'Awash in an ocean of dollars'. *FEER,* 16 Nov. 1979, pp. 66-69.
Lawrence, Susan V. 'A city ruled by crime'. 30 Nov. 2000 at http://www.feer.com/
    cgi-bin/prog/printeasy?id=67965.4775028215 (4 Sept. 2004).
Leppa, David. 'Al-Qaeda's Heathrow jet plot revealed'. *The Sunday Times,* 9 Oct.
    2005 at http://www.timesonline.co.uk/article/0,,2087-1817244,00.html
    (7 Sept. 2007).
'Lethal blast hits Philippines'. *BBC News,* 2 April 2003 at http://news.bbc.co.uk/1/
    hi/world/asia-pacific/2910073.stm (26 June 2007).
Levitch, Matt. 'Cartels lash out at Mexican crackdown on drug trafficking'.
    Christian Science Monitor, 16 May 2007 at http://www.csmonitor.
    com/2007/0516/p99s01-duts.html (21 May 2007).
Lichfield, John. 'French commandoes seize Somali pirates after yacht hostages
    freed'. *The Independent,* 12 April 2008 at http://www.independent.co.uk/
    news/world/africa/french-commandos-seize-somali-pirates-after-yacht-
    hostages-freed-808224.html (13 April 2008).
Lieberman, Joseph. 'Al Qaeda's travel agent'. *Wall Street Journal,* 20 Aug. 2007 at
    http://www.opinionjournal.com/editorial/feature.html?id=110010496
    (20 Aug. 2007).
Lim, Bo-Mi. 'Militants who seize S.Korea ship off Somalia say they're defend-
    ing against illegal fishing'. *NCTimes.com,* 5 April 2006 at http://www.
    nctimes.com/articles/2006/04/06/news/nation/16_12_004_5_06.txt (6
    July 2006).
'Limburg saboteurs had inside information'. *ICC News,* 19 June 2003 at http://www.
    iccwbo.org/home/news_archives/2003/stories/limburg.asp (10 July 2003).
Linklater, Magnus. 'Sea's treasures may no longer be with us from here to eternity'.
    The Times, 15 Feb. 2008 at http://www.timesonline.co.uk/tol/news/envi-
    ronment/article3372100.ece (16 Feb. 2008).

Lintner, Bertil. 'Arms Trade: The Phuket Connection'. *The Week*, 30 April 2000 at http://www.asiapacificms.com/articles/phuket_connection/ (13 Oct. 2005).

———. 'LTTE purchases: A link with Cambodia'. *JIR*, Dec. 1996, p. 9.

Lipowicz, Alice. 'Maritime Security: Better tracking of small craft needed'. *Washington Technology*, 29 Nov. 2007 at http://www.washingtontechnology. com/online/1_1/31884-1.html (30 Nov. 2007).

Lipton, Eric. 'Coast Gua turns its eyes underwater'. *New York Times*, 2 Feb. 2005 at http://select.nytimes.com/search/restricted/article?res=FB0F1EFC385 F0C718CDDAB0894DD404482 (2 Dec. 2005).

———. 'Trying to keep the nation's ferries safe from terrorists'. *New York Times*, 20 March 2005 at http://select.nytimes.com/search/restricted/article?res= F00A1FFE35580C738EDDAA0894DD404482 (19 March 2007).

Litterick, David. 'Petrol soars to £1 a litre amid fears of oil terrorism'. *Daily Telegraph*, 2 June 2004 at http://www.telegraph.co.uk/news/main. jhtml?xml=/news/2004/06/02/npetr02.xml (7 Sept. 2007).

'Littoral states key to Malacca safety'. *Fairplay*, 20 Sept. 2006.

Llana, Sarah Miller. 'Escalating drug war grips Mexico'. *Christian Science Monitor*, 23 May 2007 at http://www.csmonitor.com/2007/0523/p01s01-woam. html (23 May 2007).

———. 'Violent cartel culture now threatens Peru'. *Christian Science Monitor*, 3 April 2007 at http://www.csmonitor.com/2007/0403/p06s01-woam. html (23 May 2007).

———. 'With Calderón in, a new war on Mexico's mighty drug cartels'. *Christian Science Monitor*, 22 Jan. 2007 at http://www.csmonitor.com/2007/0122/ p01s04-woam.html (8 Aug. 2007).

'LNG Matthew banned from Boston'. *MarineLog.com*, 27 Sept. 2001 at http://www. marinelog.com/DOCS/NEWSMMI/MMISep27.html (3 July 2004).

Lopez, Antonio. 'Meeting force with force'. *Asiaweek*, vol. 26, no. 9, 10 March 2000 at http://www.asiaweek.com/asiaweek/magazine/2000/0310/nat. phil.mindanao.html (2 July 2007).

Lopez, Robert J.; Connell, Rich; and Kraul, Chris. 'Gang uses deportation to its advantage to flourish in US'. *Los Angeles Times*, 30 Oct. 2005 at http://www.latimes.com/news/local/la-me-gang30oct30,0,6717943. story?coll=la-home-headlines (31 Oct. 2005).

'LTTE allays shipping fears'. *TamilNet*, 12 Sept. 1997 at http://www.tamilnet. com/art.html?catid=13&artid=7319 (5 July 2007).

'LTTE attack destroys navy craft: ten missing'. *The Sunday Times* (Colombo), 23 March 2008 at http://www.sundaytimes.lk/080323/News/news003.html (25 March 2008).

'LTTE bides time to win Eelam'. *Sunday Observer* (Colombo), 30 Oct. 2005 at http://www.sundayobserver.lk/2005/10/30/fea04.html (5 April 2007).

'LTTE has arms stores in India: Report'. *Zee News,* 12 Oct. 2007 at http://www. zeenews.com/articles.asp?aid=400718&sid=NAT&sname=INDIA-NA-TIONAL-NEWS&news=LTTE%20has%20arms%20stores%20in%20 India:%20Report (13 Oct. 2007).

'LTTE human smuggling operation busted'. 18 May 2000 at http://www.priu. gov.lk/news_update/Current_Affairs/ca200005/20000518LTTE_operation_busted.htm (7 Sept. 2007).

'LTTE human-smuggling operation in Sri Lanka said foiled'. *Kyodo World News Service,* 17 May 2000.

'LTTE may get arms from S Indian hideouts – Report'. *Rediff.com,* 24 Sept. 2007.

'LTTE might be trying to acquire submarine: Report'. *Zee News,* 30 March 2007 at http://www.zeenews.com/articles.asp?rep=2&aid=362824&sid=SAS& ssid= (30 March 2007).

'LTTE shifting operations to Kerala coast: Top Navy official'. *Zee News,* 26 Nov. 2007 at http://www.zeenews.com/articles.asp?aid=409680&sid=NAT (7 Dec. 2007).

'LTTE spreading its wings in Kerala?' *The Times of India,* 6 March 2008 at http:// timesofindia.indiatimes.com/LTTE_spreading_wings_in_Kerala/article-show/2841561.cms (21 March 2008).

'LTTE terrorists have annual profit margin of US $300million'. *The Media Centre for National Security,* Ministry of Defence, Public Security, Law and Oer (Sri Lanka), 27 July 2007 at http://www.nationalsecurity.lk/fullnews. php?id=6760 (30 July 2007).

'LTTE use talks to obtain underwater scooters'. *The Island,* 17 March 2003 at http://www.island.lk/2003/03/17/news13.html (30 June 2008).

Luft, Gal 'The Palestinian Security Services – Between police and army'. The Institute for Counter Terrorism, 19 July 1999 at http://www.ict.org.il/index. php?sid=119&lang=en&act=page&id=5393&str=gal%20luft (7 Sept. 2007).

McBeth, John. 'A Futile Fight'. *FEER,* 5 June 2003.

———. 'Terrorism – Across boers'. *FEER,* 22 July 2004, p. 27.

———. 'Thailand's part-timers in terror'. *FEER,* 1 Feb. 1980, p. 27.

McCarthy, Terry. 'An invasion of paradise'. *TIME,* 8 May 2000 at http://www.time. com/time/magazine/article/0,9171,996834,00.html (31 Oct. 2006).

MacCartney, Jane. 'Asian piracy costs $25 bln a year, says expert'. *Reuters,* 11 Dec. 2002 at http://www.planetark.com/avantgo/dailynewsstory. cfm?newsid=18987 (2 Oct. 2006). Also at http://dailytimes.com.pk/default.asp?page=story_11-12-2002_pg5_16 (23 June 2007).

McCawley, Tom. 'Indonesia's terrorist hunt bears fruit'. *Christian Science Monitor,* 15 June 2007 at http://www.csmonitor.com/2007/0615/p06s01-woap. html (15 June 2007).

————. 'Sea of trouble'. *Far East Economic Review*, 27 May 2004, pp. 50-52 at http://www.feer.com/articles/2004/0405_27/p050current.html (20 July 2004).

McElroy, Damien. 'British troops track and kill al-Qa'eda escaper who taunted Americans'. *Daily Telegraph*, 26 Sept. 2006 at http://www.telegraph.co.uk/news/main.jhtml?xml=/news/2006/09/26/wiraq26.xml (7 Sept. 2007).

————. 'Saudi Arabia arrests over 100 terror suspects'. *Daily Telegraph*, 29 Nov. 2007 at http://www.telegraph.co.uk/news/main.jhtml;jsessionid=BQ0C YEVJTETWPQFIQMGSFFWAVCBQWIV0?xml=/news/2007/11/28/wsaudi228.xml (29 Nov. 2007).

————. 'UK to attack al-Qa'eda pirates'. *Daily Telegraph*, 29 Nov. 2007 at http://www.telegraph.co.uk/news/main.jhtml?xml=/news/2007/11/28/wpirates128.xml (29 Nov. 2007).

McGeown, Kate. 'Aceh rebels blamed for piracy'. *BBC News* report, 8 Sept. 2003 at http://news.bbc.co.uk/1/hi/world/asia-pacific/3090136.stm (24 April 2004).

————. 'Is this the end for Abu Sayyaf?' *BBC News*, 23 Jan. 2007 at http://news.bbc.co.uk/1/hi/world/asia-pacific/6290805.stm (28 June 2007).

McKenzie, Scott. ND. 'Vietnam's boat people: 25 years of fears, hopes and dreams'. *CNN.com* available at http://www.cnn.com/SPECIALS/2000/vietnam/story/boat.people/ (7 Sept. 2007).

McKinley, James C., Jr. 'With beheadings and attacks, drug gangs terrorize Mexico'. *New York Times*, 26 Oct. 2006 at http://www.nytimes.com/2006/10/26/world/americas/26mexico.html?scp=1&sq=With+Beheadings+and+Attacks%2C+Drug+Gangs+Terrorize+Mexico&st=nyt (15 Feb. 2008).

MacKinnon, Ian. 'Indonesian police arrest Islamist leader'. *The Guaian*, 14 June 2007 at http://www.guaian.co.uk/indonesia/Story/0,,2102474,00.html (15 June 2007).

McLaughlin, John. 'LNG is nowhere near as dangerous as people are making it out to be. Perception is the problem'. *Lloyd's List*, 8 Feb. 2005.

'Madrid bombings: 3 Moroccans held'. *CNN.com*, 24 May 2005 at http://edition.cnn.com/2005/WORLD/europe/05/24/spain.arrests/index.html (7 Sept. 2007).

Magnuson, Stew. 'Maritime domain roadmap seeks to ID all vessels'. *National Defense*, Jan. 2007 at http://www.nationaldefensemagazine.org/issues/2007/January/SecurityBeat.htm#Maritime (28 Dec. 2006).

Mahtani, Dino. 'Attacks feared on Nigerian Oil facilities'. *Financial Times*, 23 Sept. 2005 at http://news.ft.com/cms/s/598d66ee-2c52-11da-89bf-00000e2511c8.html (23 Sept. 2005).

Majtenyi, Cathy. 'Suspects in ship hijacking arrested in Somalia'. *NewsVOA.com*, 27 Feb. 2007 at http://www.voanews.com/english/2007-02-27-voa25.cfm (28 Feb. 2007).

————. 'Warship heading to ship hijacked off Somalia's northern coast'. *News-VOA.com*, 26 Feb. 2007 at http://www.voanews.com/english/2007-02-26-voa21.cfm (8 March 2007).

'Malacca sea piracy on rise'. *CNN.com*. 25 July 2004.

Malakunas, Karl. 'Armed escorts in high demand at sea'. *The Peninsula* (Qatar), 12 May 2005 at http://www.thepeninsulaqatar.com/features/featuredetail. asp?file=mayfeatures102005.xml (12 May 2005).

'Malaysia, Singapore and Indonesia implement cooperative mechanism to safegua Straits'. *Bernama*, 27 May 2008 at http://www.bernama.com/bernama/ v3/news_lite.php?id=335711 (28 May 2008).

'Malaysia to boost Malacca Strait security with 24-hour radar system'. *Channel-NewsAsia*, 11 March 2005 at http://www.channelnewsasia.com/stories/ afp_asiapacific/view/136822/1/.html (7 Sept. 2007).

'Malaysia to step up anti-piracy patrols in Malacca Strait'. *Forbes.com*, 9 Feb. 2006 at http://www.forbes.com/home/feeds/afx/2006/02/09/afx2512219.html (10 Feb. 2006).

'Malaysia warns on private marine escorts'. *MarineLog.com*, 2 May 2005 at http:// www.marinelog.com/DOCS/NEWSMMV/2005may02.html (26 Sept. 2006).

'Malaysia warns Straits gun guas'. *The Standa*, 28 April 2005 at http://www.the-standa.com.hk/stdn/std/World/GD28Wd05.html (28 April 2005).

'Malaysia's own coast guards by Nov.'. *The StarOnline*, 20 June 2005 at http://202.186.86.35/maritime/story.asp?file=/2005/6/20/maritime/ 11212046&sec=maritime (7 Sept. 2007).

Mallawarachi, Bharatha. 'Sri Lankan military investigates Indonesian ship on suspected involvement with Tamil rebels'. *Associated Press*, 26 Dec. 2007 at http://www.theacademic.org/stories/11986506090/story.shtml (27 Dec. 2007).

Malone, Robert. 'Dangerous waters'. *Forbes.com*, 25 July 2006 at http://www.forbes. com/logistics/2006/07/24/pirates-on-the-seas-cx_rm_0725pirates.html (26 July 2006).

'March 11 attackers trade drugs for explosives'. CSIS *Transnational Threats Update*, vol. 2, no. 7, April 2004.

'Maritime crime changes with time'. *Fairplay*, 3 Oct. 2006.

'Maritime piracy and terrorism are converging'. CSIS *Transnational Threats Update*, vol. 1, no. 9, June 2003.

'Maritime terrorism gains roots in Indian Ocean.' *The Times of India*, 9 Aug. 2008.

Max, Arthur. 'Crime syndicates smuggling wildlife'. *Associated Press*, 7 June 2007.

Mazzetti, Mark; and Shanker, Thom. 'Hezbollah's unexpected firepower'. *International Herald Tribune*, 19 July 2006 at http://www.iht.com/arti-cles/2006/07/19/news/missile.php (24 July 2006).

Meade, Richard. 'Cruise attack sparks UN action'. *Fairplay*, 10 Nov. 2005.

Media Centre for National Security, The (Sri Lanka). 'Indian Navy boosts its presence in the Bay of Bengal to curb LTTE'. 7 June 2007 at http://www.rnhit.com/mcns/fullnews.php?id=6138 (15 June 2007).

'Melaka Straits must be kept safe from maritime terrorism, says IGP'. *Bernama*, 12 June 2007 at http://www.bernama.com.my/bernama/v3/news.php?id=267069 (13 June 2007).

Menon, Jaya. 'Fishermen up in arms against Lankan Navy's move to lay sea mines'. *Indian Express*, 25 Jan. 2008.

'Mexican drug commandos expand ops in 6 US states'. *WorldNetDaily*, 21 June 2005 at http://www.worldnetdaily.com/news/article.asp?ARTICLE_ID=44899 (22 June 2005).

'Mexican navy reorganized for fighting drug trafficking'. *Contralinea*, 1-15- Jan. 2008 (private translation).

'Mexico drug traffickers make car bombs'. *Reuters AlertNet*, 16 July 2008 at http://www.alertnet.org/thenews/newsdesk/N16522820.htm (21 July 2008).

Meyer, Josh. 'Al Qaeda 'co-opts' new affiliates'. *Los Angeles Times*, 16 Sept. 2007.

———. 'Al Qaeda said to focus on WMDs'. *Los Angeles Times*, 3 Feb. 2008 at http://www.latimes.com/news/nationworld/world/la-fg-khabab3feb03,0,5365070.story (3 Feb. 2008).

Miexler, Louis. 'Oil Terminal attack costs Iraq $28m'. *Associated Press*, 25 April 2004 at http://www.highbeam.com/library/doc3.asp?DOCID=1P1:93821864&num=2&ctrlInfo=Round4%3AProd%3ASR%3AResult&ao= (2 July 2004).

'Militant 'planned attacks' in Gulf'. *BBC News*, 23 Dec. 2002 at http://news.bbc.co.uk/1/hi/world/middle_east/2602627.stm (23 April 2004).

'Militants set to target Niger Delta oil firms'. *Lloyd's List*, 6 Nov. 2006.

MINDEF Singapore News Release. 'Launch of the Eye in the Sky (EiS) Initiative'. 13 Sept. 2005 at http://www.mindef.gov.sg/imindef/news_and_events/nr/2005/sep/13sep05_nr.html (7 September 2007).

——— 'Launch of Trilateral Cooinated Patrols – MALSINDO Malacca Straits Cooinated Patrol'. 20 July 2004 at http://www.mindef.gov.sg/imindef/news_and_events/nr/2004/jul/20jul04_nr.html (7 September 2007).

'Mini-subs: the next terrorist threat?' *Journal of Electronic Defense*, July 2003.

Mintz, John. '15 freighters believed to be linked to Al Qaeda'. *The Washington Post*, 31 Dec. 2002 at http://www.washingtonpost.com/ac2/wp-dyn?pagename=article&node=&contentId=A56442-2002Dec30&notFound=true (14 September 2007).

Misra, Neelesh; and Singh, Rahul. 'Terror alarm along India's coastline'. *Hindustan Times*, 12 March 2007 at http://www.hindustantimes.com/StoryPage/StoryPage.aspx?id=3dfa0db9-8939-4199-b471-7ac57a81c2a6 (12 March 2007).

'Missile 'embedded in US cruise ship''. *WorldNetDaily*, 7 Nov. 2006 at http://www.worldnetdaily.com/news/article.asp?ARTICLE_ID=47257 (7 September 2007).

Mitchell, Anthony. '4 suspected Somali pirates arrested'. *Washington Post*, 27 Feb. 2007 at http://www.washingtonpost.com/wp-dyn/content/article/2007/02/27/AR2007022700371.html (28 Feb. 2007).

Mitchell, Tanya. 'Mariners face growing threat from pirates'. *Village Soup*, 29 September 2006 at http://belfast.villagesoup.com/Education/story.cfm?storyID=79082 (30 September 2006).

Mogato, Manny; and Crimmins, Carmel. 'Manila sees risk of split in Muslim rebel group'. *Reuters AlertNet*, 17 June 2008 at http://www.alertnet.org/thenews/newsdesk/MAN275800.htm (18 June 2008).

'Money talks'. *Fairplay*, 17 Aug. 2006.

Montlake, Simon. 'Ha times for pirates in busy world waterway'. *Christian Science Monitor*, 30 Oct. 2006 at http://www.csmonitor.com/2006/1030/p01s04-woap.html (30 Oct. 2006).

———. 'Japanese ship foils pirate attack'. *Guaian Unlimited*, 4 July 2006 at http://www.guaian.co.uk/indonesia/Story/0,,1812401,00.html (4 July 2006).

———. 'Pirates ahead!' *Christian Science Monitor*, 18 March 2004 at http://www.csmonitor.com/2004/0318/p13s02-woap.html?s=widep (30 Oct. 2006).

Moore, Malcolm. 'Reco copper prices power China's black market demand for hot metal'. *Daily Telegraph*, 17 June 2006 at http://www.telegraph.co.uk/money/main.jhtml?xml=/money/2006/06/17/cncopp17.xml (7 September 2007).

'Morocco 'uncovers al-Qaeda plot''. *BBC News*, 11 June 2002 at http://news.bbc.co.uk/1/hi/world/africa/2037391.stm (7 September 2007).

Moss, Michael; and Mekhennet, Souad. 'Rising leader for next phase of al-Qaeda's war'. *New York Times*, 4 April 2008 at http://www.nytimes.com/2008/04/04/world/asia/04qaeda.html?_r=1&ex=1365048000&en=523c6ab9f8d09ed0&ei=5088&partner=rssnyt&emc=rss&oref=slogin (9 April 2008).

Moulier, Philippe B.; and Casey, Ethan. 'Pirates? What Pirates?' *US News & World Report*, 23 June 1997, pp. 33-34.

'Murder of four sailors marks violent start to shipping year 2004'. *ICC News*, 13 Feb. 2004 at http://www.iccwbo.org/ccs/news_archives/2004/aceh.asp (28 April 2004).

Murphy, Dan. 'Southeast Asia easy source of Al Qaeda recruits', *Christian Science Monitor*, 9 Oct. 2002 at http://www.csmonitor.com/2002/1009/p07s01-woap.html (17 May 2008).

Murphy, Kevin. 'Hong Kong links China to bulk of sea piracy'. *International Herald Tribune*, 17 March 1994 at http://www.iht.com/articles/1994/03/17/hong_2.php (18 June 2007).

Murray, Geoffrey. '20century pirates roam the seas of Southeast Asia'. *Christian Science Monitor,* 9 June 1986 at http://www.csmonitor.com/1986/0609/opir-f.html (22 June 2007).

Murray, Leigh. 'Sri Lankan Navy destroys 2 rebel boats'. *ABC News International,* 21 Oct. 2006 at http://abcnews.go.com/International/wireStory?id=2591485 (7 September 2007).

Murray, Senan. 'The shadowy militants of Nigeria's delta'. *BBC News,* 10 May 2007 at http://news.bbc.co.uk/1/hi/world/africa/6644097.stm (22 July 2007).

Musa, Tansa. 'Cameroon says "pirates" seize six in Bakassi attack'. *Reuters AlertNet,* 11 June 2008 at http://www.alertnet.org/thenews/newsdesk/L11517901.htm (17 June 2008).

Mwakugu, Noel. 'Clan divisions behind Somali violence'. *BBC News,* 26 April 2007 at http://news.bbc.co.uk/1/hi/world/africa/6594647.stm (21 May 2007).

Mwangura, Andrew. Seafarers' Assistance Programme, Mombasa, Kenya, Press Release, 8 Feb. 2006 at http://www.ecop.info/english/e-sap-net-39.htm (7 September 2007).

Myre, Greg. 'Israel says explosives expert on fishing boat it seized'. *New York Times,* 23 May 2003 at http://query.nytimes.com/gst/fullpage.html?res=9403E0D71631F930A15756C0A9659C8B63 (7 Dec. 2007).

Narayan Swamy, M.R. 'LTTE sympathy to erode over fishermen abductions'. *Indo-Asian News Service (IANS),* 20 May 2007 at http://www.icsf.net/icsf2006/ControllerServlet?handler=EXTERNALNEWS&code=getDetails&id=34286&userType=&fromPage= (18 May 2008)..

'Nasrallah: Hostages in secure location, far away'. *YNetNews.com,* 12 July 2006 at http://www.ynetnews.com/articles/0,7340,L-3274616,00.html (7 September 2007).

Navarro, Mireya. 'Russian submarine drifts into center of a brazen drug plot'. *New York Times,* 7 March 1997 at http://query.nytimes.com/gst/fullpage.html?res=9906EFDD1130F934A35750C0A961958260&sec=&spon=&pagewanted=all (29 Feb. 2008).

'Navies to tackle Somali pirates'. *BBC News,* 2 June 2008 at http://news.bbc.co.uk/1/hi/world/africa/7432612.stm (3 June 2008).

'Navy foils arms-smuggling attempt'. *Arutz Sheva – IsrealNationalNews.com,* 22 June 2006 at http://www.israelnationalnews.com/news.php3?id=105853 (28 July 2006).

'Navy gears up for sea-borne terrorist attack'. *Rediff.com,* 29 May 2007 at http://www.rediff.com/news/2007/may/29navy.htm (30 May 2007).

'Navy overwhelmed by pirates in Malacca Strait'. *Tempo Interactive,* 30 Nov. 2006.

'Navy seizes Hizbollah bomb expert and explosives-making materials on boat'. *Israel Insider*, 23 May 2003 at http://web.israelinsider.com/Articles/Security/2326.htm (8 Dec. 2007).

'Navy will have to learn to fight terrorists and pirates: admiral'. *The Canadian Press*, 16 September 2007 at http://canadianpress.google.com/article/ALeqM-5hqeEekGvHMaif2R7eoHPC83cmQUA (16 September 2007).

'New al-Qaeda Threat: 15-ship mystery navy'. *WorldDailyNet*, 29 September 2003 at http://www.worldnetdaily.com/news/article.asp?ARTICLE_ID=34819 (2 June 2004).

'New fleet chief vows to combat piracy'. *The Jakarta Post*, 18 Feb. 2006.

Newman, Bob. 'Terrorists feared to be planning sub-surface naval attacks'. *CNSNews.com*, 3 Dec. 2002 at http://www.cnsnews.com/ForeignBureaus/Archive/200212/FOR20021203a.html (1 July 2004).

Ng, Eileen. 'Pirates attack UN ships near Indonesia'. *The State*, 4 July 2006.

'Nigeria: Report says Nigerian waters the most deadly'. *IRIN*, 27 July 2004 at http://www.irinnews.org/report.aspx?reportid=50843 (24 July 2007).

'Nigerian attack closes oilfield'. *BBC News*, 20 June 2008 at http://news.bbc.co.uk/1/hi/world/africa/7463288.stm (20 June 2008).

'Nigerian navy ousts 10 officers for smuggling oil'. *Reuters Africa*, 27 July 2007 at http://africa.reuters.com/wire/news/usnL27895536.html (30 July 2007).

'Nigerian oil fuels Delta conflict'. *BBC News*, 25 Jan. 2006 at http://news.bbc.co.uk/1/hi/world/africa/4617658.stm (1 September 2006).

'Nigeria's shadowy oil rebels'. *BBC News*, 21 Feb. 2006 at http://news.bbc.co.uk/1/hi/world/africa/4732210.stm (27 March 2006).

'No piracy in Jamaica waters, official says'. *Reuters AlertNet* 26 May 2006.

Nossiter, Berna D. 'Thai piracy against boat people seems relentless'. *New York Times*, 7 May 1980.

'Now, Habibie Inc.' *Asiaweek*, 5 June 1998 at http://www.asiaweek.com/asiaweek/98/0605/cs3.html (7 September 2007).

Obi, Ifeyinwa. 'Fish on the run: How pirates attacks on fishing trawlers hike price of fish'. *The Vangua* (Lagos), 2 March 2008 at http://www.vanguangr.com/index.php?option=com_content&task=view&id=3897&Itemid=0 (2 March 2008).

'Officer shot in piracy attack'. NUMAST *Telegraph*, vol. 31, no. 2, Feb. 1998.

'Official: Pirates were paid $1.2M ransom'. *Associated Press*, 27 April 2008 at http://edition.cnn.com/2008/WORLD/africa/04/27/pirates.spain.ap/index.html (6 May 2008).

'Officials identify al-Qaida plotters'. *Michigan Daily*, 17 September 2002 at http://media.www.michigandaily.com/media/storage/paper851/news/2002/09/17/News/Officials.Identify.AlQaida.Plotters-1412262.

shtml?sourcedomain=www.michigandaily.com&MIIHost=media.collegepublisher.com (7 September 2007).

'Oil piracy proves growing menace to tanker traffic in South China Sea'. *Oil and Gas Journal,* 18 Oct. 1999, pp. 23-25.

'Oil workers abducted in Nigeria'. ISN *Security Watch,* 12 Jan. 2006 at http://www.isn.ethz.ch/news/sw/details.cfm?ID=14305 (13 Jan. 2006).

Olatunji, Bukola. 'Operators withdraw trawlers over pirates' attacks'. *This Day* (Lagos), 4 Feb. 2008 at http://allafrica.com/stories/200802041115.html (21 March 2008).

O'Mahony, Hugh 'Mitropoulos voices fears over ISPS Code inconsistencies'. *Lloyd's List,* 30 Nov. 2006.

Omonobi, Kingsley. 'Navy arrest 236 ships for illegal bunkering, other vices in three yrs'. *Vanguar,* 18 September 2007 at http://www.vanguangr.com/articles/2002/cover/september07/18092007/f718092007.html (18 September 2007).

Ong, Graham Gera. 'A case for armed guas on ships'. *Straits Times,* 26 May 2005.

————. 'Next wave of terror targets: Will they be at sea?' *Straits Times,* 15 September 2003.

'Ongoing threat to cruise ships, The'. *Stratfor,* 14 Dec. 2005 at http://www.stratfor.com/ongoing_threat_cruise_ships (5 Feb. 2008).

'Organised crime takes to the high seas, ICC report finds'. *ICC News,* 4 Feb. 2002 at http://www.iccwbo.org/home/news_archives/2002/piracy_report.asp (28 April 2004).

Osler, David. 'Global piracy bill hits $25bn'. *Lloyd's List,* 11 December 2002.

————. 'Nato unmasks al-Qa'eda fleet'. *Lloyd's List,* 29 Nov. 2001.

————. 'Nigerian pirate attack on bulker fuels new fears'. *Lloyd's List,* 17 July 2008.

————. 'Pirates pose as Iranian officials'. *Lloyd's List,* 29 June 2006.

————. 'Pirates release Danica White'. *Lloyd's List,* 23 Aug. 2007.

————. 'Svitzer tug hijack 'linked to environmental group''. *Lloyd's List,* 5 Feb. 2008.

————. 'US Navy seizes suspect pirate vessel off Somalia'. *Lloyd's List,* 24 Jan. 2006.

O'Sullivan, Arieh. 'On gua off Gaza's coast'. *Jerusalem Post,* 5 July 2002 at http://pqasb.pqarchive.com/jpost/doc (11 May 2004).

————. 'Security forces uncover Islamic Jihad maritime unit'. *Israel Ministry of Foreign Affairs* report, 5 Feb. 2004 at http://www.israel.org/MFA/Government/Communiques/2004/Security+forces+uncover+Islamic+Jihad+maritime+uni.htm (7 September 2007).

'Outrage. Conference'. *TIME,* 6 Dec. 1926 at http://www.time.com/time/magazine/article/0,9171,722819,00.html (31 Oct. 2006).

Owen, Edward. 'Eta plot to bomb Plymouth ferry foiled'. *Daily Telegraph,* 12 July 2007 at http://www.telegraph.co.uk/news/main.jhtml?xml=/news/2007/07/12/wferry112.xml (14 July 2007).

'Owners oppose Malacca levy'. *Fairplay,* 1 Dec. 2006.

'Palestinian suicide boat attacks Israeli navy boat'. *Reuters,* 23 Nov. 2002 at http://nucnews.net/nucnews/2002nn/0211nn/021123nn.htm#331 (7 Dec. 2007).

'Palestinians and al-Qaeda bond through ship container'. 2004. *DEBKAfile,* 17 March 2004 at http://www.debka.com/article.php?aid=807 (25 Jan. 2006).

Pancevski, Bojan. 'Pirates of the Danube give shipping owners the blues'. *Sunday Telegraph,* 23 July 2006 at http://www.telegraph.co.uk/news/main.jhtml?xml=/news/2006/07/23/wdanube23.xml (23 July 2006).

'Parliament suicide attack stuns India'. *BBS News,* 13 Dec. 2001 at http://news.bbc.co.uk/1/hi/world/south_asia/1708853.stm (11 Dec. 2007).

'Paying to stay safe'. *Lloyd's List,* 12 September 2007.

Pazzibugan, Dona Z., *et al.* 'Bomb designed to burn, police say'. *The Nation,* 31 Aug. 2005 at http://news.inq7.net/nation/index.php?index=1&story_id=48580 (31 Aug. 2005).

Pennington, Matthew; and Haven, Paul. 'Experts: Mohammed arrest slowed al-Qaida'. *Washington Post,* 16 March 2007 at http://www.washingtonpost.com/wp-dyn/content/article/2007/03/16/AR2007031600394_pf.html (20 March 2006).

'Peril on the sea'. *The Economist,* vol. 369, no. 4, 4 Oct. 2003, pp. 67-68.

Perry, Alex. 'Buccaneer tales in the pirates' lair: From island hideaways brigands plague Asia's shipping lanes as they have for generations'. *TIMEasia.com,* vol. 158, nos 7/8, 20-27 Aug. 2001 at http://www.time.com/time/asia/features/journey2001/pirates.html (9 Oct. 2003).

Perry, Tony. 'Low-key war on pirates becomes more perilous'. *Los Angeles Times,* 28 March 2008 at http://www.latimes.com/technology/la-fg-pirates-29mar28,1,263399.story (19 April 2008).

'Peter Blake – Muer on the Amazon'. *Latitude 38,* Jan. 2002 at http://www.latitude38.com/features/Blake.htm (7 September 2007).

Pflanz, Mike. 'Nigerian rebels threaten new wave of kidnaps'. *Daily Telegraph,* 7 Feb. 2007 at http://www.telegraph.co.uk/news/main.jhtml;jsessionid=EAEOD2SZL5I5RQFIQMGCFGGAVCBQUIV0?xml=/news/2007/02/07/wnigeria07.xml (7 Feb. 2007).

'Phantom ship sale'. *Shiptalk.com,* 27 Nov. 2006 at http://www.shiptalk.com/index.asp?ItemID=1288&rcid=158&pcid=134&cid=158'#anch (27 Nov. 2006).

'Phantom vessels the latest tactic in Asian piracy'. *South China Morning Post,* 22 July 1994.

'Philippine blast 'extortion bid". *BBC News,* 28 March 2006 at http://news.bbc. co.uk/1/hi/world/asia-pacific/4851746.stm (7 September 2007).
'Phillipine chief says terror plot foiled against US troops'. *Associated Press,* 5 July 2007 at http://www.iht.com/articles/ap/2007/07/05/asia/AS-GEN-Philippines-Terror-Plots.php (6 July2007).
'Phillipine ferry blast kills one'. *BBC News,* 20 September 2000 at http://news.bbc. co.uk/1/hi/world/asia-pacific/933129.stm (7 September 2007).
'Phillipines, Indonesia govts warn of possible terrorist attacks'. *Bloomberg.com,* 29 Aug. 2005 at http://www.bloomberg.com/apps/news?pid=10000087&si d=aBCXEIMNfB8A&refer=top_world_news# (3 Dec. 2005).
'Philippines: New concerns arise with rebel submarine plan'. *Stratfor,* 14 March 2003 at http://www.stratfor.com/philippines_new_concerns_arise_rebel_submarine_plan_0 (4 July 2008).
'Philippines signs ceasefire with guerrilla group'. *ABC NewsOnline,* 18 July 2003 at http://www.abc.net.au/news/newsitems/200307/s905518.htm (7 September 2007).
'Piracy attacks spark crew concerns'. *Fairplay,* 5 July 2006.
'Piracy: Fishermen reluctant to go to sea'. *Bernama.com,* 21 July 2006 at http:// www.bernama.com/bernama/v3/news.php?id=209250 (22 July 2006).
'Piracy plagues Somali waters'. *Forbes,* 19 Nov. 2007 at http://www.forbes. com/2007/11/16/somalia-piracy-africa-biz-cx_1119oxfo.html (6 March 2008).
'Piracy report says Nigerian waters most deadly'. *IRINnews.org,* 23 September 2005 at http://www.irinnews.org/report.asp?ReportID=42396&SelectRegion= West_Africa&SelectCountry=NIGERIA (23 September 2005).
'Piracy resurgence feared off Somalia'. *Fairplay,* 11 Jan. 2007.
'Piracy returns to the Malacca Straits'. *Fairplay,* 10 Oct. 2006.
'Piracy suspects found guilty'. *Reuters,* 26 Oct. 2006 at http://www.news24.com/ News24/Africa/News/0,,2-11-1447_2021212,00.html (30 Oct. 2006).
'Piracy takes a higher toll of seamen's lives'. *ICC News,* 28 Jan. 2004 at http://www.iccwbo.org/ccs/news_archives/2004/Piracy_report_2003.asp (28 April 2004).
'Pirate attacks in Malacca Strait'. *BBC News,* 4 July 2006 at http://news.bbc. co.uk/1/hi/world/asia-pacific/5143858.stm?ls (7 September 2007).
'Pirate ring leader caught in Cirebon'. *Antara News,* 30 September 2007 at http:// www.antara.co.id/en/arc/2007/9/30/pirate-ring-leader-caught-in-cirebon/ (7 Oct. 2007).
'Pirates attack cruise ship'. 2005. *CBS News,* 5 Nov. 2005 at http://www.cbsnews.com/ stories/2005/11/05/national/main1015815.shtml (7 September 2007).
'Pirates attack Japanese-owned ship in Malacca Straits'. *Kyodo News,* 4 April 2005 at http://www.24hourscholar.com/p/articles/mi_m0WDQ/is_2005_April_4/ ai_n13506547 (7 September 2007).
'Pirates attack three ships off Indonesia'. *Reuters,* 5 July 2006.

'Pirates free Indonesian hostages'. *BBC News*, 19 March 2005 at http://news.bbc. co.uk/1/hi/world/asia-pacific/4363741.stm (7 September 2007).

'Pirates free Indonesian sailors'. *ABC Radio Australia*, 27 Aug. 2007 at http://www. radioaustralia.net.au/news/stories/s2016931.htm. (7 September 2007).

'Pirates halt Somali aid shipments'. *BBC News*, 21 May 2007 at http://news.bbc. co.uk/1/hi/world/africa/6675117.stm (18 July 2007).

'Pirates hijack Danish-owned ship off Somali coast'. *Associated Press*, 4 Feb. 2008 at http://www.iht.com/articles/ap/2008/02/04/africa/AF-GEN-Somalia-Piracy.php (5 Feb. 2008).

'Pirates hijack UN ship near Somalia'. *Agence-France Presse*, 26 Feb. 2007 at http://www.iol.co.za/index.php?set_id=1&click_id=87&art_id= nw20070225221636602C662354 (28 Feb. 2007).

'Pirates moving into deep sea'. *Lloyd's List*, 22 May 2007.

'Pirates open fire on cargo ship: Malaysian watchdog warns key routes threatened'. *Associated Press*, 15 May 2007 at http://www.iht.com/articles/ ap/2007/05/15/asia/AS-GEN-Malaysia-Somalia-Pirates.php (21 May 2007).

'Pirates paralyse economic activities in Ibeno'. *The Vanguard*, 13 Feb. 2008 at http://www.vanguangr.com/index.php?option=com_content&task=view &id=2201&Itemid=44 (31 March 2008).

'Pirates storm Indonesian tanker'. *BBC News* report, 14 March 2005 at http:// news.bbc.co.uk/1/hi/world/asia-pacific/4347167.stm (14 March 2005).

'Pirates used 'good conduct guide' in French yacht siege: source'. *Agence France-Presse*, 17 April 2008 at http://afp.google.com/article/ALeqM5ic4lMhcd-vj6BV5HsRB-uabBjyUmA (18 April 2008).

Pisik, Betsy. 'US sends warship against sea pirates'. *The Washington Times*, 27 Feb. 2007.

'Plane hits Milan skyscraper'. *BBC News*, 18 April 2002 at http://news.bbc.co.uk/1/ hi/world/europe/1937976.stm (7 September 2007).

Plushnick-Masti, Ramit. 'Israel: Iran aided Hezbollah attack'. *The Mercury News*, 15 July 2006.

Pook, Sally. 'It's like a vision of doomsday'. *Daily Telegraph*, 12 Dec. 2005 at http:// www.telegraph.co.uk/news/main.jhtml?xml=/news/2005/12/12/nfire12. xml&sSheet=/portal/2005/12/12/ixportaltop.html (12 Dec. 2005).

Porter, Adam. 'Global refinery shortage shifts power balance'. *BBC News*, 2 Oct. 2005 at http://news.bbc.co.uk/1/hi/business/4296812.stm (7 September 2007).

Porter, Janet. 'Maersk on course to tackle piracy'. *Lloyd's List*, 22 Jan. 2008.

Posner, Michael. 'Intelligence officers call al Qaeda nuclear threat real'. *GovernmentExecutive.com*, 2 April 2008 at http://www.govexec.com/story_page. cfm?articleid=39686&dcn=todaysnews (3 April 2008).

Preston, Julia. 'Smuggling immigrants just a sideline, court told'. *International Herald Tribune*, 24 May 2005 at http://www.iht.com/articles/2005/05/23/news/smuggle.php (7 September 2007).

'Private navies combat Malacca Strait pirates'. *WorldNetDaily*, 31 July 2005 at http://www.wnd.com/news/article.asp?ARTICLE_ID=45535 (6 Jan. 2007).

'Qaeda claims Yemen oil attacks, vows more strikes'. *Reuters*, 7 Nov. 2006.

'Q&A: Saudi oil attack'. *BBC News*, 24 Feb. 2006 at http://news.bbc.co.uk/1/hi/world/middle_east/4748978.stm (7 September 2007).

'QE2 threat and the symbolic value of cruise ships, The'. STRATFOR *Daily Terrorism Brief*, 13 April 2006.

Quezon, Manuel L., III. 'Could terrorists use the strait of disquietude to wreak havoc?' *Arab News*, 25 Match 2005 at http://arabnews.com/?page=7&section=0&article=60957&d=24&m=3&y=2005&pix=opinion.jpg&category=Opinion (30 July 2006).

'Raid disrupts Iraqi oil exports'. *BBC News* report, 25 April 2004 at http://news.bbc.co.uk/1/hi/world/middle_east/3657599.stm (25 April 2004).

Raines, Ben; and Finch, Bill. 'LNG study: explosions possible'. *Mobile Register*, 7 Dec. 2003.

———. 'Holes in LNG study'. *Mobile Register*, 4 Dec. 2003 at http://www.boerpowerplants.org/pdf_docs/Holes_quest_study.pdf (1 April 2005).

———. 'Study talks about possible LNG disaster as result of accident'. 12 July 2003 at http://www.wildcalifornia.org/cgi-files/0/pdfs/1076793906_Humboldt_Bay_LNG_Mob_Reg_Study_Possible_Disaster.pdf (7 September 2007). [Original publication unknown]

Rajan, T. 'Pirate attack? Team in S'pore will alert 14 nations'. *Straits Times*, 30 Nov. 2006.

———. 'Singapore to open anti-piracy cooination centre'. *Straits Times*, 23 Nov. 2006.

Rajoo, D. Arul. 'Foreign powers eyeing Straits of Melaka, says Chandra Muzaffar'. *Bernama*, 6 March 2008 at http://www.bernama.com/bernama/v3/news.php?id=318942 (7 March 2008).

Ramachandran, Sudha 'The Sea Tigers of Tamil Eelam'. *AsiaTimes Online*, 31 Aug. 2006 at http://www.atimes.com/atimes/South_Asia/HH31Df01.html (31 Aug. 2006).

Raman, Nachammal. 'Three nations cooinate flights to spy on Malacca pirates'. *Christian Science Monitor*, 17 Aug. 2005 at http://www.csmonitor.com/2005/0817/p10s01-woap.html?s=widep#map (30 Oct. 2006).

Ramesh, S. "Eyes in the Sky' initiative launched for Malacca Strait security'. *Channel News Asia*, 13 September 2005 at http://www.channelnewsasia.com/stories/singaporelocalnews/view/168037/1/.html (13 Oct. 2006).

————. 'Malaysia, Indonesia and Singapore set up cooperative mechanism'. *Channel NewsAsia*, 4 September 2007 at http://www.channelnewsasia.com/stories/singaporelocalnews/view/297801/1/.html (16 September 2007).

Rao, Ramadas; and Chan, Tony. 'Malacca nations shocked into anti-pirate action'. *Fairplay*, 11 Aug. 2005.

Ravid, Barak. 'Israel to UN: Hezbollah has tripled its land-to-sea missile arsenal'. *Haaretz*, 31 Oct. 2007 at http://www.haaretz.com/hasen/spages/918937.html (12 May 2008).

Rayment, Sean. 'Navy chief has 'too few ships to gua sea lanes from terrorists''. *Sunday Telegraph*, 7 September 2003 at http://www.telegraph.co.uk/news/main.jhtml?xml=/news/2003/09/07/navy07.xml. The full interview upon which this report was based was published in *Warships International Fleet Review* at www.warshipsifr.com/pages/interview_alanWest.html (7 September 2003).

————. 'SBS commander's widow to sue MOD over diving death'. *Daily Telegraph*, 27 Nov. 2005 at http://www.telegraph.co.uk/news/main.jhtml?xml=/news/2005/11/27/nsbs27.xml (7 September 2007).

'Rebel leader caught in Philippines'. *BBC News*, 9 July 2001 at http://news.bbc.co.uk/1/hi/world/asia-pacific/1429569.stm (7 September 2007).

'Rebels become Malacca pirates'. *Fairplay*, 3 Aug. 2006.

Reddy, B. Muralidhar. 'Three LTTE ships destroyed: Navy'. *The Hindu*, 12 September 2007 at http://www.hindu.com/2007/09/12/stories/2007091262771900.htm (18 September 2007).

Reece, Damian. 'Business Comment' *Daily Telegraph*, 10 Aug. 2007 at http://www.telegraph.co.uk/money/main.jhtml?xml=/money/2007/08/10/ccom110.xml (10 Aug. 2007)

Reel, Monte. 'Brazilian city wakes to prison gang's power'. *Washington Post*, 21 May 2006 at http://www.washingtonpost.com/wp-dyn/content/article/2006/05/20/AR2006052001105.html (6 Aug. 2007).

Reeve, Simon; and Foden, Giles. 'A new breed of terror'. *The Guaian*, 12 September 2001 at http://www.guaian.co.uk/wtccrash/story/0,1300,550411,00.html (3 Dec. 2005).

'Regional agreement against maritime piracy to take effect in September'. *Peoples Daily Online*, 21 June 2006 at http://english.people.com.cn/200606/21/eng20060621_275965.html (7 September 2007).

Regalado, Edith. 'NSA: RP can't police sea lanes between Mindanao, Indonesia'. *The Philippine Star*, 16 Oct. 2006.

Rennie, David. 'China oers military to wage war on killer pirates'. *Daily Telegraph*, 27 Nov. 1999 at http://www.telegraph.co.uk/htmlContent.jhtml?html=/archive/1999/11/27/wpir27.htm (17 June 2004).

Republic of the Philippines, Office of the Press Secretary. '2 Abu Sayyaf bandits in Super Ferry bombing presented to GMA'. 11 Oct. 2004 at http://

www.news.ops.gov.ph/archives2004/oct11.htm#2%20Abu%20Sayyaf (13 June 2007).

'Resentment is mounting in oil-rich Niger Delta'. *Alexander's Gas & Oil Connections*, 6 April 2005 at http://www.gasandoil.com/goc/news/nta51471. htm (23 September 2005).

Ressa, Maria. 'Bin Laden forges tactical alliance between al Qaeda and Hezbollah'. *ABS-CBN Interactive*, 18 Aug. 2006 at http://www.abs-cbnnews.com/ storypage.aspx?StoryId=47552 (22 Aug. 2006).

'Rewaing Piracy'. *Arab News*, 24 Aug. 2007 at http://www.arabnews.com/?page=7 &section=0&article=100369&d=24&m=8&y=2007 (25 Aug. 2007).

Reyes, Brian. 'Prisoner accused of Gibraltar ferry terror plot'. *Lloyd's List*, 30 March 2005.

Rice, Xan. 'How savage pirates reign on the world's high seas'. *The Observer* (London), 27 April 2008 at http://www.guaian.co.uk/world/2008/apr/27/ somalia1 (28 April 2008).

Richason, Michael. 'Crackdown on piracy'. *Asia-Pacific Defence Reporter*, Oct.-Nov. 1992.

———. 'India and China set sights on piracy'. *International Held Tribune*, 23 Nov. 1999 at http://www.iht.com/IHT/MR/99/mr112399a.html (1 May 2004).

Richason, Paul. 'China explains 'piracy attacks''. *Lloyd's List*, 18 March 1994, p. 12.

———; and Mulrenan, Jim. 'Hong Kong piracy report "updated" after withdrawal'. *Lloyd's List*, 27 May 1993.

Robinson, Simon 'Nigeria's deadly days'. *TIME*, 14 May 2006 at http://www. time.com/time/nation/article/0,8599,1193987,00.html (31 Oct. 2006).

Rogers, Paul. 'Bay at risk from chemical disaster'. *The Mercury News*, 19 Feb. 2004 at http://www.gasdetection.com/news2/mercury_news1.html (1 July 2004).

Roig-Franzia, Manuel. 'Drug trade tyranny on the boer'. *Washington Post*, 16 March 2008 at http://www.washingtonpost.com/wp-dyn/content/article/2008/03/15/AR2008031501013.html?hpid=moreheadlines (16 March 2008).

———. 'From Mexico, drug violence spills into US'. *Washington Post*, 20 April 2008 at http://www.washingtonpost.com/wp-dyn/content/article/2008/04/19/AR2008041901916.html?hpid=sec-world (20 April 2008).

———. 'Mexican drug cartels threaten elections'. *Washington Post*, 5 Jan. 2008 at http://www.washingtonpost.com/wp-dyn/content/article/2008/01/04/AR2008010403706.html (5 Jan. 2008).

———. 'Mexico's police chief is killed in brazen attack by gunmen'. *Washington Post*, 9 May 2008 at http://www.washingtonpost.com/wp-dyn/content/

article/2008/05/08/AR2008050803242.html?hpid=moreheadlines   (9 May 2008).

Rotella, Sebastian. 'Fears persist of al-Qaeda link to dive centre'. *Los Angeles Times*, 15 Feb. 2003 at http://www.cdnn.info/news/article/a030802.html (23 July 2006).

Rothman, Paul. 'Passenger ferries could be prime terrorist target'. *Access Control & Security Systems*, 1 Oct. 2003 at http://securitysolutions.com/mag/security_passenger_ferries_prime_2/ (11 June 2004) and at http://www.transportationsec.com/ar/security_passenger_ferries_prime/index.htm (7 September 2007).

'Rogue units of Sino Navy behind piracy'. *Philippine Daily Inquirer*, 21 February 1996.

'Russian oil tanker jams Suez Canal'. *MosNews*, 8 Nov. 2004 at http://www.energybulletin.net/3065.html (21 Dec. 2005).

Ryan, Margaret. 'Captain counts the cost of piracy'. *BBC News*, 2 Feb. 2006 at http://news.bbc.co.uk/1/hi/world/africa/4669050.stm (3 Feb. 2006).

Ryan, Nick. 'Wave of terror'. *The Scotsman 'Weekend'*, Aug. 1997 at http://www.nickryan.net/articles/pirates.html (7 June 2007).

'Sailors killed in Sri Lanka blast'. *BBC News*, 12 Jan. 2006 at http://news.bbc.co.uk/1/hi/world/middle_east/4605478.stm (12 Jan. 2006).

'Sailors killed in Sri Lanka blast'. *BBC News*, 11 April 2006 at http://news.bbc.co.uk/1/hi/world/south_asia/4898466.stm (7 September 2007).

Sakhuja, Vijay. 'Footing the bill'. *Shiptalk*, 17 May 2007 at http://www.shiptalk.com/index.asp?ItemID=2070&rcid=191&pcid=178&cid=191'#anch (21 May 2007).

———. 'Malacca: Who's to pay for smooth sailing?' *Asia Times Online*, 16 May 2007 at http://www.atimes.com/atimes/Southeast_Asia/IE16Ae01.html (13 May 2008).

Sale, Richa. 'Collapse of BCCI shorts Bin Laden'. *United Press International*, 1 March 2001 at http://www.highbeam.com/library/doc3.asp?DOCID=1P1:42426950&num=100&ctrlInfo=Round3a%3AProd%3ASR%3AResult (22 June 2004).

Sambandan, V.S. 'LTTE raising funds for 'final war''. *The Hindu*, 16 March 2006 at http://www.hindu.com/2006/03/16/stories/2006031605211400.htm (18 March 2006).

———. 'SLMM head, Sea Tigers meet'. *The Hindu*, 17 July 2003 at http://www.hinduonnet.com/2003/07/17/stories/2003071701801501.htm (7 September 2007).

Samuel, Henry. 2006. 'Gendarmes hunt down Riviera boat thieves'. *Daily Telegraph*, 14 July 2006 at http://www.telegraph.co.uk/news/main.jhtml;jsessionid=C40T1PPI4JBMRQFIQMGCFGGAVCBQUIV0?xml=/news/2006/07/14/wyacht14.xml (7 September).

'Save us! Save us!'. *TIME*, 9 July 1979

Sawatan, Jackson. 'Piracy Information Centre launched in S'pore'. *Bernama. com*, 29 Nov. 2006 at http://www.bernama.com/bernama/v3/news. php?id=233306 (30 Nov. 2006).

'SBS Commander killed in accident'. *BBC News*, 16 March 2005 at http://news. bbc.co.uk/1/hi/uk/4356153.stm (7 September 2007).

Schiff, Ze'ev. 'How Iran planned the Buenos Aires blast'. *Haaretz*, ND at http:// www.haaretz.com/hasen/pages/ShArt.jhtml?itemNo=273898&contrassI D=2&subContrassID=1&sbSubContrassID=0 (7 September 2007).

Schlesinger, Vivian. 'Piracy not hitting insurance rates'. *Journal of Commerce Online*, 13 Jan. 2003.

Schmitt, Eric. 'Experts see gains against Asian terror networks'. *New York Times*, 9 June 2008 at http://www.nytimes.com/2008/06/09/world/asia/09terror. html?_r=2&ref=world&oref=login&oref=slogin (9 June 2008)

———; and Shanker, Thom. 'US adapts Cold-War idea to fight terrorists'. *New York Times*, 18 March 2008 at http://www.nytimes.com/2008/03/18/ washington/18terror.html?_r=1&hp=&adxnnl=1&oref=slogin&adxnnl x=1205842477-77VrsUS5c8Apv8fyuL0LjA (18 March 2008).

'Scuba warning issued for instructors'. *Associated Press*, 27 June 2007.

Scutro, Andrew. 'Amphib lights up, but loses Somali pirates'. *Navy Times*, 7 June 2007 at http://www.navytimes.com/news/2007/06/navy_carterhall_ pirates_070605w/ (19 July 2007).

'Security experts say cruise ships a soft target'. *The Houston Chronicle*, 20 Nov. 2001 at http://www.chron.com/disp/story.mpl/special/terror/front/1139846. html (19 July 2006).

'Security stepped up after bombing of Sri Lankan port'. *Channel NewsAsia*, 19 Oct. 2006 at http://www.channelnewsasia.com/stories/afp_asiapacific/ view/236385/1/.html (7 September 2007).

Seib, Christine. 'Lloyd's flags risks to ships in Sri Lankan and Yemeni waters'. *The Times*, 22 May 2006 at http://business.timesonline.co.uk/article/0,,9063-2191412,00.html (23 May 2006).

'Seizing of the Abu Hasan, May 22, 2003'. Israel Ministry of Foreign Affairs *Press Release*, 22 May 2003 at http://www.mfa.gov.il/MFA/MFAArchive/2000_2009/2003/5/The%20Seizing%20of%20the%20Abu%20 Hasan%20-%20May%2022-%202003 (7 Dec. 2007).

Selsky, Andrew. 'Cocaine smugglers using high-tec boats'. *Associated Press*, 7 Nov. 2005 at http://www.washingtonpost.com/wp-dyn/content/article/2005/11/07/AR2005110700397.html (1 Jan. 2008).

Senanayake, Shimali. 'Bombs rock Sri Lankan port town'. *International Herald Tribune*, 18 Oct. 2006 at http://www.iht.com/articles/2006/10/18/news/ lanka.php (18 Oct. 2006).

Seper, Jerry. 'Mexican mercenaries expand base into US'. *The Washington Times*, 1 Aug. 2005 at http://www.washingtontimes.com/national/20050801-122047-2623r.htm (3 Aug. 2005).

Serrano, Richa A. 'Boer violence pushes north'. *Los Angeles Times*, 19 Aug. 2007 at http://www.latimes.com/news/nationworld/nation/la-na-boer-19aug19,0,2502235.story?coll=la-home-center (19 Aug. 2007).

'Severed head greets new troops in Mexico drug war'. *Reuters*, 12 May 2007 at http://www.reuters.com/article/worldNews/idUSN1223905320070512 (22 May 2007).

Sezer, Murad. 'Terror suspect: 'I was going to attack Israeli ships''. *USA Today*, 11 Aug. 2005 at http://www.usatoday.com/news/world/2005-08-11-turkey-terror_x.htm (14 Aug. 2005).

'Sex trade and exploitation in Batam and Bintan'. *Associated Press*, 4 Dec. 2000 at http://www.thinkcentre.org/article.cfm?ArticleID=241 (7 September 2007).

Shanker, Thom. 'A new enemy gains on the US'. *New York Times*, 30 July 2006 at http://www.nytimes.com/2006/07/30/weekinreview/30shanker.html?_r=1&ref=weekinreview&oref=slogin (31 July 2006).

Shenon, Philip. 'Threats and Responses: Terror network; a major suspect in Qeada attacks is in US custody'. *New York Times*, 22 Nov. 2002.

Sherman, Jason. 'Pentagon group details Sea Base concept'. *Defense News*, 13 Aug. 2001 at http://www.defensenews.com/sgmlparse2.php?F=archive2/20031027/atpc7674087.sgml (7 September 2007).

———. 'SOUTHCOM detects sharp boost in narco submarine fleet size'. *Inside the Navy*, 10 March 2008, p. 13.

Sherwell, Philip. 'Iranian Guas amass secret fortunes'. *Sunday Telegraph*, 19 Aug. 2007 at http://www.telegraph.co.uk/news/main.jhtml?xml=/news/2007/08/19/wiran119.xml (19 Aug. 2007).

———. 'The Royal Navy closes one of al-Qaeda's last escape routes'. *Sunday Telegraph*, 21 March 2004 at http://www.telegraph.co.uk/news/main.jhtml?xml=/news/2004/03/21/walq121.xml. (16 Aug 2004)

———; and Freeman, Colin. 'Suicide boats close oil port as 42 die in Iraq'. *Sunday Telegraph*, 25 April 2004.

'Shin Bet chief accuses Egypt of closing its eyes to Palestinian arms smuggling to Gaza. But DEBKA*file* reports its volume is dwarfed by Hizballah's illegal imports'. DEBKA*file*, 2 Oct. 2006 at http://www.debka.com/headline.php?hid=3323 (17 Oct. 2006).

'Ship hijacked as Chechen siege expands'. *CNN World News* report, 16 Jan. 1996 at http://www.cnn.com/WORLD/9601/chechen_rebels/01-16/pm/index.html (14 June 2004).

'Ship hits submerged cargo vessel'. *BBC News*, 1 Jan. 2003 at http://news.bbc.co.uk/2/hi/uk_news/2620641.stm (7 September 2007).

Shipman, Tim. 'Bin Laden sidelined as al-Qaeda threat revives'. *Sunday Telegraph*, 16 September 2007 at http://www.telegraph.co.uk/news/main. jhtml?xml=/news/2007/09/16/walq116.xml (16 September 2007).

'Shipping nations agree satellite tracking rules'. *Reuters.com*, 19 May 2006.

'Ships that died of shame, The'. *Sydney Morning Herald*, 14 Jan. 2003 at http://www. smh.com.au/articles/2003/01/13/1041990234408.html (12 May 2004).

Shuman, Ellis. 'Gaza-bound weapons arsenal seized by Israeli Navy'. *Israel Insider*, 9 May 2001 at http://www.israelinsider.com/channels/security/articles/ sec_0041.htm (8 Dec. 2007).

———. 'IDF blockades Gaza coast after encounter with terror fishing boat'. *Israel Insider*, 24 Nov. 2002 at http://web.israelinsider.com/Articles/Security/1668.htm (8 Dec.).

———. 'IDF operates against Palestinian arms smuggling attempt on Gaza coast'. *Israel Insider*, 28 Aug. 2002 at http://web.israelinsider.com/Articles/Security/1378.htm (8 Dec. 2007).

Shyamol, Nazimuddin. 'Mafia syndicates growing in Ctg port'. *The Independent* (Bangladesh), 14 May 2006.

Silvestrini, Elaine. 'Authorities want to torpedo use of drug-smuggling subs'. *Tampa Bay Online*, 26 June 2008 at http://www.msnbc.msn.com/id/25400743/ (4 July 2008).

Simpson, John. 'Death on the Amazon sheds light on modern-day piracy'. *Sunday Telegraph*, 9 Dec. 2001 at http://www.telegraph.co.uk/news/main. jhtml?xml=/news/2001/12/09/wsimp09.xml (7 September 2007).

Simpson, Sarah, 'A rise in pirate attacks off Nigeria's coast'. *Christian Science Monitor*, 20 March 2008 at http://www.csmonitor.com/2008/0320/p01s01-woaf.htm (21 March 2008).

'Singapore, Indonesia launch sea surveillance system'. *Vietnam News Agency*, 27 May 2005 at http://www.vnagency.com.vn/Home/EN/tabid/119/item-id/12243/Default.aspx (7 September 2007).

'Sipidan instructor to testify against Abu Sayyef–linked rebels'. *Cyber Diver News Network*, 24 September 2004 at http://www.cdnn.info/industry/i040924/ i040924.html (7 September 2007).

Sirilal, Ranga. 'Sri Lanka navy, air force strike at Tiger rebels'. *Reuters AlertNet*, 25 March 2008.

Sitathan, Tony. 'Cash-strapped military recipe for corruption'. *Asia Times*, 15 March 2003 at http://www.atimes.com/atimes/Southeast_Asia/ EC15Ae03.html (19 Nov. 2007).

Sivaram, Dharmeratnam. 'The Importance of 'Rearbase': Taraki, 1989'. *TamilNet.com*, 17 Feb. 2006 at http://www.tamilnet.com/art. html?catid=79&artid=17215 (7 September 2007).

'Six Lankan naval personnel killed by LTTE'. *The Times of India*, 6 Feb. 2008 at http://timesofindia.indiatimes.com/World/Six_Lankan_naval_personnel_killed_by_LTTE/articleshow/2762422.cms (7 Feb. 2008).

Slaney, Christopher. 'How they bombed Ashdod'. *Fairplay*, 8 April 2004, pp. 20-21.

'Small plane crashes into Florida building'. *BBC News*, 6 Jan. 2002 at http://news.bbc.co.uk/1/hi/world/americas/1744923.stm (7 September 2007).

Smith, Charles R. 'Al Qaeda plans scuba diver, one man submarine attack'. *Cyber Diver News Network*, 26 Aug. 2003 at http://www.cdnn.info/industry/i030826/i030826.html. Also as 'Al Qaeda plans underwater attack'. *Newsmax.com*. 26 Aug. 2003 at http://www.newsmax.com/archives/articles/2003/8/26/160951.shtml (8 July 2004). NB for access to the DHS advisory bulletin to which this report refers go to http://www.esisac.com/publicdocs/Other_Advisories/Swimmer%20Attack%20Indicators%20 and%20Protective%20Measures%20IB1.doc

Smith, Michael. 'Navy steps up al-Qaeda anti-terror patrols'. *Daily Telegraph*. 26 Nov. 2002 at http://www.telegraph.co.uk/news/main.jhtml?xml=/news/2002/11/26/navy26.xml (11 Aug. 2004).

————. 'SBS commander killed on assault exercise'. *Daily Telegraph*, 16 March 2005 at http://www.telegraph.co.uk/news/main.jhtml?xml=/news/2005/03/16/nsbs16.xml (7 September 2007).

Smucker, Philip. 'We were bombed, says oil tanker captain'. *Daily Telegraph*, 8 Oct. 2002 at http://www.telegraph.co.uk/news/main.jhtml?xml=/news/2002/10/08/wyem08.xml (7 September 2007)..

Soares, Marcelo; and McDonnell, Patrick J. 'Inmates unleash a torrent of violence on Brazilian city'. *Los Angeles Times*, 16 May 2006.

Soh, Felix. 'Straits of Malacca now free of pirate attacks'. *Straits Times*, 13 April 1996.

'Somali militiamen say US fired first'. *CBSNews*, 19 March 2006 at http://www.cbsnews.com/stories/2006/03/19/world/main1419421.shtml (25 March 2006).

'Somali pirates detained by US Navy'. *ICC-IMB*, 24 Jan. 2006 at http://www.iccwbo.org/iccffhg/index.html (7 September 2007).

'Somali pirates free Japan tanker'. *BBC News*, 12 Dec. 2007 at http://news.bbc.co.uk/1/hi/world/africa/7139897.stm (18 April 2008).

'Somali pirates release hijacked food aid ship'. *Environmental News Service*, 9 April 2007 at http://www.ens-newswire.com/ens/apr2007/2007-04-09-03.asp (15 April 2008).

'Somali pirates "received ransom onboa Spanish boat"'. *Agence France-Presse*, 29 April 2008 at http://afp.google.com/article/ALeqM5h-iNtCpgm21rOt-P78YjMJRu4bl0A (3 May 2008).

'Somali pirates seize French yacht'. *BBC News*, 4 April 2008 at http://news.bbc.co.uk/1/hi/world/africa/7331290.stm (4 April 2008).

'Somalia: Liner docks after pirate attack'. *New York Times*, 8 Nov. 2005 at http://select.nytimes.com/search/restricted/article?res=F60D17FC3E5A0C7B8CDDA80994DD404482 (7 September 2007).

'Somalia: Security Council urges action over piracy off the coast of Somalia in line with IMO assembly resolution'. *Cargo Security International*, 17 March 2006 at http://www.cargosecurityinternational.com/channeldetail.asp?cid=4&caid=6619 (18 March 2006).

'Somalia: Tension in coastal town after pirate clashes, 1 killed'. *Garowe Online*, 14 Feb. 2008 at http://www.garoweonline.com/artman2/publish/Somalia_27/Somalia_Tension_in_coastal_town_after_pirate_clashes_1_killed.shtml (19 April 2008).

'Somalia's dangerous waters'. *BBC News report*, 26 September 2005 at http://news.bbc.co.uk/1/hi/world/africa/4283396.stm (1 Oct. 2005).

'Soosai reiterates sovereign right to seas boering Tamil Homeland'. *TamilNet*, 13 May 2006 at http://www.tamilnet.com/art.html?catid=13&artid=18111 (14 May 2006).

Soufan, Ali H. 'Coddling terrorists in Yemen'. *Washington Post*, 17 May 2008 at http://www.washingtonpost.com/wp-dyn/content/article/2008/05/16/AR2008051603274.html (19 May 2008).

'South Africa, Nigeria take lead against piracy'. *Fairplay*, 22 September 2005.

'South China Sea pirates extend range'. *Lloyd's List*, 30 September 1992, p. 2.

'Spanish police find 'drugs' sub'. *BBC News*, 14 Aug. 2006 at http://news.bbc.co.uk/1/hi/world/europe/4792075.stm (15 Dec. 2007).

Speares, Sandra. 'IMB condemns pirates' release' *Lloyd's List*, 19 Oct. 1998.

Spillius, Alex. 'Americans amongst 20 hostages in resort raid'. *Daily Telegraph*, 5 June 2001 at http://www.telegraph.co.uk/news/main.jhtml?xml=/news/2001/05/28/wphil28.xml (3 July 2007).

Spurrier, Andrew. 'Anti-piracy chief calls for stronger Somalia security'. *Lloyd's List*, 10 April 2008.

———. 'France opens proceedings against Le Ponant pirates'. *Lloyd's List*, 18 April 2008).

'Sri Lanka: 20 rebels killed in sea battle'. *Rediff News*, 20 Oct. 2006 at http://www.rediff.com/news/2006/oct/20ltte.htm (7 September 2007).

'Sri Lanka attack causes carnage'. *BBC News*, 16 Oct. 2006 at http://news.bbc.co.uk/1/hi/world/south_asia/6054470.stm (18 Oct. 2006).

'Sri Lanka bans small boats totally in Colombo harbour area'. *Colombo Page*, 24 Oct. 2006.

'Sri Lanka lashes out at war reporting'. *Agence France-Presse*, 5 June 2008 at http://www.khaleejtimes.com/DisplayArticleNew.asp?xfile=data/subcontinent/2008/June/subcontinent_June155.xml&section=subcontinent (6 June 2008)

'Sri Lanka navy sinks three LTTE boats, top Tiger commander killed'. *Colombo Page*, 28 September 2007 at http://www.colombopage.com/archive_07/September2860918CH.html (29 September 2007).

'Sri Lanka says 40 rebels killed in sea battle'. *Agence France-Presse*, 26 Dec. 2007 at http://www.channelnewsasia.com/stories/afp_asiapacific/view/319261/1/.html (27 Dec. 2007).

'Sri Lankan Navy completely destroy three LTTE ships and demolish their arms shipment capabilities'. Sri Lankan Navy *Security News*, 11 September 2007 at https://www.navy.lk/index.php?id=410 (17 September 2007).

'Sri Lankan Navy plants mines along maritime boer with India'. *The Times of India*, 23 Jan. 2008 at http://timesofindia.indiatimes.com/India/Sri_Lankan_Navy_plants_mines_along_marine_boer_with_India/articleshow/2725588.cms (24 Jan. 2008).

'Sri Lankan Navy repulses LTTE attempt to destroy troop carrier, heavy fighting continues in East'. 2006. *Colombo Page*, 1 Aug. 2006.

'Sri Lankan rebels planning attack on Colombo port: report'. *Agence France-Presse*, 14 June 2007.

'Sri Lankan navy 'sinks rebel boats''. *BBC News*, 20 Oct. available 2006 http://news.bbc.co.uk/1/hi/world/south_asia/6070976.stm (7 September 2007).

'Sri Lankan Tamil Tiger ships used Indonesia as 'home base' – sources'. *The Island* (Colombo), 21 Oct. 2007.

'Sri Lanka's perspective on maritime security in the region and its relevance to the world – Sri Lanka Foreign Minister Rohitha B. *Asian Tribune*, 4 June 2007 at http://www.asiantribune.com/index.php?q=node/6006 (4 June 2007). Also at http://www.slmfa.gov.lk/index.php?option=com_content&task=view&id=874&Itemid=1 and http://www.dailynews.lk/2007/06/05/fea02.asp (4 July 2007).

'Sri Lanka's Tigers on the loose'. *The Economist Global Agenda*, 28 Dec. 2005 at http://www.economist.com/agenda/PrinterFriendly.cfm?story_id=5349948 (28 Dec. 2005).

Stables, Eleanor. 'Mines, small boats may pose threat to US ports'. *CQ Homeland Security*, 14 May 2007 at http://public.cq.com/docs/hs/hsnews110-000002511604.html (21 May 2007).

Stares, Justin. 'Brussels pushes for changes to Unclos'. *Lloyd's List*, 4 June 2007.

———. 'EU seeks to extend territorial powers'. *Lloyd's List*, 19 July 2006.

Starr, Barbara. 'Sources: Warships targeted by Al-Qaeda'. *CNN.com*, 21 Nov. 2002 at http://archives.cnn.com/2002/US/11/21/us.warships.warning/index.html (20 July 2006).

SMALL BOATS, WEAK STATES, DIRTY MONEY

Steele, John. 'The problem of policing ferries'. *Daily telegraph,* 12 July 2007 at http://www.telegraph.co.uk/news/main.jhtml?xml=/news/2007/07/12/ wferry212.xml (14 July 2007).

'Steps towas a safer strait'. *Lloyd's List,* 26 September 2006.

Sterba, James P. 'The Agony of Vietnam Refugee Boat 0105'. *New York Times,* 25 July 1979.

Stevenson, Mark. 'Mexico: Drug gangs using terror tactics'. *Associated Press,* 18 May 2007.

'Straits users welcomed to participate in maritime security – Najib'. *Bernama.com,* 18 September 2006 at http://www.bernama.com.my/bernama/v3/news. php?id=220360 (23 September 2006).

Sturcke, James. 'Herald of sea changes'. *The Guaian,* 6 March 2007 at http://www. guaian.co.uk/transport/Story/0,,2027884,00.htm (7 September 2007).

Sua, Tracey. 'For hire: Guaians of the sea'. *Straits Times,* 15 April 2005.

'Submarine carrying 3 tons of cocaine seized off Costa Rica'. *USA Today,* 21 Nov. 2006 at http://www.usatoday.com/news/world/2006-11-20-drug-submarine_x.htm?csp=34 (27 Nov. 2006).

'Submarine-like vessel transporting cocaine seized in Pacific'. *News from Russia.com,* 15 September 2005 at http://newsfromrussia.com/ usa/2005/09/15/62989_.html (15 September 2005).

'Submarine with cocaine seized off Costa Rica'. *MSNBC.com,* 20 Nov. 2006 at http://www.msnbc.msn.com/id/15811689/ (13 March 2007).

Subramanian, Nirupama. 'Disguised message by Sea Tigers might have led to ship's highjack'. *Indian Express,* 21 Aug. 1998 at http://www.indianexpress. com/res/web/pIe/ie/daily/19980821/23350404.html (5 July 2007).

———. 'SA takes stand on LTTE: Lanka rests easy'. *Indian Express,* 19 Nov. 1998 at http://www.indianexpress.com/res/web/pIe/ie/daily/19981119/32350054.html (21 September 2007).

'Suez Canal reopens after blockage'. *BBC News,* 9 Feb. 2006 at http://news.bbc. co.uk/1/hi/world/middle_east/4696678.stm (7 September 2007).

Suh, Sangwon; and Lopez, Antonio. 'Getting tough'. *Asiaweek,* vol. 26, no. 38, 29 September 2000 at http://www.asiaweek.com/asiaweek/magazine/2000/0929/nat.phil.html (29 June 2007).

Sullivan, Kevin; and Joan, Mary. 'High-tec pirates ravage Asian seas'. *Washington Post,* 5 July 1999 at http://www.washingtonpost.com/wp-srv/inatl/daily/ july99/pirates5.htm (1 May 2004).

'Survivors of pirate attack speak out'. *Associated Press,* 15 Nov. 2007 at http://www.iol.co.za/index.php?set_id=1&click_id=68&art_ id=nw20071115193145103C536207 (16 Nov. 2007).

Suryanarayan, V. 'Fishing in choppy waters'. *The Hindu,* 25 Feb. 2004 at http:// www.hinduonnet.com/2004/02/25/stories/2004022501761000.htm (2 Aug. 2006).

————. 'Prabhakaran: Back to the old game'. *The Hindu*, 1 Dec. 2003 at http:// www.hinduonnet.com/2003/12/01/stories/2003120102341000.htm (17 March 2006).

————. 'Sea Tigers – threat to Indian security'. *The Hindu*, 28 July 2004 at http:// www.thehindu.com/2004/07/28/stories/2004072802311000.htm   (2 Aug. 2006).

————. 'Sri Lanka and India's security'. *The Hindu*, 25 April 2003 at http://www. hinduonnet.com/2003/04/25/stories/2003042500251000.htm   (2 Aug. 2006).

Suryanarayana, P.S. 'India's naval surveillance a big help to Sri Lanka'. *The Hindu*, 4 June 2008 at http://www.hindu.com/2008/06/04/stories/2008060455721300.htm (5 June 2008).

'Suspected Qaeda chief cooperating'. *CBS News*, 22 Nov. 2002 at http://www. cbsnews.com/stories/2002/11/17/attack/main529656.shtml   (15   July 2006).

'Suspected Tamil Tiger suicide bombers attack Sri Lankan port'. *Channel News Asia*, 18 Oct. 2006 at http://www.channelnewsasia.com/stories/afp_asia-pacific/view/236156/1/.html (19 Oct. 2006).

Svan, Jennifer H. 'Iraq's oil industry: Guaing a nation's future'. *Stars and Stripes*, 22 Oct. 2006 at http://stripes.com/article.asp?section=104&article=3996 6&archive=true (1 Nov. 2007).

'Swiss papers accuse Tamil Tigers of using drug money for fund raising activities'. *The Sunday Times* (Sri Lanka), 20 Aug. 2000 at http://www.priu.gov.lk/ news_update/features/20000822swiss_papers_accuse_tamil_tigers.htm (7 September 2007).

'Syrian admits Israeli cruise ship plot in Turkey'. *International Herald Tribune*, 12 Aug. 2005 at http://iht.com/articles/2005/08/11/news/terror.php (14 Aug. 2005).

Taheri, Amir. 'Al Qaeda's plan B'. *New York Post*, 1 July 2008 at http://www. nypost.com/seven/07012008/postopinion/opedcolumnists/al_qaedas_ plan_b_117936.htm (3 July 2008).

Talmer, Yoni. 'IDF naval commandoes seize PA-bound weapons ship'. *Israel Insider*, 6 Jan. 2002 at http://web.israelinsider.com/Articles/Security/367. htm (8 Dec. 2007).

'Tamil rebels launch naval attack'. *BBC News*, 24 May 2007 at http://news.bbc. co.uk/1/hi/world/south_asia/6686359.stm (15 June 2007).

'Tamil Tigers humiliate India by killing Indians; Karunanidhi forced to act against pro-Tiger Vaiko'. *Asia Tribune*, 30 April 2007 at http://www.asiantribune.com/index.php?q=node/5513 (15 June 2007).

'Tamil Tigers sea HQ 'destroyed''. *BBC News*, 4 April 2007 at http://news.bbc. co.uk/1/hi/world/south_asia/6525127.stm (15 June 2007).

Tan, Abby. 'In Asian waters, sea pirates eschew eye patches, steal ships via Internet'. *Christian Science Monitor*, 13 June 1996 at http://www.csmonitor.com/cgi-bin/wit_article.pl?script/96/06/13/061396.intl.intl.4 (2 Oct. 2005).

Terror on the High Seas – A Spreading Plague'. *DEBKA-Net-Weekly* Special Report, 14 Aug. 2002 at http://www.debka.com/article.php?aid=177 (12 May 2004).

'Terror, piracy still threaten Malacca Strait – Malaysian exec'. *Agence France-Presse*, 2 September 2007 at http://globalnation.inquirer.net/news/breaking-news/view_article.php?article_id=86162 (3 September 2007).

'Terror plan in Gibraltar Strait'. *Panorama* (Gibraltar), 6 June 2002 at http://www.panorama.gi/archive/020610/updates.htm (7 September 2007).

'Terror threat from the seas real: Antony'. *Zee News*, 11 March 2008 at http://www.zeenews.com/articles.asp?aid=429644&sid=NAT (12 March 2008).

'Terror threat swells at sea'. *WorldNetDaily.com*, 8 June 2004 at http://www.worldnetdaily.com/news/article.asp?ARTICLE_ID=38835 (27 April 2005).

'Terrorism probe extends to shipping'. *American Maritime Officer*, Oct. 2001 at http://www.amo-union.org/Newspaper/Morgue/10-2001/Sections/News/foc.html (4 Oct. 2005).

'Terrorism still a threat in Malacca Strait: KL's police chief'. *JoyoNews*, 12 June 2007.

'Terrorist links to *Superferry 14* probed'. 2004. *Fairplay*, vol. 350, Issue 6271, 8 April, p. 12.

Tesoro, Jose Manuel. 'En route to Jakarta'. *Asiaweek*, 4 September 1998 at http://www.asiaweek.com/asiaweek/98/0904/cs_4_batam.html (7 September 2007).

'Thailand to join patrols of Malacca Strait to help boost maritime security'. 2007. *Associated Press*, 25 Aug. 2007 at http://www.iht.com/articles/ap/2007/08/25/asia/AS-GEN-Thailand-Malacca-Strait.php (7 September 2007).

'Thailand will join anti-piracy patrols in the Malacca Strait'. *TNA*, 17 Aug. 2007 at http://etna.mcot.net/query.php?nid=31095 (17 Aug. 2007).

Thomas, Gordon. 'Al-Qaeda's Suicide Bomber Navy Poses Real and Present WMD Threat Says Britain's Navy Chief'. *bushcountry.org*, 25 September 2003 at http://www.yourmailinglistprovider.com/pubarchive_show_message.php?globeintel+144 (4 September 2007).

Thompson, Adam. 'Drug cartels "threaten" Mexican democracy'. *Financial Times*, 13 July 2008 at http://www.ft.com/cms/s/0/9a8272f6-510d-11dd-b751-000077b07658.html?nclick_check=1 (18 July 2008).

'Three littoral states agree to set up Joint Cooinating Committee'. *Business Times*, 22 April 2006 reproduced at http://www.sof.or.jp/ocean/report_e/pdf/200604.pdf, p. 6 (7 September 2007)

'Tide of pirates, A'. *Asiaweek*, 27 May 1988, pp. 26-29.

'Tiger tricks'. *Shiptalk*, 29 May 2007 at http://www.shiptalk.com/index.asp?itemI D=2110&rcid=191&pcid=178&cid=191'#anch (29 May 2007).

'Tigers sink Sri Lanka Craft, heavy land battles erupt'. *Agence France-Presse*, 22 March 2008 at http://afp.google.com/article/ALeqM5hBuGdKdW-B53YvbuvafjBm3tR1YZg (24 March 2008)

Tighe, Paul. 'Sri Lanka destroys rebel flotilla, raids financial center'. *Bloomberg. com*, 14 September 2007 at http://www.bloomberg.com/apps/news?pid= 20601091&sid=aPNV8pNwm4iI&refer=india# (15 September 2007).

———. 'Sri Lanka says leader of Tamil rebel sea unit killed'. *Bloomberg.com*, 3 Oct. 2007 at http://www.bloomberg.com/apps/news?pid=20601080&s id=avUwaNG0xCmc&refer=asia# (8 Oct. 2007).

———. 'Sri Lanka says military destroyed Tamil rebel training base'. *Bloomberg. com*, 30 July 2007 at http://www.bloomberg.com/apps/news?pid=20601 080&sid=aBZNY6mLUNnQ# (31 July 2007).

'Timeline: The Jolo hostage drama'. *BBC News report*, 12 September 2000 at http://news.bbc.co.uk/1/hi/world/asia-pacific/917326.stm (7 September 2007).

Tobar, Héctor. 'Drug smugglers reroute shipments via Central America'. *Los Angeles Times*, 4 March 2007.

———. 'A Mexican cartel army's war within'. *Los Angeles Times*, 20 May 2007.

———. 'New phase seen in Mexico's drug war'. *Los Angeles Times*, 18 May 2008.

'Toll rises to 45 on Philippines bus bombings'. The Institute for Counter-Terrorism *Spotlight*, 28 Feb. 2000.

'Top al-Qaeda operative arrested'. *CNN.com*, 22 Nov. 2002 at http://archives.cnn. com/2002/US/11/21/alqaeda.capture/ (7 September 2007).

Torode, Greg. 'Hijacked ship might be at Chinese base'. *South China Morning Post*, 22 March 1994.

———. 'HK exposes China piracy'. *South China Morning Post*, 16 March 1994.

———. 'Probe into stolen ship racket leads to HK firm'. *South China Morning Post*, 25 July 1994.

Tran, Mark. 'Terror suspects escape US Afghan base'. *The Guaian*, 11 July 2005 at http://www.guaian.co.uk/afghanistan/story/0,,1526159,00.html (7 September 2007).

Turner, Thomas. 'Bulk carriers 'top of pirate hit list''. *Lloyd's List*, 9 May 2006.

'UK sailors captured at gunpoint'. *BBC News*, 23 March 2007 at http://news.bbc. co.uk/1/hi/uk/6484279.stm (7 September 2007).

'UN-backed project to boost safety, security in vital Malacca shipping lane'. UN News Service, 18 September 2007 at http://www.un.org/apps/news/story.asp?NewsID=23846&Cr=piracy&Cr1# (19 September 2007).

'UN: Cocaine influx could destabilise Guinea-Bissau'. *Associated Press*, 1 Nov. 2007 at http://www.iht.com/articles/ap/2007/11/01/africa/AF-GEN-Guinea-Bissau-Cocaine-Economy.php?page=2 (3 Nov. 2007).

'UN General Assembly, Department of Public Information. 'Criminal involvement by transnational, non-state actors poses major threat to international security, thi committee told'. 4 Oct. 2006 at http://www.un.org/News/Press/docs/2006/gashc3848.doc.htm (7 September 2007).

'UN Warns About Nexus Between Drugs, Crime and Terrorism'. UN Press Release SOC/CP/311, 1 Oct. 2004 at http://www.un.org/News/Press/docs/2004/soccp311.doc.htm (3 Dec. 2007).

'Unrest hits oil facilities in Niger Delta'. *New York Times,* 23 September 2005.

Urquhart, Donald. 'New Malacca pirate attacks raise concern'. *Business Times,* 5 July 2006.

———. 'Nine missing as pirates throw crew overboa'. *The Business Times On-Line Edition* 16 July 2004.

———. 'Time to close the piracy gap'. *The Business Times,* 29 Nov. 2006.

'US 7 Fleet to provide naval support for Aceh province'. *Navy Newsstand,* 1 Jan. 2005 at http://www.news.navy.mil/search/display.asp?story_id=16477 (7 September 2007).

'US attacks Somali 'militant base''. *BBC News,* 2 June 2007 at http://news.bbc.co.uk/1/hi/world/africa/6714473.stm (15 April 2008).

'US captues 13 Somali 'pirates''. *BBC News,* 19 March 2006 at http://news.bbc.co.uk/1/hi/world/africa/4822722.stm (20th March 2006).

'US claims al-Qaeda planned to crash planes in UK'. *Daily Telegraph,* (Expat edition) 22 June 2006 at http://www.telegraph.co.uk/global/main.jhtml?xml=/global/2006/06/22/uterror.xml (7 September 2007).

'US envoy in Philippines calls southern island 'Mecca of Terror''. 2005. *Xinhua. net,* 10 April 2005 at http://news.xinhuanet.com/english/2005-04/10/content_2810481.htm (7 September 2007).

'US hopes al-Qaeda captive will reveal future plots'. *USA Today,* 22 Nov. 2002 at http://www.usatoday.com/news/world/2002-11-21-al-qaeda-capture_x.htm (7 September 2007).

'US Navy captures Somali 'pirates''. *BBC News,* 22 Jan. 2006 at http://news.bbc.co.uk/1/hi/world/africa/4636588.stm (21 March 2006).

'US Navy fights pirates off E.Africa'. *CBS News,* 18 March 2006 at http://www.cbsnews.com/stories/2006/03/18/world/main1419357.shtml (7 September 2007).

'US Navy fires at Somali hijackers of Russian ship'. *Reuters,* 12 Feb. 2008 at http://www.reuters.com/article/africaCrisis/idUSL12616362 (19 April 2008).

'US Navy returns fire on suspected pirates'. *WorldNet Daily,* 18 March 2006 at http://www.wnd.com/news/article.asp?ARTICLE_ID=49338 (8 Jan. 2007).

'US port security unlikely to stop nukes: experts'. *Reuters,* 7 Nov. 2006.

'US ships block supplies to hijacked Japanese tanker'. *Agence France-Presse*, 5 Dec. 2007 at http://newsinfo.inquirer.net/breakingnews/world/view_article. php?article_id=104944 (5 Dec. 2007).

Usher, Graham Usher; and Borger, Julian Borger. 'Israel halts Palestinian arms ship'. *The Guaian*, 5 Jan. 2002 at http://www.guaian.co.uk/israel/Story/0,2763,628003,00.html (7 September 2007).

'USS Cole attack "plotter" charged'. *BBC News*, 30 June 2008 at http://news.bbc. co.uk/1/hi/world/americas/7482385.stm (2 July 2008).

'USS Cole update: Hizbollah built bomb', 21 May 2001 at http://www.newsmax. com/archives/articles/2001/5/21/71007.shtml (7 September 2007).

Valencia, Mark J. 'Mercenaries in the Strait of Malacca', *The Jakarta Post*, 28 July 2005.

Vargas, Anthony. 'JI terrorist's wife says MILF helps Abu'. *Manila Times*, 10 Oct. 2006 at http://www.manilatimes.net/national/2006/oct/10/yehey/top_ stories/20061010top5.html (13 March 2007).

———. 'Liaison team disbands, Bossi rescue snagged'. *Manila Times*, 22 June 2007 at http://www.manilatimes.net/national/2007/june/22/yehey/top_ stories/20070622top3.html (7 September 2007).

———. 'Seaborne bombers may strike in Cebu'. *ABS-CBN Interactive*, 21 Nov. 2006 at http://www.abs-cbnnews.com/storypage.aspx?StoryId=56648 (21 Nov. 2006).

Vatikiotis, Michael; and Bartholomew, James. 1992. 'Raiders of Riau: Alarming surge in attacks on shipping'. *Far East Economic Review*, vol. 155, no. 26, 2 July 1992, p. 14 at http://www.feer.com/articles/archive/1992/9207_02/ P028.html (20 July 2004).

———; and Westlake, Michael. 'Gunboat Diplomacy'. *FEER*, 16 June 1994, pp. 22-26.

Verde, Jade. 'Abu Sayyaf's Khadaffy Montaño Abubakar Janjalani'. *American Chronicle*, 13 June 2007.

Von Hoesslin, Karsten. 'Taiwan and piracy along the Horn of Africa'. *Taiwan Journal*, 24 Feb. 2006 at http://taiwanjournal.nat.gov.tw/ ct.asp?xItem=23212&CtNode=118 (15 April 2008).

Vu Kim Chung. 'Indonesian Troubles Cited for 40 Percent Rise in Pirate Attacks'. *Penguin Star*. 25 Jan. 2000 at http://www.geocities.com/TimesSquare/ Hangar/4607/00-02/PIR-indonesia-pirates.html (17 June 2004).

———. 'Thirteen Pirates Sentenced To Death'. *Penguin Star*. 22 Dec. 1999 at http://www.geocities.com/TimesSquare/Hangar/4607/00-01/PIR-13- execution.html (11 Aug. 2004).

Wadhwaney, Rohit William. 'Lankan expats 'forced to fund LTTE''. *Gulf Times*, 11 May 2006 at http://www.gulf-times.com/site/topics/article.asp?cu_ no=2&item_no=85944&version=1&template_id=57&parent_id=56 (7 September 2007).

Wagner, Breanne. 'Government lacks clear plans to ID small vessels used as terrorist weapons'. *National Defense*, Nov. 2007.

Wain, Barry. 'All at Sea Over Resources in East Asia'. *Yale Global*, 14 Aug. 2007 at
http://yaleglobal.yale.edu/display.article?id=9546 (16 Aug. 2007).

Waked, Ali. 'Hamas confirms establishment of 'navy''. *YnetNews.com*, 11 Aug.
2007 at http://www.ynetnews.com/articles/0,7340,L-3436240,00.html
(16 September 2007).

Ward, Robert. 'Piracy attacks on boxships erupt again in Santos port'. *Lloyd's List*,
17 Nov. 2006.

————. 'Piracy could cost Santos ISPS certification'. *Lloyd's List*, 9 April 2008).

Watson, Bill. 'In Search of the Trojan Horse', *Fairplay*, 8 April 2004, pp. 17-19.

'We bombed ferry claims Abu Sayyaf'. *The Nation*, 29 Feb. 2004.

'Weakened Abu Sayyaf looking for a new leader, A'. CSIS *Transnational Threats
Update*, vol. 4, no. 12, Jan. 2007, p. 6 at http://www.csis.org/media/csis/
pubs/ttu_07v4n12.pdf (3 Dec. 2007).

Webb-Vidal, Andy. 'Skimming the river in search of Farc rebels'. *Financial Times*,
8 Nov. 2005.

Weber, David. 'Illegal fishing cost Indonesia $2 billion a year: expert'. *ABC On-
line*, 12 May 2006 at http://www.abc.net.au/worldtoday/content/2006/
s1637120.htm (14 May 2006).

Weitz, Richa. 'Death of a terrorist: Abu Sayyaf's Abu Sulaiman'. *WorldPolitics-
Review*, 5 Feb. 2007 at http://www.worldpoliticsreview.com/article.
aspx?id=521 (27 June 2007).

'Well-paid fear-mongering'. *The Providence Journal*, 26 Nov. 2006 at http://www.
projo.com/opinion/editorials/content/projo_20061126_26lng.2e64d33.
html (28 Nov. 2006).

Westlake, Michael. 'Hot pursuit'. *FEER*, 16 June 1994, pp. 26-28.

'What al-Qaida could do with 'terror navy'' *WorldNetDaily*, 20 Oct. 2003 at http://
www.wnd.com/news/article.asp?ARTICLE_ID=35157 (12 June 2007).

'What if?' *The Economist*, 27 May 2006 at http://www.economist.com/business/
displayStory.cfm?story_id=2705562 (31 May 2006).

Wheatley, Jonathan. 'Gang leaders take Brazil hostage from inside jail'. *Financial
Times*, 17 May 2006 at http://www.ft.com/cms/s/76f30a68-e5d4-11da-
b309-0000779e2340.html (6 Aug. 2007).

White, Josh. 'Al-Qaeda suspect says he planned Cola attack'. *Washington Post*, 20
March 2007 at http://www.washingtonpost.com/wp-dyn/content/arti-
cle/2007/03/19/AR2007031900653.html (20 March 2007).

————; and Graham, Bradley. 'US to change tactics after Gulf attacks'. *The Washington Post*, 27 April 2004 at http://www.highbeam.com/library/doc3.as
p?DOCID=1P1:93877593&num=61&ctrlInfo=Round4%3AProd%3A
SR%3AResult&ao= (2 July 2004).

Whiteman, Tim. 'Ship held after spate of deviations'. ICC *International Cargo Crime Prevention*, vol. 5, no. 12, April/May 1988.

Whitlock, Craig. 'Homemade, cheap and dangerous: Terror cells favour simple ingredients in building bombs'. *Washington Post*, 5 July 2007 at http://www.washingtonpost.com/wp-dyn/content/article/2007/07/04/AR2007070401814.html?hpid=topnews (5 July 2007).

———. 'Probe of USS Cole bombing unravels'. *Washington Post*, 4 May 2008 at http://www.washingtonpost.com/wp-dyn/content/article/2008/05/03/AR2008050302047.html (19 May 2008).

'Who are Islamic jihad?' *BBC News*, 9 Aug. 2001 at http://news.bbc.co.uk/1/hi/world/middle_east/1005081.stm (7 September 2007).

Who's who in al-Qaeda'. *BBC News*, 27 April 2007 at http://news.bbc.co.uk/1/hi/world/middle_east/2780525.stm (7 September 2007).

Wijayapala, Ranil. 'Global community condemns LTTE suicide attack on unarmed sailors'. *Daily News* (Colombo), 18 Oct. 2006 at http://www.dailynews.lk/2006/10/18/sec02.asp (19 Oct. 2006).

———; and Manatunga, Rajmi. 2006. 'Navy foils LTTE suicide bid on Dakshina base'. *Daily News* (Colombo), 19 Oct. 2006 at http://www.dailynews.lk/2006/10/19/sec01.asp (7 September 2007).

Wilkinson, Isamba. 'Eta plot to bomb Plymouth ferry foiled in Spain'. *Daily Telegraph*, 21 June 2001 at http://www.telegraph.co.uk/news/main.jhtml?xml=/news/2001/06/20/weta20.xml (14 July 2007).

Wiltrout, Kate. 'Navy helps foil pirates' attack on merchant ships off E Africa'. *Hampton Roads Pilot*, 31 Oct. 2007 at http://content.hamptonroads.com/story.cfm?story=135890&ran=189084 (31 Oct. 2007).

Windrem, Robert. 'The frightening evolution of al-Qaida'. *MSNBC.com*, 24 June 2005 at http://www.msnbc.msn.com/id/8307333/ (30 June 2005).

Witte, Griff. 'Pakistan seen losing fight against Taliban and al-Qaeda'. *Washington Post*, 3 Oct. 2007.

Woollacott, Martin. 'The Boat People'. *The Guaian*, 3 Dec. 1977 at http://century.guaian.co.uk/1970-1979/Story/0,,106868,00.html (7 September 2007).

Woodward, Bob. 'Findings link Clinton allies to Chinese intelligence'. *Washington Post*, 10 Feb. 1998 at http://www.washingtonpost.com/wp-srv/politics/special/campfin/stories/cf021098.htm (16 June 2007).

'World, South Asia: Tamil fishermen attacked'. *BBC Online Network*, 29 September 1998 at http://news.bbc.co.uk/1/hi/world/south_asia/183050.stm (7 September 2007).

'Worrying trend as pirates turn attention to tugs'. *Lloyd's List*, 11 Dec. 2006.

'Worse Nigerian violence seen', *Fairplay*, 24 Aug. 2006.

'Wounded but still dangerous'. *Economist.com*, 14 June 2007 at http://www.economist.com/displaystory.cfm?story_id=9339835&fsrc=nwl (15 June

2007).

Wright, Robin. 'Iranian unit to be labelled 'terrorist'. *The Washington Post*, 15 Aug. 2007 at http://www.washingtonpost.com/wp-dyn/content/ article/2007/08/14/AR2007081401662.html?hpid=topnews (15 Aug. 2007).

Xavier, Nathaniel. 'No terrorism threat in Straits'. *The Star On-line*, 5 July 2004 at http://202.186.86.35/maritime/story.asp?file=/2004/7/5/ maritime/8346432&sec=maritime (20 July 2004).

Yarbro, Stan. 'Colombian jet crashes, killing 107'. *Washington Post*, 28 Nov. 1989.

'Yemen ship attack 'was terrorism'. *BBC News*, 13 Oct. 2002 at http://news.bbc. co.uk/1/hi/world/middle_east/2324431.stm#tanker (23 April 2004).

Yousafzai, Sami; and Moreau, Ron. 'Al Qaeda family feud'. *Newsweek*, 30 July 2007 at http://www.msnbc.msn.com/id/19886668/site/newsweek/ (7 September 2007).

Yusuf, Aweys Osman.'Somali pirates gather at the coastal town of Haradhere'. *Shabelle News Network*, 26 Jan. 2007 at http://www.shabelle.net/news/ ne2172.htm (27 Jan. 2007).

Zadeh, Ali Nouri. 'Iranian officer: Hezbollah has commando naval unit'. *Asharq Alawsat*, 29 July 2006 at http://www.asharqalawsat.com/english/news. asp?section=1&id=5801 (1 Aug. 2006).

Zakis, Jeremy; and Macko, Steven. 'Major terrorist plot in Singapore discovered: Al-Qaeda believed well established in the Asian region'. EmergencyNet News *Special Report*, 12 Jan. 2002 at http://www.emergency.com/2002/ Singapore_terror02.htm (23 Dec. 2007).

'Zarqari 'link to Joan rockets''. *BBC News*, 24 Aug. 2005 at http://news.bbc. co.uk/1/hi/world/middle_east/4179522.stm (7 September 2007).

Zimmerman, Peter D. 'The smoky bomb threat'. *New York Times*, 19 Dec. 2006 at http://www.nytimes.com/2006/12/19/opinion/19zimmerman.html?scp =1&sq=smoky+bomb+threat&st=nyt (12 Feb. 2008).

———; Acton, James M; and Rogers, M. Brooke. 'Seize the Cesium'. *New York Times*, 1 Aug. 2007 at http://www.nytimes.com/2007/08/01/ opinion/01zimmerman.html?_r=1&scp=1&sq=seize+the+cesium&st=nyt &oref=slogin (12 Feb. 2008).

INDEX

Camp Abu Bakar 283, 328, 329
Campbeltown 213
Cape St George 104
Caribbean 99-100, 193, 194-5, 209
Carter Hall 106, 381-2
Casablanca 348-9
Casamara 345
Cefalonia 215
Celebes Sea 76-7, 80
Central America 178-9, 193, 249, 366, 388, 397
Changco, Emilio 165
Chaumont 154
Chechens 189-90, 260
Cherry 201 309
Cheung Son 155
China 34, 56-8, 94-6, 123, 125, 126, 131, 139-43, 155-9, 161, 170, 172-7, 180, 365
Chittagong 97, 352
Cholan 351
CIA 242, 366
City of Liverpool 316
City of Poros 188-9
Claudia 345
Clinton, Bill 169-70
Coalition Task Force 102-3, 105
Coastal Road Massacre (Israel) 291
Cole 196-7, 200, 227, 230, 232, 234, 236, 280, 283, 286, 367, 368, 373
Colombia 163-4, 249, 251, 389, 399
Colombo 318, 319
*Comex Jules 354
*Comex-Joux 3 218
Comicon 165
Comité Maritime International (CMI) 20
containers 259-64, 267-8
Contras 321-2

Convention for the Suppression of Unlawful Acts against the Safety of Maritime Navigation (SUA) (1988) 18n, 188, 191-3, 195, 359
Coral Beach 296, 297
Coral Princess 78
Coral Sea 289
Cordiality 315
Corfu Channel 238
corruption 26, 28, 42, 74-6, 97, 98, 118, 121, 141-2, 161-2, 180, 379, 382
Costa Rica 249
cruise ships 78, 186-9, 201, 207-10, 233
Cuba 241, 278-9, 322
Cuban Liberation Front 278
Cyprus 289, 294

Danica White 106
Daranzali, Marmoun 348
Dardouk, Ali Mussa 302
Davao City 326, 329, 332, 339
Declaration of Paris (1856) 191
Denmark 106, 252
Dewi Madrim 159, 214
Dhahran 234
Dishman, Chris 394
Dokubo-Asari, Mujahid 115-18, 119
Don Carlos 337
Dona Ramona 339
Dondra Head 354
Dong Yih 49
Dongwon-ho 104
Doo Yang Jade 149
Dos Palmas 332, 343
Doulous 340
drug trafficking 118, 124, 163-4, 172, 174, 194-5, 248, 251, 252, 355-6, 389-90, 397, 399